EXECUTORY CONTRACTS IN INSOLVENCY LAW

EXECUTORY CONTRACTS IN INSOLVENCY LAW

A Global Guide

Edited by

JASON CHUAH

Professor of Maritime Law and Head of Department, The City Law School, City, University of London, UK

EUGENIO VACCARI

Lecturer in Law, University of Essex, UK

Edward Elgar PUBLISHING

Cheltenham, UK • Northampton, MA, USA

Published by
Edward Elgar Publishing Limited
The Lypiatts
15 Lansdown Road
Cheltenham
Glos GL50 2JA
UK

Edward Elgar Publishing, Inc.
William Pratt House
9 Dewey Court
Northampton
Massachusetts 01060
USA

A catalogue record for this book
is available from the British Library

Library of Congress Control Number: 2018967806

This book is available electronically in the **Elgar**online
Law subject collection
DOI 10.4337/9781788115520

MIX
Paper from
responsible sources
FSC® C013056

ISBN 978 1 78811 551 3 (cased)
ISBN 978 1 78811 552 0 (eBook)

Typeset by Columns Design XML Ltd, Reading
Printed and bound in Great Britain by TJ International Ltd, Padstow

CONTENTS

EXTENDED CONTENTS

PART III HYBRID LEGAL SYSTEMS

EDITORS AND CONTRIBUTORS

EDITORS

Jason Chuah is Professor of Maritime Law and Head of Department at The City Law School, City, University of London and was the holder of the Cambridge Commonwealth Trust Award, Barclays Bank Scholarship and the Cambridge Commonwealth Fellowship at the University of Cambridge. He has published well over 200 articles and is the author of ten books, including the co-authored *Encyclopaedia of Banking Law*, (with Sir Peter Cresswell, Sir William Blair, Philip Wood, Richard Hooley, George Walker, etc.) and *Butterworth's Banking Law Guide* (with Mark Howard QC and Roger Masefield QC).

Professor Chuah is editor of several international journals, including the *Journal of International Maritime Law*, *International Company and Commercial Law Review*, *International Trade Law and Regulation*, *Shipping & Trade Law*, *International Transport Law Review*, and *Finance & Credit Law*. He has served on research councils in the UK, South Africa, Canada and Colombia. His work has been cited by tribunals and institutions in the UK, US, EU and Asia.

Eugenio Vaccari is a lecturer at the University of Essex. He obtained his LL.B. from the University of Modena (Italy), a PG Cert. from the University of Bologna (Italy), his LL.M. from the LSE and he completed his Ph.D. at City, University of London.

Eugenio is a qualified Italian lawyer specialising in corporate insolvency law. He is an active member of several leading institutions in the field, including INSOL International, INSOL Europe and the Insolvency Lawyers' Association [UK]. Eugenio's main areas of interest are the theoretical and conceptual underpinnings of corporate insolvency law and the discipline of executory contracts in corporate insolvency cases.

CONTRIBUTORS

Scott Abel is a partner at Buddle Findlay, specialising in insolvency and debt restructuring, corporate and secured finance, and specialist personal property security and credit recovery advice. He advises and has acted for domestic and foreign banks, financial institutions, insolvency professionals and other organisations on receiverships, liquidations, administrations and workouts. In 2015, he became the first New Zealander to pass the INSOL Global Insolvency Practice Course and be recognised as a Fellow of INSOL International.

Vanessa Buttafuoco qualified as a lawyer in Germany in September 2016 (2. Staatsexam). She studied Law at Leibniz Universität in Hanover, Germany specialising in European Union Law and Public International Law and passed the 1. Staatsexamen in Lower Saxony in September 2012.

In 2014 she successfully completed her Master's degree (LL.M) at the London School of Economics and Political Science, specialising in European law. She currently works for Volkswagen AG in the Group Legal Department – Product Safety and Product Defense.

José Carles is a multilingual lawyer admitted to practice in Spain, shortlisted for Global Restructuring Review's 40 under 40 (worldwide, 2016). Co-founder and partner of the Spanish legal boutique Carles Cuesta Abogados (top 100 law firm worldwide in Restructuring and Insolvency, GRR 100, 2018) after his experience at Garrigues Restructuring and Insolvency team (Madrid) and UBS Investment Bank (London).

Member of the Cross-border Corporate Insolvency and Commercial Law Research Group from The City Law School (London) and of INSOL EUROPE. Master in Company Law from Centro de Estudios Garrigues and Harvard Law School, BA in Law (ICADE) and BSc in Business Administration (ICADE).

Professor in restructuring and insolvency law at ICADE, Universidad CEU San Pablo and Centro Universitario Villanueva and author of articles and reviews in specialist legal journals such as Global Restructuring Review or Anuario de Derecho Concursal (*Journal on Bankruptcy Law*).

He also has extensive experience directing and teaching programmes and seminars in prisons and detention centres aimed at social rehabilitation.

Christian Chamorro-Courtland is a Lecturer in Business Law at the University of Sydney Business School. He has a Bachelors (LL.B.) (2007) and Masters of Law (LL.M.) (2008) from King's College London (specialised in commercial and financial law), and he completed his doctoral studies in commercial, financial and banking law at Osgoode Hall Law School, York University (Canada) (2012). His Ph.D. thesis analysed the legal aspects and operations of central counterparty (CCP) clearing systems. He has nine years of international experience teaching business law subjects, including at York University, Zayed University (UAE) and Deakin University (Australia). He has special interests in CCPs and clearing and settlements systems, payment systems, fintech, consumer protection, financial regulation and legal issues concerning the international financial markets.

Carlos Cuesta is a lawyer admitted to practice in Spain, a research fellow of the Chair of Financial Markets Law of Universidad CEU, San Pablo and co-founder of Spanish legal boutique Carles Cuesta Abogados (top 100 law firm worldwide in Restructuring and Insolvency, GRR 100, 2018) after working as a lawyer in Garrigues Restructuring & Insolvency team (Madrid).

Master in Company Law from Centro de Estudios Garrigues and Harvard Law School. Legal and business studies at KÆbenhavns Universitet (Denmark), IESE Business School Fundación para la Investigación del Derecho y la Empresa. BA in Law (Universidad CEU, San Pablo).

Professor in restructuring and insolvency law at ICADE, Universidad CEU San Pablo and Centro Universitario Villanueva and author of articles in specialist legal journals and compilations such as the *Banking Market Code* (Agencia Estatal Boletín Oficial del Estado) or the *Judiciary, Notary, Registry and Doctrine Commentary on the Law on Corporations.*

He also has extensive experience directing and teaching programmes and seminars in prisons and detention centres aimed at social rehabilitation.

Rolef de Weijs is Professor of National and International Insolvency at the University of Amsterdam. He is also a Visiting Professor at Riga Graduate School of Law in Latvia.

Professor de Weijs holds a Master in law and philosophy degree from Groningen University and an LL.M. degree from Harvard Law School. He also participated in the Japan Prize Winners' Programme.

De Weijs specialises in property law, insolvency law, corporate law and corporate finance. He teaches the courses of insolvency law (insolventierecht), critical analyses of corporate finance and insolvency law and also business organization and corporate finance law as part of the Master in law and finance degree.

De Weijs practices law as an attorney and a court appointed trustee in bankruptcy at Houthoff, a law firm in Amsterdam. He is also the chair of NACIIL (Netherlands Association for Comparative and International Insolvency Law).

Indrajit Dube is a Professor in the Rajiv Gandhi School of Law at IIT, Kharagpur, India. Indrajit completed his doctorate at the University of Calcutta and has published extensively in the area of corporate law and governance. He has acted as a consultant to many government-funded bodies in India and has been a visiting academic at the University of British Columbia and the University of Western Ontario. He is also an ATEX Fellow 2018 at School of Business and Taxation, UNSW, Sydney.

Jasnica Garašić is a full Professor at the Faculty of Law of the University of Zagreb, where she teaches civil procedure law, insolvency law and arbitration law. She was granted a scholarship by the German Academic Exchange Service (DAAD) at the 'Max-Planck Institute for Comparative and International Private Law' in Hamburg and received a Ph.D. from the University of Hamburg for a thesis on international insolvency law (2004, *summa cum laude*). She was a Fulbright visiting scholar at the School of Law of the University of Texas at Austin (2007/2008).

Jasnica has been a delegate of the Republic of Croatia to the UNCITRAL's Working Group V for Insolvency Law since 2004. She cooperated with the Croatian Ministry of Justice on preparation of the Croatian Bankruptcy Acts of 1996 and 2015 as well as the Consumer Bankruptcy Act of 2015. She is a member of INSOL Europe.

Karolina Gasparkė is a Lithuanian lawyer. She holds a Master's degree in Law from Vilnius University (specialised in commercial law). She also studied law at Utrecht University, the Netherlands specialising in European Union law and public international law. Karolina did an internship in the General Court of the European Union in 2013.

Karolina is Associate at BNT Attorneys-At-Law Vilnius office (Lithuania). She specialises in the fields of commercial, corporate and insolvency law, with a special focus on cross-border insolvency. Karolina is also a member of BNT Attorneys-At-Law Insolvency and Corporate Restructuring practice group.

Before joining BNT Attorneys-At-Law Vilnius office, she practiced with another leading law firm in the Baltics. Karolina is also a board member of the Lithuanian Young Lawyers Association.

Georgi Valentinov Georgiev is Assistant Professor in Corporate and Commercial Law at Sofia University in Bulgaria. He graduated from Sofia University in 2010. In 2012 he obtained a Master's degree in international business law at King's College London where he specialised in the area of European and comparative company law and capital markets.

In 2012 Georgi was appointed as a country researcher for Bulgaria in a project of the London School of Economics and Political Science, funded by the European Commission – Study on

Directors' Duties and Liability, prepared by Professor Carsten Gerner-Beuerle, Professor Philipp Paech and Professor Edmund Philipp Schuster.

Since 2016 he has been a member of an insolvency work group at the City University, London, and Cross-Border Corporate Insolvency & Commercial Law (CI&CL) Group, London. In 2017, he was a visiting researcher at the Commercial Law Centre at Harris Manchester College, University of Oxford. His main areas of interest are Corporate and Commercial Law, Insolvency, Securities and Arbitration.

Emilie Ghio is a lecturer in law at Birmingham City University. She holds law degrees from the University of Strasbourg (France) and University College Cork (Ireland) and completed her Ph.D. in University College Cork in 2018. Her expertise lies in the field of cross-border insolvency and rescue law. Her areas of research interest include international insolvency law and legal theories, in particular the concepts of harmonisation, incrementalism and pragmatism. Emilie is a member of the INSOL YANIL board (the Young Academics Network of Insolvency Law) and a member of the advisory board of the European Commission funded JCOERE project (Judicial Cooperation supporting Economic Recovery in Europe).

Rolandino Guidotti has been Professor of Law at the University of Bologna – Department of Legal Studies since 2014 – where he teaches business, insolvency and financial market law. He was (and he still is) a member of many Research Groups both in Italy and in other European Countries.

Rolandino is the author of several books and academic articles in the area of company, insolvency, financial market and arbitration law. He regularly participates in numerous national and international conferences.

Frank Heemann is a German qualified lawyer (Rechtsanwalt) admitted to practice also in Lithuania and with more than 17 years' professional experience in consulting and representing corporate clients.

He is managing partner at BNT | Attorneys-At-Law Vilnius office (Lithuania) and the head of BNT | Attorneys-At-Law Insolvency and Corporate Restructuring practice group. Before joining BNT, Frank practiced with White & Case LLP, a globally active US law firm.

Frank specializes in insolvency and corporate restructuring, M&A and cross-border corporate advice. He is vice president of the Lithuanian board of the German Baltic Chamber of Commerce, French Foreign Trade Adviser (Conseiller du Commerce Extérieur de la France), active member of INSOL Europe, and one of The World Bank's local partners for Lithuania. Frank frequently speaks and publishes on corporate, insolvency and restructuring matters.

Jin Chun is currently Professor at the Faculty of Law, Doshisha University, Kyoto, Japan. She has taught Japanese and Chinese insolvency law, and civil procedure law. Jin Chun is a Visiting Professor, Renmin University of China (Faculty of Law), China. Jin Chun holds degrees from Renmin University of China (LL.B.), and Kyoto University (LL.M. and Ph.D. (Law)), Japan. She has worked at the Shenyang Intermediate People's Court of China after graduating from university in China and also was a Visiting Scholar at the Asian Law Centre, Melbourne Law School (Sep 2015–Sep 2017), Australia.

Her main English publications include: (with Stacey Steele) 'Some Suggestions from Japan for Reforming Australia's Personal Bankruptcy Law', 17(1) *QUT Law Review* 74, in Oct 2017; 'How technologies and innovation are driving Chinese insolvency law developments: new Supreme People's Court bankruptcy information platform', 15(1) *International Corporate Rescue (UK)*, Jan 2018; (with Stacey Steele, Andrew Goldwin et al) 'Trends and developments in

Chinese insolvency law: the first decade of the PRC Enterprise Bankruptcy Law', *The American Journal of Comparative Law* (Nov 2018).

Çağlar Kaçar graduated from Marmara University, Faculty of Law in 2009 and was called to the Istanbul Bar Association. Mr Kaçar, Partner at Kaçar Attorneys-at-Law, represents and advises multinational and domestic clients through all processes of restructuring and insolvency proceedings. He has represented significant numbers of debtors, secured and unsecured creditors, shareholders and investors in proceedings such as out-of-court debt restructuring and composition with creditors. He also assists parties in registering their claims, attending creditors' meetings and purchasing assets from the bankruptcy estates. Mr Kaçar is generally nominated by the creditors as an insolvency administrator and performs liquidation of large and medium sized corporations. He is a member of INSOL Europe.

Patrick Keinert is a German lawyer who aquired his Ph.D. in the field of comparative insolvency law at the University of Geneva, Switzerland. He studied law at the University of Heidelberg, Germany, with a focus on civil procedure law and insolvency law.

At the moment he is doing his legal clerkship in the district of the higher regional court of Karlsruhe, Germany. Before this he worked as a teaching assistant at the Department of Private International Law at the University of Geneva and for several German law firms in Stuttgart, Frankfurt and Berlin in the domains of litigation, real estate law and insolvency law. Furthermore, he was assistant editor for the *Yearbook of Private International Law*.

Felix Kernbichler studied law at the University of Vienna, where he went on to work as an Assistant Professor at the Department of Private Law. He was a Visiting Scholar at the University of California, Berkeley School of Law and received an LL.M. degree from Harvard Law School. For his dissertation on contracts in insolvency at the University of Vienna, he was awarded a Ph.D. Fellowship by the Austrian Academy of Sciences, among other academic prizes.

While working on his Ph.D. thesis, he established a Law Clinic at the University of Vienna. He now works at Herbst Kinsky Attorneys at Law in Vienna and is director of the Law Clinic at the University of Vienna.

Borhan Uddin Khan is currently a Professor in the Faculty of Law, University of Dhaka and Adviser and Adjunct Professor at the Independent University, Bangladesh. He is a former Dean of the Faculty of Law, University of Dhaka (2006–2010) and head of the Department of Law, University of Dhaka (2015–17). He holds an LL.M. in Public International Law [1990] from the London School of Economics and Political Science (LSE), University of London and a Ph.D. [1995] from the School of Oriental and African Studies (SOAS), University of London. After obtaining an LL.B. (Hons.) [1984] and an LL.M. [1985] from the University of Dhaka, he joined the same university as a Lecturer in the Department of Law in 1989 and became a Professor in 2005.

Dr Khan, among others, is a member of the Board of Advisers of the Asian Society of International Law and a former Vice President of the Asian Society of International Law (2013–2015). He is also a member of the American Society of International Law and International Law Association.

His areas of expertise include: international human rights, international humanitarian law, international refugee law and the laws of armed conflict.

Dmitry Konstantinov is Head of Insolvency and Financial Restructuring at Ilyashev&Partners Law Firm, a law firm with offices in Russia, Ukraine and Estonia. He got a specialist degree with distinction from the Russian State University of Trade and Economics and also obtained a LL.M. degree in American law from Pericles ABLE Project and a LL.M. degree in English Corporate Law from the London School of Economics and Political Science.

As a litigator, Dmitry participates in high-profile disputes; his practice is mainly focused on insolvency and banking law. He is author of more than 30 articles published by Law Journals and such sources as Forbes, Vedomosti (Russian edition of WSJ), etc.

Line Herman Langkjaer is an assistant Professor at the Department of Law, University of Aarhus. Her research focuses on International and National Insolvency Law. Line teaches insolvency law and civil procedure to bachelor and master students at the University of Aarhus.

Line obtained her Master of Law Degree from the University of Aarhus in 2008. From 2008–15 Line worked as a qualified lawyer at LETT Law Firm specialising in bankruptcy and restructuring proceedings. While practising law she was an external lecturer in Insolvency Law at Aarhus University. In 2012 she was admitted to the Danish Bar Association. In 2018 she was awarded a Ph.D. with a thesis entitled: Jurisdiction of the Danish Courts in the field of Bankruptcy – Through the lens of the European Insolvency Regulation. While writing her Ph.D. thesis Line was a visiting researcher at Humboldt Universität zu Berlin.

Line is currently vice chair in YANIL (Younger Academics Network in Insolvency Law).

Yingxiang Long is a lecturer of Harbin University of Commerce in China. She currently focuses on the reform of bankruptcy law in China. She obtained her doctorate degree from Nottingham Trent University in 2017. Before her Ph.D study, she worked in China as a law lecturer and qualified lawyer for more than four years.

Morshed Mannan (1990) is a Meijers Ph.D. candidate attached to the Company Law Department of Leiden University, where he conducts research on worker cooperatives in the platform economy. His research interests also extend to employee ownership, international labour rights, insolvency law, digital technologies, corporate social responsibility and corporate governance.

He completed his LL.M. in Advanced Studies in International Civil & Commercial Law (*cum laude*) at Leiden University, as part of which he wrote a Thesis on 'The Prospects and Challenges of Adopting the UNCITRAL Model Law on Cross-Border Insolvency in South Asia (Bangladesh, India and Pakistan)'. Prior to moving to Leiden, Morshed practised as a lawyer in Bangladesh and lectured at an Affiliate Centre of the University of London in Dhaka. Previously, he completed his LL.B. (Hons.) at the University of Warwick (Coventry, UK) in 2011 and was called to the Bar of England & Wales in 2012.

Clement Marumoagae is a Senior Lecturer at the University of the Witwatersrand, where he teaches insolvency law and procedural law. He is also a practising attorney at Marumoagae Attorneys where he specialises in family law and pension law. He has attained an undergraduate law degree (LL.B.) and Master's degree (LL.M.) in Pension Law at the University of the Witwatersrand. He has also graduated with his second Master's degree (LL.M.) in labour law at the University of North West.

Mr Marumoagae also holds a Post Graduate Diploma in Insolvency Law and Practice from the University of Pretoria as well as a Post Graduate Diploma in Corporate Law from the University of the Witwatersrand. He has published numerous articles in peer-reviewed and practice-orientated journals in the fields of pension law, labour law, insolvency law and family law.

Héctor José Miguens received his Juris Doctor Title from the Law School of the National University of Buenos Aires in 1982. He is a Specialist on Trustee in Bankruptcy, from the School of Economics of the National University of Tucumán, Argentina, in 1989, as well as Ph.D or J.S.D. with a *summa cum laude* from the Law School of the Navarre University, Spain.

An Insol International Scholar, he has published three books, co-authored 13 books and published more than 60 articles in international Law Journals. His doctoral dissertation obtained the Accesit Prize of the National Law Academy of Buenos Aires. He is Fellow of the University of Oxford, of the Max Planck Institute of Hamburg, Germany and of the Alexander von Humboldt Foundation.

At present he is an Independent Researcher of the National Council of Research and Technology in Buenos Aires, (CONICET) Argentina at the Law School of the Universidad Austral, Buenos Aires, Argentina, where he is member of the academic staff as Extraordinary Professor. He is also Professor of Insolvency Law at the Law School of the Universidad de Buenos Aires, as member of the staff of Professors of the 'Curso de Actualización en Derecho Concursal', a Postgraduate course of Insolvency Law.

José Maria Lezcano Navarro is a Panamanian Licenciado (lawyer) graduated from the University of Panama in 2007, has a LL.M. in International Commercial Law awarded by the University of Westminster in 2009, and his Ph.D. was awarded by City University London in 2014. Currently he lectures at the University of Panama and works in his law firm in Panama.

José is the author of the books: *Piercing the Corporate Veil in Latin American Jurisprudence* (2015); *Sistema Bancario Panameño* (2014); *Analisis Del Nuevo Derecho Comercial Maritimo* (2016), and contributed in the *International Company Law Handbook* edited by Roman Thomasic (2016).

Alfonso Nocilla has been an Assistant Professor at the Faculty of Law, University of Western Ontario since 2018. He teaches and researches in the areas of commercial, insolvency and restructuring law, with emphasis on comparative and empirical approaches. Prior to joining Western full time, he was a Visiting Professor and Catalyst Capital Fellow in Insolvency Law there, teaching international and comparative restructuring. He was called to the Bar of Ontario in 2012.

Loukas Panetsos is an Associate at Kyriakides Georgopoulos Law Firm, based in Athens, Greece. Loukas holds an LL.B. from the Democritus University of Thrace, an LL.M. in Corporate and Commercial Law from the London School of Economics and Political Science and an M.Sc. in Taxation from the University of Oxford. His main field of specialisation is tax law.

Loukas has authored many articles and case comments published in international and Greek law journals (e.g., *European Taxation*, *International Transfer Pricing Journal*, *Utrecht Law Review*, *Dikaio Epicheiriseon & Etairion*). Loukas is admitted to the Greek Courts of First Instance and is a member of the Athens Bar Association.

Rebecca Parry is a Professor at Nottingham Trent University, specialising in international and comparative corporate insolvency law. She teaches specialist LL.M modules in this area and she has also supervised 15 Ph.D. students to successful completion. She has a particular interest in Chinese insolvency law, having co-edited the first English language book to consider the Enterprise Bankruptcy Law 2006.

Siniša Petrović is a tenured Professor of Law at the University of Zagreb. He obtained his LL.B, LL.M and Ph.D. degrees at the Faculty of Law University of Zagreb. His former positions include Counsellor to the Special Envoy of the President of the Republic of Croatia for negotiations with international community, Vice-dean of the Faculty of Law University of Zagreb, member and vice-president of the Council for the Protection of Competition, vice-president of the Permanent Arbitration Court of the Croatian Chamber of Commerce, member of the negotiating team for negotiations on accession of the Republic of Croatia to the EU (chapters on company law, intellectual property law, right of establishment and freedom to provide services; free movement of workers) and Special Adviser to the Prime Minister for European law.

Siniša has published papers and books in the field of commercial law, company law, competition law, sports law and foreign investments.

Anna Plevri is a Lecturer of Private Law and ADR at the School of Law of the University of Nicosia. She obtained a law degree, an LL.M. (Hons) and a Ph.D. (Hons) from the Law School of Aristotle University of Thessaloniki (Greece). She has also obtained an LL.M. (Hons) on International Law from the University of Thrace (Greece). Thus, she has been trained in various law and ADR training in European countries, in the USA and in Dubai. She is an accredited Mediator (Civil, Commercial, Family, Workplace Disputes and ODR), a certified Mediator's Trainer and an Arbitrator. She is an Attorney at law, member of the Bar Association of Thessaloniki and that of Cyprus. She is an author of two books in Greek (parties in civil trials and arbitration in the energy sector) and she contributes as an author in many collaborative books, projects, reports and papers in Greek and English language. She was a Visiting Professor of the LLM in Transnational and European Commercial Law, Banking Law, Arbitration/Mediation (in English) of the International Hellenic University.

Muhammad Mahbubur Rahman is an Associate Professor at the Department of Law, University of Dhaka. He completed his Ph.D. from the School of Oriental and African Studies (SOAS), University of London and LL.M. and LL.B. (Hons) from the University of Dhaka.

Roberta Righi trained as a practicing lawyer in two different law firms in Modena, and then in 2004 she formed her own law office. Her area of expertise is international commercial law with an emphasis on international contracts and European projects; she also devotes time to civil litigation and she assists several companies in Italy with day-to-day legal matters. She is currently collaborating with the Getty Law Group PLLC, a law firm based in Lexington, KY, United States.

Roberta assists CNA, a national association representing more than 670,000 small and medium enterprises in Italy. Roberta has taught several courses for CNA Interpreta about the 'contratto di rete', and has prepared articles and publication on that matter. From December 2009 to October 2011, she served as CNA Interpreta's team leader for the group of experts in charge of presenting to the European Commission the Study 'Accounting requirements for SMEs.' Roberta was the main speaker at the final workshop held in Brussels in October, 2011, at the European Commission.

Roberta has taught numerous international commercial law and international contracts courses. She is fluent in English and Italian and has a good comprehension of French and Spanish.

Maximiliano Escobar Saavedra is a lawyer admitted to the Chilean bar, and a Commercial Law Professor at University of Concepción.

He obtained his bachelor degree from University of Concepción in 2007 and in 2010 his Master's degree with a specialization in new technologies laws and e-commerce, from Universidad Pablo de Olavide, located in Sevilla, Spain. At the same university, in 2016 he completed his doctoral studies.

Dr Maximiliano is currently the Director of the Department of Private Law at University of Concepción, which encompasses the disciplines of Civil and Commercial Law. He is a Professor for both bachelor and master students, of the different subjects that commercial law encompasses, such as insolvency law, commercial contracts, corporate law, among others. Since 2010, Maximiliano is also commercial law arbitrator.

He is the author of several articles in the field of Commercial Law, published in different national and international journals.

Mauricio Inostroza Sáez is a Professor of Commercial Law at the University of Concepción, Chile. He obtained his Law degree from the University of Concepción in 2006, and was awarded the degrees of Master in Private Law (2011) and Ph.D. (2017) by the University Carlos III of Madrid.

Mauricio is a lawyer admitted to practice by the Supreme Court of Chile in 2007. He has practised Law in Chile in the field of Commercial Law. He has published several articles in Law reviews from Chile, Venezuela, Brazil and USA in the fields of bankruptcy, unfair competition and contract law. He has also carried out research into the same topics in UNIDROIT, at the University of Rome I 'La Sapienza' [Italy], and at the National Law Center for Inter-American Free Trade [USA], where he is currently a Commercial Law Consultant.

Francisco Satiro is a Professor of Business Law at São Paulo University (USP) Law School. He specialises in corporate finance law, capital markets regulation and insolvency law. Satiro holds a Law degree and a Doctorate in Business Law, both from USP Law School. He was visiting Professor at: Universidad Javeriana – Colombia, ITAM – Mexico, FDUP – Portugal, and Centre for Transnational Legal Studies in London – UK. From 2011 to 2015, Satiro was appointed by the Ministry of Economy as a member of the National Council of Appeals of the Financial System. He was appointed in 2016 by the Ministry of Economy to draft the amendment of Brazilian Insolvency Law. He has also been a Brazilian adviser before UNCITRAL Working Groups I (micro-, small- and medium-sized enterprises) and V (Insolvency Law) since 2012. Satiro is a founding member of Satiro Law Firm.

Gelanda Shkurtaj is an academic lawyer and public notary, living in Tirana (Albania). After having accomplished her first Masters' Degree in Biology at Tirana University in 1997, she followed her studies in Law at Genoa University (Italy). She worked as a Court Expert and Technical Adviser at the General Prosecutor's Office in Liguria Region (Italy) and simultaneously she obtained the second Master's Degree in Law in 2009. In 2011 she obtained an LL.M. in Taxation Law at Genoa University. In 2012 she kept the position of Senior Project Manager at Regione Abruzzo (acting as Managing Authority) of E.U. Funds (Instrument of Pre-accession) Cross Border 2007–2013 Program. She established her notary office on 2013 in Tirana, and the main field of her activity is domestic civil law in general and in particular the implementation of contracts related to commercial and fiscal law. Since the academic year 2012–13 she has been a Lecturer of Fiscal and Business Law at the New York University and Epoka University in Tirana. She also has a Ph.D. in Legal Anthropology (2018), issued by the Academy for Albanological Studies.

Stacey Steele is an Asian law and society specialist and leading commentator on insolvency law in Japan. She has an extensive track record of delivering research outcomes based on complex cross-jurisdictional research collaborations, and is the co-editor of books on legal education in Asia (2010), internationalising Japan (2014) and match-fixing in Australia, Korea and Japan (2017) resulting from chairing international conferences, seminars and workshops. Recent publications include peer-reviewed articles on regulation and resolution of disputes about insolvency practitioner remuneration in Australia, Singapore and the UK (*Insolvency Law Journal*, 2016; *Asian Journal of Comparative Law*, 2017), insolvency practitioner regulation in Japan (*Insolvency Law Review*, 2017), personal insolvency law reform in Australia and Japan (*QUT Law Review*, 2017), and trends in Chinese insolvency law (*American Journal of Comparative Law*, 2017). Assistant Professor Steele is Associate Director (Japan), Asian Law Centre, Melbourne Law School. She holds degrees from the University of Queensland (B.A. (Jap)), Monash University (M.A. (Jap)) and the University of Melbourne (LL.B. (Hons) and LL.M. (by thesis)).

Elizabeth Streten is a Lecturer at the Queensland University of Technology (QUT) who teaches in, inter alia, insolvency and restructuring law, corporate law, contract law, commercial remedies and civil procedure. She is a member of the Law Faculty's Commercial and Property Law Research Centre. Elizabeth holds a Bachelors' degrees and a Masters' degree from QUT and is in the final months of her Doctoral degree at QUT. In July 2009, Elizabeth was awarded an IEP Award of Excellence from the Australian Restructuring Insolvency and Turnaround Association (formerly IPAA).

Elizabeth comes from over a decade practicing as an Australian lawyer in commercial litigation and insolvency, including appearances across State and Federal Courts and the High Court of Australia. Her research considers government policy, regulation and industry change at the intersection of commercial law, insolvency law, technology and business.

Jarmo Tuomisto (1952) graduated as a Master of Laws 1973. He was trained on the bench 1976–77 and received his doctoral degree in 1988. Tuomisto has served as Professor of Civil Law at the University of Turku from 1998 till his retirement in 2016. Tuomisto's main research areas are security rights and insolvency law. Among his major studies are 'Saatavan panttaus' [Pledge of Receivables] (2015), 'Takaisinsaanti' [Recovery to the Bankrupt's Estate] (3rd edition 2012), 'Sopimus ja insolvenssi' [Contract and Insolvency] (2010), Yrityskiinnitys [Floating Charge] (2007), 'Tyyppipakosta aikaprioriteettiin' [From Numerus Clausus to the principle of time priority] (1993), 'Vuokranantaja ja vuokralaisen konkurssi [Lessor and the bankruptcy of a Lessor] (1991) and 'Omistuksenpidätys ja leasing' [Retention of Title and Leasing] (1988).

Marco Verdonk LL.M. is a Ph.D. candidate and lecturer at the University of Tilburg. He holds a Master's degree in Dutch private law from the University of Amsterdam.

Verdonk specialises in property law, insolvency law and procedural law. He teaches the courses Property Law, Insolvency Law and Procedural Law. His Ph.D. research is focused on divestment clauses in executory contracts and the theoretical framework for admissibility of this kind of stipulation in case of corporate insolvency.

Eduardo G. Wanderley is a partner in BMA – Barbosa Müssnich Aragão's insolvency and restructuring group, based in São Paulo, Brazil. As co-head of the practice, he acts in high-profile court-supervised insolvency proceedings, cross-border cases, workouts and distressed investment mandates. He holds a law degree from the Federal University of Rio Grande do Sul (UFRGS) and is a Master of law by the University of São Paulo and the University of Cambridge. Wanderley acted in the most relevant court-supervised cases since the enactment of the current Brazilian corporate insolvency regime (2005), such as Varig, Parmalat, Oi, OAS, OGX, OSX, Agrenco, Grupo REDE, Abengoa, Banco Santos, Independência, UTC, PDG and others. He is frequently ranked by specialized publications as a leading bankruptcy/ restructuring lawyer and one of the most prominent of his generation. Wanderley is a member of Turnaround Management Association, American Bankruptcy Institute and is actively involved in the debates about insolvency law reform in Brazil.

Bingdao Wang completed his Ph.D. at University of Leeds in 2018. His main research interests include corporate insolvency law, corporate law and contract law. Prior to beginning the Ph.D. program, Bingdao received a LL.M. in International Commercial Law from the University of Nottingham. Based on his LL.M. comparative study of UNCITRAL Model Law on cross-border insolvency and EC regulation on insolvency proceedings, Bingdao developed his doctoral research focusing on the development and reform of cross-border insolvency law in China and Hong Kong. Bingdao will start his position as lecturer in law at Coventry University in 2019.

Jessica J. Winters is a solo practitioner with 15 years of experience. Her practice focuses generally on business services and commercial litigation, with emphasis on small business development, employment law, class action litigation, appeals, and personal injury. Jessica has extensive federal and state court litigation experience in complex cases and class actions. She is also active in the labour and employment law section of the Kentucky Bar Association and lectures several times a year on employment related topics.

Jessica is active in community and legal organisations in her hometown of Lexington, Kentucky. She co-founded Lexington's annual street art festival, PRHBTN, and through this organisation has worked to bring more than 20 world-renowned artists to Lexington to create public art through the installation of large-scale murals. Community involvement and helping others through her legal work are her core values.

Camila Hoyuela Zattera is an attorney admitted to the Chilean bar, and a Commercial Law Lecturer at University of Concepción, Chile. Camila obtained her bachelor degree from University of Concepción in 2014, and holds an LL.M in Commercial Law, with specialisation in Maritime and Transport Law, at Erasmus Rotterdam University.

Camila has published several articles in Law Journals from Chile, Italy and Portugal in the fields of corporate law, maritime law, transport law and logistics.

Katja Zdolšek is a Slovenian lawyer with a degree from University of Ljubljana (2012) and LL.M. degree in Corporate and Commercial Law from the London School of Economics and Political Science, awarded with Distinction (2014).

Katja specialises in corporate and commercial law and the related EU legislation. Before qualifying as a Slovenian attorney at law (2019), she has worked in competition law in Brussels where she trained at the European Commission and an international law firm. Katja is currently practicing law as an attorney at a business law firm in Ljubljana.

1

A THEMATIC AND COMPARATIVE CRITIQUE

Jason Chuah

BACKGROUND TO THE RESEARCH PROJECT

This peer-reviewed and edited collection of chapters sets out to detail and analyse how the different national insolvency law systems treat the matter of executory contracts. When a business becomes insolvent, that does not necessarily bring an end to the contracts that business had previously entered into but are pending performance. While the subject matter is not new, more and more jurisdictions are having to continue to evolve and reform their legal responses to the subject matter in the light of the practical and conceptual difficulties a less than flexible approach throws up. There are no easy solutions, it would appear. **1.01**

Many systems of law provide for the right of the trustee in insolvency to assume or disclaim a pre-existing contract. That right is controversial because it creates an anomaly in that the trustee appears to have been imbued with the right to speculate on the rise and fall of the relevant market and make a decision on the contract depending on which the market is heading. That, is seen by some, as flying in the face of common commercial sensibilities. After all, most legal systems do not allow a seller (for example) to speculate at the buyer's expense when they are in possession of a binding agreement. **1.02**

On the other hand, policy makers are genuinely concerned that if such a right were not to exist, that would inevitably lead to much economic waste. **1.03**

Moreover, speculation may or may not always be a relevant factor – since the market price in question may be quite stable or there are other factors to assume or disclaim the contract.

1.04 The philosophy behind this project is that lessons could be learnt from both developing and developed countries, and from small and large countries. The aim is to identify the key supporters, the stakeholders and the pull-push factors driving the agenda for reform. There will also be an analysis of the theoretical underpinnings of how the different insolvency law systems treat executory contracts and, where appropriate, policy recommendations are suggested.

1.05 In this preambular chapter, we shall draw some general observations from the country reports and comment on some of the main challenges faced by the laws of the many nations under study. There are elements in our approach in this chapter which might loosely be classed within the functional method[1] often adopted in comparative law analysis. We draw from the evidence provided by the country reports to help ascertain the impact or effects of the legal rules on the treatment of executory contracts in insolvency. However, this chapter also engages in a rule-based comparative analysis in an attempt to locate and identify the different rules and their construction within their domestic contexts. The purpose of this conjoined approach is to provide practitioners and policy makers with both a cultural and legal perspective of the research.

1.06 The functional method, of course, is not without critics;[2] however for practitioners and policy makers, it remains a useful (albeit possibly narrow) method for looking at discrete aspects of good or poor practice. For a monograph which is intended to stimulate discussion amongst policy makers

1 There is of course a great deal of literature on the method: see Ralf Michaels, 'The Functional Method of Comparative Law', *The Oxford Handbook Of Comparitive Law* (OUP 2006) 339 who provided the following list. See, e.g., for the United States, John C. Reitz, 'How to do Comparative Law', (1998) 46 *AJCL* 617; Mathias Reimann, 'The Progress and Failure of Comparative Law in the Second Half of the Twentieth Century', (2003) 50 *AJCL* 671; for France, Marc Ancel, 'Utilité et méthodes de droit compare. Eléments d'introduction générale à l'étude comparative des droits', (1971) 23 RIDC 933; idem., 'Le problème de la comparabilité et la méthode fonctionnelle en droit comparé', *Festschrift für Imre Zajtay* (J.C.B. Mohr Tubingen 1982), 1; for England, Hugh Collins, 'Methods and Aims of Comparative Contract Law', (1991) 11 *OJLS* 396; Peter de Cruz, *Comparative Law in a Changing World* (2nd edn, Routledge-Cavendish 1999) 230; for Germany, Hein Kötz, 'Comparative Law in Germany Today', (1999) 51 RIDC 753; for Scandinavia, Michael Bogdan, *Comparative Law* (Springer 1994), 59–60; for a socialist perspective, Imre Szabó, 'Theoretical Questions of Comparative Law', in Imre Szabó and Zoltán Péteri (eds), *A Socialist Approach to Comparative Law* (1977), 9, 36–38; for rise and fall in Italy, Pier Giuseppe Monateri, 'Critique et différence: Le droit comparé en Italie', (1999) 51 RIDC 989.

2 See generally Ralf Michaels (ibid.).

and professionals, aspects which borrow from the functional method might be justifiable on the grounds of convenience, focus and clarity. That said, it should be emphasised that in this chapter dealing with comparative analysis we are not merely concerned with functions of the rules but also on legal argument, interpretation and policy considerations.

An important facet of this Introduction is that as the stress is on legal themes, the subject of executory contracts would be explored without making the fine, technical distinctions between administration and liquidation. The issue of executory contracts in either of these contexts has been very ably discussed in our national reports. **1.07**

PROJECT METHODOLOGY

The chapters are grouped somewhat loosely based on the legal family they belong to – namely, civil law systems, common law systems, and hybrid systems. The contributors are asked to pay close attention to the following themes in their chapters: **1.08**

Section 1

- Which hybrid and formal procedures are available under current legislation to a company in financial or economic distress?
- Which are the requirements for triggering those procedures? If 'insolvency' is one of these requirements, is this notion provided for by the law? Who can file for these procedures (e.g., debtor only, creditors only, both and/or third parties)? Who usually institutes them?
- Do companies rely on out-of-court proceedings (e.g., direct negotiations with creditors)? Have these procedures been regulated by the legislators?
- Are there any other remarkable features of the domestic legal regime, which are relevant to mention in the introduction?

Section 2

- For each of the procedures mentioned in the first section, describe the treatment of executory contracts provided by the law. When does *pacta sunt servanda* (contracts shall be kept) apply? When does the principle of *paritas creditorum* (equal treatment of and distribution among creditors) prevail?

Do special rules apply in the insolvency context? Are executory contracts deemed to be assumed or rejected? If statutory assumption or rejection are imposed by the law, what are the consequences for the parties?

Do rules change if the debtor is either the performing or the non performing party? Do rules change depending on the nature of the procedure (either reorganisation or liquidation)? Do special rules apply depending on the nature of the contract,[3] the counterparty (public or private), its duration, or its importance for the survival of the distressed business? Can contracts be partially assumed or rejected? If no special rules apply, which is the general treatment provided in the law?

- For each of the procedures mentioned in the first section, describe the statutory treatment in insolvency law of contractual remedies agreed by the parties in solvent times.

  Are termination and acceleration clauses, sometimes referred as *ipso facto* clauses, enforceable in your country? To which extent (e.g., case-law and definition of *ipso facto* clause)? Is the same solution adopted with reference to all the procedures mentioned in the first section?

  Are other clauses with similar effects[4] valid and enforceable under current legislation? What is the courts' attitude towards these clauses?
- Are there any other remarkable features of the domestic legal regime, which are relevant to mention in this section?

Section 3

The project team was asked to consider:

- Any major reforms since the year 2000?[5]
- What is the impact of these reform (if any) on the treatment of executory contracts? Which was the position of the government, how it changed throughout the reform debate and/or years, what contributed to those changes (e.g., economic crisis, EU regulations, etc.)?
- Are new proposals of reform of the existing insolvency framework being explored?

---

3 Personal; Sale, hire-purchase and finance lease; Utilities; Labour; Pension; Financial.

4 Close-out nettings; Flip clauses; Conditional rights; Penalty Provisions.

5 Before the enactment of the Council Regulation (EC) 1346/2000 on insolvency proceedings [2000] OJ L 160 but shortly after the enactment of the UNCITRAL Model Law on Cross-Border Insolvency 1997.

In this chapter, the editor has tried to avoid making fine distinctions between liquidators, administrators, insolvency practitioners, monitors, official receivers, office holders, etc. Fine distinctions would not serve our general comparative law purposes given that different jurisdictions will have different 'officers' to deal with insolvent or virtually insolvent companies. Our object is to assess in a broad brush manner the different approaches in law and policy to how executory contracts are treated in cases of 'insolvency'. So too the term 'insolvency' would not be deeply discoursed in this text. 1.09

Prefatory observations

An immediate general observation might be made that in established common law systems, there is a good deal of disputations over what some might term the *minutiae* of the principles. In the US for example case-law seems to be divided between the right approach or test to identify what constitutes executory contracts in insolvency. Some courts prefer the so-called material breach test, first propounded by Professor Countryman[6] while others opt for the functional test. In the US prior to these two tests, commentators have tried to reason that executory contracts are property of the estate and therefore could simply be dealt with as the trustee sees fit – disclaim or assume. However, such an explanation is defective in that there are knock-on effects which could not be ignored. After all, the corporate entity in insolvency must pay for the rights it gives away or conversely, pay damages for rejecting or abandoning the contracts. 1.10

The Countryman test defines an executory contract as an agreement where 'the obligations of both the bankruptcy and the other party are so far unperformed that the failure of either to complete performance would constitute a material breach excusing performance of the other'. On the other hand, the functional test which works 'backward from an examination of the purposes to be accomplished by rejection, and if they have already been accomplished then the contract cannot be executory'.[7] 1.11

However, although there is some fretting over the definition of executory contracts, the approach in England is less conceptually oriented when contrasted against the US context. The UK Insolvency Act 1986 allows the trustee to disclaim an onerous property without needing judicial sanction.[8] 1.12

6 V. Countryman, 'Executory License Agreements in Bankruptcy', 57 *Minn. L. Rev.* 439, 460 (1973).

7 *In re Magness*, 972 F.2d 689, 693 (6th Cir. 1992); see too Jay Lawrence Westbrook, 'A Functional Analysis of Executory Contracts', (1989) 74 *Minn. L. Rev.* 227.

8 Insolvency Act 1986, s 178.

The emphasis is on the liquidator's judgment as to what is onerous, and not on any lexical discourse about the term 'executory'.

1.13 Some civil law systems in Europe tend to have specific rules relating to different types of 'executory contracts' – in Italy, The Netherlands, Finland and Spain, to name a few, there are special rules for leases, employment, real property and continuous contracts etc. where a generic definition or description of what is executory would not be sufficient. There are countries, like Finland, where a distinction is also made between divisible obligations and indivisible obligations.

1.14 In contrast, countries like Slovenia actually make an explicit definition of the term 'executory contract' in their insolvency law – the Slovenian Insolvency Act expressly defines a mutually unfulfilled bilateral contract (*executory contract*) as a bilateral contract which has been concluded prior to the initiation of insolvency proceedings, and whereby, prior to the initiation of insolvency proceedings: (i) neither the insolvent debtor nor the other party to the contract have performed their obligation on the basis of the contract, or (ii) neither of the parties has fully performed such obligations.[9] Swiss law also defines executory contracts but is more general – the Insolvency Law is only concerned with '*synallagmatic contracts which had not or had only partially been fulfilled at the time of the opening of the bankruptcy*'. By means of elimination, other forms of contractual obligations, such as a unilateral promise to provide services or money, would be excluded from the scope of 'executory contracts'. Other jurisdictions adopt the meaning of the term as provided for by their civil commercial law. In Greece for example the insolvency law simply adopts the meaning as stated in the Greek Civil Code which defines executory contracts as those that impose future rights and obligations for both contractual parties. Cyprus adopts a similar approach but places some emphasis on the failure to perform wholly the contract. Although reference is usually made in these systems to general civil law, the approach is quite pragmatic and courts do not engage in a theoretical questioning of whether a particular contractual relationship was executory or not. That matter of fact approach is also adopted in countries such as Germany, Denmark, Bulgaria, Turkey and Albania. Yet other jurisdictions do pay much attention to the conceptual definition of 'executory contracts'. In France, for instance, although there is no jurisprudence taking the sort of conceptual definitions applied by the US courts, French case law and academic commentaries suggest that it is important to identify first the performance or obligation which is characteristic of the contract. Then it follows that if the relevant characteristic obligation of a

9 See Chapter 20.

contract has already been performed before the insolvency procedure is opened, the contract would not be considered to be executory.[10] This approach appears closer to the American material breach test than the functional test, but cannot be said to be similar. The French approach starts with the construction of the agreement to ascertain the obligation on which the entirety contract sits.

In Latin America, the picture too is not uniform. Although most jurisdictions have some prescribed rules dealing with executory contracts, there is often a pragmatic acceptance as to what the term 'executory contract' means. For instance, the Panamanian legal system simply assumes that these are contracts which have not yet been performed and older legislation renders them unenforceable as soon as insolvency occurs.[11] Some other legal systems have developed a jurisprudence based on civil commercial law as to the description (not necessarily a legal definition) for the term. In Chile, for example, insolvency law practitioners and commentators take the view that executory contracts can include promises to contract but seem to exclude contracts where one party had completed performance whilst the other had not.[12] In Chile, an executory contract will lead to different implications depending on whether the insolvency procedure in question is an action for reorganisation or liquidation. Likewise, in Argentina, there are specific rules for specific types of executed and executory contractual obligations in insolvency. Broadly speaking, contracts might be classified into three groups: (a) contracts that are terminated; (b) contracts that are continuated or continuing contracts; and (c) contracts which are suspended, pending a determination as to whether they will be resolved or continued through their 'assumption' by the liquidator. Category (c) includes contracts where either party's obligations have not been fully performed.[13] Brazilian law takes a similar line whereby executory contracts can include those where neither party has fully performed their contractual obligations. **1.15**

The picture is similar in Asia – the PRC, while not expressly defining executory contracts, in providing for the liquidator's powers makes a distinction between those contracts with an obligation or part thereof to be performed by the insolvent entity and those to be performed by the other party. That appears also to be the approach taken by the common law based jurisdictions under study in this project such as Singapore, Bangladesh, India, New Zealand and Australia. These countries do not provide any explicit and **1.16**

10 See Chapter 12.
11 See Chapter 18, p 360.
12 See Chapter 7, pp 140–141.
13 See Chapter 3 generally.

detailed definition of 'executory contract', content simply with the notion of contracts with unperformed or incomplete obligations. There is no direct engagement with theory, like the US courts have been concerned with.

1.17 This leads us to the question as to whether having a definition of 'executory contract' in the context of insolvency is useful. At one level the approach should largely be about what to do with contracts calling for future performance and an overly technical characterisation of an 'executory contract' would only serve to defeat the object of the law. Legalism perhaps is not the best approach to adopt when so much of whether a future obligation should or should not be disclaimed is already a matter of business judgment.

1.18 In this context it is worth reflecting on the notion of 'adversarial legalism'; some scholars have argued that 'adversarial legalism' has in modern legal culture and history emerged as a distinctive American legal style.[14] In the context of defining the executory contract for the purposes of dealing with the liquidator's power to disclaim onerous contracts, we might be able to suggest that given that in the US, such disclaimers may routinely be challenged judicially, a particularly legalistic style which emphasises detailed, prescriptive rules, substantial transparency in legal tests and formulated principles has developed. It is undeniable in the US and parts of the common law world, normative language (such as 'you can disclaim an onerous executory contract') has to some appreciable degree been coloured now by conditionalities typified by definitions.

LIMITS ON ASSUMPTION OR DISCLAIMING OF EXECUTORY OBLIGATIONS

1.19 It is not proposed to go into depth on the subject here, given the very full explanations provided for in our country reports. The purpose here is to delineate the circumstances under which the different legal systems control the assumption or disclaiming of the executory contract following insolvency.

1.20 It might be said the legal right to assume or disclaim executory obligations is to some extent shaped by the modern tenet held in both common law and civil law countries that an insolvency event does not bring an end to the contractual relationships of the insolvent. That said, as regards assumption of the contract, in the common law tradition, it is conceivable though not commonplace that

14 See generally Robert A. Kagan, *Adversarial Legalism: The American Way of Law* (Harvard University Press 2001).

an insolvency event might be construed as an anticipatory breach which could then bring an end to the contract.[15]

On the whole the right to assume or disclaim an executory contract is a matter of private law ensuring that the liquidator or office holder has the degree of control to reorganise the company. In the case of disclaiming, it is quite clear that many jurisdictions permit the office holder to decide whether to disclaim an onerous contract based on their business judgment exercised in good faith. Judicial interference is limited as is seen quite plainly in the US, Singapore, Australia, Canada, the UK, Denmark, Turkey, Germany, France, Chile and others. However, in certain contracts, where there are important public interests at stake, the law of the land may restrict that right to assume or disclaim the executory contract. South Africa is an excellent case in point. Its political history has been such that land transfer and ownership have been highly sensitive. Its Constitutional Law hence makes it absolute that the office holder must complete the transfer of land purchased and being paid for by instalments – failure to do so would be to cause a serious injustice on those who are poor and vulnerable. Disclaiming the contract is out of the question. **1.21**

There may be less weighty reasons for curbing the right to assume or disclaim contracts. In Japan, for example, our country report highlights a Supreme Court decision where unfairness was held to be a valid reason to deny the office holder from disclaiming a contract. There, a company had paid a substantial corporate membership fee to a golf club which would be refunded in ten years' time if their membership was cancelled. The company went into liquidation and the office holder purported to disclaim all contracts with the golf club and sought a refund of the fee. The court denied the company's claim because to do so would be to cause unfair consequences on the counterparty. **1.22**

Judicial supervision in the reorganization efforts

Most legal systems, as we see, allow a good measure of discretion and business judgment for the office holder to decide whether it is in the creditors' best interest to assume or disclaim an executory contractual obligation. This editor is interested in examining and comparing the role of judicial supervision in this regard. **1.23**

The subject of judicial supervision of course is controversial. On the one hand, it is arguable that the decision to assume or disclaim is a matter of good **1.24**

15 See below.

business judgment and given the exigency of time, that discretion of the debtor should not be interfered with too easily. On the other hand, in a good number of jurisdictions the policy debate has shifted away from simply about the decision to protect creditor interest but also about the justiciability of such a decision. In matters relating to fairness and justice, it is thus contended that the discretion of the liquidator should be subject to a degree of judicial supervision. There is probably no right answer here, save the platitude that the optimal position is somewhere between the two poles.

1.25 The intention here is therefore not to look for that utopian point but simply to look at how judicial supervision should be exercised and on what grounds.

1.26 First of all, judicial supervision may actually be sought by the debtor in relation to executory contracts. In the case of Argentina, for example, in both pre-packaged reorganisation and voluntary reorganisation schemes, while the debtor is free to renegotiate the terms of the executory contract, any proposed modification must be submitted to the court for approval.[16] In the latter, (called '*Concurso Preventivo*'), differing levels of judicial supervision are applied depending on when the decision to modify/assume the contract is made. Where the decision is made by the office holder before the first 30 days since the opening of the *Concurso Preventivo*, the debtor may choose to fulfil the contract with pending reciprocal obligations. To do this, they must seek the court's approval and authorisation. The court is required to consider properly the opinion of liquidator which should be based on technical business judgment and be impartial. The court's role is thus to assess whether the decision appears to be impartial and not tempered by bad faith or manifest error of judgment. In the case where 30 days have elapsed, the third party may terminate the contract promptly or call for performance or compliance. In the first, no judicial supervision is needed. The creditor only needs to notify the debtor and trustee. In the second situation, prior judicial authorisation is required. Failure to secure judicial approval will result in the termination of the contract.[17] Naturally the 30-day threshold is a legislative compromise. However that shows that the law is not insensitive to the constraints of time and practical expediency. For clarity and certainty, if the creditor third party had taken a period of time to decide, the courts should necessarily be involved in ensuring that that decision is not unfair or impractical, and does not have too extensive a negative impact on other relationships. With the various time limits and procedural requirements, the Argentine system is one which implicitly takes the view that the lack of clarity can lead to poor, ineffectual

16 See Insolvency Act 1995, ss 71 and 75.

17 Civil and Commercial Code 2014, s 353.

judicial supervision which in turn results in poor negative restructuring or reorganisation outcomes.

It is trite to say too that a laboriously slow judicial process despite the presence of sound rules could well lead to the same negative outcomes. Indeed, our Bangladesh report highlights that proposition quite amply; although the legal rules are actually reasonably well developed having been transplanted from other parts of the common law world, the under-resourced judicial and legal system makes the judicial supervision process quite ineffectual. **1.27**

Judicial supervision might also be found not when the office holder discharges their functions, but *at an earlier point* – the time when they are appointed. In the PRC, for example, under the Enterprise Bankruptcy Act, the appointment of an administrator needs to be approved by the court. That appointment is not always a matter-of-course exercise. An indepth level of evaluation of the competencies and qualifications of the administrator is made when the official list of administrators is drawn up by a seven person special committee of the Supreme People's Court.[18] The court will decide on whether a particular administrator is appropriate for the case in question. Hence, where the case concerns wide local concerns, the court would appoint an administrator with good local experience and reputation. On the other hand, where the case concerns a large commercial entity with extensive reach, the court would look to appointing a non-local entity (usually a firm) as the administrator.[19] The administrator then assumes virtually all control over the debtor and their appointment might thus be said to reflect the court's approval of their power. **1.28**

That matter is exacerbated by the fact that under the 2006 Enterprise Bankruptcy Law, when the debtor (as against the creditor) files for bankruptcy, unlike many legal systems where the courts would merely take judicial notice of the filing, the PRC court has wide discretion not to accept the application on the basis that there is no case of bankruptcy.[20] **1.29**

18 The SPC's Regulations on Appointment of Administrators in Enterprise Bankruptcy Cases (promulgated by the SPC, effective June 1, 2007), arts 10 and 11.

19 Note The SPC Regulations on Appointment of Administrators et. al. (ibid.), art 15; also Yujia Jiang, 'The Curious Case of Inactive Bankruptcy Practice in China: A Comparative Study of U.S. and Chinese Bankruptcy Law' (2014) 34 *Nw. J. Int'l L. & Bus.* 559, 573.

20 See the PRC Enterprise Bankruptcy Law arts 2 and 7; also Lijie Qi, 'The Corporate Reorganization Regime Under China's New Enterprise Bankruptcy Law', (2008) 17 *Int'l Insolvency Rev.* 13, 15–17.

1.30 Indeed, scholarship on PRC bankruptcy law has argued that the extensive judicial discretion and intervention of government policies make the system less efficient than its counterparts elsewhere, such as in the US, Europe and the UK.[21]

1.31 In summary, it might be reasoned the role of judicial supervision while important as regards how executory contracts are to be treated in administration or liquidation, there is divergence in the policy rationale to how judicial supervision should be exercised and managed.

Ipso facto stipulations

1.32 It is widely known that *ipso facto* clauses are not treated uniformly between the different legal systems and this is properly borne out by the country reports. Some countries have had a fully aired debate about the matter of enforceability of such clauses; other jurisdictions have not tackled the matter from a policy perspective and have relied largely on general principles of law to deal with the issue.

1.33 Take Singapore, for example, lengthy debates at various policy and professional levels took place – the usual concerns were raised about whether *ipso facto* clauses which accelerate the termination of the contract would produce a deleterious effect on restructuring prospects. The discussion went on to explore whether the right provided for by these clauses should be restricted and be judicially controlled so that the management powers of the liquidator should not be unduly interfered with by the creditor who is the beneficiary of the *ipso facto* clause. There also appears to be some evidence, according to the Singapore report, that one reason why a good number of rescue proceedings fail in Singapore was because the company management refuses to engage in formal proceedings until the very last minute. Thus, if *ipso facto* clauses are unenforceable, that could perhaps induce the distressed company into starting discussions about rescue a little earlier on. However, after weighing up the pros and cons, the Singapore Government decided not to change the status quo – namely, that which mirrors the English common law position, that is to say, *ipso facto* clauses will remain valid. The main argument for keeping the status quo was that as a global financial and commercial hub, it would be insensible for Singapore as a small state to go its own way and adopt a different approach to that which has held sway in jurisdictions that have derived their laws from the English common law.

---

21 See generally Yujia Jiang, *supra* n. 19.

On the other hand, Canada and Australia have taken the confident step to depart from the traditional orthodoxy that *ipso facto* clauses, as freely entered into contractual clauses, are enforceable subject to a careful application of the legal rules on construction of contracts. Like Singapore, debates were had as to the impact, negative or otherwise, of *ipso facto* clauses. Unlike Singapore, Australia and Canada decided to legislate against *ipso facto* clauses – Canada took the step in 2009 whilst Australia, more recently in 2016/17. The Canadian experience is a little less of a stark change than the Australian in that the Canadian courts had (in the context of large insolvencies[22]) been prepared to restrict the application of *ipso facto* clauses even before the law reforms in 2009. However, the matter is properly put to rest – the new law and the Australian legislation both expressly render unenforceable those *ipso facto* clauses which allow for the termination of contracts solely on the basis of an insolvency event if a business comes under the control of an administrator or receiver or if the company is utilising draft proposed safe harbour[23] arrangements.[24] In Australia, the new law also allows 'suppliers' to apply to the court for an order to terminate the contract in circumstances of 'undue hardship'.[25] **1.34**

It is well and good for certain common law jurisdictions like Canada and Australia to take this approach – however, such reforms are themselves not without challenges, doctrinally speaking. Our Singapore report highlighted how even if *ipso facto* clauses are banned, creditors may argue that the insolvency event nevertheless constitutes an anticipatory breach of the contract. The common law jurisprudence on anticipatory breach is at best uncertain, and at worst, conflicting.[26] Thus, for a ban to work effectively, the law should ideally also remove or limit the right to claim anticipatory breach – however, the limiting of a common law general principle of contract law is not something which common law systems are generally quick to do. Having the security blanket of the status quo offered by the traditional English common law system is not necessarily a negative. Noting the case of Bangladesh, it is clear that the corporate insolvency law system in Bangladesh is very much in its infancy and having its roots in the English common law tradition means that there should not at least be a lacuna should challenges around *ipso facto* clauses surface. **1.35**

---

22 Those falling within the scope of the Companies' Creditors Arrangement Act 1985.

23 It should be noted that unlike the US Chapter 11 scheme, the Australian Safe Harbour is not a Court-controlled process. As such, there is no scope for cramming down dissenting creditors or granting super-priority status for fresh debt.

24 Australian Government Productivity Commission (n150), 32–33, 360–365.

25 Ibid.

26 As the Singapore case of *STX Mumbai* [2015] SGCA 35 demonstrates.

1.36 The Australian response however is understandable. The events leading up to the reform were significant. As is pointed out by our Australian report, the fallout from the collapse of One.tel primarily because their suppliers, Telstra and Optus, promptly exercised their rights under their *ipso facto* clauses and that quite peremptorily brought down the company in hours. Reform driven by real and significant events is of course understandable; however, it is also important to beware of any knee jerk response.

1.37 In jurisdictions where there is no specific provision for *ipso facto* clauses, one should not conclude too quickly that there is a vacuum in the law. Such a provision or at least, the utility or use of such a device may actually be dealt with by general principles. However, that reliance on general principles to resolve disputes and controversies is sometimes tempered by regard to the controversial nature of *ipso facto* clauses globally.

1.38 Take the PRC, for example, *ipso facto* clauses are not specifically recognised or unrecognised in law. Article 93 para 2 of the PRC Contract Law permits parties to agree to the conditions under which either party may bring an end to the contract. It is immediately obvious that although article 93 does not explicitly refer to *ipso facto* clauses, it could be extended to cover such clauses. There are also procedural constraints to the invoking of such a right as we see in our PRC report. Proper notice of the condition being met must be given by the person seeking to terminate the contract.[27] Moreover, the respondent may challenge the legitimacy of the purported termination in court or arbitration. In short although technically speaking such clauses do not run foul of the law, in adjudicating their legitimacy the courts would be keen to ensure that workers' rights are properly protected[28] and that the general rationale of the Enterprise Bankruptcy Law to confer sufficient discretion and management control on the administrator should not be defeated.[29] It is quite clear from the various commentaries on the subject that the controversy surrounding *ipso facto* clauses has also surfaced in the PRC. Consequently, no PRC court or arbitration will ignore the potency of such clauses in restricting the administrator's powers to continue with the contractual relationships in the commercial interest of the company and the creditors.

1.39 Noting that the PRC's insolvency system was only recently reformed in 2006 and despite the fact that commentators in the PRC have clearly and early on picked up on the problem of executory contracts and *ipso facto* clauses, one

---

27 See Contract Law of The People's Republic of China 1999, art 96.

28 See p 161.

29 See p 167.

might be critical that there is no specific treatment of the subject in the law reform. However to argue that would be perhaps unfair.

As is obvious in the case of Australia and Singapore, the matter is not resolved 1.40 – not only are there far too many uncertainties about the impact of an outright ban, problems too abound if such clauses are expressly recognised and enforced. Perhaps the matter, as far as some countries are concerned, is best left untreated at present while there is yet global consensus as to the optimal solution. That seems to be the case with countries like the PRC that have introduced reform to insolvency law in recent times such as Turkey, Croatia, Russia, Lithuania etc. In the case of Russia, there is little provision for even executory contracts more generally.

It might also be suggested that despite the lack of direct legal treatment on the 1.41 subject of *ipso facto* clauses in these countries, because of the lacuna regard may be had to public policy. In Lithuania, for example, our report tells us that *ipso facto* clauses are not banned and their enforcement has not, from available evidence, led to any unjust economic difficulties for all concerned. However, as is common with many jurisdictions the validity of the clause could ultimately be tested against the meter bar of public policy. The question is thus whether it might be argued that in a case like One.tel in Australia which led to the loss of several thousand jobs and many contracts being entirely demolished, the exercise of *ipso facto* rights might be ruled to be illegitimate under public policy considerations. From an English law standpoint, the reliance on public policy considerations in a matter which is best legislated by Parliament would clearly not be encouraged.

There is also, in some of those countries without an explicit framework for *ipso* 1.42 *facto* clauses, acknowledgement that such clauses are commonplace and would thus be permitted at least in practice, if not expressly in law. In Turkish law, for example, *ipso facto* clauses are generally acknowledged and applied in practice but the law is silent on their enforceability. Insolvency practitioners or liquidators will, guided by convention or practice, not law, approach creditors with a view to resolving potential disputes over the exercise of *ipso facto* clauses.[30] That does not however mean that there is no judicial intervention. In exceptional cases where the invoking of the *ipso facto* clause would conflict with a judicially sanctioned scheme of arrangement, the court would restrict its application by setting appropriate conditions.

30 See footnote 9 of Chapter 24 (infra).

1.43 Countries which have expressly restricted or prohibited the use of *ipso facto* clauses include the US, France, Greece, Denmark, Germany, the UAE, Canada, Australia, Austria, Spain to name a few. There are a few observations to be had. First, although in most of these countries the rationale is for the preservation of the company so as to encourage rescue, the scope of the proscription differs from jurisdiction to jurisdiction. Some countries like Austria link the prohibition on *ipso facto* clauses to an automatic stay or suspension of contracts. Others like Spain do not enforce the *ipso facto* clause but presume that the contracts shall continue to be performed until an express application is made by the liquidator or administrator to terminate an economically onerous relationship. The other party does not have the right to terminate the contract. Secondly, most of these countries provide for exceptions to the general proscription. These exceptions may lie in contractual relationships where performance is virtually uneconomic and impacts on security interests (such as close-out netting, and other financial contracts), or impinges on personal liberties (such as employment contracts, and contracts of a personal services), or is impossible (such as contracts for derivatives). Thirdly, the scope of the ban on *ipso facto* clauses is not always fully formed given that in a number of countries, the prohibition had stemmed from recent reforms. There is little clarity as to the general principles which would be taken to bear on any decision as to the scope and interpretation of the prohibition and its exceptions.

Assignment of executory contracts

1.44 A related matter is how and to what extent assignment of the executory contract to a third party should be factored in the law relating to executory contracts in insolvency. From our country reports, it is clear that not all countries have special rules dealing with assignment of executory contracts. Assignment of executory obligations has an important role alongside the provision for assumption of contracts in insolvency. It can assist in the further attempts at reorganising the corporate landscape. Where the contract is assigned (in some jurisdictions following the assumption of the contract by the liquidator), the corporate debtor might be able to avoid its contractual obligations since the performance would thence be taken over by the assignee whilst at the same time, prevent the original claimant from pursuing the legal claim against them. In the reorganisation process, it is not unforeseeable that an assignment will follow the sale of the debtor company's assets.

1.45 Often the matter is left to general law – after all, an assignment of a debt is not merely a matter of interest in insolvency law. We see this position in a number of common law countries. In the USA for example while the Bankruptcy

Code provides for the circumstances when an assignment of an executory contract would be permitted, it does not set out defining the meaning of assignment. That latter is largely a matter for general civil law of obligations. It is difficult to generalise about civil law jurisdictions – in the case of Denmark, for example, the matter of assignment of executory contracts is given extensive legislative coverage.

In the interest of the collective creditors the Danish law therefore grants the right for the debtor-in-possession to assign the continued executory contract to the buyer of the business without consent from the contracting party.[31] The right to assign can only be exercised as part of a transfer in the ownership of the business and not in a one-off asset sale. This all-or-nothing approach might be somewhat restrictive but one can understand the safeguarding and practical reasons for the constraint. After all, as the law makes explicit any such endeavour is to be for the collective interest of the creditors. The other practical constraint is that some contracts simply could not be transferred because of their distinctive, specific nature, i.e., if the contract can only be fully performed by the original contracting party. On the whole a transfer or assignment can be done without consent (save in those where by their legal nature, the contracts could not be performed by another party without cooperation and consent from the original contracting party). **1.46**

On the other hand, Russia – an assignment is permitted but its control seems very much to be a matter of judicial discretion. It appears to this editor that much of insolvency litigation in Russia is guided by legal rules which are often imprecise allowing for practical and policy considerations to be taken into account when judicial decisions are made. That seems to be the case as regards executory contracts and the matter of assignment of contracts. There is a significant degree of expectation that any scheme should pass the good faith test.[32] That is a test in the general civil law, and not some insolvency law notion. On that basis, it might be suggested that in civil law jurisdictions, at least in theory, regard may be had to notions of transparency, honesty, and loyalty to the contractual relationships. The latter is often equated also with ensuring an equilibrium in the contractual relationship or discouraging opportunism.[33] **1.47**

31 Danish Bankruptcy Act , s 14 c (2).

32 The Civil Code of Russian Federation, art 1.

33 See Saul Litvinoff, 'Good Faith' (1996) 71 *Tulane Law Review* 654, 675; Simon Whittaker and Reinhard Zimmerman, 'Good Faith', in Reinhard Zimmermann and Simon Whittaker (eds), *European Contract Law: Surveying the Legal Landscape* (CUP 2000), 7–62; Martijn W. Hesselink, 'The Concept of Good Faith', in Arthur S. Hartkamp, Martijn W. Hesselink et al. (eds), *Towards a European Civil Code-Fourth Revised and Expanded Edition*, (Kluwer Law International 2010), 619–49.

1.48 The practical difficulty is that in urgent times when a distressed company needs to be reorganised, dealing with the question of validity of the assignment after the event is usually self-defeating. A more efficient way is for the assignment to be made subject to prior judicial approval. It is however not often clear in some legal systems whether prior approval is actually required. Where permitted, it might be useful for the office holder to seek judicial approval for the purported assignment.

1.49 Practicalities undoubtedly play an important role in positing the role of assignment in a corporate reorganisation exercise. In the case of the PRC, where the law is not very explicit about the treatment of executory contracts, assignment of the contracts to third parties (subject to the governance of the general principle of good faith and Government policy) might justifiably be seen as a practical means to avoid having to litigate the niceties of executory contracts and attendant contractual stipulations such as *ipso facto* clauses. The advantage with assignment as a device to help with the reorganisation exercise is that assignment is usually properly provided for by general contract law and no change to any insolvency law is needed.

1.50 In common law countries, there is, as to be expected, varying degrees of prescription as to the scope of the power of assignment. What seems obvious is that there is due recognition of the role of assignment in the reorganisation of the distressed company. However most such assignments will require judicial supervision or approval. In Canada, for example, the law is expressed in these terms: the court 'may make an order assigning the rights and obligations of a bankrupt under the agreement to any person who is specified by the court and agrees to the assignment'.[34] Judicial approval in the Canadian context is dependent on various factors, including whether the proposed assignment is approved by the monitor, whether the assignee would be able to perform the contractual obligations and whether it was appropriate to assign the rights and obligations to that person. There is much scope thus for judicial discretion – but that is discretion guided by more general principles of creditor protection, asset protection and perhaps wider policy considerations. That said, the last is not explicitly expressed by court decisions or the legislation itself but from the tenor of the language of the law (the use of the word 'appropriate') the legislative intent is clearly not to be over restrictive as to what factors would be considered in giving approval for the assignment. Judicial

34 Bankruptcy and Insolvency Act 1985, s 84 (1). See too Companies' Creditors Arrangement Act 1985, s 11(3) where court approval for assignments in large scale insolvencies is also required.

approval however may not be required in all common law countries; however there may be grounds to challenge the assignment on equitable grounds.[35]

Both common law and civil law countries tend generally to have restrictions on what contracts could be assigned. The subject is amply discussed in our country reports. However, in the interest of completeness, the topic of anti-assignment clauses merits examination. **1.51**

At one level anti-assignment clauses might conceivably be treated as an equivalent to *ipso facto* clauses and they can certainly have a significant impact on the corporate reorganisation plans. That is especially so if the clause prevents the assignment not only of rights but also debts. Distressed companies could find it near impossible to seek receivable financing under those circumstances. In a UK context, a recent law was enacted to ban clauses which seek to prevent the assignment of receivables.[36] That law does not ban anti-assignment clauses generally, only those clauses impacting on receivables.[37] In gross, under the common law such clauses are valid. **1.52**

In the USA, 11 United States Code § 365 provides for the power of the office holder to assign the executory contract to a third party. The legal position is also that any clauses preventing the assignment would usually not be enforced. There are exceptions to the general rule. One exception arises in contracts that are not assignable to third parties *under applicable law* and the party does not consent to such assumption or assignment. There is much literature and case **1.53**

---

35 See e.g, England and Wales Insolvency Act 1986, para 74, Sch. B1 in the case of a company administrator's decision which unfairly prejudices one or a group of creditors. That said, without proper judicial guidance it is difficult to say what the scope and limits of judicial control might be.

36 Section 1 of the Small Business, Enterprise and Employment Act 2015 states:

> '(1) The appropriate authority may by regulations make provision for the purpose of securing that any non-assignment of receivables term of a relevant contract—
> (a) has no effect;
> (b) has no effect in relation to persons of a prescribed description;
> (c) has effect in relation to persons of a prescribed description only for such purposes as may be prescribed.
> (2) A 'non-assignment of receivables term' of a contract is a term which prohibits or imposes a condition, or other restriction, on the assignment (or, in Scotland, assignation) by a party to the contract of the right to be paid any amount under the contract or any other contract between the parties.
> (3) A contract is a relevant contract if—
> (a) it is a contract for goods, services or intangible assets (including intellectual property) which is not an excluded financial services contract, and
> (b) at least one of the parties has entered into it in connection with the carrying on of a business.'

37 For an account of the reasons for and against the legislative change, see Louise Gullifer, 'Should Clauses Prohibiting Assignment Be Overridden by Statute' (2015) 4 *Penn St. JL & Int'l Aff.* 47. See also Akseli Orkun, 'Contractual Prohibitions on Assignment of Receivables: an English and UN Perspective.', (2009) 7 *Journal of Business Law* 650.

law as to the meaning and scope of 'applicable law'.[38] It suffices to say that despite inconsistent judicial practice, there is inclination to construe 'applicable law' narrowly so as not to defeat the assignment of executory contracts. The US courts also make a distinction between what is non-assignable and what is non-delegable.[39] Pulley writes, 'Ostensibly, the rationale for distinguishing non-delegable, or personal service, contracts from other contracts is that these laws generally give the party receiving or rendering performance the option to refuse an alternate performer, rather than making the refusal automatic.'[40]

1.54 At this juncture it might be useful to reproduce the relevant USC provision, s 365c:

> the trustee may not assume or assign any executory contract or unexpired lease of the debtor, whether or not such contract or lease prohibits or restricts assignment of rights or delegation of duties, if—
>
> (1) (A) applicable law excuses a party, other than the debtor, to such contract or lease from accepting performance from or rendering performance to an entity other than the debtor or the debtor in possession, whether or not such contract or lease prohibits or restricts assignment of rights or delegation of duties; and
>
> (B) such party does not consent to such assumption or assignment …

1.55 In the US, there is also the vexed issue as to whether the 'applicable law' in question means that where such a law exists, not only the assignment but also the assumption of the executory contract is made impossible. Naturally the matter is largely a question of the interpretation of the US statute in question. From a functional comparative analysis, it suffices to observe that to interpret the law as extending to both assignment and assumption, from a policy standpoint, would be to place non-debtors on a stronger footing than debtors. Although that per se is not objectionable (in that the non-debtor had not asked to be made a party to the proceedings in the first place), favouring the non-debtor over debtors could well disturb the rationale which is intended to support the debtor in their reorganisation plans.[41] It would seem to permit a creditor, at will, to pull out of the contract which, under normal circumstances, had been properly assumed on the basis of a technical ban. Thus, in a majority

---

38 See generally the literature reviewed in Theresa R. Pulley, 'Limitations on Assumption and Assignment of Executory Contracts by Applicable Law', (2001) 31 *New Mexico L. Rev.* 299.

39 'At [US] common law, many courts interpreted "applicable law" under section [365](c)(1) to apply only to non-delegable, personal service contracts. Thus, even if a law existed that prohibited assignment, that law might not be sufficient to prohibit assumption and assignment under section (c)(1).' Pulley (ibid.) at p 309.

40 Ibid.

41 Ibid., at 314.

of decisions in the US, the view is that unless assignment is actually contemplated, assumption of the contract would not be prevented. That said, such a constraint does not seem to have surfaced in other jurisdictions.

In Nordic and Baltic states, there is an influential academic commentary[42] calling on the recognition of the right of the insolvent company to assign the executory contracts but subject to certain limitations. These limitations might be said to reflect an emerging consensus that such measures can assist in the reorganisation efforts of the company but should be practicable and be based on good faith. The *Nordic-Baltic Recommendations on Insolvency Law*,[43] as the commentary is titled, recommends that an assignment should be enforced when: **1.56**

- The insolvent has declared its intention that the contract should be continued (namely, the contract is assumed);
- It is reasonably clear that the assignee will be able to perform those obligations; and,
- The counterparty would not be substantially disadvantaged by the assignment.[44]

The Recommendations go on to suggest that contractual terms which seek to limit the general right of the insolvent to assume, disclaim and assign executory contracts should have no effect. Although the Recommendations do not have legally binding force, it is important to stress that in those Baltic and Nordic countries where there are no explicit provisions on the subject, these recommendations do have their origin in a good number of important commentaries and legal treatises. **1.57**

It is difficult to envisage any legal system not permitting assignment of executory contracts – however, it must not be forgotten that not all legal systems define executory contracts in exactly the same way as we have discussed above. **1.58**

Value extraction

Preserving value is clearly needful. However, in the cut and thrust corporate world there are 'investors' who seemingly step in to rescue the financially distressed company with a less than savoury agenda. These predatory investors **1.59**

42 Produced by the Nordic-Baltic Insolvency Network.

43 The Recommendations (Wolters Kluwer 2016) are available here http://www.sccl.se/wp-content/uploads/2017/04/Nordic-Baltic-Recommendations-Final-Version-bok-rotated.pdf.

44 See paras 15–16.

through setting up complex investment vehicles or arrangements may be entitled to extract in full or in part the value of their investment back and to strip the company's assets before the company eventually goes into an insolvency process. This prolonging of the company's demise and subsequently depletion of the corporate assets can undoubtedly lead to even greater damage to creditors and employees. There is little comparative law work on this subject which is increasingly troubling governments. This work goes a little distance to demonstrate that the matter of value preservation should not be considered in a discrete manner – value preservation has to be placed in a longer term context.[45] In the UK, in March 2018 a consultation was launched to invite comments on a proposal to claw back such financial gains from investors who have extracted value in this manner. The Consultation Paper gives some examples of such value extraction arrangements: management fees; excessive interest on loans, charges over company property being granted; excessive director pay or other payments; or sale and leaseback of assets.[46] These types of transactions may unfairly benefit certain parties whilst putting creditors in a worse position than they would otherwise have been in should that company subsequently become insolvent.

1.60 While it could not be said that all such rescues would fail, the UK Government is concerned that if they do fail that other creditors and other stakeholders are treated fairly and should not have to be left in a worse off position. The challenge is thus not to ban such investments (whereby the investors assume control of the company and then assume existing contracts) but to ensure that any law to claw back unfair gains made by those investors is sufficiently clear in its scope of application. It will also be needful to show that the initial investment had actually not added real value to the company – that will be highly problematic, though. The question of *real* value is always a difficult one in law. There is also the problem of how insolvency practitioners or office holders can unpick those complex value extraction arrangements. Many will be watching the developments in the UK with interest in this regard. Although the subject falls outside the scope of our project on executory contracts, it is undeniable that executory contracts form only one cog in the larger wheel of the subject of corporate rescues.

---

45 See e.g., country reports from Australia, the USA, Denmark, Germany, and Singapore to name a few.

46 Insolvency and Corporate Governance Consultation Paper 2018 https://assets.publishing.service.gov.uk/government/uploads/system/uploads/attachment_data/file/691857/Condoc_-_Insolvency_and_Corporate_Governance_FINAL_.pdf at p. 14.

CONCLUSION

This Critique has sought to draw on the rich materials the national reports have produced. It is hoped that its analysis of the key legal (as against policy) themes has gone some distance to show that despite the policy concerns about reorganisation, rescue and the preservation of value in the context of executory contracts, the legal rules can in themselves lead to results which may not sit well with the policy objectives. This analysis has also demonstrated that policy objectives can sometimes be overreached by the trustees or supervising court. In common law jurisdictions, that notably arises when highly judicialised tests are devised and applied to deal with definitions and to guide the office holder's discretion and/or judicial supervision. A highly judicialised approach could inevitably lead to confusion and causes dispute and controversies. In some civilian legal systems, on the other hand, the overreaching occurs because judicial discretion and government influence are left unbridled – as insolvency laws in a good many of civil law countries tend to be fairly perfunctory, much is left to the good sense of the supervisory tribunals. Although that has the advantage of an experienced court ensuring that good faith and neutrality are maintained, in less developed or less well resourced jurisdictions, the system may lead to unfairness or arbitrariness. **1.61**

Naturally there is no one right answer to any of the challenges discussed in this Introduction. That is very much because a solution in one jurisdiction could and would not work well in another. The fact remains that whether we are referring to a civil law country or a common law one, insolvency law interacts and intersects with different established laws, private and public. That means any solution, whether simple or complex, is likely to produce a knock-on effect elsewhere in the wider body of law. **1.62**

It is thus enriching for practitioners, policy makers and scholars of insolvency law to experiment with good practices elsewhere but they must always have an eye on the wider legal tapestry. The challenges we face are global but uniform global solutions are likely to be counterproductive unless other legal principles and rules are also properly accommodated. **1.63**

In closing, the editors are especially grateful to the project team for their sterling work in producing such a readable volume of often technical material. **1.64**

PART I

CIVIL LAW SYSTEMS

2

NATIONAL REPORT FOR ALBANIA

Gelanda Shkurtaj

A. INTRODUCTION

The latest Albanian Insolvency Law n.110, was approved by the Albanian Parliament in October 2016 ('2016 Act') and entered into power on 22 May 2017. The 2016 Act amends the former law (*Insolvency Law* no.8091/2002 as modified in 2008 – '2002 Act') which in turn had replaced an earlier one, the Law n.8017 dated 25 October 1995 ('1995 Act').[1] For several unclear reasons, which are still open to discussion, in the period 1995 to 2002 no insolvency applications have been submitted to the courts. **2.01**

One of the most likely reasons that explain the failure of the 1995 Act is related to its origin. The 1995 Act was a messy aggregation of laws taken from **2.02**

1 There are other provisions in the Albanian legal system that deal with companies in financial distress. For instance, Chapter XIX of the Civil Code provides some rules and guidance for voluntary liquidation cases. Arts 190–205 of the Law No. 9901 on Entrepreneurs and Companies 2008 'On merchants and commercial companies' ('Law on Companies') includes some disposition on the rights of the creditors of an illiquid company. The common thread of these mechanisms was their focus on liquidation. They did not and could not promote the rehabilitation or reorganization of the company in distress, even when this would have been in the best interest of the creditors on the whole.

civil law (primarily Germany) and common laws systems, which very often were in conflict between themselves. It proved ill-suited to address the needs and peculiarities of the Albanian society and business community.

2.03 Other frequently mentioned complaints deal with its content. First, the 1995 Act was simply too complicated and technical, making it difficult and uncomfortable for the Albanian legal community to implement its provisions. Secondly, unlike other jurisdictions where practitioners' commentaries are available, there was hardly any practical guidance to its implementation. As a result, all the insolvency actors worked in a vacuum, with no means of understanding the complexity of the law and its implementation.

2.04 In this context, it seems hardly surprising that there is a lack of recorded insolvency cases. Companies were liquidated according to civil law procedures, mentioned in footnote 1. As explained in that annotation, these procedures are aimed at closing insolvent companies and winding up their assets and activities, provided that creditors can agree on a distribution scheme. As the cases under the Civil Code or the Law on Companies provide little guidance for the purposes of this study, they are not mentioned in this chapter.

B. AVAILABLE PROCEDURES

2.05 According to the 2016 Act, a company is deemed to be insolvent when two situations occur: a) the company is unable to pay its debts when they fall due; or b) the company is overburdened by debts.

2.06 A company is deemed 'overburdened by debts' (balance sheet insolvency) when its liabilities toward third parties exceed the value of its assets. The evaluation of the assets is usually the work of any expert appointed by the court.[2] This is based on the market value, or contained in a specific law or normative act issued by the Government. To be relevant, this situation should affect the ability of the company to continue its usual business activity.

2.07 The 2016 Act allows companies in financial difficulties to initiate an insolvency procedure. In addition to actual inability to meet his/her debts (illiquidity), the debtor (whether a natural or juridical person) may submit a request to open a proceeding on the basis that it is probable that he/she will not be able to meet his/her obligations as they become due in the future (imminent illiquidity).

2 The appointment of the expert is previewed by the Law No. 110/2016 on Bankruptcy, art 28.

Under the current framework, only one formal procedure[3] is available to a company in financial difficulties. Once the insolvency procedure has been opened, the person in charge of the procedure (i.e., the insolvency administrator) can either: **2.08**

- propose a re-organization plan aiming for the survival of the company;[4]
- propose a sale of the company as a going-concern;
- liquidate the company's assets.[5]

(1) Eligibility requirements

To commence insolvency proceedings there should be a request or application submitted by either the debtor or the creditor to the competent court. In addition, but only with reference to legal entities, the 2016 Act allows the tax revenue office to file a petition in front of the competent court, whenever a company has incurred losses for three fiscal years in a row.[6] **2.09**

Beside the debtor and its creditors, the petition can be submitted by a member of the board of legal representative (directors) or the voluntary liquidator of a legal person. In case of partnerships, the petition can be deposited by a general partner. In particular, a member of the board is obliged to request the opening of an insolvency proceeding not later than three weeks after the legal entity has become illiquid or overburdened. **2.10**

---

3 Informal procedure is the concept previewed by, ibid., art 14, based on the request of the debtor which is already insolvent or will be insolvent in the near future.

4 As previewed by ibid., art 96, Ch I, 'Re-organization'; the bankruptcy or monitoring administrator, and the creditors holding claims representing 20 per cent or more of the total amount of claims are entitled to submit a plan of reorganization to the bankruptcy court within a month of the reporting assembly that decided for the reorganization of the debtor. The debtor may also submit a plan of reorganization together with the request for the commencement of the bankruptcy proceeding or any time after, with the time limit set in the point 1 of this article. If the creditors' assembly has under this law, mandated the monitoring or bankruptcy administrator to develop a reorganization plan, the administrator, in preparing the plan, will consider recommendations from the creditors and the debtor where there are any. If the debtor has submitted a plan within the previous 12 months which is rejected by the parties or is withdrawn by the debtor after publication of the date of the discussion assembly, the bankruptcy court shall refuse to accept a new plan by the debtor if such refusal is requested by the bankruptcy administrator or by the creditors' committee, if appointed.

5 As previewed by ibid.; the debtor may request the opening of the liquidation at any time during bankruptcy proceedings.The debtor must file for the opening of the liquidation immediately after he realizes that the reorganization plan cannot be complied with. Not filing the request will bear the same consequences as the breach to file for opening of the bankruptcy proceedings, pursuant to art 15, of this law. In the cases of point 1 and 2, of this article, the bankruptcy court will hear the bankruptcy or monitor the administrator and the creditors' committee, if there is one, before adopting the decision. Where the activity of the business has been discontinued, the bankruptcy or monitoring administrator may request the opening of the liquidation. Before adopting the decision, the debtor shall be heard by the bankruptcy court.

6 Law No. 9920 on Tax Procedures, art 104 relates to the right of the tax office to initiate the insolvency proceedings for taxpayers registered in the form of commercial companies.

2.11 The opening of an insolvency proceeding requires a decisioned step – a judicial determination. It is thus not simply an administrative act, but a reasoned decision of the competent court (called 'Insolvency Court'). The insolvency proceedings can be opened[7] only if the applicant:

- has a 'legal interest' in the proceedings;[8]
- can 'prove the validity and existence of his/her claim';[9]
- can establish that there is a 'reason' for opening proceedings;[10]
- submits the required documentation.

2.12 Any debtor can submit a request to open a proceeding ('petition').[11] The petition[12] must be accompanied by a list of available assets with a certification of their value and a list of alternative sources of income. The debtor shall also declare if the assets have been assigned as security or whether they are otherwise encumbered. The petition shall also include a list of the creditors. This list should include their names and (registered) addresses, and the amount owed to them.

2.13 Under the 2002 Act, the tax administration could request the opening of an insolvency proceedings against any taxpayer registered in the Companies' House. Such a possibility was subject to the following conditions:

- where for two years the company has registered a loss in the balance sheets deposited in the National Registration Center ('NRC');
- when the tax liabilities of this taxpayer are declared uncollectible;
- where a company declares losses of its own capital for at least three consecutive years;
- where the company has not carried out any commercial activity for at least two years after the date of enforcement of this law;
- and/or where the company has unpaid liabilities towards the tax administration for at least 2 (two) years after the date of enforcement of this law.

2.14 However, with the entrance of the new Law on Insolvency this provision has been cancelled.

---

7 Law No. 110/2016 on Bankruptcy, art 2.

8 Ibid., art 7.

9 Must provide evidence of its existence, such as the failed execution of an order to pay the debt.

10 According to Law No. 110/2016 on Bankruptcy, art 13 there are to be set out the 'reasons'.

11 Law No. 9911/2008, art 14.

12 According to the new Law the tax administration can no longer be asked to petition. As far as the creditors know the difficulties of the company (debtor) because of unapid invoices and when they enter in to one of the situations previewed by the Code of Civil Procedure, art 517.

The Insolvency Court will decide to open insolvency procedures whenever it has been proved to its satisfaction that there are proper grounds for admitting this request. As the claimant has to demonstrate that the company is unable to pay its debts as they fall due or that it is overburdened with debts, the bulk of petitions comes from debtors and creditors. **2.15**

(2) Insolvency requirement

Credit is a central feature of a modern and market economy. Without it, economic growth and expansion would be seriously hampered. However, when business organizations or natural persons become so over-indebted that their ability to participate in the market is seriously affected, it is proper that the law provides remedies to avoid systemic risks and fraudulent practices. These mechanisms should include efficient, collective actions against the debtor and its assets. **2.16**

A successful insolvency procedure frees assets for other participants in the economy. It may also involve a settlement with creditors (for instance, a debt-to-equity swap) which may preserve the operation of the distressed debtor. **2.17**

The criterion of 'insolvency' still plays a relevant role in the Albanian tradition because insolvency procedures are not seen as a turnaround process, but as mechanisms to address a situation of fully evident distress. The 2016 Act has been designed to provide these mechanisms. Article 2 of the 2016 Act provides as follows: **2.18**

- insolvency proceeding shall serve the purpose of collective satisfaction of a debtor's creditors by liquidation of the debtor's assets and by distribution of the proceeds, or, in an insolvency plan, by reaching a different arrangement, particularly in order to maintain an enterprise;
- any honest debtor shall be given an opportunity to achieve a discharge of his residual debt.

(3) Locus standi

While in theory creditors are allowed to file a petition for insolvency, in practice these procedures are commenced either by the debtor or the tax revenue authority. It is usually in the debtor's interest to initiate a procedure, as it may lead to the reorganization of the distressed corporation without the appointment of court officials to run the company. For the tax revenue authorities, under Albanian law their claims are prioritized over other unsecured creditors. Their decision to file for insolvency is motivated by **2.19** diametrically opposing reasons, as they seek to take the assets from the debtor and sell them in a quick and efficient manner.

2.20 A copy of the decision for the opening of the insolvency proceedings is sent to each of the creditors, to the debtor and to the debtors of the debtor. A copy of the decision is also sent to the QKR (NRC)[13] and is made public even at the ZVRPP (Central Office for the Registration of Immovable Properties). The decision is also published on the website of the court that has decided to open the insolvency proceedings.

2.21 The court orders that determine the opening and closure of the insolvency proceedings are also usually published in local and national newspapers. The publication includes specific information on the debtor and the business (registered office, activity, etc.).

2.22 Creditors have to submit their claims in writing to the insolvency administrator between 15 and 90 days from the date of the opening of the proceeding. The claims must be justified, and the creditor shall submit all the evidence needed to prove his claim.

2.23 The ranking of creditors is regulated by several articles of the 2016 Act, in accordance with the Civil Code.[14] The law provides that the judicial procedure shall not begin if there is insufficient money to cover the costs and expenses associated with the insolvency procedure.[15] Creditors are ranked in the following order:

- secured creditors;
- unsecured creditors;
- unsecured creditors of lower ranking;
- means of living for the debtor.[16]

---

13 National Centre of Business which is divided in National Centre of Registration and National Centre of Licence.

14 The Law no. 113/2016 published in the Official On the amendment done to the A.C.C in order to reflect the new Insolvency Law (effective starting from 22 May 2017) by providing for the following novelties: 'Changes to the ranking of payment of the creditor's claims in insolvency procedure.' The ranking provided by art 605 of Civil Code shall not be applicable to new insolvency proceedings. The Law no. 113/2016 establishes that art 607 of Civil Code: 'The creditors' right to challenge the debtor's transactions', is no longer applied in insolvency proceedings. The creditor has the right to challenge the debtor's transactions only in accordance with the respective provisions of the New Law On Insolvency.

15 Ibid.

16 This is the same for companies in Albania. Despite this, it must be said that this form is used more in cases of reorganized insolvency cases, where the creditors with voting rights are usually separated into groups of interest for the approval of the plan.

Unfortunately, this ranking has not been coordinated with the provisions in the Civil Code. As a general rule, the majority of commentators[17] agree that the Civil Code provisions should prevail over insolvency ones. Pursuant to Article 605 of the Albanian Civil Code, creditors are ranked in the following order: **2.24**

(a) credits emerging from the financial transactions being insured by encumbrance concerning the purchase price of a specific asset;
(b) credits emerging from the salaries in employment or service relations and alimonies, however, no longer than 12 months;
(c) credits of social insurance regarding the unpaid contributions along with the interest, as well as credits of employees regarding the damages sustained due to the failure of the employer to pay the above-mentioned contributions;
(d) credits emerging from the remunerations due to death or health impairment;
(e) credits of authors or their heirs concerning the remunerations emerging from full or partial alienation of their rights in the intellectual field concerning the obligations emerging during the previous two years;
(f) state credits emerging from liabilities to the budget and the credits of the state insurance institute for the mandatory insurance, set out by law;
(g) credits emerging from financial transactions, insured by encumbrance, under the criteria set out by law;
(h) credits emerging from the salaries in employment or service relations as well as alimonies beyond the limit set out at (b) above;
(i) mediation remuneration emerging from the agency contract, where it emerges during the last year of remuneration;
(j) credits secured by mortgage or lien not amounting to encumbrance, according to law, from the value of the things in mortgage or lien;
(k) credits emerging from the judicial proceedings expenses for preserving the asset and those for the executive arrangements, undertaken to the joint benefit of creditors, out of the proceeds of the sales of assets;
(l) credits granted by banks not falling under (e) above and the credits emerging out of voluntary insurances;
(m) credits for supplying seeds, fertilizers, insecticides, water for irrigation and for the works for cultivating and harvesting the agricultural products, on the annual agricultural products (yields), where the credits have been applied.

17 This is a concept taken from the reality of the courts. Even though, according to research by me, there are no articles in Albanian regarding this topic.

2.25 These are the previsions of the Civil Code, which, under the former Bankruptcy Law n. 8901/2002, was the only one aplicable for the order of the priorities in distribution and liquidations. Now, with the new reform, there are only the provisions of Article 144 of the Law N.110/2016, which lists the order of priorities as follows:

- After the fulfillment of the obligations in accordance with this law, in all cases of liquidation the process will continue with the satisfaction of the claims of the creditors in the following order:
  - secured claims secured up to the value of the property that serves as collateral;
  - claims of preferential creditors, pursuant to, this law;
  - claims of unsecured creditors;
  - claims of subordinated creditors, pursuant to, this law;
  - claims of the members of the simple society, partners and shareholders of business societies, in their capacity as such.
- The payment of creditors of the bankruptcy proceeding takes place as the claims fall due. Payment of bankruptcy creditors will be made taking into consideration the need to pay first the creditors of bankruptcy proceedings. In case of doubt, the bankruptcy administrator will set aside a monetary amount before commencing the payment of the creditors provided in point 1 of this article.

(4) Informal turnarounds

2.26 Even though there is no specific provision in the 2016 Act that regulates out-of-court solutions, it is commonly understood that debtors are free to explore these solutions before submitting a petition for insolvency.[18]

2.27 As has emerged from several conferences, workshops and seminars, as well as direct interviews with the author, insolvency administrators believe that out-of-court workouts are rarely, if ever used. A possible explanation is to be found in the circumstance that Albanian law recognizes binding effects only of those agreements signed in the course of the insolvency procedure, and ratified by the court.[19]

---

18 Under Albanian Law the parties, before presenting the petition to the competent court, try to discuss all the alternative ways for an out-of-trial agreement. When all the negotiations are exhausted, the creditor will present the insolvency petition to the court.

19 Since the first law approved by the Albanian Parliament in the field of insolvency, the competent court has always been a special unit, within the first grade courts, which was appointed to treat all insolvency cases. The establishment of a separate Court of Insolvency, entered into power with the new law of insolvency, even though it is established by law, nowadays there is still that separated section within the first grade court which face the problems.

So, while there are no specific provisions that prevent the negotiation and implementation of out-of-court reorganizations, parties are strongly incentivized to negotiate a settlement agreement within a formal insolvency procedure. Additionally, the debtor's directors can be found personally liable for corporate obligations if they do not submit an insolvency petition within 21 days from the date on which the company became insolvent. **2.28**

Once the insolvency procedure has opened, all individual proceedings are stayed, and creditors can only 'enforce' their rights/claims within the insolvency procedure. **2.29**

C. TREATMENT OF THE EXECUTORY CONTRACTS

The main object of this chapter concerns the treatment of executory contracts under the Albanian insolvency law (Articles 72–78 of the Law 110/2016). **2.30**

As has been mentioned above, the insolvency proceedings have very significant effects on the juridical and legal rights of the debtor, the creditors and any other persons involved in the process. The opening of an insolvency proceeding in Albania has the following consequences: **2.31**

- the debtor loses the power to manage or dispose of property which exists at the time the proceeding is opened or which is acquired before the proceeding is terminated;[20]
- the power to manage the property of the debtor (that becomes estate property) vests henceforth on the administrator;[21]
- all civil and executory actions against the debtor are suspended;[22]
- the administrator acquires wide-ranging powers to contest transactions entered into by the debtor prior to opening the proceeding that have resulted in diminution of the debtor's assets;[23]
- the debtor (along with members and former members of the body representing or supervizing a debtor who is a juridical person, the general partners of a partnership and employees and former employees of the debtor) becomes subject to broad disclosure and cooperation obligations.[24]

---

20 See Law No. 9911/2008, arts 67 and 68.
21 See Law No. 9911/2008, arts 67 and 116.
22 See Law No. 9911/2008, arts 71 and 74.
23 See Law No, 9911/2008, chapter 3, part 2.
24 See Law No. 9911/2008, arts 81 and 82.

2.32 One of the peculiar consequences of the opening of an insolvency proceeding is that the law grants to the insolvency administrator the right to reject certain contracts that had been signed by the parties in solvent times but that have yet to be executed.

2.33 The law speaks about the specific prohibited agreement, referring to the cases of the contracts signed by the debtor, but with a specific clause of an early termination of it, in case of a bankruptcy opening procedure. This is what the Article 73 says on the topic: 'is invalid any clause in a contract to which the debtor is a party, that provides for the early termination based exclusively due to the opening of bankruptcy proceedings'.[25]

2.34 The administrator plays a crucial role in determining the outcome of 'executory contracts'. This notion includes any contract entered into by the parties in solvent times and that, at the time of the admission of the debtor into an insolvency proceeding, still has to be fully or partially performed by one or both parties. Those are the cases of fixed date transactions executor contracts, referred to, in particular, in Article 74:

- If it was agreed that the delivery of goods was to take place at a certain time, and if such term expires after the bankruptcy proceeding was commenced, the in-kind fulfillment of those obligations may not be requested and only damages for non-fulfillment of the obligation may be claimed.
- If it was agreed that the execution of an action of a financial nature dealing with market or stock exchange prices would take place at a certain time, and if such term expires after the bankruptcy proceeding was commenced, point 1 of this article shall be equally applied. The following are considered to be actions of a financial nature:
  (a) the delivery of precious metals;
  (b) the delivery of titles or comparable rights, if there is no intention to obtain an interest in a company or to establish a long-term interest,
  (c) fulfillments in kind, which have to be executed in foreign currency or in related measurement unit as per exchange rate;
  (d) other rights to suppliers or execution in kind of a contract pursuant to (a), (b) and (c) of this point; and
  (e) financial securities according to financial legislation;
- If transactions for financial performances are combined in a frame contract or model for which an agreement has been reached that in case

25 See Performance of Legal Transactions, chapter II, art 73, p. 28.

of bankruptcy it may only be terminated in its entirety, the totality of these transactions shall be regarded as a mutual contract.

- The claim for damages for non-execution of obligations is calculated as the difference between the agreed price and the market or stock exchange price at the place and time agreed by the parties, but, not later than the fifth working day after the commencement of the bankruptcy proceeding for a contract with a determined period of fulfillment. If the parties do not reach an agreement, the second working day after the commencement of the bankruptcy proceeding shall be decisive. The other party may claim for non-execution on the contract only as a bankruptcy creditor.

In cases where there has been no execution or any kind of performance by neither the debtor nor the counterparty, the administrator can – without any time limit imposed by the law – either: **2.35**

a) opt for assuming the contract, thus forcing the other party to perform; or
b) reject the contract, thus forcing the other party to seek recovery in damages as an insolvency creditor.[26]

The Insolvency Act does not give the counterparty any right to seek the specific performance of the executory contract. This rule, however, suffers from some exceptions. For instance, pursuant to Article 89: **2.36**

> If prior to opening the proceedings, the debtor contracted to sell movable property under a retention of title sale contract and delivered the movables to the purchaser, the administrator must discharge the debtor's obligations under the contract, including the transfer of title to the purchaser when the price is tendered.

(1) Administrator's rights

In many situations, an administrator (i.e., the manager of the insolvent company) who decides to assume a contract with a counterparty would first ask for execution or performance of the debtor's obligations under the contract. However, this rule is not applicable for contracts with separate execution and when the counterparty has already executed a separate part of the contract. In this case the administrator can perform the remaining obligations in the contract without asking for execution of the debtor's obligations for that the part of the contract that has been performed. **2.37**

---

26 See Law No. 9911/2008, arts 80, 90 and 95.

2.38 This is the case of a furniture contract, which the parties expect to be executed in two different phases. Imagine that the first phase of the contract has been executed and after that, the debtor will be declared in an insolvency situation. So, the second part of furniture contract, planned to be executed during the second phase of the contract, will no longer be executed. In this case the insolvency administrator should accept, according to the contract terms, the remaining obligation, which in concrete is the loss of earnings. The contracting party is bound to his claim as an insolvency creditor, respecting the execution of these obligations.[27]

2.39 Article 87 contains special rules applicable to fixed term contracts and financial futures contracts.

2.40 As far as the periodic contracts[28] that have been implemented by the debtor's counterparty until the opening of the insolvency proceedings, these must be converted into monetary claims and are qualified as insolvency claims.

2.41 According to the Insolvency Law, contracts concluded between the debtor, in the capacity of the lessee, for the lease of immovable property or of their parts and for services to be provided related to them, shall continue to exist, in favour of the insolvency estate. The insolvency administrator, when the debtor is a lessee, can terminate the contract by notifying the other party according to the law. At the end, the 2016 Act provides that, for the service contracts, the insolvency administrator and the service provider may terminate the contract. In the case that it is the Insolvency Administrator who terminates the contract, the other party may request compensation as an insolvency creditor.

2.42 When it comes to contracts not performed by any of the parties Article 86 provides the situation when at the date of opening of the proceedings a contract between the debtor and another person has not been performed by both the parties of the contract, and in this case the administrator may opt to perform the contract or terminate it.

(a) Example

2.43 X and Y have entered into a contract under which X undertakes to sell a van to Y for a specified price. Before the van is delivered and before X pays any portion of the purchase price, an insolvency proceeding is opened involving X. As a result of Article 89, the contract is treated as no longer enforceable.

27 See Law No. 9911/2008, art 88.

28 This notion includes among others contracts where the price is paid by instalments, leasing contracts, utility contracts and contracts for the provisions of services.

However, if the administrator decides that the price to be paid for the van is below its market value, they can elect to pay the price and obtain the van. The van can then be sold by the administrator and the 'profit' is consequently added to the insolvency estate.

Limitation on administrator right under contract not performed by both parties – special contracts are contained at Article 87. These include forwarding and financial contracts[29] and contracts for the sale of movable properties by the insolvency debtor, taking into consideration the right to reserve the ownership.[30] **2.44**

D. PAST REFORMS AND CURRENT DEBATE

(1) The introduction of the Insolvency Agency

The Insolvency Supervision Agency is established pursuant to Law no. 9911, dated 23.5.2002 'On insolvency', as amended by law no. 9911, dated 19.05.2008. **2.45**

The Law 'on insolvency' basically aims to standardize the procedure of insolvency, first, supporting the commercial companies but also the financial, licensing, production and employment authorities highlighting and performing a supervisory role of these activities. The Law has defined uniform and equal rules to be applied by commercial entities for repayment of debts of debtors in a mandatory insolvency procedure. **2.46**

These amendments also introduced the establishment and operation of a special unit for the supervision of insolvency administrators, as the Insolvency Supervision Agency is. **2.47**

The implementation of mandatory rules is part of the reform for: **2.48**

- licensing administrators;
- promoting higher standards;
- maintaining the register of insolvency administrators and supervising their activity.

29 See Law No. 9911/2008, art 87.
30 Ibid., art 89.

2.49 The agency takes care that the licensed administrator performs his duties in accordance with law, the national standards of interpretation apply, as well as the Code of Ethics.

(2) The role of the Agency

2.50 The controlling role is realized through the Insolvency Supervision Agency, which, according to Article 282/3 has powers to:

- issue, revoke and renew licenses for administrators;
- organize the professional examination, maintaining the register of insolvency administrators;
- monitor their activity.

2.51 Regarding the supervisory activity, the agency ensures that licensed administrators perform their duties in accordance with the law and the national standards of the insolvency amount, as well as the Code of Ethics. The agency monitors the implementation of the law and elaborates statistical data relating to the implementation of procedures.

2.52 Amendments to the insolvency law were approved by Law n. 110 dated 27.10.2016

(3) The legal stalemate between Article 605 of Civil Code and Article 144 of the 2016 Act

2.53 As mentioned before section B(3) above, the order of priorities prescribed by the 2002 Act and the Civil Code do not match. Despite the apparent primacy of the Civil Code provisions, two conflicting rules regulate the order of preference of creditors.

2.54 In order to avoid conflict between these two provisions and provide guidance in the interpretation on the law on insolvency, the legislature added the following paragraph to Article 605 of the Civil Code: 'The order of preference foreseen by this article does not apply to insolvency proceedings, provided by a special law.'[31]

2.55 A similar clause was also added at the end of Article 607 of the Civil Code: 'This article shall not apply to insolvency proceedings, provided by a special

31 Law No. 113/2016 'For some amendments on the Law No.7850/1994, "Civil Code of the Republic of Albania", "Amended"'.

law.' As a result, this statutory amendment has addressed the existing conflict between statutory provisions, by clarifying their scope.

The legislature then focused on how to promote the use of insolvency law. As discussed under s. ... , one of the main factors for the limited use of insolvency law has been the reluctance of insolvency players to apply it. The punitive approach of the law did not favour its use by the business community, and the lack of available funds and recovery from the sale of the assets of the debtors further hampered the use of these procedures. **2.56**

To address the latter criticism, a draft bill was introduced in the Parliament to set up a special public fund to be administered by the National Agency of Insolvency.[32] This special public fund would be used to cover the costs of the procedure in cases in which the amount recovered from the sale of the debtor's assets would be insufficient to refund the insolvency administrator's expenses. **2.57**

However, a later draft repealed the introduction of the proposed fund. In cases where there is a lack of funds, the only remedy nowadays is to apply to the court for a request of a termination of the procedure. **2.58**

(4) Introduction of the Prosecutor

The Insolvency Court informs the creditors and makes a public announcement of the situation. Creditors and other concerned parties have the right, within 60 days from this notice, to appear at the Insolvency Court and oppose closure of proceedings due to lack of assets, if the debtor has assets or if further investigation is needed about assets that the debtor has transferred, which may **2.59**

32 In support of the Law No. 8901/ 2002 on Insolvency, amended by Law No. 9911/2008, it established the Agency on Monitoring the Insolvency. These amendments introduced the creation and the function of a special structure on the monitoring of insolvency administrators, so far called the Agency on Monitoring the Insolvency.

Parts of the reform are in respect of the following regulations:

- set up the Insolvency Administrators;
- promote equal standards;
- keep the register of the Insolvency Administrators and the supervise their activity.

The monitoring role will be played by the agency, which according to Article 282/3 has competences to:

- issue, retire, renew the license for the administrators.
- organize the state exam and keep the register of the insolvency administrators
- supervise their activity.

For supervision, the agency takes care to control the activity of the administrators, according to all the provisions of the law, the international standards on insolvency estate and the respect of the ethical code. The agency monitors even the application of the law and elaborate statistic data, which are related to the execution of the insolvency procedures.

be subject to avoidance action.[33] The Insolvency Court forwards the claims of the parties, which show reasonable grounds for the necessity of conducting further investigations on the operations of the debtor, to the prosecutor within five days and suspends the procedure for six months for the purpose of conducting the investigation. The Insolvency Court determines the closure of procedure due to lack of assets if:

- there are no objections to the closure of the proceedings by the opposing parties, after the expiry of the 60-day term;
- the prosecutor decides not to institute or dismiss the criminal case;
- six months have elapsed from the communication the court makes to the prosecutor about the suspension of proceedings.

(5) The role of the Insolvency Administrator

2.60 The law foresees three types of administrators: insolvency; temporary insolvency; and supervisory administrators. They all have the same status and the same selection criteria, but whom is relevant depends on the specific functions required to be performed by law and at which moment in time.

2.61 One of the elements introduced in the draft law, which was supposed to have a positive impact on businesses, was the repeal of one of the insolvency procedures, or more specifically the rate provided for in Law 9920 'On Tax Procedures in the Republic of Albania', where the tax authority was granted the right to launch insolvency procedures for defaulting companies for three consecutive years. Apparently, this proposal was not taken forward. The aim of the draft proposal was to avoid involvement in the insolvency proceedings of commercial entities that, because of the type of activity they do, are not likely to generate profits in the early years.

(6) Amendments to the Civil Procedure Code

2.62 The most important amendments to the Civil Procedure Code are related to the role of the court in an insolvency procedure.[34] Other changes are concerned with the procedure to be followed by the court when issuing enforcement orders for executive titles. These elements seem to be both important and problematic, since the issuance of the writ of execution by the court appears

33 This is the case when the court has real and concrete reasonable doubts that the debtor may transfer the properties to third parties, in order to lose trace of his properties, and not put them under the insolvency regime.

34 Law No. 114/2016 'For some amendments on the Law No. 8116/1996 "Civil Porcedure Code of The Republic of Albania", "Amended"'.

not to be a formal confirmation procedure for the enforcement of an executive title, but a procedure where the debtor in the relevant judicial process will have the opportunity to take a position in relation to the obligation he has. This issue approached from the perspective of creditors, seems to increase legal uncertainty in relation to the enforcement of executive titles.

(7) Proceedings started in other jurisdictions

Under the Albanian law, insolvency proceedings which have started in another jurisdiction are recognized by the court when: **2.63**

- the debtor has his domicile or the legal address in that other jurisdiction;
- the insolvency proceeding does not violate the principles of the Albanian Legislation, in particular the constitutional provisions.

A foreign judicial award or order would be enforceable in Albania, after the completion of the appropriate judicial proceedings in Albania, against any of the properties located in Albania according to the procedure provided by the Albanian legislation in force. So, the Albanian Court of Appeal would not enforce any foreign judgments which do not meet the conditions listed below: **2.64**

- according to the provisions in force in Albania, the dispute does not fall within the competence of the foreign court in question;
- the lawsuit and the hearing notice are not duly delivered to the absent defendant and in due time, thus depriving him of the right to a defence;
- a different judgment is rendered by an Albanian court involving the same parties, subject and dispute;
- an Albanian court is examining the same dispute before the foreign court judgment becomes final;
- the foreign court judgment becomes final contrary to the provisions of the relevant legislation; and
- the foreign court judgment is not in compliance with the fundamental principles of Albanian legislation:
- conducts a review of the foreign court judgment, but only by the procedural point of view and it does not enter into the matter of the case.

A final judgment rendered in any foreign court would be enforceable: **2.65**

- upon the completion of appropriate judicial proceedings in Albania against any of its properties located in Albania according to the procedure provided by the Albanian legislation in force, and

- if the Albanian Court of Appeal does not find any of the conditions below rendering foreign judgment unenforceable:
  - according to the provisions in force in Albania, the dispute does not fall within the competence of the foreign court in question;
  - the lawsuit and the hearing notice are not duly delivered to the absent defendant and in due time, thus depriving him of the right to a defence;
  - a different judgment is rendered by an Albanian court involving the same parties, subject and dispute;
  - an Albanian court is examining the same dispute before the foreign court judgment becomes final;
  - the foreign court judgment becomes final contrary to the provisions of the relevant legislation; and
  - the foreign court judgment is not in compliance with the fundamental principles of Albanian legislation.

(8) Concluding remarks on executory contracts and reforms

2.66 In general terms, the Albanian Law on Insolvency does not particularly focus on executory contracts, but mentions some of them, such as the fixed date transactions, rent contract, mandate, public contracts and employment contracts, as the most usual contracts of the daily business in Albania. The remarks on those executory contracts are expressed in the meaning of Article 72 of the law, where in general terms this law previews that the effects of the commencement of insolvency procedures should not affect the continuation of the contracts. In particular, this rule is very true for the employment contract, as prescribed by the Article 78 of the present Law:

- as a general rule, the opening of bankruptcy proceedings does not affect the continuation of employment contracts;
- the bankruptcy or monitoring administrator may propose the termination or the modification of employment contracts. The effect of the termination or the modification of the contracts will generally be regulated by Albanian labour law. In any case, the situation of bankruptcy is to be deemed an objective economic justification for the termination or the modification of employment contracts;
- the Bankruptcy Court shall be competent to decide on any litigation or any legal issue that arises as a consequence of the termination or modification of employment contracts.

2.67 With the specific clause that in cases determining a bankruptcy situation, there is a justification to terminate even an employment contract; but this is not the situation with public contracts, or those based under the administrative law. In the case of a public contract, there should be a public tender or a contract of concession. In the first phase, Article 77 speaks about the termination of the contract only if it is regulated by the specific law. If there is no particular provision by the public law, the mere existence of the bankruptcy is not a reason for the termination of the contract, except the real risk on the contract performance. But, the interest of a public service covers any situation, because the third paragraph of the same article asks that the public administration should adapt any measure for the execution of a basic public service, and not interrupt it because of the insolvency procedure.

- The effects of the commencement of bankruptcy proceedings on administrative contracts shall be regulated by the relevant public sector law. If no such special regulation exists, point 2 of this article will be applicable.
- The commencement of bankruptcy proceedings will not cause the immediate termination of the public contracts and concession rights. The public administration will have the right to terminate the contract or the concession right when there exist objective reasons to believe that the performance of the contract is at risk. The mere existence of bankruptcy proceedings shall not be deemed enough to terminate the contract so long as the business or professional activity is ongoing.
- When the contract refers to the execution of a basic public service, the relevant public administration shall be entitled to adopt any measures necessary to ensure the continuation of the service.

As for a mandate contract, it is automatically terminated, if the mandate has **2.68**
been given to the debtor referring to the bankruptcy estate. Thus is the provision of Article 76:

- Any contract of mandate, given to the debtor or granted by the debtor referring to the bankruptcy estate shall terminate upon commencement of the bankruptcy proceeding.
- If termination of a mandate concerning the bankruptcy estate may be prejudicial to the interests of bankruptcy proceedings, the mandate shall continue until the bankruptcy administrator is able take action over such a mandate. The party performing the mandate may claim reimbursement of his expenses incurred for such continuation as a creditor of bankruptcy estate.

So, in general terms, it is Article 72 of the present law, which talks of the **2.69**
treatment that this law makes to the executory contracts:

- When, at the moment of commencement of bankruptcy proceedings, the debtor has fully executed the obligations under a contract and the other party has not, the debtor will have the right to claim full performance. If it is the other party that has fully executed and the debtor has not, the former will have a bankruptcy claim.
- As a rule, the commencement of bankruptcy proceedings does not affect the continuation of contracts that have not been fully executed by the debtor and the counterparty to the contract. The exceptions to this rule are contemplated in this law.
- The bankruptcy administrator or the debtor, with the supervision of the monitoring administrator, may enforce the contract and claim the other party's payment or fulfilment of the obligation.
- The bankruptcy administrator or the debtor, with the authorization of the monitoring administrator, has the right to terminate the contract if it is in the interest of the bankruptcy proceedings. If the contract is terminated, both parties cease to be obliged to execute the remaining performance under the contract, and the other party shall be entitled to claim damages. The claim for damages is to be treated as an unsecured bankruptcy claim.
- The other party to the contract may require the bankruptcy administrator or the debtor under supervision of the monitoring administrator to decide whether the contract will be fully executed and notify the other party within five days. If the bankruptcy administrator or the debtor under supervision does not respond within the specified time, he will be deprived of the right to claim the performance of the contract.
- The rules above shall not apply to special provisions and contracts referred to in the subsequent articles of this chapter.

E. CONCLUDING REMARKS

2.70 It is widely accepted that a sound bankruptcy system should provide adequate protection to the interests of the creditors. For this reason, the current law has opted for the introduction in 2012 of the 'trustee' or 'insolvency administrator', with the duty to supervise the operation of the distressed debtor, promote its rescue or restructuring, or liquidate the assets. The administrator shall constantly communicate with the creditors, who in turn have set up the creditors' committee.

2.71 From the appointment of the administrator, the debtor is dispossessed from his assets/company and has a duty to cooperate with the administrator in the definition of the insolvency estate. Obviously, practice has shown many cases when debtors have taken action before initiating the insolvency proceedings to move assets, so that they are not placed under the regime of seizure by the administrator. To this end, the law has provided that all these movements should be reversed, avoided or cancelled through judicial proceedings initiated by the administrator.[35] The new 'prosecutor', introduced by the most recent 2012 reform, can also cooperate both in the investigation and potentially in the seizure phase.

The applicable law also guarantees the principle of pari passu treatment among equally ranking creditors. The Insolvency Court still retains a central role in the insolvency system. In particular, the court decides whether the administrator can propose a reorganization plan (for instance, when it appears that the creditors would reject it or when it is not 'feasible'[36]), and (if the plan has been proposed and accepted by the creditors) if this plan can be continued should the ailing debtor fail to implement it. **2.72**

In making that judgment, the Insolvency Court is guided by the purpose to promote the efficient management of the procedure and the protection of the creditors' interests from abusive practices by debtors. The system should only be used to ensure the realization of a value of an organization exceeding the value of the liquidation of its assets, in the sense that the organization is expected to be productive and successful for the process itself and for the future of debtors and creditors. **2.73**

(1) Reform of the Albanian Insolvency Law: a Comparative Study

Everybody knows that lending is a key feature of the modern market economy. However, when commercial companies or natural persons using loans are so overwhelmed that their ability to participate in an economic activity is seriously impaired or affected, it is crucial to put in motion legal mechanisms to solve the issue. The Bankruptcy Law is drafted to provide these mechanisms. The Bankruptcy Law has another public purpose encountered in many modern bankruptcy systems, which is contrary to the systematic collection and liquidation of debtor's assets in a state of insolvency and the distribution of income derived therefrom between the debtor's creditors. This purpose of the Insolvency Law provides a system in which the liquidation of **2.74**

---

35 This behaviour may give rise to criminal sanctions as well. The administrator, according to the new insolvency law, has the right to transmit the case to the prosecutor's office, in case of reasonable doubt, evidence or obligation's violation that the debtor is transferring the insolvency estate, before and after the insolvency procedures. There are four articles provided by Albanian Penal Code, 193, 194, 195, 196 which preview penalties up to seven years of imprisonment.

36 Law No. 9911/2008, art 194 (1).

debtor's assets in a state of insolvency is avoided and the debtor is given the opportunity to continue to exist and be involved in economic activity under an agreement jointly accepted by its creditors.

2.75 In the framework of further strengthening the regulatory legal framework on bankruptcy proceedings, on 27 October 2016 the Parliament of the Republic of Albania has approved the new bankruptcy law no. 110/2016. The new law, which entered into force on 22 May 2017, has as its main objective the definition of simpler, more understandable and more easily applied rules for the parties involved in the process, including but not limited to debtors, creditors, courts, bankruptcy administrators, evaluation experts, etc. Referring to a Western model in law drafting, the working group composed of local and foreign experts, at the beginning of the new law on bankruptcy, introduced through definitions the meaning of each term referred to in the law. This special provision cites definitions of the administrator, bankruptcy administrator, temporary administrator, supervisory administrator, National Bankruptcy Agency, debtor, meaning of days, expert, bankruptcy court, foreign court, bankruptcy creditor, bankruptcy proceeding creditor, insured creditor, creditor with exclusive/exceptive right, uninsured creditor, custodian, final creditors, preferred creditors, interim measures, bankruptcy amount, insolvency, participating parties, person linked with the debtor, foreign representative, conditional claim, secondary foreign proceeding, foreign proceeding, main foreign proceeding, main center of interest, discharge of outstanding liabilities, domicile/residence and location.

2.76 The new law includes the principles of applicable legislation, efficiency and transparency of information. Unlike the previous law, it mentions that the circle of subjects for which the initiation of bankruptcy proceedings may be required, includes those entities operating in strategic sectors. The general rule requires that strategic sectors, should be technically approved by virtue of a normative act of the Council of Ministers. The bankruptcy proceedings for such entities begin only in cases where the specific legislation of the relevant field where this entity operates, does not have rules defined for bankruptcy proceedings. The new bankruptcy law does not apply to insurance companies, banks, pension funds, securities investment funds and other institutions that collect deposits from the public or other financial institutions, since bankruptcy proceedings are governed by a special law.

2.77 Unlike the previous law, in the case of debtor's request, the list of documents to be filed with the court has been amended and expanded. More specifically, the debtor's report is filed, which specifies the causes of insolvency and its analysis of the business future, historical extract issued by the National

Business Centre for the debtor, balance sheet and financial statements for the last three years of the debtor's activity. If the debtor has exercised the activity for a shorter period of time, documentation is required from the date of company registration. Also, a list of movable and immovable properties is required, including the value of each asset/property at the time of purchase; the current market value if these assets were subject to revaluation; location of properties; data recorded in public registers, if these assets are subject to any legal proceedings, if any of these assets is placed as a guarantee or is subject to any liens/encumbrances and, if so, the value of the secured credit; list of current balance of cash and sources of income; list of creditors, who are natural persons, including their names, addresses, value and source of liabilities; lists of creditors who are legal persons, including their names, addresses, headquarters, names of their legal representatives, if applicable, as well as the values and source of liabilities; list of debtor's debtors, be they natural or legal persons, including their names, addresses, headquarters, values and source of loan, as well as a list of all legal proceedings where the debtor is a party as plaintiff or respondent.

As regards the obligation to file a request for the commencement of bankruptcy proceedings, the deadlines have changed as to when the bodies of the company are or should have been aware and should submit a request for the initiation of bankruptcy proceedings. More specifically, the deadline has changed from 21 days to 60 days, which is calculated from the moment when the bodies of the commercial company are or should have been aware of the company's insolvency status. **2.78**

In the previous law, the creditor's request to initiate bankruptcy proceedings was considered by the court when assessing the existence of a lawful interest by the creditor. Further, in the new law, when the creditor submits a request for the initiation of a bankruptcy proceeding, he must prove the existence of a matured and outstanding liability. The conception of the debtor's insolvency status has also changed as the new law presumes that this situation exists if the creditor has failed to collect his obligation according to the provisions referred to in Articles 517 et seq. of Civil Proceeding Code. **2.79**

Unlike the previous law when the bankruptcy temporary administrator checked the debtor's conditions as to whether or not the insolvency proceeding should be initiated, in the new law the court assesses the documentation specified in the relevant articles of the law both in the case when the claim is filed by the debtor and where the claim is filed by the creditor. If, after an overall revision of documents, the debtor's insolvency is proven, the bankruptcy court declares the commencement of the proceedings within 5 days in **2.80** the case of the debtor's request. If the claim is compliant with article 16, the bankruptcy court shall notify the debtor about the claim within five days, attaching a full copy thereof and accompanying documents in the case of the creditor's request.

2.81 Another fresh component of the law on bankruptcy is the assignment of experts from different areas to ascertain or clarify the facts, requiring special knowledge in the areas of science, technology or art, which are not covered by the specific knowledge of the administrator. In this case, the court may summon, at any stage of the bankruptcy proceedings, one or more experts if requested by the parties or, if deemed reasonable by the bankruptcy court. After assigning the expert or experts, the court assigns them the tasks and deadline within which the act of expertise should be drafted. The deadline for its preparation, as a rule, should not exceed 20 days, unless the court orders otherwise. The expert is provided with all the information of the case and cannot refuse the assigned duty without justified grounds.

2.82 In cases of the debtor's lack of property to cover the proceeding costs, the court decides on the completion of the proceeding. Before deciding on the outcome of the proceeding, the bankruptcy court issues a public announcement and informs the creditors of the situation at the National Business Centre, as well as to all public authorities whereas appropriate, the respective notes are required to be reflected according to law. Creditors and other interested parties have the right to appear before the bankruptcy court within 60 days of the notice and to object to the termination of the proceeding due to lack of assets, if they claim that the debtor has any assets or has previously concealed them. At this point, another novelty of the law is the referral of the court to the prosecutor's office of the allegations of the parties. The bankruptcy court, within five days from the expiry of the deadline for objections, communicates to the prosecutor any claims of the parties, which have reasonable grounds for the need to conduct further investigations on the debtor's actions, and suspend the proceeding for six months for conducting the investigation.

2.83 The administrative costs of the proceeding and bankruptcy proceeding costs are defined very clearly and precisely in the new law by also making a clear separation between them. The rights and obligations of the creditors and creditors' committee are clearly defined in the law, specifying the voting, opposition/challenge, participation, remuneration, announcement or the value of each vote in proportion to the total value of claims.

2.84 In the bankruptcy proceeding, the meeting for reporting purposes is the most important meeting of the bankruptcy proceeding, since in this meeting it is decided whether the debtor will be subjected to liquidation or if a reorganization plan can be applied for him. In the new law, in the case of liquidation of the debtor, a new preference order has been set on the fulfillment of creditor claims, unlike the provisions of article 605 of Civil Code.

Regarding bankruptcy proceedings with respect to foreign countries, **2.85** the provisions set out by the relevant heads of law are compliant with UNCITRAL (United Nation Commission on International Trade Law). The purpose of this part of the law is to provide effective mechanisms in international bankruptcy cases to promote the objectives of cooperation between courts and other authorities of Albania with other states involved in international bankruptcy, higher trade and investment security, fair and efficient administration of international bankruptcy cases for the protection of interests of all creditors and other interested parties, including the debtor, as well as the protection and maximization of the value of debtor's assets and the relief of the rescue of companies with financial issues, thus protecting investment and labor market.

The tenth and final part of the new law on bankruptcy other than the previous **2.86** law is the part of administrative contraventions. This part mentions the fact that filing of false statements by the debtor, members of the governing bodies, shareholders and partners or any other individual acting on behalf of the debtor will be considered an administrative violation and is punishable by a fine from the bankruptcy court amounting from 50 000 to 200 000 ALL. If false statements are filed by an individual debtor, it will be considered an administrative contravention and is punishable by the bankruptcy court by a fine amounting from 50 000 to 100 000 ALL. In addition, the concealment, transfer or alienation of assets/properties or documents from the bankruptcy or supervisory authority, custodian or bankruptcy court with a view to obstructing the bankruptcy proceeding shall be considered an administrative contravention and shall be punishable by the court by a fine from 50 000 up to 200,000 ALL.

Failure to execute bankruptcy court decisions or writs/orders by bankruptcy or **2.87** supervisory administrators, as well as failure to comply with deadlines, according to law, are considered as administrative contraventions and are punishable by the bankruptcy court with fines from 50 000 up to 200 000 ALL. Also, refusal of the bankruptcy administrator to hand over the assets/properties and documentation of the proceeding, if dismissed from office, is considered an administrative contravention and is punishable by the court by a fine from 50 000 up to 200 000 ALL. In conclusion, it is worth citing the fact that by 22.11.2017 the Council of Ministers has the obligation to draft the whole additional legal framework with new bylaws pursuant to Law 110/2016, dated

27.11.2016 'On bankruptcy'. During this period the bylaws covering insolvency are in force under the former law, as long as they are not in conflict with the provisions of new law.

2.88 The reforms on the insolvency law have been done, and are still under the particular attention of the Word Bank.

3

NATIONAL REPORT FOR ARGENTINA[1]

Héctor José Miguens[2]

A. INTRODUCTION

The origins of Argentina's bankruptcy[3] system date back to the 19th century. In 1862 the Commercial Code was put into force for the whole nation as a federal 3.01

1 This collaborative chapter has been made possible with financial aid from the Consejo Nacional de Investigaciones Científicas y Técnicas, (CONICET), Argentina, and from the Alexander von Humboldt Foundation, Germany, which funding is gratefully acknowledged. This is the translation into English of the Spanish text made by the author of the present report.

2 I am indebted to Prof. Javier Lorente for some passages of the English texts of the first part (Introduction) of this chapter.

3 In this chapter, the words 'bankruptcy' and 'insolvency' are used as synonyms to describe the procedures that deal with corporate entities.

law and, in 1869, the Civil Code was put into force as federal law as well. The original version of the Commercial Code was similar to the 1807 French Code. Therefore, it included provisions that dealt with the insolvency issues experienced, at that time pertaining, by commercial traders and corporations. The local Procedural Law of each Province dealt with the bankruptcy provisions for non-commercial entities. This Commercial Code was amended in 1889.

3.02 In 1902, Argentina passed for the first time a Bankruptcy Act with the number 4156 (the numbers of all National (Federal) Legal Acts of Argentina have begun with the number 1 since 1853 when the first Federal Constitution was approved). This Act was completely replaced by another Bankruptcy Act in 1933 (number 11719), which was again replaced in 1972 by the Bankruptcy Act no. 19551, then partially reformed by Act no. 22917 in 1983. This last Act unified all bankruptcy procedures for both commercial and non-commercial entities.

3.03 The current law was first enacted in 1995 (Bankruptcy Act no. 24522). Even though some of its sections have been reformed throughout the years (Act no. 25589 in 2002; Act no. 26086 in 2006; and Act no. 26684 in 2011), the 1995 Act conserves its original structure, and its purposes have not significantly changed in these years.

3.04 In Argentina, insolvency matters are regulated by the federal government, and they form part of the federal law (called 'derecho común' in Spanish). The same provisions are therefore applied throughout the country. This means that any local court in the country in any of the Federal Estates or 'Provinces' has jurisdiction over insolvency procedures, provided that the court has jurisdiction over Civil and Commercial Law Matters. The Insolvency Act ('Ley de Concursos y quiebras', in Spanish) was traditionally part of the former Commercial Code. The new Civil and Commercial Code of 2014 ('CCC') has not affected the main Insolvency Law institutions regulated by the 1995 Insolvency Act ('Argentine Insolvency Act', 'AIA').

3.05 The AIA outlines three statutory court-supervised proceedings that may be voluntarily commenced by a distressed company and/or natural person/consumer: (i) an 'acuerdo preventivo extrajudicial' ('APE'), a restructuring proceeding similar to a U.S. pre-packaged Chapter 11; (ii) a reorganization proceeding, called 'Concurso preventivo' in Spanish ('CP'); and (iii) a 'quiebra', or liquidation proceeding, comparable in its goals and structure to a U.S. Chapter 7, as it is performed under the control and supervision of a court for the purpose of liquidating the bankrupt's assets and distributing the proceeds among its creditors.

The characteristics and features of the Argentine proceedings are: officiousness, universality, collectiveness and equality of treatment of the creditors. In general terms the system of the AIA is regarded as a debtor-friendly regime, but there are scarce statistics on insolvency law issues in Argentina. 3.06

Local scholars have written monographs,[4] as well as articles[5] to explain the scope of Argentinian insolvency law. Noted Italian,[6] French[7] and Spanish[8] 3.07

4 Among others: Heredia, Pablo D., *Tratado exegético de derecho concursal*, Ley 24.522 y modificatorias, Comentada, anotada y concordada (ed. Ábaco de Rodolfo Depalma, Buenos Aires, Tomo V, 2005); Roitman Horacio, *Efectos jurídicos de laquiebra sobre los contratos preexistentes* (ed. Lerner, Córdoba, 1973); López de Zavalía, F., *Teoría de los contratos, Parte general* (Zavalía, Buenos Aires, 1971); Florit, S. M./Rossi, J. M., *Comentario teórico-práctico a la ley de concursos* (Ediar, Buenos Aires, 1987); AAVV., *Derecho Concursal*, (Universidad Austral-Rubinzal Culzoni, Santa Fe) (595 pages) (this is a monography on contracts and insolvency); Martín y Herrera, F., *Estudios sobre la legislación de laquiebra* (Valerio Abeledo, Buenos Aires, 1917); Holand, M., *Ley 24.522. nuevo régimen de concursos y quiebra. Análisis exegético* (ed. Juris, Rosario, 1996); Foiguel López, H. J./Donadio, J. A, *Manual de concursos*, Universidad, Buenos Aires, Tomo I. (1987); Satanowsky, I., *Tratado de derecho comercial*, Tea, Buenos Aires, Tomo 3 (1957); Fontanarrosa, R., *Derecho comercial argentino. Doctrina general de los contratos*, Zavalía, Buenos Aires (1969); Castillo, R. S., *La quiebra en el derecho argentino* (Buenos Aires, 1940); Carranza, A. S., *La nueva ley argentina de quiebras n. 11719* (El Ateneo, Buenos Aires, Tomo II, 1937); Matienzo, A. N., *Curso de quiebra* (Ghio, Buenos Aires, Tomo I, 1927); Rivarola, M. A., *Tratado de derecho comercial argentino* (Compañía Argentina de Editores, Buenos Aires, Tomo V, 1940); Maffía, O. J., *La ley de concursos comentada* (ed. Depalma, Buenos Aires, 2001); Rivera, Julio C./Roitman, Horacio/Vítolo, Daniel R., *Reformas a la ley de concursos y quiebras* (ed. Rubinzal-Culzoni, 2006), Williams, J. N., *Efectos de la quiebra respecto de los codeudores y fiadores del fallido* (Abeledo-Perrot, Buenos Aires, 1961); Quintana Ferreyra, F., *Concursos* (Astrea, Buenos Aires, Tomos I y II, 1985–1986); Parry, A. E., *Efectos de la quiebra y el concurso civil en las obligaciones y en los contratos* (ed. TEA, Buenos Aires, 1950) (764 pages); García Martínez, R., *El concordato y la quiebra* (Zavalía, Buenos Aires, Tomos II y III, 1957); Williams, J. N., *Contratos de crédito* (Ábaco, Buenos Aires, Tomos 1 y 2-B, 1984–1987); Maffía, O. J., *Manual de concursos* (La Rocca, Buenos Aires, 1997); Martorell, E. E., *Tratado de concursos y quiebras* (ed. Lexis Nexis, Buenos Aires, 2004); AAVV. Rouillon, Adolfo A. N. (dir.)/Alonso, Daniel F. (coord), *Código de Comercio, Comentado y anotado* (ed. La Ley, Buenos Aires, Tomos I, IV-A y IV-B, 2005); Rivera, Julio C./ Roitman, Horacio/Vítolo, Daniel R., *Concursos y quiebras. Ley 24.522* (ed. Rubinzal-Culzoni, Santa Fe, 1995 y 2000); Games, L./ Gerez, O./Esparza, G., *Aspectos laborales en la nueva ley de concursos y quiebras* (wd. Depalma, Buenos Airres, 1996); Baravalle, Roberto A./Granados, Ernesto I., *Ley de Concursos y quiebras, ley 24.522* (ed. Liber, Rosario, 1996); Cámara, H., *El concurso preventivo y la quiebra*, comentario ley 19.551 (ed. Depalma, Buenos Aire, 1982); Satanowsky, I., *Estudios de derecho comercial* (Tea, Buenos Aires, Tomo I, 1950); Dasso, Ariel A./Dasso, Ariel Gustavo/Dasso, Javier Aníbal, *Quiebras. Concurso preventivo y cramdown* (ed. Ad-Hoc, Buenos Aires, 1997); Rivera, Julio César, *Instituciones de derecho concursal* (ed. Rubinzal-Culzoni, Santa Fe., 2000); Martín y Herrera, F., *La convocación de acreedores en la quiebra* (Coni, Buenos Aires, Tomo II, 1923); López de Zavalía, F., *Teoría de los contratos, Parte especial* (Zavalía, Buenos Aires, Tomo I, 1976); Farina, J. M., *Rescisión y resolución de contratos (civiles y comerciales)* (ed. Orbir, Rosario, 1965); Williams, J. N., *La letra de cambio y el pagaré* (Abeledo-Perrot, Buenos Aires, 1981); Rivera, Julio César, *Cuestiones laborales en la ley de concursos*, Astrea (Buenos Aires, 1982); Armengol, M. F., *Fundamentos y crítica de la ley de quiebras* (José Tragant, Buenos Aires, 1914); Fargosi, H. P., *Cuestiones de Derecho Comercial* (ed. Jorge Alvarez, Buenos Aires, 1965); García Martínez, R./Fernandez Madrid, *Concursos y quiebras*, Contabilidad Moderna (Buenos Aires, 1976, Tomos I y II); Negre de Alonso. L. T., *Los acreedores laborales en el proceso concursal* (Rubinzal-Culzoni, Santa Fe, 1996); Fargosi, H. P., *Nuevas cuestiones de derecho comercial* (ed. Cangallo, Buenos Aires, 1971); Junyent Bas, F./Molina Sandoval C. A., *Ley de concursos y quiebras comentada* (Lexis-Nexis, Depalma, Buenos Aires, Tomo II, 2003); Obarrio M., *Estudio sobre las quiebras (anotado y puesto al día por C.C. Malagarriga)* (ed. Atanasio Martínez, Buenos Aires, 1926); Orione, F., *Exposición y crítica a la ley de quiebras* (El Ateneo, Buenos Aires, Tomos I y III., 1934–1935); Segovia, L., *El Código Civil de la República Argentina, con su explicación y crítica bajo la forma de notas* (Coni, Buenos Aires, 1981); Jorge Nicanor Williams, *Los contratos preparatorios. Su incidencia*

authors have influenced the Argentinian insolvency debate throughout the 20th century to the present. However, the subject of the treatment of

---

en el derecho comercial (Ábaco, Buenos Aires, 1978); Malagarriga, C. C., *Código de Comercio Comentado* (ed. Jajouane, Buenos Aires, 1952); Fassi, S. C./Gebhardt, M., *Concursos, Comentario exegético de la ley 19.551 con las reformas de la ley 22.917 y jurisprudencia actualizada* (ed. Astrea, Buenos Aires, 3rd ed., 1986); Malagarriga, C. C., *Tratado elemental de derecho comercial* (ed. TEA, Buenos Aires, 1952); Obarrio M., *Estudio sobre las quiebras* (Lajouane, Buenos Aires, 1895); Nougues, R. A., *La cuenta corriente bancaria*, (ed. Pannedille, Buenos Aires, 1970); Sánchez Urite, *Mandato y representación* (ed. Abeledo-Perrot, Buenos Aires, 1969); Escuti (h), I./Junyent Bas, F., *Concursos y quiebras. Reforma del Régimen concursal. Ley 24.522* (Advocatus, Córdoba, 1995); Segovia, L., *Explicación y crítica del nuevo Código de Comercio de la República Argentina* (La Facultad, Buenos Aires, tomo 3, 1933); Ruiz Guiñazú, E., *La quiebra en el derecho comercial argentina* (Juan Roldán and Cía, Buenos Aires, 1926); Lorenzetti, R. L., *Tratado de los contratos* (Rubinzal-Culzoni, Santa Fe, Tomo I, 1999); Lafaille, H., *Derecho civil. Contratos* (Ediar, Buenos Aires, Tomo I, 1953); Lorente, Javier, *La nueva ley de concursos y quiebras. Ley 24.522* (ed. Gowa, Buenos Aires, 1995); Lafaille, H., *Curso de contratos*, Ariel (Buenos Aires, Tomo III, 1928); Piantoni, M. A. (s.d.), *Las reformas contractuales en la ley 17.711 del Código Civil Argentino* (ed. Lerner, Córdoba); Solari, J. F. (s.d.), *El protesto* (ed. Abeledo Perrot, Buenos Aires); Argeri, S./Argeri Graziani, R., *El síndico en el concurso preventivo* (Platense, La Plata, 1976); Prat A. M./Zago, J. A., *El nuevo régimen de alquileres* (ed. Astrea, Buenos Aires, 1969); Rivarola, M. A., *Tratado de Derecho Comercial Argentino* (ed. Cía Arg. de Editores, Buenos Aires, Tomo V, 1940); Castillo, R., *Curso de derecho comercial* (Gaglianone, Buenos Aires, Cuatro Tomos, 1954–1957); Rocca, I./Griffi, O., *Locación mixta, divisibilidad* (ed. Ediar, Buenos Aires, 1968); Salvat, R., *Tratado de derecho civil argentino* (Contratos, ed. La Ley, Buenos Aires, 1946); Salvat, R., *Tratado de derecho civil argentino, Fuente de las obligaciones. Contratos* (La Ley, Buenos Aires, Tomos I y II, 1946); Zavala Rodríguez, Carlos Juan , *Código de Comercio y leyes complementarias, comentado y concordado* (Depalma, Buenos Aires, Tomo V, 1972); Rezzónico, L. M., *Estudio de los contratos en nuestro derecho civil* (Depalma, Tomos I y II, 1958–1959); Suárez, R. M., *Nuevo régimen de locaciones urbanas* (ed. Orbir, Buenos Aires, 1971); Salvat, R., *Tratado derecho civil argentino, Obligaciones en General* (ed. Menéndez, Buenos Aires, 1935); Argeri, S., *La quiebra y demás procesos concursales* (ed. Platense, La Plata, 1972); Farina, J. M., *Contratos comerciales modernos* (Astrea, Buenos Aires, 1999); Bunge Guerrico, H., (s.d.), *Interpretación de la ley de quiebras* (Valerio-Abeledo, Buenos Aires).

5 See, among others: Benélbaz, H., Algunos aspectos de la falencia y su vinculación con la actividad bancaria, Revista de Derecho Comercial y de las Obligaciones, 1984, 1; Bustamante Alsina, Jorge (s.d.), El boleto de compraventa inmobiliaria y su oponibilidad al concurso o quiebra del vendedor (La Ley, t. 131) 1272; Anido, C. (s.d.) Los boletos de compra venta de inmuebles. La situación del adquirente frente a la quiebra (ED t.181) 773; Balbín, Sebastián, Contratos en curso de ejecución y continuación de la actividad de la empresa en quiebra, en AAVV., Derecho Concursa (Universidad Austral-Rubinzal Culzoni, Santa Fe) 33 y ss.; Bendersky, M. (s.d.) Efectos de la quiebra sobre la compraventa inmobiliaria celebrada en instrumento privado, (La Ley, t. 120) 87; Benedetti, J. C., 'El boleto de compraventa frente a la quiebra del vendedor', (1972) Revista del Notariado, n°. 722, 525; Benedini, F., Verificación o no de los boletos de compraventa en el concurso, (2001) Rev. Doctrina Judicial, t. 2001–2, 511; Bergel, S. D. (s.d.), Efectos de la quiebra del vendedor sobre el contrato de compraventa inmobiliaria no reducido a escritura pública (El Derecho, t. 11) 580; Bergel, S. D., 'Declaración de quiebra y obligación de escriturar' (1969) Jurisprudencia Argentina, t. 1969-III, 320; Bergel, S. D. (s.d.), La situación del comprador por boleto de compraventa ante la convocatoria de acreedores del vendedor, (El Derecho, t. 37) 645; Bielsa, Rafael, 'Concesión especial del dominio público. quiebra del concesionario. Extinción de la concesión, (1930) en Cuestiones de Administración municipal, Lajouane, Buenos Aires, 130; Bono, G. A., 'El adquirente por boleto de compraventa y los acreedores del vendedor' (1995) La Ley, t. 1995-E, 743; Borda, G. A. (s.d.), 'La posesión adquirida por boleto de compraventa y la quiebra del vendedor', 96 El Derecho, 500; Conil Paz, A., 'Exigibilidad de los aportes sociales por la quiebra' (1996) La Ley, t. 1996-B, 321; Cordero, M. A., 'Los aportes irrevocables a cuenta de futuras suscripciones y la quiebra' (2001) Anuario de Derecho Concursal, Ad Hoc Buenos Aires, año 1, Doctrina General, 147; Farina, J. M. (s.d.) 'Efectos de la quiebra de una de las partes sobre el mandato y otras figuras afines' Revista Zeus, t. 14, D-57; Farina, J. M. (s.d.) 'La declaración en quiebra y los contratos con prestaciones pendientes', Revista Zeus, t. 10, D-3; Farina J.M. (s.d.), 'La quiebra y la resolución contractual por incumplimiento', Revista Zeus, t. 11, D-41;

6 See: De Semo G., *Degli effeti del fallimento sui rapporti giuridici presistenti* (Cedam, Padova, 1968); Bonelli, G., 'Gli effetti del fallimento sui contratti bileterali' (1918) Riv. Del Diritto Commerciale, n° XVI, 3 y ss.; Bonelli

executory contracts, and their performance in case of insolvency of one of the parties is largely unexplored.

G., *Del Contratto di Conto Corrente* (Vallardi, Milano, 1930); Barbero, *Il contratto tipo nel diritto italiano* (Milano, 1935); Candian, *Trattative e contratti preliminari* (Roma, 1925); Vigo, R. (, I *contratti pendenti non disciplinati nella legge fallimentare* (Giuffrè, Milano, 1989); Di Chio, G., en AAVV 'Effetti del fallimento sui rapporti giuridici preesistenti' (1979) en Commentario Scialoja-Branca, Zanichelli-Foro Italiano, Bologna-Roma; Caltabiano, A., *Il conto corrente bancario* (Cedam, Padova, 1967); Galgano, F./Bonsignori, A., 'Il fallimento de la società' (1988) en Trattato di diritto commerciale e di diritto pubblico dell'economia, Galgano F. (dir.), Cedam, Padova, Vol. X; Messineo F., *Manual de derecho civil y comercial* (Traducción de Sentís Melendo, Ed. EJEA, Buenos Aires, 1955); Vidari, E., *Corso di diritto commerciale* (5th ed. Hoepli, Milano, Tomo VIII, 1907); Vivante, C, *Trattato di diritto commerciale* (5th ed. Francesco Vallardi, Milano-Bologna, Tomo IV, 1934); De Semo, G., *Diritto Fallimentare*, (Cedam, Padova, 1968); Donati A., *Trattato del Diritto delle Assicurazioni Private* (Giuffé, Milano, 1954); Ferrara, *Teoria dei contratti* (Napoli, 1940); Fiorentino, A., *Le operazione bancarie* (Jovene, Napoli, 1964); De Sensi, V. Spunti di riflessione sulla reforma della legge fallimentare secondo il disegno di legge delega gobernativo del 24/11/2000, at http://archivioceradi.luiss.it/2004/07/27/crisi-archivio-art-8/. last visited in Noverber 29th, 2018; Gabba, F., *Contributo alla dottrina della promessa bilaterale di contratto (nuove questioni di diritto civile)* (Torino, 1912); Messineo F., *Teoría general del contrato*, Traducción de Sentís Melendo-Volterra (ed. EJEA, Buenos Aires, 1952); Bolaffio, L., *Il concordato preventivo, secondo le sue tre leggi disciplinatrici* (Unione Tipografica Editrice Torinense, Torino, 1933); Navarrini, *La quiebra*, Traducción de Hernández Borondo (ed. Reus, Madrid, 1943); Pipia, U., *Del Fallimento, del concordato preventivo e dei piccoli fallimento* (UTET, Torino, 1931); Provinciali, R., *Tratado de derecho de quiebra*, con notas de derecho español de Ramírez López, (ed. A.H.R., Barcelona, 1958); Ramírez, J. A., *Derecho concursal español, la quiebra* (Bosch, Barcelona, 1959); Pellegrino, G., *Contratti bancari e procedure concorsuali* (Cedam, Padova, 2000); Ramella, Del contratto di conto corrente, del mandato commerciale, della comissione, *Codice di Commercio Comentato*, (UTET, Torino, 1928); Ascarelli, R., *Saggi di diritto commerciale* (Giuffrè, Milano, 1955); De Semo, G., *Diritto fallimentare* (Cedam, Padova, 1967); Santarelli, U., *Per la storia del fallimento nelle legislazioni italiane dell'età intermedia* (Cedam, Padova, 1964); Fiorentino, A., *Il contocorrente* (Utet, Torino, 1957); Zanarone, G., *La resoluzione del contratto nel fallimento* (Giuffrè, Milano, 1970); Zavala Rodríguez, C. J., *Código de Comercio y leyes complementarias* (Depalma, Buenos Aires, 1966–90); Rivolta, G. C., *L'eserzicio dell'impresa nel fallimento*, (Giuffrè, Milano, 1969); Barbero, D., *Sistema del diritto privato italiano* (UTET, Torino, Tomo II., 1965); Rodríguez Rodríguez, *Derecho Bancario* (ed. Porrúa, México, 1968); Ricci, E., *Lezioni sul fallimento* (Giuffrè, Milano, 1997–1998); Pajardi, P. (a cura di), *Codice del fallimento* (Giuffrè, Milano, 1994); Satta, S., *Instituciones del derecho de quiebras*, traducción de Fontanarrosa, (ed. EJEA, Buenos Aires, 1951); Pajardi, P., *Manuale di diritto fallimentare* (Giuffrè, Milano, 1998); Fiorentino, A., Contro corrente. Contrati bancari, en Scialoja A./Branca, G. *Comentario del Codice civile*, Nanichelli, Bologna-Roma (1969); De Semo, *Trattato di diritto cambiario* (Cedam, Padova, 1963); Tedeschi, G. H, *Assicurazione e fallimento* (CEDAM, Padova, 1969); Betti, E., *Teoría general del negocio jurídico* (ed. Revista de Derecho Privado, Madrid, 1959); Bolaffio, L. 'De la quiebra', en Bolaffio, L./Rocco, U./Vivante, C. *Derecho comercial*, Ediar, Buenos Aires, Tomo III correspondiente al tomo XX de la obra general (1955); Bonelli, G., *Del fallimento (commento al Codice di Commercio)* (Vallardi, Milano, Tomos I a III, 1938–1939); Satta, S., *Diritto Fallimentare* (Cedam, Padova, 1996); AAVV., *La revocatoria fallimentare dei versamenti in conto corrente bancario* (Cedam, Padova, 1987); Bonsignori, A., Il fallimento, en AAVV. *Trattato di diritto commerciale e di diritto pubblico dell'economia*, en AAVV. Galgano, F. (ed.) (Cedam, Padova, Tomo IX, 1986); Bonsignori, A./Nardo, G./Lazzara M., *I contratti nelle procedure concorsuali* (Giuffrè, Milano, 1992); Brunetti, A., *Tratado de quiebras*, traducción de Joaquín Rodríguez Rodríguez (Porrúa, México, 1945); Cariota Ferrara, L., *El negocio jurídico* (Aguilar, Madrid, 1956); Carnelutti, F., *Studi di diritto commerciale* (Roma, 1917) 207; Messineo, F., *Manual de derecho civil y comercial* (Ejea. Buenos Aires, Tomo IV, 1955); Ciotola, E., *Le obbligazioni nel fallimento* (Società Editrice Libraria, Milano, 1936); Cuzzeri, M./Cicu, A., De la quiebra, (1954) en Bolaffio, L./Rocco, U./Vivante, C., *Derecho Comercial*, Ediar, Buenos Aires, Tomos I y II, correspondientes al vol. 18 de la obra general; De Ferra, F., *Manuale di diritto fallimentare* (Giuffrè, Milano, 1998); Ferrara (Jr.) F./Borgioli, A., *Il fallimento* (Giuffrè, Milano, 1995); Ferrarini, G., *Locazione finanziaria*, (Giuffrè, Milano, 1977); Messineo, F., *Operaciones de bolsa y banca* (Bosch, Barcelona, 1957); Ferri, G., *Manuale di diritto commerciale* (UTET, Torino, 1965); Ragusa Maggiore, G./Costa C. (1997), *Le procedure concorsuali. Il fallimento*, Utet, Torino; Lo Cascio, G., *Il fallimento e le altre procedure concorsuali* (Ipsoa, Milano, 1998); Mazzocca, D.,

3.08 By way of introduction, it is possible to say that the Italian and French statutory approaches to the definition and treatment of contracts have been adopted and adapted to national practice.[9] This chapter will describe the treatment of executory contracts under the AIA and in accordance with relevant judicial cases. It is hoped that this work will contribute to the scholar debate and literature in the field, and will provide some food for thought for regulatory reform.

B. INSOLVENCY PROCEDURES

(1) The *Acuerdo Preventivo Extrajudicial* (APE) or pre-packaged reorganization

3.09 The APE is a court-supervised procedure similar to a pre-packaged Chapter 11 case under the U.S. Bankruptcy Code.[10] It is regulated in Sections 69–76 of

Manuale di diritto fallimentare, Jovene, Napoli, 1980); Messineo, F., *Doctrina general del contrato* (Ejea Buenos Aires, Tomos I y II, 1952); Molle, G. I contratti bancari, en Cicu, A./Messineo, F., *Trattato di diritto civile e commerciale* (Giuffrè, Milano, Vol. XXXV, Tomo 1, 1966); Navarrini H., *La quiebra. Traducción española de la obra El fallimento. Estratto dal trattato teorico-pratico di diritto commerciale*, Vol. VI (Fratelli Bocca, Torino, 1926), Reus, Madrid, 1; Rocco, A., *Il fallimento. Teoria generale e origine storica* (Giuffrè, Milano, 1962).

7 See: Derrida F., *La reforme du réglement judiciaire et de la faillite* (Defrenois, Paris, 1969); Picard M./Besso, A., *Les assurances terrestres en droit francais* (ed. L.G.D.J., Paris, 1970); Escarra, *Principes de droit commercial* (Paris; Lyon-Caen, Ch/Renault, L., 1921–1936), *Traité du droit commercial*, F. Pichon, Paris, Tomo VIII; Rodière, René et al., *Faillites* (Dalloz, Paris, 1970); Thaller, E., *Traité élémentaire de droit comercial* (Arthur Rousseau, Paris, 1904); Argenson, J./Toujas, G., *Réglement judiciaire, liquidation des bienes et faillite* (Techniques, Paris, 1973); Aubry C. et Rau, C., *Cours de droit civil français* (Marchal, Billard & Cie, Paris, Tomos III y IV., 1871); Colin, A./Capitant, H., *Curso elemental de derecho civil*, traducción por Demófilo de Buen, Reus (Madrid, Tomo III, 1924); Massè, M. G., *Le droit comercial dans ses rapports avec le droit des gens et le droit civil* (Chez Guillaumien, Paris, T. II, 1862); Mazeaud, H. L., *Leçons de droit civil* (Obligations, Montchrestien, Paris, Tomo II, vol. 1, 1973); Ripert, G./Roblot, R., *Traité élémentaire de droit comercial* (Librairie Générale de Droit et de Jurisprudence, Paris, Tomo 2, 1986); Thaller, E., *Des faillites en droit comparé* (Arthur Rousseau, Paris, 1887); Percerou, J., *Des faillites et banquereutes et des liquidations judiciaires*, en Thaller, E. *Traité élémentaire de droit comercial* (Arthur Roussesau, Paris, Tomo I, 1907); Ripert, G./Boulanger, J., *Tratado de derecho civil* (La Ley, Buenos Aires, Tomo 2, 1964); Planiol, M., *Traité élémentaire de droit civil* (Librairie Générale de Droit et de Jurisprudence, Paris, Tomo 2, 1912); Pothier, R. J., *Oeuvres (annotées et mises en corrélation avec le Code Civil et la législation actuelle, par M. Bugnet)* (Videcoq, Père et Fils, Cosse et N. Delamotte, Paris, Vol. 2, 1848); Renouard, A. Ch., *Traité des faillites et banqueroutes* (3rd ed., Paris, Tomo I, 1857); Ripert, G., *Traité élémentaire de droit comercial* (Librairie Générale de Droit et de Jurisprudence, Paris, 1948).

8 See Finez Raton, J. M., *Los efectos de la declaración de quiebra en los contratos bilaterales* (Civitas, Madrid, 1992); Garrigues, J., *Tratado de derecho mercantil* (Revista de Derecho Mercantil, Madrid Tomo I, vol. 3, 1949) y Tomo III, vol. 1 (1964); Ramirez, J. A., *La quiebra. Derecho concursalespañol* (Bosch, Barcelona, Tomo II, 1998); Roca Sastre, R. M. (1948), *Estudios de derecho privado (obligaciones y contratos)*, Ed. Revista de Derecho Privado, Madrid, Tomo I.

9 Roitman Horacio, Efectos jurídicos de la quiebra sobre los contratos preexistentes (ed. Lerner, Córdoba, 1973), 241.

10 On the APE see in general: Rouillon, Adolfo A. N., *Régimen de concursos y quiebras* (17 ed. Astrea, Buenos Aires, 2016) 176–80. (Hereinafter *Régimen*); Rivera, Julio César/Roitman, Horacio/Vítolo, Daniel Roque, *Ley de Concursos y Quiebras, tercera edición actualizada* (ed. Rubinzal-Culzoni, Santa Fe (Argentina), Tomo II,

the AIA. The APE involves a restructuring agreement between the debtors and a fixed percentage of their unsecured creditors affected by the restructuring. The agreement is eventually submitted to the competent court for its approval pursuant to the AIA.

On 16 May 2002, Argentine Law No. 25589 (the 'Amendment'), which amended the AIA, became effective. The Amendment provided that the approval of an APE would bind all unsecured creditors that: (i) were creditors prior as of the date when the APE petition was filed; and (ii) were included in the APE, whether those creditors consented to the APE or not. **3.10**

While the APE can represent a useful restructuring tool in some cases,[11] the institute has been heavily criticised.[12] This is because in APEs the debtor can re-negotiate with the creditors ongoing obligations (including executory contracts) while avoiding the expenses and lengthy procedural stages that usually characterize a CP. In light of the requirement of court approval for an APE, and the many similarities with a CP, the APE proceeding is considered a 'judicial' proceeding under the Argentine Insolvency Law and has been characterized by some authors[13] as a sub-type or an abbreviated version of the CP. According to Section 69 AIA, a debtor who is in a situation of 'cesación de pagos' in Spanish (insolvency or suspension of payments) or who is undergoing economic or financial hardship of a general nature may reach an APE with their creditors and submit it for court approval. **3.11**

(2) The *Concurso Preventivo* (CP) or reorganization proceeding

The CP is a voluntary proceeding that can be triggered only by a debtor, even if any creditor with a valid and enforceable claim – whatever their nature and preference – may also file an involuntary bankruptcy petition against the debtor (Section 80 AIA). **3.12**

The main requirements a debtor must meet to seek protection under a CP are: (i) to be in situation of 'cesación de pagos' (insolvency); and (ii) to file the CP petition before a 'quiebra' (bankruptcy) is declared against the debtor (Section **3.13**

2005), 177–221; Carlos A. Molina Sandoval, *Acuerdo preventivo extrajudicial. Alternativas para la superación de las dificultades empresarias* (ed. Ábaco, Buenos Aires; Daniel Truffat, 2002), *El Nuevo acuerdo preventivo extrajudicial. Ley 25.589* (ed. Ad Hoc, Buenos Aires).

11 See Cámara Nacional de Apelaciones en lo Comercial, Sala A, 4 de octubre de 2004, *Multicanal SA s/acuerdo preventive extrajudicial*, El Dial.com

12 Some authors have criticized vigorously the APE in its present structure, e.g., Rivera, Julio César/Roitman, Horacio/Vítolo, Daniel Roque, *Ley de Concursos y Quiebras, tercera edición actualizada* (ed. Rubinzal-Culzoni, Santa Fe (Argentina), Vol. II, 2005), 177, 179, 183, 189, 192, 206–7. See also Rouillon, *Régimen* … , 179.

13 See Rouillon, *Régimen* … , 176–80.

10, AIA). In the case of a 'quiebra', the only eligibility requirement is to be in 'cesación de pagos'.

3.14 In a CP, the debtor retains the management of his assets under the supervision of the Trustee (Section 15 AIA). Despite the debtor-in-possession management, the debtor needs prior court approval to carry out certain acts (e.g., those related to recordable assets) and to perform any act other than in the ordinary course of business. Usually, it is not possible to seek ex-post approval of the case, but courts decide any issue on a case-by-case approach.

(3) The 'quiebra' or liquidation

3.15 The 'quiebra' is a typical liquidation proceeding, both voluntary and involuntary, comparable in goals to Chapter 7 of the U.S. Bankruptcy Code. It is performed under court control and supervision. Its goals are to liquidate the debtor's assets and distribute the proceeds among its creditors in proportion to their respective claims and/or credits.

3.16 Similar to the CP, the 'suspension of payments' or insolvency ('cesación de pagos') is the legal requirement for opening a 'quiebra' proceeding. This situation is described in Section 78 AIA as the state that shows that the debtor is unable to meet his obligations regularly as they become due, whatever their nature and the causes that give rise to it. In Section 79 of the AIA there is a list of events that triggers a rebuttable presumption of the existence of a situation of suspension of payment.

3.17 The 'quiebra' procedure will also be conducted and supervised by the court (a commercial trial judge) with broad powers (within the AIA) to conduct the whole proceedings. A trustee in bankruptcy is also appointed by the court. In a 'quiebra', according to Section 107 of the AIA, debtors are automatically dispossessed of the assets existing on the date of the declaration of bankruptcy, and of any other assets acquired by them until their discharge. The dispossession precludes the exercise of any disposition and/or management rights over such assets.

3.18 Once the bankruptcy and liquidation are ordered, the Bankruptcy Court has the power to declare all fraudulent dispositions of property that prejudice the debtor's assets null and void, under Sections 118 and 119 of the AIA.

3.19 In the liquidation proceeding, preferential transfers can be avoided under Section 120 of the AIA upon the application of the insolvency trustee or other parties-in-interest. The transaction must have taken place within the 'period of suspicion' ('período de sospecha'), i.e., no longer than 24 months before the opening of the bankruptcy proceeding. Before a transaction can be set aside, it must be established that: (i) the payment was made by an insolvent debtor; (ii) the transaction had the effect of preferring one creditor over another; and (iii) that the intent of the payment was to prefer the creditor to whom payment was made. The burden of proof is on the claimant.

C. TREATMENT OF EXECUTORY CONTRACTS

(1) In APEs and CPs

In APEs and CPs, the debtor can freely negotiate any modification of the terms of executory contracts ('EC') and submit them to the court, which can approve or decline the agreement, according to Sections 71 and 75 AIA, during the hearing for the judicial confirmation.[14] **3.20**

For the CP, Section 20 AIA regulates the contracts with pending reciprocal obligations in a regime similar but not identical to that regulated by Section 143.3 AIA. **3.21**

This regime distinguishes two situations: before and after the first 30 days since the opening of the CP. In the first case, the debtor may choose to fulfil the contract with pending reciprocal obligations. In order to do this, it must request and obtain the authorization of the judge and take into consideration the technical and impartial opinion of the liquidator, who acts to protect the interests of all creditors. Once compliance has been authorized, the contractor *in bonis* will be notified. The counter-party may either simply accept the contractual continuation or demand, in advance, the performance of the debtors' obligations arising from the contract, including those that should have been performed before the filing of the CP. If the bankrupt does not meet these obligations, the contract will be terminated.[15] **3.22**

After the repeal of the old Section 753 of the Civil Code and the introduction of Section 353 of the CCC, the current law prescribes a special treatment for ECs for which more than 30 days have passed without the debtor having opted for compliance. In these cases, the third party *in bonis* may: (a) terminate **3.23**

14 See, among others: See Roitman Horacio, *Efectos jurídicos de la quiebra sobre los contratos preexistentes* (ed. Lerner, Córdoba (Argentina) 1973); Pablo C. Barbieri, *Contratos y procesos concursales* (ed. Universidad, Buenos Aires, 2001); Rivera, Julio César/Roitman, Horacio/Vítolo, Daniel Roque, *Ley de Concursos y Quiebras, tercera edición actualizada* (ed. Rubinzal-Culzoni, Santa Fe (Argentina), Vol. I, 2005) 426–50.

15 Rouillon, *Régimen …* , 66–67.

the contract without requiring prior compliance, for which he must notify the insolvent and the trustee; or (b) require compliance, in which case the debtor must require prior judicial authorization if he wishes to comply. If the insolvent debtor does not wish to comply, does not request or does not obtain judicial authorization, or, for any other reasons, does not comply, the contract is rescinded.[16]

3.24 With regard to public services, Sections 20.4 and 20.5 of the AIA include a separate regime. If the bankrupt has outstanding obligations in consideration of public services used prior to the date of the opening of bankruptcy proceedings, failure to settle the outstanding bill does not result in the interruption of the service. On the contrary, the law prescribes that public services shall continue or be reactivated if interrupted. The entity providing the public service must verify its claim in the insolvency procedure according to Sections 21 and 32 of the AIA. After the opening of the CP, the provision of public services and their payment, are governed by extra-bankruptcy rules. Therefore, if the insolvent does not pay, specific rules that enable the provider to interrupt the service are applicable.[17]

(2) In 'quiebra' procedures

3.25 In quiebras, ECs are subject to Sections 143–159 of the AIA. Specific provisions for the contract of leasing are provided by a special law, number 25.248, Sections 11.2, 11.3 and 26.[18]

(3) General scheme for all contracts

3.26 Broadly speaking, contracts can be classified into three groups depending on whether, at the time of the filing, they are: (a) fully executed (AIA, Sections 147, 148, 153 and 158); (b) continued or continuing contracts

---

16 Ibid., 67.

17 Ibid.

18 Section 11.2 of the Leasing Contract Act number 25248 establishes that in the event of a tender or 'bankruptcy' of the donor, the contract will continue for the agreed term, and the borrower may exercise the purchase option in the expected time. Section 11.3. rules the case of 'quiebra' of the taker, the Trustee being able, within 60 days of the 'quiebra' declaration, to choose either continuing the contract under the agreed conditions or resolving it. In the case of the CP, the debtor may choose to continue the contract or resolve it, within the deadlines and through the procedures provided for in Section 20 of Law 24522. Once the pre-specified deadlines have elapsed without the option being exercised, the contract is deemed to have been terminated in full, and the asset must be returned immediately to the giver, by an insolvency judge order, at the request of the giver solely upon the exhibition of the contract inscribed and without need to verify the credit in the insolvency proceedings. Notwithstanding this, the giver may claim the fee accrued until the return of the good, in the CP or in the 'quiebra' proceeding and claim any other contractual rights. For other provisions on the leasing contract see CCC, Sections 1227 et seq.

(AIA, Sections 157.1 and 154); and (c) suspended, pending a determination as to whether they will be rescinded or continued through their 'assumption' by the liquidator (AIA, Sections 143.3 and 144).

For all cases that do not fit in any of these categories, the residual rule of Section 159 AIA applies. **3.27**

With specific reference to ECs, the statutory reference is represented by the three sections of Section 143, and Section 144.[19] **3.28**

The scheme of Section 143 is as follows: **3.29**

(1) If the obligation of the insolvent party is fully performed, the other party must perform his or her own obligation;
(2) If the obligation of the *in bonis* contractor is already performed, he must seek verification of the claim in the insolvency proceedings;
(3) If there are mutual obligations pending, the insolvent contractor has the right to request the termination of the contract, under Section 144 of the AIA.

The residual rule of AIA Section 159 establishes that in property relationships not expressly contemplated by insolvency or other laws, the judge must decide by applying the principles underpinning the above-mentioned rules, taking care of due protection of creditors, the integrity of the assets of the debtor and his company, the stage of the insolvency proceeding and the general interest. **3.30**

Legal scholars[20] observed that, in the first place, it is necessary to resort to analogy and then, in the absence of an analogous legal-positive norm, to the general principles inspiring the insolvency law mentioned in this chapter. These are the protection of credit, the going concern of the company, and the protection of the general interest. Unfortunately, it is often impossible to simultaneously protect all these interests. As a result, it is commonly accepted that courts have to exercise their discretion to give preference to one of them to the detriment of others, on the basis of the particular circumstances of the case to be resolved. **3.31**

---

19 Rouillon, *Régimen …* , 265–66.

20 See, among others, Rouillon, *Régimen …* , 286–7. Rivera, Julio César/Roitman, Horacio/Vítolo, Daniel Roque, *Ley de Concursos y Quiebras, tercera edición actualizada* (ed. Rubinzal-Culzoni, Santa Fe (Argentina), Vol. II, (2005) 829.

(4) Rules for reciprocal pending obligations

3.32 Section 144 of the AIA is applicable. Some authors have highlighted the differences between current Section 144 and its predecessor, Section 148 of law no. 19551.[21]

3.33 At present, the creditors or third parties concerned and the liquidator can give an opinion on the continuation or termination of these contracts. The bankrupt debtor has no standing to be heard. The current legal terminology seems to exclude the idea of incidental controversy on the subject, and the trustee (which is the same person for the CP and for the 'quiebra') assumes a role of an impartial technician instead of an opposing party. The judge can choose to follow (or not) the opinion of the trustee.

3.34 In those limited cases where Section 144 does not apply, parties can rely on Articles 147, 153 and 154 of the AIA. Some contracts have a special regime, as in the case of leasing contracts, which are subject to Sections 11 and 26 of Law no. 25248 as we have already explained.[22]

3.35 After the negotiations between the contractor *in bonis*, the trustee and other non-contracting third parties, the judge decides on the continuation or termination of the contract with reciprocal pending obligations. If the judgment is delayed by more than ten days, the contractor can request and obtain the termination of the contract. In cases of utmost urgency, statutory terms can be shortened. The contractors *in bonis* may subject their performance to the granting of additional guarantees. If they are not paid, their claims will be prioritized and they will be paid at the same time as those listed in Section 240 AIA (conservation and justice costs).[23]

(5) Contractual clauses

3.36 According to Section 145 AIA, the bankruptcy declaration renders all legal or contractual clauses that authorize the resolution for non-compliance inapplicable, unless that resolution did not actually occur or was demanded before that judgment. These clauses are commonly known as *ipso facto* clauses.

---

21 See Rouillon, *Régimen …* , 267.

22 Ibid., 267–70.

23 Ibid., 269–70.

On this topic, some authors[24] have observed that upon the submission of an insolvency petition, contracts are governed by the specific provisions of the AIA, except when it so provides. Thus, unless before the bankruptcy the contractor *in bonis* had made use of the power to terminate the contract and there had been no controversy over the exercise of such power, it will be already consolidated at the onset of bankruptcy. **3.37**

If prior to the opening of an insolvency procedure, the parties were involved in a litigation on the validity of these clauses, such litigation will follow its normal course. Only if the complaint is rejected, Section 145 of the AIA is applicable. **3.38**

(6) Preliminary contracts[25]

Pursuant to Section 146 of the AIA, promises to agree on a contract or contracts concluded without the form required by the law are unenforceable during the course of insolvency proceedings, except when the contract may be performed by the debtor and there is a judicial authorization, at the express request of the trustee and the third party. **3.39**

Section 146 of the AIA also provides that preliminary contracts for the purchase of real estates shall be valid within the bankruptcy proceedings if the buyer has paid 25 per cent of the price. **3.40**

The CCC, in Section 1171 added to this case the requirement of 'fecha cierta'[26] of the ticket in order to obtain the 'effectiveness' ('oponibilidad' in Spanish)[27] of it in the bankruptcy proceedings before the insolvency declaration.[28] **3.41**

In these cases, the judge must, whatever the destination of the property, grant to the buyer the legal title of the property once the buyer has paid the balance. In the event that the price is paid in instalments, the payment of the balance shall be guaranteed by a first-degree mortgage on the real estate property. **3.42**

---

24 Ibid. 270.

25 '*Promesas de contrato*' (namely, for example a '*Boleto de compraventa*' in Spanish). This is a preliminary contract in which the parties agree to formally execute a contract at a future point in time in a more formal document, usually a notarized document, when the law requires it, like, typically, the sales of real states. See Cabanellas de las Cuevas/Eleanor C. Hoague, *Diccionario jurídico/Law Dictionary*, Vol. 2 (ed. Heliasta, Buenos Aires, 1993) 519.

26 Date for which there is sufficient evidentiary proof as to be effective as against third parties. See ibid., 261.

27 That is quality of a transaction which creates rights against third parties. See ibid., 450.

28 See Rouillon, *Régimen*, 271–2.

3.43 Notwithstanding this favourable treatment for the buyer, if the ticket was granted within the suspect period for avoidance actions, its validity can be questioned if it is proved that the buyer knew that the debtor was in a state of cessation of payments (Sections 119 and 120 of the AIA).[29]

(7) Contracts with personal performance by the bankrupt, contracts of continuous execution[30] and normative contracts[31]

3.44 Section 147 of the AIA establishes that contracts in which the pending execution is personal and irreplaceable, as well as those of continuous execution and the normative ones, are automatically resolved upon the opening of the insolvency procedure without any exception. These contracts include contracts of mandate, bank account contracts, and agency, concession and distribution agreements.

3.45 Several authors have explained that contracts of continuous execution are those contracts in which the benefits for both parties do not occur only at specific moments in time, but throughout the duration of the contract (e.g., distribution contracts, agency, concession, franchising) or periodically according to a certain permanent need (e.g., supply contract). However, employment contracts (as defined by the Labour Contract Act, law no. 20.744 as amended, sections 4, 21 and 22) (Section 196 AIA) and the lease of properties (Section 157.1 and 157.2.) are governed by specific rules and are not always and irrevocably rescinded.

3.46 Normative contracts do not have an autonomous function. It is usually said that they serve as a framework to regulate the relationships between the parties. Examples of these contracts include bank accounts and similar contracts. For these types of contracts, Sections 380.g (power), 1441.a (commercial checking account), 1404.b (checking account), 1494.c (agency), 1509 (concession), 1522 (franchising) of the CCC are applicable, in accordance with Section 147 of the AIA.[32]

---

29 See ibid., 272.

30 '*Contrato de ejecución continuada*'.

31 '*Contrato normativo*'. That is a contract that creates rules to regulate the future conduct of the parties. See Cabanellas de las Cuevas/Eleanor C. Hoague, *Diccionario jurídico/Law Dictionary*, Vol. 2 (ed. Heliasta, Buenos Aires, 1993) 153.

32 See Rouillon, *Régimen*, 272–3.

(8) Commission or consignment contracts

The general rule is that all commission or consignment contracts are automatically terminated upon the insolvency of the principal or commission agent. Pursuant to Section 148 AIA, two specific rules for the bankruptcy of the consignee are regulated. The first establishes that if the debtor has been sold goods by the principal, he can claim the unpaid price directly from the buyer, until the concurrence of what is owed for the same operation, after hearing the trustee and with the authorization of the judge. The second establishes that if the debtor has purchased goods by the principal, the third-party seller has the power to collect directly from the principal the amount owed to the bankrupt, up to the concurrence of the unpaid price.[33] **3.47**

(9) Company contracts – law of recess

As an effect of the principle of the dispossession of the bankrupt company (Section 106 et seq. AIA), Section 149 of the AIA provides that if the right of recess is exercised by the associates when the company was in default, the partners must return all they have received for that reason pursuant to the conditions established by Section 150.2 of the EIA. Some authors believe that the two-year maximum regression period of Section 118 et seq. AIA, is not applicable, because this is not an ineffectiveness case.[34] **3.48**

(10) Non-integrated contributions to the corporation

On the one hand, Section 150 AIA establishes that the bankruptcy of the company requires the payment of the unpaid contributions for its shares by the partners. On the other hand, the law prohibits (exceptionally) the participation of unlimited liability partners (who are personally bankrupt by way of extension under Section 160 AIA) as creditors of the company. Thus, in the event of bankruptcy, the debt of the company to the unlimitedly responsible partner does not integrate that company's liability and neither does the asset of this failed partner include the credit he could have against the company.[35] **3.49**

---

33 See ibid., 274.
34 See ibid., 274–5.
35 See ibid., 275–6.

(11) Accidental corporation ('Sociedad accidental' or 'negocio en participación'[36])

3.50 The CCC in Sections 1448–1452 regulates joint ventures (or 'accidental companies' in the terminology of the previous company law in its Articles 361–366) as a kind of associative contract (CCC Sections 1442–1447). The literature in the field believes that Section 151 is applicable to accidental corporations as well.[37]

3.51 Section 151.1. AIA establishes that the declaration of insolvency against the managing partner produces the dissolution of the accidental corporation (or 'in participation'). It is also held that the other partners are not entitled to the assets subject to dispossession, as they are treated as creditors subordinated to unsecured ones (Section 240 AIA).

3.52 As the accidental or joint venture company is not a legal entity (Section 1448 of the CCC), neither are these entities subject to insolvency procedures: only the managing partner can be declared bankrupt. Third parties only acquire rights towards the managing partner, who responds unlimitedly for the entity's debts (Section 1449 of the CCC). It is unclear whether or not the managing partner's bankruptcy can be extended to other partners whose names were made public with their consent. The fact that there is no procedure against the entity means that, at least for the majority of insolvency scholars, the procedure against the managing partner cannot be extended to the other participants.[38]

3.53 With respect to other partnership agreements, these include: collaborative partnerships (CCC, Sections 1453–1462), transitory unions (Sections 1463–1469) and consortia of cooperation (CCC, Sections 1470–1478). With reference to these agreements, the grouping contract is extinguished, among other causes, by the bankruptcy of any of its participants, unless the contract allows its continuation despite such an event or the other participants decide unanimously against this outcome (CCC, Section 1461.d.). Regarding transitory union, the bankruptcy of any of the participants does not lead to the

36 '*Sociedad accidental*' in Spanish is in Argentine corporation law an unincorporated association resulting from an agreement between parties to invest capital and labour for a particular purpose. The managing investors are jointly liable for the association debts to the full extent of their personal assets, whereas the non-managing partners are liable only to the extent of their investment. Business is carried out in the name of the managing partners. See Cabanellas de las Cuevas/Eleanor C. Hoague, *Diccionario jurídico/Law Dictionary*, Vol. 2 (ed. Heliasta, Buenos Aires, 1993) 600.

37 See Rouillon, *Régimen*, 277–9.

38 See ibid., 277–8.

termination of the associative contract, which continues with the other participants if they agree on how to continue their business (CCC, Section 1469). With respect to the cooperation consortium, the CP, cessation of payments or bankruptcy of one of the members does not lead to the automatic termination of the contract, which continues with the others, except where this is factually or legally impossible (CCC, Section 1478).[39]

(12) Debentures and securities

Section 152 AIA regulates in particular the case in which the debtor has issued unpaid debentures or negotiable obligations. First, it establishes that if they have a special guarantee, the rules that regulate the mortgagee's or pledgee's rights in bankruptcy prevail over any conflicting law or agreement. Secondly, it establishes that in the case of debentures or negotiable obligations with floating or common guarantees, the trustee acts as adjunctive liquidator together with the Trustee in Bankruptcy, being able to designate the debenture holders or bondholders a representative if they had not done so before.[40] **3.54**

(13) Fixed-term contracts

In the case of fixed-term contracts, the general rules of contracts with reciprocal 'pending' obligations in Section 144 IAA do not apply. Section 153 AIA provides for the following discipline:[41] **3.55**

(A) If at the date of the declaration of bankruptcy (prior to the expiration of the contract) there are no contractual benefits in favour of any of the contractors – i.e., the insolvent party and the third *in bonis* – the contract is automatically terminated;
(B) If at the date of the declaration of bankruptcy (before the expiration of the contract), the liquidation results in a favourable difference to the contractor *in bonis*, the latter shall not wait for the agreed term and shall be entitled to claim in the insolvency proceeding the difference in its favour;
(C) If at the date of the declaration of bankruptcy (prior to the expiration of the contract), the liquidation results in a favourable difference to the insolvent contractor, the *in bonis* contractor is entitled to respect the original term of the contract. Once the maturity date has elapsed, the *in bonis* contractor cannot claim any right if, at that point, the settlement of

39 See ibid., 279.
40 See ibid., 280.
41 See ibid., 280–81.

the difference will play in its favour. If that difference still favours the bankruptcy assets, the *in bonis* contractor is only obliged to enter the lesser difference in favour of the bankruptcy estate.

3.56 Section 1429 CCC establishes that contracts entered into in a stock exchange or regulated market are governed by the rules issued by the respective authorities and approved by the control body.

3.57 There are neither specific regulations nor jurisprudence on the issue of *force majeure* in this type of contract.[42]

(14) Insurance contracts

3.58 Section 154 AIA regulates insurance contracts. This is one of the few cases of forced continuation of the contract, after the bankruptcy of one of the contractors (either the insurer or the policyholder), even against contractual stipulations to the contrary.[43]

(15) Protest of a security or negotiable instrument

3.59 Section 155 AIA regulates two cases regarding the institute of marketable securities protest. Section 155.1 establishes that in cases in which the declaration of bankruptcy exempts from the obligation to make the protest of titles, the subsequent cessation of the insolvency proceedings, whatever its cause, does not alter the effects of the dispensation. This is what authors have called extension of the dispensation of protest established in the exchange law.

3.60 Section 155.2 regulates the so-called dispensation of protest, specifically in insolvency cases, that the inefficiency and consequent restitution of what is paid in respect of these documents, under the conditions of Sections 118–122 of the AIA, produces the effects of the protest for the purposes of the actions against the other obligors.[44]

(16) Real estate leases

3.61 Section 157 of the AIA regulates the lease of properties in several sections.[45]

42 See CCC, ss 955 and 956.

43 See Rouillon, *Régimen*, 281–2.

44 See ibid., 282–3.

45 See ibid., 284–5.

With respect to the lessor's bankruptcy, the contract continues to produce all its legal effects, without the influence of the bankruptcy declaration (Section 157.1), but the lessee must pay the instalments to the trustee. 3.62

Under Section 157.2 of the AIA, in the case of the 'quiebra' of the lessee, when the property is for commercial use, Section 147 of the AIA is not applicable. If the use of the property has continued after bankruptcy, Sections 193 and 194 AIA prohibit the initial exercise of the terminating option to the contractor *in bonis* and confer on the liquidator the optional possibility of compliance or contractual resolution. 3.63

In the case of the tenant's bankruptcy in the private property market, the general principle is that the contract remains outside the bankruptcy proceedings, and will continue to be governed by commercial law. Pursuant to Section 157.3 AIA, no action for the payment of arrears due either before or after the commencement of the bankruptcy procedure can be pursued in the bankruptcy procedure. 3.64

In other bankruptcy procedures against the lessee, Section 157.4 AIA applies (irrespective of the commercial or residential nature of the contract). 3.65

(17) Life annuity agreements

Section 1599 of the CCC defines onerous life annuity agreements as those contracts whereby someone, in exchange for properties, capital or other measurable cash allowance, agrees to pay a rent to another, for the remaining duration of their lives or those of a designated person. 3.66

Section 158 of the AIA regulates both onerous and gratuitous life annuity contracts. For the first case it establishes that it is rescinded in the case of the obligor's bankruptcy. The beneficiaries have the right to submit their claims in the bankruptcy proceedings and to participate in bankruptcy for the outstanding benefits due at the date of the bankruptcy judgment and for the restitution of the 'rent price' (Section 2087 of the Civil Code of 1869, now regulated by Section 1604 of the CCC). The latter must be equal to the value necessary to constitute another similar annuity, according to the current age of the beneficiary.[46] 3.67

If the annuity was constituted gratuitously, the contract is also rescinded by the bankruptcy of the obligor. The right of the beneficiary, on the other hand, 3.68

46 See ibid., 285–6.

is limited to the verification of his claim in the bankruptcy proceedings and to the collection of benefits due until the date of the bankruptcy, without any other indemnity or obligation against the debtor for the future.[47]

(18) Contracts for the purpose of conservation and administration of property of the bankrupt debtor

3.69 Section 185 permits the trustee to enter into contracts for the preservation and administration of the dispossessed property, subject to judicial authorization. The judicial authorization may be demanded at a later stage in case of urgency. The authorization is granted only if the administration of the dispossessed properties appears in the interest of the insolvent estate and its creditors.[48]

(19) Contracts on dispossessed property (bankruptcy assets)

3.70 Section 186 of the AIA establishes the regime of contracts on dispossessed properties of the bankrupt debtor that generate a periodic net cash flow in favour of the insolvent estate. The trustee may continue to perform these contracts, provided that they do not result in the total or partial disposition of these assets, unless with authorization of the judge. This specific insolvency regime prevails over the civil and commercial law rules and therefore the trustee is not subject to the deadlines determined by civil law provisions.[49]

3.71 Section 187 AIA establishes the regime of the proposal and contracting conditions in the case of the previous Section 186 AIA. The provisions of Section 187 AIA are specifically applicable in insolvency proceedings and are explained by the precarious nature of any contract for the exploitation of assets that are destined to be liquidated. These insolvency provisions are therefore imperative and prevail over any other contractual or legal provision to the contrary.

3.72 The termination of the contract, whatever its cause (expiration of the deadlines, resolution of agreement, non-compliance, *force majeure*,[50] etc.) requires the immediate return of the asset to the bankruptcy estate. The rule also expresses that the terms in which the third party must make its rights are considered essential and the breach of it produces *ipso facto* the resolution of the contract.

---

47 See ibid., 285–6.
48 Ibid., 320–21.
49 Ibid., 321.
50 See CCC, ss 955 and 956.

The trustee has powers of control of the performance of the contractual obligations and can contract with a possible work cooperative that could take over the firm, integrated by the establishment's workers to which the goods object of the contract in question are affected, with authorization of the judge. Some or all of the workers who are members of the cooperative may voluntarily affect their unsecured labour credits in the bankruptcy, in guarantee of the contract entered into by the trustee.[51] **3.73**

(20) Lease agreements in cases of continuation of the business

Section 193 AIA states that in cases of continuation of the business operations of the bankrupt company and in which the liquidator expresses within 30 days of the bankruptcy the convenience of the liquidation of the assets as a whole unit, the lease contracts are maintained under the pre-existing conditions and the bankruptcy estate is directly responsible for leases and other future consequences. The clauses that determine the termination of the contract upon a declaration of bankruptcy are null and void. **3.74**

Regarding the lease of properties, Section 157 AIA applies. Articles 193 and 194 AIA establish an exceptional and specific rule for any lease contract in which the bankrupt debtor had been the tenant of the property and the continuation of the contract was essential for the business activity. These imperative rules prevail over any contractual clause. The contractual continuation may not exceed the legal term indicated for the liquidation of the insolvency assets according to Section 217 AIA.[52] **3.75**

(21) Mortgages and pledges on the continuation of the business operation

Section 195 AIA establishes some limitations on the rights of pledge and mortgage creditors in the event of continued operation of the company. **3.76**

(22) Employment contracts

Employment contracts are regulated by Sections 196–199 AIA.[53] The regime under the 'quiebra' is similar but not identical to the one of the CP. **3.77**

---

51 Rouillon, *Régimen …* , 322–3.

52 See ibid., 334.

53 See ibid., 336–40 for the labour law issue. See also Rivera, Julio C./Roitman, Horacio/Vítolo, Daniel R., *Reformas a la ley de concursos y quiebras* (ed. Rubinzal-Culzoni, Vol. III, 2006) 238–54; Ernesto Ed. Martorell, Concurso y quiebra de la empresa. Ley 24522. Problemática laboral (ed. La Ley, Buenos Aires, 1996); Alberto José Maza/Javier Armando Lorente, *Créditos laborales en los concursos* (2nd edn, ed. Astrea. Buenos Aires,

3.78 Pursuant to Section 196, bankruptcy does not result in the dissolution of the employment contract but in its suspension in full for the term of 60 calendar days from the date of the bankruptcy, without the right to receive wages during this period, unless effective services are rendered. After this period:

(a) If the company continues to operate (Section 191 AIA), the employment contract is partially continued. In this case, it is not necessary to verify judicially the credit for past and future earnings, according to Sections 183.2, 16.2 and 21.5 AIA. Any arrears in the payment will rank as a cost of conservation and justice, and it will be liquidated before any unsecured creditors (Section 240 AIA).
(b) If the judge decides not to continue the business operations, the contract is considered retroactively dissolved on the date of the declaration of bankruptcy. The employees have the right to collect the arrears in their wages (Sections 241.2 and 246.1 AIA) in priority over other unsecured creditors (Sections 183.2, 16.2 and 21.5 AIA).

3.79 Pursuant to Section 197 AIA, the trustee can decide, in a case of the continuation of the business activity after the bankruptcy declaration, to terminate some of the existing employment contracts. Termination of existing contracts is not possible where the business is continued by a work cooperative.

3.80 According to Section 198, the trustee must pay the wages accrued during the continuation of the business operations of the bankrupt company. These claims have a preferential ranking and they are immediately enforceable (Section 240 AIA).

2000); Francisco Junyent Bas/Fernando M. Flores, *Las relaciones laborales ante el concurso y la quiebra* (ed. Abaco de Rodolfo Depalma, Buenos Aires, 2004); Pablo C. Barbieri, *Relaciones laborales en la nueva ley de concursos* (ed. Universidad, Buenos Aires, 1996); Liliana T. Negre de Alonso, *Los acreedores laborales en el proceso concursal* (ed. Rubinzal-Culzoni, Santa Fe (Argentina), 1996); Luis M. Gámez/Oscar R. Gerez/ Gustavo A. Esparza, *Aspectos laborales en la nueva ley de concursos y quiebras (ley 24.522)* (ed. Depalma, Buenos Aires, 1996); Ricardo Willliams, *El Concurso preventivo* (ed. Plus Ultra, Buenos Aires, 1975); Horacio P. Garaguso, *Verificación de créditos. Principios y regimen en la ley 24.522* (ed. Depalma, Buenos Aires, 1997); Pablo D. Heredia, *Tradado exegético de derecho concursal* (ed. Ábaco de Rodolfo Depalma, Buenos Aires, 2000 and ss.); Francisco Junyent Bas, *Las cuesttiones laborales en el concurso y la quiebra*, (ed. Alveroni, Córdoba (Argentina), 1997); Francisco Junyent Bas, *Responsabilidad de los administradores por fraude laboral* (ed. Alveroni, Córdoba (Argentina), 2001); Julio C. Rivera, *Cuestiones laborales en la ley de concursos* (ed. Astrea, Buenos Aires, 1982); Julio C. Rivera, *Instituciones de derecho concursal* (2nd edn, ed. Rubinzal-Culzoni, Santa Fe (Argentina), 2003); Pablo C. Barbieri, *Contratos y procesos concursales* (ed. Universidad, Buenos Aires, 2001); Miguel E. Rubín, *Continuación de la actividad empresaria en la quiebra* (ed. Ad Hoc, Buenos Aires, 1991); Games, Luis M./Gerez, Oscar/Esparza, Gustavo A., *Aspectos laborales en la nueva ley de concursos y quiebras* (ed. Depalma, Buenos Aires, 1996); AAVV. Antonio Vazquez Vialard (dir), *Tratado de Derecho del Trabajo* (ed. Astrea, Buenos Aires, 1982–1996).

In this period, employment contracts are impliedly terminated by dismissal, closure of the company and acquisition of it by a third party. Both pre-bankruptcy and post-employment claims have a privilege under the terms of articles 241.2 and 246.1 for the first case and Section 240 for the second. Finally, in case of sale of the company in operation or of the transfer of the establishment as a unit, the validity of collective labour agreements (of the activity or the company) is not imposed on the buyer. **3.81**

Section 199 regulates the employment obligations of the buyer, who is not a successor to the bankrupt debtor and who will only be liable for post-bankruptcy claims and whose ownership is exclusively for workers whose employment relationship continued during the continuity of the exploitation of the company in insolvency. The pre-bankrupt employment debts or claims can only be paid with liquidated assets in the bankruptcy proceedings. **3.82**

D. REFORMS

The reforms on this matter have been few, they have been mentioned at the beginning of this work and in the main body of this chapter. There are currently no proposals of reform on the treatment of executory contracts in insolvency law. As a consequence of the last three reforms, labour cooperatives have been introduced as a contractor. **3.83**

The main reforms in the last 15 years have focused on establishing an accountable governance for ruling political parties and trade unions, especially in the aftermath of the crisis of 2001. As a consequence of this policy, reference has not been made to the documents of international or multilateral credit agencies or to other reports such as Doing Business in order to harmonise the existing law to international or regional best practices in relation to the competitiveness and appeal of the system and to the efficiency of the insolvency procedures. **3.84**

E. CONCLUDING REMARKS

This chapter has demonstrated that general civil or commercial law rules do not apply to ECs in insolvency proceedings. It is insolvency law that applies, especially with regard to the express or tacit rescission agreement (Section 145 AIA). In this way, it has been possible to unify the treatment of non-failed **3.85** third parties, in accordance with the general principle of equality of treatment of creditors (par omnium conditio creditorum).[54]

3.86 When the contract is rescinded by reason of the bankruptcy of one of the parties or by the denial of judicial authorization for its continuation, damages could not be claimed during the insolvency process. They could only be claimed or accounted for at the end of this procedure, subject to a preliminary authorisation from the court.[55]

3.87 To sum up, although in different ways, both in the CP and in the 'quiebra' case it is the judge who decides whether to terminate or perform ECs (Sections 20 and 143–145 AIA).[56] For contracts that are not subject to the AIA regime, the residual rule of Section 159 AIA is applicable.

3.88 To date, regulatory reforms have paid little consideration to international trends in the insolvency sector. Nevertheless, to improve the effectiveness and efficiency of the system, future reforms should draw inspirations from established best practices from neighbouring jurisdictions and from the United States. Additionally, to increase the attractiveness of foreign investors, more relevance should be paid to the recommendations coming from international bodies such as the World Bank or the International Monetary Fund.

---

54 See Roitman Horacio, Efectos jurídicos de la quiebra sobre los contratos preexistentes (ed. Lerner, Córdoba, 1973), 241.

55 Ibid., 241.

56 See Quintana Ferreyra, *Concursos, Ley 19.551 Comentada, Anotada y concordada* (ed. Astrea, Buenos Aires, Tomo 2, 1986) 499.

4

NATIONAL REPORT FOR AUSTRIA

Felix Kernbichler

A. INTRODUCTION

This chapter presents an overview of the Austrian Insolvency Code (*Insolvenzordnung – IO*), which was enacted in 2010. It focuses on insolvent businesses and introduces their possibilities to reorganize or to orderly liquidate in an Austrian insolvency proceeding. After providing the legal framework of the Austrian Insolvency Code, the chapter puts its main emphasis on the treatment of executory contracts in insolvency. 4.01

The legal framework of Austrian insolvency law only covers formal proceedings. There is no statute that specifically deals with out-of-court workouts. Nevertheless, out-of-court workouts are, of course, affected by the rules applicable in formal proceedings. When parties try to strike a deal in order to avoid formal insolvency proceedings, they always bargain against the law. The situation they would have to face in formal proceedings affects their bargaining power. This is a well-known, indirect consequence of insolvency law. However, insolvency law also tries to directly control behaviour outside formal insolvency proceedings. The most obvious example is avoidance provisions. A not so obvious and for Austrian insolvency law fairly new example is the treatment of executory contracts in insolvency. 4.02

B. INSOLVENCY PROCEDURES

(1) Formal proceedings

4.03 Until 2010, Austrian insolvency law offered two different proceedings, regulated by two independent statutes (*Konkursordnung – KO* and *Ausgleichsordnung – AO*). Originally, one of them was intended to be mainly for liquidation and the other one for reorganization. Liquidation proceedings (*Konkursverfahren*), however, also gave the opportunity to reorganize, and the quota you had to offer to your creditors was lower than in reorganization proceedings (*Ausgleichsverfahren*). As a consequence, liquidation proceedings were more attractive for debtors and reorganization proceedings almost irrelevant in legal practice. After a few attempts to reorganize the reorganization proceedings, the Austrian legislature laid them to rest and established a new model.

4.04 The reform in 2010 (*Insolvenzrechtsänderungsgesetz 2010 – IRÄG 2010*[1]) abolished the dual system and merged Austrian insolvency law into one statute: the new Austrian Insolvency Code. Although one statute now has to cover both liquidation and reorganization, it is based on, and for the most part is quite similar to, the old statute for liquidation proceedings. Since the old statute for liquidation proceedings already gave the opportunity to reorganize, most of its structure could be kept.

4.05 The Austrian Insolvency Code now provides for three kinds of insolvency proceedings: liquidation proceedings (*Konkursverfahren*); reorganization proceedings with self-administration (*Sanierungsverfahren mit Eigenverwaltung*); and reorganization proceedings without self-administration (*Sanierungsverfahren ohne Eigenverwaltung*). Although this might sound slightly confusing, it is possible to reorganize in all of them.

4.06 Under Austrian insolvency law, the debtor has to file an application for the opening of insolvency proceedings in two cases: (1) if it is permanently unable to pay off its debts[2] (this applies irrespective of whether the debtor is a natural person or a corporate entity); (2) if it is a corporate entity that is over-indebted[3] and there is no positive forecast.[4] Since 2010, the debtor can (but does not have to) file an application for the opening of insolvency proceedings

---

1 BGBl. I Nr. 29/2010.

2 Austrian Insolvency Code, s 66.

3 Ibid., s 67.

4 Therefore, a simple excess of liabilities over assets is, of course, no reason to file for insolvency. Nevertheless, this cannot be derived from the wording of the Austrian Insolvency Code, which only refers to over-indebtedness. This additional criterion was added by legal doctrine and adopted by the courts.

if it is imminent that it might become permanently unable to pay off its debts.[5] A creditor can file an application for the opening of insolvency proceedings if it feels that either point (1) or (2) applies.[6]

4.07 If the debtor files an application for the opening of insolvency proceedings, already attaches a reorganization plan (*Sanierungsplan*) to its application and requests that this plan shall be accepted, the insolvency proceedings have to be labelled as reorganization proceedings.[7] This legislative measure points out the positive objective of the proceedings[8] and was well received by companies and insolvency practitioners in Austria.

4.08 In cases where the debtor wants to enter into reorganization proceedings with self-administration, the debtor has to attach various documents to its application for the opening of insolvency proceedings. Most importantly, though, the debtor has to offer a quota of at least 30 per cent to its creditors,[9] compared to only 20 per cent in insolvency proceedings without self-administration.[10] The opening of reorganization proceedings with self-administration does not mean that the debtor is completely free in making its decisions: the debtor rather is supervised by a reorganization trustee and needs the approval of the reorganization trustee for certain decisions.[11] In various circumstances, the court has to strip the debtor of its self-administration right.[12] As a consequence, the insolvency proceedings have to be continued as reorganization proceedings without self-administration. In cases where the reorganization plan proposed by the debtor fails, the reorganization proceedings have to be relabelled, and continued, as liquidation proceedings.[13]

5 Austrian Insolvency Code, s 167 (2). For the advantages and disadvantages of such a provision see Horst Eidenmüller, 'Strategische Insolvenz: Möglichkeiten, Grenzen, Rechtsvergleichung' [2014] ZIP 1197. This modification, however, does not change anything for legal practice in Austria: if the debtor filed an application for the opening of insolvency proceedings before 2010, the competent courts did not check whether it was only imminent that the debtor might become permanently unable to pay off its debts or it was already unable to do so.

6 Austrian Insolvency Code, s 70.

7 Austrian Insolvency Code, s 167 (1).

8 ErläutRV IRÄG 2010, 612 BlgNR 24. GP 1 et seqq. See also Franz Mohr, 'Sanierungstendenzen in der Reform des Insolvenzrechts' in Andreas Konecny (ed), *Insolvenz-Forum 2006* (NWV 2007) 115, 118.

9 Austrian Insolvency Code, s 169 (1).

10 Ibid., s 141 (1).

11 Ibid., s 171 (1). In addition, ibid., s 172 (1) provides that certain actions are reserved for the reorganization trustee.

12 Ibid., s 170 (1).

13 Ibid., s 167 (3).

(2) Out-of-court workouts

4.09 Despite recent legislative attempts to make formal proceedings more appealing, most companies in Austria still see them as a last resort. They still fear the stigma of insolvency,[14] which comes as no surprise when you consider that even the European Commission felt the need to proclaim a second chance for entrepreneurs as a policy priority.[15] Therefore, an Austrian company in financial distress will usually try to negotiate with its main creditors (usually banks) in order to avoid the opening of insolvency proceedings. The opening of such proceedings can often be seen as a manifestation that negotiations have failed.

4.10 Austrian law does not provide a concrete legal framework for out-of-court workouts.[16] Nevertheless, such workouts are common and Austrian insolvency law even encourages them: upon the occurrence of insolvency according to the definition of the Austrian Insolvency Code,[17] Austrian law grants the debtor up to 60 days to file for insolvency.[18] This period is intended to be a chance for an out-of-court workout.[19] It can be exhausted if the debtor pursues such a workout diligently and the reorganization attempt does not appear to have no prospect of success.

4.11 In order to make up for the lack of a legal framework for out-of-court workouts, three Austrian banks and an Austrian law firm drafted non-binding guidelines for restructurings in Austria, which are based on the Statement of Principles for a Global Approach to Multi-creditor Workouts published by INSOL International in 2000. The Austrian guidelines primarily deal with the first phase of an extra-judicial restructuring, which is described as the period in which it should be determined whether there is a possibility for

---

14 This stigma does not merely exist according to conventional wisdom. Rather, the application for the opening of insolvency proceedings triggers a significant decline of the stock price. See Luís M. S. Coelho, Kose John and Richard Taffler, 'Does the Market Know Better? The Case of Strategic vs. Non-Strategic Bankruptcies' [2011] http://ssrn.com/abstract=1787197 (last accessed 2 January 2019).

15 European Commission, 'Proposal for a Directive of the European Parliament and of the Council of 22 November 2016 on preventive restructuring frameworks, second chance and measures to increase the efficiency of restructuring, insolvency and discharge procedures and amending Directive 2012/30/EU' COM (2016) 723 final.

16 Austrian law does, however, provide a legal framework for judicial reorganizations to entrepreneurs and businesses that are not insolvent. These reorganizations are governed by the Business Reorganization Act (*Unternehmensreorganisationsgesetz – URG*) enacted in 1997 and involve a court-appointed reorganization auditor. They are not mandatory and of no relevance at all in legal practice.

17 That is, as already stated above, the permanent inability of the debtor to pay off its debts or, in case the debtor is a corporate entity, over-indebtedness of the debtor and no positive forecast.

18 Austrian Insolvency Code, s 69 (2).

19 JAB IRÄG 1982, 1147 BlgNR 15. GP 21 et seq. See also Hubertus Schumacher in Robert Bartsch, Rudolf Pollak and Walter Buchegger (eds), *Österreichisches Insolvenzrecht: Kommentar II/2* (SpringerWienNewYork 2004) § 69 Rz 86 with further references.

reorganization of the debtor. These guidelines explicitly focus on restructurings in which at least three banks take part and a total volume of around EUR 30 million is involved. Since they are non-binding, only general contract law can prevent a counterparty from terminating a contract it entered into with the debtor. This situation only changes in formal insolvency proceedings.

C. TREATMENT OF EXECUTORY CONTRACTS

In many respects, the way Austrian insolvency law deals with executory contracts[20] is similar to many other jurisdictions. **4.12**

(1) Power to continue and reject contracts

Upon commencement of insolvency proceedings, the insolvency representative[21] has a right to choose whether it wants to continue to perform the contract on behalf of the debtor or reject it.[22] If the insolvency representative chooses to reject the contract, the counterparty can only claim damages. With regard to these damages, the counterparty is treated like an unsecured creditor.[23] If the insolvency representative chooses to continue to perform the contract on behalf of the debtor, both the estate and the counterparty have to fully perform the contract.[24] Claims arising from these contracts are treated as administrative expenses.[25] **4.13**

---

20 In cases where the counterparty has already fully performed its obligations prior to the opening of insolvency proceedings, the counterparty is treated like an unsecured creditor with any claims it still has against the debtor under the contract. In cases where the debtor has already fully performed its obligations prior to the opening of insolvency proceedings, the counterparty can keep the output, but also has to fully perform its obligations. This is the standard approach adopted by many jurisdictions; see UNCITRAL, *Legislative Guide on Insolvency Law* (2005) 121. For an instructive explanation of its foundations see Thomas H. Jackson, *The Logic and Limits of Bankruptcy Law* (HUP 1986) 105 et seqq.

21 Austrian Insolvency Code, ss 80 et seqq.

22 Ibid., s 21 (1). The insolvency representative does not have this right with regard to contracts that should be performed at a certain time, within a certain period or not at all (*Fixgeschäfte*) if that time or end of that period happens to be after the opening of insolvency proceedings. Austrian Insolvency Code, s 22 (1) provides that only damages for non-performance can be claimed with regard to such contracts.

23 Ibid., s 21 (2).

24 This does not apply to contracts that can be divided into severable units. Austrian Insolvency Code, s 21 (4) provides that in case both the obligations of the debtor and the obligations of the counterparty under the contract are severable and if the counterparty has already partially performed its obligations upon the opening of insolvency proceedings, it is treated like an unsecured creditor with its claim for the corresponding consideration. As a consequence, the insolvency representative may choose to continue to perform the contract without being obliged to cure past breaches. Furthermore, a breach that occurred before the opening of insolvency proceedings does not permit a counterparty to terminate a contract.

25 Special provisions exist for lease agreements (*Bestandverträge*). See Austrian Insolvency Code, ss 23 et seq and Andreas Konecny and Bettina Nunner-Krautgasser, 'Neuerungen bei Bestandverträgen durch das IRÄG 2010' in Andreas Konecny (ed), *IRÄG 2010* (LexisNexis 2010) 39.

4.14 In the past, however, the insolvency representative often did not even get a chance to choose whether it wanted to continue to perform the contract or reject it. Counterparties often decided to terminate the contract in insolvency.[26] Austrian insolvency law allowed them to effectively do so.[27] Obviously, this was a problem for the reorganization of insolvent companies.

(2) Automatic stay

4.15 The reform in 2010 altered the approach towards executory contracts in a quite spectacular fashion: in light of the worldwide economic crisis, the Austrian legislature made an attempt to aid businesses in their efforts to reorganize after they have filed for insolvency. In order to achieve its goal, it put an automatic stay of contracts in insolvency proceedings in place. In doing so, it explicitly referred to two role models:[28] the Legislative Guide on Insolvency Law published by UNCITRAL in 2005, which contains extensive advice and is intended to be used as a reference by national authorities and legislative bodies when preparing new laws and regulations or reviewing the adequacy of existing laws and regulations;[29] and the automatic stay of Chapter 11 of the United States Bankruptcy Code,[30] which is often deemed to be very debtor-friendly.[31] Similar regulations exist in other jurisdictions.[32] In addition, a report by the International Monetary Fund, which is based on a comparative

26 See for example Alexander Isola, 'Maßnahmen der IO-begünstigten Sanierung' in Kathrin Poltsch et al (eds), *Praxishandbuch Insolvenzabwicklung* (Linde 2016) 567, 570.

27 For references see Felix Kernbichler, 'Die Kündigung von Versicherungsverträgen in der Insolvenz des Versicherungsnehmers' [2011] wbl 1, 2.

28 ErläutRV 612 BlgNR 24. GP 12 et seq.

29 See General Assembly Resolution 59/40 of 2 December 2004. A short overview is for instance provided by Jean-Luc Vallens, 'Towards an Ideal System, the UNCITRAL Legislation Guide on Insolvency Law' in Henry Peter, Nicolas Jeandin and Jason Kilborn (eds), *The Challenges of Insolvency Law Reform in the 21st Century* (Schulthess 2006) 489.

30 Whether the automatic stay of Chapter 11 prohibits the termination of contracts is, however, not entirely beyond dispute. See for example 3 Collier on Bankruptcy P 362.03[5][a] (16th edn, LexisNexis 2012) with further references: '[S]ome courts appear to have held that the automatic stay does not stay termination of a contract.' An attempt at an explanation was made by Shai Schmidt, *Termination of Contracts in Bankruptcy – The Divergence in the Case Law and a Suggested Rationale* (Harvard Law School Library 2009). In favour of the view that the automatic stay of Chapter 11 prohibits the termination of contracts are, among others: David G. Epstein, Steve H. Nickles and James J. White, *Bankruptcy* (West 1993) 99; W. Homer Drake, Jr. and Christopher S. Strickland, *Chapter 11 Reorganizations* (2nd edn, West 2011) 391; Patrick A. Murphy and Eric Sagerman, *Creditors' Rights in Bankruptcy* (2nd edn, West 2012) 183; David A. Skeel, Jr. and Thomas H. Jackson, 'Transaction Consistency and the New Finance in Bankruptcy' (2012) 112 Columbia Law Review 152.

31 Even so, cf Bruce H. Mann, *Republic of Debtors: Bankruptcy in the Age of American Independence* (first published 2002, HUP 2009) 255: 'The fundamental dilemma of bankruptcy law has always been whether it is about death or rebirth. [...] The fact that it is both has never slowed debate that it should be primarily one or the other.'

32 See Restructuring & Insolvency (2018), http://www.gettingthedealthrough.com/area/35/restructuring-insolvency (last accessed 2 January 2019).

study of selected insolvency laws, emphasizes: 'if a country does not provide for the nullification of contract termination clauses upon the commencement of rehabilitation, it will be more difficult for the enterprise to rehabilitate if the contracts in question are critical'.[33]

The path the Austrian legislature took is clever: it combined the automatic stay of contracts with a prohibition of *ipso facto* clauses. My impression is that – in doing so – it brought together what belongs together. Nevertheless, the provisions did not have the impact the Austrian legislature was hoping for. The provisions simply contain too many loopholes. **4.16**

(2)(a) Stay of contracts

The Austrian Insolvency Code provides for the following automatic stay of contracts (my own translation): **4.17**

> Section 25a. (1) If the termination of a contract could jeopardize the continuation of the insolvent company, counterparties may only terminate a contract for good cause for a period of six months from the opening of insolvency proceedings. Not a good cause is
>
> 1. the deterioration of the economic situation of the insolvent company and
> 2. the lack of timely performance by the insolvent company prior to the opening of insolvency proceedings.
>
> (2) These restrictions shall not apply
>
> 1. if the termination of the contract is necessary to protect the counterparty from severe personal or economic damages,
> 2. to claims for the disbursement of loans and
> 3. to labour contracts.

(2)(b) Limitation

The problems start right at the beginning of the provision. According to the wording of the provision, the automatic stay only applies if the termination of the contract could jeopardize the continuation of the insolvent company. As a consequence, a counterparty could easily argue that the termination of one contract could not jeopardize the continuation of the insolvent company. Then, another counterparty could argue that the termination of another contract still could not jeopardize the continuation of the insolvent company. This could lead to a race for legal terminations of contracts.[34] **4.18**

---

33 International Monetary Fund, *Orderly and Effective Insolvency Procedures – Key Issues* (1999) 71.

34 See Felix Kernbichler, 'Die Gefährdung der Unternehmensfortführung in § 25a IO' [2015] ÖJZ 493, 495. Cf also Philipp Anzenberger, *Die Insolvenzfestigkeit von Bestandverträgen* (LexisNexis 2014) 85.

4.19 Most importantly, though, this limitation of the automatic stay is not necessary to protect counterparties: In order to protect them, it suffices to let them terminate a contract if the termination is necessary to prevent them from damages. Any further limitation is only an unnecessary loophole that can impair the effectiveness of the automatic stay. Therefore, the Austrian legislature should close this loophole and simply eliminate this limitation of the automatic stay.[35]

(2)(c) Breach prior to insolvency

4.20 Section 21 para 4 of the Austrian Insolvency Code provides that the continuation of contracts that can be divided into severable units does not require the cure of past breaches.[36] Nevertheless, in the past counterparties often put pressure on the insolvency representative by telling it to cure past breaches if it wanted to keep the contract.[37] If the contract was important for the reorganization of the insolvent company, the insolvency representative often had no other choice than to break the law and fulfil a claim that actually should have been treated as an unsecured claim. In 2010, the Austrian legislature took action against this misconduct and decided that lack of timely performance by the debtor prior to the opening of insolvency proceedings shall not give cause for termination of the contract.[38] In doing so, it did not follow the Legislative Guide published by UNCITRAL. Recommendation 79 of this guide says:

> The insolvency law should specify that where the debtor is in breach of a contract the insolvency representative can continue the performance of that contract, provided the breach is cured, the non-breaching counterparty is substantially returned to the economic position it was in before the breach and the estate is able to perform under the continued contract.[39]

4.21 This recommendation shows the influence of Anglo-American laws on international models.[40] Section 365 para (b)(1) of the United States Bankruptcy Code states:

---

35 Kernbichler, ÖJZ 2015, *supra* note 34, 499 et seq.

36 See in detail *supra* note 24.

37 This behaviour was observed in other countries as well. See Mark J. Roe, *Bankruptcy and Corporate Reorganization* (3rd edn, Foundation Press 2011) 342 et seqq.

38 For a more detailed analysis of this section see Felix Kernbichler, 'Insolvenzrechtliche Einschnitte in das zivilrechtliche Leistungsstörungsrecht' [2015] JBl 409, 411 et seqq.

39 UNCITRAL, *supra* note 20, 134. The remarks leading up to this recommendation sound quite different: 'There is some justification for assuring the debtor continuing access to [essential] services [such as telephone, electricity, gas, water and waste collection] without requiring cure of the breach [...], provided it can perform its post-commencement obligations' (UNCITRAL, *supra* note 20, 126).

40 Cf Christoph Thole, *Gläubigerschutz durch Insolvenzrecht* (Mohr Siebeck 2010) 637.

> If there has been a default in an executory contract [...], the trustee may not assume such contract [...] unless [he] (A) cures [...] such default [...]; (B) compensates [...] a party other than the debtor to such contract [...], for any actual pecuniary loss to such party resulting from such default; and (C) provides adequate assurance of future performance under such contract.

However, this all-or-nothing approach is not even maintained in the United States.[41] According to the critical vendor doctrine, pre-petition claims can be paid in full under certain circumstances. Judge Frank H. Easterbrook sharply criticized the approach: **4.22**

> Doubtless many suppliers fear the prospect of throwing good money after bad. It therefore may be vital to assure them that a debtor will pay for new deliveries on a current basis. Providing that assurance need not, however, entail payment for pre-petition transactions.[42]

The Austrian legislature did well to follow neither the all-or-nothing approach nor the critical vendor doctrine. Otherwise it would have legitimized how counterparties acted before the reform in 2010 and, thus, would have further complicated successful reorganizations of insolvent companies. Moreover, it would have run afoul of the core principal of insolvency law: the *par conditio creditorum*.[43] **4.23**

(2)(d) Exemptions

The Austrian Insolvency Code provides for three explicit exemptions from the automatic stay. The first one is the most important one: the automatic stay shall not apply if the termination of the contract is necessary to protect the counterparty from severe personal or economic damages. The big question is how severe the imminent damages have to be in order for the exemption to apply. The answer to this question has a massive impact on how the automatic stay is perceived by counterparties. **4.24**

Unfortunately, the Austrian legislature left the search for an answer to legal practice. Experience so far has shown that the conceivable range is remarkable. Some even argued that the exemption should only apply if the termination of the contract is necessary to prevent the counterparty from becoming insolvent as well.[44] However, prominent German insolvency law experts have already **4.25**

---

41 See Roe, *supra* note 37, 348 et seqq.

42 In re Kmart Corp., 359 F.3d 866 (7th Cir. 2004).

43 Kernbichler, JBl 2015, *supra* note 38, 413 et seq.

44 See for example Katharina Widhalm-Budak, 'Verhinderung der Vertragsauflösung und unwirksame Vereinbarungen' in Andreas Konecny (ed), *IRÄG 2010* (LexisNexis 2010) 23, 28 et seq; Andreas Konecny, 'Das Insolvenzrechtsänderungsgesetz 2010' [2010] ZIK 82, 86.

stated that an automatic stay that could lead to severe damages for counterparties would be unconstitutional.[45] This assessment also holds true for Austrian law. Therefore, the scope of the automatic stay cannot be taken to such extremes. Nevertheless, the automatic stay is generally perceived in Austria as a provision that harms counterparties. As a consequence, many still express that it is their wish to include a mechanism in a contract that helps them to terminate that contract before the opening of insolvency proceedings.

4.26 The Austrian Insolvency Code provides for two other exemptions that cause fewer problems. The exemption of claims for the disbursement of loans was incorporated because of the Austrian banks' influence on legislation. Upon closer examination, it becomes obvious that this exemption mainly exists for the avoidance of doubt. The Austrian Insolvency Code grants a right of retention to counterparties who contractually obliged themselves to perform in advance but did not know about the bad economic situation of the debtor at the time they entered into the contract.[46] If a counterparty exercises its right of retention, the exemption of the automatic stay eliminates all doubt as to the consequences: if the debtor is not able to perform or to provide securities (especially in case of loan agreements, where one party has to perform in advance to meet the purpose of the contract), the counterparty can terminate the contract.

4.27 Eventually, labour contracts are exempted from the automatic stay because they are regulated in a separate provision of the Austrian Insolvency Code.[47]

4.28 In any case, the automatic stay only applies as long as the company is a going concern. For this assessment, however, it does not matter which kind of insolvency proceedings the company is in: since a debtor can also reorganize in liquidation proceedings, the automatic stay can apply there as well.

---

45 See Wolfgang Marotzke in Godehard Kayser and Christoph Thole (eds), *Insolvenzordnung* (2016) § 112 Rz 21; Peter von Wilmowsky, 'Der Mieter in Insolvenz: Zur Kündigungssperre des § 112 InsO' [2004] ZInsO 882, 886. Cf also Hans-Georg Eckert, 'Miete, Pacht und Leasing im neuen Insolvenzrecht' [1996] ZIP 897, 898.

46 Austrian Insolvency Code, s 21 (3). In addition, the explanatory remarks on the proposal for the insolvency law reform in 2010 state that a contractual provision upon which the opening of insolvency proceedings shall trigger a switch to concurrent performance is not in conflict with the automatic stay. See ErläutRV 612 BlgNR 24. GP 13.

47 Austrian Insolvency Code, s 25. For an overview see Romana Weber-Wilfert, 'Arbeitsrechtliche Änderungen des IRÄG 2010' in Andreas Konecny (ed), *IRÄG 2010* (LexisNexis 2010) 59; Karin Ristic, 'Arbeitsrecht und Sanierung' in Kurt Lichtkoppler and Ulla Reisch (eds), *Handbuch Unternehmenssanierung* (MANZ 2010) 219; Axel Reckenzaun, 'Insolvenzarbeitsrecht aus dem Blickwinkel des Schuldnervertreters und des Insolvenzverwalters' in Bettina Nunner-Krautgasser and Gert-Peter Reissner (eds), *Praxishandbuch Insolvenz und Arbeitsrecht* (Linde 2012) 155; Isola, *supra* note 26, 582 et seqq.

(3) Prohibition of *ipso facto* clauses

In addition to the automatic stay, the Austrian Insolvency Code provides for the following prohibition of *ipso facto* clauses (again my own translation): 4.29

> Section 25b. (2) A contractual provision that terminates or gives a right to terminate a contract upon the opening of insolvency proceedings is prohibited, except in contracts listed in section 20 para 4.[48]

In corporate insolvencies, this provision can be understood as a protection of the automatic stay.[49] It should put beyond doubt that the automatic stay cannot be circumvented by an *ipso facto* clause.[50] However, the provision turned out to be probably the greatest weakness of the Austrian system to maintain contracts in insolvency. Since it only mentions the opening of insolvency proceedings explicitly, lawyers started to argue that a clause that links the automatic termination of a contract or the right to terminate a contract to the application for the opening of insolvency proceedings or a similar event must be valid.[51] Although this argument resembles the discussion in Germany,[52] such an interpretation would obviously render the prohibition of *ipso facto* clauses useless. UNCITRAL's Legislative Guide therefore goes a step further and suggests: 4.30

> The insolvency law should specify that any contract clause that automatically terminates or accelerates a contract upon the [application for commencement, or commencement, of insolvency proceedings] is unenforceable as against the insolvency representative and the debtor.[53]

48 Austrian Insolvency Code, s 20 (4) permits to exercise rights of close-out netting with regard to certain financial contracts if the parties agreed that such contracts shall be terminated and all outstanding claims shall be set off upon the opening of insolvency proceedings. The exemption makes sure that such terminations are effective.

49 The provision also applies in personal bankruptcies. However, since the Austrian Insolvency Code does not provide for an automatic stay in personal bankruptcies, the protection of debtors will be very limited in such proceedings.

50 Pursuant to Austrian Insolvency Code, s 273 (7), the prohibition of *ipso facto* clauses also applies to contracts entered before Austrian Insolvency Code, s 25b (2) came into force on 1 July 2010.

51 See Thomas Trettnak and Franz A. Höfer, 'Vertragsauflösung reloaded – Gedanken zur Vertragsgestaltung im Lichte der neuen Insolvenzordnung' [2010] ZIK 204, 205. Similarly Christian Hoenig, 'Reichweite der Vertragsauflösungssperre der IO' [2013] RdW 515, 518 et seq; Bettina Nunner-Krautgasser and Klaus Pateter, 'Die Neuregelungen über Verträge im österreichischen Insolvenzrecht' [2011] ZInsO 2068, 2073.

52 See for example Christoph G. Paulus, 'Verbindungslinien zwischen Insolvenzrecht und Privatautonomie' in Hans Prütting and Heinz Vallender (eds), *Festschrift für Wilhelm Uhlenbruck* (2000) 33, 45 et seqq; Peter von Wilmowsky, 'Lösungsklauseln für den Insolvenzfall – Wirksamkeit, Anfechtbarkeit, Reform' [2007] ZIP 553, 554.

53 UNCITRAL, *supra* note 20, 132.

4.31 This approach would certainly make it harder to terminate a contract prior to insolvency. Nevertheless, smart counterparties (or their lawyers) could still find a way: they could link the *ipso facto* clause to financial figures of the debtor which indicate that the debtor is in a weak financial position but not yet insolvent. Since they could provide for an automatic termination if these figures are met, they would not even have to monitor the debtor. They could lean back and, upon the opening of insolvency proceedings, claim that the contract is already terminated.

4.32 Accordingly, the automatic effect that an *ipso facto* clause can have is the key problem a prohibition of *ipso facto* clauses needs to solve in order to be effective.[54] To accomplish this goal, the provision has to be interpreted as follows: As from the opening of insolvency proceedings, counterparties are prohibited from invoking a clause that provides for the automatic termination of the contract prior to or upon the opening of insolvency proceedings.

4.33 Unfortunately, the current wording of the Austrian prohibition of *ipso facto* clauses does not clearly show this effect. As a consequence, the provision leaves some room for discussion. This discussion is likely to only end if the Austrian Supreme Court (*Oberster Gerichtshof – OGH*) decides on this issue or the Austrian legislature amends the provision.

(4) Timely decision

4.34 Before the reform in 2010, the insolvency representative had quite some time to decide whether it wanted to continue to perform an executory contract on behalf of the debtor or reject it: counterparties could ask the court to set the insolvency representative a deadline to exercise its right to choose to continue to perform or reject an executory contract. This deadline, however, could not be earlier than three days after the report hearing (*Berichtstagsatzung*).[55] The report hearing has to take place no later than 90 days after the opening of insolvency proceedings.[56] Obviously, waiting so long for the decision could lead to severe damages for counterparties. Until 2010, this was not a problem, because counterparties were not forced to wait: they could simply terminate the contract upon the opening of insolvency proceedings.

---

54 A contractual provision that gives a right to terminate a contract upon the opening of insolvency proceedings is a minor problem: if the automatic stay already prohibits terminating a contract just because of insolvency, a contractual clause cannot lift this prohibition. Therefore, the automatic stay actually already covers such clauses.

55 The report hearing is a meeting of the creditors in which the further course of action (continuation or closing of the company) shall be decided.

56 Austrian Insolvency Code, s 91a.

The automatic stay of contracts and the prohibition of *ipso facto* clauses (at least in theory) significantly restrict this option now. Therefore, the Austrian legislature wanted to make sure that counterparties have certainty as to the continuation of the contract.[57] A prompt decision is, so the reasoning of the legislature, particularly important if the debtor is obliged to a performance in kind and already in default with such performance. As a result, Austrian insolvency law now permits counterparties to request the insolvency representative to make a decision within five business days in such cases.[58] **4.35**

However, a prompt decision can also be important for counterparties obliged to a performance in kind.[59] If the counterparty is obliged to provide seasonal articles or other goods that perish quickly, the counterparty will want to know in a timely manner whether the debtor will still accept them. The Austrian legislature likely overlooked these cases when it drafted the provision. Since the interests of counterparties in these cases are similar to their interests in the cases the legislature covered, they should be treated equally.[60] **4.36**

The right to ask the insolvency representative to make a decision within five business days was specifically enacted for situations in which a timely decision can prevent counterparties from damages. Therefore, a counterparty can also request a prompt decision in legal practice if it is likely that the value of the performance in kind will drop quickly or if it needs to be paid quickly because it is running out of money and might become insolvent.[61] **4.37**

Irrespective of whether a counterparty is entitled to set the tight deadline or can only ask the court to set the softer deadline, Austrian insolvency law provides for a default rule: if the insolvency representative fails to decide within the specified period, the contract is treated as rejected.[62] In addition, it is worth noting that the option to request a prompt decision can often be used **4.38**

57 ErläutRV 612 BlgNR 24. GP 11. See also UNCITRAL, *supra* note 20, 125, 133.

58 The provision was heavily criticized for giving too little time to review whether the insolvent company is able to continue to perform the contract and whether this is more favourable for the estate than to reject the contract. See only Axel Reckenzaun, *IRÄG 2010 – Insolvenzordnung* (Linde 2010) 49.

59 German insolvency law addresses these situations explicitly. See German Insolvency Code (*Insolvenzordnung – InsO*), s 107 (2) sentence 2 and BT-Drucks 12/7302, 169.

60 See in more detail Felix Kernbichler, 'Privilegierte Fristsetzung nach § 21 Abs 2 IO und Haftung des Insolvenzverwalters' [2016] RdW 735, 736 et seq.

61 Ibid., 737.

62 Austrian Insolvency Code, s 21 (2).

as a way to get out of an unwanted contract because insolvency representatives will routinely decide to reject the contract[63] in order to limit their liability risk.[64]

(5) Practical consequences

4.39 The past few years have shown that there are several problems with the Austrian automatic stay. As a consequence, the stay was not really effective and insolvency representatives reported that the stay does not help them in their efforts to successfully reorganize an insolvent company. If a counterparty refuses to perform a contract, the insolvency representative hardly ever sues, because it feels that the counterparty has a good case in arguing that the stay does not apply. As a result, to date not a single dispute about the automatic stay has been brought before the Austrian Supreme Court. Only two decisions substantially deal with the prohibition of *ipso facto* clauses, but their messages are not of overwhelming importance for the general interpretation of the provision. In both decisions the Austrian Supreme Court had to solve quite specific cases: In 2013, the court had to examine an agreement upon which a bank waived a portion of a company's outstanding debts in order to facilitate an out-of-court workout. The agreement contained a clause whereby the waiver should cease to exist if the company becomes insolvent. The court ruled that the prohibition of *ipso facto* clauses does not ban this clause.[65] In a decision in late 2017, the court held that the prohibition of *ipso facto* clauses does not apply to a rule of the Austrian Football Association which provides that a club will be relegated at the end of the season if it becomes insolvent.[66] As a consequence, Austria's oldest football club, First Vienna Football-Club 1894, was relegated.

4.40 Despite the fact that the substantive shortcomings are many, the biggest problem might be a procedural one: even if the insolvency representative sues, it would not help the insolvent company to hear from a judge a year later that the stay would have applied. The only thing that would help is a preliminary

63 Cf Raoul G. Wagner, 'Hilferuf eines Masseverwalters' [2010] RdW 191.

64 This, in fact, only makes it less likely that someone will bring a claim against the insolvency representative. In order to act lawfully, the insolvency representative rather has to use the specified period to obtain as much information as possible and then choose the option that seems to be more favourable for the estate. See Kernbichler, RdW 2016, *supra* note 60, 738 et seqq.

65 See OGH 21 November 2013, 1 Ob 157/13i and my analysis: 'Unwirksamkeit eines auflösend bedingten Forderungsverzichts?' [2014] ZIK 42.

66 OGH 15 November 2017, 1 Ob 153/17g. In another quite recent decision the Austrian Supreme Court only stated the obvious by saying that the prohibition of *ipso facto* clauses only governs the termination of contracts and therefore does not apply to offers that have not been accepted by the debtor before the opening of insolvency proceedings. See OGH 27 July 2017, 4 Ob 100/17k.

injunction. The prevailing view in Austria to this point, however, is that you cannot get one for the performance of an executory contract if such performance cannot be undone.[67] The Commercial Court Vienna (*Handelsgericht Wien*) challenged this view in early 2013 and, upon the application of an insolvency representative, granted a preliminary injunction.[68] An Austrian mobile service provider had blocked the use of all phone numbers of an insolvent association. The insolvency representative successfully argued that it would be difficult to reorganize the association if it can neither make nor receive calls. Later in 2013, the case went to the Austrian Supreme Court. The Austrian Supreme Court, however, could not make any further comment on the issue: by the time the case reached the court, the company already was closed down. As a consequence, the automatic stay no longer applied. In addition, the insolvency representative had already rejected the contract.[69] In 2017, the proceedings that involved Austria's oldest football club led to a similar result. The District Court Leopoldstadt (*Bezirksgericht Leopoldstadt*) granted a preliminary injunction that temporarily saved the club from being relegated. However, as mentioned above, the Austrian Supreme Court held that the prohibition of *ipso facto* clauses does not apply in this case. Therefore, the court did not have to answer whether the provisions to preserve contracts in insolvency can be protected by a preliminary injunction.

(6) Proposal for a Directive on preventive restructuring

Upon an examination of the Austrian provisions, it becomes obvious that **4.41** there is simply too much room for arguing whether the stay applies. Therefore, it was quite a surprise to see that parts of the proposal of the European Commission for a Directive on preventive restructuring frameworks, second chance and measures to increase the efficiency of restructuring, insolvency and discharge procedures, which was published in 2016 and subject to a lively discussion in Austria, could lead to similar problems. The proposal aims at establishing 'key principles on effective preventive restructuring and second chance frameworks' in all member states of the European Union.[70] Amongst

67 See for example OGH 24 January 2006, 5 Ob 211/05y; 17 January 2012, 4 Ob 110/11x; 17 January 2012, 4 Ob 197/11s; Alfons Zechner, *Sicherungsexekution und Einstweilige Verfügung* (SpringerWienNewYork 2000) 116 et seq; Gabriela Zackl, 'Einstweilige Verfügungen und (Un-)Zulässigkeit unwiederbringlicher Eilmaßnahmen' [2005] ÖJZ 12, 18 et seqq; id., *Einstweiliger Rechtsschutz im Gesellschaftsrecht* (MANZ 2006) Rz 102; for the legitimacy of a preliminary injunction *de lege lata* Bernhard König, *Einstweilige Verfügungen im Zivilverfahren* (5th edn, MANZ 2017) Rz 2/54 et seq and 3/85 et seqq; id., 'Die Nichtrückführbarkeit einstweiliger Verfügungen' in Brigitte Schenk et al (eds), *Festschrift für Irmgard Griss* (2011) 389, 401 et seqq; Ewald Kininger, *Einstweilige Verfügungen zur Sicherung von Rechtsverhältnissen* (MANZ 1991) 42, 89 et seq.

68 HG Wien 22 January 2013, 25 Cg 3/13a-3.

69 OGH 16 October 2013, 7 Ob 164/13p.

70 European Commission, COM (2016) 723 final.

these principles is a stay of individual enforcement actions. In the final compromise text as of 17 December 2018, the intended consequences are described in Article 7 para 4 and 5 as follows:

> Member States shall provide for rules preventing creditors to which the stay applies from withholding performance or terminating, accelerating or, in any other way, modifying essential executory contracts which are necessary for the continuation of the day-to-day operation of the business, including any supplies where a suspension would lead to the debtor's activities coming to a standstill, to the detriment of the debtor, for debts that came into existence prior to the stay, solely by reason that they were not paid by the debtor. [...] Member States may provide that this paragraph also applies to other executory contracts.
>
> Member States shall ensure that creditors are not allowed to withhold performance or terminate, accelerate or, in any other way, modify executory contracts to the detriment of the debtor by virtue of a contractual clause providing for such measures, solely by reason of: (a) a request for an opening of a preventive restructuring procedure; (b) a request for a stay of individual enforcement actions; (c) the opening of a preventive restructuring procedure; or (d) the granting of a stay of individual enforcement actions as such.[71]

4.42 Just as the Austrian provision already does, the final compromise text for the Directive on preventive restructuring limits the application of the stay to essential contracts which are necessary for the continuation of the day-to-day operation of the business. Just as in Austria, this could invite counterparties to argue that their contract is not necessary for the continuation of the day-to-day operation of the business. As a result, they might be inclined to terminate the contract. Member states could work against such behaviour by making use of the opening clause of Article 7 para 4 which allows them to provide that the stay also applies to other executory contracts.

4.43 Furthermore, the final compromise text for the Directive suggests disregarding clauses that refer to a request for an opening of a preventive restructuring procedure or for a stay of individual enforcement actions, the opening of a preventive restructuring procedure or the granting of a stay of individual enforcement actions as such. Since the scope of the envisaged Directive is broader, it is a bit better than the Austrian provision against *ipso facto* clauses. Nevertheless, the main problem remains the same: no matter where the legislature draws the line, one could always draft a clause that provides for the automatic termination of the contract right before such line. Once such line is reached, one could subsequently argue that the contract is

71 http://data.consilium.europa.eu/doc/document/ST-15556–2018-INIT/en/pdf (last accessed 2 January 2019).

already terminated. Therefore, national legislatures should target this behaviour in order to provide for an effective stay. A regulation can reach this goal if it stipulates that counterparties cannot invoke a termination clause once the line drawn by the legislature is reached.

Eventually, another experience the Austrian legislature made can offer an important lesson: the Austrian legislature established a legal framework for the reorganization of debtors who are not insolvent.[72] These reorganizations are regulated by the Business Reorganization Act and involve a court-appointed reorganization auditor. They are irrelevant in legal practice. One reason could be that they do not contain a stay of individual enforcement actions. Another reason, however, could be that they are very much perceived like regular insolvency proceedings. Although they are not public, the involvement of a court might already evoke the fear of a stigma similar to the one that insolvency entails. As a consequence, entrepreneurs and businesses in financial distress rather try to resolve the situation on their own or in direct negotiations with their creditors. **4.44**

D. REFORMS

Recently, the Austrian legislature enacted another insolvency law reform.[73] It was less extensive than the reform in 2010 and did not affect any of the provisions dealt with in this chapter. Nevertheless, its goal is in line with the proposal of the European Commission: The work programme of the Austrian Federal Government for 2017/2018 contained a section captioned 'Modern Insolvency Law – Culture of Failure'. This section provided for a reform of personal insolvency aimed at enabling the debtor to quickly return to a productive occupation. The insolvency law reform in 2017 (*Insolvenzrechtsänderungsgesetz 2017 – IRÄG 2017*[74]) implemented the objectives to some extent: the duration of the procedure to skim off any income above the subsistence minimum (*Abschöpfungsverfahren*), at the end of which the debtor has to be discharged from any remaining liabilities (*Restschuldbefreiung*), was reduced from seven to five years.[75] In addition, the minimum quota of **4.45**

72 See *supra* note 16.

73 In addition, Regulation (EU) 2015/848 of the European Parliament and of the Council of 20 May 2015 on insolvency proceedings applies to insolvency proceedings opened after 26 June 2017.

74 BGBl. I Nr. 122/2017.

75 Austrian Insolvency Code, s 199 (2).

10 per cent was abolished.[76] In doing so, the Austrian legislature hoped to protect debtors from being secluded from social and economic activities.[77]

4.46 The work programme of the Austrian Federal Government for 2017/2018 also aimed at a reform of the legal framework for out-of-court restructurings. The work programme marked Brexit as a chance for Austria as a business location. The idea of the work programme was that an improvement of the legal framework for out-of-court restructurings could be a meaningful contribution in order to take this chance. One of the measures being discussed was an extension of the 60-day period to file for insolvency. However, Austria's government coalition collapsed in spring 2017, which led to early elections in autumn 2017. What will happen to the idea of an improvement for out-of-court restructurings therefore remains to be seen. The government programme of the new coalition for 2017–2022 only mentions that the Business Reorganization Act should be evaluated.

E. CONCLUDING REMARKS

4.47 In the past, the main drivers of reform were external events such as the worldwide economic crisis. Successful advocacy and the efforts of the working group of the Austrian Ministry of Justice dedicated to improving insolvency laws also played an important role in advancing Austrian insolvency law.

4.48 The next steps will depend on the new government coalition and its priorities. An extension of opportunities for out-of-court restructurings would likely have the support of companies, practitioners and banks. To what extent certain parties will support new regulations will, of course, depend on their content. In case the Austrian legislature establishes a legal framework for out-of-court workouts, it will therefore be interesting to see whether the legislature will opt for a treatment of executory contracts that is similar to the one it enacted for formal insolvency proceedings.

4.49 If the Austrian legislature decides to address the treatment of executory contracts in out-of-court workouts, it might want to draw upon the lessons learned in the last few years. The effectiveness of a system to maintain contracts clearly depends on several factors. The law should provide clear rules and a mechanism to quickly enforce them. Apart from these obvious factors,

76 For an overview of the changes see Franz Mohr, 'Neuerungen im Privatinsolvenzrecht – IRÄG 2017' [2017] ZIK 97.

77 ErläutRV IRÄG 2017, 1588 BlgNR 25. GP 1, 12.

experience in legal practice has also shown that it plays an important role in how these rules are perceived. If they give the impression that the debtor should be reorganized at the expense of its creditors, they will continue to try to terminate contracts before the opening of insolvency proceedings. How these rules are perceived mainly depends on their scope. The bigger the disadvantages that the automatic stay forces counterparties to endure are, the more likely they would try to avoid the automatic stay.

At the moment, it is fairly easy for counterparties to avoid the automatic stay **4.50** in Austrian insolvency proceedings. The current provisions simply contain too many loopholes. The good news is: they can be marked quite accurately. For the Austrian Insolvency Code, this gives every reason to hope that the legislature will see the next insolvency law reform as a chance to close those loopholes. For foreign legislatures, this can serve as an inspiration for modelling their own regulations in the future.

5

NATIONAL REPORT FOR BRAZIL

Francisco Satiro and Eduardo G. Wanderley

A. INTRODUCTION

5.01 Federal Law No. 11,101/2005, as of 9 February 2005, as amended (the 'Bankruptcy Law', 'Lei de Recuperação de Empresas e Falências' or 'LRF'), governs corporate insolvency in Brazil.[1] As a matter of legislative policy, LRF

1 Portuguese Laws (Alfonsina Ordinance: from 1500, when Pedro Alvares Cabral, a Portuguese sea captain, discovered Brazil, to 1514; Manuelina Ordinance: (1514–1603) and Filipina Ordinance (1603–1916)) applied in Brazil while it was a colony (1500–1822) and in the early decades of the Federative Republic (1889 onwards). In 1850, strongly influenced by the French Commercial Code (1808), Brazilian Empire (independent from Portugal since 1822) passed its first Commercial Code, governing commercial matters, including insolvency. In 1890, a new act on insolvency matters was issued (Decree 917/1890) to substitute the insolvency chapter of the Commercial Code (parts of which remained in force until 2002). From then on, some specific amendments changed the insolvency laws in different manners (Law 859/1902, Law 2.024/1908, and Decree 5746/1929), most of them fostered by specific policies aimed at overcoming economic crisis from time to time. Finally, in 1945, Decree-Law 7.661/1945 completely revoked the former regime and proposed a completely new framework for insolvency: liquidation proceedings ('falencia') for presumably unviable merchants and companies, and a limited composition alternative ('concordata') that was applicable and mandatory only for unsecured creditors. Although considered a technically accurate statute, Decree-Law 7.661/1945 never allowed neither efficient liquidations nor reorganization of viable companies. It remained in force for 60 years based on the resistance of most entrepreneurs who counted on 'concordata' as an alternative to keep companies (even the inviable ones) away from liquidation ('falencia') and their members' and managers' assets protected from the disregard of legal entity-type of claims, frequently applied in liquidation cases in Brazil. Judges and academics qualified 'concordata' as a 'legal benefit' ('favor legal') as it was a clear advantage without proper consideration for unsecured creditors. For more information see. Scalzilli, J. P.; Spinelli, L. F. and Tellechea, R. *Formaçao Historica do Direito Falimentar*, 2017.

aims at allowing for the reorganization of viable business and the efficient liquidation of business that should otherwise be wound-up.[2]

The country has seen in the last five years a few multi-billion court-supervised rescue proceedings, such as OGX, OSX and Sete Brasil (oil & gas); MMX (mining); OAS and Galvao (construction); Schahin (construction; oil & gas); Abengoa (power transmission); and Oi (telecom).[3] As a result, the application of the Bankruptcy Law by Brazilian courts is a 'developing work', with new trends and demands emerging as the cases become more complex. Along these lines, talks about amending LRF in academia, government and think tanks led the Ministry of Finance to set up a working group to prepare an initial draft bill of amendment, which after several modifications from its original structure was remitted to Brazilian Congress as Bill 10.220/2018 ('Bill').[4] **5.02**

The increased use of LRF over time by Brazilian companies reflects the impacts of the economic crisis that the country has been facing since 2014.[5] In most cases, however, the voluntary use of LRF by debtors is a protective measure, which typically follows unsuccessful out-of-court negotiations with local banks, bondholders and strategic suppliers. **5.03**

LRF does not provide for out-of-court arrangements and compositions in detail – though Section 167 thereof states that LRF does not affect debtors' ability to reach compositions without court supervision. However, experience shows that debtors and major creditors (mostly local banks, local or foreign bondholders) engage in out-of-court negotiations in order to avoid formal insolvency proceedings and therefore protect the company's going concern. **5.04**

Whilst this may sound counterintuitive for business reorganizations – i.e. formal insolvency proceedings should protect going concern value and not the opposite – stigma, the use of personal guarantees by shareholders (which accelerate upon the engagement of LRF), lack of available financing for **5.05**

2 Different pieces of legislation govern the insolvency of financial institutions and insurance companies (Law 6,024/74), power concessionaires (Law 12.767/12), etc. The LRF does not apply to state-owned enterprises: public companies (*empresas públicas*) or companies with private capital however controlled by governmental bodies (*sociedades de economia mista*). There is a new statute governing certain aspects of insolvency of Brazilian States (Supplementary Law 159/2017).

3 Oi Telecom is the largest Brazilian court-supervised reorganization (*recuperaçao judicial*) procedure so far, involving circa €20 billion debt.

4 On 16 December 2017, through Ordinance 467/2016, the Brazilian Ministry of Finance appointed an ad hoc group of specialists to draft a bill aimed at amending LRF. Francisco Satiro, one of the authors, lead the specialists working group.

5 In 2016, 721 Bankruptcy Liquidations were decreed, whilst 1.863 Judicial Reorganizations have been requested. See https://www.serasaexperian.com.br/release/indicadores/falencias_concordatas.htm, access on 3 February 2017.

insolvent entities, local bank policies and regulations as regards risk exposure and allocation and a certain degree of legal uncertainty with the application of LRF, all contribute to calling formal insolvency proceedings only as the last resort.

B. AVAILABLE PROCEDURES

5.06 The Bankruptcy Law contemplates three different proceedings: judicial reorganization, extrajudicial reorganization and bankruptcy liquidation, each of which is summarized below.

1. Judicial Reorganization

5.07 'Judicial Reorganization' (*recuperaçao judicial* or 'RJ') is a court-supervised debtor-in-possession reorganization proceeding.

Request for Judicial Reorganization

5.08 An application for Judicial Reorganization is only voluntary. The debtor lodges an application before the state court of its principal place of business (the 'Bankruptcy Court'), supported with the information and documentation required under the LRF (the 'Required Documentation'), which include, *inter alia*, a statement about the causes of insolvency, financial statements, balance sheets, lists of claims and creditors and other documents.

5.09 It may happen that entities belonging to the same corporate group[6] file a joint request for Judicial Reorganization. The joint request gives rise to several not fully pacified legal discussions, such as whether the assets and liabilities of the entities should be consolidated in a single package (the so-called 'substantive consolidation'); if the entities should file a single or several plans; if the creditors of one entity have the legitimacy to dispute the plan of another entity, etc.

6 LRF does not provide a definition of a corporate group. Bankruptcy cases reflect the broad definition arising from the combination of different statutes like Labour Law, Tax Law and, of course, Corporate Law. See Neder Cerezzetti, S. C. Satiro, F. A. silenciosa consolidaçao da Consolidaçao substancial in Revista do Advogado AASP, n. 131, 2016, pp. 216–23, available in: https://www.researchgate.net/profile/Francisco_Satiro/publication/311677436_A_silenciosa_consolidacao_da_consolidacao_substancial_Resultados_de_pesquisa_empirica_sobre_recuperacao_judicial_de_grupos_empresariais/links/5853ebb608ae95fd8e1ff414/A-silenciosa-consolidacao-da-consolidacao-substancial-Resultados-de-pesquisa-empirica-sobre-recuperacao-judicial-de-grupos-empresariais.pdf.

Reorganizations of groups are also a source of jurisdictional disputes. There are no express statutory provisions on cross-border insolvencies under Brazilian Law.[7] However, the Bill proposes the adoption of some of the provisions of the UNCITRAL Cross-Border Insolvency Model Law. However, the Bill is yet to be considered by the two chambers at Brazilian Congress.[8] Additionally, Brazil is not a party to international conventions or agreements providing for international cooperation mechanisms and transnational insolvency procedures in the event of insolvency involving debtors or assets located in more than one jurisdiction. Furthermore, cross-border insolvency problems were restricted to academia, and until recently there was almost no case law on cross-border insolvency in Brazil. Pre-2013, the few cases ruled by Brazilian courts were either on the (a) recognition of the effects of foreign judicial decisions in Brazilian territory (*homologaçao de sentença estrangeira*), or on the (b) recognition of Brazilian insolvency cases by other jurisdictions.[9] The first case in which foreign incorporated entities engaged LRF in Brazil was OGX (one of the most prominent RJ cases to date).[10] **5.10**

Following OGX, Brazilian courts have been keener to accept RJ requests of corporate groups with offshore affiliates with no assets, incorporated only to issue debt in order to finance Brazilian enterprises. In the OAS RJ case, the bankruptcy court of Sao Paulo granted the application of foreign affiliated companies in the RJ request filed alongside the Brazilian holding company. The court held that: **5.11**

7 For a historical background of the evolution of cross-border insolvency provisions in Latin America see Campana Filho, P. F, 'The Legal Framework for Cross-Border Insolvency in Brazil.' *Hous. J. Int'l L.* 32 (2009): 97, pp. 117–42.

8 Other bills addressing the same topic are PLC 3.741-A/2015 (http://www.camara.gov.br/sileg/integras/1473418.pdf) and PLC 1.572/11 (http://www.camara.gov.br/proposicoesWeb/prop_mostrarintegra;jsessionid=F198CCDDFA7647F0F3BE167B9B63F6A8.proposicoesWeb2?codteor=1437525&filename=SBT+1+PL157211+%3D%3E+PL+1572/2011).

9 Brazilian insolvency cases involving a Brazilian company or a group of companies based on Brazilian territory are frequently brought before U.S. courts as non-main proceedings under 'Chapter 15'. It should also be noted that during the Judicial Reorganization of Varig Airlines (2005), filed before the Court of Rio de Janeiro, the debtor filed a §304 ancillary proceeding (therefore, pre-Chapter 15) before the Courts of New York requesting the court to give comity to the Brazilian bankruptcy court and therefore extend the effects of the Brazilian moratorium to U.S. territory and protect Varig's assets (aircraft and engines) in that jurisdiction. In this case, in addition to the cross-border ancillary proceeding, there was an ad hoc cooperation among Brazilian and U.S. courts.

10 In OGX, two Brazilian companies based in Brazil and two Austrian affiliates filed for RJ in Rio de Janeiro. The court held that the Austrian affiliates could file for bankruptcy in Rio de Janeiro on the basis that (a) they were companies incorporated in Austria merely to issue international bonds to finance the Brazilian companies; (b) they had no assets; and (c) their executive officers were based in Brazil. In addition, the Brazilian court took into consideration an affidavit prepared by OGX's Austrian counsel stating that Austrian courts would give comity to the Brazilian court, recognize the Brazilian insolvency proceedings and, as a result, deny jurisdiction to institute main insolvency proceedings in Austria on the basis that (d) the Austrian companies had their 'Center Of Main Interest' (COMI) in Brazil, and (e) the LRF would treat local and foreigner creditors in the same way.

Although Brazil has not adopted the UNCITRAL Model Law for cross-border insolvency, nothing prevents that companies incorporated abroad, but with their main center of its activities in Brazil (COMI – Center of Main Interest) and unequivocally controlled by and participants of a Brazilian corporate group, file for bankruptcy according to the Law 11.101/05 before a Brazilian Court. In this case, the claimants incorporated abroad are fully controlled by OAS S/A, and act solely as fundraising companies abroad, without operational activities.

Acceptance of the case by the Bankruptcy Court

5.12 If the required documentation is in good standing, the Bankruptcy Court will typically accept the case and issue an order (the 'Acceptance Order') under which it shall:

(i) Appoint the judicial administrator ('Administrator'), who has no managerial powers over the debtor and acts solely as a supervisor of the proceeding and an assistant to the Bankruptcy Court;
(ii) Order the immediate stay of certain actions and enforcement proceedings filed against the debtor for a 180-day period;
(iii) Order the issuance of a public notice containing the summary of the mentioned decision and the list of creditors ('List of Creditors') as attached to the request for Judicial Reorganization;
(iv) Order the presentation of the reorganization plan (the 'Plan') within 60 days; and
(v) Inform creditors that they shall file proofs of claims and/or challenges to the List of Creditors before the administrator within 15 business-days.[11]

Stay period

5.13 All actions and enforcement proceedings lodged against the debtor are stayed for 180 days following the Acceptance Order, with few exceptions.

5.14 If the Plan is not approved within the stay period and unless it is not extended for an additional period at the court's discretion,[12] the creditors should be able to resume actions and enforcement proceedings, irrespectively of the stage of the negotiations concerning the Plan. In our experience, the court tends to extend the stay whenever necessary.

---

11 It is common that the publication of the list of creditors occurs after the publication of the acceptance order. Whenever that happens, the 15-day period for proofs of claims counts from the publication of the List of Creditors.

12 Which is common practice according to the dominants precedent, notwithstanding an original prohibition in LRF.

The plan

Following the Acceptance Order, the debtor will have up to 60 days to file with the Bankruptcy Court a reorganization Plan providing the means of reorganization, such as a change in the company's control or a partial sale of its assets, a debt for equity swap, mergers or leases of commercial establishments, debt rescheduling, new interest rates, etc. 5.15

A typical Plan entails some sort of debt 'hair-cut', coupled with the rescheduling of debts and the sale of assets. Plans that are more sophisticated often involve convertible instruments, so that creditors capture debtor's occasional 'upside'. 5.16

If any creditor files for a formal objection to the Plan (no matter the grounds), then the Bankruptcy Court will convey a 'General Meeting of Creditors' ('GMC'), where the creditors shall ultimately vote on the Plan divided into four classes: 5.17

(i) Holders of labour-related credits and credits resulting from on-the-job accidents;
(ii) Holders of secured credits with in rem guarantees (namely *penhor* and *hipoteca*);
(iii) Unsecured creditors;
(iv) 'Micro' and 'Small' Enterprises.[13]

All classes must approve the Plan.[14] Once approved, typically the Plan is confirmed by the Bankruptcy Court and is court-supervised for at least two years, as a rule. The non-performance of the Plan within this period should result in debtor's Bankruptcy Liquidation. 5.18

13 'Micro' enterprises are business entities with annual gross revenue lower than BRL 360,000.00 (approx. EUR 96.000), whereas 'Small' businesses have annual gross revenue between BRL 360,000.01 and BRL 3,600,000.00 (EUR 960.000), no matter the number of employees.

14 Article 45. In resolutions on the judicial reorganization plan, all classes of creditors referred to in article 41 hereof shall approve the proposal.

Paragraph 1. In each of the classes referred to in article 41, II and III, hereof, the proposal shall be approved by creditors representing over half of the total amount of the claims represented at the general meeting and, cumulatively, by a simple majority of creditors present.

Paragraph 2. In the classes under article 41, I and IV, hereof, the proposal shall be approved by simple majority of the creditors present, independently of the amount of the credit.

Paragraph 3. Creditors shall not be entitled to vote and shall not be considered for purposes of verification of the resolution quorum if the judicial reorganization plan does not alter the amount or the original conditions of payment of their claims.

5.19 Notwithstanding the foregoing, the Bankruptcy Court may 'cram-down' the Plan and confirm it in certain situations.[15]

5.20 Pre-petition claims subject to the Judicial Reorganization are novated (*novadas*) upon Plan confirmation by the Bankruptcy Court. Such novation is subject to the condition that the Judicial Reorganization is not converted into Bankruptcy Liquidation. If the debtor survives the court-supervision stage, it follows that the novation operates in full and the pre-petition claims cannot be reinstated upon an event of default under the Plan.

Filing of proofs of claims

5.21 The Acceptance Order triggers the commencement of a 15-day term for the creditors that are subject to the Judicial Reorganization to either file proofs of claims or dispute the List of Creditors.

5.22 Creditors present the proofs of claims and challenges to the Administrator, who is responsible for analysing creditor's claims and preparing a second list of creditors. The second list may be disputed by creditors before the Bankruptcy Court.

Pre-petition claims not subject to the Judicial Reorganization

5.23 Certain pre-petition claims cannot be altered by the Plan, as follows:

---

15 Article 58. The requirements of this Law having been met, the judge shall grant the judicial reorganization of the debtor whose plan has not been objected to by any creditor pursuant to article 55 hereof or has been approved by the general meeting of creditors pursuant to article 45 hereof.

Paragraph 1. The judge may grant judicial reorganization based on a plan that has not been approved pursuant to article 45 hereof, provided it has obtained, cumulatively, at the same general meeting:

I – the favorable vote of creditors representing over half the amount of all claims represented at the general meeting, independently of classes;
II – the approval of two (2) of the classes of creditors pursuant to article 45 hereof, or if there are only two (2) classes with voting creditors, the approval of at least one (1) of them;
III – in the class that rejected it, the favorable vote of over one-third (1/3) of the creditors, computed pursuant to article 45, paragraphs 1 and 2, hereof.

Paragraph 2. Judicial recovery may only be granted pursuant to paragraph 1 of this article if the plan does not entail different treatment among the creditors of the class that rejected it.

Article 59. The judicial recovery plan entails renewal of pre-petition claims, and binds the debtor and all the creditors subject to him, without prejudice to the guarantees, with due regard for the provisions of article 50, paragraph 1, hereof.

Paragraph 1. The court decision that grants judicial recovery shall constitute a judicial enforcement instrument (...) Paragraph 2. A plea may be filed against decisions granting judicial recovery by any creditor and by the Public Attorney's Office.

(i) Claims secured with fiduciary lien (*alienaçao fiduciaria*);
(ii) Claims of a lessee under a commercial leasing agreement (*arrendamento mercantil*);
(iii) Proprietary claims of an owner or committed seller of real estate whose respective agreements include an irrevocability or irreversibility clause (*promessa de compra e venda irrevogavel de imovel*);
(iv) Claims of seller under a sale agreement with retention title (*venda com reserve de dominio*);
(v) Creditor under an advance on export contract (*adiantamento a contrato de cambio* or 'ACC'); and
(vi) Tax claims.[16]

In practical terms, except as regards tax claims, debtors engage bilateral negotiations with extra-RJ creditors in parallel with the RJ proceedings. **5.24**

Post-petition claims (i.e. claims arising after a company files for RJ) are not subject to the proceedings either, and must be paid by the debtor as they fall due. **5.25**

Sale of assets

Section 60 of the Bankruptcy Law provides for the conditions under which the debtor may sell 'separate units of production' (UPIs) and branches without successor liability to the acquirer. Section 60 sales have proven to be a valuable mean to obtain new money for insolvent entities in Brazil and courts have been granting protection to such sales. **5.26**

Financing in Judicial Reorganization

In Brazil, the financing provided to the reorganizing entity is a post-petition claim in a contingent Bankruptcy Liquidation, junior to other types of post-petition claims and to creditors holding fiduciary liens and ACCs. As a result, unsecured post-filing financing is unusual. **5.27**

In addition, there is no priority during RJ for the post-filing financing provided under statutory law although priority is usually built contractually and generally approved by the Bankruptcy Court and pre-petition creditors. **5.28**

Regardless of this, post-petition financiers may profit out of converting their debt into equity if the company succeeds at negotiating attractive rates from the outset, as a condition precedent for the disbursement. This strategy has **5.29**

16 Brazilian Law prohibits tax authorities to individually negotiate with debtors.

become more frequent for medium and large companies, and a market is developing for this.

2. Extrajudicial Reorganization

5.30 The second mechanism granted to debtors by the Bankruptcy Law to pursue reorganization, the Extrajudicial Reorganization (*recuperaçao extrajudicial*), is a pre-packaged type of arrangement which is brought before the Bankruptcy Court for confirmation.

5.31 The creditors that are not subject to a plan under Judicial Reorganization, the holders of labour related claims, claims arising out of on-the-job accidents and tax claims are excluded from the Extrajudicial Reorganization.

5.32 The Extrajudicial Reorganization may precede a Judicial Reorganization and may enclose all categories of claims other than those that are excluded, some categories of creditors or even a group of certain categories. In order to bind all creditors of a certain category, approval by the holders of more than 3/5 of the amount of affected claims is necessary.

3. Bankruptcy Liquidation

5.33 Bankruptcy Liquidation ('*falencia*') is a legal proceeding which aims at marshalling and liquidating all debtor's assets, and distributing the proceeds to creditors according to a pre-established rank. A debtor may file for voluntary Bankruptcy Liquidation when it is unable to reorganize its business under Judicial Reorganization proceeding, and it is under financial and/or economic distress. Conversely, a debtor may be subject to involuntary Bankruptcy Liquidation proceedings, a more usual situation.

Exclusive jurisdiction

5.34 The State courts of the venue in which the debtor has its main business establishment or a branch (if the debtor is a foreign company) have exclusive jurisdiction to declare Bankruptcy Liquidation.

5.35 The Bankruptcy Liquidation court is indivisible and has exclusive jurisdiction over all pending actions and claims involving assets, interests and business related to the estate, with certain exceptions.[17]

17 Actions claiming a non-fixed amount shall continue at the same court where they are proceeding. Labour-related lawsuits shall be processed before the specialized courts until the respective claims have been ascertained, which shall be enrolled in the general list of creditors in the amount determined by court decision.

Consequences of the bankruptcy liquidation decree

Following the Bankruptcy Liquidation Decree ('Decree'), the debtor's debts are ascertained, the schedules are drawn up, the assets are marshalled and liquidated, and the creditors paid by apportionment, in accordance with a pre-established ranking of claims. **5.36**

The Decree will, *inter alia*: (a) set the time frame for the avoidance of preferential and fraudulent transfers; (b) specify the period for creditors to prove their claims; (c) order certain actions required to safeguard interests of the parties to the proceedings, including the preventive detention of managers when so requested on the grounds of evidence of any bankruptcy crime; (d) prohibit the performance of any act of disposal or encumbrance of the companies' assets, submitting them to prior authorization from the court; and (e) appoint the Administrator (with further powers and scope when compared to a RJ Administrator). **5.37**

Duties imposed on the debtor

The Decree imposes several duties on the bankrupt debtor and its management, including: (a) testifying/stating the (main) causes that determined the insolvency; (b) indicating the debtor's real and personal property; (c) indicating the debtor's participation in other companies; (d) disclosing and informing the debtor's bank accounts and investments; (e) disclosing ongoing proceedings in which the debtor figures as plaintiff or defendant; (f) promptly delivering all assets, company's books, papers and documents to the Administrator; and (g) promptly provide any information required by the judge, Administrator, creditors or Public Attorney's Office regarding circumstances and facts of interest to such parties. **5.38**

Management of the estate

Following the Decree, the debtor is dispossessed of its assets and management is removed and substituted by the Administrator, who shall be a reputable professional, preferably a lawyer, economist, business manager or accountant, or a specialized legal entity. **5.39**

The debtor (i.e. the bankrupt entity) will lose the right to manage and dispose of its assets and shall not do business in Brazil while the bankruptcy endures. By removing the debtor from its activities, the proceedings seek to preserve and optimize the ongoing use of the debtor's assets and resources, including intangible assets, subsequently increasing the possibility of the creditors recovering their claims. **5.40**

5.41 The prohibition of doing business in Brazil imposed by a bankruptcy decree is limited to the bankrupt entity, and should not affect non-bankrupt corporations belonging to the same corporate group.

5.42 Compensation for the Administrator is allowed by the Bankruptcy Court in an amount up to 5% of the proceeds resulting from the sale of debtor's assets. The compensation is payable after the services have been rendered, and 40% of the Administrator's compensation shall not be paid until the approval of his/her final report by the Bankruptcy Court. In practice, however, interim payments may be allowed to the Administrator by the Bankruptcy Court.

Sale of assets

5.43 The Administrator is responsible for: (a) marshalling all the assets and documents of the estate; and (b) arranging for the appraisal of assets, separately or in a block, at the place where they are situated.

5.44 The sale of assets shall start irrespective of judgments of all proofs of claims. Immediately upon scheduling of the assets, asset sales will be carried out in one of the several mechanisms of disposal provided for the Bankruptcy Law (in block or separately), which typically involve some type of competitive process seeking to maximize the proceeds for the benefit of the estate.

Creditors' rights

5.45 The following are consequences of the Decree: (a) the stay of all actions and enforcement lawsuits against the debtor, with a few exceptions; (b) the acceleration of the payment obligations of the debtor; and (c) the conversion into domestic currency of all foreign currency-denominated claims at the exchange rate prevailing on the date of Decree.

Avoidable transactions

5.46 LRF provides for several situations in which preferential or fraudulent transfers and payments made by the debtor on or within a certain period of time may be avoided by the Bankruptcy Court.

5.47 The 'lookback period' (*termo legal da falencia*) is a relevant time frame established by the Bankruptcy Court beginning as of 90 (ninety) days before (i) the date of the first valid protest for non-payment by a public notary, (ii) the date of the filing for voluntary or involuntary Bankruptcy Liquidation, or (iii) the date of the filing for Judicial Reorganization (as applicable).

Avoidable Transactions do not necessarily involve any actual wrongdoing, and may be regarded as preferential or unfair irrespectively of the intent of the parties to defraud creditors. The Bankruptcy Court may render a preferential transfer void either *ex officio* or in a lawsuit filed by any interested parties. **5.48**

Pursuant to LRF Section 129, preferential transfers are: (i) the payment of unexpired debts made within the lookback period; (ii) the payment of matured debt by any other means not provided by the agreement within the lookback period; (iii) the creation of a secured interest in debtor's property, assets or receivables for existing debts, within the lookback period; (iv) the sale of a set of operational assets as a going concern (which includes the sale of strategic or high value assets) either without the express approval or the payment of all creditors, unless the creditors do not oppose the sale within 30 (thirty) days as of the formal notification of the sale; (v) the transfer of any interest on debtors' real property after the Decree; (vi) transactions at an undervalue or gifts within 2 years before the Decree. **5.49**

Payment rank

The order of payment provided for under Bankruptcy Law, after the payment of the indispensable expenses to the administration of the proceedings with cash availabilities, is the following: **5.50**

1. Salary-related claims matured at most 3 months prior to liquidation decree, limited to five times the minimum wage per worker, paid off as soon as there is available cash;
2. Payment of the restitutions in cash (including ACC);
3. Post-petition claims;
    a. Administrator's fees and post-petition labour claims (*pari passu*);
    b. Amounts advances post-liquidation decree;
    c. Liquidation expenses;
    d. Court fees;
    e. Post-RJ and Post-Bankruptcy Liquidation Claims, in the following order: labour, secured claims with in rem guarantees, taxes, unsecured post-reorganization financing and other unsecured claims, fines and penalties and subordinated claims;
4. Labour-related (150 minimum wages, minus 5 minimum wages already paid) and credits resulting from on the job accidents;
5. Secured claims with in rem guarantees (*penhor* and *hipoteca*);
6. Tax claims;
7. Special privileged claims;
8. General privileged claims;
9. Unsecured claims;

10. Claims related to contractual penalties and fines for breach of criminal or administrative law, including tax-related fines;
11. Subordinated claims, as follows: those so provided for by law or contract, as well as the credits of partners and officers without an employment bond.

Termination of the Bankruptcy Liquidation proceedings

5.51 After all assets are sold and the proceeds distributed among the creditors, the Administrator shall submit his accounts to the Bankruptcy Court. A final report on the case states the amount of the assets and of the proceeds of their realization, the amount of the liabilities and the amount payed to creditors.

5.52 Following the submission of the final report by the Administrator, the Bankruptcy Court typically renders a decision terminating the Bankruptcy Liquidation proceedings. The statute of limitations with respect to any (outstanding) obligations of the bankrupt debtor (if any) is triggered on the date that the decision terminating the proceeding becomes final and unappealable.

Discharge

5.53 The discharge order is a final step in Bankruptcy Liquidation proceedings. In order to obtain the discharge, a debtor must meet one of following conditions: (a) the payment of all its creditors; (b) the payment of at least 50% of all unsecured claims; (c) passage of time following the termination of the Bankruptcy Liquidation proceedings, specifically (c.i) 5 (five) years if the debtor was not convicted of any bankruptcy-related crime; or (c.ii) 10 (ten) years, if the debtor has been convicted of any bankruptcy-related crime.

C. TREATMENT OF EXECUTORY CONTRACTS

5.54 This section examines the treatment of executory contracts under each of the insolvency proceedings described in the foregoing paragraphs, including related case law.[18,19]

18 For the purposes hereof 'executory contracts' are contracts that at the commencement of an insolvency proceeding have not yet been fully performed by both the insolvent debtor and the counterparty.

19 Mostly the Court of Appeals of the State of Sao Paulo ('TJSP'), the Court of Appeals of the State of Rio de Janeiro ('TJRJ') and the Superior Court of Justice ('STJ'). The first two are the busiest state courts addressing insolvency matters in Brazil, while STJ is the court responsible for, *inter alia*, settling conflicts concerning the application of federal legislation (like LRF) by state courts (like TJSP and TJRJ) throughout the country.

1. Treatment of executory contracts under LRF

The following sections of LRF deal with the matter directly or indirectly throughout the mentioned insolvency statute: 5.55

Section	Applies to	What is it about?	Connection with regime for Executory Contracts
3	RJ/RE/Bankruptcy Liquidation	Jurisdiction of the Bankruptcy Court.	Indirect
6	RJ/Bankruptcy Liquidation	Stay of actions against the debtor.	Indirect
7–20	RJ/Bankruptcy Liquidation	Filing of proofs of claims.	Indirect
22, I, b	RJ	Administrator's duty to render information to creditors.	Indirect
22, III, o	Bankruptcy Liquidation	Administrator's duty to protect and manage the estate efficiently.	Indirect
22, § 3	Bankruptcy Liquidation	Administrator's limitations on settling rights and obligations of the estate.	Indirect
27, I, c	RJ/Bankruptcy Liquidation	Committee of creditors' duty to inform the court about any violation of the law or harm to creditors.	Indirect
47	RJ	RJ's underpinning policy.	Indirect
49	RJ	Claims dischargeable in RJ proceedings.	Indirect
49, § 2	RJ	Pre-RJ obligations shall remain 'as is', except to the extent modified by the RJ Plan.	Direct
49, § 3	RJ	Protection of proprietary rights of certain creditors.	Direct
50, VII	RJ	Sale of commercial establishments (including executory contracts) as a mean of reorganization.	Indirect
59	RJ	Novation of pre-petition claims as a result of the court confirmation of the plan.	Indirect
60	RJ	Sale of 'segregated productive units' without succession liability.	Indirect
66	RJ	Prohibition of disposal of non-fixed assets without court authorisation.	Indirect
67, Sole Paragraph	RJ/Bankruptcy Liquidation	Roll-up of unsecured claims of creditors that keep on supplying to the debtor after the RJ request.	Direct
76	Bankruptcy Liquidation	Extended jurisdiction of the Bankruptcy Court.	Indirect

Section	Applies to	What is it about?	Connection with regime for Executory Contracts
77	Bankruptcy Liquidation	Acceleration of debtor's payment obligations.	Indirect
83	Bankruptcy Liquidation	Rank of pre-petition claims.	Indirect
84	RJ/Bankruptcy Liquidation	Definition and rank of post-petition claims.	Indirect
85–93	Bankruptcy Liquidation	Repossession of property.	Indirect
116, I	Bankruptcy Liquidation	Prohibition of retention rights following the Decree.	Direct
117	Bankruptcy Liquidation	The Administrator may assume or reject executory contracts.	Direct
118	Bankruptcy Liquidation	The Administrator may assume or reject unilateral contracts.	Direct
119, I to IX	Bankruptcy Liquidation	Legal regime applicable to certain executory contracts.	Direct
120	Bankruptcy Liquidation	Legal regime applicable to existing proxies.	Direct
121	Bankruptcy Liquidation	Legal regime applicable to existing bank accounts.	Direct
122	Bankruptcy Liquidation	Netting of pre-petition claims and debts.	Direct
123	Bankruptcy Liquidation	Legal regime applicable to legal entities of which the debtor was a member.	Direct
126	Bankruptcy Liquidation	Underlying police concerning situations not expressly governed by LRF.	Direct
129–138	Bankruptcy Liquidation	Avoidance of transactions.	Indirect
139–148	Bankruptcy Liquidation	Sale of assets.	Indirect
193–194	RJ/RE/Bankruptcy Liquidation	Safe harbour for debtor's obligations with financial clearance and settlement chambers.	Direct
199, §§ 1–3	RJ/RE/Bankruptcy Liquidation	Legal protection for proprietary rights of lessors of aircrafts and parts thereof.	Direct

5.56 As one can infer from the table above, there are far more sections addressing executory contracts-issues on an indirect basis than otherwise. Furthermore, the vast majority of the provisions that concern the matter directly are observed in Bankruptcy Liquidation, as opposed to Judicial Reorganization and Extrajudicial Reorganization regimes. It may seem counterintuitive that the regime for the assumption and rejection of executory contracts in a winding-up proceeding – which underpinning premise is that the business will most likely cease to exist – is more developed than the same regime for reorganization proceedings that aim to recover business. It is indeed.

Nevertheless, such a gap has been dealt with by courts on a case-by-case basis, sometimes leading to controversial results and some legal uncertainty within the scope of Judicial Reorganization proceedings (case law on Extrajudicial Reorganization is still limited on the matter and for the purposes of this chapter the same comments shall apply to either of them). **5.57**

We shall first examine the rules that deal expressly with executory contracts in Bankruptcy Liquidation, as they are more forthwith. In some situations, courts within the scope of Judicial Reorganization proceedings may broadly construe such rules; therefore, this is a useful exercise. Then, we shall consider certain relevant situations in Judicial Reorganization, which fall within the legislative vacuum that we referred to (which may apply to Extrajudicial Reorganization on the same basis), such as the assumption of executory contracts and courts' approach towards *ipso facto* clauses and the application of direct and indirect statutory provisions. **5.58**

2. Treatment of executory contracts in Bankruptcy Liquidation

The Administrator – under the supervision and authorisation of the Creditors Committee,[20] if applicable – has the prerogative of assuming or rejecting executory contracts in Bankruptcy Liquidation (LRF, Section 117). The driver for assuming contracts is 'reducing or preventing the increase of liabilities of the estate', but no clear guidance is given by LRF as to the legal meaning of the expression. However, it is fair to state that the Administrator needs to properly justify the assumption or rejection of an executory contract to the court and creditors.[21] **5.59**

Along these lines, one may infer that Section 117 prevails over *ipso facto* clauses (i.e. contractual terms providing for the automatic termination of an agreement following an insolvency event), although there is no statutory law considering such provisions invalid. **5.60**

The rejection of the contract by the Administrator gives rise to indemnification to the debtor's counterparty, which will be an unsecured claim in the **5.61**

20 Creditors Committee are not usual in Brazilian insolvency cases.

21 There are exceptions to the rule. Contracts entered into with governmental authorities, concessions and other public entities are automatically terminated upon Bankruptcy Liquidation as a matter of law. Certain kinds of joint-venture agreements, named *consorcio*, also terminate with respect to the insolvent debtor.

insolvency proceedings (Section 117, § 2). The rule is also clearly stated in Section 119, III, LRF, pursuant to which 'if the debtor fails to deliver a movable item or to provide a service sold or contracted for payment in instalments, and the Administrator rejects the contract, the claims relating to the amounts paid shall be proven in the proper class'.

5.62 The outcomes for assumed contracts are far more complicated and give rise to more legal challenges depending on the underlying situation.

5.63 Noteworthy, assuming a contract under Brazilian Law means accepting it 'as is', not only as regards its provisions but also its non-bankruptcy legal framework, including general rules and principles of Contract Law, which is mostly provided for under Brazilian Civil Code ('BCC'). Except as regards very specific situations, which will be covered later on in this chapter, LRF does not undermine the application of non-bankruptcy law to contracts assumed by the Administrator (although courts may do so on a controversial basis, especially in Judicial Reorganization).

5.64 In light of that assumption, let us first consider an executory contract whose obligations have not been performed at all by any of the parties but have been assumed by the Administrator, like a long-term legal services agreement that is engaged by one of the parties (i.e. the bankrupt debtor) by requesting for specific services from time to time. In our example, the Administrator requests a law firm to draft an opinion about a bankruptcy matter. Typically, under the relevant services agreement, the firm's lawyers would bill the services after they have been rendered, for payment in e.g. 30 days.

5.65 Now, could the law firm refuse to provide the services to the estate and, if so, on which basis? Under the assumption that non-bankruptcy law applies, the law firm could not refuse to perform its obligation, but should be able to engage BCC Section 477 and ask for a retainer fee as 'debtor's assets have reduced therefore compromising its ability to perform the obligation'.[22] Could the Administrator make the payment with absolute priority over other creditors without undermining *pars conditio creditorum*? The answer is affirmative, to the extent that such expense is 'paramount for the administration of the estate' (LRF, Section 150).

---

22 That is the application of *exceptio non adimpleti contractus* principle in an insolvency situation. We shall see in the next sub-section that courts have been undermining the application of such principle in Judicial Reorganization contexts.

Assuming that the estate fully paid for the services and now the law firm is amenable to accepting payments within 30 days. However, after additional rendered services are billed for, the estate fails to pay. What then? The firm may exercise all remedies available under the relevant agreement and the law to collect, but there is a risk that the amount is not paid immediately, but only as a post-petition claim, on the basis of Section 84, V, LRF, following the sale of assets and distributions of proceeds. 5.66

What if the debtor – that is now bankrupt – had requested the law firm to provide the services prior to the Bankruptcy Liquidation Decree, and the services were delivered back then but not paid for as a result of the Decree? Note that the services agreement is still in place, the Administrator assumed the contract and requested for additional services. Could the firm refuse to perform the assumed contract on the basis of the pre-petition event of default? As the payment of the pre-petition event of default can only be dealt by means of a distribution in the Bankruptcy Liquidation proceedings, it follows that such event cannot be invoked as an *exceptio* to avoid the performance on the basis of Section 476, BCC ('in executory contracts, none of the parties may request for the performance of the counterparty before performing its own obligation thereunder'). However, the firm could invoke Section 477 of BCC and request for a retainer fee to render post-petition services. 5.67

Now, what if the debtor had made an advance payment under the agreement prior to the Decree and the Administrator rejects the contract? Could the firm retain the payment received until the court determines the indemnification for rejection? No, as Section 116, I, LRF prohibits retention of assets belonging to the estate. Could the firm net the advance payment with the indemnification? Only if the indemnification was due and payable ('*liquida e certa*') by the time the contract was rejected; conversely, if due process is necessary to determine the amount to be indemnified, it is not suitable for netting (LRF, Section 122 and BCC, Section 369). 5.68

Let us take a step back at this point and explain the netting provisions in Bankruptcy Liquidation. As one may infer from the table above, they are only present in that winding-up proceeding and not in the reorganization proceedings. Does it mean that they only apply to the former? Not exactly, but there are good arguments (both of policy and law-in-force) to contend either position in the latter proceedings.[23] In Bankruptcy Liquidation, netting (*compensaçao*) is expressly permitted under Section 122, LRF, with the following caveats: (i) both claims and debts must be pre-petition; (ii) netting of such 5.69

23 We shall refer to discussions concerning netting in Judicial Reorganization in the next sub-section.

claims and debts must be possible under a non-bankruptcy law; (iii) claims assigned to any other creditors following the Bankruptcy Liquidation Decree cannot be net; (iv) claims that could otherwise be net but that have been assigned when the parties knew or ought to have known about the insolvency of the debtor, or with fraud or malice, cannot be net.

5.70 In furtherance of the general rules, Section 119, LRF addresses specific situations on a *numerus clausus* basis.

5.71 For instance, item I thereof provides that a 'seller cannot block the delivery of items shipped to the debtor and still in transit if prior to the bankruptcy application the purchaser had resold them, without fraud, as shown on invoices and bills of lading delivered or remitted by the seller' (i.e. a rule to protect a purchaser in good faith).

5.72 Item II states that 'if the debtor sold composite items and the Administrator rejects the contract, the purchaser may put the items already received at the disposal of the bankrupt estate, claiming damages', while item III provides that 'if the debtor fails to deliver a movable item or to provide a service sold or contracted for payment in instalments, and the Administrator rejects the contract, the claims relating to the amounts paid shall be proven in the proper class'.

5.73 Proprietary rights of a seller of a movable asset with retention of title are protected under item IV ('the Administrator (…) shall restore the movable item purchased by the debtor with title retention to the seller if the Administrator rejects the contract, requesting for the restitution of amounts paid under the agreement'.[24]

5.74 The scope of Section 119, V within the Bankruptcy Liquidation context is often doubtful, as the rule simply states that the outcome of a forward transaction with financial settlement in a non-bankruptcy scenario:

> in the event of items sold on the forward market and quoted on the stock exchange or market, and the contract is not performed by actual delivery of said items and payment of the price, the difference between the quotation on the date of the contract and at the time of exchange or market settlement shall prevail.

---

24 Differently, hire purchase agreements fall under the general provisions and will depend on the decision of the Administrator to be kept in force.

This rule has been adopted within the scope of the former insolvency statute (i.e Decree Law 7.661/45).[25] It made sense at that time because there was no provision related to exchange transactions. However, LRF has specifically defined that any transaction carried out under a regulated clearing system (including its collaterals) shall not be affected by the debtors' Bankruptcy Liquidation Decree or Judicial or Extrajudicial Reorganization procedure.[26] The integrity of the clearing system is considered to be more important than the individual interests of the creditors in Bankruptcy Liquidation.

Accordingly, Section 119, VIII protects bilateral netting agreements within **5.75** the national financial system, although allowing the non-bankrupt party to early terminate the agreement and net the claims and debts according to the clearance system rules.

Moreover, the scopes of Sections 119, VI and IX are shaped as a clear response **5.76** to the Bankruptcy Liquidations of real estate developing and construction companies (*incorporadoras*). Some iconic cases like ENCOL's bankruptcy in the 90s put at risk the investments of customers who had bought houses and apartments that have never been concluded provably as a result of fraud. The legislation applicable back then did not segregate the funds and assets concerning one given construction project from the other assets and liabilities of the developing and construction company, nor did it grant relief for customers who partially paid for their units' proprietary rights thereto. According to the former regime, if the developing and construction company went bankrupt, the customers would only have an unsecured claim for disbursed amounts, which typically was not recovered with distributions. During the early 2000s, a series of reforms in real estate legislation protected the acquirer of property in insolvency situations, including Brazilian Civil Code, Federal Law 10,931/2004 and LRF itself (note that Section 119, VI, simply calls for the application of the specific legislation: 'in the case of a real estate purchase and sale commitment, the respective law shall apply'; so does Section 119, IX: 'a segregated set of assets (*patrimônio de afetaçao*), constituted to meet a specific purpose, shall comply with the provisions of the respective laws, the assets, rights and obligations thereof continuing to be separate from those of the bankrupt estate until the advent of the respective term or until its purpose has been accomplished.'

25 The first five provisions are basically inspired by similar rules of the former law, Section 44.

26 Sections 193 and 194 are inspired by the BIS *Core Principles for Systemically Important Payment Systems*, available at https://www.bis.org/cpmi/publ/d43.pdf.

5.77 Closing out matters concerning real estate property, Section 119, VII provides that 'the lessor's Bankruptcy Liquidation does not terminate the lease agreement, and in the event of the lessee's Bankruptcy Liquidation the Administrator may terminate the agreement at any time'.

5.78 In addition, Section 120 deals with proxies in general, which are deemed revoked upon the Decree, as the Administrator takes full control of the management of the estate. On the contrary, power-of-attorneys granted to lawyers remain valid until expressly revoked by the Administrator, whilst pursuant to Section 121 all bank accounts shall be closed upon the Decree so that their balance is determined.

5.79 Finally, Section 126 contains a general guidance to the court, pursuant to which in situations not expressly governed by LRF, the judge shall decide taking into account the creditors' 'unity, universality and equal treatment', with due regard for the underpinning policy of the Bankruptcy Liquidation (maximizing assets; Section 75, LRF). The rule calls for a strict application of exceptions to the *pari passu* rule (like netting provisions), whilst it should also favour the estate in disputes concerning assets and executory contracts that are not expressly considered by LRF. Nonetheless, post-2005, although there are several court-supervised Bankruptcy Liquidation proceedings underway, few of which tested executory contracts' rules in practice.

3. Treatment of executory contracts in Judicial Reorganization and Extrajudicial Reorganization

5.80 As opposed to Bankruptcy Liquidation, the regime applicable to executory contracts in both the reorganization proceedings is vague. However, as one may infer, legal disputes involving executory contracts tend to be more often in reorganization proceedings than otherwise.

5.81 The list of legal issues is numerous. For the purposes of this chapter, we are going to focus on some of them, show how LRF and non-bankruptcy laws address the matter in abstract, and how courts tend to consider them in practice. We will make policy-related comments throughout this sub-section as well.

5.82 One fundamental question is whether the law allows the debtor to assume or reject contracts in Judicial Reorganization and Extrajudicial Reorganization. LRF says nothing about rejecting contracts, while Section 49, §2 thereof provides that 'obligations contracted prior to the Judicial Reorganization shall observe the original conditions or the conditions provided for by law (…)'. In other words, the debtor assumes executory contracts in Judicial Reorganization as a matter of law. A few questions derive from that assertion.

First, most agreements contain *ipso facto* clauses. That is a common practice in Brazil, mainly for sophisticated creditors. LRF does not provide for any express rule concerning such clauses in Judicial Reorganization.[27] However, it is evident that one company's ability to reorganize also depends upon its ability to keep strategic contracts, perhaps even more than an Administrator in Bankruptcy Liquidation may wish to keep executory contracts for the benefit of the estate. Therefore, debtors tend to request the Bankruptcy Court for injunctive relief that undermines the application of such clauses, and courts grant relief to debtors in many cases.[28] **5.83**

At least two questions derive from this issue: (i) Does the Bankruptcy Court have jurisdiction to grant such injunctive relief? And (ii) What is the legal basis (i.e. substantive law) for such relief? **5.84**

As to the first point, the extent and scope of the jurisdiction of the Bankruptcy Court in Judicial Reorganization are controversial. While Section 76, LRF provides that, for a Bankruptcy Liquidation procedure, the Bankruptcy Court is 'indivisible and has jurisdiction to hear all actions involving the debtor's assets, interests and affairs' (with a few exceptions), there is no mirror provision for Judicial Reorganization. On the contrary, LRF addresses the matter of the scope of the jurisdiction of the Bankruptcy Court in RJ sporadically (i.e. to confirm a reorganization plan; to hear challenges to the creditors' list; to authorise the disposal of non-current assets). **5.85**

Nonetheless, because LRF calls for the subsidiary application of CPC, one may argue that the Bankruptcy Court would have jurisdiction to grant injunctive relief in connection with the Judicial Reorganization, including for stalling the application of *ipso facto* clauses in executory contracts. Yet, it does not follow immediately that the Bankruptcy Court would have *prima facie* jurisdiction to rule on the merits of a case involving the termination of an executory contract in the context of RJ proceedings. **5.86**

---

27 Supporting the validity of *ipso-facto* clauses: Coelho, Fabio Ulhoa, Comentarios à nova Lei de Falencias e da Recuperaçao de Empresas 2.ed.rev. Sao Paulo: Saraiva, 2005, p. 317; against it: Kirschbaum, Deborah. IPSO Facto Clauses in Business Contracts: A Legal-Economic Analysis. Direito Gv L. Rev., v. 2, p. 37, 2006.

28 TJ-PR – AI: 12923810 PR 1292381–0 , Rapporteur: Luis Seergio Swiech, 17ª Camara Civel, Data de Published: 03/08/2015; TJSP, AI 0121739–23.2012.8.26.0000, Rapporteur Teixeira Leite, 1ª Camara Reservada de Direito Empresarial, Published. 12.3.2013; TJ-SP – AI 5017859120108260000, Rapporteur: Pereira Calças, 29ª Camara de Direito Privado, Published: 24/02/2011.

5.87 Moreover, despite jurisdiction rules not being broadly construed under Brazilian Law, conflicts of jurisdiction between Bankruptcy Courts and other venues have been ruled in favour of the former in quite a few situations, to the extent there is a risk that decisions rendered by other courts undermine the ability of the debtor to recover. Section 47 provides for a 'traditionalist'[29] approach to insolvency procedures, taking into account the interests of employees, creditors and the community, and therefore stimulating the preservation of the firm as a way to comply with its social role. For this reason, several rulings consider – whether in interim or final decisions – that the Bankruptcy Court is 'the most suitable forum' to hear the dispute – i.e. a *forum conveniens* argument – which purportedly is not usual in Brazilian Law.

5.88 As to the legal basis for undermining *ipso facto* clauses, the argument is often construed under general principles and legislative policy concerning the rescue of debtors, with express reference to Section 47, LRF. As a matter of policy, it seems evident that statutory law should address the matter specifically, and perhaps there is some judicial activism trying to adjust the system to what judges see as fair and equitable.

5.89 Another relevant aspect to the regime of executory contracts in RJ concerns how the underlying agreement continues after the Acceptance Order by the Bankruptcy Court. Like in Bankruptcy Liquidation, the contract is typically 'assumed' in its current form and LRF does not undermine the application of a non-bankruptcy legal framework. Hence, it may very well be that the debtor defaults upon the assumed executory contract post-petition, in which case the counterparty should be able to exercise all remedies under the agreement, including termination and, theoretically, enforce the jurisdiction agreement thereunder. Nonetheless, payment obligations under the same agreement existing on the date the debtor filed for RJ (due or not) are pre-petition claims that should be paid within the scope of the reorganization Plan. Furthermore, in theory, a counterparty of the insolvent company under an executory contract could invoke Section 477, BCC during RJ proceedings to refuse performance of its obligations thereunder until advance payment is made or proper guarantees granted.

5.90 In any event, LRF tries to incentivize the maintenance of executory contracts by 'rolling-up' (to a general privilege category; one position ahead of

29 Baird, Douglas G. 'Bankruptcy's uncontested axioms'. *The Yale Law Journal*, v. 108, n. 3, 1998, p. 577:

> The traditionalists believe that bankruptcy law serves an important purpose in rehabilitating firms that, but for bankruptcy protection, would fail. Jobs would be lost and communities damaged, economically and otherwise, if the protections that bankruptcy law provides were unavailable.

unsecured claims) in an occasional Bankruptcy Liquidation every R$1.00 of unsecured claim for each BRL1.00 of additional supply or services under the same conditions (Section 67, §, LRF). Also, post-petition services or supply are post-petition claims in an occasional Bankruptcy Liquidation (Section 84, V).

The market has also developed the concept that 'cooperative creditors' should be granted a more favourable treatment to their pre-petition claims in RJ vis-à-vis their peers in the same class. This is often seen by courts as a good practice, justifiable on policy grounds. **5.91**

Another relevant matter is netting. Contrary to Bankruptcy Liquidation, RJ does not expressly deal with the matter, which is deemed an exception to the *pari passu* rule. Under Brazilian Law, netting (*compensaçao*) is a manner to extinguish reciprocal obligations, which take place when two parties are simultaneously creditor and debtor of one another for obligations of the same kind and nature. Netting operates pursuant to the law, contract or commercial practices. Section 368, BCC governs legal netting and requires in furtherance of the foregoing features that the reciprocal obligations are due and payable (*liquidas, exigiveis e fungiveis*). In such scenarios, the extinguishment of both obligations operates *ipso iure*, irrespectively of the consent of the parties or acknowledgment by a court, which only declares that netting took place. Other than under BCC, a contract or the commercial practice may authorize netting however absent one of the requirements for legal netting. **5.92**

Although LRF does not expressly provide for netting within the scope of RJ proceedings, Brazilian courts have been acknowledging a creditor's right to set-off on the following basis: (i) netting operates *ipso iure* or contractually, irrespectively of any court decision; (ii) Section 122, LRF also applies to RJ and not just to Bankruptcy Liquidation; and (iii) it is unequitable to disallow netting. **5.93**

D. REFORMS

Despite general criticism about the Bill as sent to Brazilian Congress (and open to amendments as part of the legislative process), express provisions concerning the treatment of executory contracts in RJ have been added to the occasional reform package, *inter alia*: prohibition of post-RJ arguments of netting of pre-petition claims (Section 49, §6); providing that claims relating to pre-existing executory contracts whose triggering events occur after RJ are post-petition claims (Section 49, §8); allowing the debtor in RJ to reject **5.94** executory contracts (Section 49, §9); and deeming void *ipso facto* clauses (Section 49, §10).

E. CONCLUDING REMARKS

5.95 The treatment of executory contracts in LRF is somewhat dispersed and, as a matter of policy, should be improved, especially in Judicial Reorganization.

5.96 In Bankruptcy Liquidation, the existing rules seem to address most problems properly. Nonetheless, the development of a regime for executory contracts in Bankruptcy Liquidation, however relevant, loses importance when compared with the legislative vacuum in Judicial Reorganization.

5.97 It is indeed counterintuitive that reorganization proceedings, which purport to protect going-concern value, do not provide for a proper regime for executory contracts. The regime in RJ should ameliorate at least in the following points:

(1) Clearly state scope and extent of the jurisdiction of the Bankruptcy Court to solve disputes concerning executory contracts, including pre and post-petition matters;
(2) Clearly deny the enforceability of *ipso facto* clauses;
(3) Clearly govern the interaction between bankruptcy law and contractual law in a post-petition scenario, especially as regards the enforceability of contractual provisions by insolvent parties against their counterparties;
(4) Expressly govern netting within the RJ scenario;
(5) Allow for the rejection or assumption of agreements by the debtor under RJ.

5.98 Against this backdrop, the inclusion of express provisions in the Bill about executory contracts is positive. There is a growing interest in corporate insolvency matters in Brazil, and recent multi-billion dollar cases have highlighted the importance of the treatment of executory contracts. We expect that the Brazilian Congress acknowledges the relevance of a clear and express legal regime for executory contracts in insolvency settings by passing legislation that addresses such concerns accordingly.

6

NATIONAL REPORT FOR BULGARIA

Georgi Valentinov Georgiev

A. INTRODUCTION

Insolvency proceedings under Bulgarian law are governed by the Commercial Act,[1] enacted in 1991. *The Commercial Act* ('the CA') is of major significance. It regulates all general issues regarding the merchants in general and the company as a type of merchant, including, among others, its incorporation, corporate capacity, management duties, and requirements for validity of the transactions. It also governs the commercial transactions, the reorganization and liquidation procedures, as well as the insolvency proceedings and the newly introduced procedure for stabilization of a merchant. **6.01**

B. AVAILABLE PROCEDURES

There are two types of procedures available to a company in financial or economic distress: the insolvency proceedings and the stabilization procedure. The regulation of the latter entered into force on July 1, 2017. **6.02**

The transformation procedures and the liquidation are not relevant to the scope of this analysis since they achieve different goals and apply to solvent **6.03**

1 The Commercial Act promulgated SG. 48/18 Jun 1991, amended subsequently, last amendment SG. 105/30 December, 2016.

companies which should be either reorganized or liquidated. Pursuant to the CA,[2] upon opening of insolvency proceedings, the liquidation shall be stayed and terminated in case the judgment for opening of insolvency enters into force (i.e., in case the judgment has not been appealed, or when all the appeals have been dealt with by the competent court).

6.04 It is also undisputed in the law[3] that liquidation proceedings aim to satisfy the shareholders and are applicable only in the case of solvent companies. The liquidator is bound by the law to file for an insolvency proceeding if he/she finds out that the company is insolvent. It is further upheld that the satisfaction of the creditors in the liquidation procedure is only a step towards its true purpose, i.e., the distribution of the property and the assets of the liquidated company among the shareholders.[4]

(1) Insolvency proceedings

6.05 The first, and until recently the only, procedure for a company in financial distress is the 'insolvency proceeding'. This procedure is governed by the CA as amended in 1996, and it includes rules, which are substantially similar to those applied in many other European Member States.

6.06 As the legislation has evolved over the years, the regulation on insolvency proceedings in the CA is comprehensive. Recent reforms have significantly improved this procedure, as innovations have been introduced in light of the case law and the practical issues evidenced by practitioners.

6.07 Legal scholars have observed[5] that insolvency proceedings have four steps. The first is the assessment of the application for opening the procedure, in which the financial status of the debtor is analysed. The second stage entails the collection of assets by the insolvency administrator. The third is optional, as it entails the approval and execution of a scheme of arrangement (recovery plan). The last stage (which will not take place in a case of approval of scheme of arrangement) is the liquidation and sale of the valuable assets, and distribution of the proceeds among creditors.

6.08 As evidenced by section 607 of the CA, insolvency proceedings aim to provide equitable satisfaction to the creditors, while giving the opportunity to debtors

2 The Commercial Act 2016, s 272 (1).

3 Georgi Stefanov, *Commercial Insolvency* (Abagar Publishing 2014) 23; Aneta Antonova, *Liquidation of Companies* (Ciela Publishing 2009) 35.

4 Antonova, ibid.

5 Alexander Katzarsky, 'Peculiarities of the Insolvency Proceedings' (2005) 67 *Business Law Magazine* 5, 6.

to draft a rescue plan. The statute also states that in the proceedings the interests of the creditors, the debtor and his employees should be taken into consideration.

The grounds for opening of insolvency proceedings are set out in section 607a of the CA and they are two: a general one, applicable to all type of merchants (companies, sole traders, cooperatives), and a specific one, valid for capital companies only.[6] **6.09**

The general requirement for triggering of the proceedings is cash-flow insolvency (inability to meet the obligations as they fall due), which is further defined by the recently amended section 608.[7] The specific requirement is balance-sheet insolvency, also referred to as over-indebtedness. **6.10**

Three major reforms have dealt with the *cash-flow insolvency requirement*, in 2006, 2013 and 2016. By means of these reforms, the definition has been edited and broadened to enhance the enforceability of the insolvency proceedings and speed up the process of filing for insolvency. Under the CA,[8] a company is cash-flow insolvent whenever it is not able to fulfil one of the following obligations (provided that they are already due): **6.11**

- monetary obligation, due under or in relation to a commercial transaction, including its validity, performance, non-performance, termination, invalidation and dissolution or the consequences of its termination; or
- public debt to the state or the municipalities, which is related to the business activity of the company; or
- private debt to the state.

The law introduced a rebuttable presumption for cash-flow insolvency whenever it is proved that the company (the merchant) has stopped paying its creditors. Furthermore, the standstill of payments is also now presumed in a particular case – when the debtor has paid its obligations to certain creditors entirely or partially[9] there is a standstill – states the law. Until the amendments in December, 2016 the presumption was this – where there is a standstill of payments, there is a cash-flow insolvency. Following the amendments, there is **6.12**

6 Since this study is focused on executory contracts entered into by companies, this chapter focuses only on corporate debtors although the insolvency regime applies to a broad category of merchants and in certain cases even individuals. Capital companies are limited liability companies, joint-stock companies and partnerships limited by shares.

7 The last amendments were enacted in December, 2016 with State Gazette 105.

8 The Commercial Act 2016, s 608 (1).

9 The Commercial Act 2016, s 608 (3).

a new, additional presumption regarding the occurrence of the very condition of the presumption per se – standstill of payments. Therefore, the standstill of payments will be presumed when the merchant has stopped the payments. In particular, such a standstill will be always presumed in case of partial payment of debt to certain creditors or full repayment of specific creditors only.

6.13 Additionally, if the debtor has paid up or is able to pay partially or entirely only some of the creditors, insolvency *could be present*, and cash-flow insolvency presumed.

6.14 This cash-flow insolvency presumption (not for standstill) has been widely commented on by legal scholars and the judiciary. In a recent decision,[10] the Supreme Court held that the date of the commencement of the cash-flow insolvency should be determined on the basis of analysis of the overall economic situation of the debtor in light of specific ratios (coefficients) that measure criteria such as liquidity, indebtedness, and financial autonomy.

6.15 As a consequence, cash-flow insolvency is now assessed not with reference to a single default in the payments towards one creditor or the very fact of a standstill of payments, but only when the objective financial status of the debtor analysed by these ratios shows that the short-term revenues and assets are not sufficient to cover the short-term debts. It is this actual inability to fulfil the obligations which is measured in the cash-flow test.

6.16 The amendments to the CA introduced in 2016 have not affected the first two grounds to determine if a company is cash-flow insolvent.

6.17 With reference to the third one, the new law established that the actual partial or full payment to certain creditors no longer is a ground for cash-flow insolvency, but for the application of a new legal presumption. It states, that a standstill of payments *is always present* (while before the reform it was simply a possibility) whenever the debtor pays totally or partially only some creditors.

6.18 According to some authors,[11] this legal technique leads to the conclusion that in case of default of even *one* monetary obligation (or part of it) which is due, the burden of proof to disprove the presumption of cash-flow insolvency will

---

10 Judgement N° 80/08.10.2015 on commercial case N° 1565/2014, First Commercial Division, Supreme Court of Cassation (SCC); Judgement N° 33/07.09.2010 on commercial case N° 915/2009, Second Commercial Division, SCC; Judgement N° 115/25.06.2010 on commercial case N° 169/2010, Second Commercial Division, SCC.

11 Kostadinka Nedkova, 'New Presumptions for Cash-flow insolvency in the Commercial Insolvency' (2017) 2 *Commercial and Contract Law Magazine* 79.

lie on the debtor. The author concurs with the majority opinion that the reformed text is ill-suited as it mixes up the condition of cash-flow insolvency with the standstill of payments.

Furthermore, the 2016 reform introduced two new presumptions of cash-flow insolvency. **6.19**

Under section 608, subsection 2 it is assumed that the company is in default in relation to monetary obligation as described *sub* 1 where it had not filed its financial reports to the Commercial Registry for the last three years. **6.20**

The non-fulfillment of the obligation for submission of the annual financial reports, governed by The Accountancy Act,[12] is determined as of the date of the filing of the application for opening of insolvency proceedings backwards – for three years. **6.21**

Although this rule introduces severe sanctions for the debtor, this provision has been introduced in line with the recommendations from the judiciary. **6.22**

The main problem for the courts when ruling whether to approve or reject the application for opening of insolvency proceedings is to examine the actual financial status of the debtor. In most of the cases when the financial reports are not submitted to the Registrar for publication in the public Commercial Register, the debtor is able to manipulate his accounting documents and company records before or during the proceedings. This significantly hinders the work of the expert witnesses[13] appointed by the court to assess the financial status of the debtor. In addition, the lack of updated and accurate financial reports also encumbers the work of the insolvency administrator, who may not be able to determine the creditors and the amount of their claims to the extent that the first meeting of the creditors may be postponed or even cancelled. **6.23**

To conclude, to the extent to which each national legislation should regulate the insolvency proceedings in a manner providing adequate terms for their opening and conducting, as well as guarantees for the *bona fidei* participants for their rights, this new presumption for cash-flow insolvency could be considered as an adequate measure for this peculiar problem which renders the entire proceeding slow and less effective. **6.24**

---

12 The Accountancy Act promulgated SG. 95/8 December 2015, amended subsequently, last amendment SG. 97/5 December, 2017.

13 Expert witnesses are appointed in almost every such case, unless the petition appears prima facie groundless.

6.25 Section 608, subsection 4 of the CA introduces the last case in which a company can be presumed cash-flow insolvent. Cash-flow insolvency is presumed whenever the creditor who applies to open the insolvency proceeding had not been able to collect his claim entirely or partially by means of an enforcement procedure. This procedure should have lasted for at least six months from the date on which the debtor received the invitation or notification for voluntary payment.

6.26 The presumption applies if the following conditions are met:[14]

- existing enforcement procedures initiated by the creditor who filed the application for opening the insolvency proceedings, or a creditor who was adjoined by the court upon the creditor's request. If the applicant for opening of the insolvency proceedings is the debtor, this criterion is not met and the presumption is inapplicable;
- the legal entitlement upon which the enforcement procedure has been triggered shall not be subject to appeal;
- the expiration of a six-month term during which the creditor's claim had not been collected;
- the creditor's claim shall meet the requirement prescribed by section 608, subsection 1 of the CA.

6.27 The enforcement procedure should be commenced on the ground of 'an act of the creditor which is final (enforceable)'. The wording of the text is inaccurate and misleading: evidently, the enforcement procedure could not commence on an act, issued by the creditor. The Civil Procedure Code and the Tax – Insurance Procedure Code[15] govern the grounds for commencement of enforcement procedures. The notion of 'enforceable/final act' includes judgments, arbitral awards, enforcement warrants, and acts for tax revision.

6.28 It seems that this rule contradicts the presumption for standstill of payments in case of default to only one creditor, as analysed by the Supreme Court and according to which the mere default to one creditor is a valid ground to apply the presumption for cash-flow insolvency. The aforementioned conclusions of the case law are relevant also to the amended text of the CA and this begs the question what is the reason for this new approach? Why the default to one single creditor does not constitute cash-flow insolvency but the default in enforcement proceedings for six months could serve this purpose?

---

14 Nedkova, *supra* note 11.

15 The Civil Procedure Code and the Tax – Insurance Procedure Code promulgated SG. 105/29 December 2005, amended subsequently, last amendment SG. 103/28 December, 2017.

It could be upheld that the new provision of subsection 4 of section 608 of the CA governs receivables which had already been examined by the court and the judgement or the other respective act has *res judicata.* 6.29

In addition, when an enforcement procedure is unsuccessful for more than six months this could be an indication of inability for payment since the debtor is already obliged to pay – on the ground of the respective enforcement document (e.g., arbitral award, court judgment, enforcement warrant). 6.30

Notwithstanding on which of the presumptions the inability for payments is found, it should be always examined by the court whether the debtor's difficulties are temporary or his assets are sufficient to meet its debts without threating the interests of his creditors.[16] 6.31

The second, alternative ground to open an insolvency proceeding is specific, since it is applicable only to capital companies. *Balance-sheet insolvency* (or over-indebtedness) is assessed by means of a rather technical criterion that compares the assets and the debts of the debtor. Under section 742 of the CA, a company shall be deemed in over-indebtedness if its assets are insufficient to meet its financial obligations. There are no further criteria in the statutes, unlike those set out in section 19, subsection 2 of the German *Insolvenzordnung*, for example. The case law and legal literature contributed to clarify these provisions, and considered that the balance-sheet insolvency ratio could not be determined only with reference to short-term assets and liabilities. 6.32

Eligible applicants for opening of insolvency proceedings

The court cannot open the proceedings upon its own initiative. The eligible applicants for opening of insolvency proceedings are the debtor itself (the management body and the executive director), the creditors with the type of claims listed in section 608, subsection 1 (including the National Revenue Agency for the state receivables listed in this provision) who have to present evidence of the cash-flow insolvency, the partner with unlimited liability and the liquidator of the company. Under section 742 in case of balance-sheet insolvency the application for opening of insolvency proceedings could be submitted by any member of the management body. No further approval by the general meetings of the company is required.[17] 6.33

---

16 The Commercial Act 2016, s 631. It is held in the literature that this section regulates one general hypothesis for rejection of the insolvency application and it is the availability of sufficient assets for payment of the debts and the temporary character of the difficulties is a particular example of this general rule –Stefanov, *supra* note 3, 23.

17 In its recent judgment for interpretation of the law N° 5 dated December 22, 2014 the General Meeting of the Criminal Division of the Supreme Court of Cassation held that there is no need for a resolution of the

6.34 The application should be submitted within 30 days of the discovery of the insolvency or the standstill of payments. In case of default, the obliged individuals will be jointly liable vis-à-vis the creditors of the company for the damages caused by the late application or the omission to apply at all. In addition, section 227b of the Criminal Code prescribes criminal sanctions for the merchant and members of the management body who do not apply for insolvency timely. If the financial reports of the company are not published, the creditors' obligation to provide evidence to their application is waived – this is a result from the implementation of the new presumption for cash-flow insolvency, analysed above – as a result of the omission to publish the financial reports in the Company register.

6.35 It is common practice for the insolvency proceedings to be initiated by the creditors, not the debtor and such creditors are mainly banks, financial institutions and in recent cases the companies' suppliers. In the last six months two major superstore chains have gone into insolvency leaving creditors with uncollected receivables of more than EUR 50 mln.[18]

(2) The stabilization procedure

6.36 In December, 2016 a new procedure for companies in financial distress was introduced: the stabilization procedure. The law asserts that the stabilization procedure complies with the European Union Council Recommendation as of July 14 2015.[19] The new law has been enacted to address the fact that in Bulgaria, the insolvency framework:

> has been ineffective, increasing uncertainty among market participants and reducing the country's overall attractiveness to investors. Insolvencies last longer than in neighbouring countries, and the recovery rate (especially for unsecured creditors) is low. The need for an efficient framework to handle insolvencies is a topical subject due to the high indebtedness of non-financial corporations in Bulgaria, as an efficient system could facilitate the deleveraging process.[20]

---

management body of the company to authorize the submission of application for opening of insolvency proceedings since there is no such requirement in the law at all. The individuals listed in the Criminal Code will be liable for the omission notwithstanding whether there is any such resolution by the competent corporate management body under the articles of association or such resolutions was not passed.

18 The entities operating two of the major retail supermarkets chains in Bulgaria Carrefour and Picadily went into insolvency proceedings. Judgment N° 829 dated April 10, 2017, Sofia Court of Appeal, commercial case 1196 – for Picadily (which is subject to appeal) and Judgment N° 9 dated January 23, 2017, Sofia District Court, Case N° 171.

19 Council Recommendation (EC) of 14 July 2015 on the 2015 National Reform Programme of Bulgaria and delivering a Council opinion on the 2015 Convergence Programme of Bulgaria (2015/C 272/08).

20 Council Recommendation (EC) of 14 July 2015 on the 2015 National Reform Programme of Bulgaria and delivering a Council opinion on the 2015 Convergence Programme of Bulgaria (2015/C 272/08).

To address these issues, the Council recommended a comprehensive reform of the insolvency framework based on international best practice and expertise, in particular 'to improve mechanisms for pre-insolvency and out-of-court restructuring'. **6.37**

To answer this call for reforms, a new section was added into the CA. This section regulates the entire procedure of 'stabilization'. This is a court-supervised procedure where the judiciary is given considerable discretion to authorize its commencement, investigate the facts, impose interim measures, appoint trustees, and approve the stabilization plan. **6.38**

The stabilization procedure seeks to avoid the opening of insolvency proceedings by promoting an agreement between the merchant and creditors on how debts will be repaid in a situation where the business continues to operate on the market.[21] The procedure can be triggered whenever the company is in an immediate danger of cash-flow insolvency.[22] There is no reference to any balance-sheet insolvency requirement. The statute specifies that 'immediate danger' consists of any situation in which the merchant finds itself unable to pay existing obligations under section 608, subsection 1 or may stop payments within six months from filing. **6.39**

Negative requirements restrict the number of eligible applicants for the stabilization procedure. In particular, the procedure cannot be opened if there is a pending application to open an insolvency proceeding against the merchant or the company has omitted to submit its annual financial reports for the last three years.[23] Additionally, some companies such as state and municipal entities, financial institutions and insurance corporations are explicitly excluded from the list of potential applicants. **6.40**

Stabilization proceedings are designed to protect creditors' rights and interests. All of the company's creditors are entitled to take part in the procedure, including these creditors to whom the debtor provided securities for obligations of third parties.[24] The stabilization procedure should grant equal rights to all creditors belonging to the same class, i.e., with similar claims against the debtor. Non-monetary claims are converted into monetary ones on the basis of their market value as of the date of the submission of the application for stabilization. **6.41**

21 The Commercial Act 2016, s 761.
22 Ibid., s 762.
23 Ibid., s 762(3).
24 Ibid., s 766.

6.42 Merchants are only authorized to apply for the opening of a stabilization procedure. It is within the discretion of the representative of the company, e.g., the managing director, whether to apply and there is no explicit rule in the CA which restricts the power of the representative to submit the application. Namely, there is no need for a resolution of the general meeting of the company's shareholders.

6.43 The stabilization procedure is designed to satisfy all creditors while giving a last opportunity to the debtor to continue trading. The desired outcomes of the procedure are a debt restructuring and subsequent payment of all creditors, structural changes in the structure of the company and the improvement of its financial condition to the extent that cash-flow insolvency is no longer an imminent danger.

6.44 Upon filing, debtors are prevented from repaying the financial obligations that were due before the commencement of the procedure. The powers of its board of directors could be restricted, and a trustee could be appointed. Other important consequences are the prohibition to commence enforcement proceedings and the standstill of all pending procedures against the debtor.

6.45 If the stabilization plan is approved by the creditors (who vote in separate classes), it should be sent to the court for final approval. Once finally approved by the court, the plan is binding on the applicant and all of its creditors, with the sole exception of those who were not included in the list of creditors or who were not otherwise provided with the opportunity to vote for the adoption of the plan.[25]

6.46 The stabilization plan could include the sale of the entire enterprise of the company or separate parts of it.

6.47 Since the stabilization procedure has only been available since July 2017, case law on this matter is rather scarce.

(3) Out-of-court proceedings

6.48 Under the Bulgarian law, there are no other procedures for out-of-court settlement. However, under section 9 of the Obligations and Contracts Act

25 In this sense is the conclusion of Nely Madanska, *The New Amendments in the Commercial Act* (Trud I Pravo publishing 2017) 91. The author substantiates that all these are two groups of creditors who will not be affected at all by the stabilization plan, except the standstill of the enforcement procedures which could be initiated by them.

parties are free to determine the content of the contract 'insofar as it does not contravene the mandatory provisions of both the law and good morals'. Consequently, the debtor and the creditor/s can enter into any voluntary agreement to restructure the debtor's debt.

Under section 742 of the CA, in every stage of the insolvency proceedings the debtor could enter into a written agreement with all of its creditors with accepted receivables for arrangement of his pecuniary obligations. Creditors with accepted receivables are those who applied to be certified as creditors by the insolvency administrator and were included in the final list of creditors, which is subject to appeal before the court. Once a creditor is listed in the final list and approved by the court, he has all rights to vote and challenge the debts to other creditors, etc. This agreement should be further assessed by the court and upon its approval, the court will terminate the insolvency proceedings, subject to availability of pending cases for challenging of accepted receivables. Evidently, this is a voluntary settlement, which could take place only following the opening of the insolvency proceedings and the approval of the claims of the creditors by the court. It is not beyond the discretion of the court to investigate whether the terms of the agreement are in accordance with the applicable law so this option could not be classified as an out-of-court settlement. **6.49**

There are no statistics on the use of the aforementioned opportunities for voluntary settlement of the dispute between the creditors and the debtor. Anecdotal evidence suggests that they are rarely used. More frequently, the creditor who applied for opening of insolvency proceedings will settle his/her claim with the debtor before the court authorizes the opening of the procedure. **6.50**

The Bulgarian law does not regulate situations in which only one party has not fully performed its obligation as a special condition for settlement in the vicinity of insolvency. The general rules of the Obligations and Contracts Act will apply and the party will have a claim for specific performance against the party in default or the right to dissolve the contract. **6.51**

C. TREATMENT OF EXECUTORY CONTRACTS

(1) Insolvency proceedings

The right of the insolvency administrator to terminate executory contracts

6.52 The regulation of the treatment of executory contracts in the insolvency proceedings have not been amended since its enactment in 1994.[26] The provision dealing with executory contracts is only one and it is situated in the division named 'completion of the insolvency estate'. Among other measures for collection of the insolvency estate, such as collection of unpaid capital, set–offs and voidable preferences, there is an explicit provision the content of which remained unaltered since its adoption – section 644 'Termination of contract'. The systematic interpretation of the norm and its placement in this chapter of the CA leads to the conclusion that the right to terminate the contract is provided as a measure for preservation of the insolvency estate and its constitution or more precisely – its fulfillment. Under section 644 the insolvency administrator (referred in the CA as 'syndic'[27]) may terminate every contract entered into by the debtor, if it had not been executed in full or partially. In order to terminate the contract, the administrator should file a 15-day notice of termination.

6.53 Upon request by the counterparty, the insolvency administrator should respond within 15 days as to whether he will preserve the contract or terminate it. Where there is no response by the administrator, it is presumed that the contract is terminated – a silent termination is applicable in this case by virtue of the explicit provision of section 644, subsection 3 of the CA. This approach has been adopted by the legislator in order to ease the process of termination of contractual obligations in cases where the insolvency administrator failed to respond. This solution has been widely welcomed by the business community, as it takes into consideration the reality of contemporary business activity.

6.54 The general rule of the contract law is restated in section 664 – that in case of cessation of the contract the non-defaulted party has a right to indemnification for the loss suffered.

6.55 The CA furthermore stipulates that the preservation of the agreement, upon which the debtor should provide periodical payments, does not oblige the

---

26 State Gazette (Bulgaria) 63.

27 The term is specific under Bulgarian law due to the multiple functions of the syndic, but is similar to the German *Insolvenzverwalter* or *Konkusverswalter*, the Italian *curator* or the *Insolvency Representative* under the UNCITRAL Legislative guide on Insolvency Law.

insolvency administrator to pay the overdue amounts, which were due prior the date of the judgment for opening of insolvency proceedings.

Is the insolvency administrator obligated to terminate any and all contracts or are there any provisions which exclude some agreements from the scope of his powers? It is beyond dispute that the insolvency administrator has the right to terminate each and every contract but he is not bound to do so[28] – it is within his own discretion to decide, applying the principle of due care, whether the performance of the contract by both parties will be of benefit to the insolvency estate or it will endanger it in some way. Moreover, the insolvency administrator is authorized to terminate any contract by operation of the law when this appears necessary to preserve the insolvency estate, to collect and convert the assets into money and distribute them among the creditors. **6.56**

Above all, it could be stated that the executory contracts are deemed to be assumed. The opening of the insolvency proceedings does not lead *ipso facto* to termination, dissolvement or invalidation of the executory contracts. The consequences from the opening of the insolvency proceedings may vary – from restriction of the rights of the debtor to enter into new agreements, to prohibition on receiving consideration from counterparties, standstill of enforcement and court proceedings vis-à-vis the debtor etc. However, the CA does not provide for rejection of the executory contracts. Only section 644 deals with the right of the insolvency administrator to terminate them. **6.57**

The consequences for the parties are that any and all receivables, which arise out of executory contracts *following the opening* of the insolvency proceedings[29] have to be paid on the due date. **6.58**

On the contrary, all receivables of the debtor which were due *prior to the* opening of the insolvency proceedings will have to be claimed by the creditors in the stage of the proceedings for claiming and approval of the receivables. Hence the 'new' receivables, which will be those derived on the ground of the executory contracts, are excluded from the general prohibition for payment of old receivables, i.e., such as originated before the opening of the insolvency proceedings. Any act conducted in violation with the insolvency regime, is void (e.g., payment of 'old' debt to creditor, incorporation of security over an **6.59**

28 Nely Madanska, *The Syndic in the Insolvency Proceedings under the Commercial Act* (Ciela Publishing 2016) 280. The author skillfully disproves the thesis that the syndic is able to terminate only the contracts in relation to which the debtor is in default and is not authorized at all to do so with agreements with periodical payments due by the debtor. The latter statement is upheld by Georgi Horozov, 'About the right of the Syndic to Terminate an Executory Contract to which the Debtor is Party' (1996) 2 *Contemporary Law* 59.

29 This event being understood as the date of the judgment for opening of the proceedings.

element of the insolvency estate or transaction with such element which were not committed in accordance with the specific insolvency legislation).

6.60 There is no provision in the CA which renders relevant the default or non-default of the insolvent company as a criterion to be applied by the insolvency administrator when deciding whether to terminate the contract.

6.61 The intriguing issue here is the interaction between the principle *pacta sunt servanda* and the special regime established by the insolvency legislation. Furthermore, it is the conflict between the contract law principles for termination of contracts, in particular the restriction of the ability of the party in default to influence the contractual obligation and the insolvency law protection of the insolvent estate which grounded the explicit delegation of power of termination, notwithstanding the presence or lack of default by the insolvent party to the contract.

6.62 This problem was recently analysed by the Supreme Court of Cassation and was resolved with a judgment, which is mandatory for the courts and should be considered when assessing termination of executory contracts onwards. For these reasons, this judgment is worth a deeper analysis.

6.63 In case N° 3447/2015, the First Commercial Division, Supreme Court of Cassation (SCC) on which was awarded Judgment N° 212/19.01.2017 was asked to decide on the following ground: 'Is the insolvency administrator entitled under section 644 of the CA to terminate with notification an executory contract if the insolvent debtor is in default?'.

6.64 The Supreme Court emphasized the extraordinary nature of this explicitly provided authority of the insolvency administrator along with the general power to terminate, dissolve and render void the contracts entered into by the insolvent debtor. It was rightfully upheld that these particular measures for fulfillment of the insolvency estate are provided due to the unilateral change of the legal status of the insolvent company as a party to the agreement, and the necessity for the insolvency estate to cope with lack of liquidity. On the ground of the lack of any further requirements in the statute such as default of the counterparty or non-default of the insolvent company, the SCC perceived that the executory contracts could be terminated notwithstanding whether the insolvent company is in default or not. It was also argued that the explicit provision stipulating that the counterparty has a right to indemnification is additional reason to accept that there are no limits to the termination.

Since the insolvency administrator is allowed to terminate executory contracts, their partial termination should also be lawful. An example of partial termination is the termination of only specific terms of the contract, i.e., derogations or reduction of specific obligations of the debtor, of compensation for damages or other covenants, regarded as unfavourable by the insolvency administrator. **6.65**

It is noteworthy, that unlike the stabilization procedure, the termination of a contract by the insolvency administrator is *not* subject to court approval. It is entirely within the power of the syndic to terminate without any need of preliminary or *post factum* approval by the court, the creditors committee, etc. Of course, in a case of breach of the duty of care,[30] the insolvency administrator will be liable for the damages caused to the insolvent company and the creditors; he could be also sanctioned by the court by civil penalties, fines and could be dismissed. However, this will not affect the prior termination of the contract by the insolvency administrator. There are no special rules for the different kind of contracts such as lease agreements, sale, hire-purchase, labour, etc., neither is it relevant who is the counterparty. The rule is broad and covers all types of executory contracts without dividing them on the basis of their nature, the status of the parties, as clarified in the aforementioned judgment of the Supreme Court of Cassation.[31] **6.66**

The right of the creditor to set-off

It is my understanding that the set-offs conducted following the opening of insolvency proceedings do not fall within the scope of the regime of executory contracts. The main argument in favour of this conclusion is the fact that under section 645 of the CA the creditors could set-off their debts to the insolvent company only in a case where they (the receivables and the debts) were mutual, of the same kind and the creditor's claim was mature before the date of the judgment for opening of insolvency proceedings. In other cases, if the creditor's receivables became due during the insolvency proceedings or as a result of the declaring of the insolvency, or the latter caused the conversion of the two debts into such of one kind, the creditor is entitled to set-off only on the maturity date or on the date on which the conversion took place. **6.67**

Therefore, the set-off does not affect executory contracts in any way since the requirements for set-off should be present either (a) before the opening of insolvency (which does not amend the validity of content of the executory **6.68**

30 Judgement N° 212/19.01.2017 on commercial case N° 3447/2015, First Commercial Division, Supreme Court of Cassation (SCC).

31 In this regard is also Ruling N° 38/25.01.2017 on commercial case N° 1216/2016 First Commercial Division, Supreme Court of Cassation (SCC).

contract) or (b) even if this is not the case, the respective condition should be realized following the opening of insolvency proceedings or the judgment for declaring the insolvency, but again on the merits of this act and only if the requirements are met in result of the respective judgment. Hence, there is no special regime governed in the regulation of set-offs in insolvency to executory contracts but only to set-off which will be conducted during the proceedings.

(2) The stabilization procedure

6.69 As analysed in section B(2) above, the stabilization procedure is designated to avoid insolvency, and it is triggered by the court in the vicinity of insolvency upon application by the debtor. Considering the fact that the legislation on stabilization has only come into force recently, there are no case law or practical issues to be discussed on the basis of its application.

The right of the insolvent company to terminate executory contracts

6.70 As a consequence of the opening of the stabilization procedure, the court is entitled to appoint a trustee who has the right to supervise the business activity of the company. In addition, the court may restrict the discretion of the company to enter all or certain types of transactions without the consent of the trustee or in case of risk for the interests of the creditors to restrict or deprive the company from the right to manage and dispose of its assets, delegating these rights to the trustee. However, the appointment of the trustee is only an option for the court and the debtor will continue its activity under its own control unless the court rules otherwise.

6.71 As in insolvency proceedings, the opening of the stabilization procedure does not lead *ipso facto* to termination, dissolvement or invalidation of the executory contracts.

6.72 The termination procedure is similar to that in insolvency proceedings. Under section 777 of the CA upon the request of *either of the parties* the court could allow the termination of every bilateral contract to which the company is a party if it is not executed entirely or partially at the moment of the opening of the stabilization procedure. The relevant date for assessment which contract is executory is that of the court judgment for opening the proceedings.

6.73 Likewise, a right for compensation is provided for the counterparty for the damages incurred. The executory contracts are deemed to be assumed in a greater extent than in insolvency, since their termination is subject to a more complicated procedure, analysed below.

In the stabilization procedure the default of either of the parties to the executory contract is not relevant. **6.74**

There are certain distinctions between the termination of executory contracts in insolvency and in stabilization proceedings. **6.75**

First, the right for termination belongs to both parties, not only to the company in stabilization. This is a major characteristic – the legislative approach provides for equality of the parties to the agreement and takes into consideration the fact that the counterparty might be willing to dissolve the contractual relation. It is reasonable to apply such an approach since the specific nature of insolvency proceedings – to protect the creditors of the insolvency is not relevant in case of stabilization – the company is in distress but not yet insolvent and this could not justify the inequality in terms of right of termination, as it is in the insolvency proceedings. **6.76**

Secondly, the termination is a two-stage procedure supervised by the court – following the application for termination submitted by either of the parties the court has the jurisdiction to rule on it, deciding whether to terminate the executory contract or not. While doing so, the court acts with limited discretion. Section 777, subsection 2 of the CA reads as follows: the court terminates the contract only if it finds that: **6.77**

(i) the execution of the contract will hinder the fulfilment of the obligations under the stabilization plan, and
(ii) the non-execution of the contract will not cause to the counterparty more damage than ordinary in such cases.

It is subject to an assessment ad hoc by the court for each and every case whether these requirements are met. **6.78**

Relevant restrictions on fulfillment of executory contracts following the commencement of the stabilization procedure

The statute explicitly reads[32] that following the opening of the stabilization proceedings the company cannot pay its 'old' obligations (which originated and became due prior the stabilization) except those for public debts such as VAT, taxes, social insurance for employees, etc. It was pointed out above that the court has the authority to appoint a trustee and order the payments by the company in the stabilization procedure to be conducted only upon his approval. **6.79**

32 The Commercial Act 2016, s 776 (1).

6.80 Since the parties to the executory contract are allowed to terminate the contracts, their partial termination should be also lawful, subject to court approval. In my opinion, the reasoning of the SCC examined above[33] should be applied *mutis mutandis* by the court in cases initiated on application for termination of executory contracts during the stabilization procedure.

6.81 Similarly, in the regulation of the stabilization procedure there are no specific rules to the various executory contracts, nor are there explicit rules on the contractual remedies agreed by the parties prior to the stabilization procedure.

Statutory treatment of contractual remedies agreed in solvent times

6.82 In the Commercial Act, where the insolvency and stabilization procedures are regulated entirely, there are no express rules on the validity of standard and commonly used clauses such as *ipso facto* clauses, priority adjustment clauses, penalty provisions, etc.

6.83 As a general principle it could be defined that the mandatory provision on the ranking of creditors is non-negotiable and the debtor and creditor cannot rearrange the priority of the creditors, as set out in section 722 of the CA. Every provision in a contract to the contrary is null and void. However, in case of agreement between creditors with different priorities the one with higher priority in the distribution of funds (e.g,. special privilege) to transfer some portion of the received funds to the creditor with lower priority will be valid between the parties and void in relation to the debtor and every third party. The insolvency administrator will not be bound by this provision but its breach by the parties to the agreement will represent default and remedies will be due. To conclude, the rearrangement of the ranking of the creditors in insolvency proceedings is unenforceable and void, but once the distribution of funds has taken place the creditors could comply with their agreements and alter their priorities between themselves, thus exercising their priority. Penalty provisions remain unaltered by the opening of the insolvency proceedings unless they are rendered void upon claim under the special rules for contracts which detriment the creditors. In stabilization procedures the penalty provisions will also not be changed unless the stabilization plan provides explicitly for such an alteration.

6.84 *Ipso facto* clauses which trigger a certain effect upon the opening of insolvency proceedings or stabilization, are not treated as void per se. The appraisal of their validity will have to be made on an ad hoc basis of the contractual

---

33 State Gazette (Bulgaria) 63.

autonomy declared as a fundamental principle of the Bulgarian private law in section 9 of the Obligations and Contracts Act and within the restriction designated therein – 'insofar as it does not contravene the mandatory provisions of both the law and good morals'.

For example, the stipulation providing for acceleration of all payments upon the opening of insolvency or stabilization proceedings, which is standard in credit agreements, will be valid and binding since it is in accordance with the applicable law. **6.85**

The clause for immediate termination of the contract upon the occurrence of the aforementioned events should be also lawful, since this is a condition of the contract set out in advance, before the proximity of insolvency, and the parties have the authority to design their contractual relation in such a manner.[34] The options for termination of executory contracts analysed in parts (1) and (2) of this section do not restrict the parties to terminate agreements but only provide a 'shortcut' for the debtor to be able to do so due to the financial distress or actual insolvency. However, the clause for direct termination of the contract in case of insolvency or stabilization could not be deemed contradictory to the *post factum* termination (following the opening of insolvency or stabilization procedure) which is provided by operation of law. **6.86**

On the contrary, if the contract stipulates that neither party will be entitled to termination in case of insolvency or stabilization proceedings, the respective clauses will be null and void by reason of contradiction with the Commercial Act. **6.87**

Close-out netting clause

The netting clause is a clause in a financial collateral agreement or in the case of the absence of such clause, a specific provision in the legislation.[35] Bulgarian law does not contain a general netting clause, therefore if such is not agreed by the parties, it will not be relevant at all. **6.88**

The legislation is more generous on this issue – there is an explicit rule in the Financial Collaterals Agreements Act[36] which reads that in case of default the **6.89**

34 Obligations and Contracts Act 1993, s 25. The effect or the termination of a contract may be made dependent on a future uncertain event. In those cases where the party interested in its non-fulfillment has acted in bad faith in order to prevent its occurrence, the condition shall be deemed fulfilled.

35 Financial Collaterals Agreements Act 2006, s 10(2).

36 Ibid., s 13 (2).

netting clause (if agreed in the respective contract) will be applied despite the commencement of procedures such as insolvency and stabilization.

D. REFORMS

6.90 There has been no reform in the regulation of executory contracts in insolvency proceedings since 2000. As discussed above, the legislation on this issue is exiguous and has not been amended.

6.91 As regards the treatment of executory contracts in the stabilization procedure, prior to July 2017 (when the new procedure was introduced) there was no regulation on this matter at all.

E. CONCLUDING REMARKS

6.92 As a general observation it could be held that the main factor for reforms in insolvency proceedings, including the creation of new procedures for protection of companies in financial distress, is the need for compliance with the recommendations of authorities such as the European Council and the World Bank.

6.93 Furthermore, groundbreaking reforms such as the one in 2013 dealt with voidable preferences and other measures for the protection and restoration of the insolvency estate, while the case law did not provide evidence for a need for improvement of the regulation of executory contracts. The legislator dealt mainly with issues which were brought to his attention by the credit institutions such as banks and leasing companies, which suffered the consequences of the world financial crisis and its implications in Bulgarian insolvency practice. In the last 15 years the creditors were the main policy makers which initiated the debate and legislative measures to overcome the loopholes in the insolvency regulations and the parliament took into consideration their justified concerns. In doing so, the parliament developed more sophisticated criteria for opening of insolvency proceedings although acting by the principle 'attempt – error' and provided significantly more accurate and adequate rights for the interested parties to initiate voidable preferences and other claims for retrieving insolvency estate.

7

NATIONAL REPORT FOR CHILE

Camila Hoyuela Zattera, Maximiliano Escobar Saavedra and Mauricio Inostroza Sáez

A. INTRODUCTION

7.01 This chapter has been developed in the context of an international research project, with regard to the comparison of the treatment of executory contracts under insolvency law in different countries and jurisdictions. The chapter undertakes the treatment of such contracts under Chilean insolvency legislation, which has been recently amended by the introduction of laws number 20.004,[1] 20.073,[2] 20.080[3] and 20.720.[4] This major reform is a result of the

1 Law N° 20.004, entered into force on March 8th 2005, Official Gacet 39.007. This law modified law number 18.175 by extending the faculties of the Bankruptcy Superintendence ('*Superintendencia de Quiebras*') regarding its duty to supervise and inspect private bankruptcy trustees.

2 Law number 20.073, entered into force on November 29th 2005, Official Gacet 38.324. It introduced changes with regards to the agreements between the debtor and its creditors settled before bankruptcy proceedings. It widens the scope of application of the former law, by establishing that it also applies to the arrangements regulated in the title XII; and it introduces the figure of the '*experto facilitador*', who aims to facilitate these arrangements.

3 Law N° 20.080, entered into force on November 14th 2005, Official Gacet 38.320. It incorporated the insolvency legislation to the Chilean Commercial Code, in its Book IV, entitled 'Of the bankruptcy'.

4 Law N° 20.720 entered into force on January 9th 2014, Oficial Gacet 40.752. It substituted the bankruptcy procedures established in the Book IV of the Commercial Code by the reorganization and liquidation proceedings of companies and people. It also improves the role of the Superintendence, changing its name from '*Superintendencia de Quiebras*' to '*Superintendencia de Insolvencia y Reemprendimiento.*'

execution of the programme '*pro-growth agenda*' designed in response to the decreasing levels experienced by the Chilean economy. The objectives that this reform aims to achieve are to timely and efficiently encourage the effective reorganization of viable companies, to ease a fast and organized liquidation of those companies that do not hold any possibilities of subsisting and to solve personal insolvencies of those people that find themselves in a situation where they are incapable of fulfilling their obligations.[5] Moreover, the major purpose of the new legislation is to provide the people and company with efficient and nimble insolvency proceedings which will allow the usage of resources in other activities, increasing economic productivity.[6]

7.02 As a result of the aforementioned major reform, the primary legislation undertaking Chilean insolvency is law number 20.720, which regulates not only corporate but also personal insolvency. However, this research will be focused on the former.

7.03 With regards to Chilean contract law, our legal system follows a dual regulation approach, which depends on the nature of the contract. In fact, commercial contracts are regulated by the Commercial Code, whereas the Civil Code applies to civil contracts, noting that commercial acts are those listed as such in article 3 of the Chilean Commercial Code.[7] Nevertheless, some contracts are regulated by special laws,[8] while others do not have any legal regulation, which is left to the will of the parties and/or case law.[9]

7.04 An executory contract, although not defined by Chilean law, can be understood as one on which at the commencement of an insolvency proceeding, performance remains due on the part of both the debtor and the other party to the contract.[10] Moreover, this description does not include those contracts that have not yet been agreed, although the obligation to subscribe them already exists, such as preparatory contracts.[11] Furthermore, those contracts

5 Reporte División de Política Comercial e Industrial, Ministerio de Economía, Fomento y Turismo de Chile, 'Insolvencia y quiebra en Chile: principales estadísticas desde 1982 a la fecha', (2015) 3.

6 Ibid.

7 *See* Chile: Commercial Code 2009, art 3.

8 For example, the deposit contract is regulated by Law N° 18.690, and Law N° 18.101 regulates rental agreements over urban properties.

9 For example, although law number 20.720 refers to them with regards to liquidation and reorganization proceedings, leasing contracts are not regulated by law in a general way. Also, the factoring operation is also a contract which lacks from any legal regulation.

10 Thomas Jackson, *The Logic and Limits of Bankruptcy law* (Bear Books, 1986) 105.

11 Ricardo Sandoval, *Reorganización y Liquidación de Empresas y Personas* (Editorial Jurídica de Chile, 2014), 210.

where one of the parties has performed his obligation, and the other party is left with a debt, are also excluded from the abovementioned definition.[12]

B. FRAMEWORK OF AVAILABLE INSOLVENCY PROCEEDINGS

Our current legal framework regarding insolvency proceedings, is represented by law number 20.720, and offers two procedures for companies in financial distress: reorganization and liquidation.[13] **7.05**

The greatest difference between reorganization and liquidation is that the former suits viable and salvable companies, whereas the latter aims to liquidate those companies that do not hold any practical possibility of surviving. In fact, the final effect of reorganization is for credits to be remitted, novated or reagreed allowing the debtor more time to fulfil his obligations.[14] **7.06**

One of the objectives of this major reform was that insolvent companies and people would make use of both reorganization and liquidation proceedings, which did not occur under the former legislation. After more than a year of law number 20.720 being enforced, official statistics show that the major reform achieved one of its objectives. In fact, in January 2017, only three companies filed reorganization proceedings and 60 were liquidated, whereas in December 2017, 53 companies were reorganized and 10,009 liquidated.[15] **7.07**

(1) Commencement of liquidation and reorganization proceedings

Both liquidation and reorganization proceedings are triggered by the insolvency of the company. Such cause has not been legally defined, but it has been understood by the doctrine as a complex patrimonial state characterized by an imbalance between assets and liabilities in such a way that its holder is objectively incapable to fulfil his obligations.[16] A company that finds itself in such a situation can file for reorganization proceedings, but it will be required to provide documents that will provide evidence of this complex patrimonial state.[17] Regarding liquidation proceedings, article 115 gives the debtor the **7.08**

12 Ibid.

13 Law N° 20.720 also avails people in financial distress with liquidation and renegotiation proceedings.

14 *See* article 93 Law N° 20.720.

15 http://www.superir.gob.cl/informacion-y-estadisticas/informacion-y-estadisticas-ley-n-20–720/, last visited 20 November 2017.

16 Juan Esteban Puga Vial, *Del Procedimiento Concursal de Liquidación* (4 edn, Editorial Jurídica de Chile 2014) 78.

17 Law N° 20.720, arts 54 and 56.

possibility to begin his own liquidation proceedings, assuming the obligation to provide the documents mentioned in the same article, which according to the doctrine, serve to enlighten his insolvency. Moreover, article 117, establishes facts that are considered to enlighten the insolvency of the company which can be invoked by any creditor to file such proceedings. As an example of these facts, the following can be mentioned: the creditor can file liquidation proceedings if the debtor company ceases in the payment of an obligation contained in an executory instrument.[18]

7.09 Pursuant to the causes mentioned above, reorganization proceedings can only be filed by the debtor,[19] whereas the liquidation can be filed either by any creditor[20] or the debtor himself.[21] If liquidation proceedings are claimed by a creditor, the debtor can oppose them, and he can only invoke the list of defences available for executory proceedings listed in article 464 of the Civil Procedural Code.[22] The solvency of the company is not legally recognized as a defence available to the debtor, however, practice and case law have lately introduced this possibility, considering that the sole cause of liquidation proceedings is the insolvency of the debtor.[23] Once the opposition has been deduced, the judge may decide to accept it or deny it. If he accepts it, the creditor may appeal this decision, and it will be resolved by the Court of Appeal.[24] If the judge denies the opposition, he must immediately declare the liquidation of the company. The debtor may appeal this decision and it will be resolved by the Court of Appeal, however this does not suspend the proceedings before the circuit judge. This mechanism has been highly criticized by our doctrine and legal practitioners, because if the Court of Appeal takes too long to resolve the appeal, in practice we may arrive at the absurd situation where after a couple of months the Court of Appeal decided to accept the opposition, but by then the company has been already liquidated.

7.10 A debtor may judicially propose a reorganization agreement due to his insolvency, but he can also propose it at the initial hearing as an alternative to stop liquidation proceedings filed by his creditors.[25] Since this agreement has a contractual nature, it may be inefficient, because it may be declared null or defaulted. In fact, article 98 law 20.720 allows the court to declare the default of the reorganization agreement if any affected creditor claims a damage

18 *See* Law N° 20.720, art 117.
19 Juan Esteban Puga Vial, *supra* note 16, 194.
20 See Law N° 20.720, art 116.
21 See Law N° 20.720, art 115.
22 *See* Civil Procedural Code, art 464.
23 Corte de Apelaciones de Concepción, Rol 896/2016.
24 *See* Law N° 20.720, art 129.
25 *See* Law N° 20.720, art 120 (c).

occasioned by a specific breach on the part of the debtor given that one party has not performed its obligations. The court must also proceed to pronounce the liquidation of the debtor, once the default has been declared.[26] Nevertheless, when the cause of the claim is the breach of the stipulations with regard to one of the categories of the agreement, then the debtor can set aside this claim by performing such stipulations within 60 days from the notification of the claim.[27]

The processes of reorganization and liquidation are both administered by insolvency professionals, the former by a *veedor* and the latter by the liquidator. There are legal requirements to become and remain registered as a *veedor* or liquidator, which can be found in law number 20.720 in its articles 9 and 30 respectively. **7.11**

(2) Judicial and out-court proceedings

It can be said that both reorganization and liquidation are judicial proceedings since they are followed before the civil judge appointed to the circuit of the debtor. Moreover, pursuant to article 295 of law number 20.720, the incidents and the exercise of other rights that can be exercised after the constitution of the first creditor's gathering may be followed before an arbitrator. **7.12**

Nevertheless, law number 20.720 in its article 102 regulates a simplified or extrajudicial reorganization agreement between the debtor and his creditors. It is celebrated without judicial intervention, and it requires the agreement of two or more creditors who represent at least three-quarter parts of the debtors' debt.[28] Once agreed, this settlement requires judicial approval.[29] The validity and effectiveness of these agreements is subject to the general rules of contract law settled in the Chilean Civil Code. **7.13**

Moreover, companies in financial distress are free to conduct direct negotiations with their creditors before the beginning of a reorganization or liquidation proceeding. These out-court-proceedings are not specifically recognized by insolvency legislation, however they are available to the parties by virtue of general private law rules.[30] Nevertheless, parties to those agreements **7.14**

26 *See* Law N° 20.720, arts 98 and 100. Mauricio Inostroza Saez, 'Chilean law's new debtor reorganization system' (2016) 33(1) *Arizona Journal of International & Comparative Law* 287, 300.

27 *See* Law N° 20.720, art 98. Nelson Contador Rosales and Cristián Palacios Vergara, *Procedimientos Concursales* (1 edn, Legal Publishing Chile 2015) 130.

28 *See* Law N° 20.720, art 109.

29 Nelson Contador Rosales and Cristián Palacios Vergara, *supra* note 27, 135.

30 *See* Chilean Civil Code art 1545 which sets the principle of autonomy of the will of the parties.

must be careful because if certain requirements are met, these contracts may be revoked once the reorganization or liquidation proceedings begin. In fact, pursuant to article 287 cost free contracts celebrated by the debtor during the year before the commencement of the insolvency proceedings can be revoked, unless the debtor or the other party is able to prove that such a contract did not prejudice the right of the creditors.[31] Also, pursuant to article 288, contracts celebrated by the debtor during two years prior to the beginning of the reorganization or liquidation proceedings can be revoked if: (a) the party that contracted with the company in financial distress was aware of his insolvency; and (b) the contract prejudices the right of the creditors or alters the position of equality they must have during the proceedings.[32]

7.15 Notwithstanding the latter, companies in financial distress cannot conduct direct negotiations with their creditors once the reorganization proceedings have begun, by virtue of the financial protection period established in article 57 according to which no creditors can obtain a benefit in the prejudice of the rights of the others.[33] Nevertheless, articles 72 and 74 specifically regulate particular negotiations with regard to supply contracts and foreign trade operations respectively, being in any case forbidden to execute the assets of the debtor by virtue of *par conditio creditorum* principle. Direct negotiations cannot take place as soon as the liquidation proceedings begin either, in accordance with the detachment principle pursuant to which the debtor loses the administration of his goods, which remains in the hands of the liquidator.[34]

(3) Effects arising from reorganization and liquidation proceedings

7.16 Once the petition for reorganization has been declared admissible by the tribunal, the debtor enjoys of a period of financial protection, which may last 30, 60 or 90 days from the notification of the judicial resolution.[35] The main effects following from this protection period are the following: (1) all claims and actions against the debtor are suspended, with the exception of claims filed by his workers;[36] (2) all contracts subscribed by the debtor will maintain their validity and payment conditions. As a result, executory contracts cannot be unilaterally terminated, nor can the creditor demand anticipated fulfilment,

---

31 *See* Law N° 20.720, art 287.

32 *See* Law N° 20.720, art 288.

33 Nelson Contador Rosales and Cristián Palacios Vergara, *supra* note 27, 66.

34 Ricardo Sandoval López, *Reorganización y Liquidación de Empresas y Personas: Derecho Concursal* (7 edn, Editorial Jurídica de Chile 2014) 178.

35 *See* Law N° 20.720, art 57. Also, for a definition of financial protection period see N° 31 Law N° 20.720, art 2.

36 *See* Law N° 20.720, art 135. The exception comprehends only declarative claims, executory claims are in any case suspended, even when filed by the debtor's workers.

nor can he execute the contracted guarantees by cause of the reorganization agreement. If he does so, his credit will be postponed to be paid after all other creditors.[37] This effect is a manifestation of the principle *pacta sunt servanda*, pursuant to which, what has been agreed is mandatory. (3) Also, during this period the debtor loses the faculty of disposal over his property, therefore he cannot alienate, mortgage or encumber his assets with the exception of those whose disposal or sale is strictly necessary to normally develop the debtors' business.[38] (4) Moreover, once the petition for reorganization has been declared admissible by the tribunal, the right of the creditors is irrevocably fixed.[39] Thus, only those creditors whose rights are prior to the declaration of the tribunal will be considering for calculating the majorities.

With regard to liquidation proceedings, the main effects that follow from the resolution of the tribunal that has declared the liquidation of the company are the following: (1) the debtor loses the faculty of disposal over his property, therefore he cannot alienate, mortgage or encumber his assets. Thus, outside the liquidation proceedings, the property of the debtor is not available.[40] (2) Also, pursuant to article 135 of law 20.720, the right of the creditors to individually execute their credits on the assets of the debtor is suspended. Creditors can execute their credits on the debtor, but not individually; they must do it within the liquidation proceedings by verifying their credits.[41] (3) Also, according to article 136, another effect followed from the liquidation of a company is the early enforceability of the credits against the debtor. The procedural objective behind this effect is to allow all creditors, including those whose credit is not yet enforceable, to attend the liquidation procedure on equal conditions.[42] The substantive founding of this rule can be found in the Chilean Civil Code, which in its article 1496 N° 1 establishes as a cause of expiry of the deadlines, the notorious insolvency of the debtor.[43] (4) Moreover, pursuant to article 134 of law 20.720, once the liquidation has been judicially declared, the right of the creditors is irrevocably fixed. Therefore, only those creditors whose rights are prior to the declaration of the tribunal will be considered for calculating the majorities, and they will not change their qualities, i.e., a preferred credit will not lose its preference. **7.17**

37 *See* ibid., art 57(1)(c).
38 *See* ibid., art 130.
39 *See* ibid., art 134.
40 Juan Esteban Puga Vial, *supra* note 16, 404.
41 Ibid., 409.
42 Ricardo Sandoval, *supra* note 11, 38.
43 Juan Esteban Puga Vial, *supra* note 16, 402.

7.18 Most, if not all of these effects, are a clear manifestation of the *par condition creditorum* principle, which transversally inspires Chilean insolvency law, even before the major reform that recently took place.[44]

C. TREATMENT OF EXECUTORY CONTRACTS UNDER CHILEAN INSOLVENCY LAW

7.19 Before the major reform, law number 18.175 only contemplated rules relating to certain executory contracts, but it did not establish a general regime.[45] By interpreting this silence, both doctrine and case law established as a general principle that the declaration of bankruptcy is not a cause for the termination of executory contracts.[46] The current legislation, in its Chapter IV regarding liquidation proceedings, does not include a general rule in this matter. However, a recognition of this principle can be found in the provisions regulating reorganization proceedings.

(1) Reorganization proceedings

7.20 In reorganization proceedings, the principle is the maintenance and continuity of executory contracts.[47] In fact, pursuant to article 57 N° 1 letter c) of Law number 20.720, once the reorganization petition has been declared admissible, all contracts subscribed by the debtor will maintain their validity and payment conditions. Therefore, executory contracts cannot be unilaterally terminated, nor can the creditor demand its anticipated fulfilment, nor can he execute the contracted guarantees by the sole cause of the reorganization agreement. Such contracts may be unilaterally terminated by the creditor for other reasons, for example, if the debtor fails to perform his obligations.[48] If nonetheless, the creditor unilaterally terminates the contract for the sole cause of the reorganization agreement, his credit will be postponed to be paid after all other creditors.

7.21 Such a general principle is reinforced by particular rules that promote the continuity of supply contracts (article 72) and the financing of foreign trade operations (article 74).

---

44 Ricardo Sandoval, *supra* note 11, 39.

45 Ricardo Sandoval, ibid., 211; Ricardo Sandoval López, *Derecho Comercial Tomo IV* (6 edn, Editorial Jurídica de Chile 2007) 103.

46 Ricardo Sandoval, ibid., 212.

47 *See* Law 20.720, art 57(1). Also *see* Law 20.720, art 71 regarding supply contracts and art 73 regarding foreign trade agreements. Nelson Contador Rosales and Cristián Palacios Vergara, *supra* note 27, 95.

48 Juan Esteban Puga Vial, *supra* note 19, 235.

The reasoning behind the abovementioned rules is to allow viable companies effectively to reorganize their assets and stay in the market. In fact, it is of utmost importance to enable companies in financial distress to keep their supplies since it is possible for a very viable company to fail for lack of supply.[49] 7.22

By application of general contract law, it is a general rule that termination and acceleration clauses are enforceable. However, in the context of reorganization proceedings this does not apply. In fact, a clause that establishes that the contract will terminate if one of the parties becomes subject to reorganization proceedings, pursuant to article 57 is not enforceable.[50] 7.23

(2) Liquidation proceedings

Regarding liquidation proceedings, before the major reform, Chilean insolvency law did not establish a general rule applicable to executory contracts. Nevertheless, it contemplated special rules with regards to specific contracts.[51] As a result of this omission, both doctrine[52] and case law established as a general principle that the sole declaration of bankruptcy does not enable the immediate termination of executory contracts.[53] Law number 20.720, currently in force, in its Chapter IV regarding liquidation proceedings, does not include a general rule on this matter either, but the principle has been maintained. As a result, the sole declaration of liquidation does not enable the immediate termination of executory contracts.[54] 7.24

Nevertheless, and although not immediately, we can imply that the rules governing liquidation proceedings aim for the termination or anticipate the execution of executory contracts. In fact, the final purpose of these proceedings is to liquidate a company in financial distress that is no longer viable. This is the reason why law number 20.720 establishes the early enforceability and the irrevocable fixation of the credits, because it aims for the creditors to concur to the proceedings and obtain payment upon the liquidation of the assets of the unviable company. Also, pursuant to article 1489 of the Chilean Civil Code, it is perfectly possible for the compliant party to claim the resolution of a bilateral contract when the other party did not fulfil his 7.25

49 Report of the Economy Comission, Bill of the Law Number 20.720, pp. 226 and 396.

50 Juan Esteban Puga Vial, *supra* note 19, 235.

51 Ricar Ricardo Sandoval, *supra* note 11, 212.

52 Adolfo Parry, Efectos de la quiebra en las obligaciones y contratos, 212; Alvaro Puelma Accorsi, Curso de Derecho de Quiebras, (4 edn) 90, Ricardo Sandoval, ibid., 469.

53 Ricardo Sandoval, ibid., 212.

54 Ibid., 212.

obligations. This general principle receives application in insolvency law,[55] except when the unperformed contract is a purchase agreement of movable property and the sold assets are already in hands of the debtor.[56] In this respect, it must be understood that the movable property must be in physical possession of the debtor.[57] Thus, if the seller does not receive the payment, while the sold merchandise is in transit, he can file for the resolution of the contract and regain possession over the movable property.

7.26 In other words, liquidation itself does not automatically enable termination of executory contracts, but our current legal framework provides mechanisms that eventually lead to their termination or resolution of contracts and enforceability of credits.

7.27 Notwithstanding the latter, the beginning of liquidation proceedings produces other effects over executory contracts, apart from the termination. To determine such effects, Professor Ricardo Sandoval, proposes the following classification:

(1) Regarding those contracts where the debtor company is the creditor in the contract, the liquidator, acting on behalf of the creditors, is obliged to demand the performance of the contract. Such performance will naturally benefit the creditors in the liquidation proceeding.
(2) With regard to those contracts where the debtor company has assumed reciprocal obligations with the other party, a distinction shall be made: if the contract represents a benefit for the creditors, the liquidator may demand the performance of the contract if the debtor company is willing to fulfil his obligations, whereas if the contract does not represent a benefit for the creditor, the liquidator will generally abstain from demanding its performance.
(3) Finally, regarding those contracts where the debtor company is also the debtor in the contractual relationship, the other party is able to exercise several rights such as the right to demand the performance of the obligation, to request the resolution of the contract if the debtor fails to fulfil his obligations, and the right to be indemnified.[58]

Moreover, it is worth mentioning that the recognition of these rights on behalf of the counterparty implies following the general rule established in article 1489 of the Chilean Civil Code, pursuant to which the

55 Ibid., 282.
56 *See* Law N° 20.720, art 154.
57 Ricardo Sandoval, *supra* note 11, 283.
58 Ibid., 214, 215, 216 and 217.

compliant party of an unperformed bilateral contract, is able to claim the performance of the contract or its resolution in both cases with compensation.[59]

As already mentioned, although Law number 20.720 did not provide a general rule with regards to the treatment of executory contracts in the context of liquidation proceedings, it contains special rules with regards to leasing contracts. In fact, pursuant to article 225 the liquidation does not immediately enable termination of the leasing contract. The creditors must jointly adopt one of the following measures: (1) pursue the performance of the contract, according to the stipulated terms; (2) pursue the early exercise of the option of sale, in the terms originally stipulated; or (3) demand the early termination of the contract, restoring the asset that was the object of the contract. If the creditors do not choose any of these options, the legislator understands that they opt for the performance of the contract. Finally, the last part of article 225 establishes that any clause that contravenes the content of this article will not produce any effect. Before law number 20.720 came into force, there were no special rules with regard to the leasing contract, which was treated as a rental agreement.[60] It was understood that the bankruptcy trustee was substituted in the rights and obligations of the debtor, therefore in case of bankruptcy it was entirely left to the decision of the trustee to request the termination of the leasing contract. **7.28**

(3) Contractual agreements negotiated by parties in solvent times and executory contracts

Neither the former nor the current legislation include an express reference to contractual agreements negotiated by the parties in solvent times. An example of such agreements would be one that in the event of reorganization or liquidation of one of the parties, the other party would be entitled to unilaterally terminate the executory contract. In our system, to determine their validity, we must make the distinction between whether the agreement arises in the context of liquidation or reorganization proceedings. Regarding liquidation proceedings, the general rule is that such agreements are valid by application of general contract law, because in law number 20.720 there is no special rule which states the opposite. In fact, those stipulations are resolutive conditions, recognized by the Chilean Civil Code, whose statutory effect is to immediately terminate the contract without the need of judicial intervention.[61] **7.29**

59 *See* Chilean Civil Code, art 1489.
60 *See* Corte de Apelaciones de Concepción (2013) Rol 1428–2012.
61 Ricardo Sandoval, *supra* note 11, 213.

Nevertheless, as mentioned above, article 225 contains special rules regarding leasing contracts, pursuant to which liquidation does not immediately enable termination of the leasing contract and gives the creditors three options. Moreover, article 225 also establishes that any clause stipulated in the leasing contract that contravenes the content of the same article, will be considered as if it had not been written.[62] As a result, a clause which enables the immediate termination of the leasing contract once one of the parties is subject to liquidation proceedings, will be contrary to the content of article 225, and thus will be considered as if it had not been written. Before the major reform, it was very common to find clauses in leasing contracts which stipulated that the bankruptcy of any of the parties, allowed the other party to terminate the contract. Thus, the lessee was entitled to require the restitution of the asset and verify the payment of the payable instalments. Such a practice, which was legally allowed, diminished the debtors' patrimony. With regard to this subject, when law number 20.720 was being discussed, it was mentioned that giving the creditors the option to purchase the asset would produce the opposite effect, which was what law number 20.720 was aiming for.[63]

7.30 On the other hand, regarding reorganization of insolvent companies the situation is different. In fact, agreements which establish that the sole cause of reorganization of one of the parties automatically enables termination of the contract are invalid.[64] In fact, pursuant to articles 52 and 57 of Law number 20.720, all the contracts subscribed by the debtor will remain valid and maintain their payment conditions. Such rules are prohibitive, and their breach is sanctioned with nullity of the agreement or clause that contravenes it.[65] Nevertheless, it can be established that these executory contracts do terminate for reasons other than the reorganization of one of the parties, and those agreements are totally valid pursuant to general contract law.

D. REFORMS AND CONCLUDING REMARKS

7.31 Chilean insolvency law deals differently with the effects of executory contracts, depending on whether it is a reorganization or liquidation proceeding. Such differentiation relates to the objective that both these proceedings aim for, that is, reorganization aims to reorganize viable and salvable companies, whereas liquidation aims to liquidate those companies that do not hold any possibilities

62 See Law N° 20.720, art 225.

63 See the Report of the Economy Comission stated in the bill of the Law Number 20.720, 545, 828, 2159.

64 Juan Esteban Puga Vial, *supra* note 19, 235.

65 Nelson Contador Rosales and Cristián Palacios Vergara, *supra* note 27, 66.

of subsisting. In fact, for reorganization proceedings, our current legal framework establishes as an unavoidable effect the financial protection period, pursuant to which executory contracts cannot be unilaterally terminated by the sole cause of the reorganization. On the other hand, with regards to liquidation proceedings, law number 20.720 contemplates mechanisms that allow parties to terminate their executory contracts, such as the early enforceability of the credits and the irrevocable fixation of the creditor's rights. We understand that throughout these mechanisms our legal framework encourages the creditors to attend the liquidation proceedings to exercise their rights. Therefore, although in liquidation there is not a general rule with regards to executory contracts one could assume that the legislator chose for their termination.

Notwithstanding the latter, what is not clear is the quality that the creditor's rights must have in order to be exercised in insolvency proceedings. In fact, it is uncertain if these rights against the debtor must be declared or not. As a result, it is legitimate in our system to ask if the mere pretension of a right, such as a penalty clause, is enough to attend the insolvency proceedings, regardless of its judicial declaration. **7.32**

8

NATIONAL REPORT FOR CHINA

Yingxiang Long and Rebecca Parry

A. INTRODUCTION

8.01 China's legal framework has evolved rapidly in recent years to keep pace with economic development, support international commitments, and respond to the expectations of international bodies.[1]

8.02 In this context of regulatory reform, the legislature enacted the groundbreaking Enterprise Bankruptcy Law of the People's Republic of China 2006 (EBL 2006), a relatively brief statute which covers the main aspects of insolvency law, including the treatment of executory contracts. As in other jurisdictions, difficulties of executing an executory contract[2] may arise when events and changes occur, such as one or more of the contracting parties becoming trapped in financial or economic distress.[3] In such circumstance, the rigid application of the principle of *pacta sunt servanda* may lead to injustice

1 Rebecca Parry and Haizheng Zhang, 'China's New Corporate Rescue Laws: Perspectives and Principles' (2008) 8 *JCLS* 113.

2 As a starting point we take the definition of an executory contract as: '[A] contract which the obligation of both the bankrupt and the other party to the contract is so far clearly unperformed that failure of either to complete performance would constitute a material breach excusing the performance of the other': Vern Countryman, 'Executory Contracts in Bankruptcy: Part I.,' (1973) 57 *Minn.L.Rev.* 439, 460. The EBL 2006, Article 18 uses a term which may be translated as 'underperformed' contracts, which we take as functionally equivalent to the concept of executory contracts and which we discuss in further detail below.

3 On these concepts see further Douglas G. Baird, 'Bankruptcy's Uncontested Axioms' (1998) 108 *Yale L. J.* 573.

and unfairness. Consequently, it is reasonable to offer an opportunity for the parties to reconsider their intentions regarding the executory contract based on the events and changes which have occurred and to decide whether or not to continue.

This chapter sets out the Chinese approach to such contracts, initially providing an overview of the current laws, in contract law and insolvency law, before considering in more detail how the law has evolved, noting how China is moving from a position of state-control to greater private management of insolvency proceedings. This chapter suggests that the laws and legal institutions are still in need of greater development. **8.03**

(1) Rights under contract law where performance threatened by insolvency

One safeguard for the parties who are performing an executory contract lies in the Contract Law 1999, which enables the party required to perform first to 'suspend its performance if it has conclusive evidence showing'[4] that the other party's business has seriously deteriorated. **8.04**

There are two possible results after a timely notice has been made by the suspending party: **8.05**

(1) the other party may provide appropriate assurance for its performance, typically a guarantee, upon which the suspending party is expected to resume performance; otherwise
(2) the suspending party may terminate the contract. This termination can be made 'if the other party fails to regain its ability to perform and fails to provide appropriate assurance within a reasonable time'.[5]

Therefore, when financial or economic distress happens, current Chinese legislation provides an alternative for the innocent party to protect himself against the distressed party, which is known as the 'unsafe right defence' in accordance with civil law tradition. **8.06**

4 Contract Law of the People's Republic of China 1999 (中华人民共和国合同法 1999), art. 68.
5 Ibid., art. 69.

(2) Executory contracts in insolvency

8.07 Executory contracts present particular challenges in insolvency proceedings, in particular where the debtor's business activities are ongoing. In such circumstances, the principle of *paritas creditorum* (equality of creditors) prevails over conflicting individual rights.

8.08 The debtor's financial problems may be exacerbated by the performing parties in an executory contract. These creditors are only some of many unsatisfied claimants. However, because they can rely on the 'unsafe right defence' provided in terms of Article 68 and 69 of the Contract Law, they are in a comparatively better position than other unsecured creditors.

8.09 For example, take the following case: two parties (A and B) entered an executory contract and, after some time, A files for insolvency. By reason of the 'unsafe right defence' provided by the Contract Law, if the Contract Law applied, B might suspend the performance and ask for a guarantee from A over its estate property. According to Article 109 of the EBL 2006, if that fixed security was granted, B would be entitled to be paid in priority from the proceeds generated by the sale of the estate property. Therefore, other creditors would lose the opportunity to be repaid from that share of the sale proceeds. A party to an executory contract whose services are particularly valuable for the distressed debtor might use these provisions to gain leverage in any negotiation following the commencement of an insolvency procedure.

8.10 The conditions for opening insolvency proceedings are set out in Article 2 of the EBL 2006. As a general rule, the procedure can be commenced whenever 'a legal entity fails to settle its debts that are due, and if its assets are not enough to pay off all the debts or if it is obviously incapable of clearing off its debts'. A company in this position may enter liquidation or reorganization procedures under the supervision of an administrator appointed by the court.[6]

8.11 Executory contracts are expressly addressed under Article 18 of the EBL 2006, although this time in a manner favourable to the administrator. The latter is given the power to decide whether or not to terminate an executory contract. In contrast, there is no equivalent power for the other contracting party, who

---

6 EBL 2006, art. 22 '[t]he administrator shall be designated by the people's court'. Regarding the appointment process see further the 'Regulations of the Supreme People's Court on the Appointment of Administrators for Hearings on Cases of Enterprise Bankruptcy', translated by T Wang, 'Regulations of the Supreme People's Court on the Appointment of Administrators for Hearings in Cases of Enterprise Bankruptcy' (2009) 42 *Chinese Law and Government* 85 and discussed in R Parry, 'Administrator: Appointment and Remuneration' in R Parry, Y Xu and H Zhang (eds), *China's New Enterprise Bankruptcy Law* (Ashgate, 2009), Chapter 6.

is instead given a right to demand a guarantee in a case where the administrator decides to continue the contract. This Article further stipulates that '[w]here the administrator does not provide any guarantee, it shall be deemed that the contract is rescinded'. Therefore, in insolvency the key is balancing the legal right of the innocent/performing party against those of other existing creditors.

Once the insolvency petition is granted by the court, it is therefore primarily **8.12**
up to the administrator to decide whether or not to continue executory contracts. However, it is noticeable that the EBL 2006 does not offer significant protection for debtors during the period when they are applying for the opening of proceedings but before the court has determined whether to grant the petition. Furthermore, even after the insolvency procedure has commenced, the law does not exclude the possibility for the innocent party to claim the 'unsafe right defence' up until the time when the administrator communicates his decision as to whether or not to continue the contract.

In the event that the administrator decides to continue the contract, both **8.13**
contract law rules and the EBL 2006 entitle the innocent party to obtain a guarantee for the debtor's performance. This so regardless of whether the choice to perform the contract had been taken by either the administrator or the innocent party. However, there is a difference as to the period of time allowed for the administrator to make a decision.[7]

Under the EBL 2006, the administrator must communicate his decision **8.14**
within two months from the commencement of the procedure or, if the other party asks for an earlier decision, within 30 days of that request. In contrast, under the Contract Law the matter is determined by the terms of the contract or, if the contract is silent, it is likely that a reasonable time – such as 30 days – would be permitted. Therefore the other contracting party can either wait for the administrator's decision (in this case, the contract and its performance are suspended) or they can request an earlier decision. In the meanwhile, the performing party retains the right to exercise the unsafe right defence under the Contract Law. In this latter case, the administrator must respond within a reasonable time.

In the People's Republic of China ('PRC'), it is notable that there have been **8.15**
few formal insolvency proceedings since the introduction of the EBL 2006 and therefore there is little evidence of the use of the executory contract

7 Xiaowei Lan, 'Executory Contracts in Insolvency Law' (Wuhan University 2010) 1, 40–41 <http://cdmd.cnki.com.cn/Article/CDMD-10486–2010166739.htm> accessed 17 August 2017.

provisions in this context. A detailed discussion of executory contracts under the EBL 2006 is at 8.37 et seq below.

B. LEGAL FRAMEWORK

(1) Obstacles and new movements

8.16 Despite the existence of modern laws enabling the commencement of formal insolvency proceedings, the claimants may find that commencing such a proceeding is more problematic than they had expected.

8.17 China is a vast country with differing levels of economic development. Some of its coastal cities have embraced the principles and values of market economy; therefore they were ready to accept the introduction of a new bankruptcy framework. Nevertheless, the legislature was aware that the process of implementation of the bankruptcy law would have likely been long and incremental. What is surprising to observe is that even major cities have been placing limitations on the use of insolvency remedies. However, there are also signs that things are changing.

8.18 In 2002, the third civil court of Xuzhou[8] Municipal Intermediate People's Court reported that the Municipal Court had temporarily declined all applications for insolvency made by creditors, or made without approval from the local authorities.[9] This is not an isolated case, but rather can be seen as typical, even following the implementation of EBL 2006 and the *Notice of the Supreme People's Court on the Relevant Issues of Accepting Bankruptcy Cases* (《最高人民法院关于破产案件立案受理有关问题的通知》) (the 'July Notice', that was issued on July 28, 2016), which clarified many points in relation to the law and its procedures.

8.19 For example, on November 21, 2016, Guangzhou[10] Municipal Intermediate People's Court issued a document on their website stating the procedure for implementing insolvency cases. Article 3 of the document[11] noted that: (1) the

8 Xuzhou is a major city in the east of the PRC, known as a transportation hub.

9 Yingmao Tang, 'Why Do Judgment Enforcement Organizations Resolve Bankruptcy Disputes in China?' (2008) 45 *Journal of Peking University (Humanities and Social Sciences)* 12, 17.

10 It is said that Guangzhou is one of the top four cities in mainland China. It is in the south, close to Hong Kong and Macau and is important as a port and transportation hub.

11 Guangzhou Municipal Intermediate Court, 'Implementing Regulations on Insolvency Cases at Guangzhou Municipal Intermediate Court' (2016) <http://www.gzcourt.gov.cn/ck321/ck326/2016/11/21174620844.html> accessed 29 April 2017.

Basic People's Court should obtain approval from the Municipal Intermediate People's Court prior to accepting any reorganization case, compromise case or liquidation case involving a debt of over 50 million RMB, or requiring settlements for over 50 employees; and (2) the Municipal Intermediate People's Court should obtain approval from Guangdong Higher Court prior to accepting an insolvency case for reorganization, compromise, or liquidation over 100 million RMB or a required settlement for over 100 employees. It was also stated that insolvent financial enterprises (e.g., commercial banks, security companies, insurance companies and listed companies) should proceed through the court hierarchy progressively until the approval of the Supreme People's Court has been obtained.

One of the top Chinese law firms also explained from their own practical experience that the July Notice may not be implemented rigidly at the same level across the whole of mainland China.[12] Generally speaking, while further improvements have been achieved since 2016, the opening of an insolvency procedure is still a complex and lengthy procedure. **8.20**

On December 18, 2015, Chinese President Xi Jinping delivered an important speech at the fifth plenary session of the 18th CPC Central Commission for Discipline Inspection ('CCDI') in Beijing. He proposed an innovative solution to some Chinese economic issues, known as 'supply-side structural reform'.[13] There are five tasks for such reform: cutting excessive industrial capacity; destocking; de-leveraging; lowering corporate costs; and improving weak links. **8.21**

The insolvency framework is considered an important tool to cut off excessive industrial capacity, and improve the efficiency of the economy.[14] Therefore, the Supreme People's Court issued a series of documents to facilitate the submission of insolvency petitions to courts. **8.22**

12 Minny Siu and others, 'The Filing Registration System for Chinese Court Accepting Bankruptcy Filing – Latest Trends and Revelations for Automatic Early Termination in Off-the-Shelf Financial Derivatives Transactions' (*King & Wood Mallesons*, 2016) <http://www.kwm.com/zh/hk/knowledge/insights/the-prc-court-registration-system-for-bankruptcy-petitions-latest-developments-20161118> accessed 8 August 2017.

13 Huanxin Zhao, 'Xi Leads Shift from Keynesianism to 'Supply-Side' Economics' *China Daily* (Beijing, 31 December 2015) <http://www.chinadaily.com.cn/bizchina/2015–12/31/content_22877575.htm> accessed 9 August 2017.

14 Hailin Zou, 'The Application of Supply-side Structural Reform and Bankruptcy Reorganization System' (2017) *Journal of Law Application* 57, 57.

8.23 One of the structural limitations is that insolvency cases have no specific court, and are therefore generally heard by civil or economic courts.[15] Therefore, insolvency cases are not considered as a core field of activity for judges. Moreover, insolvency cases generally fail to benefit the careers of judges, as they tend to be lengthier than other cases, and require a considerable amount of time to integrate and mediate opinions from government, employees, creditors, and debtors, among others.[16] To address these issues, on June 21, 2016, the Supreme People's Court delivered a Notice called *On the Establishment of a Liquidation and Insolvency Court in the Intermediate People's Court* (《关于在中级人民法院设立清算与破产审判庭的工作方案》) (the 'June Notice'). According to the June Notice, the municipalities directly under the Central Government shall at least ensure that one of their Intermediate People's Courts shall set up a liquidation and bankruptcy court, whereas the Intermediate People's Courts situated within provincial capital cities and sub-provincial cities shall set up a liquidation and bankruptcy court. Up to February 24, 2017, there were 73 courts (four higher courts, 47 intermediate courts and 22 basic courts) nation-wide that have newly established their specific liquidation and bankruptcy division courts.

8.24 These changes seem to have produced some preliminary results. In 2016, a total of 5,665 corporate insolvency cases were opened in PRC, an increase of 53.8 per cent over 2015; a significant proportion of these petitions (i.e., 1,041) were reorganization cases. This represented an increase in the number of reorganization cases of 85.2 per cent over 2015, albeit admittedly from a low starting point. A total of 3,602 insolvency procedures were completed, up 60.6 per cent from 2015, of which 525 were reorganizations, up 43.4 per cent from 2015.[17] Therefore, considerable progress in the number of insolvency cases has been achieved in recent years, although the total number of bankruptcies remains comparatively low.

8.25 To sum up, *pacta sunt servanda* is the normal principle for contracting parties to perform their obligations under an executory contract. However, in situations of financial or economic distress, the Chinese law tends to protect the performing/innocent party. Nonetheless, if the financial distress is bad enough to lead to the formal insolvency of the company, the principle of *paritas*

15 Yingmao Tang, 'Why Do Judgment Enforcement Organizations Resolve Bankruptcy Disputes in China?' (2008) 45 *Journal of Peking University (Humanities and Social Sciences)* 12, 17.

16 Ibid.; Xiahong Chen, 'From Centre to Edge: The Issue of Staff Placement During the Evolution Chinese Insolvency Law' (2016) 4 *Journal of Gansu Political Science and Law Institute* 92.

17 Shuzhen Luo, 'The Supreme People 's Court Informs the Bankruptcy Trial' *People's Court Daily* (Beijing, 25 February 2017) <http://rmfyb.chinacourt.org/paper/html/2017–02/25/content_122162.htm?div=-1> accessed 10 August 2017.

creditorum prevails. Although there are potential obstacles for claimants who wish to commence formal insolvency proceedings in China under the EBL 2006, the obstacles may become fewer and fewer due to the needs of eliminating excessive industrial capacity and reallocation of the industrial resources.

To fully understand the current movement of legal insolvency practice, it is essential to explain the economic movement and the interaction between economic movement and development of insolvency law in the PRC. **8.26**

(2) The development of insolvency law

A number of scholars[18] believe that economic change in China has resulted in the need for an insolvency law. However, an insolvency law may serve also as the cornerstone,[19] or lead the direction, of Chinese economic reform.[20] After 1956, the PRC was a Stalinist centrally planned economy, with all corporations being state-owned.[21] In the context of centrally planned economy, the risk of failure rests with central government, rather than individual corporations and their creditors. Therefore, there was no need for insolvency in such an economy.[22] **8.27**

In 1978, China implemented a new policy, known as the 'Reform and Opening-up Policy', which transferred its economic structure from a Stalinist central planned economy to a socialist market economy,[23] which included efforts to attract foreign investors.[24] The demand for an insolvency law became more urgent following the implementation of the Reform and Opening-up Policy. In 1984, a draft group of insolvency laws was established **8.28**

---

18 Henry R. Zheng, 'Bankruptcy Law of the People's Republic of China: Principle, Procedure & Practice' (1986) 19 *VJTL* 683; Steven L. Toronto, 'Bankruptcy of Foreign Enterprises in the PRC: An Interpretation of the Rules Concerning Bankruptcy of Foreign Related Companies in the Shenzhen Special Economic Zone Note' (1990) 4 *J. Chinese L.* 277.

19 Mark E. Monfort, 'Reform of the State-Owned Enterprise and the Bankruptcy Law in the People's Republic of China' (1997) 22 *Okla. City U. L. Rev.* 1067.

20 Shirley S. Cho, 'Continuing Economic Reform in the People's Republic of China: Bankruptcy Legislation Leads the Way Note' (1995) 19 *Hastings Int'l & Comp. L. Rev.* 739.

21 In G. William Skinner and Hsieh Winston (eds), *Modern Chinese Society: An Analytical Bibliography Publications in Chinese 1644 1969 Volume 2* (Stanford Univ Press 1973).

22 Evan D. Flaschen and Timothy B. DeSieno, 'The Development of Insolvency Law as Part of the Transition from a Centrally Planned to a Market Economy' (1992) 26 *Int'l L.* 667.

23 Gordon White, Jude A. Howell and Xiaoyuan Shang, *In Search of Civil Society: Market Reform and Social Change in Contemporary China* (Clarendon Press 1996).

24 Taiming Chen, 'The Validity of China's Reform and Opening-up Policy in Quantitative Study' (2011) *Journal of Statistical Research* 54.

at national level by the relevant departments of the State Council.[25] Accordingly, the Enterprise Bankruptcy Law of the People's Republic of China (Trial) 1986 (EBL 1986), was issued on December 2, 1986 for trial implementation.

8.29 Although the EBL 1986 came into force on November 2, 1988, it unsurprisingly did not operate as a modern, market-based, bankruptcy law would be expected to operate as any procedure was conducted under heavy state-supervision. Article 43 of the EBL 1986 stipulated that 'the specific plans and steps for the trial implementation shall be stipulated by the State Council'. In other words, although insolvency was allowed for the first time by the EBL 1986, the government could still plan when, and which, state-owned enterprises were able to enter into insolvency proceedings.

8.30 The reasons for the EBL 1986 being so careful to term itself a trial version, and expressly embrace government interference in its legal articles, may be due to a variety of reasons. Article 1 of the Constitution of the People's Republic of China 1982 (Constitution 1982) stated that China was 'led by the working class and based on the alliance of workers and peasants'. It therefore proves extremely difficult to accept, from the ideological standpoint of Chinese people, that workers may lose their jobs. Moreover, Article 6 of the Constitution 1982, established two forms of ownership in China: (1) assets owned by the complete population (as represented by central government); and (2) assets owned collectively by the workers (as represented by the local authority or other institutions). Therefore, the functions of SOEs were not only limited to providing employment opportunities, but also cradle-to-grave social security to the workers and their families.[26]

8.31 As a result, were a SOE to become insolvent, the workers would not only lose their jobs, but also all social security for their families, while retired workers would also lose their future financial security, due to their retirement pensions being paid monthly by the SOEs they had formerly worked for. The EBL 1986 was therefore implemented in a modest manner, in order to eliminate some failed SOEs without resulting in too great a degree of social upheaval. In order to maintain a high level of control, insolvencies were administered under

---

25 Yanning Zhang, 'Statement of 'Enterprise Bankruptcy Law of the People's Republic of China (Draft)' by the National Economy Commission: At the 16th Meeting of the Standing Committee of the Sixth National People's Congress of the People's Republic of China on June 16, 1986' (the National Economy Commission 1986) <http://www.pkulaw.cn/fulltext_form.aspx?Db=protocol&Gid=1090519749&keyword=%e7%a0%b4%e4%ba%a7%e6%b3%95&EncodingName=&Search_Mode=accurate> accessed 26 April 2017.

26 Deborah Kay Johns, 'Reforming the State-Enterprise Property Relationship in the People's Republic of China: The Corporatization of State-Owned Enterprises' (1994) 16 *Mich. J. Int'l L.* 911.

state-control via a 'liquidation group', composed of government agencies. Nevertheless, the economy gradually developed over the years and the need for a properly functioning bankruptcy law increased, not least because the 1986 law was for SOEs only and the number of private enterprises had increased significantly. A new law was also needed in order to satisfy the demands of external bodies with whom China was establishing a relationship and which regarded a properly functioning bankruptcy law as an essential feature of a market economy, an important factor in terms of trade.

This finally led to the enactment of the EBL 2006, which came into effect in 2007, replacing the EBL 1986 and various regional bankruptcy laws. Although the concept of insolvency has been confirmed, the underlying logic and social background of the EBL 2006 has not changed fundamentally. The key driver of the insolvency law is the economic reform, especially in relation to SOEs and the core concern is the treatment of the workers of the failed companies. Therefore, the government will continue to play an important role in the insolvency practice to protect the social structure in mainland China and to further promote the economic and social development in its coastal areas.[27] **8.32**

(3) Existing procedures

The EBL 2006 identifies three insolvency proceedings applicable to enterprises: **8.33**

(1) Reorganization (Chapter 8);
(2) Compromise (Chapter 9); and
(3) Liquidation (Chapter 10).

Both reorganization and compromise are designed to rescue failing enterprises, rather than forcing them towards termination or liquidation. However, little use is made of compromise proceedings, which accordingly have received little coverage in academic papers and insolvency reports from the courts. Critics argue that compromise proceedings are unnecessary and overlap with reorganization.[28] It is also notable that it is hard for any compromise agreement to achieve the requirements expressed by Article 97 of the EBL 2006 for their approval. This threshold has been set as the consent of more than half of the creditors who are present at the creditors' meeting and who **8.34**

27 Rebecca Parry and Haizheng Zhang, 'Introduction', *China's New Enterprise Bankruptcy Law: Context, Interpretation and Application* (Ashgate 2009) 3, 3.

28 Shuguang Li and Zuofa Wang, 'The Gap Between Expectation of Legislation and Judicial Practice and Its Resolution: Empricical Analysis of Bankrucptcy Law's Three-Year Implementation' (2011) *Journal of CUPL* 58, 69.

have the right to vote, representing two-thirds or more of the total amount of unsecured claims. As compromise proceedings may vary from case to case and few common points may be found, this chapter only discusses the reorganization and liquidation proceedings.

8.35 There are a few differences according the executory contracts whether the insolvency proceeding is a reorganization one or liquidation one. In practice, the result can be the same. For example, in the *CNNC Huayan* reorganization case, the trustee continued the operations of the ailing business, including its executory contracts, while looking for potential investors.[29] Executory contracts were similarly treated in a liquidation case, *Beijing Lida Marine Biological Museum*, where the administrator was elected to continue the operation of the insolvent enterprise and packaged the profits of the company's entire property, business, and executory contracts collectively to be sold as a going-concern business through public auction.[30] Both procedures ended up in a sale, the most significant difference being that in *CNNC Huayan* the new owner continued to operate under the same name (rescue of the company), while in *Beihing Lida* the museum was re-branded (sale of the business).

8.36 Under Article 76 of the EBL 2006, an executory contract shall be performed during the period of reorganization if the contract entitles the debtor to possess any property legally. No similar provision is made for a liquidation leading to a business sale. Additionally, Article 73 of EBL 2006 also entitles the debtor's management to take over the operation and management from the administrator, which shall include the right of deciding whether to continue an executory contract or not in the proceeding of reorganization. There is no equivalent process to enable liquidation proceedings to be converted into 'debtor in possession' proceedings.

C. TREATMENT OF EXECUTORY CONTRACTS

(1) The options for administrators

8.37 Compared to the 1986 Act, the EBL 2006 contains improved provisions on the treatment of executory contracts. First, the entitlement to make the decision over the termination or continuation of the contract has been vested

29 *The Reorganization case of CNNC HUAYUAN Titanium Dioxide Co, Ltd* (Gansu Province Jiayuguan Intermediate People 's Court). (2012).

30 *The Liquidation Case of Beijing Lida Marine Biological Museum Co, Ltd* (Beijing Higher People 's Court). (2013).

in the administrator (art. 18 of the EBL 2006) rather than the liquidation team (an organ under state control), which was the choice under Article 26 of the EBL 1986.

The administrator is a new figure introduced by the 2006 law. This professional assumes a central role in insolvency proceedings under the EBL 2006. The administrator's obligations include but are not limited to: **8.368**

> (1) taking over the property, seals, account books, documents and other data of the debtor; (2) investigating the financial position of the debtor and preparing a report on such position; (3) deciding on matters of internal management of the debtor; (4) deciding on the day-to-day expenses and other necessary expenditures of the debtor; (5) deciding, before the first creditors' meeting is held, to continue or suspend the debtor's business; (6) managing and disposing of the debtor's property; (7) participating in legal actions, arbitrations or any other legal procedure on behalf of the debtor; (8) proposing to hold creditors' meetings; and (9) performing other duties that the people's court deems that he should.[31]

The establishment of an administrator system represented a significant step towards the adoption of a management system of insolvency cases more in line with the experiences of foreign jurisdictions such as the United Kingdom.[32] **8.39**

(2) The concept of executory contracts under PRC insolvency law

The EBL 2006 law innovated the notion of 'executory contract'. According to the previous law, Article 26 of the EBL 1986, '[t]he liquidation team may decide to terminate or to continue to perform the contracts that have not yet been performed by the bankrupt enterprise'. This decision now rests with the administrator. **8.40**

The 1986 provision included only those contracts that were to be performed by the insolvent party, as those contracts that were for the non-insolvent party to perform were excluded. Consequently, the liquidation team could decide to continue a contract and pay the other party in full. Such performance would reduce the value of the insolvent party's property and break the principle of *paritas creditorum*. **8.41**

The EBL 2006 classifies the treatments of unfinished contracts into three. **8.42**

---

31 The EBL 2006, art. 25.

32 Jianhua Xiao, 'Bankruptcy Administrator: Status, Powers and Duties', in *China's New Enterprise Bankruptcy Law: Context, Interpretation and Application* (Ashgate 2009) 89, 89.

8.43 First there are those contracts that have been performed by the insolvent party, and that are considered as part of the insolvent party's potential property for the administrator to claim. Then there are those that have been performed by the non-insolvent party only. They are considered as debts of the insolvent party and the administrator shall terminate those contracts and list the other parties as creditors. Finally there are those contracts that have yet to be fulfilled by both parties, which are called 'executory contracts' and whose continued performance is left for the administrators to decide.[33]

8.44 Article 18 of the EBL 2006 gives a timeline only in respect of executory contracts which have not been performed by the time that the case has been accepted by the court. Further, Article 18 of the EBL 2006 urges the administrator to notify the other party of his decision within two months from the date when the bankruptcy application is accepted. Otherwise, the contract is deemed to be terminated. In contrast, there was no such time restriction according to the EBL 1986. Further, Article 18 of the EBL 2006 entitles the non-insolvent party to make an exhortation to urge the administrator to make a decision and the time for consideration has been shortened to 30 days from the date such exhortation is made.

8.45 Besides the general rule, there are some executory contracts that are deemed to be discharged or to continue according to law. For example, according to Article 411 of the Contract Law, a commission contract is discharged when the principal or the agent enters insolvency proceedings. In contrast, Article 92 of Insurance Law of the People's Republic of China (2015 Amendment) (中华人民共和国保险法 (2015修正)) (hereinafter the 'Insurance Law 2015') stipulates that:

> [w]here an insurance company which operates a life insurance business is abolished according to the law or is declared bankrupt according to the law, it must assign its life insurance contracts and liability reserve funds to another insurance company which operates life insurance business; where it cannot reach an assignment agreement with another insurance company, the insurance regulatory body under the State Council shall designate an insurance company which operates life insurance business to accept the assignment.

As a result, administrators are not entitled to make decisions in respect of these contracts.

33 Guo Zhihui, *New Enterprise Bankruptcy Law Operation Guide and Templates of Related Documents* (China Legal Publishing House 2006) 173.

(3) The effect of continuation and termination

Previously, the second paragraph of Article 26 of the EBL 1986 only expressed the effect when the liquidation team decided to terminate a contract. In this case, where 'the other party to the contract suffers harm as the result of the termination of the contract, the amount of compensation for the harm constitutes a bankruptcy claim.' However, the treatment of the other party to an executory contract that was continued was not expressly addressed. **8.46**

In contrast, Article 18 of the EBL 2006 fills the gap and stipulates that: **8.47**

> where the administrator decides that performance of the contract is to be continued, the other party shall comply; however, the other party shall have the right to request the administrator to provide a guarantee. Where the administrator refuses to do so, the contract shall be deemed to be rescinded.

Once a decision on the continuation of an executory contract has been taken, the expense of performing that executory contract can be seen as being for the common benefit of the creditors. This reasoning supported Article 34 of the old EBL 1986, where the other party enjoyed a priority payment from the insolvent estate. Such priority has been lowered slightly in the EBL 2006. The EBL 2006 separates common benefit debts (including those arising from executory contracts) from the expenses of the insolvency.[34] Although Article 43 holds that both of them shall be paid throughout the procedure (and not at the end of it), the expenses of the insolvency proceedings shall prevail when the insolvent party's property is not enough to pay off both debts. Therefore, if the other party did not ask for a full guarantee before the performance of an executory contract, he may bear the risk to be paid with other creditors holding 'common benefit debts' of the insolvent party on a *pro rata* basis. Nonetheless, the other party still enjoys the priority over the rest of the creditors, who do not enjoy such priority. **8.48**

Little changes where an executory contract has been revoked. According to Article 53 of the EBL 2006, where an administrator or debtor revokes an executory contract according to the provisions of the law, the other party may declare his claims on the basis of his right to compensation for the damages caused by the revocation as a creditor. Therefore, the decision of whether to continue or to terminate an executory contract may not only affect the performing process of the contract but also determine the nature of the debt arising from the contract and the sequence in which the debts will be paid off. **8.49**

34 The EBL 2006, arts 41–43.

8.50 To simplify, the situation can be described as giving two alternatives: when an executory contract is chosen to be continued, the non-insolvent party will enjoy a priority ranking and a guarantee for the value of their claim, otherwise they can refuse to perform their contractual obligations. However, when an executory contract is terminated, the non-insolvent party can only claim compensation for the outstanding balance as a normal, unsecured creditor. As a result, it is easy to assume that without a material market change, the non-insolvent party is more likely to prefer to carry on with an executory contract guaranteed by property, rather than terminate it and claim for a compensation. Therefore, it is worthwhile to consider the validity and enforceability of an *ipso facto* clause under the current Chinese insolvency framework.

(4) *Ipso facto* clauses

8.51 An *ipso facto* clause 'is a provision in a contract which purports either to terminate a contract automatically or to confer on a contractor the right to terminate it when its counterparty enters into an insolvency proceeding'[35] or is in financial distress. There is no specific legal provision regarding *ipso facto* clauses in the Chinese legal system. However, the validity of an *ipso facto* clause is controversial over the world,[36] and some Chinese academics consider it invalid for derailing the administrator's option under the EBL 2006 discussed above.[37]

8.52 Specifically, there may be a distinction before and after the party in financial distress enters into an insolvency proceeding under the Chinese legal framework. According to Gao, an *ipso facto* clause which provides for termination on insolvency (not merely one which provides for termination upon a petition for insolvency) is valid before the insolvency proceeding because of the 'unsafe right' defence discussed above.[38] A more direct reason may be that the second paragraph of Article 93 of the Contract Law stipulates that '[t]he parties may agree upon conditions under which either party may terminate the contract. Upon satisfaction of the conditions, the party who has the right to terminate

35 Joanne Collett, 'Ipso Facto Clauses and the Anti-Deprivation Principle' (2010) 5 *CRI* 196, 196.

36 UK courts may have quite opposite views from US courts. However the UK Government recently indicated an intention to adopt an approach of similarity to that in the US: Department for Business, Energy and Industrial Strategy, Insolvency and Corporate Governance, Government Response (August 2018).

37 Xiaowei Lan, 'Executory Contracts in Insolvency Law' (Wuhan University 2010) 1, 45–47 <http://cdmd.cnki.com.cn/Article/CDMD-10486-2010166739.htm> accessed 17 August 2017; Zhen Gao, 'The Enforceability of Ipso Facto Clauses' (Masters, North China University of Technology 2012) 1, 8 <http://cdmd.cnki.com.cn/Article/CDMD-10009-1012389109.htm> accessed 23 August 2017.

38 Guo Zhihui, *supra* note 33, 7.

may terminate the contract'. Therefore, the parties are entitled to include a clause to terminate the contracts under the agreed conditions.

Nonetheless, there are some restrictions for the parties to excise such a right. According to Article 96 of the Contract Law, the party demanding termination shall notify the other party when the agreed condition is met. Therefore, the contract may not be terminated automatically upon one party's insolvency without notification. Moreover, '[i]f the other party objects to such termination, it may petition the People's Court or an arbitration institution to adjudicate the validity of the termination of the contract'.[39] 8.53

As a result, while in theory *ipso facto* clauses shall be enforceable before the defaulting party enters insolvency proceedings, their validity and enforceability shall be assessed on a case-by-case basis. 8.54

According to Article 126 of the Contract Law, the parties may choose foreign law to govern a foreign-related contract. For those contracts, the validity of *ipso facto* clauses depends on the governing law. However, in practice, such ascertainment can be difficult and in case of uncertainty over the applicable law, the authorized court is likely to apply local law (PRC law) instead.[40] 8.55

The relationship between the Contract Law and the EBL 2006 from the time when the defaulting party enters insolvency requires further analysis. From a hierarchical perspective, both the Contract Law and the EBL 2006 have been issued by the National People's Congress. Therefore, they are on an equal footing. However, because the EBL 2006 was issued after the Contract Law, the EBL 2006 shall prevail in case of conflict. 8.56

Further, according to the Article 52 of the Contract Law, a contract is null and void 'when violating the compulsory provisions of laws and administrative regulations'. It is arguable whether Article 18 of the EBL 2006, which entitles the administrators to choose whether to adopt a contract, is a compulsory provision that excludes the other party from terminating the executory contract, at least, not when the insolvent party fails to provide a guaranty over the performance of the executory contract. Therefore, it is hard to argue that *ipso facto* clauses are against the EBL 2006 in all circumstances. Although this article suggests *ipso facto* clauses shall be valid and enforceable by the courts, 8.57

---

39 Contract Law of the People's Republic of China, art. 96.

40 Jian Sun, 'On Implementation of Ascertainment Legislation of Foreign Law in China' (2017) 1 *Tianjin Legal Science* 60.

the legislative framework is not well-developed and risks of uncertainty should not be underestimated.

8.58 To reduce the degree of uncertainty, lawyers may advise the non-defaulting party to include grounds to terminate the contract before the defaulting party enters into an insolvency proceeding.[41] Nonetheless, such a suggestion may reduce but not fully avoid the risk of uncertainty. If the debtor makes early payment to the other party to ensure performance this may be a vulnerable transaction. For example, in terms of Article 31 of the EBL 2006, an administrator is entitled to request the court to nullify the action of paying off debts not due within one year before the people's court accepts the application of insolvency.

8.59 In conclusion, under the current Chinese insolvency framework, contracting parties have little incentives to include *ipso facto* clauses in their contracts. This is because the non-insolvent party enjoys significant protections in the law from continuing the contract. This evaluation however changes with reference to contracts negotiated in financial markets, especially swaps and derivatives.[42] As the market price of these financial instruments is subject to sudden changes, *ipso facto* clauses are extremely valued.

D. CONCLUDING REMARKS

8.60 As expressed above, the main driver of the development of insolvency law in China is the economic reform of the society. However, the barriers for further development are also related to the difficulties encountered by the country's transitioning economy.

8.61 Under current law, the rules on the treatment of executory contracts changes from the time in which the debtor is admitted into an insolvency procedure. Before that moment, the treatment is based on the principle of freedom of contracts, where parties shall perform their obligations under the agreed contract until an agreed condition for termination appears. Although contract law entitles the parties to include an *ipso facto* clause in a contract, the validity

---

41 Shaoji Ma and Naiying Xiao, 'ISDA Announces China 's Memorandum on Close-out Netting' (*King & Wood Mallesons* 2017) <http://www.chinalawinsight.com/2017/04/articles/global-network/isda%E5%8F%91%E5%B8%83%E4%B8%AD%E5%9B%BD%E6%8F%90%E5%89%8D%E7%BB%88%E6%AD%A2%E5%87%80%E9%A2%9D%E7%BB%93%E7%AE%97%E5%A4%87%E5%BF%98%E5%BD%95/> accessed 27 August 2017.

42 Acceleration clauses and close-out netting are mainly discussed with regard to insolvency of financial organizations in China in a positive way.

of such a clause is not specified and courts have yet to determine their admissibility in insolvency cases. In addition, where one party is in financial or economic distress, the other party may claim the 'unsafe right defence' and benefit from this defence if he can prove his concern.

After the acceptance of a bankruptcy case, except as otherwise stipulated by law, the decision-making right is granted to the administrator of the insolvent party. However, in practice the EBL 2006 is designed to promote an outcome similar to the contract law. It can be said that the EBL 2006 expressly ensures the substantial content of the unsafe right defence, i.e., the non-insolvent party's right to decline the performance of the terms of the contract without a property guarantee. Moreover, the non-insolvent party is also entitled to urge the administrator to make a decision within 30 days as to whether to continue the executory contract. **8.62**

As structural reforms continue, it may be anticipated that more actions will be taken by the courts to eliminate the barriers to commencing insolvency proceedings. In coming years, the number of insolvency cases is expected to grow dramatically, and a professional cohort of insolvency judges and lawyers, as well as specialist courts, is expected to rise accordingly. **8.63**

This chapter has evidenced some of the issues that need to be addressed in further laws and practice, particularly the uncertainties related to the treatment of *ipso facto* clauses. In the authors' view, without a substantial judicial reform and further support from the legislature, the development of insolvency law will only have a limited supplemental role to promote economic growth and social change. In the interim, executory contracts will tend to be assigned to a third party or continued or terminated by the reorganized debtor, as in the *CNNC* and *Beijing Lida* cases discussed above. **8.64**

9

NATIONAL REPORT FOR CROATIA

Jasnica Garašić and Siniša Petrović

A. INTRODUCTION AND INSOLVENCY PROCEDURES

9.01 There are two regular procedures available to a company in financial or economic distress under current Croatian legislation: pre-bankruptcy proceedings and bankruptcy proceedings. These two procedures are regulated by the Bankruptcy Act of 2015.[1]

(1) Pre-bankruptcy proceedings

9.02 Pre-bankruptcy proceedings are instituted to regulate the debtor's legal position and their relations with the creditors and to maintain their business operations.[2] A petition to open these proceedings may be filed by the debtor or by a creditor with the debtor's consent.[3] Such proceedings may be opened if the court has established the existence of imminent insolvency. The petitioner has to show that it is probable that the debtor will not be able to pay existing

1 *Stečajni zakon*, Official Gazette *Narodne novine* no 2015/71, 2017/104, hereinafter referred to as BA. The Bankruptcy Act regulates pre-bankruptcy and bankruptcy proceedings opened against companies and other legal entities as well as against natural persons that perform economic activities. Consumer bankruptcy proceedings are regulated by the Consumer Bankruptcy Act, *Zakon o stečaju potrošača*, Official Gazette *Narodne novine* no 2015/100.

2 Bankruptcy Act 2015, art 2 (1).

3 Ibid., art 25 (1).

obligations when they become due.[4] The statutory presumption on the existence of imminent insolvency alleviates the burden of proof for the applicant,[5] who is usually the debtor itself. Among other things, the petitioner has to attach a proposal for the restructuring plan to the petition.[6] The commercial court shall examine and establish the filed claims of creditors.[7] The creditors shall discuss the restructuring plan at the special hearing, where they also may propose changes.[8] After that the creditors shall vote on the plan.[9] If the restructuring plan has been accepted by the creditors and all other statutory preconditions have been fulfilled, the court shall confirm the pre-bankruptcy agreement.[10] The confirmed pre-bankruptcy agreement, that becomes final (*res iudicata*), is legally binding upon all creditors, except against debtor's employees, those creditors with a right for exemption of certain assets that do not belong to the debtor and creditors with a right to separate satisfaction on certain assets that belong to the debtor (creditors with security interests).[11] The goal of the pre-bankruptcy proceedings is the reorganization of the debtor. Many ideas expressed in the European Commission Recommendation of 12 March 2014 on a new approach to business failure and insolvency[12] can be found in the Croatian provisions on the pre-bankruptcy proceedings.[13]

(2) Bankruptcy proceedings

Bankruptcy proceedings are instituted to serve the purpose of collective satisfaction of a debtor's creditors by liquidation of the debtor's assets and by the distribution of the proceeds among the creditors or by reaching an arrangement in a bankruptcy plan, particularly in order to maintain debtor's business operations. Honest debtors, who are natural persons, shall be given **9.03**

4 Ibid., art 4 (1), (3) and (4).
5 Ibid., art 4 (2).
6 Ibid., art 26 (3).
7 Ibid, arts 46–51.
8 Ibid., arts 52–55.
9 Ibid., arts 56–60.
10 Ibid., art 61.
11 Ibid., art 66 (1) and (2). The pre-bankruptcy agreement also does not affect interim measures in criminal proceedings and tax procedure where abuse of law is established (ibid., art 66 (1) subparas 3–4) and so-called qualified financial contracts (ibid., art 66 para 2).
12 C (2014) 1500 final.
13 For more details see: Mihajlo Dika, 'Predstečajni postupak (Pre-bankruptcy Proceedings)' (2016) 56 Pravo u gospodarstvu, 367–425; Mario Vukelić, 'Novi Stečajni zakon – novi predstečajni postupak (New Bankruptcy Act – New Pre-bankruptcy Proceedings)' (2016) 56 Pravo u gospodarstvu, 1041–70; Ante Galić, 'Predstečajni postupak prema novom Stečajnom zakonu (Pre-bankruptcy Proceedings According to the New Bankruptcy Act)', in *Reforma Hrvatskog Insolvencijskog Prava – Novi Stečajni Zakon (Reform of Croatian Insolvency Law – New Bankrutpcy Act)*, 77–104 (Marica Kuzmić ed., 2015).

the opportunity to achieve discharge of the remaining obligations (debts).[14] A petition to open the bankruptcy proceedings may be filed by the debtor, by a creditor[15] or in certain cases by the Financial Agency (FINA).[16]

9.04 Bankruptcy proceedings may be opened if the court establishes the existence of one of three possible bankruptcy grounds: imminent insolvency; insolvency; or over-indebtedness.[17] Insolvency exists if a debtor is unable to pay their monetary obligations as they become due.[18] The statutory presumption on the existence of insolvency alleviates the establishment of this bankruptcy ground.[19] Over-indebtedness exists, if the assets owned by the debtor, who is a legal person, no longer cover their existing liabilities.[20]

9.05 In bankruptcy proceedings the petitioner is usually either a creditor or FINA. The court shall always examine and establish the claims filed by the creditors.[21] In practice, most bankruptcy proceedings are liquidation proceedings. In some rare cases, the reorganization of the debtor has been achieved by means of a bankruptcy plan. If a bankruptcy plan has been prepared by the bankruptcy administrator,[22] the creditors shall discuss this plan at the special hearing where they may also propose its changes.[23] After that, the creditors shall vote on the bankruptcy plan.[24] If the bankruptcy plan has been accepted by the creditors, the debtor has consented to it and all other statutory preconditions have been fulfilled, the court shall confirm the bankruptcy plan.[25]

9.06 The confirmed bankruptcy plan, that becomes final (*res iudicata*), is legally binding upon all the participants involved. Such a plan is effective also against the creditors who have not filed their claims, as well as against dissenting participants.[26]

---

14 Bankruptcy Act 2015, art 2 (2) and (3).

15 Ibid., art 109 (1).

16 Ibid., art 110 (1). Financial Agency (FINA) is the leading Croatian company in the field of financial mediation and the application of information technologies. Although state-owned, FINA operates on free market principles. Its position and competences are primarily regulated by the Law on Financial Agency (Official Gazette 2001/117, 2004/60, 2005/42) but also other legislative acts, including the BA, which entrust FINA with certain authorities.

17 Ibid., art 5 (1), (2) and (3).

18 Ibid., art 6 (1).

19 Ibid., art 6 (2) subparas 1–2.

20 Ibid., art 7 (1).

21 Ibid., arts 257–272.

22 Ibid., art 305 (1)–(3).

23 Ibid., arts 321–326.

24 Ibid., arts 327–332.

25 Ibid., arts 334–337.

26 Ibid., art 340 (1).

The provisions of the Croatian Bankruptcy Act on bankruptcy proceedings[27] were drafted along the lines of the German Insolvency Code[28] on insolvency proceedings. In other words, many solutions of the Croatian bankruptcy law are similar to those under the German Insolvency Code, including solutions regarding the legal effects of the opening of the bankruptcy proceedings on executory contracts. 9.07

The Croatian Bankruptcy Act regulates not only liquidation proceedings within the framework of the bankruptcy proceedings, but also reorganization proceedings by means of a pre-bankruptcy agreement within the pre-bankruptcy proceedings and by means of a bankruptcy plan within the bankruptcy proceedings. In spite of this fact, the Croatian legislator did not want to use the title 'Insolvency Act' (which, in our view, would have been more accurate) for no reason other than established tradition. 9.08

If we compare a pre-bankruptcy agreement and a bankruptcy plan as means of the debtor's reorganization then we can conclude that the statutory rules on a bankruptcy plan are more developed, detailed and precise than those on a pre-bankruptcy agreement. 9.09

Out-of-court proceedings for companies in financial or economic distress have not been regulated by the Croatian legislator. Out-of-court proceedings have been regulated only for insolvent consumers by the Consumer Bankruptcy Act 2015.[29] It is fair to assume that companies experiencing financial or economic difficulties regularly explore informal alternatives with their major creditors before filing for pre-bankruptcy or bankruptcy procedures, but there are no statistics on it. 9.10

A special reorganization procedure was implemented by the new Act on Procedure of *Extraordinary Management* in Companies of Systematic Importance for the Republic of Croatia that entered into force on 7 April 2017.[30] The goal of this Act is to maintain business operations of companies of systematic importance for Croatia which with their business independently or together with their subsidiaries or other interconnected (related) companies impact on 9.11

---

27 For more details, see Jasnica Garašić, 'Najznačajnije novine Stečajnog zakona iz 2015. godine (Most Important Novelties in Bankruptcy Act of 2015) (2017) 38 Zbornik Pravnog fakulteta Sveučilišta u Rijeci, 131–86.

28 *Insolvenzordnung*, Official Gazette *Bundesgesetzblatt I 1994*, 2866 et seq, last change, *Bundesgesetzblatt* I 2016, 3147 et seq.

29 Zakon o stečaju potrošača, Official Gazette Narodne novine no 2015/100.

30 Zakon o postupku izvanredne uprave u trgovačkim društvima od sistemskog značaja za Republiku Hrvatsku, Official Gazette Narodne novine no 2017/32, hereinafter referred to as Extraordinary Management Procedure Act (EMPA).

Croatia's economic, social and financial stability.[31] The Act applies to a joint stock company of systematic importance for Croatia (the 'Debtor') and to all its subsidiaries and other interconnected companies where it holds more than 25 per cent of shares, employing more than 5,000 employees and with balance sheet obligations exceeding 7.5 billion Kuna. The court shall open these proceedings if it is proven that the company is imminently insolvent, insolvent or over-indebted.[32] The Act is not applicable to credit companies and insurance companies.[33]

9.12 A petition to open these proceedings may be filed by the Debtor or by a creditor of the Debtor or a creditor of the Debtor's subsidiaries or other interconnected companies with the Debtor's consent.[34] Although the extraordinary management procedure is nominally a court procedure, there is a strong influence of the Croatian government in it. The extraordinary trustee, appointed by the court upon a proposal made by the Croatian government, has a central role in this procedure.[35] The extraordinary trustee shall exercise the rights, and discharge the obligations of the Debtor's bodies. His main task is to keep the business of the Debtor going and to negotiate a settlement with the creditors of the Debtor (the parent company) and of all their interconnected companies.[36] The managements of the subsidiaries and other interconnected companies of the Debtor shall not be replaced simply by reason of the filing, even if from that moment onwards they operate under the strong supervision of the extraordinary trustee.[37] The court shall examine and establish the filed claims of all the creditors.[38] If the settlement has been accepted by the creditors and confirmed by the court, it shall be legally binding upon all creditors of the Debtor and their interconnected companies, regardless of whether or not they participated in the extraordinary management procedure.[39] The extraordinary management procedure is a single insolvency proceeding that encompasses the Debtor and all their interconnected companies and actually presents a kind of substantive consolidation of all these companies involved. As such, it breaches the principle 'one debtor (company),

31 See EMPA, art 1(1).
32 See ibid., art 4 (1)–(2) and art 5.
33 Ibid., art 4 (3).
34 Ibid., art 21 (1).
35 Ibid., art 24 (1)–(3).
36 See ibid., art 12 (1)–(12) and art 43.
37 See ibid., art 13 (1)–(5).
38 See ibid., arts 32–36.
39 See ibid., art 43 (15).

one assets (insolvency estate), one insolvency proceeding'. This new controversial procedure opens many legal questions.[40] Several proposals to review the constitutionality of the Act on Procedure of Extraordinary Management in Companies of Systematic Importance for the Republic of Croatia have already been submitted to the Constitutional Court of the Republic of Croatia.

The Croatian Civil Obligations Act[41] contains general rules for the situation where only one party has not fully performed their obligations. **9.13**

B. TREATMENT OF EXECUTORY CONTRACTS

(1) Pre-bankruptcy proceedings

The provisions of the Bankruptcy Act on pre-bankruptcy proceedings do not address directly executory contracts. Nevertheless, when we consider the legal effects of pre-bankruptcy proceedings on these contracts, we have to take into account the following statutory provisions. **9.14**

During the time between filing the petition to open the pre-bankruptcy proceedings and the day of issuing the decision on opening of these proceedings, the debtor may make only those payments that are necessary to operate the business on a regular basis.[42] If a custodian has been appointed, he is bound to control (supervise) the debtor's business, especially his financial operations.[43] Each filed claim, including claims of creditors from executory contracts, may be disputed (denied) by the debtor, the appointed custodian or another creditor.[44] During the time between the day of opening of the pre-bankruptcy proceedings and the day of their conclusion the debtor may make only payments that are necessary for the business on a regular basis and fulfil obligations from the new loans that are necessary for the continuation of the debtor's business. In that period the debtor cannot fulfil obligations that arose and became due before the opening of the pre-bankruptcy proceedings, with the exception of any claim from the employees and those payments that are classified as necessary for business on a regular basis according to special **9.15**

40 For more details, see Jasnica Garašić, 'Izvanredna uprava države nad povezanim društvima (Extraordinary Management of the State in Interconnected Companies)' (2017) 57 Pravo u gospodarstvu, 5–29.

41 *Zakon o obveznim odnosima*, Official Gazette *Narodne novine* nos 2005/35, 2008/41, 2011/125, 2015/78. See Civil Obligations Act, arts 342 and 360.

42 Bankruptcy Act 2015, art 29 (1)–(2).

43 Ibid., art 24 (5).

44 Ibid., art 147.

laws.[45] In that period, it is not allowed to initiate legal suits, enforcement proceedings, administrative proceedings and securement proceedings against the debtor. If these proceedings have already been commenced, they shall be stayed (discontinued) by the day of the opening of the pre-bankruptcy proceedings.[46] The confirmed pre-bankruptcy agreement that became final (*res iudicata*) is legally effective against all creditors, except against debtor's employees, creditors with a right for exemption of certain assets that do not belong to the debtor and creditors with a right to separate satisfaction on certain assets that belong to the debtor.[47]

(2) Bankruptcy proceedings

9.16 The legal effects of the opening of bankruptcy proceedings on executory contracts concluded by the debtor prior to the opening of the bankruptcy proceedings are regulated in Articles 181–197 of the Croatian Bankruptcy Act.

9.17 The solutions envisaged in these statutory provisions reflect the intention of the Croatian legislator to find a balance between the necessity to protect the bankruptcy estate or to allow reorganization of the insolvent company on one hand and the necessity to protect legitimate interests of the counterparty in an executory contract on the other hand.

(a) General treatment

9.18 The basic rule that determines the legal effects of the opening of the bankruptcy proceedings on executory contracts is the following. If the debtor and his counterparty have not performed, or have not performed completely a bilateral (mutual) contract at the time of opening of the bankruptcy proceedings, the bankruptcy administrator, a practitioner appointed by a court, may perform the contract instead of the debtor and claim the other party's consideration.[48] In other words, in this situation the bankruptcy administrator may choose between assumption and rejection of the executory contract.

9.19 If both parties, the debtor and his counterparty, have completely performed their obligations, the opening of the bankruptcy proceedings shall not affect such an executed contract, unless it is concluded and performed to the

45 Ibid., art 67 (1)–(2).
46 Ibid., art 68 (1)–(2).
47 Ibid., art 66 (1)–(2).
48 Ibid., art 181 (1).

detriment of creditors of the bankruptcy proceedings and a legal basis for bankruptcy avoidance proceedings exists.[49]

The bankruptcy administrator does not have a right to choose between assumption and rejection of a contract when one of the parties, either the debtor or his counterparty, has completely performed their obligations prior to the opening of the bankruptcy proceedings. Such a contract and transactions in connection with it can also be contested, if a legal basis for bankruptcy avoidance proceedings exists. 9.20

In a situation where only the insolvent debtor has completely performed the contract prior to the opening of the bankruptcy proceedings, the bankruptcy administrator may not reject the contract only due to the opening of the bankruptcy proceedings. He may claim the counterparty's consideration for the bankruptcy estate and enforce all contractual performance claims according to the rules of general law of obligations. He may also use non-performance remedies foreseen by general law of obligations, including termination of the contract and damages claims.[50] According to the Croatian law, all rights of the corporate bodies of the debtor who is a legal person shall be transferred to the bankruptcy administrator by the opening of the bankruptcy proceedings.[51] The administrator shall act as a legal representative of the debtor. The corporate bodies of the debtor shall lose their right to represent the debtor. A legal person shall retain its legal capacity until dissolution. Among other things, the bankruptcy administrator is bound to see to it that the claims of the insolvent debtor are satisfied.[52] 9.21

In a situation where only the counterparty has completely performed the contract prior to the opening of the bankruptcy proceedings, the bankruptcy administrator may also not reject the contract. The counterparty's performance claim against the debtor shall be converted into a monetary claim[53] and if it has been filed with the bankruptcy administrator and established (determined) at the examination hearing, it can be satisfied as a claim of a creditor of the bankruptcy proceedings[54] *pro rata*. The same is true for any damages claims of the counterparty for non-performance. 9.22

49 Insolvency avoidance powers are regulated in ibid., arts 198–215.
50 Civil Obligations Act, arts 360–362.
51 Bankruptcy Act 2015, art 159 (1).
52 Ibid., art 89 (1) no 6.
53 Ibid., art 144.
54 Ibid., art 137 (1).

9.23 As we have said, only in the situation where both parties, the insolvent debtor and his counterparty, have not performed, or have not performed completely a mutual contract at the time of the opening of the bankruptcy proceedings, may the bankruptcy administrator decide whether he will assume (continue) or reject such an executory contract.

9.24 In a case of partial performance of the contract prior to the opening of the bankruptcy proceedings, the contract shall be divided into executed and executory part, and the bankruptcy administrator may decide only on assumption or rejection of the executory part of the contract.[55] The executed part of the contract shall not be affected by the opening of the bankruptcy proceedings, unless there is a legal basis for avoidance proceedings.

9.25 The bankruptcy administrator should assume only those executory contracts whose continuation is beneficial to the bankruptcy estate and reject any executory contracts whose continuation is detrimental to it. That is the basic criteria for his decision whether a particular executory contract is to be assumed or rejected.

9.26 The administrator has an express statutory duty to proceed with consciousness and care and, in the manner of a good manager, to see to it that the commenced and unfinished transactions of the debtor are finished and that actions necessary to prevent damage to the debtor's assets are carried out.[56] If the debtor's business is being continued, the bankruptcy administrator is bound to conduct that business conscientiously.[57]

9.27 An executory contract cannot be partially assumed or rejected. It can be assumed as it was concluded between the debtor and the counterparty. If it is not beneficial for the bankruptcy estate, such a contract should be rejected and the bankruptcy administrator may offer a new contract to the same counterparty with provisions that are more favourable to the bankruptcy estate.

9.28 Croatian bankruptcy law does not prescribe the need for a court's examination of the bankruptcy administrator's decisions on assumption or rejection of executory contracts as a rule. However, if a particular executory contract would present a transaction of particular importance to the bankruptcy proceedings, the bankruptcy administrator is bound to acquire the previous consent of the

55 For more details, see Mihajlo Dika, 'Pravne Posljeduce Otvarana Stecajnoga Postupka (Legal Consequences of the Banktruptcty Proceedings)' (2002) Zagreb, 83–5.

56 Bankruptcy Act 2015, art 89 (1) no 5.

57 Ibid., art 89 (1) no 7.

creditors' committee[58] or in some cases even the consent of the creditors' meeting (assembly)[59] for such a legal transaction. The bankruptcy court may, following a proposal made by the debtor or a certain number of creditors, temporarily suspend the proposed assumption of the legal transaction and convene the creditors' meeting (assembly), which will be empowered to decide on whether to continue or reject the contract.[60] The absence of consent of a creditors' body for the undertaken transaction shall not make such a transaction invalid,[61] but it may represent a cause of personal liability for the bankruptcy administrator acting in breach of it.[62] Bankruptcy administrators must have a professional liability insurance policy like attorneys at law.[63]

The counterparty has a legitimate interest to know in good time, whether the bankruptcy administrator will assume or reject the executory contract. However, the bankruptcy administrator usually needs some time in order to decide whether the particular executory contract is beneficial to the bankruptcy estate or not. The law has tried to accommodate these opposing interests by prescribing that the counterparty can call upon the bankruptcy administrator to make a statement regarding the assumption or rejection of the executory contract. In that case, the administrator is bound to inform the counterparty immediately, at the latest after the reporting hearing, by means of registered mail, whether he intends to request performance of the contract. As an exception, if the counterparty would suffer substantial damage by waiting until the reporting hearing, the bankruptcy administrator is bound to reply within eight days, by means of registered mail, if he intends to request the performance (fulfilment) of the contract. If the bankruptcy administrator fails to do so, he shall not be entitled to request the performance of the contract.[64] 9.29

In bankruptcy proceedings with a debtor-in-possession (personal management of the debtor), the right of the bankruptcy administrator to choose between assumption and rejection of executory contracts shall be exercised by the debtor-in-possession. The debtor-in-possession shall exercise this right in agreement with the appointed custodian (trustee).[65] It is important to point out that obligations, which are not the result of regular business activities may be accepted by the debtor-in-possession only with the custodian's consent. 9.30

58 Ibid., art 230.
59 Ibid., arts 231–233.
60 Ibid., art 231(2).
61 Ibid., art 234 (1).
62 A bankruptcy administrator is liable for the damages that have resulted from wrongful violation of his duties, to all parties in the proceedings (ibid., art 92 (1)).
63 Ibid., art 81 (4).
64 Ibid., art 181 (3) and (4).
65 Ibid., art 165.

The debtor-in-possession may not accept the obligations resulting from his regular business activities if the custodian objects to such obligations.[66] The debtor-in-possession shall also be bound to obtain the consent of the creditor's committee for undertaking legal transactions of particular importance for the bankruptcy proceedings.[67]

9.31 Provisions included in the executed contracts as well as in executory contracts might be invalid under the rules of general law of obligations. Contract stipulations that exclude or limit the application of the Bankruptcy Act in advance have no legal effect.[68] The executed contracts as well as executory contracts may be contested under the rules of bankruptcy law, if a legal basis for bankruptcy avoidance proceedings exists.[69]

9.32 The same rules on the treatment of executory contracts apply irrespectively of whether the debtor is the performing or the non-performing party, and on the nature of the procedure (liquidation or reorganization). In Croatian bankruptcy law there are no special rules for such executory contracts where the counterparty is a public person (i.e., the state or any legal entity that exercises public powers). However, there are a few special rules regarding some long-term contracts or contracts that were concluded for an indefinite time, such as rental contracts, leasing contracts, and employment contracts. The rules on the treatment of executory contracts apply only to the executory contracts concerning the property which belongs to the bankruptcy estate.

Assumption of executory contracts

9.33 If the bankruptcy administrator assumes an executory contract and requests performance for the bankruptcy estate, the counterparty shall have the position of creditor of the bankruptcy estate. It means that the claims of the counterparty in connection with this assumed contract shall constitute obligations of the bankruptcy estate.[70]

9.34 The costs of the bankruptcy proceedings[71] and other obligations of the bankruptcy estate shall be settled first from the bankruptcy estate as they become due.[72] In other words, claims of the counterparty in an executory

66 Ibid., art 361 (1).
67 Ibid., art 362.
68 Ibid., art 197.
69 Ibid., arts 198–215.
70 Ibid., art 156 (1) no 3.
71 The costs of the bankruptcy proceedings, e.g., include: costs of the court in bankruptcy proceedings; remuneration and expenses of the temporary (interim) bankruptcy administrator; the bankruptcy administrator and the members of the creditor's committee (ibid., art 155).
72 Ibid., art 154 (1 and 2).

contract shall always be satisfied prior to the creditors of the bankruptcy proceedings. Only if the costs of the bankruptcy proceedings and the other obligations of the bankruptcy estate are fully covered, can proceeds be distributed to the creditors of the bankruptcy proceedings, according to their statutory ranking. Creditors of the bankruptcy proceedings usually receive only a small portion of their original claim, as they shall be satisfied only *pro rata* from the distribution of the proceeds.

If after the assumption of the executory contract, the bankruptcy administrator fails to fulfil the obligations of the bankruptcy estate, the counterparty is entitled to use the non-performance remedies envisaged by the general law of obligations, including termination of the contract and damages claims against the debtor. The counterparty may enforce their claims in court by bringing an action against the debtor. The automatic stay of legal suits (litigation) and enforcement actions against the bankruptcy debtor does apply to the creditors of the bankruptcy proceedings,[73] but not to the counterparty of an executory contract legally assumed by the bankruptcy administrator for the claims arising from that particular contract.[74] **9.35**

The Croatian Bankruptcy Act foresees a personal liability of the bankruptcy administrator in the case of non-performance of the assumed executory contract due to insufficient funds of the bankruptcy estate. However, the administrator shall not be liable for the damage the counterparty has suffered, if the administrator at the time of the assumption of the executory contract could not have foreseen that the bankruptcy estate would not be sufficient for the performance of the contract.[75] **9.36**

Special rules apply to divisible contracts. If the performances owed are divisible and the counterparty has partly fulfilled their performance at the time of the opening of the bankruptcy proceedings, the counterparty may realize their claim for counter-performance which corresponds to their partial performance as a creditor of the bankruptcy proceedings, even if the bankruptcy administrator assumes the contract. Due to the non-fulfilment of their claim for counter-performance from bankruptcy estate, the counterparty shall not be entitled to demand the return of the value added to the debtor's assets **9.37**

73 See Civil Procedure Act, art 212 (5), *Zakon o parničnom postupku*, official gazette *Narodne novine* nos 1991/53, 1992/91, 1999/112, 2001/88, 2003/117, 2005/88, 2007/2, 2000/84, 2008/96, 2008/123, 2011/57, 2013/25 and ibid., art 169 (1)–(9).

74 Ibid., art 170 (2).

75 Ibid., art 92 (4).

by their partial performance prior to the opening of the bankruptcy proceedings.[76] Only claims that correspond to the counterparty's partial performance to the bankruptcy estate *after* the opening of the bankruptcy proceedings may be satisfied as obligations of the bankruptcy estate.

Rejection of executory contracts

9.38 If the bankruptcy administrator rejects the performance of an executory contract, the counterparty's consideration claims remain unenforceable. These claims became unenforceable at the moment of the opening of the bankruptcy proceedings. Nevertheless, the counterparty is entitled to their claim based on debtor's non-performance and potential damages only as a creditor of the bankruptcy proceedings.[77]

9.39 The counterparty must file their claim with the bankruptcy administrator, so that this claim can be examined and established (determined) at the examination hearing in the bankruptcy proceedings.[78] If the claim is established (determined), it shall be satisfied in the distribution phase *pro rata*, according to the level of priority granted to the claimant by the law.[79]

9.40 The automatic stay of legal suits and enforcement against the bankruptcy debtor applies to all creditors of the bankruptcy proceedings, including the counterparty from the executory contract, which the bankruptcy administrator has rejected. Only in the situation where the claim of a creditor of the bankruptcy proceedings is disputed, shalll the court direct the creditor to commence or continue an earlier legal suit against the debtor in order to establish (determine) the disputed claim.[80]

9.41 The rule referred to above with reference to contracts with divisible performances also applies in a situation where the bankruptcy administrator has opted for rejection of an executory contract.[81]

(b) Special rules for certain types of contracts

9.42 The Bankruptcy Act contains special rules on the legal effect of the opening of bankruptcy proceedings on certain types of contracts, because the bankruptcy

76 Ibid., art 183.
77 Ibid., art 181 (2).
78 Ibid., art 257.
79 Ibid., art 273.
80 Ibid., art 266. A claim that was disputed (denied) in the bankruptcy proceedings may also be established (determined) in arbitration proceedings (ibid., art 268 (1)–(6)) or within mediation procedure (ibid., art 262 (1)–(8))
81 Ibid., art 183.

administrator's general right to choose between assumption and rejection of executory contracts in the case of these certain types of contracts does not contribute enough to the necessary balance between the interests of the insolvent debtor or the bankruptcy estate on one hand, and the interests of the counterparty on the other.[82]

Fixed date transactions, financial performances and qualified financial contracts with fixed date

If a contract related to the delivery of goods that have a market price or a price based on a stock exchange established a fixed time or fixed time period for performance, and this time or period occurs after opening of the bankruptcy proceedings, performance may not be claimed, but only compensation for non-performance.[83] **9.43**

The same rule applies if a fixed time or a fixed time period has been set for performance of a financial transaction that has a market price or a price based on a stock exchange, and this time or period occurs after opening of the bankruptcy proceedings.[84] For example, this is the case if a financial contract deals with delivery of precious metals or securities, performances in foreign currency, options on financial assets, derivatives, financial collateral, etc.[85] The bankruptcy administrator's right to choose between assumption and rejection of the contract is excepted in these cases. **9.44**

Nevertheless, if transactions regarding financial performances are combined in a framework contract that provides that, in case of the breach of the contract provisions, the contract may be terminated only uniformly, all these transactions shall be regarded as one mutual contract, which is subject to the bankruptcy administrator's right to opt for assumption or rejection of that contract.[86] **9.45**

The compensation for non-performance shall be equal to the difference between the contractual price and the market or stock price valid at the place of performance on the second working day after opening of the bankruptcy proceedings for contracts with the fixed time of performance. The other contractual party may settle their claim for such compensation only as a **9.46**

82 Ibid., arts 182–196.
83 Ibid., art 182 (1).
84 Ibid., art 182 (2).
85 Ibid., art 182 (3) subparas 1–5.
86 Ibid., art 182 (4).

creditor of the bankruptcy proceedings (*pro rata* satisfaction according to the statutory ranking rules).[87]

9.47 The Bankruptcy Act 2015 introduced a new rule according to which the opening of the bankruptcy proceedings does not in itself affect qualified financial contracts,[88] if the contractual parties have agreed on netting. The compensation for non-performance may be claimed in accordance with the content of the contract. If after the netting of mutual claims the bankruptcy debtor still has outstanding obligations towards the creditor, the latter may settle a claim for the non-netted amount in the bankruptcy proceedings only as a creditor of the bankruptcy proceedings.[89]

Sale, hire-purchase and finance lease contracts

9.48 Sales contracts and hire-purchase contracts are subject to the general rules on effects of the opening of the bankruptcy proceedings on executory contracts, including the rules on contracts with divisible performances.

9.49 In order to diminish the risk of insolvency, parties may stipulate security rights. In particular, reservation of ownership (retention of title) for movable goods and so-called *predbilježba* for immovables are common for these types of contracts. There are special rules for these security rights in case of bankruptcy proceedings.

9.50 If prior to the opening of the bankruptcy proceedings, the debtor has sold a movable item under a retention of title agreement and has transferred the item into the buyer's possession, the buyer may claim performance of the sales contract. The same applies if the debtor has charged himself with further obligations towards the buyer and has failed, completely or partially, to fulfil them.[90] In such a situation, the bankruptcy administrator may not exercise his right of choice between assumption and rejection of such contract. On the contrary, if the debtor has bought some movable item prior to the opening of the bankruptcy proceedings with the retention of title and possession of the movable item was transferred to the debtor by the seller, the bankruptcy

---

87 Ibid., art 182 (5). For more details, see Dika, *supra* note 57, at 76–82.

88 The following contracts shall be regarded as qualified financial contracts: financial contracts where one of the parties is a credit institution, a financial institution, an investment company, a leasing company, a management company, an alternative investment fund management company, a pension company or an insurance company and by which obligations that occur have to be fulfilled at a fixed time or within a fixed period, independently of whether they have been concluded under condition or not (ibid., art 182 (7)).

89 Ibid., art 182 (6).

90 Ibid., art 185 (1).

administrator shall have the right to choose between assumption or rejection of such contract.[91]

If *predbilježba* (a preliminary inscription understood as a form of priority notice) was entered into the land register in order to secure a claim to grant or terminate a right in the debtor's real estate or in a right registered for the benefit of the debtor, or in order to secure a claim to alter the contents or priority of such right, the creditor may claim satisfaction of their claim as a creditor of bankruptcy estate. The same applies in cases where the debtor has undertaken additional obligations with respect to the creditor and has failed, completely or partially, to fulfil them.[92] In such a situation, the bankruptcy administrator may not exercise his right to choose between assumption or rejection of the underlying sales contract. These rules apply according to *predbilježba* entered into the register of ships, register of ships under construction or into the aircraft register.[93] **9.51**

Finance lease contracts are not affected by the opening of the bankruptcy proceedings against the lessor, if the leased asset was transferred as a security to a third party (usually a bank) who had financed their acquisition or production.[94] **9.52**

Operational lease and rental contracts

Operational lease contracts and rental contracts that concern movables are subject to the general rules on effects of the opening of bankruptcy proceedings on executory contracts. **9.53**

The Croatian Bankruptcy Act includes special rules for operational lease contracts and rental contracts that concern immovables, in order to support the possibility of restructuring i.e., reorganization of the bankruptcy debtor or to alleviate the sale of rented or leased property. **9.54**

These contracts that concern real estate and premises do not cease to exist by the opening of bankruptcy proceedings, independently of whether the bankruptcy debtor is a landlord/a lessor or a tenant/a lessee.[95] Claims arising before the opening of the bankruptcy proceedings as well as damages for premature termination of such a contract may be brought by the counterparty only as a **9.55**

91 Ibid., art 185 (2). For more details, see Dika, *supra* note 57, at 88–92.
92 Ibid., art 184 (1) subparas 1 and 2.
93 Ibid., art 184 (2). For more details, see Dika, *supra* note 57, at 85–88.
94 Ibid., art 186 (1) subpara 2.
95 Ibid., art 186 (1).

creditor of the bankruptcy proceedings.[96] Claims arising after the opening of the bankruptcy proceedings shall be considered liabilities (obligations) of the bankruptcy estate.

9.56 The Bankruptcy Act especially protects the debtor who is a tenant or a lessee. If at the time of the opening of the bankruptcy proceedings the debtor as a tenant or a lessee has entered the real estate or premises, the bankruptcy administrator may terminate a rental or lease contract, without regard to the agreed duration, but within the notice period provided by the statute. If the administrator terminates the contract, the counterparty may claim damages for premature termination only as a creditor of the bankruptcy proceedings.[97] If at the time of the opening of the bankruptcy proceedings the debtor has not yet entered the real estate or premises, the bankruptcy administrator as well as the counterparty may withdraw from the contract. If the administrator withdraws from the contract, the counterparty may claim damages for premature termination of the contract only as a creditor of the bankruptcy proceedings. Each party shall within 15 days inform the other party, at its request, whether they intend to withdraw from the contract. If they fail to do so, they lose the right to withdraw.[98]

9.57 The law prohibits the termination of the rental and lease contracts after a petition for the opening of the bankruptcy proceedings has been filed against the debtor, who is a tenant or lessee. The contracts in such a case may not be terminated due to a default in the payment of rental or lease fees arising before the opening of the bankruptcy proceedings or due to the deterioration of the debtor's financial situation.[99]

9.58 If the bankruptcy debtor is a landlord or a lessor, the bankruptcy administrator may terminate the rental or lease contract according to the notice period provided by the statute, without regard to the agreed duration.[100] The Bankruptcy Act also has a few rules for a situation where the debtor as landlord or lessor assigned their future claim to rental or lease fees to a third party prior to the opening of bankruptcy proceedings.[101] If the bankruptcy administrator has sold real estate or premises let by the debtor, and if the third person as purchaser replaces the debtor as a party of the rental or lease

96 Ibid., art 186 (2).
97 Ibid., art 187 (1) subparas 1 and 2.
98 Ibid., art 187 (2) subparas 1–2.
99 Ibid., art 190.
100 Ibid., art 188 (4).
101 Ibid., art 188 (1), (2) and (3).

contract, the purchaser may terminate the rental or lease contract according to the notice period provided by the statute.[102]

Employment contracts

Opening the bankruptcy proceedings does not result in the automatic termination of employment contracts or service contract where the debtor is the employer.[103] Despite that, the law considers that the opening of bankruptcy proceedings is a special justified reason to terminate them.[104] **9.59**

After the opening of bankruptcy proceedings, both the bankruptcy administrator, acting on behalf of the debtor-employer, and the employee may cancel the employment contract, regardless of the agreed duration of the contract, and of the statutory or contractual provisions on protection of the employee. The notice period shall be one month, unless a statute provides for a shorter period.[105] If the employee believes that the termination of his employment contract is not legally valid, he may demand protection of his rights according to the provisions of the Employment (Labour) Act[106,107] **9.60**

As an aspect of the social protection of workers, the Agency for Insurance of Workers' Claims in Case of Employer's Bankruptcy shall pay the value of employees' salaries for the last three months before the opening of the bankruptcy proceedings instead of the debtor-employer and put itself in a position of a creditor of the bankruptcy proceedings in the concrete bankruptcy proceedings for those paid claims.[108] The additional three salaries of employees that have been earned before the opening of the bankruptcy proceedings shall be settled as costs of the bankruptcy proceedings.[109] The rest of salary claims and other claims regarding income based on employment, to which the rights have been acquired before the opening of the bankruptcy proceedings may be brought by an employee only as a creditor of the bankruptcy proceedings. In other words, these claims can be satisfied only *pro rata* from the distribution of the proceeds. But these claims are privileged because they are claims of the first higher payment rank.[110] **9.61**

---

102 Ibid., art 189. For more details, see Dika, *supra* note 57, at 96–114.

103 Ibid., art 191 (1).

104 Ibid., art 191 (2).

105 Ibid., art 191 (3).

106 *Zakon o radu*, Official Gazette *Narodne novine* no 2014/93.

107 Bankruptcy Act 2015, art 191 (4).

108 See Act on Insurance of Workers' Claims in Case of Employer's Bankruptcy, arts 2(a) and 3 (1) nos 1–4 para 2, *Zakon o osiguranju potraživanja radnika u slučaju stečaja poslodavaca*, Official Gazette *Narodne novine* nos 2008/86, 2013/80, 2015/82.

109 Bankruptcy Act 2015, art 155 (2).

110 Ibid., art 138 (1).

9.62 The bankruptcy administrator may, with the consent of the bankruptcy judge, enter into new, temporary employment contracts in order to finish the commenced business activities and prevent the occurrence of damage. These contracts may be agreed without the limitations prescribed by the general law on employment for the temporary employment contracts.[111] In that case the administrator shall determine the salaries and other income based on employment, with the consent of the bankruptcy judge, and in accordance with the statute and the collective agreement.[112] The salaries and other income based on employment, to which the rights have been acquired after the opening of the bankruptcy proceedings, shall be settled as obligations of the bankruptcy estate. In other words, the employees shall have the position of creditors of the bankruptcy estate for these claims.[113]

9.63 The employees' rights regarding participation in management (decision making) cease to exist by the opening of the bankruptcy proceedings. Agreements made with employees' council shall not bind the bankruptcy administrator.[114]

Pension contracts

9.64 The Croatian Bankruptcy Act does not contain special rules on pension contracts.

9.65 Neither pre-bankruptcy proceedings nor bankruptcy proceedings may be opened against the Pension Insurance Institution of Croatia.[115]

Utility contracts

9.66 There are no special rules in the law for utility contracts, i.e., for contracts that deal with supply of electricity, gas, water, etc. and that are usually contracts of indefinite duration. These contracts are subject to the general rules on the effects of the opening of the bankruptcy proceedings on executory contracts, including the rules on contracts with divisible performances.

Agency contracts, management contracts, power of attorney

9.67 Any debtor's mandate concerning the assets to be included in the bankruptcy estate shall expire upon the opening of the bankruptcy proceedings.[116] If the

---

111 Ibid., art 191 (5).

112 Ibid., art 191 (6).

113 Ibid., art 191 (7). For more details, see Dika, *supra* note 57, at 114–22; Jelena Čuveljak, 'Utjecaj otvaranja stečaja na prava iz radnog odnosa (Impact of the Opening of Bankruptcy Proceedings on Rights from Employment)' (2010, no 3) Pravo i porezi, 19–30.

114 Bankruptcy Act 2015, art 192.

115 Ibid., art 3 (2), (3).

116 Ibid., art 193 (1).

mandatary, who, without his fault, did not know of the opening of the bankruptcy proceedings, continues the agreed activity, it shall be considered that the mandate is still in force.

In such a case, the claims of the mandatary related to the continuation of activities shall be satisfied as claims of a creditor of the bankruptcy proceedings.[117] **9.68**

The mandatary is bound to continue with the activities in order to prevent the occurrence of damage, even after the opening of the bankruptcy proceedings, until the moment when the bankruptcy administrator is able to take care of such activities. The claims of the mandatory related to such continuation of activities shall be settled as obligations of the bankruptcy estate.[118] **9.69**

The presented rules accordingly apply to managerial contracts.[119] **9.70**

A proxy granted by the debtor with respect to the assets included in the bankruptcy estate shall expire upon the opening of the bankruptcy proceedings. The presented rules on mandate shall be applied accordingly to the proxy.[120] **9.71**

Expiry of offers

Offers made to the debtor, as well as offers made by the debtor, shall lose their validity on the day of the opening of bankruptcy proceedings, unless they have been accepted before that day.[121] **9.72**

(3) Extraordinary Management Procedure

The provisions of the Act on Procedure of Extraordinary Management in Companies of Systematic Importance for the Republic of Croatia do not address directly the treatment of executory contracts. Despite that, there are some its rules that we have to take into account when we consider legal effects of the opening of extraordinary management proceedings on the rights of creditors from the executory contracts. **9.73**

The extraordinary trustee shall undertake all actions necessary for the ordinary course of business of the Debtor (the parent company), including the necessary **9.74**

117 Ibid., art 193 (2) subparas 1 and 2.
118 Ibid., art 193 (3) subparas 1 and 2.
119 Ibid., art 195.
120 Ibid., art 196 (1) and (2).
121 Ibid., art 194.

payments, especially towards the employees of the parent and connected companies, regardless of the day when the claims of employees in connection with employment arose.[122] The extraordinary trustee shall be bound to acquire the consent of the creditor's committee for legal transactions regarding the disposal of real estate properties, shares in interconnected companies or in other companies and for the transfer of an economic unit whose value exceeds 3,500,000.00 Kuna.[123] The management in the Debtor's subsidiaries and its other interconnected companies may undertake only actions that are necessary for the ordinary course of business of these entities. For any other measure, the previous consent of the extraordinary trustee has to be acquired.[124] With previously acquired consent of the creditors' committee, the extraordinary trustee may take new financing in the name and on behalf of the Debtor in order to mitigate a systemic risk, continue the business operations, preserve the assets or make payments in the ordinary course of business. The claims of these new creditors shall have a higher rank in comparison to other creditors, with the sole exception of claims of the existing and former employees. In case of subsequent bankruptcy proceedings, these new creditors shall have the legal position of the creditors of the bankruptcy estate, what means that their claims shall be satisfied before the claims of bankruptcy creditors.[125] The management in the Debtor's subsidiaries or other interconnected companies have also authorization to take new financing, but only with the previous consent of the extraordinary trustee.[126] Further, the extraordinary trustee is authorized, with the previous consent of the creditors' committee, to pay due claims that arose before the opening of extraordinary management proceedings, if it is necessary in order to mitigate a systemic risk, continue the business operations, preserve the assets or make payments in the ordinary course of business.[127] The management in the Debtor's subsidiaries and other interconnected companies have the same authorization of making such payments for creditors of its company, if the extraordinary trustee gave his consent for it.[128] The claims of financial and credit institutions and claims of holders of securities are not considered as claims that can be paid in the ordinary course of business, except when they participate in a new financing.[129]

9.75 During the time between the day of the opening of extraordinary management proceedings and the day of their conclusion it is not allowed to initiate legal

122 EMPA, art 12 (7).
123 Ibid., art 12 (8).
124 Ibid., art 13 (4).
125 Ibid., art 39 (1) and (3).
126 Ibid., art 13 para 4 in connection with, art 39 (1) and (3).
127 Ibid., art 40 (1).
128 Ibid., art 40 (2).
129 Ibid., art 40 (4).

suits, enforcement proceedings, administrative proceedings and securement proceedings against the Debtor, its subsidiaries or its other interconnected companies. If these proceedings have already been commenced, they shall be stayed (discontinued) by the day of the opening of the extraordinary management proceedings.[130] The Bankruptcy Act shall be accordingly applied on the legal consequences of the opening of extraordinary management proceedings, including rules on executory contracts, unless otherwise provided by the EMPA.[131]

C. PRE-INSOLVENCY AGREED CONTRACTUAL REMEDIES

(1) Pre-bankruptcy proceedings

The Bankruptcy Act does not have explicit provisions on effects of the opening of the pre-bankruptcy proceedings on the pre-insolvency agreed contractual remedies. In our opinion, any contractual clause that circumvents statutory rules which limit the debtor's duty to fulfil his obligations during the pre-bankruptcy proceedings[132] and that modifies the statutory effects of a pre-bankruptcy agreement,[133] would be null and void – these statutory rules of the Bankruptcy Act are *ius cogens* and they have to be respected. **9.76**

(2) Bankruptcy proceedings

Contractual provisions that suspend or limit the application of statutory provisions of the Bankruptcy Act shall have no legal effect.[134] That is the explicit rule of the Bankruptcy Act. Therefore, pre-insolvency agreed contractual remedies that would, for example, exclude or restrict the bankruptcy administrator's right to choose between assumption and rejection of the executory contracts or which would exclude the administrator's statutory right to terminate a certain type of contract, would have no legal effect. **9.77**

(a) Termination and acceleration clauses

The Bankruptcy Act does not have an explicit rule on permissibility of termination and acceleration clauses, sometimes referred to as *ipso facto* clauses. **9.78**

130 Ibid., art 41 (1) and (2).
131 Ibid., art 37 (1).
132 See the Bankruptcy Act 2015, art 29 paras 1–3 and also, art 67 paras 1–2.
133 Ibid., art 62 (1).
134 Ibid., art 197.

9.79 A termination clause, a contractual provision that provides for the termination of the contract referring to the opening of the bankruptcy proceedings, would be, in our opinion, generally speaking null and void. Specifically, such a termination clause would circumvent the bankruptcy administrator's right to choose between assumption and rejection of an executory contract.

9.80 An acceleration clause, a contractual provision that provides for the acceleration of all payments owed by the debtor to a creditor referring to the opening of the bankruptcy proceedings, would be, in our opinion, generally speaking also null and void. Such a clause would as well circumvent the administrator's right to choose between assumption and rejection of an executory contract.

9.81 Unfortunately, this is mainly a doctrinal debate as courts in Croatia have yet to decide cases that deal with these issues.

(b) Close-out netting provisions

9.82 The Bankruptcy Act explicitly allows netting agreements,[135] so that close-out netting clauses may be regarded as valid and enforceable.

(c) Flip clauses

9.83 The Bankruptcy Act does not contain explicit provisions on permissibility of a ranking agreement between the (later insolvent) debtor and a creditor that would foresee a lower ranking of claims of the creditor.

9.84 The Bankruptcy Act also does not contain explicit provision on permissibility of ranking agreements among creditors which would allow *inter se* ranking swaps.

9.85 There are no published court decisions in Croatia that address these issues.

(d) Conditional rights

9.86 The Bankruptcy Act does not explicitly address the clauses where parties agree that the debtor will be deprived of property or certain rights upon the opening of the bankruptcy proceedings. In our opinion such clauses would be null and void, if they circumvent the bankruptcy administrator's statutory powers on executory contracts.

135 Ibid., art 182 (6) and (7).

(e) *Penalty provisions*

Contractual penalties that would exclude or restrict the bankruptcy administrator's statutory powers regarding executory contracts would be, in our opinion, null and void. **9.87**

(3) Extraordinary management procedure

The Act on Procedure of Extraordinary Management in Companies of Systematic Importance for the Republic Croatia does not include explicit provisions on the treatment of pre-insolvency contractual remedies. What we said about statutory treatment of contractual remedies agreed by the parties in solvent time regarding the opening of bankruptcy proceedings, we can accordingly say for their treatment in the case of the opening of extraordinary management proceedings. Namely, the Bankruptcy Act shall subsidiarly apply in the extraordinary management proceedings.[136] **9.88**

D. REFORMS

Special provisions on the legal effects of the opening of the bankruptcy proceedings on the executory contracts have existed in the Croatian bankruptcy law for decades, even during the socialism, when the Republic of Croatia was a part of Socialist Federal Republic of Yugoslavia.[137] **9.89**

Most of the rules on executory contracts in the bankruptcy proceedings that exist under the current Croatian Bankruptcy Act of 2015 have already been included in the Croatian Bankruptcy Act of 1996.[138] **9.90**

The new Bankruptcy Act 2015 only introduced additional rules on the permissibility of netting agreements and rules according to which the opening of the bankruptcy proceedings does not affect the so-called qualified financial contracts that are defined by this statute.[139] The introduction of these rules was suggested by the representatives of the credit institutions in the Working Group of the Ministry of Justice that was entrusted with the task to draft the new bankruptcy bill. **9.91**

---

136 EMPA, art 37 (1).

137 See for example Act on Compulsory Settlement, Bankruptcy and Liquidation, arts 93, 108–111 and 119. *Zakon o prisilnoj nagodbi, stečaju i likvidaciji*, *Official Gazette of the Socialist Federal Republic of Yugoslavia* no 1989/84.

138 *Stečajni zakon*, Official Gazette *Narodne novine* nos 1996/44, 1999/29, 2000/129, 2003/123, 2006/82, 2010/116, 2012/25, 2012/133.

139 Bankruptcy Act 2015, art 182 (6) and (7).

9.92 Unfortunately, the Government's Explanation of the Final Proposal of the Draft of the Bankruptcy Act[140] does not provide any evidence that the Working Group, which was preparing the new law, took into consideration complex questions of the legal permissibility of the pre-insolvency agreed contractual remedies discussed in the previous section.

9.93 During preparations of the new Bankruptcy Act, the legal experts of the World Bank had a meeting with the members of the Working Group of the Ministry of Justice and gave their opinion on the proposed solutions of the new law, but primarily concerning the pre-bankruptcy proceedings.

9.94 The new Bankruptcy Act of 2015 was drafted in a hurry before the election. In our opinion, it leaves much room for further elaboration and improvement. This in particular appears to be the case for the provisions on pre-bankruptcy proceedings. The practitioners are also not satisfied with this law. Therefore, we can expect that changes and amendments to the Bankruptcy Act will soon follow. This would then also be an opportunity to introduce explicit and precise rules on treatment of pre-insolvency agreed contractual remedies.

9.95 The Act on Procedure of Extraordinary Management in Companies of Systematic Importance for the Republic of Croatia was written in an even greater hurry and without the advice of insolvency law experts. The authors believe that this Act does not give adequate rules and solutions in situations where a group of companies faces insolvency. The Act breaches some of the most important principles of civil, company and insolvency law,[141] and as such should be replaced with a complete new legal framework that would properly regulate insolvency within a group of interconnected companies.

E. CONCLUDING REMARKS

9.96 The main 'drivers' of reform in the area of the bankruptcy law or insolvency law in Croatia are neither a need to secure international funds or political support, nor a desire to boost national competitiveness and international attractiveness.

9.97 The principal motive for the reform is the necessity, perceived by the legal and business community, to have good and efficient insolvency procedures. This

140 *Vladino Obrazloženje Konačnog prijedloga Stečajnoga zakona*, Klasa: 022–03/14–01/183, Ur. broj: 65–15–07 od 14. 5. 2015.

141 See Garašić, *supra* note 42, at 5–29.

necessity is accentuated in a situation where the country's economy is struggling in the aftermath of the financial crisis.

The principal supporters of the reform are often academics and bankruptcy **9.98**
judges as well as banks.

Of course, as a member state of the European Union, Croatia must always **9.99**
respect legal sources of the European Union law and follow recommendations of the EU-bodies and development in all areas of its law, including insolvency law.

In our opinion, Croatia has a good general framework of rules on the **9.100**
treatment of executory contracts in the bankruptcy proceedings. Statutory improvements are desirable in the area of the pre-bankruptcy proceedings, because the effects of the opening of these proceedings on the debtor's contracts could be better regulated. Statutory improvements are also desirable with reference to the treatment of the pre-insolvency agreed contractual remedies, in order to enhance legal predictability and certainty. Completely new rules are necessary regarding insolvency of a group of interconnected (related) companies, including the rules that would regulate executory contracts in such a situation.

10

NATIONAL REPORT FOR DENMARK

Line Herman Langkjaer

A. INTRODUCTION TO THE AVAILABLE INSOLVENCY PROCEDURES

10.01 In 1872 the first systematic overall insolvency regulation was introduced in Denmark. The bankruptcy act of 1872 was based on insolvency principles which were developing all over Europe and highly influenced by the Norwegian bankruptcy act of 1863 and the Prussian *konkursordnung* of 1855. Insolvency law was – and still is – basically considered a public aid to creditors faced with a debtor in distress and the regulation has been based on the principle of *creditor autonomy*.[1] By the late 50s it was concluded by the Danish parliament that the insolvency law was out of date and a new bankruptcy act was introduced in 1977 still focusing on the creditors with a focus on reducing

1 Udkast til lov om gaeldsordning udarbejdet af den ved kgl. Resolution af 8. august 1930 nedsattekommission, 164, Report from Konkursrådet, *Betænkning* om konkurs og tvangsakkord (Betænkning nr. 606, 1971), 33.

administrative costs, abandoning several privileges and introducing a more efficient system of avoidance rules where bad faith is usually not required.

There are two collective formal insolvency procedures available for a distressed business in Denmark and both are governed by the Danish Bankruptcy Act (DBA):[2] '*Bankruptcy proceedings*' and '*Restructuring proceedings*'.[3] Both proceedings are commenced by a court order on the basis of a petition presented by either the debtor or a creditor.[4] **10.02**

'*Bankruptcy*' is the main insolvency procedure, and approximately 97 per cent of all formal insolvency procedures commenced in Denmark are bankruptcy procedures.[5] Bankruptcy is basically a liquidation procedure where the debtor's assets are liquidated and the proceeds are distributed between the creditors. The overarching purpose of 'bankruptcy' is to maximize the recovery rate for the creditors. **10.03**

The '*Restructuring proceeding*' was introduced in 2011 for the purpose of rescuing viable businesses through a restructuring plan encompassing either a business transfer of the debtor's assets or a compulsory composition.[6] The proposed plan *may* also consist of various initiatives such as downscaling, debt-for-equity conversion or appointment of a new management. The proposal must be approved by the creditors and ratified by the bankruptcy court.[7] A ratified proposal binds all creditors, consenting and non-consenting (cram-down effect). If the plan is not approved by the creditors within 11 months of the filing for restructuring, a bankruptcy proceeding is automatically opened against the debtor.[8] **10.04**

---

2 Consolidated Act No 11 of 6 January 2014, Bankruptcy Act, with later amendments, 'Danish Bankruptcy Act' ('Konkursloven'), (herinaftaer DBA).

3 Judicial debt relief is available as a formal procedure for natural persons.

4 Where a creditor files a petition for 'restructuring' it requires consent from the management of the debtor, cf. DBA, s 11 (4) and DBA, s 11 (5). If this cannot be achieved, the administrator must take over the management during the restructuring procedure or the petition must be converted to a petition for bankruptcy instead.

5 Ernst and Young: Rekonstruktion, *Hvordan virker reglerne i praksis*, September 2014.

6 DBA s (10) and Report from Konkursrådet, Betænkning om konkurs og tvangsakkord (Betænkning nr. 1512, 2009), 248 and 256. The definition of a business transfer is much like the definition in Council Directive 2001/23/EC of 12 March 2001, art 1.

7 DBA, s 13 d and DBA, s 13 e (1). The proposal will be ratified unless errors in the procedure or proposals have been of material importance to the result of the voting, if the proposal is contrary to rules of law or if a creditor has been giving advantages outside the restructuring. If the terms of the proposal are disproportionate to the debtor's financial position, the court will also deny ratification.

8 Ulrik Rammeskow Bang-Pedersen, *Rammeskow Bang-Pedersen, Højlund Christensen, Sommer Jensen, Jul Madsen og Kærsgaard Mylin*: Rekonstruktion – teori og praksis (1st supp, 1st edn, Jurist- og Økonomforbundets Forlag, 2011), 435. In contrast, in 2000 the average length of the bankruptcy proceedings was 21.6 months, see more: Prime Minister's secretariat: 'Bilag om behandling af konkursboer' http://www.stm.dk/multimedia/Bilag_om_behandling_af_konkursboer_9.pdf last accessed 5 December 2018.

(1) Actors in the proceedings

10.05 The bankruptcy estate is administered by the administrator ('*Kurator*') who is appointed by the bankruptcy court. The administrator has exclusive powers to manage and realize the estate, i.e., whether the realization of the debtor's assets – both secured and non-secured – should be done as a business transfer as a going-concern or a piecemeal sale.[9]

10.06 In the restructuring proceeding the debtor is still in possession of his assets. The bankruptcy court appoints a restructuring administrator ('*Rekonstruktør*') who facilitates, assists and supervises the debtor under the procedure and a restructuring accountant ('*Tillidsmand*') who prepares and approves financial material for supporting the procedure.[10] The debtor is not entitled to enter into any transactions of *material significance* without the consent of the restructuring administrator during the proceedings, and on approval by the creditors the restructuring administrator can take over the management and control of the business.[11]

(2) Requirements

10.07 The overall substantial requirements for entering into one of the two formal procedures are generally the same.[12] The debtor must be *insolvent*. Insolvency is defined as 'when the debtor is unable to meet its liabilities as and when they fall due, unless such inability must be deemed to be only temporary'.[13] The insolvency definition is based on a cash flow analysis.

10.08 There is no formal obligation for the debtor to file for bankruptcy or restructuring but hesitation to do so can result in liability for the management.[14] Liability may occur if the management continues to operate a business at a time where it should be evident that the business is insolvent and continued operation will result in loss for the creditors.[15]

---

9 If, however, a secured creditor will not receive total fulfillment by the realization of the secured assets, he must accept the sale. Since 2005 it has been possible to secure assets by a floating charge and the creditor who has secured his assets by a floating charge plays an major role in the bankruptcy proceedings.

10 DBA, s 11 a (1).

11 DBA, s 12 a.

12 On procedural requirements see, DBA, s 7, DBA, s 11 and DBA, s 22 and 23.

13 DBA, s 17(2).

14 Consolidated Act No. 1089 of 14 September 2015 on Public and Private Limited Companies, s 361 ('*Selskabsloven*').

15 For more recent examples, see case law from the Supreme Court: UfR2015.2075H; UfR2015.257 and UfR1998.1137H.

(3) Out-of-court restructuring

Out-of-court proceedings are used quite significantly as an alternative to the formal proceedings.[16] The exact numbers of out-of-court restructuring procedures is uncertain since an out-of-court proceeding is not automatically known to the public. However, fairly large companies have undergone informal restructuring in recent years. **10.09**

An out-of-court restructuring is not supervised by the court and is basically an agreement between the debtor and the participating creditors. Such an agreement has no cram-down effect on the non-participating creditors. In contrast to the formal proceedings, the success of an out-of-court proceeding relies on the creditors' will to participate. The out-of-court proceedings are in principle purely governed by ordinary contractual regulation and not the DBA. Against this backdrop out-of-court proceedings are considered much more flexible than the formal restructuring procedure. This flexibility facilitates that an out-of-court restructuring plan can be designed on a more individual basis. However, the flexibility and lack of court supervision may also involve risks for both the management and the advisers during the proceedings. **10.10**

As only contractual law governs the out-of-court proceedings, the principle of *paritas creditorium* does not as a principle rule the possible outcome. In reality it is, however, hard to imagine that creditors will accept a differentiation of the treatment of creditors unless solid reasons dictate such a solution.[17] **10.11**

The out-of-court proceedings do not prevent the creditors from enforcing their individual rights but a stay of execution can be, and is often, agreed upon by the parties. **10.12**

B. TREATMENT OF EXECUTORY CONTRACTS

Historically, the treatment of executory contracts was already included in the first Danish Bankruptcy Act of 1872. The regulation on executory contracts has however undergone significant changes in 1977 and more recently in 2011. **10.13**

---

16 Report from Konkursrådet, *Betænkning om rekonstruktion mv* (Betænkning nr. 1512, 2009), 25.

17 Christian Jul Madsen, *Rammeskow Bank-Pedersen, Højlund Christensen, Sommer Jensen, Jul Madsen og Kærsgaard Mylin*: Rekonstruktion – teori og praksis (1st sup, 1st edn, Jurist- og Økonomforbundets Forlag, 2011), 40.

10.14 The opening of insolvency proceedings does at least in theory not automatically affect the executory contracts agreed upon prior to the opening of insolvency proceedings. An executory contract is not automatically terminated or suspended by the opening of the insolvency proceedings. Enforcement measures are, however, stayed as is the case of all claims against the debtor.[18]

(1) Regulation on executory contracts in DBA

10.15 The treatment of executory contracts is regulated in the DBA. The legal framework grants rights to both the estate and the counterparty.[19] The possibility to exercise these rights has the practical consequence that the executory contracts are widely affected by the insolvency proceedings. The framework purportedly ensures that the estate maintains the legal position which the debtor had prior to the commencement of insolvency proceedings to the benefit of the interest of the creditors.

10.16 The rights granted by the DBA concern only mutual contracts which have not yet been performed by the debtor. In theory it is of no importance whether the counterparty has performed or not but the nature of a contract which has been performed by the counterparty results in a slightly different treatment to these contracts as seen below.

10.17 The core element of the legal framework is the permission for the estate/debtor-in-possession to assume/continue the beneficial contracts and reject the contracts which do not represent economic value for the creditors.

10.18 The legal framework in DBA is striving to balance between the interest of the creditors and the interest of the concerned counterparty; however, as seen below, it is quite easily observed that the legal framework does favour the interest of the creditors.

(2) Assumption of executory contracts

10.19 The administrator has a right on behalf of the estate to choose which – if any – of the debtors' contracts are to be assumed.[20] The choice will be based on an assessment of the economic value of the contract for the estate. If the administrator has assumed a contract which later proves to be detrimental to the creditors he can be held personally liable if he has acted in bad faith or

---

18 DBA, s 31.

19 DBA, chapter 7 and DBA, s 12 o.

20 DBA, s 55 (1).

negligently but the administrator enjoys a fairly large margin of business discretion and liability only rarely occurs.[21]

Some contracts cannot be assumed by the estate due to the character of the contract or due to statutory provisions outside insolvency law.[22] The DBA does not give an exhaustive list or even exemplify which contracts are to be exempted, but contracts that require the debtor's personal qualifications to perform in accordance with the contract as well as loan agreements are listed in the preparatory works as examples of contracts that will be exempted.[23] **10.20**

The administrator assumes a contract by declaration or by conduct.[24] Case law shows that assuming a contract by conduct requires a certain element of active involvement from the estate, i.e., the active use of rental goods.[25] **10.21**

The administrator is not obliged to exercise his right to assume and in general there is not a time limit to do so.[26] This leaves the counterparty hanging in uncertainty. Out of interest to the counterparty the administrator is obliged to decide whether or not he will exercise the right to assume by a request of the counterparty. The decision must be made without undue delay.[27] In most cases notice should be given within a week, however, this is dependent on the complexity and character of the contract. If the counterparty according to the contract is to deliver perishable goods, the notification by the administrator should, for instance, be given immediately. A contract is deemed to be rejected if the administrator does not exercise his right to assume within the time limit. **10.22**

In business tenant lease contracts where the debtor is the non-performing party, the counterparty has no possibility to retain his performance and the administrator is therefore obliged to give notice immediately after the counterparty has requested him to do so. If the administrator fails to do so, remuneration from the time of the commencement of the bankruptcy and until notification on non-assumption will be treated as administrative expenses.[28] **10.23**

---

21 The liability will be based on non-statutory tort law based on a general negliance standard.

22 DBA, s 53. Statutory provisions that cause a contract to be exempted from assumption are rare but can e.g., be found in Consolidated Act No 251 of 21 March 2017 on Securities Trading. ('*Værdipapirhandelsloven*').

23 Report from Konkursrådet *Betænkning om konkurs og tvangsakkord* (Betænkning nr. 606, 1971), 120–21.

24 Ibid.

25 In a Supreme Court ruling the use of a leased real estate in a time period of two months was not considered enough to declare assumption by conduct; see UfR2005.3090H.

26 For employment contracts, some construction contracts and business tenant contracts the regulation is slightly different.

27 DBA, s 55 (2).

28 DBA, s 62.

10.24 Time limits on notification agreed upon prior to the insolvency proceeding are in general upheld as long as the time limit allows the administrator reasonable time to assess the particular contract. Such time limits are seen in standard agreements, i.e., AB 92 regarding contractual contracts.[29]

10.25 Employment contracts are treated slightly different than other contracts. Notification on assumption of an employment contract must be given by the administrator as soon as possible. If the administrator has not notified the employers two weeks from the date of the commencement of the bankruptcy, claims for remuneration from the commencement date and until the date of the notification will be treated as administrative expenses, regardless of whether or not the employer has been working for the estate.[30]

(3) The effects of the assumption of a contract

10.26 Once a contract has been assumed, the estate becomes liable for the performance of the contract as a whole. All claims of the counterparty incurred in performing the contract will be treated as administrative expenses.[31]

10.27 This includes all types of contractual claims, i.e., remuneration (considerations) and damages, and is not limited to the future performances on the contract.[32] Pre-commencement claims relating to the contract will also be treated as administrative expenses. Claims that normally would be treated as ordinary unsecured claims are in this way elevated to priority claims. This effect of assumption necessitates the administrator to carefully assess the contract and especially carefully examine whether the debtor has breached the contract prior to commencement. Administrators have, due to the risk of elevating major claims to administrative expenses, shown some reluctance to assume a contract.

10.28 When a contract is assumed, the estate must perform according to the stipulated terms of the contract.[33] As a safeguard for the counterparty it is therefore not possible to partially assume a contract.[34] The rationale for this rule is that the agreed terms of the contract must be seen as a result of a

---

29 AB92 – General conditions for the provisions of works and supplies within building and engineering, s 42(2).

30 DBA, s 63.

31 DBA, s 93(3).

32 Cf. UfR1955.1009H and Kim Sommer Jensen, *Rammeskow Bang-Pedersen, Højlund Christensen, Sommer Jensen*: Konkurs (1st supp, 1st edn, Jurist- og Økonomforbundets Forlag 2014) 307.

33 As a supplementary protection for the counterparty a right to require adequate security for the performance of the contract, cf. DBA, s 57.

34 DBA, s 56 (1).

negotiation process between the parties, and the estate should not be able to retain the benefits of a contract without accepting the burdens.

To avoid the counterparty exercising his contractual rights, i.e., termination of the contract, the estate must perform according to the contract but also cure breaches relating to the time prior to the opening of the insolvency.[35] **10.29**

The effects of assumption of a contract where the parties have agreed upon periodical payments by the debtor (*'Continuous contracts'*), i.e., contracts on electricity supply, insurance or lease contracts are slightly different than the effects of assuming other executory contracts. Only considerations arising for services rendered after the issuance of the commencement order are treated as administrative expenses.[36] Obligations prior to this will be treated as if the contract was not assumed. **10.30**

The limitation reduces the reluctance shown by the administrators to assume the most necessary contracts since it reduces the immediate cost relating to assumption of such contracts. According to the *travaux preparatoires* the interest of the counterparty is adequately protected since the assumption of a continuous contract does not result in an additional burden to the counterparty since all additional costs for the counterparty will be treated as administrative expenses.[37] Based on the *pari passu principle*, consideration relating to performance prior to the commencement of a continuous contract is treated like all other claims on the estate.[38] The limitation is presumably not only applicable to the considerations. Also a claim for damages which arose before the opening of insolvency will presumably be treated as if the contract was not assumed.[39] **10.31**

It is also possible for the estate to assume a 'continuous contract' temporarily. The estate is entitled to step back from an assumption causing only consideration claims arising from the time of the commencement of the bankruptcy **10.32**

35 DBA s 58 (2).

36 DBA s 56 (2).

37 Report from *Konkursrådet* (Betænkning nr. 606 of 1971 om konkurs og tvangsakkord), p. 123.

38 Contrary to regular contracts, continuous contracts are per se severable so accepting a partial performance by the bankruptcy estate is not considered an extra burden for the counterparty, cf. Report from Konkursrådet, *Betænkning om konkurs og tvangsakkord* (Betænkning II 606, 1971), 123.

39 Neither statutory law nor case law has provided any answers. The prevailing opinion in legal literature argues for such a limitation. For a detailed discussion in Danish see; Kim Sommer Jensen, *supra* note 32, 309–12. Lars Lindencrone Petersen and Anders Ørgaard: *Konkursloven med kommentarer*, (1st supp, 13 edn, Karnov Group 2016) 504, ctr. Bernhard Gomard, *Obligationsret, 3. del, ved Torsten Iversen*, (1st supp, 2nd edn, Jurist- og Økonomforbundets Forlag 2009) 49.

order and until the termination to be treated as administrative expenses.[40] This right to step back from the assumption makes it financially possible for the estate to assume contracts that are normally non-terminative, i.e., financial leasing contracts.

(4) Protection of the counterparty in the DBA

10.33 The DBA gives the 'upper hand' to the estate. The opening of the insolvency proceeding leaves the counterparty in an uncertain position. Will the estate assume the contract or will the counterparty be left with nothing but an unsecured claim?

10.34 To alleviate the position for the counterparty, the DBA sets out a few legal rights for the counterparty.

10.35 As mentioned above, in theory the insolvency proceedings do not affect the existing executory contracts. The counterparty is therefore entitled to perform according to the contract. But the counterparty cannot enforce his claim against the debtor and cannot demand performance by the estate. To minimize the risk to the counterparty who has not yet performed, the DBA entitles the counterparty to retain his performance until adequate security is delivered by the estate and the estate has declared that it will assume the contract.[41] In practice the opening of insolvency therefore suspends the performance of the executory contracts.

10.36 Even when the estate has assumed the contract and claims are elevated to priority claims, supplementary protection is given to the counterparty.

(5) The effects of non-assumption (rejection of the contract)

10.37 When the administrator does not assume a contract or when the time limit initiated by the counterparty has passed, the counterparty is entitled to terminate the contract and file a claim for non-performance of the contract notwithstanding the normal contractual requirements to termination are not fulfilled.[42] Hence, the rejection of the contract does not automatically result in termination or expiration of the contract.

---

40 DBA, s 55 (3).

41 DBA, s 54 and DBA, s 58, cf. Kim Sommer Jensen, *supra* note 32, 313.

42 DBA, s 59 (1), cf. Bernhard Gomard, Obligationsret, 3. del, ved Torsten Iversen, (1st supp, 2nd edn, Jurist- og Økonomforbundets Forlag, 2009) p. 40. If the counterparty has already performed he is, however, not entitled to terminate the contract but is entitled to claim damages, cf. DBA, s 59 (3).

The counterparty might not always want to terminate the contract in spite of the debtor's insolvency and the non-assumption notice from the administrator. While the rejection does not oblige the counterparty to terminate the contract, claims relating to the contract will remain ordinary unsecured claims and the counterparty cannot demand performance of a non-assumed contract unless the goods subject to the contract are in the care of the estate and can be identified.[43] **10.38**

(6) Long-term contracts and indefinite contracts

As seen above the non-assumption of the contract does not automatically expire or terminate the contract. When the counterparty terminates the contract, the legal effects thereof will in general be determined by contract law. **10.39**

Exemption to this is given by the DBA section 61 (1) which grants the administrator the right to terminate a contract upon giving *usual* or *reasonable* notice even if a longer notice or irrevocability has been agreed upon under the contract. The reduced termination paves the way in a reduction of the creditor's claim in the estate. This right can be exercised irrespective of the estate's assumption of the contract or not. The provision plays a key role towards reducing claims relating to business tenant lease contracts and employment contracts where long notices often occur. **10.40**

It can be difficult to establish what the usual or reasonable notice is for a given contract. Guidelines for this evaluation can be found in legislation such as the Salaried Employees Act[44] or in 'standard contracts' for certain types of contracts. It is worth noticing that the provision has no practical effect on financial leasing contracts since their non-terminate clauses are considered usual and reasonable.[45] **10.41**

The possibility for the estate to reduce the agreed notice is only applicable upon contracts that govern a so-called *'continuous legal relationship'* such as lease contracts, employment contracts, etc.[46] Exempted also are contracts where the **10.42**

---

43 In this case the counterparty will be seen as the beneficial owner who's right to segregate the assets is governed by DBA, s 82. For more details see; Kim Sommer Jensen, *supra* note 32, 330.

44 Consolidation Act No. 81 of 3 February 2009 on the legal relationship between employers and salaried employees (*'Funktionærloven'*), with further amendments.

45 DBA, s 98, however, governs that certain claims under a lease agreement that are equivalent to interest accrued after the date of the bankruptcy order are considered deferred claims.

46 *Konkursrådet* is proposing to eliminate the possibility to use section 61 on employment contracts, see more: Report from Konkursrådet,*Betænkning om ansattes retsstilling under insolvensbehandling* (Betænkning 1555, 2015).

agreed notice is safeguarded against the debtor's creditors by registration in the land register or other similar registrations in public registers.

10.43 The counterparty can be entitled to file a claim for damages due to the shortened notice.[47] The practical use of this right is very limited and is only applicable if the result of the termination will lead to the unjust treatment of the counterparty.

(7) Mandatory rules

10.44 The provisions on executory contracts in DBA are considered mandatory. Contractual clauses entered by the parties prior to the opening of insolvency proceedings that exclude or limit the rights given to the administrator (*ipso facto* clauses) cannot be enforced by the counterparty.[48] Consequently, the administrator may assume an executory contract notwithstanding an *ipso facto* clause.

10.45 An *ipso facto* clause becomes unenforceable but not invalid in the event of insolvency proceedings and can be seen as a protection of the interest of the collective creditors. A debtor in the negotiation process of the contract will naturally safeguard his own rights but there is hardly any certainty that a debtor will have an interest in protecting the later estate and therefore other creditors' interest.[49]

10.46 An exemption to the mandatory character is found in the Danish regulation on Close-out netting agreements which are regulated in the Danish Capital Markets Act.[50] Close-out netting agreements entered into before the insolvency proceeding can be enforced by the counterparty.[51] However, a contractual clause where all payments under a derivative or financial agreement are suspended in case of insolvency is not necessarily binding for the estate.

(8) Executory contracts in restructuring proceedings

10.47 The restructuring procedure was introduced into Danish law in 2011 to encourage the rescue of viable businesses while safeguarding the interest of the creditors. The purpose of the procedure thereby differs from the bankruptcy

47 DBA, s 61 (3).

48 Report from Konkursrådet, *Betænkning* om konkurs og tvangsakkord (Betænkning nr. 606, 1971),121.

49 Ibid.

50 The Danish Capital Markets Act implements the EU Collateral Directive.

51 The Danish Capital Markets Act, s 206 (1). See more on close-out netting in Danish law, Ulrik Rammeskow Bang-Pedersen, *Slutafregning* (1st supp, 1st edn, Thompson Gad-Jura 2005).

proceeding and this difference is reflected in the treatment of executory contracts in *restructuring*. Although there are many similarities between the two sets of regulation, the intention of rescuing the business results in more extensive rights for the debtor-in-possession.[52]

(9) Continuation of the executory contracts

Prima facie, contrary to the situation in the bankruptcy proceedings the debtor is still in possession of his assets and the commencement of the restructuring proceedings does not trigger a change of the contractual parties. Contracts, however, are not automatically continued but the DBA grants a similar right for the debtor-in-possession to continue an executory contract.[53] **10.48**

The competence of choice is entrusted to the debtor-in-possession but he must have an explicit consent from the restructuring administrator.[54] **10.49**

Differentiating from the regulation in bankruptcy the DBA grants the right for a debtor-in-possession to *re-establish* contracts which have been terminated by the counterparty.[55] Contracts can be *re-established* up until four weeks after the termination. Where the counterparty has acted in accordance with the termination, the right to re-establish is extinguished i.e., if the counterparty has already sold or leased the concerned object to a third party. **10.50**

(10) The effects of continuation

The effects of the continuation are quite similar to the effects of the assumption in the bankruptcy proceeding.[56] The rights and liabilities remain the same after the continuation of the contract and the claims according to the contract will be treated as preferential claims according to the DBA section 94. **10.51**

---

52 Some executory contracts fall out of the scope of the regulation in the DBA due to the character of the contract or due to statutory provisions outside insolvency law, DBA, s 12.

53 DBA, s 12 o (1).

54 DBA, s 12 o (1) See more on the requirements of the consent – Kim Sommer Jensen, *Rammeskow Bank-Pedersen, Højlund Christensen, Sommer Jensen, Jul Madsen og Kærsgaard Mylin*: Rekonstruktion – teori og praksis (1st sup, 1st edn, Jurist- og Økonomforbundets Forlag 2011), 338 and DBA, s 12 o (3).

55 DBA, s 12 o (1).

56 Report from Konkursrådet, Betænkning om rekonstruktion (Betænkning nr. 1512, 2009), 228 and Kim Sommer Jensen, Rammeskow Bank-Pedersen, Højlund Christensen, Sommer Jensen, Jul Madsen og Kærsgaard Mylin: Rekonstruktion – teori og praksis (1st sup, 1st edn, Jurist- og Økonomforbundets Forlag 2011), 345–57.

10.52 The success of the restructuring procedure normally presupposes that the debtor can continue its operations as before the commencement of the procedure. Continued operations require a certain cash flow. Given the purpose of the procedure, the DBA prohibits the counterparty to demand additional security such as demanding provision of security for performing according to the contract, withholding its performance or demanding performance prior to its due date.[57] Employers are, however, entitled to demand security for the next payment falling due.[58]

10.53 Where the debtor chooses not to continue the contract, the counterparty is entitled to terminate the contract according to the DBA section 12 r (1).

(11) Assignment of contracts

10.54 As stated above the restructuring of an insolvent debtor involves either a business transfer or a compulsory composition. To maximize the price of the business when transferred as part of a business rescue it is of extreme importance that key contracts can be part of the transferal.

10.55 In the interest of the collective creditors the DBA therefore grants the right for the debtor-in-possession to assign the continued executory contract to the buyer of the business without consent from the contracting party.[59] The right to assign can only be exercised as part of a business transfer and not in a one-off asset sale. All continued contracts can be transferred without consent apart from contracts where such a transfer would be contrary to the legal nature of the contract, i.e., if the contract can only be fully performed by the original contracting party.

10.56 Not only does this right for the debtor-in-possession secure the value of the on-going business, it also quickens and eases the negotiating process since the seller does not need to secure the consent from the contracting parties.

C. LEGISLATIVE REFORMS SINCE 2000

10.57 One significant reform has been introduced to the insolvency regime in Denmark since 2000 – the introduction of the restructuring procedure in

57 DBA, s 12 q.
58 DBA, s 12 q (2).
59 DBA, s 14 c (2).

2011. Current reforms are possibly on their way based on the EU directive on preventive restructuring frameworks.[60]

(1) Introducing the restructuring procedure in 2011

10.58 The restructuring proceeding was introduced in 2011. The reform was politically initiated by an action plan launched in 2003 by the Ministry of Economics and Business Affairs on improving the framework conditions for entrepreneurs.[61] The action plan aimed for Denmark being a top performing entrepreneurial society to secure further growth.[62] The existing legal framework on insolvency law was seen as a limiting factor on the willingness to take risks which was stated as essential to promote an entrepreneurial society.[63] Through changes in insolvency law the government intended to encourage restarters to conduct business in Denmark.

10.59 As is the tradition in relation to amendments in Danish insolvency law, a standing expert committee on insolvency law ('*Konkursrådet*') drafted a proposal and an explanatory report.[64] The proposal was also subject to a public consultation procedure. However, the impact of the consultation was fairly insignificant. In relation to the treatment of executory contracts the original proposal only underwent a few alterations based on a statement from 'Finance and Leasing, The Association of Danish Finance Houses'.[65]

10.60 Although the original intention from the government was seen as a way of promoting the entrepreneurship and encouraging restarters, it follows from the explanatory report by the expert committee that the new legal framework intended to support the rescue of viable but insolvent businesses but not necessarily the debtor behind it. The maximization of the recovery rate is still seen as the main purpose of the procedure and the amendments in the treatment of executory contracts should be seen in this view.[66]

---

60 As of 22 November 2016 a new EU directive had been proposed by the European Commission. See COM(2016) 723 final. Since the proposal is based on Arts 53 and 114, and not Title V of part three of the Treaty on the Functioning of the European Union, the final directive will have effect in Denmark.

61 Report from Konkursrådet, Betænkning om rekonstruktion (Betænkning nr. 1512, 2009), 14.

62 Ministry of Economic and Business Affairs, The action plan for entrepreneurs (2003), p. 6, available at: http://www.stm.dk/multimedia/Handlingsplan_for_iv_rks_ttere.pdf accessed 8 September 2017.

63 Ministry of Economic and Business Affairs, *The action plan for entrepreneurs* (2003), 12, available at: http://www.stm.dk/multimedia/Handlingsplan_for_iv_rks_ttere.pdf accessed 8 September 2017.

64 Members of *Konkursrådet* are appointed by the Ministry of Justice and the current members are lawyers, judges, accountants and academia.

65 The Association of Danish Law Firms stated more profound changes to the proposals but these were not implemented in the final draft. See more: http://www.danskeadvokater.dk/Hoeringssvar.aspx?ID=19057&Action=1&NewsId=12841&currentPage=43&PID=39735, accessed 8 September 2017.

66 Report from Konkursrådet, Betænkning om rekonstruktion (Betænkning nr. 1512, 2009), 56.

(2) Changes in the treatment of executory contracts in 2011

10.61 The reform in 2011 brought significant changes to the treatment of executory contracts in insolvency procedures. Most importantly the implementation of the above-mentioned rights to continue the debtor's contracts in the restructuring procedure, including the possibility to re-establish already terminated contracts and the possibility to step back from an assumed or continued contract.

10.62 Based on the explanatory works the reform had no intention of harmonizing the existing law with international regulation. However, a comparative study served as an inspirational background but no references in the report were made to foreign regulation.

(3) Future reforms of the insolvency framework

10.63 *Konkursrådet* published a report on the treatment of employers in insolvency law in 2015. *Konkursrådet* proposes significant changes in the treatment of employers in insolvency, including a financial limit on the current preferential status of employment contracts. Major objections from labour unions were presented to the Ministry of Justice in June 2015 and the current status of the proposal is unknown.[67]

10.64 By a mandate from the Ministry of Justice of 14 May 2014 *Konkursrådet* was (again) asked to propose changes in the current insolvency legislation to promote the conditions for restarters. The report was to be finished by October 2015 but is currently still in the process.

D. CONCLUDING REMARKS

10.65 The treatment of executory contracts in Danish insolvency law is based on a balance between the interest of the collective creditor interest (the estate) and the interest of the counterparty. Recent reforms appear to favour the interest of the estate by granting rights for the estate that the debtor did not have

67 See more: Confederation of Professionals in Denmark (FTF) and The Danish Confederation of Professional Associations Consultation (Akademikerne) Report of 25 June 2015, http://www.ac.dk/media/510936/hoeringsvar-fra-akademikerne-og-ftf-vedr-hoering-om-ansattes-retsstilling-unde.pdf. accessed 8 September 2017.

beforehand to maximize the recovery rate for the creditors and to make a rescue of a viable business possible.

11

NATIONAL REPORT FOR FINLAND

Jarmo Tuomisto

A. INTRODUCTION AND AVAILABLE PROCEDURES

(1) Insolvency proceedings available to companies in financial or economic distress

11.01 In Finland, there are two different legal procedures to be used by companies in financial or economic distress. The traditional one is bankruptcy, which nowadays is regulated in the Bankruptcy Act.[1] The bankruptcy[2] proceedings aim at liquidation of the company, though selling the business of the company as a going concern is, of course, one possible and usually the best solution from the point of view of all stakeholders. In bankruptcy, all debts originating from the time before the proceedings are, as far as possible, paid according to the prevailing order of preference.

1 In Finnish: Konkurssilaki; Act 120/2004 with its subsequent amendments. An unofficial translation of this act is to be found in the address: http://www.finlex.fi/fi/laki/kaannokset/2004/en20040120.pdf last accessed 11 December 2018.

2 In accordance with the customary Finnish legal terminology, the term bankruptcy refers in this report to insolvency proceedings of commercial entities as well as private persons.

The newer procedure available in Finland is based on the Restructuring of Enterprises Act.[3] The restructuring of enterprises aims at helping the company out of its economic or financial crisis, but even this procedure can, in certain irregular cases, end up with selling the property of the company. The latter alternative is at hand, if it becomes apparent after the commencement of the proceedings that the economic or financial problems of the company cannot be resolved using other means provided by the Restructuring of Enterprises Act and the assets of the company or a material proportion of these assets can be transferred to a new owner as a separate entity following the rules of the said act.[4] Some property of the company can, of course, be sold also as a part of normal restructuring measures. **11.02**

When the restructuring proceedings have started, creditors can neither collect money nor take security from the debtor. Nor can they terminate debtor's contracts on the grounds that the debtor has not paid the debt originating from the time before the proceedings. These kinds of interdictions, which can be temporarily imposed before the court decision on starting the proceedings, aim at giving time to find ways for restructuring the operations of the company and arranging its debts. In the restructuring programme, which is meant to be approved at the end of the court procedure, money debts can be arranged basically in four ways, which are: (1) a change of the payment schedule of a debt; (2) an order that payments made by the debtor shall first be considered as payments against the balance of the debt and only later as payments against credit costs; (3) a reduction in the obligation to pay credit costs relating to the remaining credit period; and (4) a reduction in the principal of the unpaid unsecured debt. **11.03**

Both the bankruptcy proceedings and the restructuring proceedings are largely based on creditor autonomy. The court has, nevertheless, many important controlling functions and, during the restructuring proceedings, the debtor retains authority to undertake measures that are not unusual or have extensive consequences, with due note of the extent and nature of the activities of the debtor. **11.04**

---

3 In Finnish: Laki yrityksen saneerauksesta; Act 47/1993 with its subsequent amendments. An unofficial translation of this act is to be found in the address: <http://www.finlex.fi/fi/laki/kaannokset/1993/en199300 47.pdf> last accessed 11 December 2018.

4 Restructuring of Enterprises Act, s 7 (3).

(2) The requirements for triggering an insolvency proceeding

11.05 The company as well as every one of its creditors – including all public and private entities – can petition for bankruptcy, and both these alternatives are in common use. A creditor may petition for bankruptcy, if its claim against the debtor: (1) is based on a *res judicata* judgment or a judgment, decision or other ground for enforcement that can be enforced like a *res judicata* judgment; (2) is based on a commitment signed by the debtor and not contested by the debtor with obvious justification; or (3) is otherwise so clear that its validity cannot justifiably be doubted.[5]

11.06 A company may be declared bankrupt, if it is insolvent.[6] Insolvency means that the company is otherwise than temporarily unable to repay its debts as they fall due. The Bankruptcy Act also contains rules about when a company is presumed to be insolvent.[7] The company is deemed to be insolvent, first, if the company declares itself to be insolvent and there are no special reasons for not accepting that declaration. Thus, the bankruptcy petition is normally accepted, if the company itself is the petitioner or if the petitioner is some creditor of the company and the company admits to being insolvent. Unless it is otherwise proven, the company is also deemed be insolvent if: (1) the company has discontinued its payments; or (2) it has been determined in enforcement proceedings during the six months preceding the filing of the petition for bankruptcy that the company cannot repay some of its claim in full; or (3) the company has not repaid a clear and due claim of its creditor within a week of the receipt of a reminder and the creditor files its petition for bankruptcy within three months after that.

11.07 Restructuring procedure may be commenced basically on three grounds.[8] The first case is when at least two creditors, whose total claims represent at least one-fifth of the company's known debts and who are not, in a way specifically defined in the Act, closely related to the company, file a joint application with the debtor or declare that they support the debtor's application. In this case, the court starts the procedure without examining whether the economic or financial situation of the company actually is so severe that restructuring is needed. Even a so-called probable creditor, i.e., a party for whom the insolvency of the debtor would probably cause financial loss on grounds other than partnership or shareholding, can be one of the petitioners, not however

5 Bankruptcy Act, s 7(2).
6 Ibid. chapter 2, s 3(1).
7 Bankruptcy Act, chapter 2, s 3.
8 Restructuring of Enterprises Act, s 6.

any creditor with a claim contested as to its basis or a claim essentially contested as to its amount or a claim otherwise unclear.[9]

The second case is when the company is insolvent and the restructuring programme will probably remedy the insolvency and prevent its recurrence in a short period. The application may be filed by the company or its creditor(s) or probable creditor(s). Insolvency is defined in the act similarly as in the Bankruptcy Act.[10] **11.08**

Even if the above mentioned criteria are not fulfilled, the restructuring procedure can be commenced on the grounds that the company is facing imminent insolvency. Even in this case, the company as well as its creditor(s) or probable creditor(s) can apply for the restructuring procedure. The restructuring proceedings on the basis of imminent insolvency shall, however, be commenced on the application of a creditor or probable creditor only if this is necessary in order to secure a considerable financial interest of the applicant or in order to prevent such an interest from jeopardy. **11.09**

In practice, the application for restructuring proceedings is usually filed by the company itself on grounds of insolvency or imminent insolvency. **11.10**

(3) Other general questions concerning Finnish insolvency proceedings

Finnish companies rely also on out-of-court proceedings, but there is neither legislation nor statistics concerning these proceedings. These kinds of proceedings, usually led by the biggest creditors, are taken care of without publicity and it is, therefore, very difficult to reliably estimate their frequency. The lack of publicity is also the main advantage of these proceedings. The biggest problem, on the other hand, is that all creditors are not bound by the agreement thus reached. **11.11**

B. TREATMENT OF EXECUTORY CONTRACTS

(1) Treatment of executory contracts in bankruptcy

The treatment of executory contracts in insolvency depends mainly on the type of the insolvency proceedings and the type of the contract. When it comes to **11.12**

9 The claim of a probable creditor does not have to be due or even definitely come into existence. The definition of probable creditor is to be found in the Restructuring of Enterprises Act, s 5.

10 Restructuring of Enterprises Act, s 3 (1).

bankruptcy proceedings, we nowadays have a general rule in chapter 3 section 8 of the Bankruptcy Act. This rule is to be applied when any special provisions are not given.

11.13 According to the wording of the aforesaid provision, the bankruptcy estate has a general power to commit to the contracts entered, but not performed, by the debtor before the bankruptcy proceedings.[11] If the debtor has performed before the proceedings, the bankruptcy estate can simply adhere to the contract and there is no need to commit to it. If only the other party has performed before the proceedings, this party is, however, normally in the position of a common bankruptcy creditor and neither in this case is there any need to commit to the contract. Commitment to the debtor's contract would, actually, mean ungrounded favouring of the debtor's contracting party. So the rule in chapter 3 section 8 of the Bankruptcy Act applies, despite its wording, only to contracts, which have not been fully performed by either the insolvent debtor or its counterparty before the commencement of bankruptcy.

11.14 The power of the bankruptcy estate to commit to the debtor's contracts is general by its nature, as mentioned above.[12] This power must, however, be used only when it is in the best common interest of all bankruptcy creditors. The estate administrator shall, therefore, use that power only if this is advantageous to the bankruptcy creditors. Neither shall the creditors' meeting decide to commit the estate to the debtor's contracts in other cases. Namely, the decision of the creditors' meeting can be overturned by the court if it is conducive to confer unjust advantage to a creditor or someone else at the expense of the bankruptcy estate or another creditor.[13]

11.15 There are also certain other exceptions to the bankruptcy estate's power to commit to the debtor's contracts. According to the provision of the Bankruptcy Act mentioned above, the debtor's contracting party may, namely,

11 The estate administrator, appointed by the court in the beginning of the bankruptcy proceedings, is competent to decide on matters of the current administration of the bankruptcy estate and on measures that cannot be delayed without causing harm to the bankruptcy estate. In other kinds of cases, only the creditors' meeting can decide to commit the estate to the debtor's contract. The debtor loses its authority over the assets of the bankruptcy estate in the beginning of the bankruptcy proceedings. See the Bankruptcy Act, chapter 3, s 1, chapter 14, s 8 and chapter 15, s 1.

12 Thus, the bankruptcy estate may commit, for instance, to basically all service and utility contracts, public procurement contracts, financial contracts and even preliminary contracts. The bankruptcy estate must fulfil the contract by itself, if the contractual rights and obligations are not, according to law or contract terms, transferable. The bankruptcy legislation does not make any exception from the general norms concerning the contracting party's right to transfer the contract or, e.g., to use a sub-contractor.

13 Bankruptcy Act, chapter 15, s 10. Bankruptcy matters are handled by the general courts (in first instance the District Courts) with three legally trained members present. The restructuring proceedings, on the other hand, are concentrated in certain District Courts in order to guarantee sufficient expertise in these rarer issues.

terminate the contract if it is of a personal nature or there is some other special reason for which it cannot be required that the other party would stay under that contract with the bankruptcy estate. This rather ambiguous expression is clarified in the *travaux préparatoires* of the Bankruptcy Act.[14] According to them, the contracting party can prevent the bankruptcy estate from committing to the contract because of its personal nature, for instance, in cases where the performance of the contract is essentially based on the personal contribution, knowledge and/or skills of the debtor. Other reasons for which the other party need not remain in a contractual relationship with the estate, according to the *travaux préparatoire*, are that the companies are in a particularly close relationship (such as a franchise relationship) or that the other party's brand carries special value which might be harmed by the continuance of business trading relations with the bankruptcy estate. Well-founded suspicions concerning the technical abilities of the bankruptcy estate to perform according to the contract could entitle the other party to refuse continuing business relations with the bankruptcy estate. This may be the case, e.g., when a construction company becomes bankrupt in the starting phase of a building project.

Any Supreme Court ruling concerning the bankruptcy estate's right to commit **11.16**
to the debtor's contracts according to chapter 3 section 8 of the Bankruptcy Act are, regrettably, not available. These kinds of disputes must, of course, be solved very hastily and cannot have years of court proceedings. Amicable settlements of disputes are, therefore, highly esteemed.

The bankruptcy estate is not obliged to announce on its own initiative whether **11.17**
the estate is willing to commit to the debtor's contract or not. Instead, the other party may raise the issue to the bankruptcy administrator. The administrator must answer 'within a reasonable time' if the estate wants to commit to the contract. What is a reasonable time depends on the circumstances of the case. One essential factor to be taken into account is, of course, the need of the other party to get a fast response or decision. According to the *travaux préparatoires*, the time limit can vary from a few days to a month.[15] The bankruptcy estate is also obliged to deliver an acceptable security for the performance of the contract, if it wants to commit to the contract.

The other party is entitled immediately to terminate the contract if the **11.18**
bankruptcy administrator does not answer in due time and post an acceptable security for the performance of the contract. The other party is also entitled to damages for a breach of contract but he or she is then in the position of a

14 Government proposal to Parliament concerning reform of the bankruptcy legislation (26/2003) 55.

15 Ibid., 54–55, 77.

common bankruptcy creditor, which normally means that he or she will get only a small fraction of the claim.[16]

11.19 If the bankruptcy estate commits itself to the debtor's contract, the estate is obliged to fulfil that contract normally. The obligations based on the contract are, in this case, obligations of the estate, not obligations of the debtor. This means that those obligations must be fulfilled before the bankruptcy creditors get their share. If the performance of both the debtor and the other contracting party is divisible, e.g., a contract concerning delivery of electricity or water or delivery of bulk merchandises in various part deliveries or a contract of lease, the bankruptcy estate is, however, not obliged to fulfil the contract to the part which relates to time before the bankruptcy.[17] For instance, the bankruptcy estate is not obliged to pay for water, electricity or merchandise delivered before the bankruptcy or to pay rent for the time before the bankruptcy. These kinds of claims are normal claims in bankruptcy. If the contract is not divisible, e.g., a building contract or a contract of sale of a machine which is to be delivered in various part deliveries, the bankruptcy estate is obliged to fulfil the whole contract, and even regardless of which party of the contract is in bankruptcy.

11.20 The provision in chapter 3 section 8 of the Bankruptcy Act contains the general rule which is to be applied when there is not any special provision concerning the impact of bankruptcy on the contractual relations of the debtor. There are, however, various *special provisions*, which in variable degrees modify the rules described above.

11.21 For instance, according to chapter 7 section 8 of the Employment Contracts Act[18] both the bankruptcy estate of the employer and the employee are entitled to terminate the employment contract in 14 days after the notice. The salary as well as other benefits of the employee during those 14 days is to be paid by the bankruptcy estate.

11.22 According to section 39 of the Act on Lease of Business Premises,[19] the bankruptcy estate of a lessee is entitled to commit to the contract in one month after the landlord has asked for it. If the bankruptcy estate wants to commit, it is not obliged to deliver any security to the landlord. The landlord

16 Ibid., 54.

17 Ibid.

18 In Finnish: Työsopimuslaki; Act 55/2011 with its subsequent amendments. An unofficial translation of this act is to be found in the address: http://www.finlex.fi/fi/laki/kaannokset/2001/en20010055.pdf last accessed 11 December 2018.

19 In Finnish: Laki liikehuoneiston vuokrauksesta; Act 482/1995 with its subsequent amendments.

is supposed to be protected by the ongoing right to file for eviction if the rent is not paid appropriately by the bankruptcy estate. The same kind of provision is to be found in the Act on Residential Lease[20] and in the Act on Lease of Land,[21] whereas according to the Insurance Contracts Act,[22] the bankruptcy of the insured does not, as such, affect the insurance as long as the insurance premium is properly paid.

In chapter 5 sections 8 and 9 of the Bankruptcy Act, there are special provisions concerning the impact of a buyer's bankruptcy on a contract of sale of movable property with retention of title clause.[23] The bankruptcy estate of the buyer has the right to commit to the contract by notifying the seller. The notice must be given within a reasonable time after the seller has requested payment or the return of the movable. The estate is not obliged to deliver any security to the seller. The estate has also the right to redeem the sales article at once by paying the full amount due to the seller, less the interest and the other costs of the credit for the remaining credit period. Finally, the estate has even the right to cancel the contract, in which case the seller may be liable to return all or part of the payments made by the buyer before the bankruptcy. **11.23**

The impact of a buyer's bankruptcy on a contract of sale of real property with retention of title clause is regulated in chapter 2 sections 28 and 29 of Code of Real Estate.[24] The bankruptcy estate of the buyer must deliver an acceptable security for the payment of the purchase price in a reasonable time after an exhortation to pay. If the security is not delivered or the estate does not pay the price according to the original terms, the seller may cancel the contract of sale. **11.24**

One thing which ought to be taken into consideration is, additionally, the rules of property law. Especially many rights of use remain in effect notwithstanding the bankruptcy of the owner of the encumbered object. These kinds **11.25**

20 In Finnish: Laki asuinhuoneiston vuokrauksesta; Act 481/1995 with its subsequent amendments. An unofficial translation of this act is to be found in the address: http://www.finlex.fi/fi/laki/kaannokset/1995/en19950481pdf last accessed 11 December 2018.

21 In Finnish: Maanvuokralaki; Act 258/1966 with its subsequent amendments.

22 In Finnish: Vakuutussopimuslaki; Act 426/2010 with its subsequent amendments. An unofficial translation of this act is to be found in the address: http://www.finlex.fi/fi/laki/kaannokset/1994/en19940543pdf last accessed 11 December 2018.

23 The retention of title clause does not affect the buyer's legal status in the bankruptcy of the seller. The buyer may claim delivery if the sold property was appropriately identified before the commencement of the bankruptcy.

24 In Finnish: Maakaari; Act 540/1995 with its subsequent amendments. An unofficial translation of this act is to be found in the address: http://www.finlex.fi/fi/laki/kaannokset/1995/en19950540.pdf last accessed 11 December 2018.

The retention of title clause does not affect the buyer's legal status in the bankruptcy of the seller. The buyer is fully protected against the creditors of the seller when the bill of sale is signed.

of contracts may cease to be in effect as a consequence of the realisation of the debtor's property but until then they often automatically stay in force. This applies, for instance, to the contracts concerning lease of land or premises.

11.26 There are no special rules concerning the effects of bankruptcy on contractual relations which would depend on the counter-party (public or private) or duration of a contractual relation or importance of a contract for the survival of the distressed business.

(2) Treatment of executory contracts in restructuring proceedings

11.27 The position of executory contracts in restructuring proceedings is substantially different from the one in bankruptcy. The restructuring proceedings affect in various ways the position of money creditors, as described above at the beginning of this chapter. There is an explicit provision in the Restructuring of Enterprises Act stating that the commencement of restructuring proceedings shall have no effect on the existing undertakings of the debtor, if not otherwise provided in this Act.[25] This means, first, that even contracts which constitute a money payment obligation of the company under restructuring basically stay in force as far as they are not arranged in the restructuring programme using the above mentioned means of restructuring. The only exceptions to this rule are (a) different kinds of contracts of hire or lease, (b) contracts of employment and (c) contracts concerning a performance which cannot be deemed a regular part of the activities of the debtor.[26] The hirer or lessee company under restructuring may terminate all kinds of contracts of hire or lease on a two-month notice. Also all employment contracts can be terminated on a shorter notice than usual, if the restructuring of the employer company presupposes it. If the performance of a contracting party cannot be deemed a regular part of the activities of the debtor and if this contract is, at the time of the commencement of the proceedings, on both sides unfulfilled, the administrator shall on the request of the contracting party state whether or not the debtor will keep to its part of the contract. If the answer is in the negative or if it is not given in a reasonable time, the other party has the right to cancel the agreement.

11.28 Secondly, contracts which do not oblige the company to money payment but to other kind of performance, will stay unchanged in force despite the restructuring proceedings. If the company was, for instance, obliged to deliver some merchandise or to take care of some building project, this contract will

25 Restructuring of Enterprises Act, s 15(1).

26 Restructuring of Enterprises Act, s 27 and the Employment Contracts Act, chapter 7, s 7.

stay valid despite of the restructuring process. The idea of this rule is to keep the business of the company running as normally as possible, while the money debts of the company are, on the other hand, rearranged as much as necessary. The common rules concerning anticipatory breach of contract are, nevertheless, in force even during the restructuring proceedings. Thus, the commencement of restructuring proceedings may *in casu* demonstrate that the company under restructuring will be unable to fulfil its contractual obligations. However, the restructuring proceedings are not, as such, regarded as a sufficient proof of the company's incapacity to fulfil its obligations.[27]

There are no special rules concerning the effects of restructuring proceedings on contractual relations which would depend on the counter-party (public or private) or duration of a contractual relation or importance of a contract for the survival of the distressed business. **11.29**

(3) Contractual remedies agreed by the parties in solvent times

There has been a well-established opinion in the legal literature that the parties of a contract may not directly regulate the legal status of their creditors.[28] This means that contract clauses, which in practice affect only the position of the parties' creditors, are invalid. That view was clearly accepted in the Supreme Court decision 1994:35. In this case, there was a provision in the employment agreement which entitled the employee to extra-large damages if he would be dismissed on grounds of his employer's bankruptcy. According to the Supreme Court, the parties had tried to harm the position of third parties with a contractual provision, and the court found that provision inefficient. **11.30**

The above mentioned opinion was further confirmed during the preparation of the new bankruptcy legislation. In the *travaux préparatoires* of the Bankruptcy Act, it is clearly stated that the provision in chapter 3 section 8 of the Bankruptcy Act concerning the power of the bankruptcy estate to commit to debtor's contracts is peremptory by its nature and this power cannot, therefore, be excluded or diminished by contract clauses.[29] The latest phase in this development is the Supreme Court decision 2016:100. According to this decision, it is not decisive whether the parties actually intended to regulate only the position of their creditors. It is, instead, relevant whose position a **11.31**

27 Government proposal to Parliament concerning legislation of restructuring of enterprises (182/1992) 32–33.

28 See e.g., Jarmo Tuomisto, *Vuokranantaja ja vuokralaisen konkurssi* (Lessor and Bankruptcy of Lessee) (Lakimiesliiton kustannus 1991) 272–78; Risto Koulu, *Immateriaalinen varallisuus konkurssissa* (Immaterial Property in Bankruptcy), (WSOY Lakitieto 2003) 263–69; Jarmo Tuomisto, *Sopimus ja insolvenssi* (Contract and Insolvency) (Lakimiesliiton Kustannus 2010) 124–27.

29 Government proposal to Parliament concerning reform of the bankruptcy legislation (26/2003) 54.

contract clause in reality affects. If a contract clause in reality affects only the status of creditors, it is invalid.

11.32 Termination clauses, acceleration clauses and similar *ipso facto* clauses affect in practice only the position of bankruptcy creditors. They are, therefore, not applicable in bankruptcy.[30] The situation is, however, different, if the termination or acceleration or similar legal effect has occurred, e.g., on grounds of a contract clause concerning the effects of imminent insolvency of a contract party, already before the commencement of the bankruptcy proceedings, i.e., the moment when the court declares the company bankrupt. In this case, one can, on good grounds, assert that the contract clause has, in a relevant manner, regulated not only the legal relations between the contracting parties, but also the legal status of their creditors. In lack of precedents, it is, however, difficult to exactly define when a contract clause does, relevantly enough, regulate also the legal relations between the contracting parties. If this kind of clause is considered valid, the only conceivable means for the creditors to annul the effects of the clause are to be found in the Act on Recovery to the Bankruptcy Estate.[31] The recovery for the bankruptcy estate is, however, very seldom possible in these kinds of cases.

11.33 The question of effectiveness or ineffectiveness of different kinds of *ipso facto* clauses in the restructuring proceedings is more open, especially because there is no case law concerning this procedure. Same kinds of arguments should, however, apply also to this case: the parties of a contract should not negatively regulate the legal status of third parties, e.g., legal status of their creditors.

11.34 In practice, many companies use standard terms which fail to conform to chapter 3 section 8 of the Bankruptcy Act and the idea of the peremptory nature of that provision. Some of these standard terms have even been drafted by notable business unions.

C. REFORMS

11.35 The Restructuring of Enterprises Act was enacted 1993 during a severe economic crisis in Finland. At the same time the renewal of bankruptcy

30 The same applies to set-off clauses used in order to widen a bankruptcy creditor's right to set-off. A certain exception to this can, however, be seen in the validity of close-out netting clauses in accordance with Directive 98/26/EC of the European Parliament and of the Council of 19 May 1998 on settlement finality in payment and securities settlement systems [1998] OJ L 166/45 and Directive 2002/47/EC of the European Parliament and of the Council of 6 June 2002 on financial collateral arrangements [2002] OJ L 168/43.

31 In Finnish: Laki takaisinsannista konkurssipesään; Act 758/1992 with its subsequent amendments.

legislation had been under discussion for more than a decade. The bankruptcy legislation was out of date and, due to countless partial reforms, technically poor. The reform of restructuring legislation was, however, considered more urgent, and thus the new Bankruptcy Act was not enacted until year 2004.

Preparation of the new bankruptcy legislation started in cooperation with Sweden, Denmark and Norway as early as the1970s. During the preparation, attention was, of course, paid to international instruments such as the EU legislation (especially Council Regulation (EC) 1346/2000 of 29 May 2000 on insolvency proceedings [2000] OJ L 160/1) and for instance the UNCITRAL's Model Law On Cross-border Insolvency. National requirements together with Nordic traditions were, however, clearly the starting point in the preparation work. **11.36**

The Bankruptcy Act 2004 was prepared by a working group set by the Ministry of Justice. The group consisted of officials of the Ministry, judiciary and administration, but during and after the preparation by the working group a large number of different kinds of interest groups were, naturally, consulted. **11.37**

The proposition of the working group was largely welcomed by the different interest groups heard during the various stages of preparation, and it is practically impossible to name some decisive interest group in this process. The weightiest discussions concerned questions like the position of security creditors or banks' right to set off. The provision concerning bankruptcy estate's right to commit to the debtor's contracts was not largely contested. The Ministry of Transport and Communications, which often represents the state as a customer in large building projects, criticised the conception of the peremptory nature of the provision in chapter 3 section 8 of the Bankruptcy Act. The Finnish Association for Industrial Property Rights was doubtful as to whether this provision would be appropriate when it comes to industrial property rights, for instance, licence agreements. The association recommended a special provision for those kinds of situations and preferred that the bankruptcy estate of a licensor should, under certain circumstances, be liable to continue the licence agreement. Other interest groups heard during the preparation were, however, seemingly happy with the proposed provision or did not comment on it at all. **11.38**

The Bankruptcy Act meant a total reform of the bankruptcy legislation, although the new legislation is, of course, partly based on Finnish – and Swedish – traditions during centuries. As one novelty, the Bankruptcy Act contains the above described general provision concerning executory contracts. **11.39**

11.40 After the enactment of the Bankruptcy Act, the Restructuring of Enterprises Act has been critically reviewed by a working group set by the Ministry of Justice. This revision led in 2007 to many amendments in the act, but these amendments did not affect the rules concerning executory contracts. Later, also the Bankruptcy Act has been reviewed by a similar working group, but this working group did not propose any reforms in the provisions concerning executory contracts of the debtor.

D. CONCLUDING REMARKS

11.41 Economic objectives like safeguarding the credit trade, industry and employment are, obviously, central driving forces of reforms of the insolvency law. This connection is especially clear in Finland when it comes to the Restructuring of Enterprises Act. This Act was exceptionally quickly prepared during the economic crisis in which Finland was living at that time. The aim was to prevent unnecessary bankruptcies by creating better tools for the arrangement of debts and other restructuring arrangements after the former legislation had proven to be quite insufficient. In the main, the representatives of major creditors like banks, insurance companies and tax authorities have shown interest in the preparation of insolvency legislation, but the development of this legislation is in the wider interest of the society.

11.42 Legislation in other Nordic countries has been the most important foreign source of ideas in the preparation of the Bankruptcy Act. The Chapter 11 procedure of the US Bankruptcy Code was probably one of the central foreign models in the preparation of the Restructuring of Enterprises Act.

11.43 The treatment of executory contracts in bankruptcy has not changed dramatically during recent years. The most important novelty was the general provision in chapter 3 section 8 of the Bankruptcy Act, which has essentially clarified the legal situation. This provision is, however, largely based on the ideas previously manifested in various special provisions, case law and literature. The idea of the peremptory nature of the rules concerning executory contracts in bankruptcy is not new as such, but this conception has been essentially confirmed by the case law and the *travaux préparatoires* of the Bankruptcy Act.

11.44 The restructuring of enterprises can be seen as a totally new procedure in Finland and therefore also the treatment of executory contracts in restructuring proceedings is a new problem. The status of executory contracts in restructuring proceedings is, however, basically clear: the debt arrangements and other restructuring arrangements affect only money creditors of the company. Other kinds of contracts stay unchangeably in force, because the company is supposed to continue its functions as normally as possible. The peremptory nature of that rule is, however, rather unclear because of a lack of case law.

12

NATIONAL REPORT FOR FRANCE

Emilie Ghio

A. INTRODUCTION: AVAILABLE INSOLVENCY PROCEDURES IN FRANCE

12.01 Corporate insolvency law is an old legal subject in the French legislative system, having its origins in Roman law. Before the introduction of the Commercial Code of 1807, although bankruptcy law evolved over time, it was mostly of a purely coercive nature. Even with the promulgation of the 1807 Code, French bankruptcy law still severely punished bankrupts, since the bankruptcy procedure consisted of arresting and imprisoning the defaulting person, and selling his assets in order to pay back his debts.

12.02 The Law of 4 March 1889 introduced the procedure known as judicial liquidation. This procedure was more flexible and it coexisted with the stricter coercive procedure for a while. The latter was reserved for dishonest traders, whereas the former was available to honest bankrupts, who could save their businesses through debt forgiveness from their creditors.

In 1967, the Law of 13 July[1] considerably transformed the corporate insolvency landscape by dissociating the fate *of* the company from that of its management. The roots of modern insolvency law were also laid down, where a 'twin-track' system[2] was implemented. A business could either be rescued or liquidated. In the 1980s, three new insolvency laws were passed, one of which introduced a pre-insolvency process for the first time.[3] These laws placed the focus on reorganisation, rather than liquidation. They introduced alert procedures, designed to oblige managers of a company showing signs of weakness to explain how they were planning on resolving growing difficulties. **12.03**

Finally, the year 2000 marked the promulgation of the new Commercial Code, which reconsolidated insolvency laws, as part of the bicentenary celebrations of the great codification project inaugurated by Napoleon. The provisions relating to French insolvency proceedings have since been codified under Articles L610–1 to L680–7 of the French Commercial Code ('*Code de Commerce*'). In France, companies encountering financial difficulties are offered two paths to deal with their distress: liquidation or restructuring. The French insolvency test is a pure cash flow test, i.e., a company is declared insolvent ('*en état de cessation de paiements*') when it is unable to meet its current debts out of its current assets. **12.04**

(1) Liquidation and rehabilitation proceedings

Liquidation proceedings ('*liquidation judiciaire*')[4] aim at liquidating a company through the sale of its business, or each of its assets individually, when there is no prospect of recovery. Liquidation proceedings are opened either when rescuing the company seems to be impossible or after the court orders a sale plan of the debtor's assets in the context of failed restructuring proceedings. **12.05**

Liquidation proceedings last until the sale of the company's business or assets generates no more proceeds. However, no later than two years after the judgment ordering liquidation was made, any creditor can apply to the court to request the closing of the liquidation procedure. **12.06**

Additionally, a simplified form of liquidation proceedings is available for small businesses, which can last no more than one year. **12.07**

1 Law N°67–563 of 13 July 1967.

2 See P. Omar, 'A Reform in Search of a Purpose: French Insolvency Law Changes (Again!)' (2014) 23 *International Insolvency Review* 201, at 201.

3 Law N°84–148 of 1 March 1984; Law N° 85–98 of 25 January 1985 focused on insolvency law; and Law N°85–99 of 25 January 1985 regulated office-holders.

4 Commercial Code, arts L640–1 *et seq.*

12.08 *Rehabilitation proceedings* (*'redressement judiciaire'*)[5] are rescue proceedings, available to insolvent, yet still operating, debtors, in order to rescue the going concern of the business. In contrast to safeguard proceedings (described below) which can be opened at the discretion of the management at a preventive stage, filing for rehabilitation proceedings must be done no later than 45 days following the date at which the enterprise becomes insolvent, unless conciliation proceedings are ongoing.[6] A rehabilitation plan (*'plan de redressement'*) may provide for a debt restructuring; a recapitalisation of the company; a debt-for-equity swap; and/or the sale of assets or some parts of the business. If the company is later deemed unviable, the court can convert rehabilitation proceedings into liquidation proceedings.

(2) Pre-insolvency proceedings

12.09 *Safeguard proceedings* (*'procedure de sauvegarde'*)[7] were introduced in 2005 and were constructed on the model of Chapter 11 of the US Bankruptcy Code. The procedure was designed as an anticipatory rescue procedure. The idea behind the introduction of such procedure was to shift the emphasis on rescue to a time before the debtor becomes insolvent. Article L620–1 of the French Commercial Code sets out the qualifying criteria for commencing safeguard proceedings. Since the Ordinance of 2008, safeguard proceedings can be 'open on request by the debtor … who, without being in a payment failure situation, can show that he is encountering difficulties which he is not in a position to overcome.' As a result, the debtor does not need to show that the financial difficulties he is experiencing will lead to a payment failure situation.[8] Therefore, safeguard proceedings are voluntary proceedings,[9] available to a debtor who is solvent. They lead to a 'continuation' plan for the company. The purpose of the safeguard procedure is the reorganisation of the business to allow for the continuation of the economic activity, the maintenance of employment and the settlement of liabilities.[10]

5 Ibid., art L631–1.
6 Ibid., art L631–4.
7 Ibid., arts 620–1 *et seq.*
8 However, some commentators have noted that the amendment of the entry criterion is more theoretical than actual, since the debtor must still prove financial difficulties to the court: See J-L. Vallens, 'Flexibility in France' Eurofenix 2009 (Summer), at p. 22.
9 Ibid., art 620–1.
10 Ibid.: 'afin de permettre la poursuite de l'activité économique, le maintien de l'emploi et l'apurement du passif.'

12.10 *Accelerated safeguard procedure* (*'procedure de sauvegarde accélérée'*) (AS),[11] introduced by the Ordinance of 2014,[12] is a particular type of safeguard proceeding, to be implemented on an accelerated basis. It is available to a debtor who is going through a conciliation procedure and has drawn up a restructuring plan which would have sufficient support from the creditors such that it is reasonably likely to be adopted on an expedited basis, i.e., a maximum of three months.[13]

12.11 *Accelerated financial safeguard* (*'procedure de sauvegarde financière accélérée'*) (AFS)[14] is similar to the AS but applies to restructurings involving only financial debts and therefore, affects financial creditors only. Designed as a 'pre-pack' variation of the safeguard, the procedure is available to debtors who have initiated conciliation proceedings, who can demonstrate that they qualify for the opening of a safeguard procedure and who are required to have creditors' committees formed for the purposes of approving a rescue plan.[15] A rescue plan is required that is believed to be supported by a majority of financial creditors and/or bondholders. The court takes into consideration the views of the conciliator on the progress of the conciliation and the likelihood of adoption of the draft plan by the relevant parties.[16] The objective of the procedure is to provide for the elaboration of a fast reorganisation plan with a limited impact on commercial partners. It is a middle ground between an out-of-court procedure (*'procedure de conciliation'*) and a safeguard proceeding since it allows for the restructuring of some of the company's debts, without a stay on all of the creditors' claims.

(3) Out-of-court proceedings

12.12 *Mandat ad hoc* proceedings[17] are flexible proceedings. A debtor can apply to the court to request the appointment of a *'mandataire' ad hoc* charged with facilitating and supervising negotiations with the debtor's main creditors. The debtor continues to manage his business without being divested and the tasks of the *'mandataire' ad hoc* are decided by the court according to the specific needs of the debtor. The *ad hoc* mandate is a very flexible procedure, free from many legal formalities. The objective is to invite the main creditors to consider debt rescheduling or debt cancellation or the injection of new financing into

11 Ibid., arts L628–1 *et seq.*
12 Ordinance n°2014–326 of 12 March 2014, 'portant réforme de la prévention des difficultés des entreprises et des procédures collectives'.
13 Commercial Code, art L628–8.
14 Ibid., arts L628–9 *et seq.*
15 Commercial Code, Article L628–1.
16 Commercial Code, Article L628–2.
17 Ibid., arts L611–3 *et seq.*

the business. There is no statutory limit for the process, and the *mandataire* does not have any management responsibility. An *ad hoc* mandate does not have any cram-down effect and does not trigger an automatic stay on enforcement action.

12.13 *Conciliation* proceedings[18] are voluntary proceedings, open when a debtor facing 'legal, economic or financial difficulties'[19] and who has not been insolvent for more than 45 days requests the appointment of a conciliator to assist it in reaching an agreement with its main creditors and contractual partners. The procedure cannot be opened for longer than four months[20] and the conciliator's duty is to reach an amicable agreement between the company and its main creditors in order to end the business's financial difficulties.[21]

12.14 If an agreement is reached, it may be acknowledged by the President of the Commercial Court giving legal force to the agreement, or approved by the court if:

- the debtor is still solvent or the agreement puts an end to the debtor's insolvency;
- the terms of the agreement ensure the continuity of the business;
- the agreement does not harm the interests of non-signatory creditors.[22]

(4) General comments and other remarkable features of the French regime

12.15 Historically, French insolvency law has generally been quite debtor-friendly, geared towards the rescue of ailing businesses and the preservation of employment, often prioritised over the situation of creditors.[23] Over the last 20 years in particular, several reforms have been passed, introducing new restructuring procedure and updating existing ones in order to make them more efficient. The focus has increasingly been placed on urging companies to be aware of arising financial difficulties and to act to remedy the situation at an early stage.[24] However, a shift in the debtor-creditor balance has now occurred.

---

18 Ibid., arts L611–4 *et seq.*

19 Ibid., art L611–4: 'les débiteurs … qui éprouvent une difficulté juridique, économique ou financière'.

20 Ibid., art L611–6.

21 Ibid., art L611–7.

22 Ibid., art L611–8.

23 See R. Parry, 'Introduction' in K. Gromek Broc and R. Parry (eds.), *Corporate Rescue in Europe: An overview of Recent Developments from Selected Countries in Europe* (Kluwer Law International, 2004), at p. 1.

24 M. Campana, 'A Critical Evaluation of the Development and Reform of the Corporate Rescue Procedures in France' in K. Gromek and R. Parry (eds.), *Corporate Rescue in Europe: An overview of Recent Developments from Selected Countries in Europe* (Kluwer Law International, 2004), at p. 34.

Creditors' rights have been advanced as they now play a more active role in (pre-) insolvency proceedings.

The use of out-of-court proceedings has been stimulated by recent reforms, such as the Ordinance of 2014 and the Law No. 2016–1547 dated 18 November 2016. In 2015, the French National Institute of Statistics and Economics Studies (INSEE) reported the altogether decline of insolvency and restructuring procedures over the last five years: generally, INSEE reported the opening of 57,844 restructuring proceedings, of which 2,400 were out-of-court proceedings (160 rehabilitation and safeguard proceedings for companies over 50 employees),[25] an increase of 3 per cent compared to 2015. In 2016, 1,293 '*sauvegardes*' were opened (against 1,647 in 2014; and 1,516 in 2012); 17,288 '*redressements judiciaires*' (against 18,205 in 2014; and 18,726 in 2012); and 39,263 '*liquidations judiciaires*' (against 43,156 in 2014; and 41,817 in 2012). **12.16**

B. TREATMENT OF EXECUTORY CONTRACTS IN FRANCE

(1) General remarks about executory contracts

The French Commercial Code does not provide a definition of the concept of executory contracts and therefore, case law and academic discourse have played an important role in shaping its definition over time.[26] For an existing contract to be executory, one must look at the obligation *characteristic* of the contract. Indeed, it is argued that certain obligations define certain contracts, e.g., a sale contract is defined by the obligation to transfer ownership and a loan contract by the obligation to transfer funds. If the relevant characteristic obligation of a contract has already been performed before the insolvency procedure is opened, the contract is not deemed executory.[27] Generally, the trend in the legislature's treatment of executory contracts over the years has been to strengthen the position of counterparties. **12.17**

25 See Stéphanie Chatelon and Arnaud Pédron, 'Insolvabilité : Actualités au niveau européen et état des lieux en France' (2017) Deloitte Taj.

26 A. Bac, De la notion de contrat en cours et de ses grandes consequences, notamment pour les cautions, (JCP E I. 2000) 22.

27 See e.g., Cass. Com. 2 March 1993, Case no. 90–21353, Rec. Dalloz 1993, p. 572; Cass. Com. 28 February 1995, Case no. 94–12108, JCP E 1995, I, 487, n°11.

12.18 Executory contracts are mostly dealt with in Articles L622–13 and L641–11–1 of the Commercial Code. Article L622–13 generally applies to reorganisation proceedings, whereas Article L641–11–1 applies to liquidation proceedings. However, these provisions are very similar.

(2) Executory contracts in French insolvency proceedings

12.19 Insolvency proceedings do not result in the automatic termination of the debtor's executory contracts.[28] Therefore, the Commercial Code requires the counterparty to perform its obligations, irrespective of the debtor's failure to perform his before insolvency proceedings were open.[29] Hence, executory contracts remain binding on both parties pending their assumption or rejection by the insolvency official.

12.20 Under French law, no distinction is made between contracts concluded for a fixed or indefinite term. Additionally, the relevant court has discretion to decide which executory contracts are necessary to safeguard the business and can therefore sell them as part of the going concern.[30]

(2)(a) Provisions regarding executory contracts in restructuring procedures

12.21 *Preventive proceedings (ad hoc and conciliation proceedings):* Article L611–16 provides that any contractual clause increasing the obligations of the debtor or limiting his rights by the sole reason of opening an *ad hoc* or conciliation procedure is deemed null and void. Apart from such provision, there are no specific rules regarding executory contracts in *ad hoc* or conciliation proceedings.

12.22 *Reorganisation proceedings (safeguard and rehabilitation):* Article L622–13 I protects executory contracts in safeguard proceedings, notwithstanding any legal or contractual provisions to the contrary. As a result, an executory contract remains in force and the debtor's counterparty must perform the obligations arising under the contract despite the non-performance of the debtor's obligations.[31]

28 Commercial Code, art L622–13 I. See also E. Jouffin, Le sort des contrats en cours dans les entreprises soumises à une procédure collective, (Préf. Ch. Gaval-DA., LGDJ, 1998); Cass. Com. 8 March 2017, n°15–21.937.

29 Ibid.

30 Commercial Code, art L642–7.

31 R. Dammann, 'Le sort des contrats en cours dans les procédures de sauvegarde, de redressement judiciaire et de liquidation judiciaire', 41 Journal des sociétés.

(2)(b) Assumption and rejection of executory contracts

Article L622–13 II states that the decision to assume or reject the contract is taken by the insolvency officer alone. The insolvency official can request the counterparty to perform its obligations under the executory contract in exchange for the performance of the debtor's post-petition obligations, subject to the debtor having sufficient funds to perform these obligations.[32] Pursuant to article L622–13 III 1° of the Commercial Code, the counterparty can require the administrator to give his opinion on the continuation of an executory contract, which will be automatically terminated if left unanswered for longer than one month. **12.23**

Regarding termination of executory contracts, pursuant to Article L622–13 II of the Commercial Code, the administrator must apply to the court to terminate an executory contract if the debtor's funds prove insufficient to pay the next term. Early termination of executory contracts results in damages which constitute pre-petition claims.[33] **12.24**

Article L622–13 III 2° also provides that an executory contract can be automatically terminated if the counterparty does not agree to continue such contract.[34] **12.25**

Finally, Article L622–13 IV provides that the decision to reject executory contracts can be made only by the relevant insolvency court (*'juge-commissionnaire'*) on application by the insolvency official. Since the termination would result in a loss to the counterparty, the insolvency official's power to reject a contract is limited by two conditions: (1) it must be necessary for the restructuring of the debtor; and (2) it must not adversely impact the interests of the counterparty.[35] **12.26**

In the case of liquidation proceedings, Article L641–11–1 III 3° adds that an executory contract is automatically terminated by the insolvency official without application to the court if the debtor's sole obligation was the payment of a sum of money. **12.27**

---

32 Commercial Code, art L622–13 II.

33 Ibid., art L622–13 V.

34 Pursuant to art L622–13 II, only the officer has the power to make the decision to assume a contract: counterparties do not have a veto power. However, in a case where a fixed-term contract stated that it would be automatically renewed unless one of the parties sent a termination notice, the Supreme Court in France ruled that the counterparty was entitled to rely on that termination provision, notwithstanding the officer's powers to assume the contract (Cass. Com. 30 October 2000, case N° 97–21339).

35 Commercial Code, art L622–13 IV.

(2)(c) Special types of contracts

12.28 Certain types of executory contracts are deemed to justify special treatment in insolvency proceedings.

Sale contracts, hire-purchase, and finance lease contracts

12.29 There is no special statutory regime regarding sale contracts: if a sale contract ceases to be executory, the seller's claims for non-payment are converted into unsecured insolvency claims. Additionally, the French Supreme Court ('*Cour de cassation*') has held that life annuity sales contracts ('*vente en viager*') are not executory contracts if the ownership of the good was transferred to the buyer before insolvency proceedings were opened.[36]

12.30 A hire-purchase contract ('*vente à temperament*') is deemed executory if the ownership of the asset or the payment of the last instalment has not been transferred. However, the Commercial Code does not provide for specific rules regarding these types of contract, therefore they are governed by the general regime described above.

12.31 Special rules apply to lease contracts ('*contrat de bail*') regarding the termination of leases pertaining to property assets rented or used by the debtor in the course of his business.[37] The termination of this type of contract occurs either (i) on the date when the lessor is informed by the insolvency official of his decision not to assume the lease contract;[38] (ii) when the lessor requests the termination of such a contract on the basis of a default payment after the opening of insolvency proceedings;[39] (iii) the absence of activity during the observation period in the rented property does not lead to the automatic termination of the lease, notwithstanding clauses to the contrary.[40]

---

36 Cass. Com. 28 February 1995, Case N° 94–12108.

37 P. Roussel Galle, *Les nouveau régimes des contrats en cours et du bail* (Rev. Proc. Coll., janvier-février 2009), 55; B. Saintourrens, 'Le régime du bail commercial après la réforme des procédures collectives (loi du 26 juillet 2005 de sauvegarde des entreprises)', (2005) 10 Loyers et copr.; C. Saint-Geniest and A. Colin, *Bail et entreprises en difficulté: les apports de la loi du 26 juillet 2005 ou l'incidence de la loi de sauvegarde des entreprises sur la situation des bailleurs*, (Rev. Loyers, 2006) 862; R. Castel and A. Romain-Huttin, 'Le bail commercial à l'épreuve des procédures collectives', (2010) 48 RLDA 65; F. Auque, *La résiliation du bail commercial en cas de procédure de sauvegarde ou de redressement judiciaire du bailleur*, (RJ com. 2005), 478; F. Barat, 'La levée d'option d'achat du crédit-bail par le preneur soumis à une procédure collective après l'ordonnance du 18 décembre 2008', (2010) RLDA 99; Cass. Com. 17 Février 2015, n°13–17.076.

38 Commercial Code, art L622–14 1°.

39 Ibid., art L622–14 2°.

40 Ibid., art L622–14.

Utilities

No specific rules apply to utilities contracts in the Commercial Code. The general regime governing executory contracts applies. 12.32

Employment contracts

Articles L622–13 VI and L641–11–1 VI specify that they do not apply to employment contacts, to which general rules of employment law apply. In pre-insolvency proceedings, the general regime of French employment law applies, which affords a high level of protection to employees who cannot be dismissed freely by the debtor. Dismissals are allowed either for economic reasons or for misconduct and a formal procedure must be followed by the employer. Special rules apply for certain types of employees[41] and businesses of a certain size may be obliged to redistribute employees made redundant.[42] 12.33

In insolvency proceedings – either restructuring or liquidation – employment contracts are ruled by a unique combination of general law and special insolvency provisions. General provisions of employment law remain applicable with respect to dismissal for misconduct in insolvency proceedings. However, special insolvency rules apply regarding dismissals for economic necessity. Regarding procedural rules, the insolvency officer must first consult the employee representatives and inform the French labour administrator and second, apply to the insolvency court, in order to dismiss the employees.[43] On a substantive level, dismissals for economic necessity are allowed only if they are 'urgent, unavoidable and indispensable'.[44] The intention of the legislator is clearly that such layoffs remain exceptional during insolvency proceedings. 12.34

Additionally, the Commercial Code directs the court to take into account the impact of such a decision on employment, when deciding on a sale of the business as a going concern[45] or the adoption of a restructuring plan.[46] 12.35

Finally, French law also confers a specific status on unpaid salaries and other employees' claims arising before the commencement of the insolvency proceedings. As a consequence, employees are given a preferential right[47] on movable and immovable properties owned by the insolvent employer, which 12.36

41 E.g., employee representatives, Labour Code, art L2411–1; women who are pregnant or on maternity leave: Labour Code, art L1225–4.
42 Labour Code, art L1233–61.
43 See e.g., Commercial Code, art L631–17.
44 Ibid.
45 Ibid., art L642–5.
46 Ibid., art L631–19.
47 Ibid., art L625–7.

comprise wages, paid leave and severance payment for the termination of the labour contract and dismissal compensation.

Pension contracts

12.37 Subscriptions to compulsory complementary pension programmes meet the definition of executory contracts. If insolvency proceedings are opened against the company, the pension institution as well as the insolvency official can terminate the pension contracts within three months after the proceedings are opened. The debtor can be reimbursed the part of pre-paid premium which corresponds to the lapse of time during which risks were not covered.[48] The French Social Security Code ('*Code de la Sécurité Sociale*') also states that insolvency proceedings against pension organisations can be either requested by the dedicated supervisory authority ('*autorité de contrôle prudentiel*') or after such authority has been consulted.[49]

Financial contracts

12.38 Directive 2002/47/EC, amended by Directive 2009/44/EC, governs the treatment of financial collateral contracts. A European measure was deemed necessary in this legal area in order to promote the smooth functioning of the capital markets, and the conclusion reached was that financial transactions should not be affected by the opening of insolvency proceedings. The French legislator implemented the European provisions in the Financial and Monetary Code ('*Code Monétaire et Financier*'). Article L211–36–1 II of the Financial and Monetary Code provides that the rules governing assessment, set-off and termination of financial contracts are enforceable against third parties, even if insolvency proceedings have been initiated against the parties.

(3) Statutory treatment of contractual remedies

(3)(a) Ipso facto *clauses*

12.39 Under French law, termination and acceleration clauses, also called *ipso facto* clauses, are not automatically considered null and void. However, Article L622–13 I (and Article L641–11 I regarding liquidation) of the Commercial Code states that indivisibility or termination clauses, or clauses allowing rescission of an executory contract cannot be triggered by the opening of insolvency proceedings, whether liquidation or reorganisation proceedings, except for employment and fiduciary contracts.[50]

48 Social Security Code, art L932–10.

49 Ibid., art L951–2.

50 Commercial Code, arts L622–13 VI.

The French Commercial Code goes further in the case of reorganisation proceedings, stating that the opening of such proceedings does not lead to the triggering of acceleration clauses, under which sums of money to be paid, or other obligations to be performed, become payable and due immediately.[51] The Commercial Code provides that these clauses are deemed non-existent ('*non-écrites*'). **12.40**

(3)(b) Close-out netting provisions

Close-out netting is permitted under French law and close-out netting provisions are governed by Article L211–36–1 II of the Financial and Monetary Code, regarding their assessment, set-off and termination. **12.41**

(3)(c) Flip clauses

Such clauses are not addressed by the Commercial Code, which deals with termination clauses only.[52] **12.42**

(3)(d) Flawed/conditional rights

Since the commencement of insolvency proceedings has no effect on termination clauses, contractual terms which attempt to achieve the same result are also deemed null and void.[53] As a result, a counterparty cannot request the debtor to pay any amounts due prior to the beginning of the insolvency proceedings before he agrees to perform his own obligations,[54] regardless of any clause in the contract requiring such payment as a pre-condition of his performance. **12.43**

(3)(e) Liquidated damages/penalty provisions

The French Supreme Court has held that a clause determining the amount of damages due in the event of a breach of contract is enforceable. If the counterparty is not compensated as a result of the opening of insolvency proceedings but instead, as a result of the insolvency official's decision to reject an executory contract, neither the *pari passu* principle, nor the general rule **12.44**

---

51 Ibid., art L622–29.

52 There is no case law on the validity of such clauses under French law so far. Issues surrounding flip clauses have mainly been addressed by English and US courts in the late 2000s. See *Perpetual Trustee Company Ltd v BNY Corporate Trustee Services Ltd* [2009] EWHC 1912 (Ch) and *Lehman Bros. Special Fin. Inc. v BNY Corporate Tr. Servs. (In re Lehman Bros. Holdings Inc.)*, 422 B.R. 407 (Bankr. S.D.N.Y. 2010). These conflicting decisions expose the differences in approach in both jurisdictions and therefore highlight the lack of harmonisation across jurisdictions in terms of the enforcement of such clauses.

53 Cass. Com. 2 March 1993, Case No. 90–21849; Cass. Com. 19 December 1995, Case no. 93–20398.

54 Cass. Com. 3 April 2011, Case No. 10–19463 JCP E 2004, p. 1713.

nullifying termination clauses can support the invalidity of a liquidated damage clause.[55]

C. REFORMS

(1) Major reforms of French insolvency law to date

12.45 *2000:* The new Commercial Code came into force, reconsolidating insolvency and restructuring law, in its Book VI. In 2003, insolvency practice was modernised, and insolvency law was later reformed in 2005.

12.46 The principal innovation of this law was the introduction of safeguard proceedings, modelled on Chapter 11 proceedings but incorporating some specifically French characteristics. It also introduced the *ad hoc* representative.

12.47 However, the changes brought in by the Law of 2005 did not have the expected impact and the French government quickly realised that the new safeguard procedure was not as attractive as it had hoped, with just over 500 procedures being opened in each of the first few years after the 2005 law came into force.[56] On the other hand, the number of conciliation and *ad hoc* proceedings increased and 2,500 procedures were reported annually, compared to 1,500 procedures before the Law entered into force.[57]

12.48 *Law n°2008–676 of 4 August 2008* on the Modernisation of the Economy (‘*Loi de modernisation de l'économie*’) was passed and enhanced most of the insolvency procedures contained within Book VI of the Commercial Code, especially pre-insolvency and out-of-court procedures. *Ordinance n°2008–1345*[58] which followed was a response by the French legislator to the Law of 2005 and to the practical difficulties encountered by companies since the introduction of the safeguard proceeding. The Ordinance is principally aimed at making the safeguard proceedings more accessible and clarifying the rules governing such

55 Cass. Com. 13 June 2006, Case No. 05–14138.

56 See T. Montéran, ‘Pour améliorer le droit des entreprises, osons la réforme’ (2008) 24 Gazette du Palais 3. More precise statistics are quoted by M-H. Monsèrié-Bon and C. Saint-Alary-Houin, ‘La loi de sauvegardes des entreprises: nécessité et intérêt d'une réforme annoncée’ (2008) 14 Recueil Dalloz 941, noting 500 procedures in 2006 and 506 in 2007.

57 T. Montéran, ibid.

58 See Ordinance N°2008–1345 of 18 December 2008. An account of these reforms can be found in P. Omar, ‘French Insolvency Law: Remodelling the Reform of 2005’ (2009) 6 *International Company and Commercial Law Review* 225; P. Omar, ‘Preservation and Pre-Packs à la Française: The Evaluation of French Insolvency Law after 2005’ (2011) 8 *International Company and Commercial Law Review* 258.

procedure. Additionally, it liberalised the *ad hoc* and conciliation proceedings by making them more flexible.

Law n°2010–1249 of 22 October 2010: In the wake of the global financial crisis, the French legislator focused on the financial and banking sector and introduced a pre-pack procedure through the AFS procedure.[59] **12.49**

With the multiplication of the reforms and the coming into force of new insolvency and pre-insolvency procedures, French insolvency law modernised its insolvency law to focus on restructuring viable companies. However, the continued impact of the global financial and the Eurozone crises led to continuous underemployment and the incapacity of successive governments to turn the economy around. These factors led to a review of the commercial legislation, including insolvency law, by the government in 2012.[60] In its report accompanying the reformed legislative text, the government explained that the new legislation was geared towards improving the existing procedures' efficiency.[61] The report listed the main objectives of the new law as (i) the need to efficiently foresee the worsening of businesses' economic conditions; (ii) the need to improve the protection afforded to creditors; and (iii) the necessity to improve procedural insolvency rules to ensure 'greater security, simplicity and effectiveness'.[62] **12.50**

Ordinance n°2014–326 of 12 March 2014[63] extensively reformed French bankruptcy law with a view to: (1) favouring preventative measures; (2) strengthening the efficiency of pre-insolvency proceedings; and (3) increasing the rights of creditors in insolvency proceedings. **12.51**

The text of the Ordinance is quite lengthy and extensive, with 117 articles regarding insolvency provisions contained in the Commercial Code and other texts. Importantly, two new restructuring procedures were introduced: the '*sauvegarde financière*' and the '*rétablissement professionnel*'.[64] These procedures **12.52**

59 Law N°2010–1249 of 22 October 2010, see arts 57–58.

60 See P. Pétel, 'Entreprises en Difficulté: encore une réforme' (2014) 18 Entreprises et Affaires 20.

61 Rapport au Président de la République relative à l'ordonnance N°2014–326 du 12 Mars 2014 portant réforme à la prévention des difficultés des entreprises et des procédures collectives.

62 'Améliorer les règles de procédures pour plus de sécurité, de simplicité et d'efficacité'.

63 Ordinance N°2014–326 of 12 March 2014, 'portant réforme de la prévention des difficultés des entreprises et des procédures collectives'.

64 Ibid., at Chapter IV, Section 3, 'Dispositions relatives au rétablissement professionnel'. A physical person debtor who has not been the subject of insolvency proceedings and has not employed anyone within the past six months, and who owns assets not exceeding an amount to be determined by subsequent decree may request to open a '*rétablissement professionnel*' rather than judicial rehabilitation or liquidation. The procedure is opened for a period of four months and does not result in the debtor losing control of his assets. Although

are conditional upon the opening of another insolvency proceeding before they can be commenced: conciliation proceedings for the financial safeguard and liquidation proceedings for the '*rétablissement professionnel*'.

12.53 The reform of 2014 also introduced a pre-pack sale plan in conciliation proceedings, i.e., the option for the court-appointed official to draft a partial or total sale plan of the business as a going concern, which would ultimately be implemented in safeguard, rehabilitation or liquidation proceedings. The main objective of this reform was to speed up the duration of insolvency proceedings and shorten the period during which the company is undergoing insolvency proceedings, in order to preserve the value of the business which is to be sold.[65]

12.54 The Ordinance of 2014 extensively reformed most of the provisions of the Commercial Code contained in Book VI.

12.55 *Law n°2015–990 of 6 August 2015* ('*Loi Macron*') was designed to promote economic growth, activity, and equal opportunity. Some notable features of this law include the creation of specialised insolvency courts for large cases[66] and the power of courts to dilute or compel divestiture of shareholder interests in reorganisation proceedings ('cram down').[67]

12.56 Additionally, *Ordinance 2015–1024 of 20 August 2015* implementing various European financial provisions[68] was also adopted, which aimed at strengthening the framework regarding resilience in times of financial crises, and at promoting the rescue of financial institutions, prior to any grant of public aid.

12.57 *Law n°2016–1547 of 18 November 2016* on the Modernisation of 21st Century Justice[69] focused on the promotion of the rescue culture; the enhancement of confidentiality; the ring-fencing of new monies during restructuring; and the improvement of transparency and impartiality.[70]

---

claims against the debtor are not suspended, the supervising judge may, at the request of the debtor, order the rescheduling of amounts due for a period of four months.

65 The first pre-pack sale plan was implemented in June 2015 when the business and assets of NextiraOne, a spin-off of Alcatel-Lucent, were transferred (alongside all of its 1,400 employees) to a purchaser only one month after the opening of rehabilitation proceedings.

66 Law N°2015–990, at Chapter V, Section 1. See Commercial Code, Article L721–8.

67 Commercial Code, art L631–19–2.

68 Ordonnance 2015–1024 of 20 August 2015 'portant diverses dispositions d'adaptation de la législation d'adaptation de la législation au droit de l'Union européenne en matière financière'.

69 Law N°2016–1547 'de modernisation de la justice du XXIè siècle'.

70 Law N°2016–1547 of 18 November 2016, at Article 99 IV 1°; Article 99 III; Article 99 VI 2°, Article 99 IV 3° a); Article 99 VI 1° a°. See also Commercial Code, Article L621–1; Article L611–3; Article L611–6; Commercial Code, Article L611–11; Article L642–2; Article L621–4; Article L641–1.

Regarding the latest French reforms in the insolvency and restructuring area, it is noticeable that the laws of 2014, 2015 and 2016 extensively reformed the field. There is no pending legislation to further reform the French insolvency provisions and the current focus of future reforms is on civil and employment law. It is yet to be seen how any of these current reforms will affect the French restructuring practice. **12.58**

(2) Influences behind the reforms

Political actors have strongly influenced the various reforms of insolvency and restructuring law in France: Law n°2015–990 of 6 August 2015 was named after the then French Minister for the Economy and the Bill preceding Law n°2016–1547 of 18 November 2016 was named after the then Minister for Justice Christiane Taubira. **12.59**

Additionally, the influence of the government can be seen in the format of the instruments passed over the last few years to reform French insolvency law. Indeed, Article 38 of the French Constitution allows the government to regulate some aspects of the law, notably in order to promote the use of preventive measures under Book VI of the French Commercial Code. This is done through ordinances, which are statutory instruments issued by the Council of Ministers in areas of law which are usually reserved for parliamentary legislation. **12.60**

Additionally, the influence of external actors has increased over the years: business unions, such as SOS Entrepreneurs, advocated the introduction of a pre-pack procedure modelled on Chapter 11 of the US Bankruptcy Code to help companies in financial distress to negotiate with their creditors before the opening of a formal insolvency procedure. As a result, business unions were pleased with the creation of a pre-pack and other procedures such as the Accelerated Safeguard procedure. The impact of these business unions and other entrepreneurial actors can also be seen in the introduction of various devices asserting the role of managers, and implementing a debtor-in-possession regime in certain insolvency proceedings. The impact of the banking and lending sector as well as certain type of creditors, such as secured creditors, has led to a rebalancing of powers for the benefit of creditors, giving them an increased role in insolvency proceedings. **12.61**

The role of the negotiation process and lobbying activities before a bill is passed into law has been promoted over the years, since it is argued that laws regulating insolvency proceedings have traditionally been drafted by bureaucrats, unaware of the reality of business life. As a result, the Bill preceding Law **12.62** n°2005–845 of 26 July 2005 for example was deemed to neglect two of the important underlying elements which make a strong insolvency legislation: the promotion of a relationship of trust between stakeholders and of confidentiality of the proceedings. Following intense lobbying activities, mainly by business unions and the lending sector, the French Parliament amended the text and the procedure introduced, relying on the intervention of an *ad hoc* official, is now used in major insolvency cases. The impact of main players in the area of insolvency is therefore extremely useful in shaping efficient laws.

12.63 However, the introduction of new reforms every few years has also been deemed to increase the complexity of the law of insolvency, which sometimes has been criticised as been drafted for the benefit of large companies, rather than for small and medium enterprises, which compose the bulk of companies in France.

(3) Impact of such reforms on executory contracts provisions.

12.64 *Law n°2005–845 of 26 July 2005:* the most notable features of the Law of 2005 concerning executory contracts are:

(a) Article 24 of Law n°2005–845 amended Article L622–6 of the Commercial Code, adding that when insolvency proceedings are opened, the debtor needs to give a list of the executory contracts to the insolvency official.
(b) Article 29 of Law n°2005–845 amended Article L622–13 of the Commercial Code, providing that the counterparty can be awarded damages if the insolvency official does not continue the contract.
(c) Article 9 of Law n°2005–845 amended Article L611–12 of the Commercial Code, stating that creditors who have invested new money into the debtor company or performed essential executory contracts in order to support the continued activity of the debtor as a going concern after the opening of an insolvency proceedings are offered super-priority ranking in conciliation and safeguard proceedings.
(d) Regarding insurance contracts, prior to the Law of 2005 and in accordance with Article L113–6 of the Insurance Code (‘*Code des Assurances*’), the insurer had the right to terminate the insurance contracts in progress on the day of the opening of insolvency proceedings, without having to justify its termination. This article was modified by Law n°2005–845 and insurance contracts are now subject to the general regime applied to executory contracts.

(e) It is also Law n°2005–845 which created specific provisions for certain types of contracts, such as lease agreements for buildings used in relation with the business.

Generally, Law n°2005–845 was quite favourable to the debtor company regarding executory contracts. **12.65**

Ordinance n°2014–326 of 12 March 2014: regarding executory contracts, the Ordinance of 2014 generally provided that the payment of debts arising after the judgment opening insolvency proceedings must be made on their due date if they arose from an executory contract accepted by the insolvency professional.[71] **12.66**

Article 14 added a new Article L611–16 which provided that clauses modifying the conditions of performance of an executory contract, to the detriment of the insolvent debtor opening a restructuring procedure, are deemed non-existent, as well as those imposing the financial burden of the clause on the debtor only. **12.67**

The Ordinance introduced the Accelerated Safeguard and therefore added some provisions regarding executory contracts under such procedure,[72] notably the possibility for the insolvency professional to ask the insolvency judge to terminate the contract if it is not excessively detrimental to the counterparty.[73] **12.68**

Law n°2016–1547 of 18 November 2016: Article 99 of Law n°2016–1547 contained the amendments regarding executory contracts. Generally, Article L641–13 of the Commercial Code, as amended by Law n°2016–1547 of 18 November 2016 reformulates the concept of claims arising under an executory contract. Previously, the law provided that claims arising from an executory contract after the opening of insolvency proceedings had a preferential status, if the executory contract had been accepted by the liquidator. However, this led to confusion in cases where liquidation proceedings were opened following the opening or a restructuring procedure. Such claims could not have a preferential status since the executory contract was not accepted by a liquidator. Article 99 V of Law n°2016–1547 of 18 November 2016 corrected this gap and the word 'liquidator' was removed from the text.[74] Article L641–13 I of the Commercial Code now provides that preferential **12.69**

71 Ordinance N°2014–326, at Article 68, modifying Commercial Code, art L641–13.

72 Commercial Code, art L622–13 III.

73 Commercial Code, art L622–13 IV.

74 Law N°2016–1547, art 99 VI, §1, c.

claims are those arising from an executory contract accepted in a restructuring or liquidation procedure.

(4) General trends in French reforms

12.70 Generally, the rate at which reforms of French insolvency law have been passed has intensified since the economic crisis of 2008–2009. The French regime has shifted towards offering more protection and advantages to creditors. Indeed, the reform of 2014 undoubtedly improved the situation of creditors in particular by (a) relaxing the formality surrounding creditors' claims; (b) offering creditors the right to propose their own restructuring plan (or a counter-proposal to a debtor's plan); and (c) giving creditors a bigger role to play in insolvency and restructuring proceedings.

12.71 On the other hand, however, the successive reforms have also promoted the rescue of viable companies, therefore enhancing the options offered to the debtor, notably by abolishing the obligation of debtors to settle due debts in one payment following the opening of safeguard proceedings, by accelerating the liquidation procedure and importantly by creating the '*rétablissement professionnel*' proceeding which leads to a cancellation of debts altogether.

12.72 French insolvency law is now providing more rules governing out-of-court workouts, in particular provisions aiming at anticipating the debtor's financial difficulties, by implementing various alert procedures, which can be triggered by different actors such as the statutory auditor,[75] the employees' council,[76] the shareholders,[77] the President of the Court.[78]

12.73 Interestingly, since the beginning of the financial crisis in 2008, restructuring cases have mostly been negotiated through amicable and out-of-court proceedings,[79] which have now become the customary proceedings for negotiations between the various stakeholders in an insolvency case. The introduction of pre-pack proceedings over the last few years has contributed to this development, by promoting the use of pre-insolvency, amicable and out-of-court procedures, considered more efficient than traditional insolvency proceedings.

---

75 Commercial Code, arts L234–1 *et seq.*

76 Labour Code, art L2313–14.

77 Commercial Code, art L223–36.

78 Ibid., art L611–2 I.

79 See M. Guillonneau, J-P. Haehl and B. Munoz-Perez, 'La prévention des difficultés des entreprises par le mandat ad hoc et la conciliation devant les juridictions commerciales de 2006 à 2011', Rapport de Recherche, Ministère de la Justice (2013).

The repeated reforms introduced following the economic and financial global crisis have greatly modernised French insolvency law, improving the flexibility of out-of-court and pre-insolvency proceedings and creditors' rights. Creditors, notably new investors, are now offered a greater role in their debtor's insolvency proceedings, allowing for negotiations to be conducted more efficiently. 12.74

(5) The European context underpinning French reforms

The latest French insolvency reforms have been prompted by several European measures pushing the member states to modernise their rescue regimes. Such instruments comprise notably the European Commission Recommendation on a New Approach to Business Failure,[80] the European Insolvency Regulation Recast 2015[81] and the Proposal for an insolvency Directive of 22 November 2016.[82] 12.75

Such documents generally advocate the strengthening of pre-insolvency proceedings and the rescue culture and for more convergence of the member states' insolvency and restructuring laws since 25 per cent of European insolvency proceedings have cross-border effects.[83] The Recommendation of 2014 in particular, has had a great influence on the French insolvency and rescue law regime, notably visible with the reform of 2014. Indeed, as explained above, the Ordinance of 2014 extensively reformed the legislation with a view to favouring reorganisation at a preventive stage, strengthening the efficiency of out-of-court proceedings and increasing the rights of creditors in insolvency proceedings. 12.76

Generally, the insolvency benchmark has improved over the crisis period in France, following the extensive reforms in this area. France, therefore, offers various preventive restructuring procedures and over the years, has introduced a debtor-in-possession regime, a cram-down element, a moratorium on enforcement actions and the possibility for debtor for equity swap into its legislation. As a result, France has a number of procedures that already satisfy the provisions set out in the Proposal for a Preventive Restructuring 12.77

80 Council of the European Union, Comission Recommendation of 12.3.2014 on a new approach to business failure and insolvency (C(2014) 1500 final).

81 European Parliament and Council Regulation (EU) 2015/848 on insolvency proceedings (recast) of 20 May 2015, OJ L141/19.

82 Proposal for a Directive of the European Parliament and of the Council on preventive restructuring frameworks, second chance and measures to increase the efficiency of restructuring, insolvency and discharge procedures and amending Directive 2012/30/EU [2016].

83 European Commission Staff Working Document, Impact Assessment accompanying the document Revision of Regulation (EC) No 1346/2000 on insolvency proceedings, SWD(2012) 416 17.

Directive.[84] However, improvements could be made: Doing Business Report states that France scores 11 (out of 16) for the strength of its insolvency framework.[85] Additionally, in Europe, between 30 and 90 per cent of debts owed to creditors are paid back by debtors and 78 per cent of debts are repaid by French debtors.[86]

12.78 Finally, regarding the international context, the adoption of the UNCITRAL Model Law on Cross-Border Insolvency has been discussed but, for the time being, no steps have been taken to implement it in France.

D. CONCLUDING REMARKS

12.79 Since the start of the global financial and economic crisis in 2008–2009, French insolvency law reforms have intensified. Law n°2005–845 of 26 July 2005 set off a new approach to regulating insolvency and rescue law in France, promoting restructuring provisions. Three years later, Law n°2008–676 of 4 August 2008 on the Modernisation of the Economy fulfilled the promise inscribed in its name, by strengthening most of the insolvency provisions contained in Book VI of the Commercial Code. Two years later, Law n°2010–1249 of 22 October 2010 focused on enhancing procedures afforded to financial and banking institutions.

12.80 Another shift occurred in 2014, first with the choice of format of instruments adopted. Indeed, the passing of ordinances as opposed to laws showed the involvement of the Government in the reform activity, as well as the urgency of such modernisation. Second, Ordinances n°2014–326 of 12 March 2014 and n°2015–1024 of 20 August 2015 extensively reformed the substance of insolvency and restructuring law by promoting preventive measures. Finally, Law n°2016–1547 of 18 November 2016 on the Modernisation of 21st Century Justice continued on such path by promoting the rescue culture.

12.81 The main drivers behind the most recent reforms have been the lending sector and business unions. Their lobbying activities resulted in the introduction of more efficient pre-insolvency and out-of-court proceedings, as well as an increase in the creditors' role. Additionally, such reforms have been driven by

---

84 Proposal for a Directive of the European Parliament and of the Council on preventive restructuring frameworks, second chance measures, insolvency, and discharge procedures and amending Directive 2012/30/EU [2016] COM723 final.

85 The World Bank, 'Doing Business: Measuring Business Regulations'. Available at http://www.doingbusiness.org/en/data/exploreeconomies/france/resolving-insolvency#DB_ri lst accessed 10 December 2018.

86 See Stéphanie Chatelon and Arnaud Pédron, *supra* note 19.

the developments at European level, in particular the European Commission Recommendation on a New Approach to Business Failure 2014, as well as the general convergence of national insolvency regimes happening across the EU member states. As a result, France has now become more competitive in the EU, offering attractive and efficient insolvency and restructuring proceedings to French and European companies facing financial distress.

Finally, regarding the evolution of the treatment of executory contracts, the general trend has been to increase the protection afforded to debtors' counterparties. **12.82**

All the aforementioned reforms have improved the balance between debtor and creditor protection: France is now a more investor-friendly jurisdiction, while debtors benefit from a more sophisticated set of tools. **12.83**

13

NATIONAL REPORT FOR GERMANY

Vanessa Buttafuoco

A. INTRODUCTION

13.01 The current legal sources of insolvency law in Germany are the Insolvency Act (*'Insolvenzordnung'*, InsO), which entered into force in 1999 after a major reform of the system, and its Implementing Law (EGInsO). Further insolvency regulations are contained in other laws, for example, in the German Civil Code (BGB) and the Commercial Code (HGB). They cover in particular the duty to lodge the application for insolvency and the personal liability of the debtor's representative bodies.

13.02 The primary objective of insolvency proceedings, pursuant to Section 1 of the InsO, is to fulfil the claims of the creditor by utilizing the debtor's assets. In principle all creditors are treated equally. The purpose of the procedure is to pay to all the creditors at least a small proportion of their debts. The underlining principle is the *par conditio creditorum*. In order to prevent a few creditors from consuming the last remaining assets of the debtor, insolvency proceedings forbid the individual creditors the independent execution in the assets in favour of a coordinated overall execution.[1]

1 Reinhard Bork, *Einführung in das Insolvenzrecht* (7th edn, Mohr Siebeck, Tübingen 2014).

The insolvency proceedings are mostly procedural, although they are also intended to establish the claims lodged. The entry into the insolvency table is the basis for enforcement after the conclusion of the proceedings. The InsO also regulates the impact on the private rights of the parties concerned. This applies in particular to the handling of contractual relationships and to the contestation of legal transactions, which have been carried out before the opening of the insolvency proceedings. **13.03**

B. AVAILABLE PROCEDURES

The InsO establishes different insolvency procedures. The Main Procedure ('*Regelinsolvenzverfahren*') is ruled in Section 11 InsO.[2] A procedure aimed specifically at the restructuring of the debtor's company is the Insolvency Plan Procedure ('*Insolvenzplanverfahren*'), ruled in Sections 217–269. In a similar direction goes the Self-Management Procedure ('Eigenverwaltung') ruled in Sections 270–285.[3] **13.04**

Out-of-court proceedings are not possible for company insolvency but only for cases of consumer bankruptcy, as ruled in Section 305 (I) 1. **13.05**

(1) The main procedure – *Regelinsolvenzverfahren*

An insolvency procedure is divided into two sections: the opening procedure and the subsequent, actual insolvency proceedings. **13.06**

a. The insolvency application

The insolvency proceedings are initiated only on application in accordance with Section 13 (1) 1. As a possible debtor in insolvency proceedings, Section 11 cites natural and legal persons, as well as companies without legal personality, e.g., open commercial partnership, limited partnership and civil society. The application must be submitted to the competent district court as an insolvency court (Sections 2 and 3). **13.07**

The debtors and their creditors are, pursuant to Section 13 (1), entitled to lodge an application for insolvency. In the case of legal persons and companies without legal personality, every member of the representative body (managing director, board member) and every personally liable partner is entitled to **13.08**

2 All following Sections without any specification of the Act are of the InsO.
3 Klaus Reischl, *Insolvenzrecht* (3rd edn, Müller, Heidelberg 2014) 3.

apply. According to Section 15a InsO, legal persons and companies without legal personality, in which no shareholder is personally liable, such as a GmbH & Co. KG, even have a duty to lodge an application for insolvency in due time. This is due to the fact that only limited liability is available to such creditors, since no shareholder is personally liable.[4]

b. The insolvency reason

13.09 The essential prerequisite for opening insolvency proceedings is the existence of an insolvency reason. The InsO provides in Sections 17–19 for three: insolvency ('*Zahlungsunfähikeit*'), imminent insolvency ('*drohende Zahlungsunfähigkeit*') and over-indebtedness ('*Überschuldung*').

Insolvency

13.10 Section 17 (2) defines '*insolvency*' as the incapacity to meet its own due payment obligations. Such an incapacity exists if the payment obligations exceed the available or readily available cash. The payment due date is primarily determined by the provisions of the BGB, but the claim must also be seriously demanded by its holder.[5] This is the case when the creditor has expressly demanded the fulfilment of his claim. Exceptions are hereby made to demands, which are deferred, or whose non-fulfilment is temporarily tolerated, for example when the creditor has not solicited fulfilment from the debtor. The feature of 'soliciting' thus, serves only the purpose of exempting those claims that are actually deferred – that is to say, even without any legal will to bind or discernible explanation.[6]

13.11 The value of the non-fulfilled liabilities must be at least 10 per cent of the total liabilities, in order to differentiate the insolvency from a temporary liquidity reduction. In addition, the lack of liquidity must have been present for at least three weeks.[7] Pursuant to section 17 (2) 2, the insolvency of the debtor is presumed when the latter has ceased payments. Such a suspension of payments shall be deemed to exist, if the conduct of the debtor suggests the persistent inability to pay a substantial portion of the debts.[8]

---

4 Ulrich Foerste, *Insolvenzrecht* (6th edn, C. H. Beck, München 2014) 91.

5 Bundesgerichtshof: *IX ZR 63/08*. In: Neue Zeitschrift für Insolvenz- und Sanierungsrecht 2009, S. 471 (472) and Mock, Sebastian: *§ 17*, Rn. 117. In: Wilhelm Uhlenbruck, Heribert Hirte, Heinz Vallender (Hrsg.): *Insolvenzordnung: Kommentar*. 14. Auflage. Vahlen, München 2015.

6 Bundesgerichtshof: *IX ZR 63/08*. In: Neue Zeitschrift für Insolvenz- und Sanierungsrecht 2009, S. 471 (472–473).

7 Ludwig Häsemeyer, *Insolvenzrecht* (4th edn, Carl Heymanns, Köln 2007) 7.20–7.21.

8 Ibid.

Imminent insolvency

The '*imminent insolvency*', defined in Section 18, is open to the debtor as a special insolvency reason. The aim of the scheme is to provide the debtor with an incentive to lodge the insolvency application as early as possible in order to promote an effective procedure.[9] This reason is blocked for the creditors, to prevent them from putting pressure on the debtor with the threat of an insolvency application based on forecasts.[10] **13.12**

An application for imminent insolvency is justified, in accordance with Section 18 (2), if the debtor can foresee that his means of payment, including all credit lines and comparable values, are not sufficient to meet his obligations within a reasonable period of time.[11] The law does not define the duration of this projection period. The current jurisprudence assumes that this period may not exceed 12 months. The newer jurisprudence of the Federal Supreme Court (BGH) requires that the application be filed with corresponding proof.[12] **13.13**

Over-indebtedness

The requirement of '*over-indebtedness*', regulated in Section 19, comes into consideration only in the case of legal persons or in the case of partnerships in which no shareholder is a natural person. Like the obligation to submit the application for insolvency (Section 15a) this additional reason arises from the fact that only a limited amount of liability is available to the creditors.[13] Under Section 19 (1), the debtor is over-indebted if his assets no longer cover the existing liabilities. This over-indebtedness is determined by establishing a balance sheet, which is used to compare the liabilities and the assets of the debtor. Subsequently, a forecast of the success of a possible continuation of the company is to be prepared.[14] **13.14**

c. The examination of the application

The insolvency court will subsequently examine if the application is admissible and substantiated. The application is substantiated if at least one of the three causes of insolvency is present and the insolvency assets cover the costs of the proceedings (Section 26). The insolvency assets are the total assets which the debtor owns at the time of the opening and which he obtains during the **13.15**

9 Rolf Leithaus: *§ 18*, Rn. 2. In: Dirk Andres, Rolf Leithaus, Michael Dahl (Hrsg.), *Insolvenzordnung: (InsO); Kommentar* (3rd edn, C. H. Beck, München 2014).

10 Ulrich Foerste, *supra* note 4, 113.

11 Ludwig Häsemeyer, *supra* note 7, 7.22.

12 BGH, 05.12.2013 – IX ZR 93/11.

13 Rolf Leithaus, *supra* note 9.

14 Ulrich Foerste, *supra* note 4,116–19.

proceedings (Section 35). If the assets do not cover the costs of the proceedings the application is rejected for lack of assets.

13.16 In the period leading up to the decision on the application, the insolvency court has the duty to take measures to secure the insolvency assets so that these cannot be further reduced during the hovering period (Section 21). The appointment of a provisional insolvency administrator may be considered as such a measure. In addition, a prohibition of execution could be imposed against the debtor and foreclosures against him may be prohibited or temporarily interrupted.

d. Opening decision

13.17 If the opening requirements are met, the court decides to open the insolvency proceedings and makes the decision public in accordance with Section 30 (1). In addition, the insolvency administrator is appointed. As a rule, the provisional insolvency administrator takes the position of the final insolvency administrator.[15] The creditors are requested to assert their claims and security rights within a specified period (Section 28). The report deadline and the examination date are also set.

e. Effects of the opening of the proceedings

13.18 As soon as the insolvency proceedings are opened, the debtor is deprived of his administration right. Disposal authority over his assets is transferred to the insolvency administrator for the protection of the insolvency estate, although the debtor remains the owner of the assets (Section 80 I). The insolvency administrator is immediately obliged to take possession of the assets belonging to the estate (Section 148 (1)). Likewise, the debtor cannot carry out any legal proceedings with effect for the insolvency estate. According to Section 81, dispositions, which the debtor undertakes over the insolvency estate objects after the opening of the proceedings, are ineffective. For the purposes of effective measure protection, the standard covers any legal action by the debtor at the expense of the assets, including rescues, contestations, deadlines or trials.

13.19 During the period of insolvency proceedings, insolvency creditors may exclusively claim their claims, pursuant to Section 87, as insolvency claims. Compulsory enforcements are excluded pursuant to Section 88. To this end, they must register their claims in writing with the insolvency administrator in accordance with Section 174 I 1.

---

15 Ibid., 97.

f. The reporting meeting

The insolvency administrator creates lists of the objects and financial assets as well as of the creditors. These have to be presented to the court no later than one week before the reporting date and the parties have a right to view them (Sections 151–154). At the reporting meeting, the insolvency administrator reports on the economic situation of the debtor to the creditors' meeting, explaining the possibility of a restructuring for the company and an insolvency plan (Section 156). **13.20**

The creditors, the debtor, the administrator and the creditors' committee previously appointed by the insolvency court (Section 74) compose the creditors' meeting, which is headed by a judicial officer. It decides, on the basis of the report, on the progress of the insolvency proceedings (Section 29 (1) 1), in particular about the decommissioning or continuation of the company (Section 57). **13.21**

g. The claims inspection

After the registration of the claims, pursuant to Section 174, the insolvency administrator submits a formal check to each claim form. He checks whether the application is duly filed, and whether the reason and the amount are indicated in the application. In the event of a formal error the application will be rejected. Otherwise, the administrator shall enter the application into the claim table. Before the table is open to all parties for inspection (Section 175), the Insolvency Court re-examines the admissibility of the individual applications on the basis of the aforementioned criteria. **13.22**

At the examination date, the registered claims are examined within the framework of a creditors' meeting (Sections 29 (1) 2 and 176). If neither the administrator nor a creditor contradicts a claim, it is deemed to be established and is entered in the ranking and amount table (Section 178). In the case of a contradiction, a distinction is made between an enforceable and a non-enforceable claim. In the case of an enforceable claim, that is, where an enforceable judgement or an executable deed had already been issued before the opening of the proceedings, it is up to the contestant to pursue the contradiction. In the case of a non-enforceable claim, the creditor may bring an action for determination before the court (Section 179–186). **13.23**

h. Exploitation of the assets

Afterwards the administrator may, without the consent of the creditors' meeting, sell commercial goods individually or auction them. If he plans to sell the company, he shall, in accordance with Section 160, have the consent of the **13.24** creditors' committee or, if the latter is not appointed, the creditors' meeting. The divestment means that the company is no longer an insolvency factor, but the sale will increase the value of the insolvency estate. Special features apply to the exploitation of objects, which are subject to segregation rights. The right to segregate gives the holder the right to be satisfied before all the other creditors.[16]

13.25 The exploitation of the assets can, thus, be carried out in different ways: in the case of liquidation, the entire debtor's assets are utilized in the context of foreclosures or private sales. The creditors are satisfied with the revenues of the liquidation. The restoration, on the other hand, assists the preservation of the company: it aims at making the undertaking viable again in order to satisfy the creditors with the profits generated.[17]

i. The distribution

13.26 If the assets are converted into money, the 'insolvency estate liability' is dealt with first. This covers the costs of the insolvency proceedings (Section 53), i.e., the remunerations of the provisional and the final administrator as well as the court costs (§ 54).

13.27 Afterwards, the 'insolvency creditors' will be satisfied. These are creditors who acquired a claim against the insolvency estate during the proceedings, such as suppliers who were to supply the insolvent company to continue their own production (Section 55).[18] Finally, the other creditors, whose claims existed at the time the proceedings were opened, are satisfied from the remaining funds (Section 38).

13.28 According to Section 195, the creditors' committee assumes the task of determining the quota. At the examination date, the administrator creates a list of claims to be taken into account during the distribution, the insolvency table (Section 188). After the exploitation of the insolvency estate has ended, the final distribution is made in accordance with Section 196 with the consent of the insolvency court.

j. Closing of insolvency procedures

13.29 After completion of the final distribution, the court closes the proceedings (Section 200). Once these have been closed, the creditors can, in principle,

16 Ulrich Foerste, *supra* note 4, 368.

17 Heinrich Friedhoff, *Sanierung einer Firma durch Eigenverwaltung und Insolvenzplan.* In: Zeitschrift für Wirtschaftsrecht 2002, 497.

18 Klaus Reischl, *supra* note 3, 392.

assert their remaining claims without limitation, for example by way of individual enforcement. The enforcement is then carried out with an enforceable extract from the insolvency table, which has judicial power in the procedure (Section 201). The insolvency table is a list of all registered and audited receivables of the insolvency creditors prepared by the insolvency administrator in accordance with Section 175. Whether and to what extent the determined receivables from the insolvency table will be paid out will be determined by the insolvency rate at the latest at the conclusion of the insolvency proceedings. This depends on how much mass is available to satisfy the creditor's claims.

However, enforcement cannot be carried out from the table entry after the insolvency proceedings have been closed if the debtor himself has denied the existence of the claim. In such a case, in order to obtain a title for enforcement after the insolvency proceeding has been terminated, the creditor has to bring an action for a declaratory judgment against the debtor (Section 184). If, at the time of the opening of the insolvency proceedings, a legal dispute was already pending against the debtor, the creditor must resume the proceedings and change the action for payment to an action for a declaratory judgment. In the event of a successful judgment, the creditor can then execute even after the insolvency proceedings have been terminated. **13.30**

In practice, enforcement after the end of the proceedings is often not possible: natural persons can apply for the residual debt exemption in the context of the insolvency proceedings. If the court grants such a sentence, enforcement is no longer possible (Sections 291 and 294). If the debtor is a legal person who no longer has any assets after the insolvency proceedings have been carried out, the debtor shall be extinguished *ex officio* in accordance with Section 394 (1) 2 FamFG, so that any claims shall become irrelevant. **13.31**

(2) The insolvency plan – *Insolvenzplanverfahren*

Within the regulatory process, the insolvency regulation provides the newly created instrument of the insolvency plan (Sections 217–234). Within this framework, the parties can reach agreements differing from the regulatory procedure in several ways. In particular, an arrangement for maintaining the company can be made. Following the acceptance of the insolvency plan by the creditors, the Insolvency Court decides on its confirmation (Section 248). In the context of this decision, which is *ex officio*, the court also checks whether the lack of consent from creditor groups (Section 245) is to be replaced. **13.32**

13.33 The plan must be rejected *ex officio* if the provisions on the content and the procedural treatment of the insolvency have not been complied with according to a substantial point and the deficiency cannot be remedied (§ 252). A further reason for failure is that the plan is unfair, in particular by favouring an interested party over the others (Section 250 No. 2). Unfair and therefore void would be the assumption of an insolvency plan by means of a purchase, which offers particular advantages to individual creditors.[19] This would be the case, for example, if a creditor or a third party acquires the other creditor's claims at a price in excess of the quota provided for in the submitted insolvency plan and, with the majority of votes so obtained, effects acceptance of the insolvency plan.[20]

(3) The self-administration procedure – *Eigenverwaltung*

13.34 In the case of the self-administration procedure, no insolvency administrator will be appointed. Instead, the debtor carries out the procedure for which he retains his power of disposal. However, he is supervised by an administrator, appointed by the court, in his business activities, pursuant to Section 270.[21]

13.35 The self-administration procedure is of little importance in practice: since it entered into force in March 2012, just 2.7 per cent of the companies' insolvency activities in Germany were carried out by self-administration. There is, however, one exception: in the case of large-scale enterprises. One-third of the 50 largest insolvency proceedings since 2012 were carried out in self-administration. Smaller companies seem to have problems with the more complex application process; more and more self-administration applications fail: since 2012, more than 40 per cent of the self-administration procedures applied for have ended in '*Regelinsolvenzverfahren*'.[22]

C. EXECUTORY CONTRACTS AND CONTRACTUAL REMEDIES

13.36 At the opening of proceedings, the debtor is typically in contractual relations with other persons. If the creditor has already provided his service in full under a mutual contract, such as a purchase, lease or work contract, his claim is a

19 Dirk Andres,*§ 250*, Rn. 8. In: Dirk Andres, Rolf Leithaus, Michael Dahl (Hrsg), *supra* note 9.

20 Nils Derksen, Die Unternehmenssanierung innerhalb und außerhalb der Insolvenz (Nomos 2016) 138.

21 Helmut Zipperer, *§ 270*, No. 12. In: Wilhelm Uhlenbruck, Heribert Hirte, Heinz Vallender (Hrsg.), *Insolvenzordnung: Kommentar* (14th edn Vahlen, München 2015).

22 Strategieberatung Boston Consulting Group: https://www.finance-magazin.de/strategie-effizienz/unternehmensstrategie/insolvenzrecht-unternehmen-tun-sich-mit-esug-schwer-1346599/.

claim for the insolvency estate. If the debtor has fully performed, the insolvency administrator may request the creditor to pay the amount back.

The processing of open legal relationships is a core problem in insolvency proceedings. According to the InsO, the legal situation of the debtor is treated differently, depending on the kind of legal relationship. **13.37**

(1) The insolvency administrator's right of choice and executing contracts

A general rule for the execution of mutual contracts, which is quite relevant in practice, is Section 103, which grants the insolvency administrator a right of choice with regard to the fulfilment of certain contracts. The application of Section 103 presupposes that a mutual contract is not fully fulfilled by either party by the time of the opening of the insolvency procedures. **13.38**

All contractual obligations, which are subject to a dependency relationship (synallagma), fall under the scope of Section 103 InSO, unless there are special regulations. These include purchase, exchange, and work contracts, but also competition agreements and settlements. **13.39**

Service contracts are subject to the special provisions of Sections 108, 113: contracts of employment with insolvent workers remain unchanged. However, employment contracts with insolvent employers can be terminated prematurely by the administrator (Section 113 (1)). For rent and leasing contracts of the debtor, Sections 108 and 109 contain special rules. However, they relate only to rental and lease agreements on immovable objects or rooms. For leasing or leasing contracts on vehicles, therefore, the applicability of Section 103 shall remain.[23] Mandates ordered by the debtor and proxies granted by the debtor with respect to the property forming part of the insolvency estate are extinguished according to Sections 115 (I) and 117 (I). The details are comprehensively regulated in Sections 104–118 InsO. **13.40**

If the insolvency administrator chooses the fulfilment of the contract, the creditor must provide the service and may demand the counter-performance from the debtor. According to Section 55 (1) No. 2, this claim has the quality of an insolvency estate claim, which means that the administrator can ask for performance and the creditor can only file an insolvency claim for the payment. If the administrator chooses the rejection of the contract, the **13.41**

---

23 Münchener Kommentar Insolvenzordnung – Huber, §103 No. 75 and 78.

creditor cannot demand its fulfilment, but can only file a claim for non-fulfilment, for example, on the loss of profit, as an insolvency claim.

13.42 Over a long period of time, the effect of the opening up of insolvency procedures on executing contracts was highly controversial.

13.43 Previously, the jurisprudence assumed that the reciprocal claims expire and arise through the choice of the administrator (extinction theory).[24] This view has earned criticism from the legal scholars.[25] The main argument against the extinction theory is provided by Section 201, which stipulates that the claims can again be enforced against the debtor after the closing of the insolvency proceedings. This presupposes that the requirements in the process are not extinguished but are only hindered in their enforceability.[26]

13.44 Therefore, the jurisprudence has disregarded the extinction theory and now argues that the claims arising from contracts of the debtor are not extinguished but are hindered in their enforceability with the opening of proceedings. If the administrator opts for the fulfilment, the claims become enforceable again. In doing so, they receive the quality of original insolvency estate claims and liabilities (quality leap theory).[27] This quality leap is beneficial for the insolvency estate, because it shakes off the opposing rights of the contracting party. Offsetting would fail according to Section 96 (1) No. 1 and the assignment according to Section 91.[28]

13.45 For certain types of contracts the norms following Section 103 contain special provisions restricting the option rights of the insolvency administrator. Some regulations relate to long-term debt obligations, such as tenancy and lease contracts, as well as employment contracts. In particular, the latter are protected in a special way, for example through insolvency and unemployment benefits as well as through the participation of the workers' council in the case of operational changes.[29]

---

24 BGHZ 116, 156 (158), BGHZ 135, 25 (26–27).

25 Häsemeyer, *supra* note 7, 20.07 and 20.23. Nerlich/Römermann/Tintelnot, Insolvenzordnung, Kommentar 25 Auflage 2013, §103 No. 60.

26 Klaus Reischl, *supra* note 3.

27 Bundesgerichtshof: IX ZR 313/99. In: Neue Zeitschrift für Insolvenzrecht 2002, S. 375. Bundesgerichtshof: IX ZR 51/02. In: Neue Zeitschrift für Insolvenzrecht 2003, S. 491. Dirk Wegener: § 103, No. 133. In: Wilhelm Uhlenbruck, Heribert Hirte, Heinz Vallender (Hrsg.), *supra* note 5.

28 Reinhard Bork, *supra* note 1, 157.

29 Ibid., 167–81.

(2) Contractual remedies – insolvency-related clauses

Contracts often contain provisions, which allow the dissolution of the contract in the event of payment-stop, insolvency or opening of the provisional insolvency proceedings. Such insolvency-related clauses may give the contracting party a right to terminate without notice or a right to rescind the contract, or place the contract under the condition of insolvency-related circumstances. The opinions on the effectiveness of these clauses have been quite different in the past years. **13.46**

In its judgment of 15 November 2012, the Federal Court of Justice (BGH) apparently put an end to the conflict of views on the effectiveness of dissolution-clauses ruling that insolvency-related dissolution-clauses are ineffective, unless a corresponding possibility for the dissolution of the contract is specifically provided for by the law.[30] **13.47**

The BGH defines insolvency-related solution clauses as clauses according to which 'a party is granted the right to rescind the contract in the event of payment-stop, insolvency-application or opening of the insolvency proceedings'.[31] It has been highly controversial in the literature to determine whether such insolvency-dependent solutions are effective. **13.48**

The lower courts, prior to the BGH judgment, had followed in many parts of the literature so far advocated opinion, according to which such clauses were effective.[32] This view argues in particular with the deletion of Section 137(2) in the government draft, which explicitly provided for the ineffectiveness of the clauses of dissolution. The deletion, according to this view, implies that the legislature wanted the permissibility of insolvency-related solution clauses. In addition, Section 112, which provides for a lock-up clause for leasing contracts for pre-insolvency payments, would be obsolete if dissolution clauses were in any event ineffective. Moreover, Section 119 would not be infringed, since the clause of the dissolution relates to the existence of the contract, but not to its execution, in the sense of Sections 103 and following. The insolvency administrator has only the choice to take over the contract as **13.49**

---

30 BGH judgment of 15.11.2012 – IX ZR 169/11.

31 Ulrich Foerste, *supra* note 4, 97.

32 OLG München, ZInsO 2006, 1060, 1062; MünchKomm-InsO/Huber, aaO § 119 Rn. 28 ff; ders. in Gottwald, *Insolvenzrechtshandbuch* (4th edn § 35 Rn) 13; Flöther/Wehner in Ahrens/Gehrlein/Ringstmeier, InsO, § 119 Rn. 2; FK-InsO/Wegener, 6. Aufl., § 119 Rn. 4 ff, 9, aber anders für Energielieferungsverträge Rn. 8; Zeuner in Leonhardt/Smid/ Zeuner, InsO, 3. Aufl., § 119 Rn. 12; von Wilmowsky, ZIP 2007, 553, 554 ff.

agreed between the parties, that is, with all the dissolution clauses and the right to cancel the other party's rights.[33]

13.50 With the ruling, the BGH joined the opposite opinion. According to the BGH these clauses violate Section 119. This section states that contractual agreements obstructing or making the provisions set in Sections 103–118 less effective are void. Ergo, insolvency-related clauses are void since they obstruct the purpose of the insolvency administrator's options under Section 103. Insolvency-independent solution clauses, which relate to non-insolvency-specific circumstances such as default, other contractual infringements or the asset deterioration of the debtor, on the other hand are permissible,[34] since they are not directed to the objective of undermining the option of the insolvency administrator. An insolvency-related solution clause, on the other hand, is linked to a date defined by the insolvency order.

13.51 Insolvency-related dissolution clauses are in any case ineffective if a suitable solution is not already provided for in a special law. The deletion of Section 137(2) in the government draft does not imply that insolvency-dependent clauses are effective. Insolvency-related solution clauses would prevent the right of the insolvency administrator in accordance with Section 103 even before the insolvency, and would therefore be ineffective according to Section 119. Section 103 is concerned with the protection of the insolvency estate and has to work even before the opening of the insolvency proceedings, in order to avoid an idle running of the election right in practice. If the contract were to be favourable for the insolvency estate, the unilateral dissolution would have anti-remedial effects. Section 105 is intended to enable the insolvency administrator to continue to pursue contracts for the supply of goods or energy during the insolvency proceedings under the same conditions as before. The creditor, too, is not thereby unduly burdened because his claim from the unresolved contract is an insolvency estate claim at the time of the performance.[35]

13.52 The clarity provided with this judgment has though somewhat faded by means of another judgment by the BGH from April 2016.[36]

13.53 The subject of the decision was the use of a contract fulfilment guarantee, which would enable the insolvent applicant to secure the fulfilment of his

---

33 Ibid.

34 BGH judgment of 15.11.2012 – IX ZR 169/11, No. 21.

35 Ibid.

36 BGH judgment of 07.04.2016 – VII ZR 56/15.

claims up to an amount of 10 per cent of the contract sum. The contract on the establishment of a commercial building had been stipulated between the parties with inclusion of the Construction Tendering and Contract Regulation (VOB/B). Section 8 (2) 1 VOB/B states that:

> the customer may terminate the contract if the contractor stop his payments, the Insolvency Proceedings (Sections 14–15 InsO) or a comparable legal procedure are initiated by him or by the client or another customer or the opening of the proceedings is rejected due to lack of assets.

The BGH argues that the principle laid down in Section 8 (2) 1 VOB/B is an insolvency-related dissolution clause, which could at least indirectly affect the right to vote of the insolvency administrator according to Section 103 InsO. However, this would not be contrary to Section 119, since the client's contractual right to termination corresponds to the particular interests of the parties involved in the construction. The BGH emphasizes that the personal characteristics of the contractor, such as expert knowledge, performance and reliability, are so important to the client that he cannot be expected to continue the contract with the insolvency administrator if he does not want to. An insolvency administrator, on the other hand, cannot rely on the trust required to fulfil a building contract in the same way, since he will regularly depend on the involvement of third parties, such as suppliers of goods, subcontractors and banks, which often because of their own claims towards the contractor will not be available for further cooperation. **13.54**

In this respect, the client in a building contract differs in principle fundamentally from other creditors, since he regularly has a serious interest in the early solving of the contract in the case of a solicitation application and to assert the damage caused to him by the otherwise allocation of the remaining work. **13.55**

Section 8 (2) 2 VOB / B also does not deviate from the legal model of Section 649 BGB, which rules the Right of Dissolution for the customer in work contracts, since this clause does not regulate the legal consequences of a free right of termination of the client but the legal consequences of a termination for an important reason. The contractor's own insolvency application constitutes an important reason because the contractor can no longer guarantee the proper fulfilment of the contract. The trust relationship required for the continuation of the construction contract is thereby permanently undermined. **13.56**

The decision is quite surprising, because the jurisprudence indicated that Section 8 (2) VOB / B was deemed to be invalid. But the BGH clarified that the decision of the IX. Zivilsenat, which denied the effectiveness of a solution **13.57** clause in favour of an energy supplier in the event of the customer's insolvency, is limited to contracts for the continuous supply of goods or energy. For construction practice, the decision means in any case a relief and more planning security.

D. REFORMS

13.58 The German Insolvency System runs through a long-term and multi-stage reform process which started with the implementation of the InsO in 1999.

13.59 With the 'Act for the further facilitation of the rehabilitation of enterprises' (ESUG), which has been in force since 2012, the economic conditions for the rehabilitation of distressed enterprises are to be improved. The process of insolvency is to be understood now more as a real 'opportunity for rehabilitation'.

13.60 Currently undergoing the legislative process is the law on corporate insolvency. Its aim is to prevent the friction losses of an insolvency-related break-up of groups and to safeguard reorganization chances. By means of special rules of jurisdiction and reference, the possibility of appointing an administrator for several procedures and the introduction of a separate coordination procedure, these procedures should be better coordinated. On 29 September 2015, the Federal Cabinet launched a draft law aimed at improving the legal certainty in the case of contestations under the InsO and under the Law of Contestation. The draft aims to relieve economic traffic and workers of legal uncertainties arising from the current practice.[37]

13.61 But more importantly in the context of insolvency related dissolution clauses, on 22 December 2016, the German Bundestag decided to amend the InsO with a change of Section 104.[38] A new Section 104(4) clarifies that for the deliveries of goods and financial performances with a market or stock exchange price, which were agreed to take place exactly on a definitely fixed date or within a definitely fixed period the parties may enter into agreements

---

37 http://www.bmjv.de/DE/Themen/FinanzenUndAnlegerschutz/ReformInsolvenzrecht/ReformInsolvenzrecht_node.html. 1488117239798 [last accessed 11 December 2018].

38 https://www.bgbl.de/xaver/bgbl/start.xav?startbk=Bundesanzeiger_BGBl&start=//*%5B@attr_id='bgbl116s3147.pdf'%5D#__bgbl__%2F%2F*%5B%40attr_id%3D%27bgbl116s3147.pdf%27%5D__1488117239798 [last accessed 11 December 2018].

on the contractual termination of the contract before the opening of insolvency proceedings, in particular when the application is submitted.[39] Furthermore, the parties may in the future determine the amount of the claim using the market or stock exchange price, by means of substitute transactions or by means of a method guaranteeing the appropriate valuation of the transaction. The creditor can assert this claim as an insolvency creditor pursuant to Section 104(5). According to a new Section 104(1) sentence 2, it will not be possible for financial service providers, when creditors, to claim the fulfilment of the contract. Only the damage claim for non-fulfilment may be possible.

According to the new Section 104 (1) 3, options and other rights to deliver goods at a fixed market or stock exchange price are included in the financial services. According to the formal justification, this applies in cases in which the market provides assurance for an integral and transparent price formation on the basis of regulatory requirements outside securities trading law, for example in the case of wholesale energy markets. **13.62**

Insolvency-dependent clauses in energy supply agreements or trade agreements are, thus, just as effective as the formation of a termination amount. With the new regulation it will be easier for German banks, but also the German energy industry, to be able to separate from their contractual partner in the event of insolvency. **13.63**

The starting point for this reform was the decision of the BGH of 9 June 2016.[40] According to the judgment, agreements for the settlement of financial market contracts are ineffective in so far as they provide for legal consequences in the event of the insolvency of a contracting party, which deviate from Section 104. The BGH considers that insolvency-related dissolution clauses, which permit a termination of the contract in the event of the occurrence of insolvency-related situations, are ineffective deviations from the insolvency-based regulatory model. The draft bill states that the judgment affects 'all the customary framework contracts for the aggregation and settlement of financial market contracts to which German insolvency law would apply in the event of insolvency'.[41] **13.64**

39 http://www.bundesgerichtshof.de/DE/Bibliothek/GesMat/WP18/I/InsO_EGZPO.html [last accessed 11 December 2018].

40 BGH Judgment of 9 June 2016 – IX ZR 314/14.

41 See the government draft p. 1, available at: http://www.bundesgerichtshof.de/SharedDocs/Downloads/DE/Bibliothek/Gesetzesmaterialien/18_wp/InsO_EGZPO/rege.pdf?__blob=publicationFile [last accessed 11 December 2018].

13.65 According to the legislature, the verdict of the BGH poses 'threats to the international competitiveness of German institutions and market participants and to the stability of the German financial system'.[42] These are to be repelled by the new law, which creates legal regulations for the clarification of the insolvency resistance of liquidation-netting clauses. In essence, paragraph 104 is supplemented by a number of clarifying sentences, which are no longer intended to be interpreted as in the aforementioned judgment – the draft law is thus against the judgment of the BGH.[43]

13.66 The new law means that the typical large-scale creditors from the banking and energy sector will have ample opportunity to withdraw quickly from a bankruptcy situation. This, of course, has a significant impact on companies threatened by insolvency in the sense that, for example, credit lines and energy supply contracts can be unilaterally resolved without a deadline. This means that companies can be cut off from a part of the basic supply for their business operations during the crisis.

13.67 This also contradicts the actual purpose of the protection function of the insolvency proceeding in so far as the insolvent company is actually protected against insolvency-induced contract terminations. It is necessary to preserve the core of the company affected by the insolvency, thus also securing jobs. However, if, for example, the supply of energy is discontinued, the operational work of the company is severely restricted, if not excluded. This means that there is hardly any way of continuing the operation without disturbing the (provisional) insolvency proceedings and of initiating the necessary reorganisation measures.

13.68 Above all, this approach also leads to an unequal treatment of creditors. Those creditors who do not have the possibility of extraordinary, one-sided contract resolution may experience disadvantages in the insolvency proceedings, as the performance of the company concerned can be (severely) restricted.

13.69 The fact that this reform advantages a specific set of creditors can also be seen by an analysis of the opinions presented during the public consultations. In favour of the changes in the law were the opinions of the German Credit

---

42 Ibid., 6.
43 Ibid., 7.

Management,[44] of the Institute for International Private Law and Comparative Law University of Bonn[45] and of the Association German Gas and Electricity Trader.[46]

A more critical stand on the other hand has been taken by the Federal Lawyer Chamber,[47] the Association of German Insolvency Administrators,[48] the Institute for Insolvency Law – Humbold University Berlin,[49] the Institute for International and European Insolvency Law – University of Cologne[50] and Federal Working Group of the Insolvency Courts.[51] **13.70**

The chance of obtaining satisfactory quotas for all creditors is thus reduced.[52] **13.71**

E. CONCLUDING REMARKS

Insolvency related dissolution clauses are fundamentally anticompetitive. As a rule, the job of insolvency administrators is made more difficult if they cannot insist on the fulfilment of pre-existing contracts concluded by the debtor. Inversely, the ineffectiveness of the dissolution clauses regularly prevents creditors from walking away from contracts that are favourable to the debtor and which could be vital for the continuation of the business in the short term. **13.72**

44 Stellungnahme die Deutsche Kreditwirtschaft 11 October 2016, available at: http://www.bundestag.de/blob/478350/db8a9072b05439a437bda41a909cd29a/die_dk_koehling-data.pdf [last accessed 11 December 2018].

45 Stellungnahme Uni Bonn – Institut für Internationales Prvatrecht und Rechtsvergleichung, Prof. em. Dr. Johannes Köndgen, available at: http://www.bundestag.de/blob/479334/188f01eefbf1ecb161f1ad707b3e0b60/koendgen-data.pdf [last accessed 11 December 2018].

46 Verband Deutscher Gas und Stromhändler http://www.bundestag.de/blob/479224/cf19f1938cd8f183c69c63b74e5b95d5/efet_liesenhoff-data.pdf [last accessed 11 December 2018].

47 Stellungnahme Bundesrechtsanwaltskammer November 2016 http://www.bundestag.de/blob/479154/6642c37dcf9da50fb667cef1b4f4efd3/brak_floether-data.pdf. [last accessed 11 December 2018].

48 Stellungnahme Verband Insolvenzverwalter Deutschland http://www.bundestag.de/blob/479336/3b989d5d5626b908cfcabd75ab0d3be4/vid_niering-data.pdf [last accessed 11 December 2018].

49 Stellungnahme Humbold Unversität zu Berlin, Lehrstuhl für Bürgerliches Recht, Zivilprozess- und Insolvenzrecht sowie Römisches Recht, Prof. Dr. Christoph G. Paulus, available at: http://www.bundestag.de/blob/478800/16c05b98e8a0be31198fe500e60fdf94/paulus-data.pdf [last accessed 11 December 2018].

50 Universität zu Köln Rechtswissenschaftliche Fakultät – Institut für Internationales und Europäisches Insolvenzrecht, Prof. Dr. Christoph Thole http://www.bundestag.de/blob/479158/c2ba13de152b957a7ed1f4613a1757f4/thole-data.pdf [last accessed 11 December 2018].

51 Stellungnahme Bundesarbeitskreiskreis Insolvenzgerichte http://www.bundesgerichtshof.de/SharedDocs/Downloads/DE/Bibliothek/Gesetzesmaterialien/18_wp/InsO_EGZPO/stellung_bakinso_aendvorschl.pdf?__blob=publicationFile[last accessed 11 December 2018].

52 For more information on consultations: http://www.bundesgerichtshof.de/DE/Bibliothek/GesMat/WP18/I/InsO_EGZPO.html [last accessed 11 December 2018].

13.73 As indicated in the official justification of the law by the German Government, the main drivers of reform might have been to boost national competitiveness and international attractiveness of the financial and energy sector.[53]

13.74 The driving principles of the German insolvency system though, are the equal treatment of creditors (*par condition creditorum*) and the restoration function. The rules set out in Sections 103 and 119 aim at the observance of these principles. The administrator's right to choose helps him in the quest of the restoration of a company so that its creditors will be satisfied on equal terms.

13.75 The BGH decision on the validity of Section 8 VOB and the change of Section 104 carve out special treatment for specific sectors in the industry. The reaction of the building industry and the opinions in the public consultation openly show how strong these special treatments have been advocated by the relevant sectors, albeit at the expense of the underlining principles of the insolvency system and of the other creditors who cannot profit from these special rules.

13.76 Considering the pressure from the industry sector, it might become a trend to expand the validity of contractual remedies agreed by the parties in solvent times at the expense of the Insolvency Administrator's right to choose, hence to the expense of all other creditors.

---

53 See the government draft p. 7, available at: http://www.bundesgerichtshof.de/SharedDocs/Downloads/DE/Bibliothek/Gesetzesmaterialien/18_wp/InsO_EGZPO/rege.pdf?__blob=publicationFile [last accessed 11 December 2018].

14

NATIONAL REPORT FOR GREECE

Loukas Panetsos

A. INTRODUCTION TO GREEK INSOLVENCY LAW

The roots of Greek Insolvency Law date back to the beginnings of the Modern Greek State, when the French-inspired 'Commercial Act' (*Emporikos Nomos*) was introduced. The insolvency system of *Emporikos Nomos* has been in place, with many amendments, until 2007, when the new Bankruptcy Code (hereinafter 'GBC') came into force.[1] **14.01**

The Greek legal community uses the term 'bankruptcy'[2] instead of the term 'insolvency'.[3] Thus, the main insolvency law statute, Law 3588/2007, is called 'Bankruptcy Code'.[4] The justification of this terminological choice derives **14.02**

1 Law 3588/2007.
2 In Greek 'πτώχευση', pronounced 'ptohefsi'.
3 In Greek 'αφερεγγυότητα', pronounced 'aferegiotita'.
4 In Greek 'Πτωχευτικός Κώδικας', pronounced 'Ptoheftikos Kodikas'.

from the fact that traditionally the *Emporikos Nomos* focused on post-insolvency and liquidation procedures and did not include any provisions for the preservation of the business of the insolvent debtor.[5] As a result, the judiciary still plays an important role in all stages of the insolvency procedure.[6] For the purposes of this chapter, to refer to corporate cases the term 'insolvency' will be used instead of the term 'bankruptcy'. Yet, it should be noted that the use of the term 'insolvency' is rather limited in Greek terminology, and the term 'bankruptcy' is the formal one (corresponding to the British term 'insolvency').

(a) Application

14.03 The GBC applies only to legal persons with an economic scope and sole proprietorships.[7] Thus, individuals, such as those exercising liberal professions, are excluded from the application of the GBC. Individuals or corporate persons with no economic scope are only subject to the provisions of the Code of Civil Procedure regarding 'mandatory (or else 'individual') enforcement'. Further, there is a separate procedure for households in economic distress.[8]

14.04 The critical point from a time perspective in the Greek insolvency system is the so-called 'declaration of insolvency', which is triggered by the 'cessation of payments'.[9] A cessation of payments exists when the debtor is unable to perform her due monetary liabilities in a general and permanent manner. Both creditors and the debtor can request the opening of insolvency proceedings if there is a cessation of payments, while it is possible for the debtor to initiate such a process when the cessation of payments is imminent, or upon submitting a restructuring plan. On the other hand, the end of the insolvency procedure is mainly reached either by the ratification of a restructuring plan, or the liquidation of all assets.[10]

(b) The actors of insolvency

14.05 Currently, there is no formal insolvency procedure where the Civil Courts have no role, although recently a new out-of-court non-insolvency mechanism

5 Perakis, *Bankruptcy Law* (Nomiki Vivliothiki, 2012, in Greek) 8.

6 Greece does not have separate insolvency or commercial courts; instead, specific departments of the civil law courts deal with insolvency law issues (i.e. the locally competent Multi-member Courts of First Instance).

7 GBC, art 2.

8 Law 3869/2010.

9 GBC, art 3.

10 Perakis, *supra* note 5, 447; GBC, arts 125 and 132.

has been introduced for the settlement of sustainable business debts.[11] Such a mechanism is available only to the companies and individuals falling under the scope of GBC. The insolvency proceedings take place before a Court of First Instance composed of three judges, one of which is appointed as a 'judge-rapporteur' and has a closer supervision of the insolvency procedure.[12] The court appoints an 'insolvency administrator' or 'insolvency syndic' for managing the business of the insolvent debtor and conducting the insolvency proceedings, a post now reserved for specially qualified professionals, called 'insolvency practitioners'.[13] The creditors are organized through forming the 'creditors' meeting', being comprised of all the creditors.[14] The creditor's meeting can elect to appoint a 'creditors' committee' for coordinating the creditors.[15]

B. THE INSOLVENCY PROCEDURES

The GBC provides for two main insolvency procedures: the 'rehabilitation procedure' and the main insolvency procedure, which can be combined with the 'restructuring plan' procedure. Of these two procedures, the latter is a pure post-insolvency procedure while the former is in fact a pre-insolvency procedure.[16] It should be noted that both these procedures can only be initiated through court proceedings. However, informal out-of-court agreements regarding the restructuring of nearly insolvent businesses are common in practice and usually involve banking institutions, which are frequently the most important creditors.[17] Yet, the recently amended[18] rehabilitation procedure is based, to a certain degree, on out-of-court procedures. **14.06**

(a) The rehabilitation procedure

The 'rehabilitation procedure' can be initiated both by the debtor and or/the creditors with whom a pre-pack agreement has been reached.[19] Under the **14.07**

11 Law 4469/2017.

12 GBC, arts 4 and 7, known as the 'Multi-member Court of First Instance'.

13 GBC, art 63 as amended by the art 3, para 7a of the Law 4446/2016; the profession of the 'insolvency practitioner' is regulated by the Presidential Decree 133/2016.

14 GBC, art 82.

15 GBC, art 85.

16 Christoph Paulus, Stathis Potamitis, Alexandros Rokas andIgnacio Tirado, 'The Bankruptcy Law as one of the Main Market Economy Pillars – Critical Review of the Greek Bankruptcy Law' (2015), *21 Dikaio Epichiriseon & Etairion (Business and Company Law)* 1065, 1068 (in Greek).

17 Alexandros Rokas, 'Attempts of Reorganization and Mediation in the Modern Bankruptcy Law' [2010], http://www.syneemp.gr/?pgtp=1&aid=1262250672 (in Greek).

18 Law 4446/2016.

19 GBC, art 99.

current regime, the debtor can conclude a pre-pack agreement with creditors representing 60 per cent of the liabilities and 40 per cent of the secured ones,[20] and submit it to the Bankruptcy Court for ratification.[21] Further, if the debtor is insolvent, they can also submit concurrently a petition for declaration of insolvency. Such a petition can also be submitted by the creditors.

14.08 The court can either ratify the pre-packed agreement, or reject the petition. If accepted by the court, the pre-packed agreement has a cram-down effect and binds the non-consenting creditors. The scope of the rehabilitation procedure is to restructure the debtor's business and allow them to renegotiate their liabilities without commencing a formal insolvency procedure. For this reason, it has become relatively popular and has been used by some important companies in distress.[22] Moreover, its introduction after the Greek sovereign debt crisis is one of the factors explaining why the number of formal insolvency procedures has not increased during the last years.

14.09 The recent amendment of Law 4446/2016 has slightly limited the in-court proceedings, by abolishing some of them, as an attempt to reduce the inefficiencies of previous regime. Nevertheless, the role of the in-court-proceedings still remains important.

(b) The main insolvency procedure and the restructuring plan

14.10 The main insolvency procedure, which can be combined with the restructuring plan procedure, commences when a debtor is declared insolvent.[23] The debtor has an obligation to file a petition for the declaration of insolvency 30 days after the cessation of payments takes place, a possibility that is also granted to creditors.[24] The debtor can also submit a proposal for a restructuring plan, together with the petition for the declaration of bankruptcy.[25] If the court accepts the petition, it should declare the debtor insolvent, appoint

20 GBC, art 100.

21 GBC, art 99(3).

22 Andreas Aggelidis, 'Strict and Misguided Critic on Article 99' (Kathimerini, 13 July 2013, in Greek). The most famous case is the rehabilitation procedure of 'Marinopoulos SA', one of the largest hypermarket chains in Greece, with operations in other South-eastern European countries and a former joint venture of Carrefour SA (until 2012). The rehabilitation procedure of Marinopoulos SA was approved by the 8/2017 decision of the Multimember Court of First Instance of Athens, and the ownership and control of the company passed to one of its main competitors, Sklavenitis SA. See: http://www.naftemporiki.gr/story/1194067/athens-court-oks-highly-anticipated-marinopoulos-supermarket-rescue-plan.

23 GBC, art 3.

24 GBC, art 5.

25 GBC, art 108 (2).

an insolvency administrator and seal the assets of the debtors.[26] Also, third-party individual enforcement actions are put on an automatic stay.[27] However, this stay does not cover secured creditors, with certain exception.[28]

The restructuring plan, which is an alternative to the liquidation of debtor's assets, is the Greek equivalent of the Chapter 11 of the US Bankruptcy Code.[29] A proposal for a restructuring plan can be submitted within three months of the declaration of the insolvency[30] and should be approved by the majority of the creditors, representing 60 per cent of the liabilities and 40 per cent of the secured ones,[31] while it also has a cram-down effect towards the non-consenting creditors.[32] If the restructuring plan is not approved by the court, or not submitted, then the normal bankruptcy procedure is continued. In short, the main stages of main bankruptcy procedure are the verification of the claims of the creditors that have announced them,[33] the liquidation of the assets[34] and the distribution to the creditors.[35] **14.11**

(c) Synopsis

The Greek insolvency law system is based on the interaction between the debtor, the creditors, the Bankruptcy Court and the insolvency administrator. There are no formal out-of-court procedures. The two formal procedures are the pre-insolvency rehabilitation procedure and the main insolvency procedure, which can be combined with the restructuring plan procedure. **14.12**

C. THE TREATMENT OF EXECUTORY CONTRACTS

The general principle that underlies the treatment of executory contracts in the insolvency proceedings is that the outstanding executory contracts (i.e., those that are still existent at the time an insolvency procedure begins) are preserved after the declaration of the insolvency, although it is possible to be terminated if the GBC provides so.[36] **14.13**

---

26 GBC, art 7 (1).
27 GBC, art 25 (1).
28 GBC, art 26 (2).
29 Perakis, *supra* note 5, 373.
30 GBC, art 108 (2).
31 GBC, art 108 (3).
32 GBC, art 125 (1).
33 GBC, arts 93 et seq.
34 GBC, arts 135 et seq.
35 GBC, arts 153 et seq.
36 GBC, art 28.

14.14 Since the late 19th century, the Greek Supreme Court, *Areios Pagos*, has ruled that the declaration of insolvency does not terminate an executory contract of the insolvent party.[37] Nevertheless, until 2015, the prevailing '*pacta sunt servanda*' principle could be circumvented through *ipso facto* clauses, which used to be included in contracts concluded by sophisticated creditors.[38] After the amendment of the GBC by Law 4336/2015, *ipso facto* clauses are in principle prohibited, although there are certain exceptions. This development was praised by the Greek academic community, although some concerns have been expressed.[39] Yet, the new provisions have not been subject to a systematic study by domestic scholars.

14.15 Under the Greek Civil Code, executory contracts are those that create rights and obligations for both contractual parties.[40] Thus, their fundamental characteristic is the 'exchange' of obligations between the parties. Executory contracts can be categorized as permanent or instant.[41] Contracts which are executed over a long period of time are characterised as permanent, while those which are executed or performed instantly or within a short time are deemed to be instant contracts.[42] This distinction is important for insolvency law purposes. Our analysis focuses on permanent executory contracts, whose existence is threatened by *ipso facto* clauses.

(a) Instant executory contracts

14.16 Instant executory contracts are not terminated upon the declaration of insolvency, unless a specific provision provides so, but they become inactive.[43] The insolvency administrator has to make a business decision regarding whether the execution of an instant executory contract is in favour of the insolvent debtor.[44] Thus, the trustee is given the 'option' to execute certain instant executory contracts.[45] In such a case, the claims of the creditors are considered as being born after the declaration of the insolvency.[46]

---

37 Areios Pagos 1890/1890, A΄ Themis 87; Perakis, *supra* note 5, 291.

38 Christoph Paulus, Stathis Potamitis, Alexandros Rokas and Ignacio Tirado, *supra* note 16, 1078 (in Greek).

39 Alexandros Rokas, 'The Recent Amendments to the Bankruptcy Procedure by Law 4336/2015' (2015), Chronika Idiotikou Dikaiou (Chronicles of Private Law) 657, 658 (in Greek).

40 Civil Code, arts 374 et seq.

41 Apostolos Georgiadis, *Law of Obligations – General Part*, (Dikaio & Oikonomia P. N. Sakkoulas, 1999, in Greek) 57

42 Ibid., 51.

43 Lambros Kotsiris, *Bankruptcy Law* (Ekdoseis Sakkoula, 2011, in Greek) 366.

44 Perakis, *supra* note 5, 293.

45 GBC, art 29.

46 Perakis, *supra* note 5, 221.

If the insolvency administrator considers that the execution of an instant executory contract is not in favour of the insolvent debtor, then he can either refuse the execution, or not exercise the option of article 29. In such a case, the creditors are given the possibility to ask for the execution of the instant executory contracts setting a reasonable deadline. When this deadline expires, they can withdraw from the contract, and their claims are considered as being born before the declaration of insolvency.[47] **14.17**

(b) Permanent executory contracts

Under the current wording of the GBC, permanent executory contracts are not terminated automatically upon the declaration of insolvency, unless specific legislation provides so.[48] This means that *ipso facto* clauses are in principle prohibited, except for certain types of executory contracts, such as financial contracts or executory contracts of a personal nature. For this reason, we can further categorize the permanent executory contract among the following types: **14.18**

- general executory contracts, subject to the rule that they can be terminated automatically only if provided by the law. *Ipso facto* clauses are not permissible,[49] but the administrator has the same power to accept or reject them pursuant to article 29. When the rejection occurs sometime after the commencement of the insolvency procedure, the performing party has the right to seek the payment for the goods and services provided after the commencement of the procedure in priority as administrative expenses over other unsecured creditors;
- financial contracts are not subject to this restriction. Thus, *ipso facto* clauses are permitted. Also, clauses allowing the amendment of financial executory contracts are permitted too;[50]
- executory contracts of personal nature are terminated automatically if the debtor is a contractual party;[51]
- automatic termination or *ipso facto* clauses are permitted if provided by specific legislation;[52]
- employment contracts are not terminated upon the declaration of insolvency. Yet, special rules apply for their subsequent treatment;[53]

47 Ibid., 295.
48 GBC, art 31.
49 GBC, art 31(1).
50 GBC, art 31(1).
51 GBC, art 32(1).
52 GBC, art 32(1).
53 GBC, art 34.

- special rules apply in the case of sales contracts where the seller maintains the ownership of the sold goods (contracts with a title retention clause), until he receives the full consideration for the sale. Unlike other jurisdictions and real estate securities, these contracts don't have to be registered;[54]
- special rules apply for setting-off executory contracts with claims from other contracts, where the insolvent debtor is a creditor and the creditor is a debtor.[55]

(c) The general principle regarding *ipso facto* clauses

14.19 As already mentioned, the general rule is that the treatment of permanent executory contracts is not influenced by the declaration of insolvency and that they are preserved in force after this event. Until 2015, *ipso facto* clauses were permissible and common in practice. The only grounds for the trustee to refuse the application of an *ipso facto* clause could derive from the good faith provision of article 281 of the Civil Code.[56] *Ipso facto* clauses have been prohibited since 2015, when the GBC was amended by the Law 4336/2015, in order to comply with international practice, focusing on the preservation of the business of the insolvent debtor.[57] Yet, the prohibition of *ipso facto* clauses does not exclude the right of the creditors to terminate an executory contract during the insolvency procedure.[58] This means that the declaration of insolvency may constitute a contractual legitimate ground for terminating a fixed-term executory contract, while permanent executory contracts can be terminated without cause.[59] Thus, a delicate line has to be drawn between automatic termination of an executory contract due to a contractual *ipso facto* clause, which is prohibited, and the right for the debtor and their legal representative to terminate an executory contract during the insolvency procedure, which is still permitted. The distinction is important, because if an executory contract is terminated after the declaration of insolvency, the claims

---

54 GBC, art 35; As a rule, contracts with a title retention clause are not required to be registered, although such registration is optional under the Law 2844/2000, art 10: see Perakis, *supra* note 5, 311.

55 GBC, art 36.

56 Perakis, *supra* note 5, 301.

57 Explanatory Report of Law 4336/2015.

58 GBC, art 32(1); Georgios Michalopoulos and Lia Athanasiou, 'The treatment of the Licence of use of Commercial Trademarks after the insolvency of the Licensee' (2016) 22 *Dikaio Epichiriseon & Etairion (Business and Company Law)* 993, 999.

59 Rokas, supra note 39; Kotsiris, supra note 43, 370.

of the creditor from the filing of the petition are considered as born after the declaration of insolvency.[60]

14.20 Although contractual *ipso facto* clauses are prohibited, this general rule is subject to certain exceptions. The first exception is statutory *ipso facto* clauses, which are valid.[61] Examples of statutory *ipso facto* clauses can be found in the Civil Code,[62] leasing contracts[63] or in public procurement legislation.[64] The second exception can be found in financial contracts, which can include contractual *ipso facto* clauses. Financial contracts are those that have as scope banking, credit, and investment or insurance services.[65] Thus, financial contracts are granted a 'safe harbour' in the insolvency procedure, contrary to what happens in general executory contracts. The third important exception applies to executory contracts of personal character.

(d) The executory contracts of personal character

14.21 The treatment of executory contracts of personal character has been controversial in academic literature. The GBC does not define the content of executory contracts of personal character (*intuitus personae*); yet, such should be characterized the executory contracts that create relationships between the contractual parties that require a unique personal nature and trust.[66] For this reason, the disruption of this personal link results in the discontinuity of the executory contract.[67]

14.22 According to the jurisprudence, the personal character (*intuitus personae*) of the executory contract is determined either by the nature of the contract (i.e., mandate contract), the will of the contractual parties or the existence of an *ipso facto* clause.[68] The last factor, i.e., the existence of an *ipso facto* clause, should not be considered as valid after the amendment of 2015 by Law 4336/2015, since they are generally prohibited by the law. Thus, after the 2015 introduction of a general prohibition on the use of these clauses, the personal

60 Michail-Theodoros Marinos, 'Permanent Executory Contracts of "Personal Character" during Bankruptcy (BC, art 31(2)) – a critical approach with the example of the patent license' (2013), *Epitheorisi Emporikou Dikaiou (Commercial Law Review)* 791, 794 (in Greek).

61 GBC, art 31(1).

62 Civil Code, art 726 (mandate contract); Civil Code, art 883 (novation contract, or anweisung).

63 Law 1665/1986, art 4(3).

64 Law 4412/2016, art 167(1).

65 Explanatory Report of Law 4336/2015.

66 Explanatory Report of Law 3588/2007.

67 Ibid.

68 Multi-member Court of First Instance of Thessaloniki 2202/2014; Multi-member Court of First Instance of Peiraeus 922/2013; Multi-member Court of First Instance of Peiraeus 1822/2013; Multi-member Court of First Instance of Ilia 100/2012; Multi-member Court of First Instance of Athens 459/2012.

character of a contract should be assessed primarily by the nature of the contract or the will of the parties. The most typical examples of executory contracts of personal character are banking contracts such as a joint credit account[69] or a credit card account,[70] which imply a relationship of trust between the contractual parties.

14.23 There is a strong debate on the legal effect of the statutory provision that the declaration of insolvency constitutes a '*material ground*' for the termination of executory contracts of personal character. The case law and the majority of the literature support that the provision of article 31 paragraph 2 of the GBC constitutes a statutory *ipso facto* clause and that these contracts are terminated automatically upon the declaration of insolvency, irrespective of whether their performance would be in the interest of the creditors as a whole, the debtor or the counter-party.[71] However, a minority view claims that the executory contracts of personal character are not terminated automatically, but they are moved to a phase of 'liquidation' where the obligations of the parties have been extinguished, yet they are still existent.[72] According to this minority narrative, article 31 paragraph 2 does not contain a statutory *ipso facto* clause, but only a legitimate material ground to terminate a contract, or the right to agree a contractual *ipso facto* clause.[73] Nevertheless, the minority view is not accepted by the jurisprudence.

(e) Employment contracts

14.24 GBC contains special provisions for the treatment of dependent employment contracts. The default rule is that the employment contracts are preserved, although it is possible for them to be terminated by the insolvency administrator.[74] However, the trustee may face restrictions in employment law regarding the number of employment contracts he can terminate.[75]

14.25 All the employees' claims accrued before the declaration of insolvency, as well as the claims from the notice of termination of contract are considered as

69 Multi-member Court of First Instance of Peiraeus 1822/2013; Multi-member Court of First Instance of Ilia 100/2012.

70 Multi-member Court of First Instance of Athens 459/2012.

71 Multi-member Court of First Instance of Thessaloniki 2202/2014; Multi-member Court of First Instance of Peiraeus 922/2013; Multi-member Court of First Instance of Peiraeus 1822/2013; Multi-member Court of First Instance of Ilia 100/2012; Multi-member Court of First Instance of Athens 459/2012; Perakis, *supra* note 5, 299; Spyridon Psichomanis, 'Bankruptcy Law and Law of Regulating the Liabilities of Over-debt Natural Persons', (Ekdoseis Sakkoula, 2012, in Greek), 311.

72 Marinos, *supra* note 60.

73 Ibid.

74 GBC, art 34, paras 1, 2.

75 Perakis, *supra* note 5, 303.

pre-insolvency claims. On the contrary, all entitlements for work carried out after the declaration of insolvency are considered as born after the declaration of insolvency, and paid in preference to other creditors as administrative expenses.[76] Thus, the employees have preferential treatment compared to other creditors, whose contracts have been terminated during the insolvency, a policy decision explained by social, political and economic considerations.[77]

(f) Other provisions

Finally, GBC has some miscellaneous provisions regarding the treatment of executory contracts. First, the insolvency administrator can transfer the executory contracts that are not terminated to third parties, if it is in favour of the creditors.[78] The consent of the other contractual party is required; otherwise the trustee may ask the court to order the transfer of the contract.[79] Secondly, as a default rule, the sale contracts with retention-of-title clauses are preserved.[80] If the insolvent debtor is in possession of the goods and the trustee does not exercise the option to execute the contract, the seller has the right to isolate the goods from the assets of the insolvent debtor.[81] Finally, the declaration of insolvency does not affect the rights of the contractual parties for setting-off their claims, while over-the-counter derivatives, claims from clearing houses and close-out netting are subject to their own specific legislative treatment.[82] **14.26**

(g) Synopsis

As a general principle, *ipso facto* clauses are not valid in Greek Insolvency Law. **14.27** However, this general rule is subject to many exceptions, concerning certain special types of executory contracts, such as financial contracts or contracts of personal character. Further, the relative novelty of the legislative amendments means that there is little guidance from the judiciary on the treatment of contracts which feature *ipso facto* clauses.

76 GBC, art 34, paras 4, 5.
77 Perakis, *supra* note 5, 304.
78 GBC, art 33, para 1.
79 GBC, art 33, para 2.
80 GBC, art 35, para 1.
81 GBC, art 35, para 2.
82 GBC, art 36; Law 3156/2003, art16; Law 3301/2004, art 7.

D. MAJOR REFORMS IN THE GREEK INSOLVENCY LAW

14.28 Greek insolvency law has experienced many reforms during the 21st century. In essence, its modern life begins in 2007, when the insolvency law provisions of the old *Emporikos Nomos* and other legislative acts were replaced by the new GBC. However, the GBC of 2007 has been amended many times since then.[83]

14.29 The most important reforms were launched in three stages: the first was the replacement of conciliation procedure by the rehabilitation procedure;[84] the second was the general prohibition of the *ipso facto* clauses and the reform of the rehabilitation procedure;[85] while the third was the abolition of the special liquidation procedure, the partial reform of the rehabilitation procedure, as well as a reform in the general nature of the insolvency process.

(a) A timeline of the recent reforms

14.30 Before 2007, the Greek insolvency law system was based on an amalgam of the archaic *Emporikos Nomos* and many quasi-insolvency procedures.[86] The old system, designed in the beginnings of the 19th century and reformed in 1878,[87] was not appropriate for the current needs of the Greek economy. The long life of the *Emporikos Nomos* had created many conflicts with later statutory provisions.[88] Further, it did not have sufficient provisions for the restructuring and recovery of the insolvent business.[89]

14.31 The new GBC introduced many innovations. First, it codified the insolvency legislation in a uniform statute. Secondly, it introduced two procedures aimed at the recovery of the insolvent business: the reconciliation procedure and the restructuring plan procedure, based on foreign models. Also, the special liquidation procedure was introduced, targeting larger businesses. Thirdly, it had a friendlier approach towards creditors compared to the old regime.[90] It

---

83 GBC has been amended by the following Acts: 3858/2010, 4013/2011, 4055/2012, 4072/2012, 4336/2015 and 4446/2016.

84 Law 4013/2011.

85 Law 4336/2015.

86 Perakis, *supra* note 5, 17.

87 Georgios Sotiropoulos, 'The New Bankruptcy Code: from the Bankruptcy to the Rehabilitation of Greek Bankruptcy Law' (2008), *Chronika Idiotikou Dikaiou (Chronicles of Private Law)* 289 (in Greek).

88 Eleftherios Skalidis, 'A Dialectic Approach of the Bankruptcy Court' (2010) Epitheorisi Trapezikou Axiografikou and Chrimatistiriakou Dikaiou (Review of Banking, Securities and Stock Exchange Law) 405, 406 (in Greek).

89 Perakis, *supra* note 5, 7.

90 Sotiropoulos, *supra* note 87.

has to be noted that this reform was the product of a long series of preparatory work and two drafting committees, which led to a long Preparatory Report.[91]

The pre-insolvency reconciliation procedure, which was French-inspired,[92] proved very popular (5,000 procedures were opened) but also ineffective (only 20 were ratified).[93] The reason for this paradox was that this procedure was very friendly to debtors, providing for enhanced protection against individual claims and enabling free riding and possibilities for abuse. For this reason, this procedure was replaced by the rehabilitation procedure, which had the same object as the reconciliation procedure, but focused on saving the business.[94] The rehabilitation procedure was further reformed recently,[95] reducing the in-court proceedings, in order to make this procedure more efficient. **14.32**

The main insolvency procedure and the restructuring plan have also been subject to reforms, although fewer than those related to the rehabilitation procedure. After the recent amendments by Law 4446/2016, the main insolvency procedure has become more flexible and has been aligned with the changes in the pre-insolvency rehabilitation procedure. Further, the insolvency administrator, who used to be chosen among lawyers, should now be a qualified insolvency practitioner. **14.33**

(b) The drivers for reform

The seminal reform of the Greek insolvency law system that was initiated by the Law 3588/2007, was long-awaited. However, the preparatory committee drafted the GBC in a very short time, without engaging into any substantial debate and little coordination with the academic and business community.[96] The introduction of the GBC was a necessity requested by the reality, the judiciary, the legal and academic community, as well as the business sector, since the old system was based on grounds rooted in the 19th century. After the enactment of law 3588/2007, reforms have been sporadic and not driven by a systemic attitude. The main drivers for reform have been internal, with the need to provide remedies to the decreased efficiency of the system, and to reduce the number of cases in front of the courts. **14.34**

91 Ibid., 297; Perakis, *supra* note 5, 16.

92 Ibid, 298.

93 Georgios Sotiropoulos, 'Issues of the Business Restructuring Law' (2012), *Epitheorisi Emporikou Dikaiou (Commercial Law Review)* 803, 805 (in Greek).

94 Ibid., 803.

95 By Law 4446/2016.

96 Sotiropoulos, *supra* note 87.

14.35 Yet, another factor has partially influenced these subsequent reforms. The global financial crisis hit Greece particularly hard. This prompted the International Monetary Fund and the European Union to financially support the country and its sovereign debt on more than one occasion.

14.36 The triumvirate of the IMF, the European Commission and the European Central Bank (called – in a rather derogatory way – 'troika' or 'the institutions' after 2015) has requested several reforms in the process of providing financial support to the country. These reforms have also affected, to a certain extent, the Greek insolvency legislation.

(c) The reform in the treatment of executory contracts and *ipso facto* clauses

14.37 As has been already mentioned, the current treatment of executory contracts and *ipso facto* clauses dates back to 2015. This reform was part of the measures that were introduced during the third Greek bailout.[97] Thus, the prohibition on the enforcement of *ipso facto* clauses stems from proposals by the IMF and the EU.

14.38 This ban on *ipso facto* clauses had been supported by the majority of academic literature; thus, the amendment of Law 4336/2015 was widely welcomed.[98] However, there are some proposals by academics for loosening the absolute prohibition of *ipso facto* clauses in order to provide flexibility,[99] although such discussion is only theoretical. Yet, the academic literature has not approached the prohibition of *ipso facto* clauses under the light of its economic consequences.

(d) Quantitative and qualitative studies regarding the Greek insolvency law system

14.39 The many reforms of the Greek insolvency law system are mainly justified by the general assumption that it is inefficient. This is evident in the annual 'Doing Business 2016' report, issued by the World Bank, where all countries are ranked according to the ease of doing business, taking into account ten criteria, among them resolving insolvency. Greece ranks 61th in the general

97 Law 4336/2015.

98 Paulus, Potamitis, Rokas and Tirado, *supra* note 16, 1078.

99 Rokas, *supra* note 39, 658.

index, and 52nd in the resolving insolvency index.[100] The average duration of an insolvency procedure is estimated at 3.5 years, costing 9 per cent of the estate of the insolvent business and recovering only 35.6 cents on the euro to the creditors.

Greece has a particularly low recover rate, compared to the 73 per cent which is the OECD average. Compared to the 2007 rankings, Greece has a far better standing in the general index (it used to be 109th), but worse in the closing a business index (it used to be 34th, while the average time was 2.0 years, the cost of the insolvency at 9 per cent and the recovery rate at 46.3per cent).[101] Thus, from a quantitative perspective, the reforms after 2007 have not performed well. **14.40**

On average, between 2004 and 2014, 1,061 decisions per year have been issued by the courts that involve insolvency proceedings.[102] Of them, 914 (i.e., 86.1 per cent) have accepted the petition to begin an insolvency proceeding, while only 457 such petitions result in a declaration of insolvency (i.e., 50 per cent of the petitions have been approved). Overall, the average amount of liabilities that was approved by the courts per year was 470,421,026 €, while 1,265 employees have a claim against the insolvent business. **14.41**

What seems paradoxical is that the economic recession after 2008 has not resulted in a significant rise in the number of insolvency proceedings (335 declared insolvencies in 2014, the minimum of a decade, against 612 in 2005, which was the maximum). There are two interpretations for this outcome. First, after 2007, many businesses chose the available pre-insolvency procedures. Also, since the Greek insolvency procedures are rather slow and inefficient, many businesses do not attempt to begin court proceedings in the first place. These numbers show that despite the frequent reforms after 2007, the Greek insolvency system has not become more efficient. **14.42**

(e) Conclusion

The Greek insolvency law system, rooted in the early 19th century, was substantially reformed in 2007 with the introduction of the GBC. After 2007, **14.43**

100 The World Bank, 'Doing Business 2017 – Greece' (2017), available at http://www.doingbusiness.org/~/media/WBG/DoingBusiness/Documents/Annual-Reports/English/DB17-Report.pdf.

101 The World Bank, 'Doing Business 2007' (2007), available at http://www.doingbusiness.org/~/media/WBG/DoingBusiness/Documents/Annual-Reports/English/DB07-FullReport.pdf last accessed 1 December 2018.

102 Hellenic Statistic Authority, 'Declared Bankruptcies of Businesses, 2004–2014' [2016], available at http://www.statistics.gr/documents/20181/62b27c79-7871-4d1c-afea-2a22bbbbe969 last accessed 1 December 2018.

at least six reforms have been enacted, having a sporadic, rather a systematic character. The main driver for reform is the underperformance of the Greek insolvency system, although some factors have influenced the legislative decisions (as it is the case with the prohibition of *ipso facto* clauses, which was part of the third bailout programme).

E. CONCLUDING REMARKS

14.44 This chapter has examined the treatment of executory contracts and *ipso facto* clauses by Greek law, under the spectrum of the general insolvency law system. In Part A, this chapter referred to the main characteristics of Greek insolvency law, which is still characterized by the prevalence of official court proceedings, although it has copied many foreign models (e.g., the rehabilitation and the restructuring plan procedure). In Part B, it discussed the treatment of executory contracts and *ipso facto* clauses. As a principle, *ipso facto* clauses are prohibited, although there are exceptional rules for specific categories of contracts. However, this general prohibition has been very recently added to the GBC. Part C briefly presented the major reforms in the field of insolvency law during the 21st century, focusing on the developments after the introduction of the GBC.

14.45 The Greek insolvency law system reflects many of the deficiencies of the domestic markets and the malfunctioning judiciary. Further, its performance has not been improved during the last years. One of the most important factors for this evolution is the economic recession that has affected Greece after 2009. However, the insolvency law reforms have not contributed, in quantitative terms to the efficiency of the insolvency procedures. For this reason, there is a tendency to reduce the in-court proceedings, which was evident in the latest reform. Moreover, a new non-insolvency out-of-court mechanism for the settlement of sustainable business debts has recently been introduced, with no evidence of its efficiency.[103] Yet, such developments cannot be assessed in the short term. It should be noted that the recent reforms in the field of insolvency law, which aim at the improvement of the quantitative figures of its performance, are products of external influence (IMF and EU institutions) related to the Greek sovereign crisis, rather than a result of internal proposals. Thus, the insolvency law reforms should be seen as part of the general reforms undertaken by Greece in the course of the three bailout programs, aiming at the liberalization of its economy.

103 Law 4469/2017.

Regarding the Greek treatment of executory contracts and *ipso facto* clauses, the current *status quo* is a characteristic case of a legal transplant, as is the case with most recent legislative amendments. Therefore, although it follows the international trends, the Greek position was not a product of an internal debate, but a measure, which was part of the commitments of the Greek Government for the third bailout programme. The background of the introduction of the general prohibition of the *ipso facto* clauses does not suggest that it was not necessary.[104] On the contrary, it is a measure expected to bring the Greek insolvency law system closer to its American and Western-European models, enhancing the legal certainty of the actors involved in the insolvency proceeding. Yet, it is an example of the sporadic and non-systematic nature of the reforms of the Greek insolvency legislation. Due to the very recent introduction of this reform, it is difficult to assess already the practical implications of this measure, although it seems that it fills a gap in the former regime. **14.46**

104 Perakis, *supra* note 5, 301.

15

NATIONAL REPORT FOR ITALY

Rolandino Guidotti

A. INTRODUCTION AND AVAILABLE PROCEDURES

1. Introduction

15.01 The current Italian Insolvency Law – as amended by the decree March 14th 2005, n. 35,[1] the legislative decree January 9th 2006, n. 5, and the legislative decree September 12th 2007, n. 169 – contains significant elements of discontinuity compared to the former Bankruptcy Law of 1942.[2] This discontinuity will be even more marked if the government implements the guidelines

1 Transposed into Law 14th May 2015, n. 80.

2 In this chapter the terms Bankruptcy Law (b. law) is used with reference to the Royal Decree March 16th 1942, n. 267, Provisions on Bankruptcy, arrangement with creditors, arrangements with creditors, temporary receivership and compulsory winding-up, where not otherwise specified.

included in the recently enacted Law known as '*Rordorf Reform*',[3] as this chapter explains in Section C.[4]

Starting in 2005 the old provisions were profoundly altered to favour the restructuring of distressed but viable entities. In particular, the new rules dramatically improved the procedure known as 'Arrangements with Creditors', whose structure is loosely based on the U.S. Chapter 11. **15.02**

Further worth mentioning is the introduction of the 'Arrangements with Creditors with Business Continuity'[5] in 2012,[6] alongside new rules according to which the debtor can file a petition for an arrangement (so called 'in white' or 'incomplete' petition) reserving the right to lodge the proposal and the plan at a later stage.[7] **15.03**

The statutory favour towards the use of Arrangements with Creditors ended abruptly in 2015, following some concerns on the abusive use of these mechanisms. That year marked the introduction of new eligibility requirements for the admission to Arrangements with Creditors based on Liquidation. Nowadays it is necessary that the debtor ensures the payment of 100 per cent of the senior/preferential debts and 20 per cent of the unsecured debts to be admitted to the procedure, while creditors have been given the right to submit rival proposals and rival bids.[8] **15.04**

At the time of writing, ailing companies have the opportunity to choose among a wide variety of procedures to liquidate or turn around their business. **15.05**

These include: Out of Court Compositions with Creditors, Attested Plans for Restructuring,[9] Agreements for the Restructuring of Debts,[10] Agreements for **15.06**

---

3 On this global reform see Alberto Jorio, Introduzione generale alla disciplina delle crisi di impresa, in Alberto Jorio and Bruno Sassani (eds), Trattato delle procedure concorsuali, I, Introduzione generale – (Il fallimento, Giuffrè, Milan, 2014) 3; Federica Pasquariello, Italian Bankruptcy Code moving Towards a Reform Era, (Il diritto fallimentare e delle società commerciali, 2016) 347 ff.; and Section D of this chapter.

4 It is the Law October 19th 2017, n. 254.

5 Bankruptcy Law, art 186.

6 Decree 22th June 2012, n. 83, transposed into Law 7th August 2012, n. 134.

7 Bankruptcy Law, art 161, Application for admission to an Arrangement with Creditors, § 6.

8 On this topic see Rolandino Guidotti, '*Le soluzioni della crisi dell'impresa in Italia: il concordato preventivo dopo la riforma dell'estate 2015*', in Miguel Pestana de Vasconcelos (ed.), Recuperação de empresas e insolvência. As experiências italiana, espanhola e portuguesa, Euriconv, Porto, 2016, 29–41.

9 Bankruptcy Law, art 67 (3) (b).

10 Ibid., art 182. Within the Italian legal system the agricultural entrepreneur is not subject to bankruptcy or other insolvency proceedings applicable to the commercial entrepreneur (Italian Civil Code, art 2221). There is an exception regarding Agreements for the Restructuring of Debts (art. 23, § 43, of the Law decree of 6 July 6th 2011, n. 98, transposed by the Law of July 15th 2011, n. 111); however, the agricultural entrepreneur may

Restructuring of Debts Involving Financial Entities,[11] Agreements with Tax Authorities (Tax Settlements),[12] Arrangements with Creditors,[13] Extraordinary Administrations for large Undertakings in State of Insolvency,[14] Bankruptcy[15] and Enforced Judicial Liquidations.[16]

15.07 Some of these procedures can be considered Formal Insolvency Procedures, according to the definition adopted by the European Union.

15.08 Presently, the most important and widely used procedures are Bankruptcy (i.e., *fallimento*) and Arrangement with Creditors (i.e., *concordato preventivo*).

15.09 Both these procedures contain rules on the treatment of executory contracts. However, given the different goals pursued by each of these procedures, the relevant rules are substantially dissimilar.

15.10 The goal of Bankruptcy under Italian law is only the liquidation of the assets of the company (*rectius*: Bankruptcy is a liquidation and a compulsory winding-up procedure).

15.11 Accordingly, while the latest reforms focused on granting a second chance to a distressed company or some of its entities/divisions, Bankruptcy continues to be used to maximize the assets of the company for the benefit of its creditors.

15.12 The primary goal of the Arrangement with Creditors is instead the preservation of the company or its business, even if liquidation remains a legitimate outcome of this procedure.

15.13 Obviously, the two opposite goals affect the treatment of executory contracts. Different rules apply depending on whether a liquidation or a reorganization proceeding is commenced. From the debtor's perspective, executory contracts acquire a particular relevance especially in business reorganization, while they play a lesser role in liquidation procedures.

---

use the over-indebtedness procedures, provided by the Law January 27th 2012, n. 3, which are applicable to entities not subject to bankruptcy.

11 Ibid., art 182 *septies*.

12 Ibid., art 182 *ter*.

13 Ibid., art 160.

14 Legislative decree July 8th 1999, n. 270; on this topic recently see: Fabrizio Di Marzio and Franceso Macario, 'Amministrazione straordinaria delle grandi imprese in stato di insolvenza', in Alberto Jorio and Bruno Sassani (eds), *Trattato delle procedure concorsuali*, V, Giuffrè, Milan, 2017, 601 ff.

15 Bankruptcy Law, art 1.

16 Ibid., art 194.

The main characteristics of the treatment of executory contracts in the above-mentioned procedures will be outlined in the following paragraphs, and some suggestions will also be offered about how the current global reform may affect the evolution of these rules. **15.14**

The discipline of these contracts is affected by two preliminary considerations: **15.15**

- when the idea of *pacta sunt servanda* (or 'bargains must be kept') must yield to the principle of *paritas creditorum* (or 'equal treatment of creditors');
- which parties in the contract deserve additional protection.

Both Bankruptcy and Arrangement with Creditors are judicial procedures that are provided for by the court, which outlines the general structures of the process and controls its evolution. **15.16**

It is necessary to point out that the judicial authority, when carrying out this function, is not acting, as is usual in civil jurisdiction, to solve a contrast between two opposite parties. Instead this is a function of a managerial character in a proceeding focused on its specific goals. **15.17**

In the following paragraphs, the term Bankruptcy will describe a liquidation proceeding, which can be used by a large number of creditors, including companies. The reason for choosing this word instead of liquidation is because this is the term used under the current Italian Law to make reference to liquidation proceedings. Bankruptcies can be commenced by both individuals and companies (*rectius*: natural persons, legal persons or other entities which may be subject to bankruptcy while carrying out commercial activity[17]) even if it is acknowledged that in other jurisdictions the term 'bankruptcy' only refers to liquidation proceedings that involve individuals. **15.18**

It is impossible to translate the word *fallimento* with the English notions of 'Insolvency' or 'Insolvency Procedure': the Italian Bankruptcy is based on **15.19**

17 According to the Bankruptcy Law, art 1 only enterprises (mainly individuals and companies) that conduct business activity, with the exclusion of public bodies, are subject to the provisions on Bankruptcy and Arrangement with Creditors. Those enterprises are not subject to the provisions on Bankruptcy and Arrangement with Creditors only if they can demonstrate all the following requirements: (*a*) having possessed total assets, calculated on an annual basis, not exceeding €300,000 in the three financial years preceding the date of the filing of the Bankruptcy petition or since the commencement of its activities if this period is lesser; (*b*) having achieved, in any manner, results in the three financial years prior to the date of filing of the Bankruptcy petition or since the commencement of its activities if this period is lesser, total gross revenues calculated on an annual basis not exceeding €200,000; (*c*) having total debts, including debts that are not yet due, not exceeding €500,000.

different eligibility criteria and specific characteristics that will be briefly explained in the next Section.

2. The Bankruptcy procedure in Italy

15.20 Bankruptcy is a procedure available to entities carrying out commercial activities (under Italian Law small entities are excluded). It is intended to satisfy creditors by the means of the liquidation of the debtor's assets.

15.21 The main objective of Bankruptcy is to grant protection to the rights of the creditors and to maximize their return, especially when compared to the ordinary individual execution proceedings.

15.22 Under article 51 of the Law, entitled 'Prohibition of individual enforcement and preventive actions', unless otherwise provided, from the day of the Bankruptcy order no individual enforcement or preventive actions (including those regarding claims becoming due during the Bankruptcy) can be brought or continued against the assets included in the Bankruptcy estate.

15.23 With the discipline of Bankruptcy, the legislature nevertheless tried to preserve the integrity of the ailing company. As a result, sales of individual assets are permitted only if the sale of the entire company and/or its divisions would not be in the best interests of the creditors.

15.24 The primary concern of the Italian Bankruptcy Law is to guarantee the rights of the creditors. The goal is thus to assure the creditors the maximum return on their claims in the shortest possible time.

15.25 In the Italian Bankruptcy procedure, a court-appointed administrator runs the proceedings.

15.26 The administrator (alternatively called official receiver or trustee in Bankruptcy) is responsible for the insolvent assets. He/She performs all the operations of the procedure under the supervision of the Bankruptcy judge and the committee of inspection with respect to their assigned functions.[18]

15.27 The administrator personally performs the functions of his/her office, but he/she may delegate specific operations.[19] The administrator has full autonomy in the management of the case.

---

18 Bankruptcy Law, art 35.

19 Ibid., art 32.

The committee of inspection is the body representing the creditors. It supervises the work of the administrator, authorizes actions and expresses opinions in the cases provided by law or at request of the court or the bankruptcy judge.[20] **15.28**

B. TREATMENT OF EXECUTORY CONTRACTS

1. General treatment of executory contracts in the Bankruptcy procedure

In the discipline of the Bankruptcy procedure, the principal rule that deals with pre-existing legal relationships is article 72 b. law.[21] **15.29**

There are also some specific rules on single contracts: these include, among others, rules on real estate contracts where the building is yet to be built or completed[22] or sales with retention of title clauses.[23] In addition, outside the Bankruptcy Law, specific contracts are also subject to specific rules. **15.30**

The general rule is that, upon filing, the enforceability of executory contracts is suspended and the Law gives the administrator the power to assume or reject them. **15.31**

Indeed, the general rule states that, when one of the parties is declared bankrupt, if a contract is still not performed or not entirely performed by both parties, the performance of the contract remains suspended. **15.32**

The contract remains suspended until the administrator, with the authorization of the committee of inspection, declares that he/she is succeeding to the contract on behalf of the bankrupt entity. **15.33**

Only if the administrator declares that he/she is succeeding into the contract, is the preliminary authorization of the committee of inspection required. Only in this last case does the Bankruptcy procedure assume all the relevant obligations. **15.34**

---

20 Ibid., art 41.

21 On this topic see: Massimo Franzoni, 'I contratti pendenti nel fallimento', in Gregorio Gitti, Francesco Delfini and Daniele Maffeis (eds), *Studi in onore di Giorgio De Nova*, II (Giuffrè, Milan, 2015) 1351 ff.

22 Bankruptcy Law, art 72.

23 Ibid., art 73.

15.35 The administrator, however, is free to decide to reject the contract; in this case the authorization of the committee of inspection is not necessary.

15.36 The decision of the administrator is not subject to any time limits. However – as a counterweight – the other contracting party (the *in bonis* party) may bring an action against the administrator, obliging the Bankruptcy judge to set a deadline, of not more than 60 days, for the administrator to reach a final decision.

15.37 If the deadline expires with no reply from the administrator, the contract is considered to be dissolved.

15.38 Regarding this general rule we can observe that:

(*a*) the Law attributes to only one of the parties to the contract (i.e., the Bankruptcy entity), the discretionary power to dissolve it;
(*b*) the other party is penalized;
(*c*) the reason for this discipline – which clearly favours the Bankruptcy estate – can be found in the need to preserve and promote the collective interest of creditors;
(*d*) the choice of the administrator must be determined after having considered the interests of the creditors as a whole.

15.39 This discipline reflects the Bankruptcy policy that a debtor should have the ability to abandon burdensome contracts while retaining beneficial contracts, if this is in the best interest of creditors.

15.40 In the Bankruptcy procedure one relevant exception to this rule is the situation (not really frequent) in which the court establishes the provisional trading of the bankrupt enterprise.

15.41 Indeed, with the Bankruptcy order – or at a later time – the court may order the enterprise to continue all its activities, or those of specific branches, if a suspension of the activities could lead to serious damage to the value of the company or the business, and provided that the continued activity does not negatively affect creditors.

In this last case, the general rule is replaced by the provisions that outstanding contracts shall continue to be performed by both parties unless the administrator opts for suspending their performance or rejecting them.[24] **15.42**

In this situation the general rule of article 72 b. law applies again when the Bankruptcy judge orders the cessation of the provisional trading of the bankrupt's enterprise. **15.43**

2. The most significant specific contracts

Under Italian Law there are particular rules for specific pre-existing legal relationships/contracts. The most significant rules concern real estate to be built, finance lease, sale with retention of title, contracts with continuous periodic performance, business lease agreements, property lease agreements, procurement contract, insurance contract and stock market forward contract. **15.44**

2.1 Real estate to be built

There is a specific discipline for this kind of contract,[25] to be more precise for the contract whose objective is the future transfer of the ownership of a building not yet fully completed. This discipline is not applicable, however, in the case of a building already completed. **15.45**

Regarding this contract the Law provides that the decision on the dissolution or the continuation of the contract is not (only) given to the administrator, but to both parties. The decision of any of them binds the other. **15.46**

According to article 72 *bis* b. law, after the declaration of Bankruptcy, this type of contract is also dissolved if the purchaser, a natural person, has claimed back from the guarantor the sum paid to the constructor, and has so informed the administrator. Obviously, this must happen before the administrator announces his/her decision to perform or reject the contract. **15.47**

The case-law underlined the peculiarity of the above-mentioned discipline with respect to article 72 b. law by affirming that article 72 *bis* b. law provides a special legal framework for executory contracts regarding real estate to be built which grants to the promisee buyer particular instruments of protection, **15.48**

24 Ibid., art 104 (7) (b).
25 Legislative decree June 20th 2005, n. 122.

such as the constructor's guarantee.[26] Therefore this discipline is special and it waives the one set out in article 72 b. law.[27]

15.49 The Law is clearly intended to protect the buyers of the building to be built, in order to avoid the risk that, during the period between the conclusion of the contract and the purchase of the property, the Bankruptcy of the seller might prevent the purchase and at the same time cause the buyer to lose the funds already paid as a deposit.

15.50 For this reason, the buyer is not forced to respect or wait for the decision of the administrator. On the contrary, the buyer can anticipate the decision of the administrator by executing the guarantee that covers the amount deposited when the parties signed the contract. This can be done by a written communication to the administrator, thus obtaining the dissolution of the contract by the initiative of the buyer.

2.2 Finance lease

15.51 Under Italian Law, the finance lease is a contractual form that features manifold variations of structure and content. Its discipline is included in article 72 *quarter* b. law.

15.52 This type of contract had – and still has – enjoyed a significant success in the market. Similarly to the Anglo-Saxon experience, this contract is autonomously regulated by the Law,[28] and it is primarily used in financial transactions.

15.53 In the event of the Bankruptcy of the user/lessee, the general rule[29] is applicable to finance lease agreements with the following further specifications.

15.54 If, within the Bankruptcy proceeding of the user, the provisional trading is allowed by the court;[30] the agreement continues to be performed unless the administrator declares his/her intention to dissolve it.

15.55 In the event of the dissolution of the agreement, the grantor/lessor has the right to obtain the asset, and he/she is obliged to pay to the Bankruptcy administrator the difference (if any) between the price obtained by the sale of the asset and the residual capital credit.

---

26 Art 2, § 1, Legislative decree June 20th 2005, n. 122.

27 Court of Brescia May 23th 2014, in *Fallimento*, 2015, 480 ff.

28 Law August 4th 2017, n. 124, art 1, §§ 136–140.

29 Bankruptcy Law, art 72.

30 According to Bankruptcy Law, art 104.

The grantor/lessor has the right to be included in the list of Bankruptcy creditors[31] if the price of the sale does not cover the entire amount of the credit claimed at the date of the Bankruptcy order. **15.56**

To the contrary, in the event of the Bankruptcy of the lessor, the agreement remains valid and enforceable. The lessee maintains the right to purchase the assets after the expiry of the agreement, subject to the payment of lease rentals and the previously agreed price. **15.57**

2.3 Sale with retention of title

This is a contract expressly disciplined by the Italian Civil Code[32] characterized by the fact that the ownership of the asset remains with the vendor, while the possession of the asset is immediately transferred to the purchaser, even if the payment occurs by instalments. **15.58**

According to article 73, § 2, b. law the Bankruptcy of the vendor does not constitute grounds for the dissolution of the contract. **15.59**

According to the case-law the peculiar discipline provided by the article 73, § 2, b. law, is justified by the fact that in this contract the effect of the transfer of the property, although it is postponed and subject to the full payment of the price, is already binding between the parties, and therefore the seller is obliged to deliver the goods, and from that moment, pursuant to article 1523 Civil Code, the buyer bears the risks in case the good perishes.[33] **15.60**

Otherwise, according to article 73, § 1, b. law in the event of the Bankruptcy of the purchaser, if the price is to be paid at a future time or in instalments, the administrator may succeed to the contract with the authorization of the committee of inspection. **15.61**

In this case, the vendor may request a deposit/guarantee if the administrator does not immediately pay the price with a discount at the legal interest rate. **15.62**

If the administrator withdraws from the contract, the vendor must return the instalments already paid, subject to the right to fair payment for the use of the item. **15.63**

---

31 Bankruptcy Law, art 96.

32 Civil Code, arts 1523–1526.

33 Court of Rome, January 26th, 2007, in *Fallimento*, 2007, p. 592 ff.; Supreme Court, December 22th 2005, n. 28480.

2.4 Contracts with continuous or periodic performance

15.64 Contracts with continuous or periodic performance guarantee, in the modern economy, the continuity of the supply of raw materials, commodities, energy and services between the parties at an agreed price.

15.65 With regard to this type of contracts, the case-law has specified that every single delivery or supply of the performances satisfies an autonomous interest of the creditor, so with reference to the same contract with Continuous or Periodic Performance, it is not identifiable as a single performance but a plurality of performances, even if the plurality of the performances is related to the same contract which is the source of the obligation.[34]

15.66 According to article 74 b. law on so-called 'rolling contract', if the administrator succeeds in a contract of this type, he/she is obliged to pay in full the price of the deliveries already made or the services already performed after the opening of the formal insolvency procedure.

15.67 The case-law specified that the choice of the administrator to succeed in the contract does not necessarily require the written form, but it may be tacit and presumed by conclusive facts, as long as those facts are unequivocal.[35]

15.68 The rule only regulates the case in which the administrator of the Bankruptcy estate is the beneficiary of the supply or the service, and he/she decides to succeed in the contract.

15.69 In any other case, the general treatment of executory contracts (described in Section B (1)) applies.

2.5 Business lease agreements

15.70 After the Bankruptcy order against any of the parties of the business lease agreement,[36] the general rule is that the contract continues to produce its effect among the parties (art 79 b. law).

15.71 In other words, bankruptcy does not represent a reason to dissolve these contracts, but both parties may withdraw within 60 days by paying a fair indemnity to the counterparty.

---

34 Supreme Court, May 22th 1996, n. 4715.

35 See ibid.

36 On this topic for the *in bonis* situation, see Italian Civil Code, arts 2555–2562.

In the case of disagreement between the parties concerning the amount of the indemnity, this is determined by the bankruptcy judge after hearing the arguments of the parties involved. 15.72

The compensation/indemnity due to the administrator has a preferential right and is governed by article 111 b. law. 15.73

2.6 Property lease agreements

The discipline is different in the event of the Bankruptcy of the lessor or the lessee. 15.74

In the first case,[37] the Bankruptcy of the lessor does not cause the dissolution of the property lease and the administrator succeeds in the contract. 15.75

If the agreement is set to expire after more than four years from the Bankruptcy order, the administrator has the power to withdraw from the agreement within one year of the Bankruptcy order. The withdrawal produces effect only after four years from the Bankruptcy order. 15.76

The administrator has to pay to the lessee a fair indemnity for the early withdrawal.[38] 15.77

In the second case,[39] i.e., the Bankruptcy of the lessee, the administrator may withdrawal from the agreement at any time, by paying the lessor a fair compensation for advance withdrawal; in this last case obviously the indemnity has a preferential right.[40] 15.78

In the event of disagreement between the parties regarding the amount of the indemnity, this is determined by the bankruptcy judge after hearing the arguments of the parties involved. 15.79

---

37 Bankruptcy Law, art 80 (1) and (2).

38 The case-law specifies that even in the case of a Bankruptcy of a property leased for hotel use, whose contract the administrator succeeded to the landlord according to art 80 b. law, recognizing the right of pre-emption to the tenant, the latter may exercise the aforementioned right every time the auction price has become definitive: Supreme Court, January 28th 2013, n. 1808.

39 Bankruptcy Law, art 80 (3) (b).

40 Under ibid., art 111.

2.7 Procurement contract

15.80 The rules on the private procurement contract differ depending on the characterization of these contracts. Special rules apply if the subjective qualities of the contractor have been the determining reasons for the contract (*intuitus personae*).

15.81 When the personal qualities of the parties are not crucial,[41] the administrator of the insolvent party has the right to terminate the contract or to assume it. In the latter case, he/she needs the authorization of the committee of inspection. The procurement contract is automatically terminated if the administrator does not inform the other party within 60 days from the opening of the procedure that he/she wants to assume the contracts, and if he/she does not offer proper guarantees on the future performance to the performing party.

15.82 In the other case,[42] the Bankruptcy of the contractor dissolves the contractual relationship only if the subjective quality of the contractor was the determining grounds for the contract, unless the other party agrees to continue the relationship.[43]

2.8 Insurance contract

15.83 In this case, the rules[44] are as follows:

(a) unless agreed otherwise, the Bankruptcy of the insured party does not dissolve the insurance contract covering damages; except in the case of a considerable aggravated risk which arises as an effect of the bankruptcy order;
(b) if the insurance contract continues, the insurer's claim for unpaid premiums must be fully satisfied, even if the due date of the premium is before the bankruptcy order.

15.84 This discipline is an exception to the general rule in order to ensure that the assets of the bankrupt entity remain fully insured during the development of the procedure.[45]

15.85 In application of these principles, waiving the general rule (art 72 b. law), the case-law affirmed that in the case of bankruptcy of the insured, the insurance

---

41 According to ibid., art 81 (1) (b).
42 Ibid., art 81 (2) (b).
43 These provisions apply to the regulation on procurement contracts for public work.
44 Bankruptcy Law, art 82.
45 Supreme Court, April 4th 2013, n. 9676.

contract continues *ope legis*, and the administrator replaces the insured and assumes all the obligations.[46]

2.9 Stock Market forward contract

For this kind of contract there is a specific discipline that aims to eliminate from the assets of the Bankruptcy procedure any risk linked to the price fluctuation; indeed it is believed that this risk is incompatible with the goal of the Bankruptcy that in Italian Law is the liquidation (see Section A (1)). **15.86**

According to the Law[47] if the term expires after the bankruptcy order of one of the contracting parties, the Stock Market forward contract is dissolved on the date of the bankruptcy order. **15.87**

The difference between the contractual price and the value of the items or the securities at the date of the bankruptcy order is paid to the Bankruptcy proceeding, if the bankrupt claims a credit; or, in the opposite case, the bankrupt is included in the list of approved claims. **15.88**

For the reasons indicated above the case-law foster the application of the article 76 b. law to the largest possible number of stock market contracts,[48] as for example the swap contract,[49] the domestic currency swap,[50] the option on futures contracts and the option on currency.[51] **15.89**

3. The arrangement with creditors based on liquidation

This is a very important proceeding; as mentioned before, the goals of the arrangement with creditors – a satisfactory and preservation procedure – can be either the restructuring or the liquidation of the company or its business; and these two objectives can be pursued within the same procedure. **15.90**

During this procedure – unlike what happens in the Bankruptcy – the debtor remains in possession of his/her assets and continues the activity of the enterprise under the control of the court-appointed receiver. **15.91**

---

46 Ibid.
47 Bankruptcy Law, art 76.
48 Court of Appeal Milan, October 17th 1986, in *Banca borsa e titoli di credito*, 1986, II, p. 62 ss.
49 Court Florence, January 15th 1998, in *Fallimento*, 1998, p. 857 ff.
50 Court Turin, April 4th 1998, in *Fallimento*, 1998, p. 857 ff.
51 Court Turin, January 23th 1998, in *Fallimento*, 1998, p. 534 ff.

15.92 The goals pursued by the Law are in this case carried out without depriving the debtor of the management of his/her assets and the management of the enterprise.

15.93 Indeed, his/her activities and decisions are subject to a series of controls to avoid abusive behaviour.

15.94 The arrangement with creditors includes four principal steps (the first of which is optional):

(a) the proceeding may commence with the filing of an 'incomplete' petition in which the court is asked to establish a deadline for the presentation of the complete petition and the remaining documents required by the Law. The debtor obtains manifold advantages from submitting an 'incomplete' petition. These include, among others, the temporary protection of the debtor during the phase of preparation of the final petition (i.e., the automatic stay);
(b) the 'complete' petition for the access to the procedure shall be filed alongside the request to the court for the admission to the procedure. This petition contains: (1) the proposal directed at creditors, which can include quantitative and qualitative terms, as well as time deadlines for satisfying the creditors; and (2) the plan. In other words, the complete petition includes a description of all the activities that the debtor intends to implement in the plan, if approved by the creditors. The plan must be accompanied by, among the other things, a report by an independent professional attesting the truth of the company records and the feasibility of the proposed plan;
(c) the assembly of the creditors called to vote on the proposal. A proposal is considered to be approved if it is supported by both the majority of the impaired creditors and the classes admitted to the vote;
(d) the ratification of the agreement, i.e., the moment in which, if there have been no objections, the court[52] verifies the regularity of the procedure and the result of the vote of creditors. The decision to ratify an agreement cannot be appealed to a higher court.

52 In a very important decision the Supreme Court held that the courts cannot evaluate either the economic, or the general feasibility of the plan. Their powers are limited to determine if the plan meets the legal and substantive requirements set out in the law. See Supreme Court January 23rd 2013, n. 1521.

4. The arrangement with creditors on a going concern basis

To facilitate the preservation of viable but distressed companies or businesses, the Italian legislature introduced a new procedure, called 'Arrangement with Creditors on a Going Concern Basis'.[53] **15.95**

The model for this procedure is the discipline of the arrangement with creditors described above, but this type of arrangement is less frequently used than the liquidating arrangement. **15.96**

The goal of this special procedure[54] is to maintain the business operation while searching for a buyer, or for the approval of a restructuring plan. **15.97**

To reach this target, the Italian Bankruptcy Law grants additional powers and prerogatives to the debtor. **15.98**

However, the legislature requests additional guarantees about the seriousness and practicality of the restructuring plan: **15.99**

(a) the plan must include – on top of the usual requirements – an analytical indication of the expected costs and revenues, the necessary financial resources and the respective financing mechanisms;
(b) the independent professional must certify that the continuation of the business under the planned arrangement (on a going concern basis) is instrumental to ensure a better satisfaction of the creditors.

5. The executory contracts in the arrangements with creditors

In the discipline of the Arrangement with Creditors the principal rule which regulates the effects on executory contracts is article 169 *bis* b. law.[55] **15.100**

According to the Law, executory contracts are contracts in which the obligations have not been performed or not fully performed by both parties. **15.101**

---

53 On this topic see Fabrizio Di Marzio, 'Introduction to the Arrangements with Creditors with Business Continuity', in Michele Vietti, Francesco Marotta and Fabrizio Di Marzio (ed.), *The Italian Change for Restructuring* (Giuffrè, Milan, 2014) 273 ff.

54 Bankruptcy Law, art 186.

55 On the topic of Arrangement with Creditors, the Supreme Court has recently affirmed that the non-declaration of costs or expenses for the dissolution or prosecution of executory contracts represents a violation of the informed consent – which must obviously be complete – of the creditors that vote for the proposal of the Arrangement (Supreme Court September 4th 2017, n. 20719).

15.102 Considering this point of view, therefore, the notion of pending contracts in article 169 *bis* b. law is comparable to that of pending relationships provided in article 72 b. law.

15.103 The admission itself to the procedure does not change the discipline of the executory contracts.

15.104 But with the (incomplete or complete) petition or with a separate request, the debtor may at any time ask for the authorization to dissolve the executory contracts.

15.105 This request is addressed to the court or, once the debtor has been admitted to the procedure, to the Bankruptcy judge who supervises the Arrangement with Creditors.

15.106 The executory contracts are dissolved from the date of the aforesaid specific petition.

15.107 Only at the debtor's request, suspension of a contract may be authorized for no longer than 60 days; and the latter period may be extended once only for the same period.

15.108 Obviously, the suspension or the dissolution of the contracts might cause prejudice to the other party.

15.109 In the above-mentioned cases, the other party shall be entitled to compensation amounting to the damages due for non-performance. The debt in question shall be paid as an old debt existing prior to the Arrangement with Creditors. These debts are then without priority for the procedure.

6. The executory contracts in the arrangements with creditors on a going concern basis

15.110 Article 186 *bis*, §§ 3, 4 and 5, b. law. regulates the treatment of executory contracts in the Arrangement with Creditors on a Going Concern Basis.

15.111 This article applies without prejudice to article 169 *bis* b. law, and the admission to this sub-procedure does not suspend and/or dissolve the executory contracts, even if the counterparty is a governmental authority.

Furthermore, according to these rules the debtor (admitted to this type of Arrangement) may continue to perform contracts with governmental authorities and participate in public tenders, if it complies with specific terms stated in the Law. **15.112**

C. REFORMS

1. The global 'Rordorf Reform'

As indicated in the introductory paragraph (Section A(1)), the Law concerning the business crisis should be completely reformed in the near future. **15.113**

At this precise moment, while almost all the European Union countries have recently adopted new insolvency laws, the Italian Law – in its general structure – dates back to 1942. **15.114**

It is now a widespread opinion that in Italy a complete reform of the entire Insolvency Law is necessary, not only for substantial reasons but also for the country's image. **15.115**

Moreover, the frequent reforms which have occurred recently, as illustrated in the previous paragraphs, have created significant difficulties in the application of the law because – in a civil law legal system – the continuous modifications of the rules hinder the establishment of an established and uniform case-law. **15.116**

Considering these aspects, the need was: **15.117**

> from all the scholars and the operators, to adopt an approach to reform which is no longer episodic and directed only to deal with the emergency, but [an approach to reform which is] systematic and organic, in order to shed clarity on a system that has become too confused.[56]

In this process, the Italian legislature will have to take into account the European Union legislation and in particular: **15.118**

- the Regulation (EU) 2015/848 of the European Parliament and of the Council of May 20th, 2015 on insolvency proceedings;

---

56 See the Reports on the Bill n. 3671, presented by the Minister of Justice to the Chamber of Deputies on March 11th, 2016, 2.

- the Commission Recommendation of March 12th, 2014 on a new approach to business failure and insolvency.

15.119 The Italian Legislature will also have to consider the model law on insolvency elaborated by the United Nations Commission on International Trade Law.[57]

2. The general principles

15.120 Among the general principles indicated in the Act of the Parliament that delegated the government to reform the Insolvency Law,[58] it is worth mentioning some lexical terminological innovations, such as:

(a) the replacement of the word 'bankruptcy' with 'Judicial Winding-up Procedure' in accordance with a trend already observed in other European civil law countries (France, Germany and Spain). This change is justified by the need to avoid the negative and disparaging meaning that is traditionally associated with the word 'bankruptcy'. In fact, as any business activity implies a certain degree of risk and uncertainty, the unfortunate outcome (failure) may not be dependent on the entrepreneur's ability. As a result, the use of the word 'bankruptcy' can be inappropriate;
(b) to distinguish the concepts of crisis and insolvency, and to identify the crisis as a probability of future insolvency.

15.121 Furthermore, from the general point of view, the upcoming legislation:

(a) will give priority to the proposals that intend to overcome the crisis and ensure the business continuity, even by means of a different entrepreneur, as long as these proposals ensure the best satisfaction for the creditors;[59]
(b) will consider the judicial winding-up (which should replace the current 'bankruptcy' procedure) as a last resort mechanism;[60]
(c) will ensure the specialization of the judges involved in insolvency procedures and the improvement of their skills.

---

57 UNCITRAL.
58 Rordorf Reform, art 2 (it is the Law October 19th 2017, n. 155).
59 Rordorf Reform, art 2 (g).
60 Rordorf Reform, art 2 (g).

3. The crisis of groups of companies

It is obviously not possible in this chapter to analyse more thoroughly the general aspects of the reform, but it must be pointed out that great importance is given to the necessity to establish rules on the crisis of the groups of companies that today are outside the scope of the Italian insolvency legislation. **15.122**

As a matter of fact, it is obvious that in this situation the crisis and/or the insolvency have features that are specific. **15.123**

In an effort to address this issue, the European legislation introduced some provisions in the above-mentioned EU Regulation 2015/848 on cross-border insolvency. **15.124**

Therefore, the upcoming Law should provide not only rules to allow a unitary procedure for the insolvency of the companies which are part of the same group, but also rules to establish reciprocal information duties in case of a separate procedure taking place before different courts. **15.125**

In particular, with reference to the unitary procedure of the group's arrangements with creditors: **15.126**

(a) it should be provided that a single court shall handle the procedure and that a single receiver must be appointed by the court;
(b) the presentation of a unitary proposal for the recovery of the 'group crisis' will regulate intra-group operations and transactions to preserve the business continuity, and to guarantee the protection of the shareholders and of the creditors of each company part of the group.

Also, with regard to the unitary procedure of the judicial winding-up of the group, the Law is expected to identify only one competent judicial authority and court-appointed administrator. **15.127**

The government, among other things, will also have: **15.128**

(a) to identify the criteria to proportionally allocate the costs of the proceeding among the companies part of the group;
(b) to grant to the court-appointed administrator certain powers to be exercised in respect also to the non-insolvent companies.

4. The judicial winding-up procedure

15.129 Regarding the judicial winding-up procedure which, as mentioned above, should replace the current Bankruptcy procedure, it should be based on the following fundamental principles:

(*a*) first, the strengthening of the powers of the court-appointed administrator, who has acquired a leading role (*dominus*) in the judicial winding-up procedure, and whose action will be more effective and trustworthy through a series of measures including: (1) a more stringent regulation of incompatibilities of offices[61] in the event of subsequent insolvency proceedings; (2) the definition by law of the minimum content of the liquidation plan; (3) the possibility for the court-appointed administrator to file or continue specific lawsuits if they can be beneficial to the insolvent estate;

(b) to limit the grounds for avoidance actions that aim at invalidating the debtor's acts carried out before the beginning of the procedure;

(c) regarding the examination of claims, innovations should be introduced to ensure that this phase is governed according to the criteria of promptness and concentration. These criteria consist in: (1) facilitating the presentation of the creditors' claim application online, and restricting the possibility to submit late claims; (2) examining each credit to be off-set[62] within the insolvency procedure;

(d) regarding the liquidation of the assets, the Law is intended to introduce procedures inspired by the maximum transparency and efficiency to be pursued also through the use of the most modern technologies.

15.130 The entire administration of the liquidation is supposed to ensure the utmost surveillance, transparency and disclosure also through the use of the system so-called 'Common', which is based on three fundamental principles:

- the introduction of a unified national online market for the assets to be sold;
- the possibility accorded to creditors to purchase such assets if specifically authorized;
- the establishment of one or more funds to manage the unsold assets.

---

61 For example, between court-appointed receiver and court-appointed administrator in the event of passage from Arrangements with Creditors to judicial winding-up.

62 Bankruptcy Law, art 56:

> [c]reditors have the right to offset claims that they assert against the bankrupt with their debts to the bankrupt, even where such debts are not due before the Bankruptcy order. Nevertheless, claims not immediately due are not offset if the creditor has acquired the credit by an act *inter vivos* after or in the year before the Bankruptcy order.

The Law also introduces some modifications with regard to the Release of the Debtor procedure.[63] The most significant innovations seem to be: 15.131

(a) to extend the discharge of debt to companies – and therefore not only to natural persons as in the present provisions – if it is demonstrated that the directors or (in case of partnership) the partners, are worthy;
(b) to provide types of automatic discharge of the debtor in small value insolvency cases, unless the creditors express their opposition.

Specific guiding principles and criteria are also provided to integrate the discipline of the executory contracts as set in the current article 72 b. law (Section B(1)). 15.132

Integrations to the current discipline shall principally concern: 15.133

(a) the limitation of the liquidation expenses only to the period following the continuation and/or replacement of the court-appointed administrator, and therefore only and exclusively to the credits acquired during the course of the proceeding (with the exception of the credits prior to the admission to the procedure, unless other special rules provide so). This measure obviously aims at reducing the liquidation expenses that often compromise the expectations of the general body of creditors;
(b) with regard to the contracts in which debtor's personal qualities are a determining element for the performance of the contract, the automatic termination is provided, unless the other party agrees to the continuation of the contract despite the debtor's insolvency procedure.[64]

The discipline of the executory contracts is therefore unlikely to be revolutionized. 15.134

Also, according to the reform, the basic philosophy will remain unchanged, so the liquidation function of the proceeding must be realized not only through the monetary conversion of the debtor's assets (tangible and intangible) but also through the handling of all legal relationships resulting from the executory contracts. 15.135

---

63 For the current situation on this topic in Italian Law see: Rolandino Guidotti, 'L'esdebitazione del fallito', in Riccardo Borsari (ed.), *Crisi dell'impresa, procedure concorsuali e diritto penale dell'insolvenza*, (Padua University Press, Padua, 2015) 97 ff.

64 With a mechanism similar to the one referred to in art 81, § 2, b. law mentioned above (Section A (2.7.)).

15.136 As explained in the Report on the Reform Bill of the Law,[65] with reference to the contracts, the liquidation function of the insolvency proceeding is indirectly expressed as a criterion of orientation for the court-appointed administrator's choices or as a basis for the effects required by law on the single contractual relationship.

5. The reform of the Arrangements with Creditors

15.137 Regarding the reform of the Arrangements with Creditors, the future legislature seems, in general, willing:

(a) to allow the arrangements with creditors to have only a liquidation purpose; (1) when there are external resources that are considerably increasing the creditors' satisfaction; (2) when the payment of at least 20 per cent of the total amount of unsecured claims is guaranteed;
(b) to redefine the method to verify the reliability of the company data reported in the proposal and its feasibility, by identifying the powers of the court in this regard;
(c) to eliminate the assembly of the creditors by providing online procedures to allow creditors to discuss the proposals and to express their vote;
(d) to review the current rules of executory contracts, with reference to their possible stay and dissolution, the role of the receiver appointed by the court, and the competence to determine the indemnity;[66]
(e) to provide detailed rules on the implementation of the plan, including the possibility for the court to entrust the implementation of the proposal to a third party;
(f) to integrate the provisions regarding the arrangements with creditors having the aim of the business continuity, by providing that the rules will apply: (1) even when there is an ongoing business lease; as well as (2) when the arrangements with creditors provide, beside the business continuity, also the liquidation of the assets that are non-functional to the enterprise.

15.138 In case the enterprise subject to the arrangements with creditors is a company, the legislature should also consider:

(a) to set rules to place on the bodies of the company the obligation to promptly implement the proposal once it has been endorsed by the court; such rules should also provide that in the event of dilatory or obstructive

65 Report on the Reform Bill of the Law, 11.
66 Rordorf Reform, art 6 (1) (i).

behaviour, the implementation of the proposal may be entrusted to a provisional administrator;

(b) to coordinate the rules of the arrangements with creditors regarding the companies with the rules on transformation, merger and division.

D. CONCLUDING REMARKS

Under Italian Law, there is not a unified treatment of the executory contracts when the debtor enters into a formal insolvency proceeding. Depending on the procedure and its goals, different rules apply. **15.139**

For instance, in the Arrangement with Creditors on a Going Concern Basis, since the Law obviously focuses on the continuation of the business activity (more than in the other formal procedures) the debtor, rather than the creditors, is given large discretion to determine the outcome of the executory contract. **15.140**

On the contrary, in the Bankruptcy procedure the general rule is that, upon filing, all executory contracts are suspended. This is because the law gives the administrator the power to assume or reject the same executory contracts. **15.141**

It is, therefore, necessary to point out that the Italian insolvency law is under review from a global viewpoint. The Italian Parliament has recently approved the 'Rordorf Reform'.[67] **15.142**

This new discipline, as we have seen, might foresee corrections and integrations for the rules on executory contracts, in both Bankruptcy and Arrangement with Creditors, but it is possible to say that the structure of the Law, and its principles will, probably, not change on the topic of executory contracts. **15.143**

The principal innovations on the global 'Rordorf Reform' – as noted above – will concern: **15.144**

67 A bill was approved by the House of Deputies on February 1st 2017, and was transmitted to the Senate. The Senate in the meeting of October 11th 2017, approved the same text which is composed of 16 articles subdivided in three Chapters: the first one (arts 1–2) on the general dispositions, the second (arts 3–15) outlines principles and directive criteria for the reform of the crises and insolvency procedures, and finally, the third (art 16) is dedicated to financial matters. The government, within 12 months, must adopt one or more decrees for the implementation of the Law, obviously following the principles and the directive criteria of the Parliament. The Law was approved on October 19th 2017.

(a) the Judicial Winding-up Procedure– which will replace the Bankruptcy procedure – the integration of the current rules (see Section C (5)), with:
   (1) in case of prosecution or subentry of the administrator in the executory contracts, the limitation of the liquidation expenses to exclusively credits created during the Liquidation procedure (not to previous credits, except the special disposition of other Laws);
   (2) the dissolutions of personal contracts, which do not continue without the agreement of the counterparty (specifically, the contract based on the *intuitus personae*, such as those of proxy and employees), for which must be written a similar rule to that currently contained in the current discipline of the procurement contract;[68]

(b) regarding the discipline of the arrangement with creditors, the specification of the rules on executory contracts, referring to their possible suspension or dissolution, and the rules on the court-appointed receiver.[69]

15.145 The global reform intervenes realistically not only on the insolvency discipline but also on the discipline contained in the Civil Code that concerns, directly or indirectly, the crisis of companies.

15.146 Among these, it is fundamental to highlight the important provision[70] that obliges the future legislature to set rules regarding organizational systems directed to promptly discover and take action in case of a crisis situation, in order to avoid the loss of continuity of the business. According to this new rule, the individual entrepreneur or the board of directors will have to rapidly adopt the instruments indicated in the Law in order to resolve the crises and recover the business continuity.

15.147 These principles, which are probably already implicit in the current Italian Company Law, will be expressly codified in the near future. Therefore, they will become mandatory both for the individual entrepreneur and for the organ of the company, so they will impact all types of entities that conduct commercial activities.

15.148 The works on this Reform are still in progress.

---

68 Rordorf Reform, art 7 (6) (a) and (b).

69 Ibid., art 6 (1) (1) (i).

70 Ibid., art 13 (1) (b).

16

NATIONAL REPORT FOR JAPAN

Jin Chun and Stacey Steele

A. INTRODUCTION

The treatment of executory contracts and *ipso facto* clauses is a controversial issue in contemporary debates about Japanese insolvency law. Wide-sweeping procedural and legislative reforms undertaken between 1996 and 2005 focused on fundamental structural and procedural problems which had built up over decades and were ripe for review after the collapse of the bubble economy in the early 1990s. **16.01**

While the reforms addressed aspects of the treatment of executory contracts, the reforms did not significantly develop the statutory law in relation to *ipso facto* clauses. This chapter provides a summary of the current state of play in Japan in relation to executory contracts and *ipso facto* clauses. **16.02**

The chapter is divided into four parts. First, it presents an overview of the key Japanese corporate insolvency proceedings. Secondly, the chapter examines the general rule applying to executory contracts under those proceedings and analyses key statutorily determined exceptions to that rule, including certain exceptions introduced during the most recent legislative reforms. Thirdly, the chapter examines the treatment of *ipso facto* clauses in winding up and reorganization proceedings in Japan. As this analysis shows, judicial interpretations play a significant role when it comes to the treatment of *ipso facto* **16.03** clauses in the absence of clear statutory provisions. Fourth and finally, the chapter examines the most recent reform debates and highlights the desire among reformers to reach consensus before moving forward, as well as the crowded reform agenda, which arguably led to the failure to resolve outstanding matters in this area from a statutory perceptive.[1]

B. INSOLVENCY PROCEDURES

16.04 Japan's corporate insolvency law framework is a flexible regime encompassing a number of choices for debtors and creditors.[2] The framework is supported by a well-trained judiciary and sophisticated insolvency profession who are typically qualified lawyers with deep experience in restructuring and workouts and a keen understanding of international developments, at least amongst elite levels.[3] Courts continue to play an important role in formal insolvencies, but recent data suggests that formal filings by enterprises have decreased to pre-reform levels for some proceedings.[4]

16.05 The key formal insolvency proceedings available to enterprises are set out in the Bankruptcy Act (*Hasan hō*, Act No. 75, 2004, 'BA'), Corporate Reorganisation Act (*Kaisha kōsei hō*, Act No. 154, 2002, 'CorpRA') and Civil Rehabilitation Act (Act No. 225, 1999, 'CivRA'). The overall framework of the bankruptcy procedure is still heavily influenced by 19th Century German

1 This chapter uses translations from the Japanese Ministry of Justice's *Japanese Law Translation Database System* unless otherwise noted. The term executory contract is used in this chapter to refer to '*sōmu mirikō keiyaku*', although the System also uses '*sōmu keiyaku*' which is translated as 'bilateral contracts'. See Ministry of Justice, Japan, Japanese Law Translation Database System, 2017, http://www.japaneselawtranslation.go.jp/dict/list?re=02&dn=1&x=0&y=0&ky=bilateral+contract&co=1&x=0&y=0) last accesssed 3 December 2018. The translations contained in the System are unofficial and are for reference only. See Ministry of Justice, Japan, Japanese Law Translation Database System, 2017, http://www.japaneselawtranslation.go.jp/?re=02 last accesssed 3 December 2018. To the extent that any law or regulation is considered in light of any legal issue or dispute, readers should consult the original texts published in the Official Gazette.

2 For a detailed analysis of Japan's insolvency law framework, see Stacey Steele and Chun Jin, 'Insolvency', CCH Japan Business Law Guide, Loose-leaf, last updated 2015. On the reform process, see also: Stacey Steele, 'Appointing and remunerating insolvency practitioners in Japan: the roles of Japanese courts' (2017) 26(1) *International Insolvency Review* 82, 118. Bankruptcy and civil rehabilitation discussed in this chapter also apply to individuals. For a recent analysis of Japanese personal insolvency law, see Stacey Steele and Chun Jin, 'Reforming personal bankruptcy law in Australia: reflections from experience of insolvency law in Japan' (2017) 17(1) *QUT Law Review* 74, 96.

3 On Japanese insolvency practitioners, see: Steele, above n 2.

4 During the period from 1 January to 31 December 2016, there were 8,164 enterprise bankruptcy cases, one corporate reorganization case, and 246 ordinary (enterprise) civil rehabilitation cases. Teikoku Databank, *Tōsan shūkei*, undated, https://www.tdb.co.jp/tosan/syukei/16nen.html last accesssed 3 December 2018. For reasons for the decline in formal insolvency proceedings and rise of informal workouts, see: Takashi Sonoo, 'Hōteki seiri to shiteki seiri wa kongo doko ni mukau no ka – Tōsan jiken genshō no haikei to shōrai tenbō' (Background and future trends in the situation of insolvency cases: where are formal workouts and informal workouts going now?) (2016) 2050 Kinyū hōmu jijō 6, 10.

legislation on which the old bankruptcy act was based, and the corporate reorganisation procedure was historically based on the US Chapter 11 procedure, which also influenced the otherwise indigenously formulated civil rehabilitation procedure.

Reformers considered consolidating the legislation into a single code similarly to the US Bankruptcy Code, but events such as the Asian Financial Crisis in 1997 led to a decision to quickly produce a procedure which could benefit small–medium enterprises and thus the civil rehabilitation proceeding was enacted first. Subsequent legislation followed, but the various procedures were never collected into one code. There are also special procedures in separate legislation for liquidation of a solvent company, financial institutions and insurance companies. Further, Japan has special provisions dealing with cross-border insolvencies set out in the Act on Recognition of and Assistance for Foreign Insolvency Proceedings (*Gaikoku tōsan shori tetsuzuki no shōnin enjo ni kansuru hōritsu*, Act No. 129, 2000). The Act is generally consistent with the UNCITRAL Model Law on Cross-Border Insolvency. Certain provisions of the Civil Code (Act No. 89, 1896, 'Civil Code') and Commercial Code (Act No. 48, 1899, 'Commercial Code') are also relevant to the treatment of executory contracts and *ipso facto* clauses. **16.06**

The new Bankruptcy Act became effective in 2005. A local district court[5] will order commencement of a proceeding, and appoint a trustee (BA Arts 78, 79), if one of three causes of bankruptcy is evidenced: inability to pay debts as they fall due (*shiharai funō*, BA Art 15(1)); suspension of payment of debts (*shiharai teishi*, BA Art 15(2)); or liabilities exceeding the value of assets in the case of a juridical person (*saimu chōka*, BA Art 16(1)). Commencement does not bind secured creditors (BA Arts 95, 465(1)) and petitions are typically filed by debtors. **16.07**

The Civil Rehabilitation Act became effective in 2000. It was designed as a fast and simple rescue procedure for small- and medium-sized enterprises to enable a debtor to rehabilitate by performing a rehabilitation plan that has the approval of a majority of unsecured creditors and the court (CivRA Art 1). Civil rehabilitation is prima facie a debtor-in-possession ('DIP') proceeding and petitions are usually filed by debtors (CivRA Art 21), but the court may appoint a supervisor or investigator (CivRA Arts 54(1) and 62(1)) and a **16.08**

5 Typically insolvency cases are commenced in a debtor's local district court. While there are not special bankruptcy courts in Japan, the key District Courts such as Tokyo and Osaka have specialized insolvency divisions which are experienced in handling these types of cases. District courts in Japan have the busiest jurisdiction and deal with a wide range of disputes; they are typically the court of first instance for all matters in Japan. Exceptions include the specialist IP High Court.

supervisor is typically appointed. Secured creditor's with a right of separation (*betsujōkensha*) are not automatically stayed (CivRA Art 53), but a court may order a stay on a case-by-case basis and there are special provisions providing for the extinguishing of a security interest in certain circumstances (*tanpoken shōmetsu seikyū seido*) (CivRA Arts 148–153).[6]

16.09 The Corporate Reorganization Act came into effect in 2003 and applies to large stock corporations (*kabushiki gaisha*) with a significant economic and social impact. The procedure reflects aspects of Chapter 11 of the US Bankruptcy Code. Debtors typically petition the court and must show that there is a risk that: (a) an act or cause of bankruptcy may occur; or (b) the debtor will face significant difficulty in continuing its business if the debtor pays its debts that are due (CorpRA Art 17(1)). Secured creditors are automatically stayed on commencement of a reorganization proceeding (CorpRA Art 47(1)) and may be subject to cram-down under the reorganization plan. The court must appoint a trustee (CorpRA Art 67; compare CivRA Art 68(1)), although reforms in 2005 allow officers of the company, including managers, to be appointed as trustee in some cases (CorpRA Arts 67(3), 100). Reorganization plans must be approved by various groups of creditors depending on content. Typically, the various groups are made up of similarly placed creditors: secured creditors, priority unsecured creditors, unsecured creditors (which typically includes claims such as taxes and employee wages), and subordinated unsecured creditors (CorpRA Art 168). Approved reorganization plans must also be confirmed by the court.

16.10 Prior to legislative reforms in the 2000s, Japan arguably favoured private workouts based on so-called main bank intervention and administrative guidance from relevant government ministries. In September 2001, coinciding with legislative reform efforts, Japan adopted the Guidelines for Out-of-Court Workouts (*Shiteki seiri ni kan suru gaidorain*, 'Corporate Guidelines') modelled, in part, on the London Approach and INSOL International's Statement of Principles for a Global Approach to Multi-Creditor Workouts.[7] The use of informal workouts based on written rules for large corporations was further encouraged by the introduction of the Special Certified Dispute Resolution Procedure (*tokutei ninshō funsō kaiketsu tetsuzuki*), more commonly known as Business Revitalization ADR (BRADR), which was established in 2007. BRADR draws on the Corporate Guidelines, and the procedure is designed to

6 Stacey Steele, 'Too hot to handle: Extinguishing secured creditors' interests in insolvency under Japan's civil rehabilitation law' (2003) 8(16) *Journal of Japanese Law* 223, 248.

7 See Stacey Steele and Chun Jin, 'Insolvency', CCH Japan Business Law Guide para 19–620, Loose-leaf, last updated 2015.

be driven by an accredited independent committee of insolvency practitioners rather than a main bank.[8]

C. TREATMENT OF EXECUTORY CONTRACTS

(1) General rule in relation to the treatment of executory contracts

The general rule in relation to the treatment of contracts gives a trustee or DIP a choice when one party to a contract commences an insolvency proceeding and both parties to the contract are yet to perform the whole or part of an obligation under that contract. The trustee or DIP may exercise a right to assume the debtor's obligation and demand performance of that obligation from the other party or, alternatively, extinguish the contractual relationship by exercising a right of cancellation (BA Art 53(1); CivRA Art 49(1); CorpRA Art 61(1)). The trustee and DIP's right to cancel the contract under Japanese law should be contrasted with the approach under the US Bankruptcy Code of rejecting performance. This difference means that the claim of the party which has already partially performed the contract may be treated differently under Japanese law when considered from an American law perspective, as discussed below. **16.11**

(1)(a) Consequences for the parties where the general rule applies

Based on the general rule, a trustee or DIP may assume contracts which are advantageous to the estate, and cancel those contracts with are disadvantageous. If a trustee or DIP chooses to assume a contract, the other party's claim becomes an administrative expense claim (*zaidan saiken*, BA 148(1)(7); or *kyōeki saiken*, CivRA Art 49(4) and CorpRA Art 61(4)). An administrative expense will be paid in preference to other unsecured creditors, but not secured creditors. Where a debtor already owes an obligation to the other party to the executory contract before the contract is assumed and is yet to perform the whole or part of the obligation, the administrative expense ranking will extend to these sums although some commentators criticize this approach. It is necessary to obtain the court's approval if assumption is chosen in the case of a bankruptcy proceeding (BA Art 78(2)(9)) or cancellation is chosen in the case of a civil rehabilitation or corporate reorganization proceeding (CivRA Art 61(1)(4); CorpRA Art 72(2)(4)). If a trustee or DIP chooses cancellation, the **16.12**

8 Practitioners must be certified under the Act on Promotion of Use of Alternative Dispute Resolution (*Saiban gai funsō kaiketsu tetsuzuki no riyō no sokushin ni kansuru hōritsu*, Act No. 151, 2004, the so-called 'ADR Act') by the Ministry of Justice and the Ministry of Economy, Trade and Industry (ADR Act Art 2). The Japanese Association of Turnaround Professionals (JATP) is the only organization approved to date.

contractual relationship is extinguished. Where damage to the other party arises as a result of the cancellation, that party has a right to make a claim for compensatory damages as a bankruptcy creditor (Civil Code Art 545(3); BA Art 54(1)). However, unlike the approach under the US Bankruptcy Code, if the other party has already partially performed the contract, then their right to be restored their original position (*genjō kaifuku seikyū ken*) under the Civil Code (Art 545(1)) will be treated as a right to demand a return of the property[9] or an administrative expense claim (BA Art 54(2); CivRA Art 49(5); CorpRA Art 61(5)). As a consequence, this enhanced protection for the creditor *in bonis* has the effect of restricting the margin of discretion of the trustee/DIP.

16.13 Generally speaking, creditors' claims in Japan have the following priority in insolvency proceedings: secured claims; administrative expenses (including some taxes and certain employee claims); priority claims (including other taxes and certain other employee claims); general unsecured claims or so-called bankruptcy claims; subordinated bankruptcy claims; and contractually subordinated bankruptcy claims. Accordingly, claims which are classified as an administrative-type expense rank highly and before general unsecured claims.

16.14 To provide certainty to parties, Japanese law provides a mechanism under which the counterparty may force a trustee or DIP to confirm her or his intention. The counterparty may give a notice to the trustee or DIP stipulating a reasonable time for a response, typically one month, and if the trustee or DIP has not indicated whether the contract will be assumed or cancelled within that period the following results ensue. In the case of a bankruptcy proceeding, the contractual relationship will be deemed to have been cancelled by the trustee (BA Art 53(2) first paragraph). In the case of a civil rehabilitation or corporate reorganization proceeding, the trustee or DIP will be deemed to have lost the right to cancel the contract, and the contract will be assumed (CivRA Art 49(2); CorpRA Art 61(2)).

16.15 There is no clear provision, however, which stipulates the scope of a cancellation. Commentators are divided as to whether a trustee or DIP may completely cancel a contract, or whether just that part of the contract which is yet to be performed by both parties.[10]

9 Otherwise known as a right of segregation (*torimodoshi ken*) (BA Art 62; CivRA Art 52; CorpRA Art 64). Bankruptcy Act, Art 62, for example, provides that the commencement of a bankruptcy proceeding does not affect rights to property that is inadvertently included in the bankruptcy estate but does not belong to the bankrupt.

10 Kazuhiko Yamamoto et al, *Tōsanhō gaisetsu* [Overview of insolvency law] (2nd edn, Kōbundō, 2010), 210.

(1)(b) Objective of the general rule

Commentators disagree when it comes to explaining the objective of the general rule in relation to the treatment of executory contracts in Japanese insolvency law. This discussion focuses on debates in relation to the treatment of executory contracts under the Bankruptcy Act, noting that the arguments were and are similar when it comes to their treatment under the Civil Rehabilitation Act and Corporate Reorganization Act. **16.16**

Traditionally, most commentators focused on so-called fairness between the parties.[11] According to this view, a counterparty is at a disadvantage where both parties are obliged to perform obligations at the same time under the executory contract, but the counterparty's right simply becomes a general unsecured claim in bankruptcy if the bankruptcy trustee decides to assume the contract. In this scenario, there is no guarantee that the counterparty's rights will be completely satisfied. Moreover, the trustee still receives complete performance. Accordingly, to maintain fairness between the contracting parties, the counterparty's right should be treated as an administrative expense claim. Further, to ensure that the bankruptcy proceeding is completed smoothly, only the trustee, and not the counterparty, is given a right to assume or cancel the contract. **16.17**

An alternative view, known as the 'Professor Ito argument' after a leading insolvency law professor formerly at the University of Tokyo, is focused on restoring the counterparty to its original position.[12] Where a trustee chooses to cancel a contract and the contractual relationship is extinguished, the general rule is that the counterparty has a right to be restored to the counterparty's original position (Civil Code Art 545(1) main paragraph). The counterparty's right arises because of the exercise of the right of cancellation by the trustee in the trustee's special capacity. Accordingly, fairness requires that the party's claim in the bankruptcy proceeding should be treated as a right of segregation or administrative expense claim (BA Art 54(2)). Professor Ito's argument emphasizes the trustee's special function and consistency with substantive law rather than the disadvantage to the counterparty per se. **16.18**

(1)(c) Exceptions to the general rule

There are exceptions to the general rule under Japanese insolvency law. A trustee or DIP's right of assumption or cancellation may be denied by the **16.19**

11 Makoto Ito, *Hasanhō minji saiseihō* [Bankruptcy Law and Civil Rehabilitation Law] (3rd edn, Yūhikaku, 2014), 350.

12 Ibid., 351.

courts, for example. In a leading Supreme Court of Japan case, the court suggested that a bankruptcy trustee might not be permitted to exercise the right of cancellation where it would give rise to 'significantly unfair consequences to the other party'.[13]

16.20 The court found that the issue of whether significantly unfair consequences will arise needs to be considered in the context of various factors, including: 'the content of the payment which is required to restore both contractual parties to their original positions due to the cancellation'; the extent to which the counterparty will be disadvantaged by simply giving that party a right to demand compensatory damages; and 'whether the unperformed obligations on the bankrupt's side are merely collateral to the main or core essence of the executory contract'. In this case, Company A paid an initial joining fee of 23,000,000 yen to a Company Y which operated a golf course in 1991. Under the rules of the club, the joining fee would be returned if A lost its membership status, but the fee would only be returned after ten years elapsed if membership was lost within a decade of joining. In 1992, A was declared bankrupt. In 1996, A's bankruptcy trustee informed Y of the trustee's intention to cancel the membership contract and demand repayment of the joining fee.[14] The court did not recognize the cancellation of the membership contract in these circumstances.

(2) Special rules for certain types of contracts

16.21 There are also a number of provisions in relation to the insolvency of one party supported by basic laws such as the Civil Code and Commercial Code which provide for exceptions depending on the particular type of contract. Some exceptions to the general rule were introduced or clarified by the most recent substantial reforms to the insolvency legislation during the 1990s–2000s. The reforms reflected a desire to deal with areas of the law where the application of the general rule in respect of executory contracts was perceived by commentators and interested parties as undesirable on the basis of the character and type of contract, and long-standing debates suggested a need for reform.

(2)(a) Rental contracts: when a lessor commences an insolvency proceeding

16.22 In the case of a lessor's (*chintai'nin*) insolvency proceeding, new provisions were introduced as part of the law reforms in the 1990s–2000s. The general

13 See Supreme Court of Japan 29 February 2000 *Minshū* Vol. 54 No. 2 at 553 in Makoto Ito and Junichi Matsushita (eds), *Tōsan hanrei hyakusen* [One hundred insolvency judgements] (5th edn, Yūhikaku, 2013), 162.

14 It is not clear from the judgement why the trustee waited until 1996 to claim cancellation.

rule no longer applies to a leasehold right (*chinshakuken*) established under a lease agreement (*chintai shaku keiyaku*) which has been perfected and is thus able to be asserted against any third party such as an assignee (BA Art 56(1); CivRA Art 51; CorpRA Art 63). The reform reflects the desire to restrict a trustee's right to cancel such a contract and make insolvency laws consistent with substantive law which strongly protects perfected leasehold rights and lessees.[15] Perfection in this context includes registration of a building (*chijōken butsu*) which is on leased land even if the lease itself is not registered, and circumstances where a building which is subject to a building lease is occupied even if that building lease is not registered.[16] Accordingly, the exception has broad application. If rent is paid in advance, the lessee's right to use and profit-making will be treated as an administrative expense claim (*zaidan saiken*, BA Art 56(2)); or *kyōeki saiken*, (CivRA Art 51; CorpRA Art 63). Moreover, the lease contract will not be cancelled such that the lessee may continue to enjoy its right of use and profit-making despite the landlord's insolvency.[17]

(2)(b) Licensing contracts

Similarly, the general rule for the treatment of executory contracts will not apply to licensing where royalties are paid in return for a right to continuous use where a licensor commences an insolvency proceeding if those rights have been perfected. Instead, the provisions relating to insolvency of a lessor which were introduced by the 1990s–2000s reforms as discussed above will apply. Accordingly, the contract will be assumed by the trustee (BA Art 56(1); CivRA Art 51; CorpRA Art 63). **16.23**

The reforms reflect the view that cancelling a licence contract in a licensor's insolvency would have a significant detrimental effect on the licencee, and thus it is better to restrict a trustee's cancellation right. In practice, however, many licence contracts are not perfected, and some commentators argued in favour of providing further protection. Based on discussions in the Working Group on the Patent System within the Intellectual Property Policy Sub-Committee of the Ministry of Economy, Trade and Industry's Legislative Advisory Council (*shingikai*), an automatic perfection system (*tōzen taikō seido*) was established in 2011 by amendment to the Patent Act (*Tokkyo hō* Act **16.24**

---

15 Yamamoto et al, above n 10, 214. There is a distinction between leases which may be perfected by, e.g., registration such as tenancies. In relation to finance leases, please see the section [Judicial guidance on the treatment of *ipso facto* clauses in Japan] below.

16 See Act on Land and Building Leases (*Shakuchi shakuya hō* Act No. 90, 1991) Arts 10(1) and 31(1) respectively.

17 Hideki Ogawa, *Ichimon ittō atarashii hasanhō* [New bankruptcy law: one question at a time] (Shōjihōmu, 2004), 85.

No. 121, 1959, Art 99). This later reform overcomes the problem of lack of perfection from an insolvency perspective and highlights the need for various ministries in Japan to be involved to achieve insolvency law reform.

(2)(c) Hire-purchase and finance lease contracts

16.25 Hire-purchase agreements which include retention of title provisions allow a purchaser to receive the relevant property before payment of the full purchase price, and provide the seller with a security interest in respect of the purchase price. In other words, hire-purchase agreements which provide for payment by installments for movable assets such as automobiles and machinery (*kappu hanbai keiyaku*), typically include a provision such that the seller retains the ownership rights in the relevant asset until full payment has been made. Although there are different opinions among scholars, the Supreme Court of Japan found that the relevant asset should be perfected by registration or some other method for the seller to be treated as a secured creditor.[18]

16.26 The general rule does not apply in the case of a purchaser's insolvency based on the views of commentators[19] which are supported by judicial decisions.[20] This approach is based on the interpretation of the content of the agreement which concludes that the seller's obligation to transfer ownership is fulfilled at the time that the relevant property is given to the purchaser if the contract provides that the ownership right in the relevant property transfers to the purchaser upon payment of the full purchase price. Accordingly, the seller's right will be treated as a secured claim in an insolvency proceeding.

16.27 Full pay-out type finance lease contracts where the full purchase price will be paid during the lease period have been considered by the Supreme Court.[21] Where a user of the goods commences an insolvency proceeding, the general rule for the treatment of executory contracts has been held not to apply to such lease contracts. The Supreme Court emphasized the economic substance of these contracts which provide a financial benefit, and therefore found that the

---

18 Supreme Court of Japan, 4 June 2009 *Minshū* Vol. 64 No. 4, 1107.

19 Makoto Ito, above n 11, 347.

20 In respect of reorganization proceedings, see Osaka High Court, 27 September Showa 59, Hanta 542, 214; Yoshimitsu Aoyama et al, *Tōsanhō hanrei hyakusen* [One hundred insolvency judgements] 3rd edn, Yūhikaku, 2002), 162.

21 Finance lease contracts refer to agreements under which a lease company purchases machinery or other goods from a supplier and then leases those goods to the user in return for a periodic payment. For case law, see: Makoto Ito et al, *Jyokai hasanhō* [Articles and commentaries on bankruptcy law] (2nd edn, Kōbundō, 2014) 491; Supreme Court of Japan, 14 April Heisei 7 *Minshū* Vol. 49 No. 4, 1063 (in Makoto Ito and Junichi Matsushita (eds)), *Tōsan hanrei hyakusen* (5th edn, Yūhikaku, 2013), 150 (in relation to corporate reorganization proceedings), Supreme Court of Japan, 16 December Heisei 20 *Minshū* Vol. 62 No. 10, 2561 (in Makoto Ito and Junichi Matsushita (eds), *Tōsan hanrei hyakusen* [One hundred insolvency judgements] (5th edn, Yūhikaku, 2013), 154 (in relation to civil rehabilitation proceedings).

lease company should be treated as a secured creditor. Many academics support the arguments reflected in the Supreme Court's decisions, but arguments in favour of applying the general rule of executory contracts to finance leases are still made on the basis that they are similar to typical leasehold agreements and should not be treated as akin to a security interest.[22]

(2)(d) Utility contracts

Executory contracts such as agreements for electricity, gas, water and fuel, which are necessary to the everyday life of the user, are known as *keizokuteki kyūfu wo mokuteki to suru sōmu keiyaku* or 'bilateral contracts for continuous performance'. A counterparty is not entitled to refuse to supply these types of services after the commencement of an insolvency proceeding in respect of a user on the basis that the user did not pay for those services prior to the user becoming insolvent (BA Art 55; Civil RA Art 50; Corp RA Art 62). Any claim for payment in relation to supply during the period after filing a petition and prior to the commencement of the proceeding will be treated as an administrative expense claim (*zaidan saiken*, BA article 55(2); or *kyōeki saiken*, CivRA Art 50(2); CorpRA Art 62). Contracts for the supply of raw materials and maintenance services are also considered by some commentators to fall within the definition of 'bilateral contracts for continuous performance'.[23] **16.28**

(2)(e) Employment contracts and insolvency of corporate employers

There are special provisions in the Civil Code in the case of the bankruptcy of an employer. Both the employee and bankruptcy trustee have the right to cancel the contract (Civil Code Art 627), and neither party may make a claim for compensatory damages based on the cancellation by the other party (Civil Code Art 631). The rationale for this position is that if the employer becomes bankrupt: first, the bankruptcy trustee does not need to receive the employee's labour; and secondly, the employee should not be bound to the employment contract because the employee needs to find a new job as soon as possible. In the case of termination, employees will receive the protections under in the Labour Standards Act (*Rōdō kijun hō* Act No. 49, 1947). Notice periods for restructuring and payment of allowances will apply, for example (Labour Standards Act, Art 20). There are no special provisions in the Civil Rehabilitation Act or Corporate Reorganization Act, and if a civil rehabilitation or corporate reorganization proceeding is commenced in respect of an employer, **16.29**

---

22 Makoto Ito, above n 11, 283. Ito argues that the general rule for the treatment of executory contracts should apply to full payout-type finance lease, and full payout-type finance lease contracts should not be treated as giving lease companies a security interest.

23 Katsumi Yamamoto et al, *Hasanhō minji saiseihō gairon* [Outline of Bankruptcy Law and Civil Rehabilitation Law] (Shōjihōmu, 2012) 230.

employment contracts will be dealt with in accordance with the general rule for the treatment of executory contracts (Civil RA Art 48; CorpRA Art 61).

(2)(f) Construction contracts

16.30 Construction contracts may be divided into situations where the contractor is insolvent and situations where the client is insolvent.

16.31 There are no special rules in relation to the insolvency of a construction contractor in the insolvency legislation. The courts, however, have developed criteria in case law in relation to bankruptcy proceedings. If the work to be performed by the contractor may be completed by an alternative provider, in principle the general rule will apply.[24] To the extent that the content of the contract for work may not be performed by an alternative provider, however, the general rule will not apply. In such cases, it would be necessary for the debtor itself to complete the work in the same way as would be the case for an employment contract. In the case of civil rehabilitation and corporate re-organization proceedings, however, this distinction does not apply, and the general rule for the treatment of executory contracts will apply.

16.32 The general rule does not apply in the case of a bankruptcy of the party who has ordered the works. Rather, the Civil Code provides that the contractor, and not only the trustee, has a right to cancel the contract on the commencement of a bankruptcy proceeding in respect of a party ordering works (Art 642(1)). The policy behind this provision focuses on protecting the contractor who has the obligation to perform the future work. Claims for damages suffered as a result of the cancellation of the contract are not permitted, however, where the contractor cancelled the contract; such damages claims are only permitted if the trustee cancelled the contract (Civil Code Art 642(2)). This aspect of the Civil Code treatment of construction contracts which denies the counterparty a right to claim damages was controversial during the reform process.[25] In the case of civil rehabilitation and corporate reorganization, these special provisions from the Civil Code do not apply, and the general rule for the treatment of executory contracts applies.

(2)(g) Financial contracts

16.33 There are special provisions in relation to financial contracts known as *shijō no sōba ga aru shōhin no torihiki ni kakawaru keiyaku* or contracts for a transaction

24 Makoto Ito and Junichi Matsushita (eds), *Tōsan hanrei hyakusen* [One hundred insolvency judgements] (5th edn, Yūhikaku, 2013), 160.

25 Makoto Ito, above n 11, 272.

of goods with a market quotation on the insolvency of one of the parties. These contracts will be deemed to be cancelled.

16.34 The amount of damages, to the extent not specified by the exchange or market, shall be the difference between the market price and the contract price at the time of the commencement of the insolvency (BA Art 58(2); Civil RA Art 51, CorpRA Art 63). Until the reforms to insolvency laws in the 1990s–2000s, the scope of the equivalent provision was limited to a sale of goods on an exchange market (*torihiki no sōba no aru shōhin no baibai*). After the reforms, the terminology was expanded to refer to contracts for transactions of goods with a market quotation and the requirement for the sale to occur on an exchange market was dropped. Reflecting international trends, the insolvency legislation now confirms the validity of close-out netting clauses in derivative financial contracts (BA Art 58(5); CivRA Art 51; CorpRA Art 63).[26] The provision is supported by legislation passed in 1998 which also clarified the treatment of such contractual provisions.[27]

(2)(h) Mandate contracts

16.35 A mandate contract (*i'nin keiyaku*) refers to a contract such as an agreement for engaging a legal representative. There are no special provisions in the Bankruptcy Act in relation to mandate contracts. Because a mandate is based on a relationship of trust, the Civil Code provides that the relationship of trust is broken if one party becomes bankrupt and the mandate relationship is thus extinguished (Art 653(2)). The Civil Code approach is not applicable in the case of civil rehabilitation and corporate reorganization, however, where the general rule applies. Accordingly, a trustee or DIP may choose to cancel or assume a mandate contract in those proceedings (CivRA Art 49; CorpRA Art 51). The current majority view amongst commentators is that a mandate relationship as between a company and its directors does not end on the bankruptcy of the company or a director, and the Civil Code position does not apply.[28]

---

26 Hideki Ogawa, above n 17, 97.

27 See Stacey Steele, 'Japan's bankruptcy safe harbour provisions and repurchase agreements: A commentary and annotated translation of the "Act Concerning Close-out Netting of Specified Financial Transactions Undertaken by Financial Institutions etc."' (2010) 30 *Journal of Japanese Law* 175, 202, http://www.zjapanr.de/index.php/zjapanr/article/viewFile/348/366. On the Japanese derivatives market generally, see Annelise Riles, *Collateral Knowledge: Legal Reasoning in the Global Financial Markets* (University of Chicago Press, Chicago, 2011).

28 In relation to the nature of a contract as between a company and its directors, see also Companies Act (*Kaisha hō*, Act No. 86, 2005) Art 330.

(3) Treatment of *ipso facto* clauses

(3)(a) Judicial guidance on the treatment of ipso facto *clauses in Japan*

16.36 *Ipso facto* clauses are commonly found in the types of executory contracts discussed in the first part of this chapter in Japan. The clauses typically give a counterparty the right to cancel a contract without notice to the other party on the occurrence of events such as filing for commencement of an insolvency proceeding or a suspension of payments (*shiharai teishi*).[29] The post-reform insolvency legislation in Japan, however, is still silent on the treatment of *ipso facto* clauses in insolvency proceedings despite consideration of the issue during the reform process. Instead, practitioners rely on two key decisions from Supreme Court of Japan from 1982[30] and 2008[31] for guidance in this area of the law.[32] In both cases, the Supreme Court emphasized the importance of the legislative aims and objectives of corporate reorganization and civil rehabilitation proceedings, and denied the effectiveness of the *ipso facto* clauses.

16.37 In the first case, machinery was purchased by the debtor under a hire-purchase agreement which included a retention of title clause. The machinery was considered indispensable for the continuation of the enterprise. The agreement provided that if any promissory note issued by the purchaser was dishonoured or any grounds for the filing or commencement of any insolvency proceedings in respect of the purchaser should occur, the seller may exercise its right to cancel the contract without notice and demand the return of the machinery. The purchaser filed for corporate reorganization and the seller sought to cancel the agreement based on the *ipso facto* clause. Citing the objective set out in Article 1 of the Corporate Reorganization Act, the Supreme Court found that such a clause, 'impairs the aim and purpose of

---

29 Bankruptcy Act, Art 15(2) provides that a debtor who has suspended payments will be presumed to be unable to pay debts (*shiharai funō*) and thus a ground for commencement of bankruptcy will exist in respect of that debtor if there has been a suspension of payments. Accordingly, in Japan if a contract includes suspension of payments as an *ipso facto* clause trigger, the right to cancel the contract potentially occurs much earlier than the time of actual filing of a petition to commence a bankruptcy proceeding.

30 Supreme Court of Japan, 30 March 1982 *Minshū* Vol. 36 No. 3, 484. Makoto Ito and Junichi Matsushita (eds), *Tōsan hanrei hyakusen*, Yūhikaku, 2013, 154. An unofficial translation of this case may be accessed at Group for International Insolvency Law, Transparency of Japanese Law Project, 'Rehabilitation Proceedings', Kyushu University, para 4.12, http://www.law.kyushu-u.ac.jp/~tomeika/insolvency/4_Rehabilitation.html.

31 Supreme Court of Japan, 16 December 2008, Third Petty Bench. Makoto Ito and Junichi Matsushita (eds), *Tōsan hanrei hyakusen* [One hundred insolvency judgements] (Yūhikaku, 2013) 152.

32 Decisions from district courts both support and deny the effectiveness of *ipso facto* clauses. In Japan, there is no strict rule of precedent, although most judges will follow a higher court decision to ensure consistency, which is a key concept of the rule of law in Japan. Moreover, judges are also inclined to follow higher court decisions because of their training, socialization and from the perspective of career advancement. Accordingly, the decisions from Japan's highest court, the Supreme Court of Japan, are important statements of the law in this area.

corporate reorganization proceedings which purport to maintain and rehabilitate the business of a company in difficulty while coordinating the interests of the creditors, shareholders and other interested parties'. Accordingly, the Supreme Court upheld the lower court's decision that the purported cancellation of the sale and purchase agreement by the seller was ineffective.

The second case involved a so-called full-payment-type finance lease agreement. The agreement included a special provision which entitled the lease company to cancel the agreement without notice if the user was the subject of a petition to commence an insolvency proceeding. After a petition and order for commencement of a civil rehabilitation proceeding in respect of the user, the lease company sought to rely on the provision in the agreement to cancel the contract and demand return of the lease property. The Supreme Court found that the leased property was indispensible to the rehabilitation of the debtor and to uphold the cancellation of the contract would not give effect to the aims and objectives of the civil rehabilitation proceeding. Furthermore, the right to demand the return of the leased property meant that the leased company had an interest akin to a security for the receipt of any future lease payments or liquidated damages. **16.38**

Despite both cases supporting the reconstruction aims and objectives of the corporate reorganization and civil rehabilitation proceedings, the cases leave room for conjecture as to the treatment of *ipso facto* clauses in Japan as the academic commentary discussed in the next section suggests. Both cases, for example, deal with retention of title rights and finance-type leases, and thus may be limited in application to those cases dealing with these types of atypical security (*hi'ten-gata tanpo*). Accordingly, the facts also need to be considered in light of the debates presented below in relation to the enforcement of security rights. Moreover, it is not clear if the same reasoning would be applied in cases dealing with other types of contracts or other types of proceedings such as a bankruptcy proceeding. **16.39**

(3)(b) Commentary on the treatment of ipso facto *clauses in Japan*

Consistent with other jurisdictions with a civil law tradition, this area of the law highlights the important role played by academic commentary in the development of Japanese legal thinking where there are legislative gaps. The various academic commentators compete for recognition and their theories are studied by law students and practitioners, until potentially consensus eventually solidifies behind one line of thinking which may ultimately be codified or adopted in a judicial decision from a superior court. Traditionally, almost all academic commentary in Japan supported the view that freedom of contract operates before the commencement of an insolvency proceeding and *ipso facto* **16.40** clauses were considered valid based on this line of thinking.[33] Contemporary commentary, however, acknowledges that reorganization may be difficult if *ipso facto* clauses are recognized, especially if a contract which is necessary to the reorganization is cancelled. Further, giving effect to *ipso facto* clauses undermines the principle that only the trustee or DIP should have a right to cancel an executory contract. Accordingly, the contemporary view is that the effectiveness of *ipso facto* clauses should be restricted in an insolvency proceeding at least to some extent.

16.41 There are various views about the scope of any restrictions and the detailed reasoning differs depending on the commentator, but the views of key commentators in Japan may be divided into four main groups. A first group emphasizes the principle that only the trustee or DIP should have a right of cancellation in relation to executory contracts which remain unperformed. Accordingly, the effectiveness of *ipso facto* clauses should be denied regardless of whether the proceeding is a reorganization or liquidation-type proceeding.[34] A second group suggests that *ipso facto* clauses should be invalid regardless of the type of insolvency proceeding because they offend the principle of equality among creditors. They argue that the effect of *ipso facto* clauses is to give certain creditors an advantage over others, and the bankruptcy estate will simply be administered to pay these creditors.[35] Another group takes the view that protecting the assets necessary for the reorganization of the enterprise is paramount. Proponents of this view support upholding the effectiveness of *ipso facto* clauses in the case of liquidation-type proceedings, but argue that the effectiveness of these clauses should be denied in respect of reorganization-type proceedings.[36] A fourth group argues that the effectiveness of these types of provisions should only be denied in the case of corporate reorganization proceedings, because the exercise of security rights is already restricted in those proceedings. Accordingly, *ipso facto* clauses would be effective in bankruptcy and civil rehabilitation proceedings which do not automatically restrict the exercise of a security right. This line of thinking views the exercise of an *ipso facto* clause as akin to the exercise of a security

33 Ibid., 153.

34 Makoto Ito, above n 11, 358; Makoto Ito, *Kaisha kōseihō* [Corporate Reorganisation Act] (Yūhikaku, 2012) 277.

35 Morio Takeshita, *Tanpoken to minji shikkō tōsan tetsuzuki* [Security interests: civil execution and insolvency proceedings] (Yūhikaku, 1990) 311; Hironori Mizumoto, *Keiyaku no jiyū to tōsan kaijo tokuyaku no kōryoku* [Freedom of contract and the effectiveness of special provisions for cancellation on insolvency], (Kumamoto hōgaku, N117, 2009) 7.

36 Hiroaki Tominaga, *Kakushu no keiyaku no shori* [Treatment of various types of contracts], in Takashi Sonoo et al (eds), *Shinpan hasanhō* [New edition of the Bankruptcy Law] (Seirinshoin, 2007) 210.

right in practice and does not sit well with the Supreme Court's conclusion from 2008 analysed above.[37]

(3)(c) *Conditional rights and penalty clauses*

While not technically considered to be *ipso facto* clauses, provisions placing various obligations on a debtor which do not amount to cancellation of the contract may be found in practice in Japan. It is also common for contracts to provide for penalties (*iyakukin jyōkō*) and compensatory damages upon the cancellation of a contract. Decisions from lower courts, for example, have upheld special provisions in a fixed-term building lease agreement which entitle a counterparty to cancel a contract to the extent that the counterparty pays an amount equivalent to the rent due during the remaining rental term. Similarly, a clause providing for the payment to the lessor of an amount of compensatory damages equivalent to the rental amount which would have been payable in future until the property was returned at the end of the rental agreement has also been upheld.[38] **16.42**

D. REFORMS

At the beginning of the comprehensive reforms to the insolvency law framework in 1996, there was an opportunity to substantially reform the law in relation to the general rule relating to executory contracts, and the treatment of certain special contracts and *ipso facto* clauses.[39] As the discussion above highlights, however, statutory reforms in relation to *ipso facto* clauses were not achieved. Moreover, the reforms in relation to executory contracts focused on the treatment of special contracts rather than a fundamental shift in the priority of counterparties once a decision to assume or cancel a contract was made by a trustee or DIP. **16.43**

(1) Reforms in respect of executory contracts

According to the members of the subcommittee established to consider insolvency law reform in 1996, consideration was given at the time of the reforms to amending the general rule in relation to the treatment of executory contracts to move away from the concept of cancellation by adopting the US **16.44**

37 Kazuhiko Yamamoto, *Tōsan shorihō nyūmon* [Introduction to insolvency workout] (4th edn, 2012) 82.

38 Makoto Ito, above n 11, 278. Yamamoto, et al, above n 10, 242.

39 Makoto Ito et al, *Shinhasanhō no kihon kōzō to jitsumu* [Fundamental structure and practice of the new Bankruptcy Law] (Yūhikaku, 2007) 271.

concept of 'rejection'.[40] No consensus among various key commentators was reached, however. There was significant debate about the prospect of a counterparty simply having an ordinary unsecured claim, particularly where there was already partial performance by the counterparty.[41] As noted above, the current law provides for a right to restore the counterparty to its original position under Civil Code (Art 545(1)) such that they are treated as having a right of segregation or an administrative expense claim (BA Art 54(2); CivRA Art 49(5); CorpRA Art 61(5)). Accordingly, reforms to the priority of treatment of a counterparty after cancellation were not realized.

16.45 Reforms in relation to certain special contracts, however, were implemented and reflected an updating of the insolvency law framework to take into account international and domestic community expectations, modernization and realities of trade and finance, and existing substantive law principles.[42] The situation in relation to leasehold contracts was clarified, for example. Finance lease contracts discussed above, however, are still not the subject of specific legislative provisions despite suggestions that the situation be statutorily clarified. In the case of finance leases, insolvency law reformers found it difficult to update the insolvency law framework due to outstanding issues relating to substantive laws such as the Civil Code which does not include any provisions about the definition of finance lease contracts.[43] A lack of a clear definition makes it difficult to establish specific provisions within the insolvency law framework. Accordingly, the reformers ultimately considered as acceptable the position that these types of contracts and issues should continue to be dealt with in light of judicial decisions.

16.46 In the end, there was no fundamental change to the general rule in respect of the treatment of executory contracts, and the ability of the trustee or DIP to assume contracts which are advantageous to the proceeding or cancel those contracts that are disadvantageous continues. In relation to a number of special contracts, such as lease agreements, service agreements, insurance agreements, licence agreements, and close-out netting arrangements, however, certain reforms were achieved including as discussed above. To be successful, any future reform movement in this area will need to focus on achieving consensus amongst the various industry representatives' perspectives and evidence the need for special rules in the insolvency law framework which diverge from substantive law principles.

---

40 Ibid., 271.
41 Ibid., 271.
42 Ibid., 272.
43 Ibid., 305.

(2) Reforms in respect of *ipso facto* clauses

During the comprehensive reforms of the 1990s–2000s, there was also consideration of the legislative approach to the restriction of the effectiveness of *ipso facto* clauses. As the analysis above demonstrates, however, there is still no consensus in relation to the approach set out in the two key Supreme Court decisions. Even to the extent consensus could be achieved with respect to the restriction of *ipso facto* clauses in the limited context of corporate reorganization proceedings, it was not possible to establish parameters in relation to issues such as the scope of contracts which would be included in any restriction. Limiting the effectiveness in civil rehabilitation proceedings was also controversial. As noted above, some commentators were of the view that an *ipso facto* clause should be effective if the clause is essentially a clause which facilitates enforcement by a secured creditor, because secured creditors are not automatically drawn into a civil rehabilitation proceeding.[44] Accordingly, it was difficult to establish a predictable, standard criteria for the invalidity of *ipso facto* clauses and the reforms did not confirm a legislative approach to the restriction of the effectiveness of *ipso facto* clauses.[45] **16.47**

(3) Principal supporters of the reforms

The comprehensive reforms to the Japanese insolvency law framework which began in 1996 were the result of the establishment of an *ad hoc* Insolvency Law Subcommittee within the powerful Legislative Advisory Council (*Hōsei shingikai*) after consultation with the then Minister of Justice that same year. The Legislative Advisory Council is a permanent consultative body established in 1949.[46] When the government is planning legislative reform in respect of civil, criminal or other law, it will always consult the Legislative Advisory Council and it is customary for the government to respect the opinions of the Council as much as possible. In the case of insolvency law, the Insolvency Law Subcommittee considered the various opinions of experts in the area, including their own, and sought public comment on a draft outline and consultation draft of the revised insolvency legislation. Afterwards, the Insolvency Law Subcommittee decided on a draft bill after deliberation among the Subcommittee members. **16.48**

44 Ibid., 279.

45 Ibid.

46 The Council was established under the Legislative Advisory Council Order (Government Ordinance No. 134, 1949). The current Legislative Advisory Council Order is as amended on 7 June 2000.

16.49 Accordingly, the deliberations of the Insolvency Law Subcommittee have substantial weight. The Subcommittee was led by Professor Morio Takeshita and made up of other academics specializing in insolvency law and civil procedure law, insolvency law practitioners, judges, representatives of the Ministry of Justice, and other stakeholders such as the Ministry of Economy, Trade and Industry. Such consultative bodies often perform important consensus building and drafting roles when legal reforms are considered in Japan and thus these stakeholders, particularly academics from leading universities, have an important role in legislative reform in Japan generally.

E. CONCLUDING REMARKS

16.50 As this chapter demonstrates, Japan's insolvency law reforms in the 1990s–2000s considered the treatment of executory contracts and *ipso facto* clauses in detail with differing results. Statutory provisions were revised to reflect international trends and contemporary debates in Japan focused on establishing fairness between the parties to executory contracts. Accordingly, certain provisions were introduced restricting the general rule which enables a trustee or DIP to exercise a right of cancellation with respect to executory contracts. For policy reasons, for example, the right to cancel a lease or hire-purchase agreement has been restricted. On the other hand, a counterparty's exercise of a right to netting in certain types of financial contracts has been clarified and confirmed in accordance with international precedents.

16.51 The reform processes in the 1990s–2000s did not, however, introduce legislative provisions in relation to the treatment of *ipso facto* clauses. Based on key Supreme Court decisions and contemporary commentator views, however, the effectiveness of *ipso facto* clauses is generally considered to be restricted in Japan at least in the case of corporate reorganization and civil rehabilitation proceedings. There are still strong supporters, however, of balancing the fairness between creditors, and the principle of limiting the right to assume or cancel a contract to a trustee and DIP in insolvency proceedings. Moreover, there is still a desire to respect the principle of freedom of contract.[47] Given these tensions, there is likely to be continued debate in relation to the treatment of *ipso facto* clauses in future in Japan before any further substantial reforms are possible.[48]

47 Morio Takeshita et al (eds), *Daicomentaaru hasanhō* [Key commentaries on bankruptcy law] (Seirinshoin, 2007) 127 (written by Junichi Matsushita).

48 Yamamoto et al, above n 10, 240.

17

NATIONAL REPORT FOR LITHUANIA

Frank Heemann and Karolina Gasparkė

A. INTRODUCTION

Two laws set out the main body of rules for insolvencies in Lithuania, including rules for the treatment of executory contracts.[1] The Enterprise Bankruptcy Law[2] (EBL) provides rules for insolvency procedures that are aimed at dividing proceeds among the debtor's creditors and that eventually lead to the liquidation and deregistration of the debtor.[3] The Enterprise Restructuring Law[4] (ERL) aims at rescuing businesses facing temporary financial distress. **17.01**

1 With regard to the situation the past, cf. D(1) below.

2 Enterprise Bankruptcy Law of Republic of Lithuania (*Lietuvos Respublikos įmonių restruktūrizavimo įstatymas*) 20 March 2001, No. IX-216 as last amended on 15 October 2015. In contrast to some other jurisdictions, Lithuanian legal acts use the term 'bankruptcy' to refer not only to individuals but also to companies. For the purpose of this study we will use 'insolvency', except when referring to the name of the laws.

3 Except for cases of composition with creditors.

4 Enterprise Restructuring Law of Republic of Lithuania (*Lietuvos Respublikos įmonių bankroto įstatymas*) 20 March 2001, No. IX-218 as last amended on 16 December 2014.

B. INSOLVENCY PROCEDURES

(1) Insolvency procedures under the EBL

17.02 Insolvency proceedings falling into the scope of the EBL are subdivided into formal and informal proceedings, the latter being referred to as extrajudicial proceedings. The EBL establishes two types of formal proceedings: standard and simplified proceedings.

(a) Scope of the EBL

17.03 The EBL applies to all legal persons registered in Lithuania, 'except for budgetary institutions, political parties, trade unions, religious communities'.[5] However, separate laws establish specific rules in certain areas for insolvency proceedings of some legal entities such as banks,[6] credit unions,[7] insurance companies[8] as well as other legal entities that may be established by other laws.[9] The EBL then applies to the extent that no specific rules are set out in separate laws. The EBL does also not apply to the extent that it contradicts the Law on Financial Collateral Arrangements[10] and the Law on Settlement Finality in Payment and Securities Settlement Systems[11] which implement Directive 2002/47/EC[12] and Directive 98/26/EC[13] into Lithuanian law.[14] However, EBL rules apply in a subsidiary way to those cases that do not fall within the scope of the above-mentioned laws and directives.

5 EBL, art 1 (2).

6 Law on Banks of the Republic of Lithuania (*Lietuvos Respublikos bankų įstatymas*) 30 March 2004, No. IX-2085.

7 Law on Credit Unions of the Republic of Lithuania (*Lietuvos Respublikos kredito unijų įstatymas*) 21 February 1995, No. I-796.

8 Law on Insurance of the Republic of Lithuania (*Lietuvos Respublikos draudimo įstatymas*) 18 September 2003, No. IX-1737.

9 EBL, art. 1 (2) (3). The provisions of other laws regulating the activities of companies, the creditor's right to satisfaction of claims as well as right to take measures to recover debts, set-off, taxes and other compulsory payments in the course of insolvency process under the EBL are applied to the extent they do not contradict the provisions of the EBL.

10 Law on Financial Collateral Arrangements of the Republic of Lithuania (*Lietuvos Respublikos finansinio užtikrinimo susitarimų įstatymas*) 15 April 2004, No. IX-2127.

11 Law on Settlement Finality in Payment and Securities Settlement Systems of Republic of Lithuania (*Lietuvos Respublikos atsiskaitymų baigtinumo mokėjimo ir vertybinių popierių atsiskaitymo sistemose įstatymas*) 5 June 2003, No. IX-1597.

12 Directive 2002/47/EC of the European Parliament and of the Council on financial collateral arrangements [2002].

13 Directive 98/26/EC of the European Parliament and of the Council on settlement finality in payment and securities settlement systems [1998].

14 EBL, art 1 (4).

(b) Right to request the opening of proceedings under the EBL

The following persons may request the opening of proceedings under the EBL: creditor(s),[15] the head of the debtor[16] (i.e., its director or similar person), and liquidators.[17] These persons may file an opening petition to the court provided at least one of the following conditions[18] is met: 17.04

- the debtor failed to pay in due time remuneration and other employment-related payments to its employee(s);[19]
- the debtor failed to perform its contractual obligations in the ordinary course of business (for example, failed to pay for goods or to redeem a loan);[20]
- the debtor failed to pay in due course either taxes and other compulsory contributions prescribed by law or other awarded amounts;[21]
- the debtor had insufficient assets or income to meet the requests of its creditors in an executory procedure.[22]

Despite that, creditors intending to initiate an insolvency proceeding against the debtor must first set an additional term of at least 30 days for the debtor to meet its overdue obligations.[23] Only after the expiry of this term may the creditor bring an insolvency petition to the competent court. 17.05

(c) Grounds for opening of proceedings under the EBL

The occurrence of any of the following circumstances allows the court to approve an insolvency petition: 17.06

- a situation of 'insolvency', as defined by the EBL;[24]
- the debtor's failure to pay salary and other remuneration to its employee(s);[25]

15 Ibid., art 5 (1) para 1.
16 Ibid., para 2.
17 Ibid., para 3. The liquidator has to file a claim for insolvency in cases where a solvent liquidation procedure was initiated but the company subsequently was found to be insolvent.
18 Ibid., art 4.
19 Ibid., art 4 (1).
20 Ibid., art 4 (2).
21 Ibid., art 4 (3).
22 Ibid., art 4 (5).
23 Ibid., art 6 (2).
24 Ibid., art 9 (7) para 1 alternative 1.
25 Ibid.

- the debtor's inability to perform its obligations in the ordinary course of business.[26]

17.07 'Insolvency' is defined by the EBL as:

> the state of an enterprise when it fails to discharge its obligations (pay debts, carry out works paid for in advance) and the overdue liabilities of the enterprise (debts, unperformed works) are in excess of half of the value of the assets entered in the enterprise's balance.[27]

17.08 Under the EBL, in addition to the opening ground 'insolvency', other grounds can lead to the opening of proceedings even if the conditions for 'insolvency' are not met, namely if the debtor fails to pay remuneration to its employees or is not or will not be able to meet its obligations in the near future. In legal literature,[28] the additional circumstances mentioned in the law are criticized for not being necessarily or sufficiently related to the insolvency of the company.[29] Lithuanian courts have not turned a deaf ear on the legal community's complaint, and have recently started to take a more pragmatic approach in determining when a company can be admitted to a liquidation procedure. According to current court practice, liquidation proceedings can be opened under the EBL only if there is sufficient evidence that the company is insolvent.[30] Recent case law indicates that courts in this context do not assess if the company fulfils the criteria of 'insolvency' as defined in the EBL but rather take a more liberal approach when assessing the facts of the case at hand in order to determine if insolvency proceedings should be opened.[31]

---

26 Ibid., art 9 (7) para 2. This ground is related to instances, when 'the enterprise has publicly announced or notified the creditor (creditors) in any other manner of its inability or lack of intent to discharge its obligations' as previously stated in EBL, art 4 (4) that is inapplicable as of 1 January 2016, in conjunction with Conclusion on amendments of EBL, arts 8, 10, 11, 23, 33 of the draft law of 30 September 2015, No. P-108–27 issued by the Economic Committee of the Parliament. However, the ground set forth in art 9 (7)) is not sufficient for the court to open insolvency proceedings without examining and analysing the financial situation of the debtor. The Review of the case law of the Lithuanian Supreme Court of 30 April 2015 regarding legal rules applicable to the initiation of the bankruptcy and restructuring proceedings No. AC-41–1 (Teismų praktika. 2015, 41) 644–692.

27 EBL, art 2 (8).

28 S. Kavalnė, R. Norkus, et al., *Bankroto teisė*: vadovėlis, Antroji knyga (Justitia 2011) 83–7.

29 For instance, under the current regulation of the EBL it is sufficient for the employee to initiate insolvency proceedings against the debtor which is late paying the remuneration by one day and does not face financial difficulties.

30 The Review of the case law of the Lithuanian Supreme Court regarding legal rules applicable to the initiation of the bankruptcy and restructuring proceedings No. AC-41–1. (Teismų praktika. 2015, 41) 644–92.

31 Ibid.

(d) *Simplified insolvency procedures under the EBL*

Simplified procedures are applied when the court makes a sufficiently justified assumption that the debtor either has no assets or that its assets will be insufficient to cover the legal and administrative expenses of the proceedings.[32] In such cases, the court recommends that the person who filed the petition pays a deposit in order to enable the court to open the simplified insolvency proceedings.[33] **17.09**

Simplified insolvency procedures must not exceed one year.[34] All proceeds from the sale of the debtor's assets are first used to cover the expenses incurred by the court as well as other administrative expenses.[35] All remaining proceeds from the sale are allocated to satisfy the claims of the debtor's employees first, and then to all other unsecured creditors.[36] The expenses incurred by the respective person who paid the deposit to the court are covered only if funds remain in the estate after satisfaction of the employee-related claims. To the extent the person that paid the deposit for opening of proceedings does not receive satisfaction on his expenses, he is entitled to claim damages from the manager of the debtor for late filing for insolvency.[37] **17.10**

(e) *Composition with creditors*[38]

One way to end an insolvency procedure under the EBL is the conclusion of a composition agreement between the debtor and its creditors. The proposal for a composition can be submitted by the debtor's creditors, owner(s) or its **17.11**

32 In practice the 'sufficiently justified assumption' is based on the accounting documents and related information made available to the judge by the company's management and/or accountant.

33 Under the current legislation, such a deposit must not exceed 9500 EUR.

34 EBL, art 13^1 (1).

35 Ibid., art 13^1 (5).

36 Ibid., art 13^1 (7).

37 Ibid., art 10 (11). In comparison to 2015, the number of simplified insolvency proceedings increased by 62.9 per cent and amounted to 1083 simplified proceedings commenced in 2016. In the context of all insolvency proceedings, the simplified proceedings amounted to 40.24 per cent in 2016. Details on the statistics can be found in The Authority of Audit, Accounting, Property Valuation and Insolvency Management under the Ministry of Finance of the Republic of Lithuania 'Review of Processes of January–December of 2016 of Bankruptcy and Restructuring of Legal Entities and Bankruptcy Processes of Natural Persons' (title translated from Lithuanian language) 1 February 2017, No. (6.13) D4–535, 2–3.

38 In practice, the number of compositions is increasing, even though it has not yet become widely used. For instance, there were 11 insolvency proceedings terminated due to composition agreements with creditors signed in 2015. This number increased by 15 in 2016. For the moment, there is only one composition agreement with creditors being signed in 2017. The Authority of Audit, Accounting, Property Valuation and Insolvency Management under the Ministry of Finance of the Republic of Lithuania 'Review of Processes of January – December of 2016 of Bankruptcy and Restructuring of Legal Entities and Bankruptcy Processes of Natural Persons' 1 February 2017, No. (6.13) D4–535, 2–3.

administrator.[39] The EBL sets out minimum requirements for the composition agreement, and has to be approved by creditors with claims of at least two-thirds of all claims on the day of signing the agreement. The composition comes into force after having been approved by the court,[40] or, in case of extrajudicial proceedings, by a notary public.[41]

17.12 There are a number of open questions related to composition agreements. In particular neither the law nor court practice provide clear guidance on whether creditors that have not filed their claims in the proceedings may participate and become parties to the composition agreement, and whether a court-approved composition agreement binds also creditors that did not vote in favour of the composition agreement or did not even participate in the proceedings.[42]

(f) Extrajudicial insolvency proceedings

17.13 Extrajudicial insolvency proceedings as an informal type of insolvency proceeding are specific in that the creditors have the power to decide on the questions that in case of formal insolvency proceedings are the competence of the court.[43] Extrajudicial procedures can be opened provided that two preliminary conditions are met.

17.14 First, there must be no litigation in the courts against the debtor with regard to pecuniary claims. Secondly, there must be no ongoing enforcement proceedings against the debtor under enforcing orders issued by courts or any other institutions.[44]

17.15 In order to open an extrajudicial insolvency procedure, the debtor must convene a meeting of all its creditors (including tax and public authorities) during which a decision must be taken to open the proceedings. The decision to carry out extrajudicial insolvency procedures requires an affirmative vote by the creditors whose claims in terms of value account for at least three-quarters of the amount of the company's liabilities on the day of the adoption of the opening decision, including those claims which have not yet matured.[45] In case the statutory majorities are not achieved, creditors as well as the manager

39 EBL, art 28 (1).
40 Ibid., art 29 (4).
41 Ibid., art 29 (6).
42 V. Mikuckienė, 'Opportunities of Amicable Settlement in Insolvency Proceedings' (2007) Jurisprudencija 5, 95.
43 EBL, arts 12 et seq.
44 Ibid., art 12 (1).
45 Ibid., art 12 (4).

of the company may file a petition to the court in order to open formal insolvency proceedings against the debtor, without the 30-day compulsory notice mentioned above.[46]

In practice extrajudicial insolvency proceedings amount to only 6.5 per cent of the total proceedings opened in 2016.[47] However, their use seems to be on the rise, as their number increased by 69.9 per cent in only one year.[48] **17.16**

(2) Insolvency procedures under the ERL

The ERL defines 'enterprise in financial difficulties' as an 'enterprise unable to discharge its obligations and reduce losses which, without assistance rendered by creditors, would force it to terminate its activities and go bankrupt'.[49] Restructuring of such an enterprise is understood as a 'set of measures/ procedures intended to preserve and/or develop activities of an enterprise experiencing financial difficulties'.[50] **17.17**

The main tool for rescuing a company in financial distress is the implementation of a restructuring plan approved by the creditors. **17.18**

(a) Scope of the ERL

The ERL applies to all legal persons in financial difficulties which are registered in Lithuania,[51] 'except for budgetary institutions, political parties, trade unions, religious communities and associations, credit institutions, payment institutions, electronic money institutions, insurance and reinsurance companies, management companies, investment companies and intermediaries of public trading in securities'.[52] **17.19**

---

46 Ibid., art 12 (5) in conjunction with art 6 (1). See also above in (2) Right to request the opening of proceedings under the EBL.

47 The Authority of Audit, Accounting, Property Valuation and Insolvency Management under the Ministry of Finance of the Republic of Lithuania Review of Processes of January – December of 2016 of Bankruptcy and Restructuring of Legal Entities and Bankruptcy Processes of Natural Persons 1 February 2017, No. (6.13) D4–535, 4.

48 Ibid. This increase of popularity during 2016 is explained by changes to the appointment system of insolvency administrators. As of 1 January 2015 the bankruptcy administrator is selected randomly by a computer program (reference is made to Selection Rules for Bankruptcy Administrators as approved by Government Order No. 647 of 9 July 2014). The random appointment order is not applicable to the extrajudicial proceedings where the creditors may choose and appoint the administrator themselves from the official list (EBL, art 13 (2)). This right for creditors to propose an administrator existed also for standard EBL proceedings before the mentioned changes to the law.

49 ERL, art 2 (1).

50 Ibid., art 2 (3).

51 Ibid., art 1 (3).

52 Ibid., art 1 (3), (4).

(b) Right to request and grounds for the opening of proceedings under ERL

17.20 According to the ERL, only the debtor is entitled to request the opening of formal proceedings under the ERL. Restructuring proceedings can be opened only when *all* of the following preconditions are met:

- the debtor faces financial difficulties or there is a real possibility that it will face financial difficulties within the next three months;[53]
- the debtor has not discontinued its activities;[54]
- no insolvency proceedings are opened against the debtor;[55]
- the debtor was established at least three years before the date of filing of a petition to open restructuring proceedings;[56]
- at least five years have passed from the coming into effect of a court's previous decision to close the debtor's previous restructuring proceedings.[57]

(c) Types of proceedings under the ERL

17.21 Restructuring proceedings may only be formal[58] proceedings under the ERL. Yet, the ERL offers in addition to the standard proceedings a simplified restructuring procedure which can be opened if the debtor's restructuring plan is drawn up prior to the filing of the petition to the court for opening of the proceedings.[59]

(d) Informal restructuring proceedings

17.22 In practice, there are also informal restructuring proceedings involving negotiated solutions with creditors. However, these procedures fall outside the scope of the ERL and the jurisdiction of the courts. They allow for a more flexible approach to restructurings. On the other hand, creditors and the

---

53 Ibid., art 4 (1).
54 Ibid., art 4 (2).
55 Ibid., art 4 (3).
56 Ibid., art 4 (4).
57 Ibid., art 4 (5).
58 Recent statistics confirm that formal restructuring proceedings play no significant role in practice. For instance, there were only 16 companies undergoing restructuring proceedings during the first half of 2016 while the number of opened insolvency proceedings under the EBL during 2016 exceeded 2600 (Data according to Lithuanian Official Statistics Portal (accessible via http://osp.stat.gov.lt/en/) accessed 23 March 2017). Considerably long restructuring proceedings, complicated and complex decision-making, lack of restructuring plans of adequate quality are named as some reasons for the limited attractiveness of restructuring proceedings. To illustrate this, the statistics show that during the period between 2001 and 2016 there were only 424 restructuring proceedings opened, from which only 40 were completed successfully. National Audit Office of Lithuania. Performance Audit Report for Management of Enterprise Restructuring Process 2015, No. VA-P-20-12-14, executive summary in English is accessible via:
59 ERL, art 10 (1).https://www.vkontrole.lt/audito_ataskaitos_en.aspx?tipas=15 accessed 23 March 2017.

debtor cannot rely on a structured proceeding supervised by a court or an insolvency/emergency administrator.

No reliable statistics are available on the number and use of informal restructurings. Based on publicly accessible sources and the author's own experience, they do not play any noteworthy practical role in Lithuania. 17.23

C. TREATMENT OF EXECUTORY CONTRACTS

Lithuanian law accepts the general principal of freedom of contract. Valid contracts concluded in compliance with the law are binding on the parties (*pacta sunt servanda*).[60] Insolvency proceedings under the EBL and the ERL, however, can affect the rights and obligations under the agreements in general and of executory contracts in particular, i.e., contracts that at the commencement of an insolvency proceedings have not yet been fully performed by both the insolvent debtor and the counterparty.[61] 17.24

(1) Insolvency proceedings under the EBL: impact on executory contracts

(a) General

The coming into force[62] of the decision to open insolvency proceedings under the EBL has certain general effects on the debtor's contractual rights and obligations. These effects are independent from the type of EBL proceeding. First and foremost, the debtor is prohibited from settling financial obligations which had not been settled before the opening of insolvency proceedings, including the payment of interest and contractual penalties.[63] Creditors are prohibited from enforcing their claims in or out of court. Set-offs are prohibited, except for set-offs of certain tax-related claims and made by the respective state authorities to the extent such set-offs are permitted under the applicable tax laws.[64] 17.25

Even before the coming into force of the opening decision, the courts usually apply interim protective measures which aim at protecting the debtor's estate 17.26

60 Civil Code of the Republic of Lithuania (*Lietuvos Respublikos civilinis kodeksas*) 18 July 2000, No. VIII-1864, art 6.200 1).

61 Neither the EBL nor the ERL contain definitions of executory contracts.

62 The decision comes into force if the appeal period has expired or appeals against the opening decision have been dismissed with binding effect by the Court of Appeal.

63 EBL, art 10 (7) para. 3.

64 Ibid.

for the case that proceedings will be opened. For this, interim protective measures are applied once the court formally accepts a petition to open proceedings under the EBL. The effect is that during the period in which the court examines the conditions and grounds for the opening of the proceedings, creditors may not start or continue measures to enforce titles against the debtor.[65] In such a case, all enforcement proceedings against the debtor are suspended until the court's decision to open or not to open the proceedings comes into effect.[66]

17.27 The mere opening of insolvency proceedings does not, however, automatically terminate contracts. Rather, the EBL provides different rules for the termination of: (i) employment contracts; (ii) contracts with the management; and (iii) other contracts (e.g., rental, lease, sale/purchase). These rules apply irrespective of the type of proceedings under the EBL. As mentioned above,[67] the regime under the EBL does not apply to financial collateral arrangements after Directive 2002/47/EC and Directive 98/26/EC were transposed into Lithuanian law. This also means that opening of insolvency proceedings does not have an impact on financial collateral arrangements.

(b) Employment contracts[68]

17.28 The insolvency administrator has to notify employees about the termination of an employment contract within three business days after the decision to open insolvency proceedings becomes final and binding; 15 business days after such notice, the insolvency administrator must terminate the employment contracts.[69]

(c) Contracts with the management of the debtor

17.29 The management loses its powers after the decision to open insolvency proceedings comes into force. Upon a 15-day written advance notice, the insolvency administrator has to terminate employment or civil contracts with the board members and the head of the company.[70]

65 Ibid., art 9 (3).

66 The interim protective measures do not apply to the public sale of pledged/mortgaged property if the public sale was announced before the opening of insolvency proceedings (EBL, art 9 (3), art 33 (4)).

67 See above (a) Scope of EBL.

68 Noteworthy is a particularity under the EBL: the Creditors' Assembly may vote to limit the validity of a collective agreement concluded in the insolvent company (EBL, art 10 (7) para 3, art 23 para (8)). Due to the lack of practical relevance and absence of the case law with regard to such distinction of collective agreements from the general regulation, this study does not analyse them in more detail.

69 EBL, art 19 (1).

70 Ibid., art 10 (7) para 2.

(d) Other contracts

The insolvency administrator is obliged and entitled to examine agreements concluded by the debtor prior to insolvency, including executory contracts. The administrator in exercising his duty must decide on further performance or rejection of the debtor's executory contracts the performance dates of which have not yet expired.[71] The EBL sets a term of 30 days during which the administrator must exercise his duty and in which he must notify the intention to terminate a contract. This term starts once the opening decision comes into force.[72] This rule generally applies to all agreements (including lease contracts, contracts for use), except for employment contracts and contracts based on which the debtor has a right against the counterparty.[73] **17.30**

The underlying justification of this exception is said to be that the administrator would not act in the interest of the estate and its creditors if by terminating a contract he waived a debtor's right with economic value that could be exercised without economic disadvantage for the estate.[74] **17.31**

With regard to the application of the general rule, published Lithuanian case law lacks coherence and is quite fragmented. Decisions of relevance to the topic rendered by courts so far do not provide clear guidance. One common denominator of most decisions appears to be the courts' emphasis placed on the duty of the administrator to evaluate whether the continuation of the contract is likely to be favourable for the estate, that is, in the interests of the creditors.[75] However, case law has not, as yet, developed reliable criteria on how to treat particular types of executory contracts and the termination right under the EBL of the administrator (or the debtor‘s counterparty) with regard to such contracts. **17.32**

---

71 EBL, art 10 (7) para 4.

> If within 30 days from the entry into force of the ruling to initiate bankruptcy proceedings the administrator notifies the persons concerned that he will not execute the contracts which have been entered into by the enterprise and whose period of execution has not yet expired, the aforementioned contracts (including lease and loan for use contracts), except for employment contracts and contracts from which the rights of claim of the enterprise in bankruptcy arise, shall be deemed to have expired …

72 In a case where the management of the debtor violates its obligation to fully handover to the administrator the corporate files and documents then the mentioned 30-day term does not start before the documentation for a respective contract has been handed over to the insolvency administrator. EBL, art 11 (5) para 13, art 17, art 10 (7), para 4.

73 EBL, art 10 (7), para 4.

74 S. Kavalnė, R. Norkus, et al., note 28, 135–8.

75 Decision of Lithuanian Supreme Court of 30 October 2013, civil case No. 3K-3–521/2013; decision of Lithuanian Supreme Court of 16 November 2012, civil case No. 3K-3–493/2012; decision of Lithuanian Court of Appeal of 29 September 2016, civil case No. 2A-578–464/2016.

17.33 Legal literature is also scarce on this topic. However, one available source gives clearer guidance for the application of the administrator's power to terminate contracts, in particular with regard to severable contracts. It argues that for cases where the performance of an executory contract is severable (e.g., certain supply of services like electricity, construction works) and the further performance of the contract is essential and beneficial for the debtor, the administrator is said to have the power to request the performance of the contract.

17.34 If the administrator decides to continue such a contract, the counterparty may also request performance in full from the estate for the part of the contract continued after the opening of insolvency case. For the remaining part, that is, the part that relates to the (non)performance before the opening of the proceedings, the counterparty cannot impose the original obligation on the debtor, but would have to file a normal insolvency claim. The supporters of this solution argue that the EBL prevents the performance of obligations that arose before the opening of the insolvency case.[76]

17.35 Whenever the insolvency administrator informs the interested parties (counterparties) within the 30-day term of the decision not to perform a contract, then this contract is deemed to have terminated on the day of the coming into effect of the opening decision. If a contract is deemed to be terminated then the affected counterparty may file its claim (for damages)[77] which, once approved, can expect satisfaction according to the general rules on ranking of creditors (see below B.II.).[78]

17.36 Based on the above, one can conclude that executory contracts continue to be in force unless the insolvency administrator validly exercises his/her right to terminate the contract or, alternatively, an *ipso facto* clause leads to the termination of the agreement.[79]

(e) Ipso facto *clauses*

17.37 Lithuanian law does not expressly prohibit *ipso facto* clauses, that is, clauses that would trigger an automatic termination or grant termination or other right to the counterparty for the case that the company runs into financial

---

76 S. Kavalnė, R. Norkus, et al., note 28, 137–8; EBL, art 10 (7) para 3.

77 Ibid., 135–6; Civil Code of the Republic of Lithuania (*Lietuvos Respublikos civilinis kodeksas*) 18 July 2000, No. VIII-1864, art 6.256(2).

78 cf. EBL, art 10(7) (4), see below (f) Satisfaction of claims in the proceedings under the EBL.

79 Ibid.; With regard to the ranking of claims, cf. EBL, art 10(7) (4); Note also, that in case the management of the debtor violates its obligation to fully hand over to the administrator the corporate files and documents then the mentioned 30-day term does not start before the documentation for a respective contract has been handed over to the insolvency administrator.

difficulties or restructuring proceedings are initiated or opened against the company. Thus, it does not prohibit clauses that would lead to an automatic termination of the agreement or establish a termination right for the debtor's counterparty if certain, agreed conditions related to the (imminent) insolvency of one or both of the parties are met (e.g., deterioration of financial situation of the company, filing a petition for insolvency, opening decision or similar).

However, as mentioned above, the EBL also obliges the insolvency administrator to examine agreements and, where permitted, to terminate contracts.[80] Owing to this, one can argue that the insolvency administrator may challenge the termination of a contract under an *ipso facto* clause by claiming that the *ipso facto* clause/termination of the contract is in conflict with the Lithuanian imperative rules and/or public order and that the right of the administrator to decide on the fate of executory contracts should prevail, including the right to insist on the performance of the contract.[81] However, there is no published case law dealing with this topic in the context of proceedings under the EBL, neither was this topic for such scenarios comprehensively analysed in legal literature. In practice, *ipso facto* clauses are used and creditors like leasing companies exercising rights under *ipso facto* clauses do not seem to face significant problems. **17.38**

(f) Satisfaction of claims in the proceedings under the EBL

Under the EBL, claims of secured creditors[82] enjoy priority over all other claims, including employment and tax-related claims, but their priority is limited to the proceeds of the sale of the debtor's pledged assets. After the secured creditors, claims are satisfied according to rank in the following way: **17.39**

Claims of employees relating to employment relations, claims for the compensation for damage due to an accident at work; and certain claims for payment for agricultural produce purchased for processing.[83] **17.40**

---

80 EBL, art 17.

81 S. Barakauskas, 'Influence of Judicial Procedures of Company Rescue on Contractual Relationship: Importance on Preserving Contracts' (2015), Teisė, ISSN 1392–1274 101.

82 'Creditor's claims secured by pledge and/or mortgage' are defined as:

> the right acquired by the creditor (holder of the pledge, mortgage creditor) under a pledge agreement or a registered mortgage bond or pledge note, in the event of the enterprise's default to fulfil the obligation secured by pledge and/or mortgage, to request in the manner prescribed by this Law that the pledged assets be sold and his claims be satisfied from the proceeds and, in the event of failure to sell the pledged assets, that the assets be transferred into his ownership

(EBL, art 2(7)).

83 EBL, art 35 (2).

17.41 Claims for taxes and other duties, excises and remittances into the state budget.[84]

17.42 All the remaining creditors.[85]

17.43 The creditors' claims are satisfied in two stages. During the first stage, they are satisfied in accordance to the sequence mentioned above, not including the interest and default interest. During the second stage, the remaining part of the creditors' claims (that is, interest and default interest) are satisfied according to the same order of priority, provided that there are enough funds to meet all requests.[86]

17.44 Even though secured claims are ranked as priority claims under Lithuanian law, the enforcement of a pledge and/or mortgage is delayed in case of insolvency of the debtor due to the need to adhere to formalities of public auctions as well as related disputes and deduction of legal and administrative expenses from the proceeds from the sale of security.[87]

(2) Insolvency proceedings under the ERL: impact on executory contracts

(a) General

17.45 The commencement of a restructuring proceeding determines some restrictions on the ability of the debtor to dispose of his assets.[88]

17.46 Upon receiving a petition to initiate restructuring proceedings, the court may apply and usually applies interim protective measures such as, for instance, the seizure of the debtor's assets or the suspension of enforcement from the debtor's property. Interim protective measures stay in effect, unless changed or revoked by the court, until the date of coming into effect of the court decision to approve or reject the debtor's request to commence a restructuring proceeding.[89] As from the day of the court's decision to open restructuring proceedings, recovery actions of creditors from the seized assets of the debtor

---

84 Ibid., art 35 (3).

85 Ibid., art 35 (4).

86 Ibid., art 35 (1).

87 Ibid., art 36 (1).

88 The ERL expressly states that it does not apply to the extent that it contradicts the Law on Financial Collateral Arrangements and the Law on Settlement Finality in Payment and Securities Settlement Systems which implement Directive 2002/47/EC and Directive 98/26/EC into Lithuanian law (ERL, art 1 6)). This also means that opening of restructuring proceedings does not have an impact on financial collateral arrangements.

89 ERL, art 7 (1) (3).

are stayed.[90] The decision to open restructuring proceedings, once in force, has the following effects:

- prohibition of performance of any pecuniary obligation (including the payment of interest, default interest and compulsory payments as well as debt recovery) which was not settled before the coming into effect of the opening decision;[91]
- suspension of calculation of interest for all the liabilities of the debtor which accrued before the date of coming into effect of the court's decision to initiate the enterprise restructuring proceedings, except for the calculation of interest for the late payment of salary to employees;[92]
- suspension of recovery under enforcement orders as well as by way of set-off.[93]

The mere opening of restructuring proceedings does not, however, automatically terminate contracts concluded by the debtor. **17.47**

(b) Treatment of contracts

For the restructuring, the debtor is obliged to prepare a restructuring plan. Among other elements, the restructuring plan must state which of the contracts concluded before the opening of the restructuring proceedings are to be terminated.[94] Also, the plan must explain the anticipated or proposed consequences of such a termination.[95] Thus, when drafting the restructuring plan, the debtor may propose to terminate contracts that are not beneficial for the further operations of the debtor. The claims of the creditors, including the claims for damages for non-performance of contracts, are to be satisfied by the company according to the approved restructuring plan which must adhere to certain statutory requirements for the ranking of the creditors' claims (see below).[96] **17.48**

(c) Ipso facto *clauses*

Lithuanian law does not *expresis verbis* prohibit *ipso facto* clauses The same arguments mentioned in the EBL section with reference to the opportunity and validity of these clauses are applicable here. Noteworthy is a recent judgment of the Lithuanian Supreme Court where the court recognized the **17.49**

90 Ibid., art 7 (2).
91 Ibid., art 8 (1),(2).
92 Ibid., art. 8 (2).
93 Ibid., art 8 (3).
94 Ibid., art 12 (2) para 5.
95 Ibid.
96 cf. ERL, art 13, see (d) Satisfaction of claims in the proceedings under the ERL.

enforceability of an *ipso facto* clause with a termination right based on the filing for restructuring proceedings as a valid ground to terminate the contract despite the fact that the restructuring administrator disputed the termination.[97]

17.50 In this respect, it is also worth noting that the interim protective measures usually applied during the plan-preparation period do not ensure that assets owned by a creditor (and not by the debtor) will remain in the debtor's possession and thus can be used for the restructuring. This causes uncertainty for the debtor as there is no legal tool that would prevent third-party owners from repossessing their assets that might be essential for a successful restructuring of the debtor. For example, a leasing company would not be prevented from repossessing leased trucks from the debtor that runs a transport business and would need the vehicles to perform its activities as result that which in line with the current case law of the Lithuanian Supreme Court.[98]

17.51 In light of this background and the current case law of the Supreme Court, it appears that there is little room for the administrator to challenge the validity and enforceability of *ipso facto* clauses based on his general right to decide the fate of executory contracts.[99]

(d) Satisfaction of claims in the proceedings under the ERL

17.52 The ERL establishes a slightly different creditor ranking system compared to the EBL. As in insolvency proceedings under the EBL, secured creditors enjoy priority when it comes to the satisfaction of claims.[100] After the secured claims are satisfied[101] from the proceeds of the sale of the debtor's pledged assets, the remaining claims are satisfied according to ranks as follows:

1. Claims of employees relating to employment relations as well as claims for the compensation for damage due to an accident at work and certain claims for payment for agricultural produce purchased for processing. These are paid alongside with secured claims not exceeding the value of the pledged assets which are not sold during the restructuring.[102]

---

97 Decision of Lithuanian Supreme Court of 8 May 2015, civil case No. 3K-3–261–421/2015.

98 The Decision of the Supreme Court of the Republic of Lithuania of 26 April 2011, No. 3K-3–209/2011. The Supreme Court in this case confirmed the creditor's repossession right according to which owners are free to vindicate their owned property from the debtor undergoing restructuring proceedings during the opening period in which the restructuring plan has not been approved.

99 S. Barakauskas, note 81.

100 ERL, art 13 (1).

101 Where the proceeds of the sale of the pledged assets are insufficient, the remaining amount of unsatisfied claims shall be satisfied second in line, as specified in EBL, art 13 (4).

102 Ibid., art 13 (3).

2. All the remaining claims, except for:
3. The claims of the shareholders of the debtor who became creditors prior to initiation of the restructuring proceedings and who (alone or together with other shareholders) control the debtor under restructuring.[103,104]

Claims of creditors who provide financing for the restructuring are satisfied before the claims mentioned in no. 2 above, to the extent they are not secured by a mortgage or pledge.[105] **17.53**

The creditors' claims are satisfied in the same two stage approach described with reference to the procedures under the EBL.[106] **17.54**

D. REFORMS

(1) General

Since the restoration of Lithuania's independence in 1990, there have been three versions of Enterprise Bankruptcy Laws (EBL 1992,[107] EBL 1997[108] and EBL 2001) and two versions of laws on restructuring (Law on Corporate Capital Rescue and Restructuring 1998[109] and ERL 2001), as well as subsequent amendments to both laws. **17.55**

The EBL 1997 clarified the definitions and legal grounds for the opening of insolvency proceedings. It also introduced the priority of secured creditors, whereas under the previous EBL 1992 claims of secured creditors were satisfied in a rank lower than employment related claims.[110] Amendments to the EBL made in 1997 were to a great extent influenced by the Convention concerning the Protection of Workers' Claims.[111] **17.56**

---

103 Ibid., art 13 (4).
104 Ibid., art 13 (6).
105 Ibid., art 13 (5), art. 12 (2) No 7.
106 Ibid., art 13 (2). Note that these stages are not applicable to the claims of secured creditors. See also above in (f) Satisfaction of claims in the proceedings under the EBL.
107 Enterprise Bankruptcy Law of the Republic of Lithuania (*Lietuvos Respublikos įmonių bankroto įstatymas*) 15 September 1992, No. I-2880.
108 Enterprise Bankruptcy Law of the Republic of Lithuania (*Lietuvos Respublikos įmonių bankroto įstatymas*) 17 June 1997, No. VIII-270.
109 Law on Corporate Capital Rescue and Restructuring 20 October 1998, No. VIII-900.
110 S. Kavalnė, R. Norkus, et al., *Bankroto teisė*: vadovėlis, Pirmoji knyga, note 28, 193.
111 Convention concerning the Protection of Workers' Claims in the event of the Insolvency of their Employer 1992, No. 173.

17.57 In 2001, the Lithuanian Ministry of Economy proposed to the Parliament a draft law of the new EBL. It is important to note that the EBL 2001 clarified the definition of 'insolvency'.[112] Compared with the insolvency definition provided in the EBL 1997 under which the company was insolvent when its financial obligations were equal or exceeded its assets, the EBL 2001 lowered the criteria for characterizing a company as insolvent. This amendment was expected to favour earlier and more timely restructuring, and thus an increase in the satisfaction rate of the creditors' claims. However, at that time it was criticised by Lithuanian Free Market Institute who expressed concern that even solvent companies could fall under the broader definition of insolvency.[113]

17.58 The EBL 2001 was strongly influenced by the intended accession by Lithuania to the EU. Changes to the previous regulation took into consideration PHARE experts', the EU Commission's and The World bank's experts' recommendations.[114] There was also a need to harmonize the procedures under the EBL with the newly adopted Lithuanian Civil Code and the Law on Companies. The ERL 2001 changed the rescue procedure that had been in place before.[115]

(2) Reforms in the context of executory contracts from 2000

17.59 Analysing the rules of the treatment of executory contracts established in the current EBL and its predecessor of 1997, the reform of the treatment of secured creditors stands out clearly from other amendments.

17.60 The EBL 1997 obliged the insolvency administrator to file a claim with the court for challenging pledge/mortgage contracts if these had been concluded more than 30 days after the conclusion of the loan contract, unless the underlying loan contracts had already stated the need to provide security and the specifications of the security to be pledged/mortgaged.[116] Moreover, the EBL 1997 stipulated that pledge/mortgage contracts were void if they had

---

112 Under the first version of the EBL 2001 which since then has been amended, insolvency of the company was defined as a state of a company when it fails to discharge its obligations to its creditor(s) within three months after the due date and such obligations exceed half of the value of the assets entered in the company's balance.

113 Data accessible via the webpage of Lithuanian Free Market Institute: http://www.llri.lt/naujienos/ekonomine-politika/bendroji-ekonomine-politika/analize-del-imoniu-bankroto-istatymo-ir-imoniu-restrukturizavimo-istatymo-projektu/lrinka accessed 23 March 2017 (in Lithuanian language only).

114 S. Kavalnė, R. Norkus, et al., *Bankroto teisė*: vadovėlis, Pirmoji knyga, note 28, 194.

115 Ibid., 195.

116 EBL 1997, art 21 (3).

been concluded at a time when the debtor was already insolvent.[117] The above regulation was replaced by the EBL 2001 establishing a more liberal regime for secured creditors. Even though there is only very scarce publicly available data nor protocols of the Parliament with regard to the groups and main drivers behind these changes implemented in the EBL 2001, there is strong reason to believe that the changes in treatment of secured contracts were substantially lobbied by banks and other financial institutions after the market of loans had increased during the 1990s.[118]

After 2001, all reforms with regard to executory contracts have been rather cosmetic. More meaningful reforms in other areas (e.g., qualification and selection of administrators, right to appeal decisions, appointment of the administrators, administration costs) were often driven by the aim to prevent abuse and to increase transparency, also to simplify and shorten proceedings as well as to reflect EU rules and international best practices.[119] **17.61**

Currently, there are no noteworthy proposals to reform the existing framework of insolvency laws in the context of executory contracts. Neither major reforms nor significant initiatives to improve the current regulation appear currently on the legislature's agenda. However, there has been – at least on a regional, cross-border level – a private initiative supported by practitioners and other stakeholders to harmonize the existing insolvency laws in the Nordic and the Baltic States. Recommendations for insolvency laws have recently been published as the result of the five-year work of the Nordic Insolvency Network. These recommendations are available in English language and include a section on the treatment of executory contracts in insolvency.[120] They are heavily influenced by the respective laws, practice and experiences in the Nordic countries, in particular Sweden, Finland, Norway and Denmark. Unfortunately, they have not, as yet prompted debates at the legislative level. **17.62**

117 Note that under EBL 1997, art 2 (8) the definition of an insolvent company was determined when its financial obligations were equal to or exceeded its assets.

118 Statistics regarding financial sector are available via the webpage of Lithuanian Bank: http://www.lb.lt/kredito_istaigu_apzvalgos_2 accessed 23 March 2017 (in Lithuanian language only).

119 Such as, e.g., UNCITRAL model law on Cross-Border Insolvency.

120 *Nordic-Baltic Recommendations on Insolvency Law* (Wolters Kluwer 2016). The network consisted of practitioners and stakeholders from Denmark, Norway, Sweden, Finland, Estonia, Latvia and Lithuania. Section IV (pp 27–31) contains detailed 'proposals for the treatment of the debtor's contracts', including the insolvent side's right to choose between continuation and rejection, the counterparty's right to request a decision, general effects of the continuation decision, the insolvent side's right to request limited future continuation, the counterparty's right to request security, the counterparty's right to terminate, limitations of the counterparty's contractual right to terminate or accelerate the contract, the insolvent side's responsibility for the performances obtained and consumed after the commencement decision and the insolvent side's right to assign the debtor's contracts. The Recommendations are available here http://www.sccl.se/wp-content/uploads/2017/04/Nordic-Baltic-Recommendations-Final-Version-bok-rotated.pdf [last viewed 23 March 2017].

E. CONCLUDING REMARKS

17.63 Lithuania's accession to the European Union, the legislature's willingness to comply with the international rules and principles of the UNCITRAL Model Law on Cross-Border Insolvency[121] and the need to fill the gaps and imperfections of previous legislation have been and continue to represent the main drivers for reforms of the otherwise young Lithuanian insolvency framework.

17.64 Further analysis of the reforms in the field of the treatment of executory contracts leads to the belief that some noteworthy changes have been suggested, supported or at least welcomed by banks and other financial institutions, in particular due to the increase in the market of loans which followed the collapse of the Soviet Union and the socialist economy. This seems to be the case in particular with regard to the regulation of treatment of secured creditors under the current versions of the EBL and the ERL.

17.65 Other important amendments to the insolvency laws were mainly influenced by the interest of the legislator to make insolvency proceedings more cohesive, efficient and transparent, boosting Lithuanian attractiveness in the international market.

17.66 It is, however, remarkable that current Lithuanian statutory law offers a rather rudimentary set of rules for the treatment of executory contracts in insolvency proceedings (both under the ERL and the EBL). Compared to other jurisdictions (such as, e.g., Germany), Lithuanian law lacks detailed rules for the treatment of, for example, severable contracts, retention of title, lease agreements with a differentiation of the debtor being a tenant or landlord, and contracts with continuous obligations. Case law is developing and providing some guidance in certain areas, as in the case of *ipso facto* clauses. However, case law is still relatively scarce, and occasionally inconsistent and dogmatically incoherent.

121 Available, alongside with the Guide to Enactment and Interpretation, at: <http://www.uncitral.org/pdf/english/texts/insolven/1997-Model-Law-Insol-2013-Guide-Enactment-e.pdf> [last viewed: 8 December 2017].

18

NATIONAL REPORT FOR PANAMA

José Maria Lezcano Navarro

A. INTRODUCTION

Every dynamic economy must have appropriate tools to deal with economic reversals. Insolvency law is one of these tools. It is therefore in the primary interest of its citizens that a developing country like Panama has an efficient insolvency regulation. **18.01**

In principle, a dynamic economy demands an efficient legal framework. However, the case of Panama is special. Panama has experienced noticeable economic growth over the last couple of decades. Consequently, commercial regulation has been updated over the past 20 years. The new Insolvency regulation, *Ley 12 de mayo de 2016* (*LA LEY*), is the most recent development.[1] **18.02**

Originally, Insolvency law was a subject regulated in the Code of Commerce, in its *Libro Tercero*.[2] This code was enacted in 1917 and was the first Panamanian law dedicated to the regulation of commerce.[3] For 100 years, the **18.03**

1 See, Ley No 12 de jueves 19 de mayo de 2016, que establece el régimen de los procesos concursales de insolvencia y dicta otras disposiciones. Gaceta Oficial 28036-B.

2 The Panamanian Codes are structured in: *Libros, Títulos, Capítulos* and *Secciones*.

3 Panama was a Spanish Colony from 1501 until 1821. Afterwards it became part of Colombia. However, due to political tensions Panama became independent from Colombian in 1903. Our legal system is heavily

rules contained in the *Libro Tercero* have represented the foundation for all insolvency proceedings. Certainly, the *Libro Tercero* provided the methods to deal with insolvency. However, the *Libro Tercero*, in this author's opinion, had two big flaws: it did not include any reorganization process and its provisions on cross-border cases were vague and general in nature.

18.04 *LA LEY* not only addresses these flaws. It also identifies a series of fundamental principles that should underpin the law, and which should be used as a guidance in domestic procedures. Indeed, LA *LEY* yields dramatic changes in Panamanian commercial law.

18.05 Panama, as any other jurisdiction, has developed its own commercial regulations. However, the development of new regulations, such as *LA LEY*, has been promoted by a variety of factors. The globalization of commerce has introduced new players who advocate for changes in the law. Multinational companies and trade associations among others play a key role in the way international markets have been shaped. They unarguably have a degree of influence over the development of domestic policies. This is due to the fact that commercial law and all related areas have been developed in accordance with the needs of the market.

18.06 Multinational companies highly praise the development of a uniform legal framework for commerce. A uniform legal framework reduces issues like 'forum shopping' and facilitates the solution of conflicts related to trade. The United Nations Commission for Trade and Development of Commercial Law (UNCITRAL) has achieved uniformity through its provision of 'Model Laws' in different areas,[4] with the objective to aid the development of a standard framework. Insolvency has been one of the areas addressed by the UNCITRAL and not only Panama, but also other countries in the Latin American region have followed the UNCITRAL MODEL LAW on insolvency.[5]

18.07 Insolvency has proven a difficult subject to harmonize; this has been the case particularly in Latin America, a region known for territorialism and national protectionism.[6] This is a fact that has an impact in international contracts.

---

influenced by Spanish doctrine and codes. However, since the independence from Colombia, Panamanian law makers have tried to develop law according to Panamanian needs.

4 www.uncitral.org/uncitral/en/about_us.html [last visit 12 December 2017].

5 http://www.uncitral.org/uncitral/en/uncitral_texts/insolvency/1997Model.html [last visit 18 April 2017].

6 See, M. Rowat, Reforming Insolvency Systems in Latin America. *Public Policy for the Private Sector* (Note No 187) June 1999. Available at http://siteresources.worldbank.org/EXTFINANCIALSECTOR/Resources/282884-1303327122200/187rowat.pdf [last visit 18 April 2017].

Indeed, the lack of uniformity regarding insolvency law creates complications in cross-border cases, and in particular those that include ongoing executory contracts between parties based in different jurisdictions.

Latin American countries have modified their insolvency regulation gradually.[7] Panama joined this wave of reform with its recent enactment of *LA LEY*. The objective of this chapter is to present the rationale behind *LA LEY*, its innovations and the impact on executory contracts. The treatment of executory contracts in the new Panamanian insolvency regulation is a subject worthy of attention because it is one of the most important changes in the Panamanian insolvency regime. **18.08**

To achieve the objective, this chapter has been divided into three parts. The first part will address the rationale of the law and the most relevant changes. In the opinion of the author, as mentioned above there are three relevant changes: the introduction of reorganization; the creation of the insolvency courts and the amendments to the management of cross-border insolvency cases; and the recognition of foreign judgements. In addition, this section will address the proceedings available for a business in distress. The second part will list the procedures available to a business in distress under Panamanian law. The third and final part addresses the effect of the new law on executory contracts. **18.09**

(1) Rationale of the law and subsequent innovation

The previous insolvency law was 'pragmatic.' It punished the debtor and gathered the assets to pay the creditors in accordance with the '*par condition creditorium*' principle. Indeed, it was an insolvency regulation created to accommodate the needs of the Panamanian economy 100 years ago. In the past, being a newborn republic, Panama had a small population and poor port infrastructure. The railway and the canal were not under Panamanian administration and there was no manufacturing industry. However, over 100 years a lot has changed. **18.10**

Nowadays, the Panama Canal is under Panamanian administration and its income is an important source of revenue.[8] Additionally, modern transport and communication infrastructures have been built across the country and the **18.11**

7 Since the late 1990s Latin American countries such as Costa Rica, Argentina, Peru and Colombia among others have engaged in the reform of their insolvency regime. See, ibid.

8 The Panama Canal and port infrastructure represent 20 per cent of the Panamanian Gross domestic production. See: http://www.amp.gob.pa/newsite/spanish/home_mirror.html [last visit 18 April 2017].

Panamanian financial centre is regarded as one of the most solid across the Latin American region. These are some of the most significant innovations that have allowed Panama to thrive as a 'service economy'. Certainly, as a small country with few mineral resources Panama had to focus on developing its service sector if it wanted to succeed in the global market. However, the drawback of the Panamanian strategy is the dependency on foreign capital.

18.12 Panama has a 'service economy' that depends on foreign capital in order to grow. Therefore, the legal framework has been gradually amended to stimulate foreign investment. Codes have been modified and new laws have been enacted, but the dramatic changes in our commercial code have occurred in the last decade.[9] One of the most notable changes has been the enactment of *LA LEY*, which derogates the previous regulation contained in the Commercial Code and modifies Panama's insolvency regime. However, what is the rationale behind it?

18.13 *LA LEY* was created to provide a friendly environment for foreign investors. Consequently, it can be argued that foreign investors influenced the development of the new insolvency act. Indeed, innovations such as the process of reorganization, the creation of insolvency courts and a review of cross-border insolvency rules are some of the aspects that reveal the influence of foreign investors in the new Panamanian insolvency law.

18.14 First, the process of reorganization creates an opportunity to rescue a business. Consequently, the invested capital is less likely to be lost. Second, insolvency courts are especially employed as a special branch to deal with this subject. The mere existence of an insolvency court creates a degree of trust in the judicial system. In addition, it prevents insolvency proceedings stagnating in ordinary courts. Third, the new cross-border insolvency rules bring certainty to the subject, something not fully developed in previous regulation. These three aspects support the following fact: the objective of *LA LEY* is to encourage foreign investment, by providing protection for foreign capital. As a country that depends on foreign capital, Panama needs to create a 'legal environment' where foreign investors can feel safe. To understand how the above-mentioned innovations help to achieve this objective, each one shall be briefly explained.

---

9 Besides insolvency law, the Panamanian policy has also enacted the *Ley 56 de 2008 sobre comercio maritimo*, which is a regulation that updates Panamanian regulation on carriage of goods by sea, freight contracts, marine insurance and other aspects regarding maritime commerce. Another example is the Panamanian Arbitration Law, *Ley 131 de 2013 sobre arbitraje*, which also updates the Panamanian approach on arbitration. These are some examples of recent changes that have had an impact on the Panamanian legal framework for commerce.

(2) Reorganization

Reorganization proposes to re-establish the economic stability of a business in order for the business to continue its operations. This practice can be implemented to aid a distressed business and prevent its collapse. Modern insolvency regulations tend to offer reorganization as an alternative to liquidation, especially when the rescue of the business as a going concern appears in the best interest of the majority of creditors.[10] It is widely accepted that a statutory framework which pursues the rescue of viable businesses and the efficient liquidation of unviable ones is more likely to promote the growth of the country's economy, and its attractiveness to foreign investors. **18.15**

In the past, Latin American countries did not pursue the goal of rescuing or restructuring businesses. Rather the preferred choice was to favour the liquidation of assets to pay as many creditors as possible.[11] Indeed, this approach had resulted in a negative stigma over insolvent businesses. **18.16**

Globalization has obliged Latin American policy makers to reconsider their insolvency regulation. As a result, the reform of insolvency laws across Latin America in general has been triggered since the late 1990s with the introduction of reorganization being one of the most dramatic changes due to a push for a culture of preservation over the previous tendency for the immediate liquidation of the business.[12] **18.17**

The enactment of *LA LEY* introduces the concept of 'reorganization', which is a pillar in achieving the objective of *LA LEY*: the protection of the creditors' interests, the protection of employment generated by the business and above all protection of the national economy.[13] *LA LEY* achieves these objectives by the creation of a friendly framework where the insolvent debtor (in good faith) can request protection and assistance to save the business. Moreover, *LA LEY* encourages the insolvent debtor to present proposals to save the business.[14] **18.18**

---

10 See, Rowat, *supra* note 3.

11 See, J. Queiroz, 'An Overview of Recent Bankrupcy Reforms in Latin America' (2007) 26 (3) *America Bankrupcy Institute Journal*.

12 Ibid.

13 Artículo 1: El régimen concursal de insolvencia regulado en esta ley tiene por objeto la protección del crédito y de los acreedores, a través del proceso de reorganización, a fin de garantizar la recuperación y conservación de la empresa eficiente, como unidad de explotación económica y fuente generadora de empleo, mediante una liquidación pronta y ordenada de la empresa eficiente.

14 See, La Ley, art 36.

18.19 Certainly, the introduction of the reorganization process breaks with the traditional 'seize and liquidation of assets' approach. This statement is supported in Article 1:

> ... its *objective is to protect creditors by using the reorganization process* to save and keep the business operating as an efficient source of capital and jobs; *or* by implementing *seizure and liquidation* of assets in an efficient manner.[15]

18.20 It can be noted that *LA LEY* establishes reorganization as the first approach to protect creditors, which is a fact that strengthens the objective of this regulation. This is a change that also has an impact on the treatment of executory contracts, which is a subject addressed later in this chapter.

(3) Insolvency courts

18.21 In Panama, insolvency is a subject considered '*de orden publico*'. This means the Panamanian State can intervene when there is a threat to the public interest. Certainly, State intervention in economic affairs has been discussed throughout the twentieth century. However, national economy is a subject of public interest. If there is a threat to the economy, the State has a duty to protect public interest. Insolvency law is part of the mechanism used by the Panamanian authorities to safeguard the '*orden publico*'. *LA LEY* in its Article 2 points out: 'The contents of the law are "*de orden publico*", the objective is to protect the national economy, creditors, jobs and the free market. *Private agreements cannot override the law and the competence of national courts.*'[16]

18.22 That Article not only asserts the importance of the law but also that the State preserves its authority on the subject by restricting arbitration. Certainly, *LA LEY* does not address arbitration but '*restricts the use of private agreements*'. Nowadays, arbitration clauses are a key element in almost every commercial relationship. This is because commerce cannot be stagnated; controversies derived from commercial relations demand a quick response that cannot be provided by national courts. The Panamanian policy maker is aware of this fact. However, the Panamanian policy maker is also aware that insolvency is a subject '*de orden publico*'. An arbitration clause cannot affect ongoing insolvency proceedings. At the same time, to address some of the concerns

---

15 See, *supra* note 10.

16 Articulo 2: Las disposiciones de esta ley son de orden público y tienen como fin proteger y asegurar el orden económico nacional, los acreedores, las fuentes de empleo y el proceso de libre competencia económica, así como acrecentar la riqueza nacional.

No serán oponibles los acuerdos privados relativos a la sustracción de ley y jurisdicción.

stemming from the business community, the legislator decided to create a separate system of courts run by highly skilled judges: the insolvency courts.

Insolvency courts are indeed an important part of insolvency proceedings. However, the validity and enforceability of arbitration clauses is still contentious in cross-border cases. What is the position of the Panamanian authority? *LA LEY* has been in force since January 2017 and consequently it is too early to give an opinion about Panamanian insolvency courts and the effects *LA LEY* has on arbitration clauses. Whether the Panamanian insolvency courts fulfill the objective is something that can be answered in a few years from now. At this moment, this author is limited to celebrate this innovation, which in theory should make insolvency proceedings more efficient. **18.23**

The importance and complexity of insolvency proceedings demand an efficient judicial system. Therefore, *LA LEY* has created insolvency courts, which have exclusive competence over insolvency issues.[17] *LA LEY* creates the *Cuarto Tribunal Superior* (which functions as a Court of Appeal) and the *Juzgado de Circuito de Insolvencia* (which is equivalent to a First Instance Court).[18] **18.24**

In addition to the creation of insolvency courts, *LA LEY* has modified some aspects of procedural law applicable to insolvency proceedings. It has to be pointed out that insolvency courts are special tribunals, whose judges, in theory, receive special judicial training on the subject. However, in Latin America, a problem has been the inadequate judicial training regarding insolvency.[19] Panama is no exception on this issue and *LA LEY* does not seem to provide a solution. A personal criticism of *LA LEY* is the fact that the Panamanian policy maker does not request a judge or officer with special knowledge on insolvency. *LA LEY*, in the criteria for the selection of insolvency judges, only demands a candidate with general studies regarding commercial law.[20] This is a delicate matter because insolvency is a subject that cannot be taken lightly. Judges and officers with no specialized knowledge on **18.25**

17 See, La Ley, arts 17, 21 and 26.

18 The Panamanian system is divided into Civil Courts, Criminal Courts, Administrative Courts and Labor Courts. Regarding first instance courts, we have *Juzgados Municipales* and *Juzgados de Circuito*. The competence of each of these courts will be determined by factors such as amount of the claim, e.g., a credit below 2,500 U.S. Dollars will be competence of a *Juzgado Municipal*. Over 2,500 U.S. Dollars will be competence of the *Juzgado de Circuito*. The *Tribunal Superior* operates as a second instance court. The Panamanian court system cannot be explained in a footnote. However, if the reader wants to know more about the Panamanian court structure he/she look for the Panamanian procedural Code (*Código Judicial*). See, Codigo Judicial de la Republica de Panama. Gaceta Oficial 24.384 de 10 de septiembre de 2001.

19 See, Rowat, *supra* note 3.

20 See, La Ley, art 18.

the subject are a potential hindrance to the establishment of a sound framework for insolvency. If Panama wants to compete at global level, the Panamanian insolvency framework needs well-prepared judges capable of protecting public interest and in turn enabling global competitiveness. As a personal observation, the lack of qualified insolvency lawyers can be attributed to factors such as the possibility to practice as a lawyer without the need for a formal qualification beside the law degree. Certainly, this is a concern and insolvency courts are one of the areas that may be affected by this situation. However, this law has only just been passed and consequently members of these new courts have not yet been appointed. Therefore, it is too early to pass an opinion about the members, which will be appointed. A later law reform may establish a stricter criterion not only for the selection of insolvency judges, but also for the practice of law in Panama.

(4) Cross-border insolvency

18.26 The concept of cross-border insolvency refers to any case where a debtor has assets in more than one jurisdiction, therefore assistance is required during its reorganization or winding-up process. Other cross-border issues arise whenever two or more insolvency proceedings against the same debtor take place simultaneously in more than one jurisdiction; or whenever a creditor or a person with a recognized legal interest request to participate in an insolvency proceeding in a foreign jurisdiction. This is a commercial law occurrence derived from the internationalization of commerce, which has undeniably affected Latin America. Latin America depends on international commerce. Consequently, one must pay special attention to reforms regarding insolvency regimes across the entire region and in particular regarding cross-border insolvency.

18.27 Insolvency, as is the case with many other areas of commercial law, has been difficult to harmonize. However, due to an increase in international commerce, the legal community discussed strategies to facilitate it, and the recognition of foreign judgments in national courts. One of the most achievable results has been the adoption of the Model Law on Cross-Border Insolvency (1997).

18.28 This is a document drafted by the United Nations Commission on International Trade Law, and has served as the template on which most Latin American jurisdictions have restructured their approach to cross-border insolvency. This fact has contributed to the gradual development of a uniform approach in relation to cross-border insolvency.

The previous Panamanian insolvency regulation largely followed the Latin American trend regarding insolvency proceedings, based on territoriality and sovereignty. Nonetheless, Panama differs from other Latin American jurisdictions due to its particularly strong dependency on foreign capital. For that reason, the previous regulation did not ignore the subject of cross-border insolvency but the contents on the subject were laconic. *LA LEY* innovates because it revamps the Panamanian approach to cross-border insolvency. However, this has not been done from scratch. The Panamanian policy maker has supported the development of this subject on the Model Law on Cross Border Insolvency (1997). **18.29**

It can be considered that the current Panamanian approach to cross-border insolvency is based on characteristics promoted by the Model Law; for example, access and participation, legal certainty, protection of investment, enforcement and equal distribution of assets. These characteristics not only allow the creation of a more efficient insolvency law but also promote cooperation in cross-border insolvencies: **18.30**

- *access and participation*: *LA LEY* provides opportunity to foreign creditors to access asset recovery and asset protection mechanisms that are available under the Panamanian insolvency regime.[21] A foreign court can request assistance from the Republic of Panama and the Panamanian court may request assistance from a foreign State regarding a pending action under insolvency law.[22] It recognizes that insolvency proceedings in Panama may be taking place in Panama and a foreign jurisdiction simultaneously. *LA LEY*, in addition, allows foreign creditors to file insolvency proceedings in Panama.[23] The new Panamanian approach to cross-border insolvency is a body of law that intends to present Panama as a jurisdiction that cooperates on judicial matters;
- *legal certainty*: This is a key element for a healthy economy. Legal certainty encourages investors because it guarantees the protection of capital. An efficient approach on cross-border insolvency aids to reinforce legal certainty. *LA LEY* addresses matters such as the prevalence of international treaties over domestic law and reinforces the commitment Panama has to fulfil its international obligations.[24] In addition, regarding matters such as foreign representatives and creditors,

21 See, La Ley, art 219.
22 See, La Ley, art 217.
23 See, La Ley, art 221.
24 See, La Ley, art 213.

LA LEY includes a chapter on their rights and duties.[25] Concerning proceedings, matters such as priority, competence and legal resources are methodologically addressed;[26]

- *enforcement and equality regarding distribution of assets*: This is a characteristic that strengthens legal certainty. Nonetheless, *LA LEY* is cautious regarding the distribution of assets in cases of parallel proceedings in order to avoid discrimination towards creditors from another jurisdiction. Throughout the section dedicated to cross-border insolvency, *LA LEY* creates the grounds for cooperation for most circumstances that could occur during the proceedings. However, the distribution of assets tends to give preference to creditors under Panamanian law. This is derived from Panamanian practice. Indeed, it can be considered as inherited from the previous regulation, but it is not necessarily a negative feature. Creditors who start insolvency proceedings in Panama, whether it is the main process or not, require protection of their credit. Foreign claims may affect domestic claims. Certainly, foreign creditors have a right over the assets located in Panama and the law establishes grounds for the payment of foreign claims but Panamanian practice has established an order of payment in which domestic claims have priority;
- *protection of investment*: *LA LEY* grants foreign creditors equal rights with local creditors regarding the filling of proceedings in Panama. A legal representative can request (in a Panamanian court) the commencement of insolvency proceedings against the debtor in Panama. The law gives foreign creditors equal access to insolvency tribunals. In other words, foreign creditor(s) who file insolvency proceedings will receive the same treatment as domestic creditors. It is important to point out that this regulation only applies to assets located in the territory of Panama, not assets in other jurisdictions.

18.31 The Panamanian policy maker has worked on improving the approach to cross-border insolvency. The need for foreign investment can be considered as one of the main motives for this improvement. This new approach to cross-border insolvency creates an environment of legal certainty, something underdeveloped in the previous regulation, solely for the purpose of attracting foreign investment.

25 See, LA LEY-Titulo III-Capitulo II sobre acceso de los Representantes y los Acreedores Extranjeros a los Tribunales de la Republica de Panamá.

26 See, *LA LEY-Titulo III-Capitulo III* sobre Reconocimiento de un Proceso Extranjero y Medidas Otorgables.

B. AVAILABLE INSOLVENCY PROCEDURES

As evidenced in the first section, the new Panamanian regulation on insolvency introduced the reorganization process as an alternative to liquidation. Therefore, reorganization and liquidation can be regarded as the options offered to a business in distress by the new Panamanian law. The main differences between these procedures lay on facts such as: objective, the circumstances that triggered the process and the anticipated effect over the business in distress. **18.32**

(1) Objective

Although both proceedings focus on the payment of creditors, the objective of reorganization is the recovery of the business, which is an objective that differs from liquidation.[27] If a business is viable, the payment to creditors is more probable. On the other hand, liquidation is a process based on the gathering of assets in order to pay as many creditors as possible. **18.33**

(2) Circumstances that trigger the process

Reorganization and liquidation are triggered by the insolvency of a business. However, the circumstances that justify the use of each proceeding are different. On the one hand, the reorganization process can be requested by a debtor or a creditor whenever the debtor is not able to pay debts, or if a situation of insolvency is unavoidable.[28] On the other hand, *liquidacion forzosa*[29] needs to be requested by the creditor and needs to be based on circumstances such as the impossibility of the debtor to honour debts or the impossibility of locating the debtor.[30] **18.34**

(3) Effect over the business in distress

As has been pointed out, reorganization is a process that intends to recover the business in distress. In order to achieve this objective, the law establishes mechanisms such as the protection of assets and the preservation of executory **18.35**

---

27 See, La Ley, art 4 (2) (18).

28 See, La Ley, art 27.

29 *LA LEY* addresses two types of liquidation. On the one hand, the debtor can request liquidation. This is known as *Liquidacion Voluntaria*. On the other hand, if the debtor's behaviour threatens the creditor's stability, the creditor can request the insolvency judge to force the liquidation of the business in distress.

30 See, La Ley, art 80.

contracts (a subject addressed later in section C below). These mechanisms allow the existence of resources to apply the proposed strategy to recover the business. Liquidation, in contrast has a different effect. The insolvency judge will freeze any existent assets and will restrict the business in distress from making new commercial relationships that will demand a payment from the pool of assets.

18.36 In addition to the mentioned proceedings, the law also provides a cross-border insolvency regulation that deals with businesses that have assets and activities in more than one country.

C. TREATMENT OF EXECUTORY CONTRACTS

18.37 The term 'executory contract' refers to a type of contract that at the commencement of a formal insolvency proceeding has not yet been fully performed by both the insolvent debtor and the counterparty. This type of contract is common in the practice of commercial activities. However, if the business were to become insolvent, what would be the fate of these contracts?

18.38 Each legal system has a unique approach in dealing with executory contracts. Some jurisdictions like Panama have traditionally paid little attention to these issues. Indeed, the previous Panamanian insolvency regulation declared executory contracts null the moment the debtor was declared insolvent. Unless the debt was secured, the affected party had to present their claim together with other creditors.

18.39 This 'careless' treatment of executory contracts was due to the approach based on 'creditors' wealth maximization'. As has been pointed out, the Panamanian insolvency regime focused on the immediate seizure and liquidation of assets. However, *LA LEY* has not only changed the Panamanian insolvency regime, but has also had a dramatic impact on the treatment of executory contracts.

(1) Executory contracts and reorganization

18.40 The introduction of reorganization has offered an opportunity to introduce a new statutory treatment of executory contracts, as their preservation is sometimes seen as an essential element to promote the turnaround efforts of an insolvent business. As they are required in order to keep a business operational during the reorganization process, the law prescribes that they cannot be terminated by the creditor.[31]

It is important to point out that the law confers wide discretionary powers to the administrator, as outlined in Article 47 of *LA LEY*. This is due to the fact that the administrator will carry out the reorganization plan. In order to achieve successful reorganization, the law empowers the administrator to deal with matters such as credit records, confidential documents and executory contracts. Regarding executory contracts, the administrator has the authority to encourage the negotiation between the debtor and a creditor in circumstances concerning executory contracts, whether there are changes regarding terms or the termination of the contract. It is a function of the administrator to aid the parties to reach an agreement that will be beneficial for the reorganization process. **18.41**

It can be appreciated that the Panamanian policy maker gives power and freedom to the administrator, in order to aid the insolvency judge. However, this cannot be considered a *carte blanche* for the administrator. *LA LEY* has established means of judicial supervision, such as the administrator's requirement to submit monthly reports to the insolvency judge, and the obligation to report to the insolvency court any irregular behaviour from the debtor.[32] As a personal observation, the obligation to submit reports can be regarded as an **18.42**

31 See, La Ley, art 39.

Artículo 39. *Protección financiera concursal.* Mientras esté vigente la protección financiera concursal:

1. No podrá iniciarse ningún proceso ejecutivo, ejecución de cualquier clase, restitución de bienes o lanzamiento en contra del deudor, salvo lo dispuesto en esta Ley. Para tal efecto, quedarán suspendidos los términos de prescripción.
2. Todos los contratos suscritos por el deudor mantendrán su vigencia y condiciones de pago. En consecuencia, no podrán terminarse anticipadamente en forma unilateral, exigirse anticipadamente su cumplimiento o hacerse efectivas las garantías contratadas, invocando como causal el inicio de un proceso concursal de reorganización.

   Sin embargo, quedará suspendida la exigibilidad de los intereses, legales o convencionales, salvo los correspondientes a los créditos con garantía real. La suspensión durará hasta que la Junta apruebe el Acuerdo de Reorganización, en que podrá establecer condiciones sobre la tasa de interés aplicable o el cobro, total o parcial, en cada caso.
3. El deudor no podrá ser incapacitado o inhabilitado para contratar con las entidades estatales por someterse al proceso concursal de reorganización, ni esta situación podrá invocarse como causal de resolución administrativa del contrato.

   El juez de la causa declarará la nulidad de las actuaciones surtidas en contravención a los numerales 1 y 2 de este artículo, por auto que no admite recurso alguno.

In the underlined paragraph it can be appreciated that the Panamanian legislator establishes the basis on which the reorganization process is carried out. In some circumstances the preservation of certain contractual relationships is essential for the business to operate, therefore achieve the objective of the reorganization process.

32 La Ley, art 47 (4) (6).

initiative of the Panamanian policy maker to create an environment of trust on the Panamanian insolvency process.

(2) *Proteccion Financiera Concursal*

18.43 The new treatment of executory contracts can be appreciated in Article 39, which addresses the '*Proteccion Financiera Concursal*'. This is a measure applicable to business subjected to a reorganization process, which prevents the liquidation of assets and suspends legal proceedings against the debtor among other acts that may affect the reorganization process. Among the benefits of the *proteccion financiera concursal* is the prevention of executory contracts from becoming null. The article forbids unilateral termination of the contract or advanced payments. The rationale of this measure is on the preservation of assets until the trustee or debtor has assessed whether the contract shall be assumed or subjected to renegotiation.

18.44 In regard to executory contracts *LA LEY* is cautious as it restricts the possibility to amend the terms and conditions of ongoing contracts.[33] This can be considered as a measure to protect the assets and determine the reorganization strategy that will be applied. Nonetheless, there is an exception to this restriction, where renegotiation is allowed if it is necessary for a successful reorganization process.[34]

(3) Specific contracts

18.45 *LA LEY* not only addresses the subject of executory contracts in a general manner, but also addresses some specific contracts, such as:

Property lease contracts

18.46 *LA LEY* blocks eviction or termination unless circumstances recognized by the law are present.[35] This type of contractual relationship receives attention because a business cannot operate without some level of infrastructure. Although the law prevents the parties from terminating the contract once the reorganization process has started, *LA LEY* provides protection for the

---

33 See, La Ley, art 39.

34 *LA LEY* has not only introduced provisions regarding executory contracts in order to aid the reorganization process but it additionally provides an alternative for the creditor. The creditor, for example, can request (from the insolvency judge) the termination of the contract due to circumstances such as the nonpayment, and his/her credit will be added to the pool of assets. See, La Ley, arts 43 and 44.

35 In art 45 *LA LEY* protects the landlord by allowing the termination of a tenancy agreement if rent has not been paid. The process of reorganization cannot be used to justify the non-payment. The law allows the restitution of the asset to the landlord.

landlord. For example, if the landlord is not paid during the reorganization process, they can request the termination of the tenancy agreement and the restitution of the asset.[36]

Employment contracts

It must be pointed out that *LA LEY* does not include special rules on employment contracts, a factor that can be attributed to the fact that reorganization intends to recover financial stability. To recover financial stability, the administrator must be free to reduce the workforce in excess. This measure has its legal support in Panamanian Employment Law, which includes the cases in which an employment contract can be terminated. Among these causes there is the circumstance of the employer's insolvency. **18.47**

While allowing insolvent debtor to terminate employment contracts may do little to preserve jobs, this solution is in line with the achievement of the primary goal of the reorganization procedure, i.e., the rescue of the business. Panamanian policy makers were primarily concerned with the need to facilitate reorganization when they drafted *LA LEY*,[37] and the treatment of employment contracts is in line with their policy goals. **18.48**

Contracts with retention of title clauses

This type of contract is addressed by *LA LEY* in both proceedings (reorganization and liquidation). Regarding the reorganization process, *LA LEY* prevents the restitution of goods that are vital for the business to achieve a successful reorganization.[38] The exception lies in the lack of payment. The liquidation process, on the other hand, establishes the immediate restitution of goods to the creditor that is vested with title of property over the goods.[39] **18.49**

Service and utility contracts

Service and utility contracts, like any other contractual relationship necessary to achieve a successful reorganization, will be valid. The rescission of the contract can be requested by the creditor based on circumstances such as nonpayment. **18.50**

36 See, *supra* note 26.
37 See, Codigo de Trabajo de La Republica de Panama. Publicado en la gaceta oficial 17.040 de 18 de febrero de 1972 Articulo 213.
38 See, La Ley, art 45.
39 See, La Ley, art 105.

Contrato de fideicomiso (trust)

18.51 In Panama the *Fideicomiso* is a contract equivalent to the Anglo-American trust. One party named *fideicomitente* transfers assets to another party called *fiduciario*, for the latter to have custody and administer the assets in favour of a *beneficiario*.[40] This type of contract is addressed by la *LA LEY* in the section about liquidation, in which it is stated that the assets under the custody of a *fiduciario* cannot be counted in the pool of assets because these assets cannot be considered as part of the debtor's capital.[41] In the section regarding reorganization, this contract is not mentioned. However, it can be considered that this contract will continue despite of the reorganization process because these assets are not part of the resources at the disposition of a business in distress.

Public procurement contracts

18.52 Although the debtor is under a reorganization process, *LA LEY* does not restrict them from the procurement of contracts with the government.[42] This position on public procurement can be supported by the fact that under reorganization, the business is still operational. Moreover, the procurement of contracts with the government can be part of a strategy for the business reorganization. However, in situations regarding liquidation, the position is different. A business in distress cannot be part of any contractual relationship from the moment liquidation is declared.

Financial contracts

18.53 *LA LEY* addresses the effect of reorganization on financial contracts. Indeed, this type of contract cannot be ignored because it is common in contemporary business. *LA LEY* establishes that financial contracts cannot be terminated on grounds of reorganization. In addition, any interest rate will be suspended until a reorganization plan has been drafted.

(4) Executory contracts and cross-border insolvency

18.54 *LA LEY* serves as a strong foundation for the development of an efficient legal framework for insolvency. Nevertheless, it must be observed that reorganization is a new concept not only in Panama but also across Latin America. As personal observation of the author, the subject of cross-border insolvency

40 See, La Ley, art 126.
41 Ibid.
42 See, La Ley, art 39 (3).

appears focused mainly on liquidation in a cross-border context. The section on this subject has specific provisions concerning cooperation for seizure, liquidation and distribution of assets. This leads to the idea that the parties in executory contracts will look for the termination of the contract in a cross-border context. This is a personal observation. As has been pointed out in this chapter, *LA LEY* is new and more time is needed in order to appreciate its effects better.

D. REFORMS AND CONCLUDING REMARKS

Latin America has been pushed to change conservative and territorial regulation in favour of more flexible and cooperative rules due to the globalization of commerce. Panama, as any other country in the region, has also been obliged to reform its legal framework gradually. However, unlike other Latin American countries, Panama does not have natural resources or industry. Therefore, foreign capital is necessary for the economy to grow. In order to motivate foreign investors, changes such as the reform of the insolvency regime have been made. Indeed, Panama's need of foreign capital can be considered as the key factor for the development of *LA Ley 12 de mayo de 2016*. **18.55**

LA LEY is not a brief addition to the previous regulation; rather it has changed the entire Panamanian approach towards insolvency. Innovations such as the introduction of the reorganization process, the formation of insolvency courts and the revamp of cross-border insolvency regulation are the three most important contributions made through *LA LEY*. Moreover, with the introduction of reorganization, executory contracts have gained importance. The previous regulation established the immediate termination of any contract and the creditor had to present their claim with the rest of the creditors. *LA LEY* sets aside this approach and supports the continuation of executory contracts as a means to aid the reorganization of an insolvent business. **18.56**

As a personal observation of the author, the fact that the new insolvency law has been developed is something positive about Panama. Law is developed in accordance the needs of a society. In the case of Panama, social, economic and political changes have happened recently. For that reason, law has been recently adapted. **18.57**

For academic purposes, Panama's insolvency regime is an interesting case study due to the characteristics of the Panamanian system and the impact of **18.58**

LA LEY. The insolvency regime is new at the time this chapter was written. Thus, a few more years are needed in order to see the effects that *LA LEY* has over the Panamanian commercial legal framework.

19

NATIONAL REPORT FOR THE RUSSIAN FEDERATION

Dmitry Konstantinov

A. INTRODUCTION

In the Soviet era, Russia did not accept any business law concepts; thus, the first insolvency regulation in contemporary Russia was introduced only in 1992. Currently, insolvency in the country is regulated by Insolvency Law 2002[1] and the number of rulings of the Supreme Court of the Russian Federation (*Верховный Суд Российской Федерации*). **19.01**

B. INSOLVENCY PROCEDURES

Russian companies in distress can commence any of the following five insolvency procedures: the preliminary procedure (observation control); three reorganization procedures (external control; economic recovery; and comprehensive agreement); and liquidation. The only procedure available to credit institutions is liquidation. It is also noticeable that in Russian Insolvency Law **19.02**

1 Insolvency (Bankruptcy) Law of Russia 2002 (Федеральный закон от 26.10.2002 № 127-ФЗ «О несостоятельности (банкротстве)).

special rules apply to individuals, credit organizations, developers, pension funds and some other organizations.

19.03 According to official statistics for the period 2010–13[2] the vast majority of insolvencies ended up in liquidation. Economic recovery was applied in approx. 0.2 per cent of insolvencies and external control in less than 2 per cent of all formal insolvency cases recorded for the period.

19.04 Any insolvency proceedings might be initiated by a creditor, the debtor or the authorities. A creditor is entitled to file an insolvency petition if his claim is supported by the court order; however, this condition does not apply when the creditor is a bank, which is only required by the law to make a public announcement about the petition. Tax authorities might also file an insolvency petition without the prior need for a court order if the debt is based on any kind of tax duty.

19.05 The debtor may submit an insolvency petition if future default seems likely. This faculty becomes a legal imposition whenever he realizes that, by paying one creditor, all or substantially all the other creditors will go unpaid. Equally, the debtor is obliged to submit a petition if: the disposal of his assets would prevent any payments to all or substantially all the remaining creditors; the debtor cannot pay its debts as they fall due (cash flow insolvency); his assets exceed the liabilities (balance sheet insolvency); or the authorized body of the debtor has decided to file such a petition. If the court grants the petition, the procedure usually triggered is 'observation control', unless the debtor was already in voluntary liquidation at the time of the filing (in that case, the petition triggers a liquidation procedure).

19.06 Out-of-court proceedings seem to be even rarer than formal restructuring procedures. Russian law does not regulate workouts even though there are some provisions outside insolvency law that facilitate negotiations and debt renegotiation. There is no statistic on the frequency of out-of-court proceedings; therefore it is inappropriate to speculate on their use as it is impossible to provide a realistic estimate.

19.07 Anecdotally, it is possible to observe that Russia does not have a strong tradition in promoting a rescue culture, either within or outside courts. In this

2 Information about Hearing Insolvency Cases by Commercial Courts of Russia in 2010–2013 (*Информация о рассмотрении арбитражными судами Российской Федерации дел о несостоятельности (банкротстве) в 2010–2013*) <http://www.arbitr.ru/_upimg/A0397A1AFD76C6B4E3082E213B98BB5D_11.pdf> last accessed 5 December 2018.

context, it would be surprising to observe massive numbers of out-of-court proceedings. This may not be the case for large corporations, as they are able to hire international experts. These practitioners would conduct the workout or the formal proceeding according to international best practices, at least insofar as possible. At the same time, recourse to specialized assistance for 'zombie'[3] or distressed enterprises is precluded to the majority of businesses, which do not have the money to hire expert turnaround professionals (even if they acknowledged the need for support, which represents a questionable assumption in the Russian tradition).

(1) Observation control

Observation control is the formal procedure that is usually triggered by the filing of an insolvency petition. The procedure might be described as a preliminary one, but in fact observation control is unique and it is not fully comparable to the preliminary proceedings that exist in other European jurisdictions. **19.08**

The first consequence associated with the admission of the petition is the recognition of a 'breathing space' to the company and its administrators. This would allow them to 'observe' its financial performance, in order to choose the most appropriate course of action. The insolvency petition might be filed if the following conditions are met: the debtor has a debt equal or higher than 300,000 rubles, and the debt has been due for more than three months. **19.09**

All contractual claimants shall file a petition within the insolvency case (art 63 of Russian Insolvency Law). Upon appointment, the insolvency practitioner (IP) shall publish all the information about the opening of the procedure (art 68 of Russian Insolvency Law); after the publication creditors have 30 days to file a claim (art 71 of Russian Insolvency Law). **19.10**

The opening of the procedure determines a stay on all judicial actions against the debtor. Equally, individual executions against the debtor shall be postponed and liquidation of shareholders' shares is forbidden. Set-off is equally forbidden if it results in a modification of the creditors' ranking, and no interests or penalties are recognized if the debtor fails to meet its monetary obligations after the filing. **19.11**

3 Zombie companies are indebted businesses that, although generating cash, after covering running and fixed costs (such as wages, rates, rent), only have enough funds to service the interest on their loans, but not the debt itself. As such, they generally depend on banks (creditors) for their continued existence, effectively putting them on never-ending life support.

19.12 The claimants, whose claims are admitted, participate in the first meeting of creditors. The role of the meeting is to determine the next phase of the process: either reorganization (in any of the forms prescribed by the law) or liquidation. The creditors' committee is also responsible for appointing the insolvency practitioner.[4] The claims of these creditors are included in the register, which is updated throughout the next phase of the procedure up until the time the IP announces the distribution of the assets.

19.13 Only monetary claims give creditors the right to participate in the creditors' meeting and therefore influence the decisions taken by the IP. If a creditor has a non-monetary claim, such as a demand of specific performance under a contract, the claim is heard outside the insolvency case, albeit exceptions apply.[5]

(2) Economic recovery

19.14 Economic recovery is the procedure based on plan of recovery which might be offered to the company's creditors by either the debtor's shareholders or any interested parties (if the plan is secured). The procedure allows the owners of the company to finance the debts in accordance with the plan to avoid the liquidation.

19.15 As a legal consequence of the procedure, all monetary claims against the debtor can be filed only within the insolvency case (art 81 of Russian Insolvency Law), the freezing orders are possible only within the insolvency case and penalties based on previous contracts are not applied.

(3) External control (external administration)

19.16 External control is the procedure which replaces the directors of the debtor with an IP. The IP is responsible for recovering the debts of the company.

19.17 The external control might result in the full recovery of the financial conditions of the debtor and/or the cancellation of the insolvency procedure after all debts have been paid. If that outcome is not achievable, the external control procedure may result in either a comprehensive agreement or a liquidation. The automatic stay of monetary obligations of the debtor is also applied.

---

4 Insolvency practitioners in Russia are professionals licensed by the Ministry of Economic Development; at the same time insolvency practitioners are obliged to be members of an association (a self-regulated organization) of insolvency practitioners.

5 Ruling of Commercial Court of Murmansk Area (*Арбитражный суд Мурманской области*) [2015] in case no A42–276/2014.

(4) Comprehensive agreement

Comprehensive agreements might be signed any time by the majority[6] of the creditors (clause 1 of art 150 of Russian Insolvency Law); such an agreement might include restructuring the debts and/or decreasing their amount by means of any solution (provided that it is not against public policy). The comprehensive agreement shall be approved by the court; when it does, the insolvency ends (clause 4 of art 150 of Russian Insolvency Law); such check is limited to formalities. **19.18**

(5) Liquidation

Liquidation is the final procedure. It is followed by the cancellation of the company from Companies' House. The goal of the procedure is to collect assets and monetize their value. If, once the administrative claims have been paid, there is still money left, this will be distributed to the creditors. **19.19**

This procedure seriously affects the autonomy of the contracting parties. **19.20**

The opening of any insolvency liquidation determines that all existing monetary obligations are due to be paid, but penalties and fines determined by the breach of the conditions in the contract are not enforceable. Any enforcement against the property of the debtor by third parties is no longer possible apart from within the insolvency case. All freezing orders are eliminated, and the execution of debtors' contracts is possible, but only in accordance with the insolvency regulation. **19.21**

C. TREATMENT OF EXECUTORY CONTRACTS

Overall, Russian Insolvency Law does not describe the situation when a debtor has not fully performed a non-monetary obligation. The main regulation in the field is article 102 of Russian Insolvency Law, which gives the IP the right to refuse execution of a contract which is not beneficial for the debtor (quite similar to, e.g., German law[7]). This prerogative applies only to certain insolvency procedures, namely external control and liquidation. This right can **19.22**

---

6 Majority of creditors in this case means majority of creditors in accordance with the register of creditors and supported by all security creditors.

7 Dennis Farber, Niels Vermunt and Kathleen van der Linde, eds. Oxford. *Treatment of Contracts in Insolvency.* (2013), 199.

be exercised only in particular circumstances (described below), and within a limited timeframe (three months after the beginning of the procedure).[8]

19.23 The law does not grant similar rights to the IP in charge of the 'observation control' procedure. As 'observation control' is simply a preliminary and temporary procedure, the legislator considered that it would have been inappropriate to grant the right to unilaterally modify the obligations of the parties in performing contracts at that stage.

19.24 There are no limitations for the execution of non-monetary obligations; however, new contracts must be approved by the insolvency practitioner.[9] In fact, execution of contracts, which do not create a monetary duty for the debtor under supervision does not meet any obstacles.

19.25 'Economic recovery' is a rehabilitation procedure. The main consequence of the opening of this procedure is that the contract's performance is frozen or suspended. Upon commencement of the procedure, all monetary claims against the debtor shall be filed only within the insolvency case. The execution of any monetary demands against the debtor is suspended unless the claim was submitted before the filing of the petition and it is based on labour entitlements, damages or compensation. Liquidation of shareholders' shares is forbidden, as well as set-offs that modify creditors' ranking, while no penalties are applied to the debtor if he fails to perform monetary obligations. There are some limitations for entering into new contracts, but execution of the existing contracts is not affected, provided that the contract does not fall in any of the exceptions mentioned in this paragraph, and that the performance of the contract is in the best interest of the company and its reorganization.

19.26 'External control' is a procedure that has the most far-reaching consequences. Once this procedure begins, the directors of the company cease to have any powers and can no longer legally represent the company. All documentation and property of the debtor shall be transferred to the IP. The freezing orders made on behalf of creditors are lifted, and any further freezing orders against the debtor could only be made within the context of the insolvency. Payments to the creditors are possible only through insolvency, and all monetary claims against the debtor shall be filed only as creditors' claims.

19.27 Liquidation is the final and the most frequent insolvency procedure. After the liquidation starts, all obligations of the debtor are due to be paid, any penalties

8 Insolvency Law, art 102.
9 Insolvency Law, art 64.

are not calculated, and any relocation of debtor's assets is possible only in the course of insolvency (frequently at an auction). The forced performance of debtor's obligations is forbidden, all monetary claims against the debtor shall be filed only to the insolvency case, and the freezing orders made on behalf of creditors are revoked.

(1) Rejection of executory contracts by the insolvency practitioner

The IP appointed for external control or liquidation is entitled, in the three months after the procedure starts, to reject any executory contract signed by the debtor if any of the following conditions are met: (1) the contract has not been entirely executed; and (2) it creates obstacles to the potential recovery of the debtor; or (3) is more harmful than beneficial to the debtor than the comparable contracts (art 102 of Russian Insolvency Law). **19.28**

The rule is applied to cases where the debtor's obligations are either monetary or non-monetary.[10] This concept is substantially similar to the liquidator's right to terminate a contract under section 178 (2) of the Insolvency Law of England and Wales and under § 103 of German Insolvency Code. Unlike these foreign jurisdictions, the Russian law prescribes peculiar grounds for terminating an executory contract. **19.29**

Some questions arise in practice – for example, whether a contract might be terminated if it has been partially performed. The law says that a contract cannot be terminated if executed, but it does not cover the situation in which parties have partially performed their obligations. Currently, there is a dearth of clear guidance from the judiciary. **19.30**

Some academics argued that the IP cannot terminate a contact if it has been fully performed by both parties; in all other cases the contract might be stopped.[11] However, the majority of researchers agree that a contract, which has been partially performed, might be cancelled; Brusko B.V. agrees that such a contract might be cancelled, but he mentions that the IPs' right to abandon a partially performed contract is not fair and potentially harmful for business.[12] **19.31**

---

10 Ruling of Arbitration Court of Moscow Circuit (*Постановление Арбитражного суда Московского округа*) [2014] in case no A41–28207/2013.

11 M. Telyakina, 'Commentary to Federal Law on Insolvency (bankruptcy) dated 26 October 2002' (*Телюкина. М. Комментарий к Федеральному закону от 26 октября 2002 «О несостоятельности (банкротстве)*) (2003) 107.

12 B.V.Brusko, 'Defense In Insolvency Law' (*Бруско Б. Защита в банкротном праве*) (2006) 72.

19.32 Little guidance can be drawn from practice either. Generally, performance of the contract is considered to represent an obstacle to the termination of the contract only when the contract has been fully performed by the debtor, as the IP cannot terminate the obligation which has been performed. For example, in a ruling of the Supreme Commercial Court[13] it was held that 'termination of the contract under article 102 of Insolvency Law should target obligation of the debtor in the part which has not been performed by him yet'.

19.33 However, the lower courts do not always follow this reasoning. In a more recent ruling[14] the court did not accept the rejection of an assignment agreement made by an IP since the debtor had partially performed their part of the agreement.

19.34 Court practice suggests that there are some contracts, which cannot be terminated. In fact, it is commonly accepted that an insolvency practitioner cannot cancel unilateral contracts such as bank guarantees.[15] The same rule applies to pledge agreements.[16]

19.35 If the IP starts an action to cancel the contract, the burden of proof for him is quite complicated. Such claims often fail as the liquidator cannot provide the court with sophisticated evidence.[17]

19.36 Insolvency practitioners sometimes terminate most of the debtor's contract to avoid having to engage in any business activities; in the author's opinion, this course of action is far from ideal. The wording of article 102 of Russian Insolvency Law is problematic, because it significantly limits the right of the IP to refuse to perform a contract which is not in the interests of the insolvent estate by not clearly stating under which conditions the contract might be rejected.

---

13 Ruling of Supreme Commercial Court (*Высший Арбитражный Суд Российской Федерации*) [2012] in case no A70–6266/2011.

14 Ruling of the Arbitration Court of Moscow Circuit [2016] in case no A41–78652/2014.

15 Ruling of Supreme Court of Russia [2016] in case no A43–5154/2015.

16 Ruling of Plenary Meeting of the Supreme Commercial Court of the Russian Federation (*Постановление Пленума Высшего Арбитражного Суда Российской Федерации*) [2009] 58, cl 8.

17 Ruling of Supreme Court of Russian Federation [2016] N 305-ЭС16–3756 in case N A40–23990/2015; Ruling of Supreme Court of Russian Federation [2015] N 307-ЭС15–15143 in case N A26–8058/2014.

(2) Performance of the executory contracts

The Russian Insolvency Law does not cover situations when the IP has not refused to perform a contract. Such contracts are governed by non-insolvency regulations. **19.37**

If under the contract, the debtor holds the property which belongs to the creditor, the latter might bring a claim to get the possession of that property; such a claim is to be heard outside the insolvency case. However, it is noticeable that in individual bankruptcy cases, article 213.11 of Russian Insolvency Law states that a vindication claim against the property of the insolvent individual shall be heard within the insolvency procedure. **19.38**

In cases where the creditor has no *actio in rem*, and the IP has not cancelled the contract, there are no legal grounds for the debtor to avoid performance of the contract. But two elements should be taken into consideration. **19.39**

First, if the debtor does not perform its obligation, the creditor only has a remedy in insolvency (i.e., he can only file a claim for the value of the goods/services provided). Under article 393 of Civil Code of Russian Federation (*Гражданский кодекс Российской Федерации*), the debtor shall compensate all losses caused by non-performance or not appropriate performance of the obligation; in the case of insolvency such damages might be brought in the insolvency case. Only claims based on actual damages are considered to be regular claims ranked equally with other unsecured claims (art 137 of Russian Insolvency Law). The creditor may also claim expectation and punitive damages, but they rank lower in priority, as they are paid only after the debtor has fully paid all other unsecured claims. Thus, once the IP has decided not to pay for the services or good provided, the negative consequences of such non-performance are very limited for the insolvent estate. The only risk for the liquidator is that such a claim might be treated as a cost incurred by him and then would rank higher than unsecured creditors' claims. However, the IPs' liability is usually found only with reference to contracts made after the opening of the insolvency proceeding. **19.40**

Secondly, the debtor in liquidation is not expected to continue business activities. If the performance of the contract requires the debtor to carry on with its business activities, the IPs may refuse to perform the contract as they see fit. The Supreme Court of Russia[18] held that the: **19.41**

18 Ruling of Supreme Court of Russian Federation [2016] no 307-ЭС14-8417 in case N° A21-2012/2008.

final goal of liquidation is proportional distribution of debtor's assets to creditors. Even though the insolvency practitioner shall discover and collect debtor's assets to distribute to creditors, the Russian Insolvency Law does not ban the debtor from carrying on trading. Behaving reasonably and in the good faith, the insolvency practitioner should define the best liquidation strategy for the debtor, and, inter alia, validate whether it is reasonable to continue business activities of the debtor.

19.42 In other words, the IP should check before assuming a contract whether the continuation of the business activities, and the performance of the executory contract would result in a higher return for creditors. Only in this case, has the liquidator the discretion to accept and perform an executory contract.

19.43 In our view, these rules actually mean that the IP should terminate the contract whenever it is not profitable. This contradicts the general principles of Russian civil law, such as the obligation to execute rights in good faith (art 1 of Russian Civil Code) and proper execution of the contract (art 309 of Russian Civil Code). As insolvency law deals with cases where the debtor is in general unable to meet all its obligations, it is not surprising that these general principles of civil law are derogated.

19.44 As we mentioned above, Russian Insolvency Law does not contain general rules for executory contracts in insolvency; but there are, of course, some exceptions. Chapter 9, §7 of Russian Insolvency Law creates the special insolvency regime for building contracts. Article 201.5 of Russian Insolvency Law states that the opening of a liquidation procedure against a developer allows its creditors (i.e., those who put down money for the construction of residential apartments) to reject such contracts. However, if the contract has not been rejected, the creditors can demand specific performance from the debtor. Such demands are to be included in the special register of creditors. Such a register includes only demands referring to developer's obligation to build and deliver the residential units, and it sits alongside the register of monetary creditors. The request shall be definitely met if, as part of the reorganization proceeding, it has been decided to continue the debtor's business.

19.45 Executory contracts, as well as any other contracts of the debtor, might be challenged by the IP. The grounds for challenging transactions in Russian Insolvency Law are varied. In particular, a transaction might be challenged if the price is not fair to the debtor (sub. 1, art 61.2 of Russian Insolvency Law), if it was made with intent to harm the creditors (sub. 2, art 61.2 of Russian Insolvency Law) or if it gives any preferences to a creditor. The Russian Insolvency Law allows challenges not only to the validity of the contracts but also to their performance. In other words, if an IP cannot cancel the contract or avoid its performance under any of the conditions mentioned above, he might be entitled to challenge *post factum* the performance with an avoidance action. This circumstance represents an additional argument to amend article 102 of Russian Insolvency Law, to give the IP more discretion to avoid the debtor's contracts.

D. REFORMS

Overall, the treatment of executory contracts in insolvency in Russia has drawn significantly from foreign statutes, primarily German insolvency law. Russian insolvency law was introduced much later than other insolvency statutes from its European neighbour. As a result, the Russian lawmaker at first opted to transplant – with minimum amendments – statutes and provisions already enforced in other jurisdictions. **19.46**

Despite the contradictory and controversial treatment of executory contracts in insolvency, there is little debate on reforms aimed at changing the existing stratified and non-unitary discipline. The reform debate so far is primarily focused on more general aspects, such as proposals to promote a rescue culture in the country and a wider use of rehabilitation procedures. Other issues frequently mentioned in regulatory debates include the limited powers of insolvency practitioners, the characterization of the insolvency regime (either pro-debtor or pro-creditor), and the liability of former management. **19.47**

Officially there is no discussion about reform of insolvency procedures. In 2014 the Russian Government approved the road map of insolvency law reform,[19] which does not propose to amend insolvency procedures. The reform concerns only observation and financial recovery, and how these procedures should be modernized to increase their use and effectiveness. **19.48**

However, there is a discussion among academics. For example, V. Popondopulo argues that only liquidation and comprehensive agreement should be used as formal insolvency procedures, but other less formal procedures such as out-of-court tools should be used.[20] **19.49**

19 Directive of the Government of the Russian Federation (*Распоряжение Правительства Российской Федерации*) [2014] no 1385-р.

20 V. Popondopulo, 'Some Problems of Insolvency Law Reform' (В.Ф. Попондопуло. Некоторые проблемы совершенствования законодательства о банкротстве. Журнал предпринимательского и корпоративного права) (2016) *Journal of Commercial Law* 1.

19.50 To sum up, article 102 of Russian Insolvency Law seriously limits the right of any IP to reject the debtor's contracts. It also creates legal uncertainty in the implementation phase.

19.51 Courts can sanction a rejection of an executory contract only in external control and liquidation procedures, and only when certain conditions are met. The existing burden of proof for IPs is quite hard, as they are required to ascertain and demonstrate to the satisfaction of the court that a contract creates an obstacle for the financial recovery of the debtor.

19.52 As it appears, part of the problem for the implementation of this test in liquidation cases is that the provision was initially applied only to 'external control' cases. And when the lawmaker extended its scope to include liquidation cases, it did not prescribe different, more tailored requirements. The problem might be solved if the liquidator was given the right to reject any contracts that are economically harmful for the debtor.

19.53 Secondly, the law remains silent as to when a contract might be challenged, but cannot be rejected. Following the formal logic of law, the IP should perform such a contract and then challenge the transaction, which would be costly and not effective. It seems that the IP should have the right to postpone performance of such contracts to challenge them.

19.54 Thirdly, the Russian Insolvency Law *de facto* encourages insolvency practitioners to break the contracts that they consider to be against the interests of the debtor, but that they would fail to challenge in front of the court.

E. CONCLUDING REMARKS

19.55 To conclude, it is possible to observe that Russian Insolvency Law generally does not regulate executory contracts in insolvency. It only prohibits the execution of debtor's monetary obligations other than those which have the potential to facilitate and maximize the distribution to the creditors. Nevertheless, insolvency practitioners in external control and liquidation have a limited right to reject a contract which is not profitable for the debtor. Apart some particular exceptions, performance of other executory contracts is regulated by the non-insolvency law.

19.56 If, as a result of the contract, the debtor possesses property of the creditor, the latter has the right to demand this property. If under a contract the debtor shall perform any other obligations and the contract has not been cancelled by the IP, the debtor theoretically can perform such an obligation. However, in liquidation the debtor's business activities are limited by the final goal of the procedure and for the creditor there is no real mechanism to encourage the debtor to perform the obligations.

20

NATIONAL REPORT FOR SLOVENIA

Katja Zdolšek

A. INTRODUCTION

20.01 The general legal framework of insolvency proceedings in Slovenia is laid down by the Financial Operations, Insolvency Proceedings and Compulsory Winding-up Act (hereinafter: Insolvency Act),[1] which regulates the proceedings available to companies in distress and their legal consequences.[2] The Insolvency Act provides two main types of formal proceedings available to companies in a state of insolvency, namely the *corporate bankruptcy proceedings*

1 Financial Operations, Insolvency Proceedings and Compulsory Winding-up Act (Zakon o finančnem poslovanju, postopkih zaradi insolventnosti in prisilnem prenehanju, Uradni list RS, št. 13/14, as amended).

2 The origins of Slovenian insolvency law go back to 1781, when, as a member of the Austro-Hungarian Empire, Slovenia adopted the first 'Austrian' Insolvency Act. The Austro-Hungarian insolvency legislation was also the basis for the insolvency legislation adopted later by the Kingdom of Yugoslavia of which Slovenia was a member state. As a part of the Socialist Federal Republic of Yugoslavia (1943–91), the Slovenian economy underwent several drastic changes ranging from a mixture of planned socialist economy and market socialist economy to socialist self-management regime, all of which were reflected in the insolvency legislation (or lack thereof). As an independent state Slovenia adopted its first insolvency legislation in 1993 in the form of the Compulsory Composition, Bankruptcy and Liquidation Act which aimed to facilitate the country's transition to a free market economy. With the aim of providing a comprehensive legal framework and aligning the rules of insolvency law with the needs of a developed market economy, Slovenia adopted the Financial Operations, Insolvency Proceedings and Compulsory Winding-up Act in 2008, which, subject to several changes, is in force today. (For more information on the history and the origins of Slovenian insolvency law see Jaka Cepec: Ogledalo slovenskega insolvenčnega prava: pravno-empirična analiza učinkovitosti insolvenčnih postopkov nad gospodarskimi družbami v Sloveniji, Ekonomska fakulteta, 2016).

and the *compulsory settlement*. As of 2013, the Insolvency Act also establishes a preventive restructuring procedure for companies in distress that have not yet reached the point of insolvency but are expected to do so within a period of one year. Apart from insolvency proceedings applicable to companies, the Insolvency Act also regulates other insolvency proceedings, namely personal bankruptcy proceedings[3] and bankruptcy of an estate of a deceased person.[4]

The first phase of every formal insolvency proceeding is the preliminary proceeding, the purpose of which is for the competent court to establish whether the statutory conditions to commence the main insolvency proceedings are met. The preliminary proceedings are initiated by a motion filed by an eligible proposing party (hereinafter: eligible petitioner). In order to trigger the main proceedings, the eligible petitioner will have to prove the necessary substantive conditions, notably that the company is in a financial state of insolvency or, in the case of preventive restructuring, that it is likely to become insolvent within the period of one year. Insolvency is defined by the Insolvency Act[5] as a financial situation where the debtor is either: (i) for a longer period of time not able to settle all their liabilities falling due within such a period of time (hereinafter: continuous cash-flow insolvency); or (ii) long-term balance-sheet insolvent (hereinafter: long-term balance sheet insolvency). **20.02**

The burden of proving the company's position of continuous cash-flow insolvency is alleviated by several legal presumptions established by the Insolvency Act. Notably, a company is presumed to be insolvent if the corporate bankruptcy proceedings are initiated at its own motion. **20.03**

Further, a company shall be, unless proven otherwise, considered to be in a position of continuous cash-flow insolvency in the following instances:[6] **20.04**

- If it is more than two months in arrears in meeting one or more liabilities exceeding in total 20 per cent of the amount of its liabilities shown in the last published annual report, or
- if the funds in the company's bank accounts are insufficient for executing an enforcement order by the court or realising an enforcement draft, and such a situation continues without interruption for a period of 60 days or with interruptions for more than 60 days of the last 90-day period, and

3 Insolvency Act, s 5.11.
4 Ibid., s 5.12.
5 Insolvency Act, art 14.
6 Insolvency Act, art 14.

such a situation continues on the date prior to lodging the petition for the initiation of insolvency proceedings, or

- if the company does not have any bank accounts opened with payment services providers in the Republic of Slovenia, and if it has not settled its liabilities under an enforcement order within 60 days of the date when the enforcement order became final.

20.05 An additional set of presumptions applies to companies regarding which compulsory settlement or simplified compulsory settlement proceedings have already been carried out and a final confirmation of the compulsory settlement has already been issued by the court. Such a company shall, unless proven otherwise, be considered as continuously cash-flow insolvent if it has delayed for more than two months with:

- payment of its liabilities set forth in the creditors decision on compulsory settlement or simplified compulsory settlement, confirmed by the court; or
- payment of its liabilities to creditors holding the right to separate satisfaction that arose prior to the commencement of compulsory settlement or simplified compulsory settlement proceedings to creditors with the right to a separate settlement; or
- the scheduled implementation of other financial restructuring measures defined by the financial restructuring plan.

20.06 Further, it is irrefutably presumed that a company is continuously cash-flow insolvent if it is in default, for over two months, with either:

- payment of employees' wages up to the value of the minimum wage; or
- payment of taxes and social contributions which have to be paid on behalf of the employees by the employer.

20.07 It is presumed, unless proven otherwise, that a company is in a state of long-term balance sheet insolvency if:

- the total amount of its liabilities exceeds the value of its assets, or
- the net loss of the current year, together with the transferred losses, amounts to one-half of the registered capital, and such loss cannot be offset by the profit brought forward or reserves.[7]

---

7 Subject to rules laid down by the Companies Act (Zakon o gospodarskih družbah, Uradni list RS, št. 65/09, as amended) regarding the offsetting of losses by profits brought forward and reserves. See: Nina Plavšak, *Uvodna pojasnila k Zakonu o finančnem poslovanju, postopkih zaradi insolventnosti in prisilnem prenehanju (ZFPPIPP)* (GV Založba 2008) 33.

As soon as the company reaches the point of insolvency, it is bound by the principle of equal treatment of creditors.[8] Opening the main insolvency proceedings, however, gives rise to several additional legal consequences for the insolvent debtor and its creditors, depending on the type of the formal procedure triggered. In preliminary proceedings the court shall, on the basis of the evidence provided by the eligible petitioner, decide on whether the company is indeed insolvent and whether other substantive and procedural requirements to open the insolvency proceedings are met. The beginning of the main insolvency proceedings is marked by the publication of the court's decision. **20.08**

B. CORPORATE BANKRUPTCY PROCEEDINGS

Corporate bankruptcy proceedings are formal proceedings carried out in the interest of creditors to receive payment of their claims against an insolvent debtor in accordance with the principle of equal treatment and distribution among creditors. The repayment of creditors is achieved by realising the company's assets which form the bankruptcy estate. **20.09**

The motion to initiate corporate bankruptcy proceedings can be filed by these categories of eligible petitioners:[9] (i) the insolvent company itself (the debtor); (ii) a shareholder of the debtor who is personally liable for the debtor's liabilities; (iii) a creditor who demonstrates the probability of their existing claim against the debtor and the circumstances of the debtor's delay of more than two months in payment of such claim; and (iv) Public Scholarship, Development, Disability and Maintenance Fund of the Republic of Slovenia[10] that demonstrates the probability of a claim of employees against the debtor and the circumstances of the debtor's delay of more than two months in payment of such claims. **20.10**

In order to initiate the corporate bankruptcy proceedings, the eligible petitioner will have to demonstrate that the company is insolvent. Once the court issues the decision starting the main corporate bankruptcy proceedings, an administrator will be appointed to take over the management of the company. **20.11**

8 Insolvency Act, art 24.

9 Ibid., art 231.

10 Public Scholarship, Development, Disability and Maintenance Fund of the Republic of Slovenia (*'Javni jamstveni, invalidski in preživninski sklad Republike Slovenije'*) is a public fund established with the purpose of, inter alia, providing compensation for workers who lose their employment as a consequence of their employer's insolvency.

The creditors will have limited time to register their claims in order to receive payment from the bankruptcy estate. A company in bankruptcy proceedings shall only be allowed to undertake those business risks that are essential for the repayment of the creditors.[11] Once the bankruptcy estate is realised and the creditors are repaid, the company is dissolved.

(1) Compulsory settlement proceedings

20.12 Unlike the bankruptcy proceedings, the compulsory settlement procedure is aimed at restructuring the debt of the insolvent company in a way that does not result in liquidation of the company. The procedure is built on the principle of balancing the interests of the creditors to enforce their claims and the interests of the insolvent debtor to financially restructure and remain a going concern. According to the Insolvency Act,[12] the purpose of the compulsory settlement proceedings is to carry out financial restructuring of the insolvent company while ensuring that: (i) the existing shareholders maintain a share in the company the value of which does not exceed the value of the remaining assets they would have received had the company entered into corporate insolvency proceedings; (ii) the creditors secure better conditions for payment of their claims than they would have in corporate bankruptcy proceedings; and (iii) the company or its viable part remains a going concern.

20.13 The motion to initiate compulsory settlement proceedings can, pursuant to the Insolvency Act,[13] be filed by (i) the debtor and (ii) a shareholder of the debtor who is personally liable for the company's liabilities. Compulsory settlement proceedings regarding a medium or large company may also be initiated by creditors holding financial claims[14] in the aggregate value of at least 20 per cent of all debtor's financial liabilities.[15]

20.14 In order to initiate the compulsory settlement proceedings, the eligible petitioner needs to prove the following substantive requirements:

---

11 Insolvency Act, art 228.

12 Ibid., art 136. The article was recently (2013) amended to reiterate the absolute priority rule in compulsory settlement proceedings.

13 Ibid., art 139.

14 The Insolvency Act distinguishes between financial and non-financial claims (operating claims), whereby financial claims are claims based on loan agreements, bank guarantee agreements, financial leasing agreements or similar agreements concluded with banks or other financial institutions as well as other loan agreements (see Insolvency Act, art 20 (a)).

15 Insolvency Act, art 221 (j).

- the debtor is insolvent;
- the compulsory settlement proposes to the creditors to reduce their ordinary claims or postpone their payment in accordance with the principle of equal treatment and is in compliance with certain other provisions of the Insolvency Act;[16]
- there is at least a 50 per cent chance that the proposed financial restructuring shall result in the debtor's short-term and long-term solvency;
- there is at least a 50 per cent chance that by confirming the proposed compulsory settlement the creditors of the company shall secure better conditions of payment than if the company entered into corporate bankruptcy proceedings.

The first and the last two conditions are confirmed by a certified business evaluator who reviews the proposed restructuring plan and prepares a report. In cases where the conditions are met, the certified business evaluator shall give an unqualified opinion confirming that the substantive requirements for compulsory settlement proceedings are met. **20.15**

If the conditions are fulfilled, the court will issue a decision opening the compulsory settlement proceedings and appoint an administrator[17] to supervise the process. The proposed compulsory settlement is part of the company's financial restructuring plan concerning the restructuring of claims against the company. The final decision on these restructuring measures is therefore made by the creditors' vote on the approval of the proposed compulsory settlement.[18] In cases where the compulsory settlement is approved, the creditors shall only be entitled to receive payment of their claims in accordance with the new conditions established by the compulsory settlement. The compulsory settlement is then confirmed by a decision of the court and becomes enforceable thereafter. Where the creditors do not approve the proposed compulsory settlement, the court shall, subject to few exceptions, immediately issue a decision opening corporate bankruptcy proceedings.[19] **20.16**

16 Ibid., arts 142 and 143.

17 Administrators are private individuals appointed and supervised by the Ministry of Justice. Once they are appointed by the court to act in particular insolvency proceedings they, according to the Insolvency Act, art 97, become a body in insolvency proceedings, executing its competencies stipulated by law, with the aim of protecting and realising the interests of creditors.

18 Insolvency Act, art 200.

19 Ibid., art 208.

(2) Preventive restructuring proceedings

20.17 The 2013 amendment of the Insolvency Act introduced a new type of proceedings available to large, medium and small companies[20] in distress that have not yet reached the point of insolvency but are likely to do so within a period of one year.

20.18 The proceedings of preventive restructuring are conducted for the purpose of allowing a soon-to-be insolvent debtor to carry out financial restructuring based on the agreement with its creditors. The preventive restructuring proceedings can only be initiated by the debtor itself, however, only with consent of a certain proportion of its financial creditors.[21] In order to trigger the restructuring proceedings, the debtor will have to show that it is likely to become insolvent within a period of one year, which shall be presumed, if the debtor obtains consent to initiate the proceedings from creditors holding at least 30 per cent of the value of all financial claims against the company.[22] The court's decision of commencement of the preventive restructuring proceedings has a *standstill* effect on all financial claims contained in the debtor's list of financial claims presented to the court. Such creditors are barred from initiating any enforcement or interim security proceedings with respect to these claims for a period of three–five months, depending on the company's size.[23] Within this time frame, the company will need to reach an agreement with creditors holding at least 75 per cent of the value of unsecured financial claims as well as the same proportion of those holding secured financial claims against the company.[24] Notably, the beginning of the preventive restructuring proceedings shall have no *standstill* or other effects on financial collaterals subject to the Financial Collaterals Act[25,26] as well as any claims secured by such collaterals unless the holder of the collateral agrees with the restructuring.[27]

20.19 The restructuring agreement between the debtor and its creditors is a central part of the preventive restructuring procedure. The relevant section of the Insolvency Act is built on the principle that detailed regulation of neither the

---

20 Like compulsory settlement proceedings, these proceedings may not be conducted regarding certain types of companies (i.e., banks, insurance companies, brokerage companies and certain other financial institutions), see Insolvency Act, art 44 (b) (1) (3).

21 Creditors holding at least 30 per cent of the aggregate value of financial claims listed in the debtor's list of financial claims, certified by an appointed auditor (Insolvency Act, art 44 (h) (2) (3).

22 Insolvency Act, art 44 (d).

23 Ibid., art 44 (m) and (n).

24 Ibid., art 44 (o).

25 Financial Collateral Act: Zakon o finančnih zavarovanjih (Uradni list RS, št. 67/11, as amended).

26 The Act defines financial collaterals as the transfer of a financial instrument, cash or credit claim for the purpose of insurance, as well as a lien on a financial instrument, cash or credit claim.

27 Insolvency Act, art 44 (l) (4).

negotiations between the debtor and its creditors nor the content of the restructuring agreement is necessary.[28] A restructuring agreement is essentially a contract between the company and its creditors and is therefore subject to the general rules of Slovenian contract law, apart from certain specific rules provided by the Insolvency Act. Further, there is no requirement for the court to confirm the content of the restructuring agreement, as it becomes legally binding on the parties when the agreement is executed.[29] The court's decision approving the restructuring agreement is only necessary in cases of so-called *compulsory restructuring*, where the debtor wishes to make the restructuring measures binding also on the financial creditors[30] that have not (voluntarily) entered into the agreement. In such a case, the agreement shall be examined by an auditor and shall only be approved by the court if it is in compliance with the principle of equal treatment.[31] The effects of this court-confirmed restructuring agreement on non-consenting creditors only concern the restructuring measures;[32] any other agreed obligations of creditors towards the debtor have no effect on the non-consenting creditors. Conversely, any rights granted to creditors by the agreement, extend to non-consenting creditors as well.[33]

(3) Out-of-court restructuring

Slovenian insolvency legislation does not specifically regulate out-of-court restructuring agreements. However, pursuant to the general principles of civil law and subject to the provisions of the Code of Obligations companies may negotiate and enter into agreements with their creditors to restructure the claims against the company. Such restructuring agreements may be entered into well before the company reaches insolvency and may be used to restructure financial as well as non-financial claims. **20.20**

Several advantages of out-of-court restructurings have been noted, mostly corresponding to the practical drawbacks of the formal insolvency proceedings that became more apparent during the financial crisis. It has been argued that the courts simply lack the capacity efficiently to process the increased numbers of initiated insolvency proceedings which results in excessive length of these **20.21**

28 Nina Plavšak, *Uvodna pojasnila k Zakonu o finančnem poslovanju, postopkih zaradi insolventnosti in prisilnem prenehanju (ZFPPIPP)* (GV Založba, 2014).

29 Ibid., 18.

30 Only financial claims can be the subject of compulsory restructuring.

31 In addition, the court shall also verify if other conditions for the validity of the agreement have been fulfilled (Insolvency Act, art 44 (o)).

32 Available restructuring measures for unsecured financial claims are the reduction of the value of the claim and postponing the maturity date. Secured financial claims can be subject to postponing the maturity date and changes of the interest rate.

33 See: Nina Plavšak, 'Postopek preventivnega prestrukturiranja' (2014) Pravna Praksa, št 3.

proceedings. Compulsory settlement proceedings have also been considered too expensive and elaborate, which makes them particularly unfit for smaller businesses that make up for over 90 per cent of all companies in Slovenia.[34] Further, it has also been pointed out that out-of-court restructuring may secure better payment conditions for creditors and allow companies to restructure in good time prior to insolvency.[35] These concerns were, to some extent, addressed in 2013 when the legislator introduced a simplified compulsory settlement procedure[36] available to micro companies and sole traders and a preventive restructuring procedure available to small, medium and large companies. Certain companies, however, may still prefer out-of-court restructuring compared to the preventive restructuring regulated by the Insolvency Act as the former allows more flexibility. Notably, formalised preventive restructuring proceedings, like corporate bankruptcy and compulsory settlement, begin with a court decision that is published on the website of the Agency for Public Legal Records (AJPES),[37] while out-of-court restructuring may be conducted without notifying the public.

C. TREATMENT OF EXECUTORY CONTRACTS

(1) The general regime for treatment of claims arising from contracts

20.22 Obligations arising from contracts where one party has not (fully) performed their obligations are subject to the general regime for treatment of claims provided by the Insolvency Act. In cases where the only non-performing party to the contract is the insolvent company, a general regime will apply to the outstanding claim of the performing party towards the non-performing debtor.[38] The Insolvency Act regulates several legal consequences affecting the claims from the moment when the main insolvency proceedings are commenced. With the initiation of the corporate bankruptcy proceedings and the compulsory settlement proceedings: (i) claims of creditors against the insolvent debtor and counterclaims of the insolvent debtor against such creditors are set-off; (ii) non-monetary claims against the debtor are converted to monetary claims; (iii) periodic claims are converted into lump-sum claims; (iv) claims

34 According to the information published by the Agency of the Republic of Slovenia for Public Legal Records and Related Services (AJPES), in 2015 94.4 per cent of all Slovenian companies qualified as *micro* companies.

35 See e.g.: Mag. Mojca Kunšek, 'Z zunajsodnim prestrukturiranjem do večje gospodarske aktivnosti' (2013) Pravna Praksa, št. 38, 22.

36 See: Nina Plavšak, 'Poenostavljena prisilna poravnava' (2013) Pravna praksa, št. 23, 6.

37 https://www.ajpes.si/ [last accessed 11 December 2018].

38 Naturally, insolvency proceedings will have no impact on a situation where the insolvent debtor has fully performed its obligations and holds a claim against the non-performing party to the contract.

expressed in foreign currency are converted to euros. With the beginning of the corporate bankruptcy proceedings, the contractual or statutory interest rate applicable to a claim changes to the statutory interest rate. As of 2004, however, claims arising from financial collateral agreements subject to the Financial Collaterals Act are exempted from some of these aforementioned legal effects.[39]

In order to enforce their claims in corporate bankruptcy proceedings or in compulsory settlement proceedings, creditors need to register their claims within a statutory time limit. With respect to corporate bankruptcy proceedings the Insolvency Act distinguishes between several types of claims and establishes an absolute priority rule. Claims secured with the right to repayment from certain assets (right to separate satisfaction[40]) are repaid from these assets, which do not form a part of the general bankruptcy estate.[41] Once the bankruptcy estate is realised, it is first used to repay the costs of bankruptcy proceedings, which also include the performance of executory contracts.[42] Priority,[43] ordinary and subordinated claims[44] are repaid subsequently from the remaining bankruptcy estate in the aforementioned order, in accordance with the absolute priority rule and the principle of *paritas creditorum*.[45] **20.23**

(2) Treatment of executory contracts by the Insolvency Act

Executory contracts are defined by the Slovenian Insolvency Act as mutually unfulfilled bilateral contracts. A bilateral contract is a contract whereby each party to the contract is liable to perform an obligation as debtor, and is at the same time as creditor entitled to demand the other party to perform their obligation. This definition is in line with the concept of bilateral contracts as established by the Slovenian Code of Obligations.[46] According to the second paragraph of Article 24 Insolvency Act, a mutually unfulfilled bilateral **20.24**

39 According to art 11, the financial collateral agreements and on its basis acquired rights, including the right to enforce the collateral shall remain in force even after the beginning of the bankruptcy or compulsory settlement proceedings. The rights acquired under such contract remain in force also with respect to will remain in force as regards interest that have not yet fallen due (until the date of the initiation of compulsory settlement or bankruptcy proceedings). According to art 12, the agreement on close-out netting contained in a financial collateral agreement remains valid even in the case of compulsory settlement or bankruptcy proceedings.

40 Insolvency Act, art 20 defines secured claims as claims secured by the right to separate satisfaction.

41 See rules on payment of claims from the separate distribution estate in Insolvency Act, art 371.

42 Insolvency Act, art 355 (3) (2).

43 Ibid., art 21 establishes eight categories of priority claims, most of them relating to either claims of employees, taxes and other contributions or restructuring loans backed by a state guarantee.

44 As defined by ibid., art 21.

45 Ibid., art 359 (3).

46 Nina Plavšak, *Uvodna pojasnila k Zakonu o finančnem poslovanju, postopkih zaradi insolventnosti in prisilnem prenehanju (ZFPPIPP)* (GV Založba 2008), 39.

contract (*executory contract*) is a bilateral contract which has been concluded prior to the initiation of insolvency proceedings, and whereby, prior to the initiation of insolvency proceedings: (i) neither the insolvent debtor nor the other party to the contract have performed their obligation on the basis of the contract, or (ii) neither of the parties has fully performed such obligations.

20.25 The Insolvency Act contains certain special provisions concerning the treatment of executory contracts. These provisions form a special regime and exempt the executory contracts from the general treatment of claims in insolvency proceedings.

20.26 Disapplication of the general rules of corporate bankruptcy proceedings to executory contracts leads to two important consequences:

- non-monetary claims from executory contracts shall not be converted into monetary claims;[47]
- claims and counterclaims of parties to the contract shall not be set-off *ex lege*.[48]

20.27 Further, the creditors' claims against the debtor arising from the executory contract are not affected by the general rules on payment of creditors' claims from the bankruptcy estate.[49] The creditor maintains its right to demand full performance of obligations from the executory contract as they fall due. Creditors' claims arising from executory contracts do not need to be registered and are treated in the same way as claims that originate from the period after the initiation of bankruptcy proceedings, namely the costs of the proceedings. The creditor is only obliged to notify the bankruptcy administrator of the existence of their claim arising from an executory contract.[50] Providing that the bankruptcy estate is sufficiently large, these claims will be repaid in full, based on the rules on payment of the costs of bankruptcy proceedings.[51]

20.28 The Insolvency Act establishes three types of legal consequences that, subject to certain conditions, affect the executory contracts at the beginning of corporate bankruptcy proceedings: (i) the creditor obtains the right to deny their performance of the contractual obligation; (ii) the creditor loses their

---

47 As otherwise prescribed by Insolvency Act, art 253.

48 As otherwise prescribed by ibid., art 261.

49 Second paragraph of Insolvency Act, art 265.

50 The creditor is obliged to notify the administrator about the existence of such a claim within three months from the initiation of corporate bankruptcy proceedings and is liable for any damages and costs if he/she fails to do so (Insolvency Act, art 265 (4)).

51 Ibid., art 354.

right to demand the fulfilment of the contract when the insolvent debtor delays its performance; (iii) the debtor obtains the right to withdraw from the contract when such withdrawal is beneficial for the repayment of its creditors.

In contractual relationships where the debtor's creditor is obliged to first perform its obligation under the executory contract, a provision of the Insolvency Act[52] awards such a creditor the right to withhold its performance until such time as the debtor either fulfils its part of the obligation or provides appropriate collateral.[53] **20.29**

According to the general provisions of contract law, if a party to a bilateral contract fails to perform its obligations, the other party may either demand the performance or withdraw from the contract.[54] The Insolvency Act rescinds such right of a creditor to demand performance from the debtor in a situation where (cumulatively): (i) the performance of obligations by a specific deadline is an essential component of the contract; (ii) the deadline for the performance expires after the initiation of the corporate bankruptcy proceedings against the debtor; and (iii) the debtor fails to perform the obligations by the stipulated deadline. In such cases, the contract shall be terminated *ex lege* and the creditor shall not have the right to insist on the debtor's performance.[55] **20.30**

According to Article 267 of the Insolvency Act,[56] with the beginning of the corporate bankruptcy proceedings, the insolvent debtor gains an additional statutory right to withdraw from an executory contract. In order for the withdrawal to be effective, it needs to be approved by the court and delivered to the counterparty within three months from the beginning of the corporate bankruptcy proceedings.[57] **20.31**

The main purpose of the corporate bankruptcy proceedings is to realise the bankruptcy estate in order to repay the creditors. The right of the debtor to withdraw from the executory contract based on this specific provision of the Insolvency Act therefore has to be interpreted as one of the means to achieve this purpose. It follows that the courts shall approve the debtor's exercise of the right to withdraw from the executory contract if such withdrawal secures **20.32**

---

52 Ibid., art 266 (1).

53 This provision is equivalent to the general provision of the Code of Obligations (art 102) concerning situations where performance of obligations by one party becomes uncertain due to financial or other serious difficulties.

54 Code of Obligations, art 103.

55 Insolvency Act, art 266, para 2.

56 Ibid., art 267, para 1.

57 Ibid., para 2.

more favourable conditions for the payment of the creditors.[58] For example, this will generally be the case when the debtor's claim to the counterparty is non-monetary and the debtor would otherwise first have to pay a sum of money from the bankruptcy estate in exchange for the goods which would then have to be sold and their value distributed to the creditors.

20.33 In cases where the debtor's claim arising from the contract towards the counterparty is monetary, an assessment of whether the debtor's withdrawal from the contract is beneficial for the payment of the creditors needs to take into account the extent to which both parties have already performed their obligations under the contract. If the parties have predominantly performed their obligations, the debtor's withdrawal from the contract is unlikely to be to the benefit of its creditors. As a consequence of withdrawal, each party would have to return whatever they have received on the basis of the terminated contract, meaning that a monetary payment from the bankruptcy estate would have to be made to the other party to the contract. In cases where the debtor is under the contract obliged to sell certain goods to the counterparty, and the goods are already in the debtor's possession, withdrawal from the contract is unlikely to be to the benefit of the creditors as the goods would in any event need to be sold as a part of the bankruptcy estate. It follows that in cases where the obligation of the counterparty towards the insolvent debtor is monetary, debtor's withdrawal from the executory contract is likely to be approved by the court in two instances: (i) when the debtor's obligation under the contract is to provide a certain service performance of which would go beyond the completion of necessary operations as defined by the Insolvency Act;[59] and (ii) when the debtor's obligation under the contract is the provision of goods which the debtor does not yet possess and cannot manufacture within the scope of completion of necessary operations.[60]

20.34 The courts have so far been firm in holding that the bankruptcy administrator needs to clearly demonstrate the benefits of terminating an executory agreement under Article 267 of the Insolvency Act in order to obtain the court's approval.[61]

20.35 As a consequence of the debtor's withdrawal from the executory contract, the legal basis for the fulfilment of contractual obligations ceases to exist and,

---

58 Ibid., art 267 (4).

59 Ibid., art 316.

60 Nina Plavšak, 'Razmerje med ločitveno in izločitveno pravico pri gradnji in prodaji stanovanj', (Pravni Letopis, 2011) 97.

61 See, e.g., the decisions of the High court in Ljubljana: VSL sklep Cst 52/2015, dated 17.2.2015 and VSL sklep Cst 78/2016, dated 9.2.2016.

according to the general provisions the Code of Obligations, the parties are obliged to return whatever they have already received on the basis of the terminated contract.[62] These mutual claims for the return of what has been given as a partial performance of the contract shall be set-off according to the general rules on the setting-off of claims at the initiation of bankruptcy proceedings.[63] If the creditors claim for the return of partial performance is not (entirely) set-off, they will need to register the remaining claim in bankruptcy proceedings and this remaining claim shall be paid from the bankruptcy estate in accordance with the general rules and on the basis of the principle of equal treatment of creditors.

In compulsory settlement proceedings, executory contracts are treated in a similar manner. According to a provision of the Insolvency Act,[64] executory contracts are not affected by the consequences that the initiation of compulsory settlement proceedings generally has on creditors' claims.[65] The claims arising from executory contracts are therefore at the beginning of the compulsory settlement proceedings (i) not converted into monetary claims and (ii) are not set-off against each other. Further, the court-confirmed compulsory settlement and the restructuring measures set out therein have no effect on the claims arising from executory contracts. Consequently, after the compulsory settlement is confirmed by the court, the party to the executory contract may still claim from the debtor performance of its obligations in full. **20.36**

In the same way as in corporate bankruptcy proceedings, in compulsory settlement both parties to the executory contract maintain their rights to withdraw from the contract based on the general rules contract law and the Code of Obligations. According to the provisions of the Insolvency Act,[66] with the beginning of the compulsory settlement proceedings, the insolvent debtor obtains an additional statutory right to withdraw from an executory contract. In order for the withdrawal to be effective, it needs to be approved by the court and delivered to the counterparty within a month from the beginning of the compulsory settlement proceedings. **20.37**

The exercise of such a withdrawal right in the context of compulsory settlement proceedings constitutes one of the restructuring measures. The approval of the court shall only be granted if such withdrawal is necessary for implementing the financial restructuring according to the proposed **20.38**

---

62 Code of Obligations, art 190.
63 See Insolvency Act, arts 268, para 2 and 3 and 261.
64 Ibid., art 165 (1).
65 See ibid., arts 161–164.
66 Ibid., art 165, para 2.

financial restructuring plan. The exercise of the withdrawal right must therefore be included in the proposed financial restructuring plan together with the description of its effects on the implementation of the financial restructuring.[67]

20.39 In a similar manner to corporate bankruptcy proceedings, after the withdrawal from the contract, the mutual claims for the return of what has been given as partial performance of the contract shall be set-off according to the general rules on the setting-off claims at the initiation of compulsory settlement proceedings.[68] If the creditors claim for the return of partial performance does not (entirely) cease to exist due to the setting-off, the outstanding claim is not affected by the restructuring measures established by the confirmed compulsory settlement.[69]

(3) Enforceability of contractual clauses agreed in solvent times

20.40 Unless the debtor exercises its right to withdraw from the contract on the basis of Article 267 of the Insolvency Act, an executory contract remains valid and the debtor is obliged to perform its obligations in line with the provisions of the contract. The other party maintains its right to demand the performance of the contract in accordance with the contractual clauses agreed therein. In particular with respect to termination rights, the courts have noted that Article 267 of the Insolvency Act establishes an additional right for the insolvent debtor to withdraw from an executory contract due to insolvency proceedings without prejudice to any other statutory or contractual grounds to terminate the contract.[70] After the initiation of the insolvency proceedings, both parties to the executory contract maintain their rights to withdraw from the contract based on the rules of contract law as well as any right to terminate the contract specifically agreed between the parties.

20.41 When the contract is terminated by the debtor pursuant to Article 267 of the Insolvency Act or due to debtor's non-performance of its obligations by the stipulated deadline pursuant to Article 266 of the Insolvency Act, the other party to the contract shall maintain its right to claim damages and/or a

67 Nina Plavšak, *Uvodna pojasnila k Zakonu o finančnem poslovanju, postopkih zaradi insolventnosti in prisilnem prenehanju (ZFPPIPP)* (GV Založba 2008) 141.

68 See Insolvency Act, art 167, para 2 and 3 in connection with Insolvency Act, art 164.

69 Ibid., art 167, para 4.

70 See, e.g., decision of the High Court in Maribor VSM Sklep I Cpg 224/2017, dated 9.11.2017.

contractual penalty for the termination of the contract.[71] Although such claims for damages or penalty originate from the period after the initiation of corporate bankruptcy proceedings, according to the specific provision of the Insolvency Act, they need to be registered within one month. These claims are paid from the bankruptcy estate according to the general rules applicable to ordinary claims based on the principle of equal treatment of creditors. In case of compulsory settlement proceedings, claims for damages and/or contractual penalty arising from the termination of the contract by the debtor pursuant to Article 167 of the Insolvency Act are affected by the restructuring measures established by the confirmed compulsory settlement.

D. MAJOR REFORMS

The Insolvency Act was adopted in 2007 and became effective on October 1, 2008. It replaced two pieces of legislation formerly regulating financial operations of businesses and insolvency proceedings, the Compulsory Composition, Bankruptcy and Liquidation Act[72] adopted in 1993 and the Financial Transactions of Enterprises Act[73] of 1999. The Insolvency Act was adopted in the period when, after having gained its independence in 1991, the Slovenian market was still adapting to the new conditions of a free market economy. The new Insolvency Act was drafted with the aim of providing a comprehensive legal framework and aligning the rules of insolvency law with the needs of a developed market economy. The UNICITRAL's Legislative Guide on Insolvency Law as well as the IMF's recommendations for orderly and effective insolvency procedures[74] were taken into consideration when preparing the new legislation.[75] **20.42**

Since 2008 seven amending Acts have been adopted to introduce changes to the Insolvency Act. Despite these frequent amendments, the core principles governing the Insolvency Act, namely: (i) the principle of equal treatment of creditors; (ii) the principle of ensuring the best conditions for payment of **20.43**

71 See also: Nina Plavšak, 'Razmerje med ločitveno in izločitveno pravico pri gradnji in prodaji stanovanj' (2011) Pravni Letopis , 97.

72 Compulsory Composition, Bankruptcy and Liquidation Act: Zakon o prisilni poravnavi, stečaju in likvidaciji, Uradni list RS, št. 67/93, as amended.

73 Financial Transactions of Enterprises Act: Zakon o finančnem poslovanju podjetij, Uradni list RS, št. 54/99, as amended.

74 Orderly and Effective Insolvency Procedures Key Issues Legal Department International Monetary Fund 1999.

75 See: Nina Plavšak, *Uvodna pojasnila k Zakonu o finančnem poslovanju, postopkih zaradi insolventnosti in prisilnem prenehanju (ZFPPIPP)*, (GV Založba 2008) 20.

creditors; and (iii) the principle of promptness of insolvency proceedings, have been maintained throughout the reforms.

20.44 The first major reform was introduced in 2010,[76] encouraged by the changes in the economic conditions in the market. In preparation for the reform, the Ministry of Justice launched a large expert consultation and received input from the courts, the Chamber of Administrators of Slovenia, individual administrators, the Tax Administration of the Republic of Slovenia, the Chamber of Commerce and Industry of Slovenia, the Chamber of Craft and Small Business of Slovenia, the Bank Association, individual banks and other financial institutions as well as private individuals. The reform featured a number of procedural and technical solutions, aimed at improving the efficiency of insolvency proceedings, and good practice of the administrators. With the purpose of enabling more efficient restructurings of otherwise viable businesses in distress, the reform introduced, in the context of compulsory settlement proceedings, the option of share capital increase through contributions.[77]

20.45 Major reforms continued in 2013 when, as a result of two years of preparation and expert consultation,[78] the fifth amendment of the Insolvency Act was passed. Informed also by the 2012 findings of the *Vienna Initiative*,[79] the reform continued to provide solutions aimed at greater efficiency of restructuring and preserving viable parts of the businesses. Notably, the amendment introduced a simplified compulsory settlement procedure[80] available to micro companies,[81] requiring faster and less expensive means of restructuring.

---

76 Act Amending the Financial Operations, Insolvency Proceedings and Compulsory Dissolution Act (ZFP-PIPP – C): Zakon o spremembi Zakona o finančnem poslovanju, postopkih zaradi insolventnosti in prisilnem prenehanju, Uradni list 126/07.

77 See Insolvency Act, art 199 (a).

78 Input was received from: the Chamber of Commerce and Industry of Slovenia, the Chamber of Craft and Small Business of Slovenia, the Bank Association, the Slovenian Chamber of Commerce, the Supreme Court of the Republic of Slovenia, the State's Attorney of the Republic of Slovenia, the Chamber of Administrators of Slovenia, the Association of Creditors in bankruptcy proceedings, the Bank of Slovenia, the Slovenian Bar Association, the Managers' Association of Slovenia, High Court in Celje, the Administrative Court of the Republic of Slovenia, the Slovenian Association of Judges, the Commission for the Prevention of Corruption, and Holding Slovenske elektrarne d.o.o (a state-owned power generation company).

79 European Banking Coordination 'Vienna' Initiative, Working Group on NPLs in Central, Eastern and South-Eastern Europe, March 2012.

80 Insolvency Act, art 221 (a)–(g).

81 Micro companies represent the majority of Slovenian economy. They are defined by Companies Act as companies which meet two of the below criteria:

- the average number of employees in the financial year does not exceed ten,
- net sales revenue does not exceed EUR 700 000, and
- the value of assets does not exceed EUR 350 000.

Further, several measures strengthening the position of creditors in compulsory settlement proceedings were introduced, including the possibility to initiate a debt-to equity swap and take over the management of the company's business.[82]

Less than six months later, the sixth amendment Act was passed, introducing several measures facilitating more effective restructuring of medium and large companies. The preparation of the amendments included a consultation with the IMF representatives who had provided comments on the outline of the reform. Most notably, the amendment introduced the preventing restructuring procedure, described in section B.2 above, and further strengthened the position of creditors in compulsory settlement proceedings by reiterating the absolute priority rule and enabling financial creditors to initiate compulsory settlement proceedings against a large or medium company.[83] **20.46**

The latest amendment of the Insolvency Act was passed in 2016 and reinstated that the simplified compulsory settlement proceedings are only available to micro companies[84] and extended the right of creditors to initiate compulsory settlement proceedings even against small companies. **20.47**

Despite the numerous and frequent reforms of the Slovenian insolvency legislation, treatment of executory contracts has remained relatively uncontroversial. Since the adoption of the Insolvency Act, only one substantial amendment has so far been made concerning the treatment of executory contracts in corporate bankruptcy proceedings. The 2013 reform concerned the situation when the insolvent debtor terminates the contract based on Article 267 of the Insolvency Act and the mutual claims between the parties to return whatever they have already received on the basis of the terminated contract are set-off. Prior to the 2013 amendment the remaining claims against the debtor that did not cease to exist due to the setting-off were not required to be registered and were treated in the same way as the costs of the proceedings. The current solution makes such claims, as well as claims remaining after the termination of the contract based on the general rules of contract law, subject to the general regime of treatment of claims in corporate **20.48**

82 Insolvency Act, art 199 (b) and (c); Some of these amendments were advocated by the Bank Association (Združenje bank Slovenije).

83 See also: Marko Zaman, 'Pravne možnosti upnikov v postopku prisilne poravnave nad srednjo in veliko družbo' (2014) Podjetje in delo, št. 6–7, 976 See also: Nina Plavšak, 'Novosti ureditve stečajnega postopka v noveli ZFPPIPP-F' (2014) Pravna Praksa, št. 2, 10 and Nina Plavšak, 'Preostale novosti ureditve postopka prisilne poravnave v noveli ZFPPIPP-F' (2013) Pravna Praksa, št. 49–50, 8.

84 In the 2013 amendment, the option of simplified compulsory settlement proceedings was extended also to small companies at the initiative of the Chamber of Commerce and Industry of Slovenia. The 2016 amendment rescinded this possibility to prevent financial holding companies from misusing it.

bankruptcy proceedings.[85] It could be argued that the described amendment was to some extent initiated by the Chamber of Administrators of Slovenia[86] who, during the 2013 reform, asserted that the previous regime had favoured certain creditors and had created uncertainty for others as to how much would be left in the bankruptcy estate after the fulfilment or termination of the executory contracts.[87] In the legislative proposal by the Ministry of Justice, the change in question was explained as necessary to align the provision with the principle of equal treatment of creditors.

E. CONCLUDING REMARKS

20.49 It seems that the numerous amendments of the Slovenian insolvency legislation can be, to a large extent, attributed to the fact that Slovenia had entered the financial crisis with a new Insolvency Act that had only come into force in October 2008. Since then, most efforts have been put into improving the efficiency of the insolvency proceedings and providing businesses in distress with the means of financial restructuring. A large and diverse number of contributors participated in the reforms through working groups and public consultations. It can be observed that when preparing the amendments, the Ministry of Justice first turned to the courts for feedback. Other influential entities seem to be the Chamber of Commerce and Industry of Slovenia and the Chamber of Craft and Small Business of Slovenia that have, inter alia, advocated efficient means of restructuring for companies and maintaining viable parts of businesses to the benefit of the economy. The interests of creditors are most strongly represented by the Banks Association of Slovenia that has initiated several notable changes in the compulsory settlement procedure. Another entity that seems to be gaining importance is the Chamber of Administrators[88] which has so far provided a variety of initiatives, ranging from promoting equal treatment of creditors in the context of executory contracts to forwarding the interest of the employees in the 2013 reform.

---

85 See Insolvency Act, art 268, paras 4 and 7.

86 Zbornica Upraviteljev Slovenije.

87 See Proposal of the Act Amending the Financial Operations, Insolvency Proceedings and Compulsory Winding-up Act : Predlog Zakona o spremembah in dopolnitvah Zakona o finančnem poslovanju, postopkih zaradi insolventnosti in prisilnem prenehanju – 2012–2030–0053–nujni postopek – novo gradivo št. 1, available at: http://www.insolvinfo.si/download/razno/ZFPPIPP-16.4..pdf [last accessed 11 December 2018].

88 Established as a part of the 2010 amendment of the Insolvency Act to promote professionalism and good practices of the administrators in insolvency proceedings.

It can be concluded that the main drivers of the recent reforms of Slovenian insolvency legislation seem to be the efforts to improve the effectiveness and efficiency of insolvency proceedings to the benefit of the economy. The legislator has displayed a clear preference for financial restructuring and preservation of viable businesses over dissolving the companies in bankruptcy proceedings. The general public has devoted a lot of attention to the length and the costs of Slovenian insolvency proceedings. According to the Doing Business Report,[89] however, the length of insolvency proceedings in Slovenia is within the average and the proceedings are one of the least expensive. Interestingly, treatment of executory contracts has so far remained relatively uncontroversial. This might also be due to the numerous prominent reforms concerning financial restructuring measures and procedures that have captured most of the attention of the interested parties. **20.50**

89 Doing Business 2014, Understanding Regulations for Small and Medium-Size Enterprises, http://www.doingbusiness.org/reports/global-reports/doing-business-2014 [last accessed 11 December 2018].

21

NATIONAL REPORT FOR SPAIN

José Carles and Carlos Cuesta

A. INTRODUCTION

(1) Available insolvency procedures in Spain

21.01 Under the Spanish insolvency regime, the '*concurso de acreedores*' is, after 2003, the only formal insolvency procedure. Nevertheless, since 2009, Spanish Insolvency Law has undergone several reforms to introduce new hybrid, pre-insolvency procedures: (i) the negotiation proceedings (commonly referred to as '*preconcurso*') in order to reach a refinancing agreement and/or early arrangement with creditors; (ii) the Court-approval of refinancing agreements ('*homologación*'); and (iii) the out-of-Court payment arrangements with creditors ('*acuerdo extrajudicial de pagos*'). All of them are, indeed, considered collective proceedings by the Spanish law and, accordingly, they have been included in the list of insolvency proceedings that shall be automatically recognized across Europe under the European Insolvency Regulation on insolvency proceedings (recast).[1]

In 2016, 3,872 Spanish companies underwent a formal insolvency proceeding.[2] Out of these, the vast majority (75.16 per cent) were small businesses with a turnover of less than one million Euro, 11.62 per cent had a revenue of one to two million Euro, 8.06 per cent were among two to five million Euro and only 5.16 per cent exceeded the five million Euro turnover. **21.02**

(2) Requirements for insolvency procedures in Spain and rules for petition

In accordance with article 2 of the Act 22/2003, dated 9 July 2003, on Insolvency (*'Ley 22/2003, de 9 de julio, Concursal'*, hereinafter 'the Spanish Insolvency Act'), the objective premise to open any of these proceedings is the occurrence of an 'event of insolvency'. This is defined by the law as the situation in which the debtor is no longer able to duly fulfil their overdue payment obligations ('current insolvency'). In the event of current insolvency, the insolvent business has the legal obligation to file an insolvency petition (or to commence any of the the hybrid alternatives) within two months from the date it is aware, or should have been aware, of its insolvency situation (Spanish Insolvency Act, article 5). **21.03**

Companies undergoing imminent as opposed to current insolvency – that is to say, those companies that foresee they will not duly fulfil their obligations in the short term – may file for these proceedings but do not have the legal obligation to do so. **21.04**

If the debtor voluntarily petitions for a formal insolvency proceeding, the general rule is that the directors temporarily retain the rights to manage and dispose of the aggregate assets of the company, subject to the supervision of the Court-appointed insolvency practitioner (IP) (Spanish Insolvency Act, article 40.1). **21.05**

When the petition is submitted by a creditor, the applicant needs to prove that a previous enforcement proceeding was unsuccessful (totally or partially) because the Court could not seize enough assets to repay the creditor. **21.06**

1 Regulation (EU) 2015/848 of the European Parliament and of the Council on insolvency proceedings (recast) [2015] L 141, annex A.

2 Data for companies (insolvent individuals with business activity have been excluded). INE, 'Estadística del Procedimiento Concursal (EPC). Cuarto trimestre de 2016 y Año 2016. Datos provisionales' (Notas de Prensa, 7 February 2017).

Otherwise, the creditor has to prove to the satisfaction of the court that one of the 'external facts' that establish a rebuttable presumption of 'insolvency' has occurred (Spanish Insolvency Act, article 2.4). These 'external facts' include: (i) a general default in the company's payment obligations; (ii) pending seizures with an overall effect on the company's assets; (iii) unlawful removal of hasty or ruinous liquidation of its assets; or (iv) a generalized breach of the payment obligations against the Social Security and/or tax authorities or against the business' labour force. Besides, the creditor shall file the necessary evidence of his claim.[3]

21.07 When a creditor files for the *concurso de acreedores* of an insolvent business, the general rule is that the Court-appointed IP replaces the company's directors in the management and disposal of the aggregate assets of the company (Spanish Insolvency Act, article 40.2). This has important consequences regarding the director's liability, as in these cases it is clear that the insolvent company did not comply with their petition obligation within two months from the date they should have been aware of their insolvency situation.[4]

21.08 Creditors can only file a petition to commence a formal procedure. They cannot file for any of the hybrid pre-insolvency procedures. Usually, the petition for a *concurso de acreedores* is filed by the insolvent business. In 2016, creditors only filed 7 per cent of the insolvency formal procedure petitions.[5]

(3) Out-of-court workouts and hybrid pre-insolvency proceedings in Spain

21.09 Before the 2009 reform,[6] there were no statutory alternatives in Spain to the formal *concurso de acreedores*. Companies experiencing a current insolvency situation that tried to avoid the opening of a formal insolvency proceeding by direct negotiations with their creditors faced the risk that any of their creditors could file an insolvency petition. Additionally, their directors could incur personal liability for not filing voluntarily for insolvency in due time (unless a waiver was formally signed by the creditors).

---

3 Case law has repeatedly declared that creditors are entitled to petition for insolvency of the insolvent debtor even in the event the insolvent company denies the claims (contingent claims). AAP Madrid, s 28, 8 May 2008 (Air Madrid Líneas Aéreas, S.A. insolvency proceedings) and AAP Madrid, s 28, 28 June 2010 (Nozar, S.A. insolvency proceedings) are clear at this respect.

4 The insolvency proceedings are presumed to be tortious, among other causes, when the debtor has 'breached the duty to petition for a declaration opening the insolvency proceedings' (Spanish Insolvency Act, art 165.1.1º). Official translation from Spanish to English from the Ministry for Justice, *Traducciones del derecho español: Act 22/2003, dated 9th July, on Insolvency* (Boletín Oficial del Estado, 2015).

5 Above note 2.

6 Royal Decree-Law 3/2009, dated 27 March 2009, on urgent tax, financial and insolvency measures considering the evolution of the economic situation.

Despite the risks associated with out-of-Court workouts, negotiations were common in Spain due to the social stigma attached to *concurso de acreedores* (over 90 per cent of the companies which filed for formal insolvency proceedings are finally liquidated[7]). In fact, the explanatory memorandum to the Spanish Insolvency Act (Section I) states that: 21.10

> Hoy por hoy, la mayor parte de los concursos que se tramitan concluyen con la liquidación de la empresa, el cese de actividades y el despido de los trabajadores. Realidad que tensiona el sistema legal, al que se acude menos y, en su caso, más tarde que en otros países, habida cuenta del estigma que pesa todavía sobre el concurso, como consecuencia de una concepción histórica y cultural, y sin que haya conseguido aumentar el grado de satisfacción de los acreedores ordinarios.[8]

Barcelona's Commercial Court number 9 has defined this stigma in the following terms:[9] 21.11

> (...) the stigma related to insolvency that, unfortunately, prevails in our country versus other neighbour countries, in which the insolvency proceedings culture is far more developed. The wrong belief that exists in Spain or such a negative perception of the insolvency proceedings causes this companies' reticence to filing their insolvency proceedings on time, reaching an extreme situation, without cash, having destroyed the goodwill, etc. and making their recovery impossible in most cases.

One of the main concerns of the Spanish legislator in the past years has been, indeed, to encourage risk-free negotiations by means of the new hybrid pre-insolvency proceedings, to avoid the perverse effects that this social stigma of formal insolvency procedures causes to the business.[10] 21.12

---

7 Esteban van Heemen Almanzor, *Estadistica Concursal. El concurso de acreedores en cifras. Anuario 2016* (Colegio de Registradores de la Propiedad, Bienes Muebles y Mercantiles de España, 2016) 40. The percentage of Spanish companies whose insolvency proceeding finished in liquidation amounted to 92.8 per cent in 2009, 88.6 per cent in 2010, 90.2 per cent in 2011, 93.1 per cent in 2012, 92.1 per cent in 2013, 90 per cent in 2014, 89.4 per cent in 2015 and 91.4 per cent in 2016.

8
> Nowadays, the vast majority of insolvency proceedings finish with the company being wound up, the activity ceasing and the labour force being dismissed. This reality is in tension with the legal system itself, less used than in other countries and, when used, later, taking into account the stigma that there still is on the concurso due to a historic and cultural understanding and to the satisfaction of ordinary debtors not being achieved.

This is the translation in English of the Spanish text made by the authors of the present chapter.

9 *Bank of America Merril Lynch International Limited v Hotel Diagonal 205*, S.A. [2015] AJM B 6/2015, 20 January 2015 (CENDOJ 08019470092015200005). This is the translation in English of the Spanish text made by the authors of the present chapter.

10 José Carles Delgado, 'Avances legislativos en las soluciones extrajudiciales al concurso de acreedores' in *Las medidas preventivas de conflictos jurídicos en contextos económicos inestables* (J. Bosch 2014).

(4) General rule for contracts in which only one party has not fully performed its obligations

21.13 At the time the opening of the insolvency proceeding is declared by the Commercial Court, if one party has not fully performed its obligations under a contract, the Spanish law prescribes distinct consequences depending on whether the non-performing party is either the insolvent business or the counterparty (Spanish Insolvency Act, article 61.1). Case law has clarified that to determine if a contract is still executory/pending, parties have to look at the main mutual obligations, not necessarily at the accessory ones.[11]

21.14 If the non-performing party is the insolvent business, then the principle of *paritas creditorum* applies, and the creditor will have the right to see his claim included in the aggregate liabilities of the insolvency proceedings, together with the claims of the rest of the creditors.

21.15 If the non-performing party is the counterparty, the opposing principle of *pacta sunt servanda* applies and, therefore, the counterparty has the obligation to fulfil its obligation as if there had been no insolvency proceedings (if it consists of a payment obligation, it will be included under the aggregate assets of the insolvency proceedings).

B. BANKRUPTCY PROCEDURES

(1) Treatment of executory contracts

(a) General rule under formal insolvency proceedings in Spain: pacta sunt servanda

21.16 On the one hand, hybrid pre-insolvency procedures do not have immediate consequences on the ongoing contractual obligations between the insolvent company and the counterparty.[12] Therefore, the 'business as usual' approach

---

11 Francisco de P. Blasco Gascó, *Declaración en concurso y contratos. Resolución sin incumplimiento e incumplimiento sin resolución* (Tirant lo Blanch 2009) 30–34. The author analyses the case of a purchase of machines (main obligation) with maintenance obligations after the purchase (accessory obligation). The fact that the counterparty had provided the insolvent company with the machines but still had to comply with maintenance obligations was considered as full performance because the main obligation was complied with.

12 A specific legal regime on contracts for companies under insolvency proceedings is provided under the Spanish Insolvency Act only for companies which have been declared under the formal insolvency proceedings *concurso de acreedores* (Spanish Insolvency Act, Title III on the 'Effects of the insolvency proceedings declaration', Chaper III, 'On the *effects of contracts*'). No specific regime is provided, nevertheless, for pre-insolvency proceedings, which means that during the pre-insolvency stage contracts are ruled by the general provisions on contracts under Spanish Law.

applies in this period, although creditors' rights to initiate or continue enforcement actions against the debtor may be limited under certain circumstances.

On the other hand, the opening of formal insolvency proceedings in Spain does not affect the validity of executory contracts. This is in line with the general aim of preservation of companies under the Spanish system[13],[14] and the principle of continuation of the business activity performed by companies after the commencement of the procedure (Spanish Insolvency Act, article 44.1). Thus, the insolvent estate cannot unilaterally terminate executory contracts, and the obligations arising from them are considered 'administrative expenses' (Spanish Insolvency Act, article 61.2). This means that if payments still have to be made by the insolvent business to comply with its obligations under an executory contract, they will be made at their due date following a 'business as usual' implied rule. **21.17**

The Barcelona's Court of Appeal[15] has justified this approach by reference to the principles of justice and fairness that should underpin business relationships. Consistently, the same rules apply even in the event of liquidation (Spanish Insolvency Act, article 147). **21.18**

(b) Termination due to breach of contract

As explained, a party cannot terminate a contract on the sole grounds of a formal insolvency procedure of its counterparty. Nevertheless, both parties are **21.19**

---

13 In fact, the explanatory memorandum of the Spanish Insolvency Act states (Section VI) that:

> The arrangement with creditors is the normal solution of the insolvency proceedings, which the law incentives with certain measures (...). The aim of preservation of the professional or business activity of the debtor may be fulfilled through an arrangement with creditors. A viability plan will be attached to the arrangement proposal.

and (Section VII) that '(...) the law tries to preserve businesses or business units'. This is the translation in English of the Spanish text made by the authors of the present chapter.

14 Rafael Fuentes Devesa, 'Artículo 61. Vigencia de los contratos con obligaciones recíprocas' in LEFEBVRE – El Derecho (ed), *Ley Concursal Comentada* (2nd ed., LEFEBVRE – El Derecho 2016).

15 *Banco Santander, S.A. v Tecnicart Aplicacions Tècniques del Cartró* [2011] SAP Barcelona, Section 15, 9 February 2011 (CENDOJ 08019370152011100214). Barcelona's Court of Appeal stated that:

> Article 62.2 of the Spanish Insolvency Act refers to reciprocal obligations and to the fact that they are pending fulfilment by both parties. It implies that contractual obligations pending fulfilment are interrelated, in a way in which the obligations of one party have this functional link to the other party's obligations. It would then be unfair to require the fulfilment to the other party if the obligation of the insolvent debtor were only to be recognized as a claim in the creditor's list. These reasons of justice do not exist when the contract does not have this functional interrelation, because the obligations pending fulfillment by one of the parties (in this case, the insolvent debtor) have no causal link with the obligations that could arise in the future to the other party.

This is the translation in English of the Spanish text made by the authors of the present chapter.

entitled to terminate a contract if the other party does not comply with its obligations under the contract (Spanish Insolvency Act, article 62).

21.20 The breach of the contract must have taken place after the formal insolvency declaration (otherwise, the rules previously referred in this chapter would apply). However, if the contract consists of an ongoing performance, a breach on the part of the insolvency business that happened before the opening of the insolvency proceedings would also entitle the counterparty to terminate the contract.

21.21 It is therefore possible to observe that insolvency rules on the treatment of executory contracts do not differ significantly from the general precepts under the Spanish Civil Code.[16] The main difference has to do with the nature and enforceability of compensation claims. In fact, any claim arising from the termination of a contract with an insolvent company shall be filed before the Commercial Court under which the insolvency proceedings is being administered. The '*concurso*' Commercial Court is the Court that could best analyse if each specific termination claim (filed by third parties or by the insolvent business) is in the best interest of the insolvency proceedings or if, on the contrary, fulfilment of the contract in the best interest of the insolvency proceedings should apply.[17]

21.22 Regarding the effects, termination will automatically extinguish the pending obligations. If there were obligations that were due by the insolvent business but not complied with, Spanish Law foresees different consequences depending on the moment the contract was breached (Spanish Insolvency Act, article 62.4). If the breach took place prior to the opening of the insolvency proceedings, a claim of the performing counterparty will be recognized in the creditor's list subject to the *paritas creditorum* rule. However, if the breach happened after the opening of the *concurso*, the creditor will be paid in priority against the aggregate assets (pre-deductible claim, not subject to the *paritas creditorum* rule). In both cases, damages may be awarded to the counterparty when appropriate.

(c) Termination or fulfillment in the best interests of the insolvency proceedings

21.23 One of the most relevant effects of the opening of formal insolvency proceedings is the possibility for the insolvency administrator to request either the

---

16 Royal Decree dated 24 July 1889 (Spanish Civil Code), article 1.124 allows the performing party to terminate contracts with reciprocal obligations in the event of breach of the other party's obligations. The performing party may choose from requiring the fulfillment or the termination of the contracts with the damages that may have been caused, together with the interest accrued.

17 Aurora Martínez Flórez, 'Resolución por incumplimiento (art. 62)' in Rojo-Beltrán, *Comentario de la Ley Concursal, Tomo I* (1st ed., Thomson Civitas 2004).

compulsory termination of the executory contract (even if there is no legal cause for termination because the counterparty has not breached) or its compulsory continuation (even if there is a breach from the insolvent company).

The grounds for this request are the best interests of the insolvency proceedings or '*interés del concurso*' (Spanish Insolvency Act, articles 61.2.2° and 62.3, respectively). **21.24**

(d) Termination in the best interests of the insolvent estate

The termination of an executory contract will be deemed convenient to the best interests of the insolvent estate when the creditors that are subject to the *paritas creditorum* rule will obtain a higher return of their claims than in the event of compliance with the contract. **21.25**

Aurora Martínez Flórez explains[18] that the following criteria should be considered to determine the cases when compulsory termination applies. First, the IP shall consider profit and the cash inflow and outflow derived from the executory contract itself, as well as the profit derived from other sectors of the business that require this contract to be executed to operate (even if, considered alone, the contract is not profitable). Second, the IP shall consider the effects that a potential liquidation would have on the assets that, due to the termination of the executory contract, would compose the insolvent business's assets. If the value of the assets under a liquidation scenario would be lower than the consideration for the contract, the latter shall be performed. Third, if the contract deals with the supply of essential goods or services for the insolvent estate, the IP shall compare the conditions of the ongoing executory contracts with the potential terms of a contract that he or she would be able to get from the market for the supply of goods and services of comparable nature. Fourth, the IP should consider if the performance of the executory contract would facilitate the negotiations with the creditors, or if it is likely to yield a better solution in a liquidation scenario.[19] Lastly, the IP shall consider if termination would result in an award for damages to the performing counterparty and its likely magnitude. **21.26**

Termination in the best interest of the insolvent estate is pursued whenever the IP wants to get rid of 'economically undesirable contracts'.[20] The **21.27**

18 Aurora Martínez Flórez, 'Vigencia de los contratos con obligaciones recíprocas (art. 61)' in Rojo-Beltrán, ibid.

19 Sebastià Roca Roquer, 'Consideraciones en torno a la Ley Concursal 22/2004' in *Actualidad Civil número 9* (LA LEY 2005) also refers to the 'interest of the insolvency proceedings' in similar terms.

20 José Ramón García Vicente, 'Comentarios al artículo. 61 LC' in Bercovitz Rodríguez Cano, *Comentarios a la Ley Concursal, Tomo I* (1st ed., Tecnos 2004) 699.

counterparty's performance of its portion of the contract, and its compliance with the freely negotiated terms and conditions is immanent. In the words of Ana Moreno Sánchez-Moraleda:[21]

> Así, la resolución concursal de un contrato pendiente de cumplimiento se justificaría en 'interés del concurso', por cuanto éste podría menoscabar el patrimonio concursal, resultar perjudicial al desarrollo del concurso y no aportar ningún beneficio económico: por los sacrificios correspectivos, por el plazo de duración, por la misma materia a la que se refiere o por las garantías anejas, o por otros motivos.

21.28 Only the insolvent company (if under a supervision regime) or the insolvency practitioner (if under a substitution regime) may request this termination. Thus, the performing counterparty or any of the debtor's creditors are not entitled to request the termination of the contract in the interest of the insolvency proceedings.

21.29 A summary hearing takes place before the Commercial Court under which the insolvency proceeding is being followed in which the parties may reach an agreement on the termination and its effects. If no agreement is reached, the same Commercial Court will decide on the matter under a separate insolvency procedural plea.[22]

21.30 In order to compensate the performing and 'innocent' counterparty, the Spanish Insolvency Act provides that both the restitution obligations and/or damages that arise from the termination shall be pre-deducted and, therefore, be paid directly from the insolvent company's assets.

(e) Fulfilment in the best interests of the insolvent estate

21.31 Insolvent companies may not only terminate contracts in the best interests of the insolvency proceedings. They can also invoke best interests of the *concurso* when there is cause for termination (i.e., when the insolvent companies have breached an executory contract after the opening of the proceedings) in order for the contract to be kept. Logically, the fulfilment of the insolvent company's

---

21 Ana Moreno Sánchez-Moraleda, Los efectos de la declaración de concurso en los contratos bilaterales (Tirant lo Blanch 2010) 225:

> Thus, the termination of an executory contract under an insolvency proceedings would be justified in the 'best interest of the insolvency proceedings', as the contract could reduce the assets of the insolvent debtor, be detrimental to the development of the proceedings and do not result in any economic profit. This could happen because of the correspondent sacrifices, because of the duration of the contract, because of the object itself of the contract or for any guarantees linked to it, or for any other reasons.

This is the translation in English of the Spanish text made by the authors of the present chapter.

22 The 'interest of the insolvency proceedings' must be duly identified and proved. Enrique Sanjuan Muñoz, *Concurso de acreedores en el sector de la construcción* (1st ed., Tirant lo Blanch 2008) 189.

obligations shall also be pre-deductible and, therefore, not subject to the *paritas creditorum* rule. This means that any payments due by the insolvent debtor (even if they were due before the opening of the '*concurso de acreedores*') have to be made in full in order for this compulsory fulfilment to be applicable.[23]

(f) Rehabilitation of some specific contracts in Spain

Insolvency receivers may reinstate loans and credit contracts if the breach took place less than three months before the opening of the insolvency proceeding and if the debtor pays all the arrears to the counterparty. The creditor may oppose the rehabilitation if it had already filed a claim against the insolvent company and/or any co-debtors and guarantors (Spanish Insolvency Act, article 68). Similar provisions are found for purchase contracts by instalments (Spanish Insolvency Act, article 69). **21.32**

The insolvency practitioner may assume urban leasing contracts[24] (and even stop evictions) if all the unpaid rents and pending obligations (including the costs of the legal actions of eviction which are stopped) are paid to the lessor (Spanish Insolvency Act, article 70). **21.33**

In all these cases, in order to rehabilitate the contract, payments to the counterparty must be pre-deducted and directly paid from the insolvent business' assets. **21.34**

(2) Termination clauses and contractual remedies agreed by the parties in solvent times

The rather strict application of the pacts sunt servanda rule to determine the treatment of executory contracts in insolvency explains why clauses that trigger termination of the contract solely upon the opening of formal insolvency proceedings (commonly known as *ipso facto* clauses) shall be deemed void (Spanish Insolvency Act, article 61.3). **21.35**

---

23 Rafael Bonardell Lenzano, *Régimen de los contratos sinalagmáticos en el concurso* (1st ed., Tirant lo Blanch 2007).

24 Juan Madrazo, 'Enervación del desahucio en arrendamientos urbanos (art. 70)' in Rojo-Beltrán, n 17, explains that rustic leases (as opposed to urban leases) are excluded from the possibility of rehabilitation. Nevertheless, other authors such as Ana Moreno Sánchez-Moraleda (n 20) consider that the option of rehabilitation of the lease contract should also exist for rustic leases as:

> there is no reason that would justify that in the case of rustic leases or enterprises or businesses not located in a city and therefore, their leases not considered legally as urban, the opportunities of the business shall be worse than they would be in the case of the lease of an office, commercial property or industrial warehouses, for example.

This is the translation in English of the Spanish text made by the authors of the present chapter.

21.36 These clauses are quite common in financial contracts.[25] Since 2003, these clauses are deemed non-existent.[26]

21.37 The Supreme Court has clarified that the general unenforceability of *ipso facto* clauses is not comparable to not exercising an option under 'option sale' contracts. In fact, the counterparty to the insolvent company may not wish to exercise the option after the other party is formally declared insolvent because it has the right to do so under the option contract itself.[27]

21.38 Setting-off of debts and claims of the insolvent company is not valid under the Spanish system (as, evidently, it would go against the *paritas creditorum* rule). However, if the conditions for setting-off the synallagmatic claims already existed prior to the opening of the insolvency proceeding the parties shall be entitled to set-off (Spanish Insolvency Act, article 58). This is very relevant in the case of commercial current account contracts ('cuenta corriente mercantil'), through which parties that reciprocally and regularly provide for products and/or services to each other have agreed on a regular set-off. In this case, the claims of the creditor against the insolvent company would set-off with the debts and, therefore, only the claims that were not set-off in the last regular set-off date would fall under the *paritas creditorum* rule. These contracts clearly reduce the risk of a creditor against insolvency of the counterparties. Some Spanish legal scholars[28] and some rulings[29] also apply this set-off rule to connected transactions or '*ex eadem causa*' claims.

21.39 Cross-default clauses (those that trigger the termination of a contract if other contracts with third parties are breached) are accepted in Spain even in the

25 Ana Moreno Sánchez-Moraleda, Los efectos de la declaración de concurso en los contratos bilaterales (Tirant lo Blanch 2010) 225.

26 Specific exceptions under special legislation may be of preferential application. For example, Royal Decree-Law 5/2005, dated 11 March 2005, on urgent reforms to incentive productivity and for the improvement of public procurement is of preferential application to swap contracts.

27 Immochan España, S.A.U. v Llanera Urbanismo e Inmobiliaria, S.L.U. and Llanera, S.L. [2013] STS, 26 February 2013 (CENDOJ 28079110012013100130).

28 In this respect, Iván Jesús Trujillo Díez, *Los Efectos del Concurso sobre el Contrato de Cuenta Corriente* (1st ed., Aranzadi 2003):

> In fact, according to some scholars, the requirement of reciprocity in the claims to be compensated would not only mean that each debtor is, at the same time, creditor of the counterparty, but also that both claims arise from different title deeds. If both claims arised from the same title deed, then we would not be talking about compensation itself but about a sinalagmatic relationship. If we apply this thesis to the insolvency proceedings, 'ex aedem causa' claims could then be compensated. Nevertheless, it would not technically be considered a compensation but a simple clearing or deduction in order to calculate the ultimate result of a single legal relationship.

This is the translation in English of the Spanish text made by the authors of the present chapter.

29 *Inversiones, Terrenos y Servicios, S.A. v Bestin Supply Chain. S.L.* [2011] SAP Barcelona, Section 15, 6 September 2011 (CENDOJ 08019370152011100453).

event of insolvency.[30] Nevertheless, fulfilment of the contract in the best interests of the '*concurso*' may be imposed even if a valid cross-default clause has been agreed on.

Penalty provisions included in contracts with the aim of agreeing on a fixed amount of damages in the event of breach (in Spain, the nature of these clauses is to substitute any valuation of the damages) are also accepted. Whether the agreed amount is paid in preference to other contractual creditors or not depends on whether the breach occurred before or after the opening of the insolvency procedure. **21.40**

The existence of penalty clauses is one of the criteria that the IP has to consider when deciding whether to terminate an executory contract. In any case, the Commercial Court shall analyse the penalty agreed on and will have the authority to adjust it. **21.41**

(3) Special rules depending on the specific nature of some contracts

(a) Contracts with the public sector

Companies under a formal insolvency proceeding are prohibited from being a party in public procurement contracts.[31] However, if an arrangement with the creditors has been approved by the Court as part of the insolvency procedure, the insolvent company will be eligible again to enter into contracts with the public sector.[32] **21.42**

(b) Employment contracts and top management contracts

The most relevant provision for insolvent companies is that the insolvency Court will hear any proceedings for material amendment of collective working conditions (including cases of collective suspension, collective dismissal, etc.) once the insolvency proceeding is formally declared (Spanish Insolvency Act, article 64). **21.43**

---

30 *Natixis Lease, S.A. v Grúas Industriales Salamanca, S.L.* [2012] AP Salamanca, Section 1, 17 October 2012 (CENDOJ 37274370012012100642) and *Natixis Lease, S.A. v Grúas Duero, S.L.* [2012] SAP Salamanca, Section 1, 19 October 2012 (CENDOJ 37274370012012100697).

31 The Spanish Insolvency Act refers to special legislation. In this regard, Law 9/2017, dated 8th November, on Contracts of the Public Sector, article 71.1.c) or Law 33/2003, dated 3rd November, on Assets of the Public Administrations, art 94.

32 Antonio Fernández, Adrián Thery, José Carles, 'La aprobación judicial acelerada de la propuesta de convenio (AJM 1 Barcelona 27.9.2010 y SJM 1 Barcelona 29.10.2010)' in Anuario de Derecho Concursal number 25 (Civitas, 2012).

21.44 The insolvency practitioner may suspend or terminate top management contracts (Spanish Insolvency Act, article 65). In this case, the Commercial Court may limit the dismissal compensation (even if previously agreed on in the top management staff contract).

C. MAJOR REFORMS IN SPAIN SINCE 2000

(1) The Spanish Insolvency Act from 2003

21.45 The Spanish Insolvency Act, which dates back to 2003, introduced a single formal insolvency procedure in place of four different insolvency proceedings that co-existed until then (out of these procedures, only two applied to companies).[33] It also replaced the existing insolvency rules included in the Spanish Civil Code, the Spanish Commercial Code (both from the eighteenth century) and the Law for Payment Suspensions, dated 26 July 1922. Despite that reorganization effort, the effect of insolvency on some contracts is still determined by special laws.

21.46 The unavailability of hybrid pre-insolvency proceedings and the social stigma associated to formal proceedings pushcd companics to assumc unncccssary risks and pursue direct out-of-Court negotiations even in cases of current insolvency and financial distress. Also, most companies only filed for formal proceedings when multiple attempts at negotiation had failed. Not surprisingly, the most common outcome for formal insolvency proceedings is still liquidation, which accounts for more than 90 per cent of the cases.

(2) Further major reforms and the introduction of hybrid pre-insolvency proceedings in Spain

21.47 Since its adoption in 2003, the Spanish Insolvency Act has been amended roughly 30 times.[34] One of the most frequently mentioned explanations for this regulatory frenzy has been the need to promote the rescue of companies hit by the effects of the global financial crisis (2008–10).

33 The explanatory memorandum to Act 22/2003, dated 9 July 2003, on Insolvency relates, under Section II, that 'The diversity of insolvency proceedings being left behind (...) was due to the tendency for simplifying the procedure'. This is the translation in English of the Spanish text made by the authors of the present chapter.

34 *Ley Concursal Comentada* (2nd ed., Lefebvre – El Derecho 2016).

By means of the 2009 reform to the Spanish Insolvency Act,[35] the Spanish Government introduced, through the urgent procedure, the first of the hybrid pre-insolvency-proceedings: the negotiation procedure, aimed at reaching an early arrangement with creditors. This meant that a simple communication to the Commercial Court (*preconcurso*) granted the applicant an extra four-month term to negotiate with creditors. The formal procedure should have been used either in cases of failure of these negotiations, or to certify and give effect to the arrangement with the creditors. The submission of this communication resulted in an automatic stay of all executory proceedings, and prevented a declaration of insolvency. **21.48**

Although the *preconcurso* was literally only meant for companies that had initiated negotiations to reach an early arrangement with creditors, in practice, this negotiation period was also used, when possible, to remove the insolvency and/or to reach out-of-Court refinancing agreements (which logically included new guarantees in favour of the banks upon request of the banks) that avoided the insolvency proceeding. Nevertheless, Commercial Courts were declaring rescinded refinancing agreements on the grounds of being detrimental to the aggregate assets of the insolvent company (due to the new guarantees), which led to financial institutions not entering into new refinancing agreements with insolvent companies.[36] **21.49**

As banks withdrew their support from companies seeking to restructure their business by means of a *preconcurso* and refinancing agreements, the legislature in 2009 introduced further regulatory reforms to protect refinancing agreements. In the government's view, these reforms should have stimulated the national economy, allowed fresh money in the system and avoided, when possible, the closing of businesses (Spanish Insolvency Act, current article 71 *bis*). **21.50**

In 2011,[37] refinancing agreements were formally included under the scope of the *preconcurso* together with the negotiations for an early arrangement with creditors (that is to say, the Insolvency Act itself made it clear that the four-month term could also be used for this purpose, as it had been happening in practice since 2009). In addition, the 2011 reform extended the effects of refinancing agreements to some non-participating parties through their Court-approval or '*homologación*' (Spanish Insolvency Act, current Additional **21.51**

35 Above note 6.

36 Jesús Quijano González, 'El contexto, las claves y los aspectos principales del sistema 'concursal' español en las sucesivas reformas' in *Hacia un nuevo paradigma del derecho europeo de insolvencias. Sistemas jurídicos a debate* (EuriConv 2016).

37 Act 38/2011, dated 10 October 2011, on reform of the Spanish Insolvency Act.

Provision 4).[38] Later reforms also protected businesses negotiating refinancing agreements against enforcement measures under certain circumstances.

21.52 Refinancing agreements and their Court-approval were introduced in the Spanish system to offer a solution that was requested by financial creditors (mainly banks and financial institutions). Therefore, this procedure is useful to companies whose liabilities mainly comprise financial creditors, but not to those with mainly commercial debts.

21.53 Out-of-Court payment arrangements or '*acuerdos extrajudiciales de pagos*' were created in 2013 and later reformed in 2015.[39] In these procedures, the Business Registrar appoints a mediator and the law grants protection against enforcement measures up to a period of three months under certain circumstances. If no arrangement is reached, the business or the mediator shall petition for a formal insolvency procedure together with a proposal for an early arrangement with creditors or a liquidation plan.[40]

21.54 The advantages of hybrid insolvency procedures are clear. Unlike formal insolvency procedures, hybrid procedures have no direct consequences on the management and disposal rights of the directors of the business. Hybrid procedures are simpler, they cost less, last a shorter period and avoid the social stigma of formal insolvency procedures (*preconcurso* may even be confidential if requested by the business). Nevertheless, the fact that the time for negotiations is so limited could be a disadvantage as negotiations with creditors usually last longer.

21.55 Finally, the fact that the required support from creditors is higher under out-of-Court payment arrangements[41] than under formal proceedings has resulted in the latter procedures not being very popular for businesses in Spain.[42]

---

38 The recent '*homologación*' of Spanish corporation ABENGOA (Auto from Sevilla's Commercial Court number 2, 6 April 2016) has increased the popularity of this measure.

39 Act 14/2013, dated 27 September 2013, on support to entrepreneurs and their internationalization introduced a new *Título X* (arts 231–242) to the Insolvency Act to regulate this procedure, later reformed by Royal Decree-Law 1/2015, dated 27 February 2015 and Act 25/2015, dated 28 July 2015, both on second chance mechanism, reduction of financial liabilities and other social measures.

40 Spanish Insolvency Act, art 242.2.1º.

41 For example, under formal insolvency proceedings, creditors that hold 50 per cent of the ordinary liabilities are entitled to agree on a stay of up to five years and/or a reduction of 50 per cent binding the rest of the ordinary creditors (Spanish Insolvency Act, art 124.1.a). However, under out-of-Court payment arrangements, 60 per cent is required for a stay of maximum five years and/or a reduction of up to 25 per cent (Spanish Insolvency Act, art 238.1.a).

42 Statistics referred to year-end 2015 from the Business Registrars reveal that, since its creation in 2013, only 30 businesses filed for this proceedings. Esteban van Hemmen Almanzor, 'Estadística Concursal. Anuario 2015' (Colegio Registradores de la Propiedad, Bienes Muebles y Mercantiles de España, 2016).

It is also appropriate to observe that the aforementioned discipline of executory contracts applies only to companies that undertake a formal insolvency procedure. Therefore, a 'business as usual' rule applies to companies under hybrid pre-insolvency proceedings, with only seizure of assets under enforcement proceedings being restricted. **21.56**

(3) Reforms regarding executory contracts

Prior to 2003, Spanish Law did not foresee a specific provision on the effects of the opening of an insolvency procedure in executory contracts.[43] For contracts that had been fully complied with by one of the parties, the rule was similar to the current one. **21.57**

Nevertheless, there was no general rule on the termination of executory contracts either as there were only some particular provisions on the effects of specific contracts in different laws.[44] Some contracts terminated automatically upon the opening of the insolvency proceedings (e.g., mandate with retribution) while some others continued in a 'business as usual' rule (as the insurance for damages). For those contracts for which there was no specific legal provision (most of them), *ius electionis* of the IP applied. That is to say, the IP had the capacity to choose whether to assume or reject executory contracts to which the insolvent company was a party.[45] **21.58**

As explained in this chapter, this *ius electionis* rule was substituted in 2003 by the general *pacta sunt servanda* rule for executory contracts. The explanatory memorandum of the Spanish Insolvency Act refers that this general principle is completed with 'flexible formulas in the best interests of the insolvency proceedings and safeguarding the interests of the counterparty'. **21.59**

Since 2003, no major legal reforms have affected this general rule, although case law has redefined the concept of 'reciprocal pending obligations', which has led to some specific contracts not being considered executory and therefore, falling under the regime foreseen under article 61.2 of the Spanish Insolvency Act.[46] **21.60**

---

43 The explanatory memorandum of the Spanish Insolvency Act referred that the previous regime on the effects of the opening of an insolvency proceeding on contracts was one of the most deficiently regulated matters regarding Insolvency Law.

44 Above note 17.

45 Above note 21, 127.

46 IP of *Salmantina de Formularios, S.A. vs. Banco Espirito Santo, S.A., Sucursal en España* [2016] Supreme Court (Civil Section), 2 November 2016 (CENDOJ 28079110012016100629) regarding leasing contracts in the following terms:

21.61 After the 2003 reform, there have been no major reforms on the regime of executory contracts.[47] Indeed, the major reforms that have had an impact on contracts in Spain have been the reforms that we have described in the previous section regarding new pre-insolvency proceedings. It is clear that avoiding a formal insolvency procedure entails avoiding applying the *concurso* rules to the fulfilment and/or termination of contracts, which is in itself a remarkable change in everyday practice. In addition, the whole new regulation of refinancing agreements introduced after 2009, required by financial institutions in order to provide new fresh money into the system, has had a significant impact in Spain.

21.62 Analysing the explanatory memorandums of the reforms, we can imply that the main reasons behind these reforms have been to keep businesses alive, to adapt the Spanish economy and its business landscape to the global economic crisis, to increase productivity and to foster entrepreneurship and international attractiveness.

21.63 In the near future, we can expect further reforms of the hybrid insolvency proceedings in order to adapt to the needs of the Spanish economy, contribute to decrease the social stigma regarding insolvency, and increase the success of restructuring measures. These are, yet, unresolved issues in Spanish insolvency.

21.64 One of the latest reforms of the Spanish Insolvency Act[48] authorized the Spanish Government to draft a consolidated text of the Spanish Insolvency

---

> La interpretación que ha de darse a la nueva redacción del art. 61.2 de la Ley Concursal, y en concreto al último inciso en el que hace mención a los contratos de arrendamiento financiero, es que si del análisis del concreto contrato de leasing concertado por la concursada resultan obligaciones pendientes de cumplimiento también para el arrendador financiero tras la declaración de concurso, será aplicable el régimen previsto en dicho precepto para la resolución en interés del contrato de leasing pendiente de cumplimiento por ambas partes. Pero no puede entenderse (...) que dicha modificación legal tiene por consecuencia atribuir en todo caso al contrato de leasing la naturaleza de contrato de tracto sucesivo en el que las obligaciones a cargo de las partes subsisten a lo largo de la vigencia del contrato, sea cual sea la regulación convencional que resulte de las cláusulas del contrato suscrito por las partes.

The cited ruling from the Supreme Court insists on the relevance of the pending obligations of leasing contracts at the time of the *concurso* declaration to be considered executory: if the pending obligations from the leasor are only accessory or secondary then the leasing contract cannot be considered executory. A case-by-case analysis will be needed in order to consider the relevance of the pending obligations of each party.

47 Act 38/2011, dated 10 October 2011, on reform of the Spanish Insolvency Act introduced a nuance on the termination of leasing contracts in the best interest of the insolvency proceedings (which would apply only if the pending obligations from both parties are 'main' obligations under the leasing contract): the plaintiff must file, together with the claim, a valuation from an independent expert on the leased goods, that the Commercial Court may take into account when awarding damages.

48 Law 9/2015, dated 25 May 2015, on urgent measures on insolvency matters.

Act. The Ministry for Justice thus ordered[49] the creation of a special panel to draft a proposal of the law. This panel has recently produced a proposal,[50] dated 6 March 2017, which did not introduce almost any modifications to the regime of executory contracts (except of a new systematization of the previous provisions). Minor changes are proposed basically regarding:

(i) the possibility for the insolvency receivers to reinstate not only loans and credit contracts but also 'other financing agreements' if the breach took place within the three months prior to the insolvency proceedings opening and if all the sums owed are paid to the counterparty;
(ii) a new obligation of the insolvency receivers towards the notification of the rehabilitation of urban lease contracts to the leasor;
(iii) the procedure and effects of material amendment of collective working conditions (i.e., the proposal clarifies that the effects of the ruling issued by the insolvency proceedings Court are constitutive).

As it can be implied, no great modifications of the current regime of executory contracts for insolvent companies are expected in Spain in the short term. **21.65**

D. CONCLUDING REMARKS

One of the main purposes of Spanish Insolvency Law, although not so often achieved in practice, is the survival of businesses. Therefore, 'business as usual' is behind the Spanish Insolvency Act as well as the 'contracts shall be kept' general rule for executory contracts. **21.66**

This general rule is, however, flexible enough to increase, *de facto*, the survival chances of the insolvent company. The Spanish Insolvency Act provides for exceptions that entitle the insolvent business to terminate or preserve contracts in the best interests of the insolvency proceedings or that allow it to rehabilitate contracts even when they have been breached prior to the opening of the '*concurso de acreedores*'. In these cases, the interests of the performing **21.67**

---

49 Order of the Ministry for Justice dated 20 January 2016, by which a special panel is created to draft a proposal for consolidated text of Insolvency Law under the Commercial Law section of the General Codification Commission.

The panel was composed of Ángel Rojo Fernández-Río (President), Carmen Alonso Ledesma, Alberto Arribas Hernández, Esperanza Gallego Sánchez, Enrique García García, Enrique Piñel López and Juana Pulgar Ezquerra.

50 Ministerio de Justicia, Secretaría General Técnica, Comisión General de Codificación (6 March 2017) <http://www.mjusticia.gob.es/cs/Satellite/Portal/1292428364645?blobheader=application%2Fpdf&blobheadername1=Content-Disposition&blobheadername2=Grupo&blobheadervalue1=attachment%3B+filename%3DPropuesta_de_Real_Decreto_Legislativo_por_el_que_se_aprueba_el_T>, accessed 30 July 2017.

counterparty are also preserved as the law provides that the sums that will have to be paid to that counterparty (either as damages in case of termination or as amounts owed in case of rehabilitation) are to be prededucted and paid directly (therefore, not subject to the '*paritas creditorum*' rule).

21.68 Recent modifications to the Spanish Insolvency Act (those after 2003), as well as the ones expected in the short term, do not include relevant new provisions regarding the specific regime of executory contracts. Nevertheless, the fact that Spanish Law has provided, since 2009, for new hybrid pre-insolvency proceedings (to which the specific regime for executory contracts for insolvent businesses does not apply) indicates that the Spanish system believes in a 'business as usual' rule under insolvency situations in order to achieve its main goal: the survival of Spanish businesses.

22

NATIONAL REPORT FOR SWITZERLAND

Patrick Keinert

A. INTRODUCTION AND AVAILABLE CORPORATE INSOLVENCY PROCEDURES

(I) Preface and *sedes materiae*

Swiss insolvency law is primarily regulated by the Swiss Debt Enforcement and Bankruptcy Law (Bundesgesetz über Schuldbetreibung und Konkurs (SchKG)) from 11th April 1889. A number of provisions may also be found in the Law of Obligations (OR). Interestingly, in Switzerland, insolvency procedures are carried out by public 'debt prosecution and bankruptcy offices'.[1] There are three types of independent insolvency proceedings: a liquidation procedure (Konkursverfahren, art. 159 ff. SchKG), a composition agreement 22.01

1 SchKG, art. 2, also Valentin Rétornaz, 'International Cooperation in Bankruptcy: It Is Time To Lift The Swiss Isolation' (2013/2014) 15 YbPIL 573, 578. Exceptionally, a private person may be appointed as administrator, SchKG, art. 237 para. 2.

procedure (Nachlassverfahren, art. 293 ff. SchKG), and a stay of insolvency proceedings (Konkursaufschub, art. 725a OR).[2]

(II) Liquidation procedure (Konkursverfahren)

22.02 The aim of the liquidation procedure is the winding up of the debtor.[3] When a liquidation procedure is opened, the debtor's company shall be shut down immediately, unless the creditors' assembly delegates the running of the business to the administrator.[4] The commencement of the liquidation procedure must be published, among others in the Commercial and Land Registers.[5]

1. Reasons for application by creditors

22.03 After unsuccessful foreclosure of a debtor listed in the Commercial Register, creditors may file for a liquidation procedure.[6] Creditors may also file for a liquidation if the debtor's residence is unknown, the debtor escapes from his debts or has hidden assets in the foreclosure, or the debtor has ceased payments.[7]

2. Reason for application by the debtor

22.04 The debtor may declare his inability to pay (insolvency) in order to open the liquidation procedure (art. 191 SchKG). It is necessary for the debtor to be illiquid and unable to fulfil his upcoming financial obligations. There is no statutory requirement for the liabilities of the debtor's company to exceed the assets thereof.[8]

3. Reasons for opening the proceedings ex officio

22.05 Finally, the liquidation procedure may be opened *ex officio*.[9] For instance, corporate businesses shall be covered by this provision if their liabilities exceed their assets. They are required to notify the court if their balance sheet shows

2 Cf. concerning the composition agreement and the stay of insolvency proceedings in detail Franco Lorandi, 'Sanierung mittels Konkursaufschub oder Nachlassstundung: alte und neue Handlungsoptionen' in Thomas Sprecher (ed.), *Sanierung und Insolvenz von Unternehmen V: das neue Schweizer Sanierungsrecht* (Schulthess 2014) passim.

3 Philipp Weydmann, *Zweiseitige Verträge im Konkurs einer Vertragspartei* (Druck Franz Renggli 1958) 23 who describes the aim of the liquidation procedure in the 1950s: 'the ultimate goal of the procedure is to convert the bulk into cash. […]' (This is an English translation of '*Endziel des Verfahrens ist Versilberung der Masse […]*' by the author of the present report).

4 SchKG, arts 223, 237 para. 3, no 2.

5 Ibid., art. 176.

6 Ibid., arts 39, 159 ff.

7 Ibid., art. 190.

8 Swiss Federal Supreme Court, 15.6.2010, 9C_145/2010, E.4.2.

9 SchKG, art. 192.

that the claims of the company's creditors are not covered, whether the assets are assessed at going-concern or liquidation value.[10] The court then verifies the debtor's over-indebtedness before liquidation *ex officio* is permitted.[11] Insolvency may indeed briefly precede over-indebtedness – in this case the debtor shall declare an inability to pay under art. 191 SchKG (cf. A., II., 2.).

(III) Composition agreement procedure (Nachlassverfahren)

The second procedural instrument aims at reorganisation: the composition agreement aims to settle the debts. The potential to avoid liquidation by means of a settlement deal was expressly included in the SchKG from the very beginning of the law's existence.[12] Nevertheless, the first clear legislatory intention to facilitate company reorganisation came in the partial revision of the SchKG dating from 16.12.1994, entering into force on 1.1.1997.[13] After the *Swissair* insolvency case in 2001, the legislator focused yet again on reforming the law concerning reorganisation (cf. C., I. and II.).[14] **22.06**

An expert commission, set up during the legislative process, concluded that the existing insolvency law was capable of promoting the rescue of distressed yet viable businesses. Accordingly, it recommended just a small number of isolated reforms.[15] **22.07**

The proposals were adopted on 21.6.2013 and entered into force on 1.1.2014.[16] The reformed law facilitates the access to and the conclusion of a composition agreement. Moreover, the reform introduced in Swiss law an automatic provisional moratorium similar to the automatic stay under U.S. law **22.08**

10 OR, art. 725, para. 2; Swiss Federal Supreme Court, 14.4.1978, BGE 104 IV 77, E.3.d.

11 Swiss Federal Supreme Court, 16.12.2011, 5A_517/2011, E.3.2.

12 Hans Hanisch, 'Krise des Insolvenzrechts – Einige rechtsvergleichende Beobachtungen' (1977) Basler Juristische Mitteilungen 161, 174 f. The legal situation was similar to the old German law of 1928 which was considered unsatisfactory.

13 Law from 16.12.1994, entering into force 1.1.1997 (AS 1995, 1227; BBl. 1991 III 1); Message to the parliament concerning the modification of Debt Enforcement and Bankruptcy Law, 8.9.2010, 10.077, BBl. 6455, 6459; David Rüetschi, 'Das neue Sanierungsrecht : ein Rückblick auf die Entstehungsgeschichte' in Thomas Sprecher, Brigitte Umbach-Spahn and Dominik Vock (eds), *Sanierung und Insolvenz von Unternehmen V: das neue Schweizer Sanierungsrecht* (Schulthess 2014) 8.

14 Concerning the reform in detail, ibid.; also concerning the deficits of the Swiss reorganisation law Franco Lorandi, 'Vorgeschlagene Änderungen zum Sanierungsrecht' (2011) Blätter für Schuldbetreibung und Konkurs 95, 95 and 96 ff.; Daniel Hunkeler, 'Neues Sanierungsrecht verabschiedet – voraussichtliches Inkrafttreten bereits am 1. Januar 2014' (8. Juli 2013) Jusletter, Rz. 1 f.

15 Associated report concerning the draft, revision of the Debt Enforcement and Bankruptcy Law (SchKG): Reorganisation procedures (Bern, December 2008) 4; Message to the parliament concerning the modification of Debt Enforcement and Bankruptcy Law, 8.9.2010, 10.077, BBl. 6455, 6456.

16 AS 2013, 4111.

(arts 293a–293d SchKG).[17] Since such a moratorium does not necessarily lead to a composition agreement or liquidation, it is also possible to use the moratorium purely as a means to defer payment. Thus, the moratorium is intended to confer on the company sufficient time to renegotiate existing contracts with its creditors and suppliers.[18]

1. Involved persons and composition procedure stages

22.09 (I) Upon application, the procedure features an immediate provisional moratorium which may last up to four months (art. 293a para. 1, 2 SchKG). Usually, the court appoints a provisional administrator in order to examine the economic situation of the debtor and the potential for reorganisation (art. 293b para. 1 SchKG). If the provisional administrator concludes that there are reasonable chances of success to restructure the business in the provisional moratorium period, the procedure will then continue with the appointment of a definite administrator and the moratorium shall be extended for a further four to six months (art. 294 para. 1 SchKG).

22.10 In cases where the chances of reorganisation appear minimal, the court converts the composition agreement procedure into a liquidation procedure (arts 294 para. 3, 296b SchKG).

22.11 The moratorium applies to all pending suits, including but not limited to executory ones against the assets of the debtor.[19] The provisional moratorium does not affect claims secured by a land charge.[20]

22.12 During the composition procedure, the debtor may continue his business activities.[21]

22.13 (II) In the meantime, the composition agreement has to be negotiated and accepted by the creditors: Either the majority of the creditors representing two-thirds of the claims or a quarter of the creditors representing three-quarters of the claims are necessary (art. 305 para. 1 SchKG).

---

17 Message to the parliament concerning the modification of Debt Enforcement and Bankruptcy Law, 8.9.2010, 10.077, BBl. 6455, 6456; Hunkeler (Fn. 14) Rz. 5.

18 Cf. debate in the Swiss National Council on 16.4.2013, AB 2013 N 611.

19 Daniel Hunkeler, 'Das revidierte schweizerische "Nachlassverfahren" – der Insolvenzplan schweizerischen Rechts' (2000) ZInsO 369, 369.

20 SchKG, art. 297.

21 Ibid., art. 298.

(III) The court has then to confirm the composition agreement.[22] Therefore the value of the provided performances of the debtor has to be in an appropriate relation to his possibilities; the claims of privileged creditors have to be satisfied and secured as well as the shareholders have to contribute appropriately to the reorganisation (art. 306 SchKG). **22.14**

(IV) Finally, the agreement is enforced. The composition procedure is led by an administrator and the court.[23] **22.15**

2. *Application for composition*

If the petition for a composition agreement is submitted by the debtor (art. 293 lit. a SchKG), he shall not necessarily prove that the business is insolvent or near insolvency. He shall only demonstrate to the satisfaction of the court that the business is in a situation of crisis, and that it has the potential for being reorganised. **22.16**

The procedure may also be triggered by any creditor (under the same conditions as that of filing for a liquidation procedure) and *ex officio*, for instance when the court forwards a liquidation application to the competent court for composition.[24] **22.17**

3. *Types of composition agreements*

The ordinary composition agreement (art. 314 SchKG) provides the deferment of claims or a *pro rata* release of the creditor's claims. Debt equity swaps may also be included.[25] Therefore, the content of the composition agreement is restricted. Alternatively, the total assets of the debtor may be assigned to the creditors in a composition agreement with assignment of assets (art. 317 SchKG). The power of disposal passes to the creditors in the moment the composition agreement is legally binding (art. 319 SchKG). The creditors resign their claims not covered by the debtor's assets. **22.18**

(IV) Stay of insolvency proceedings (Konkursaufschub)

The third instrument, the stay of insolvency proceedings (Konkursaufschub), has also been designed to support the reorganisation of the debtor. The instrument is codified outside insolvency law, in the Code of Obligations (OR). **22.19**

---

22 Ibid., art. 306 para. 1.
23 Hunkeler, (Fn. 19) 369.
24 Ibid., arts 173a, 293.
25 Ibid., arts 314 para. 1bis, 318 para. 1bis.

22.20 Typically, the court commences insolvency proceedings after notification of over-indebtedness (see above, cf. art. 725 para. 2 OR). If there is a potential for financial restructuring, the court may stay the insolvency proceedings on application by the board of directors or by a creditor (art. 725a OR).[26] The stay of insolvency proceedings may be accompanied with measures to preserve the company's assets like the protection against debt enforcement or the prohibition against entering into new liabilities. Moreover, an administrative receiver may be appointed. In contrast to the composition agreement, here the aim is complete debt settlement.

(V) Evaluation

22.21 Although reorganisation is valued as a purpose of Swiss insolvency law, the legal literature contends that the existing mechanisms may fall short of achieving the desired goal.[27] Extensive mechanisms to facilitate early reorganisation or to discharge the debtor do not exist under Swiss law. Notwithstanding the general possibility for out-of-court debt settlements, there are no legal rules facilitating such procedures.

22.22 Swiss insolvency law is still based on a law which is more than 100 years old and one which has only seen relatively minor adjustments ever since. Theoretically, it is possible to switch between the aforementioned procedures.[28] However, this is factually restricted at the moment the liquidation procedure starts since business activities usually must be ceased.[29] In the relevant legal literature, authors tend to bemoan the lack of any uniform insolvency procedure such as that which exists in Germany.[30] In their view, such a procedure would facilitate the switch between liquidation and reorganisation.

22.23 Statistics seem to confirm the doctrinal analysis. In 2015, 13,082 liquidation procedures were completed in Switzerland; but there are no federal statistics on the composition procedure. Looking for instance at the Swiss canton of Bern, statistics show that composition agreements represent a neglectable portion of overall insolvency procedures. In 2015, there were only 128 composition agreement procedures as opposed to 1,551 liquidation cases.

---

26 Stock company: OR, art. 725a; Ltd.: OR, art. 820; cooperative: OR, art. 903; foundation: OR, art. 84a.

27 Lorandi, 'Vorgeschlagene Änderungen zum Sanierungsrecht' (Fn. 14) 99; Hans Caspar von der Crone, Bettina Kopta-Stutz and Loïc Pfister 'Some Theses Concerning Modern Swiss Reorganization Law' in: Henry Peter, Nicolas Jeandin and Jason Kilborn, *The Challenges of Insolvency Law Reform in the 21st Century – Facilitating Investment and Recovery to Enhance Economic Growth* (Zurich, Schulthess, 2006), 518.

28 SchKG, arts 309, 332.

29 Hunkeler, (Fn. 19) 371 f.

30 Ibid., 374.

B. TREATMENT OF EXECUTORY CONTRACTS

(I) Historical background of the administrator's right to determine execution of the contract

Legal provisions concerning the treatment of executory contracts are very rare in Swiss insolvency law. The core provision is art. 211 para. 2 SchKG – compared to other jurisdictions a very short one: **22.24**

> However, the bankruptcy administration is entitled in the debtor's stead to fulfill synallagmatic contracts which had not or had only partially been fulfilled at the time of the opening of the bankruptcy. The other party to contract may demand that security be furnished.[31]

The administrator's right to decide on the fate of an executory contract is a fundamental rule of Swiss insolvency law. As such, it is an independent rule – not just an exception – to art. 211 para. 1 SchKG which regulates the conversion of the creditor's claims to monetary claims. Art. 211 para. 1 SchKG concerns the settlement in the insolvency procedure, whereas para. 2 is related to execution of the contract (after assumption).[32] The first draft of the SchKG however intended a more detailed provision, including legal consequences in case of rejection of the contract.[33] The last reform from 1994 then introduced art. 211 para. 2bis SchKG – a new provision for financial contracts – and modified the wording of the old paragraph 2 insignificantly without introducing any material amendments.[34] The administrator's right to determine execution of the contract essentially corresponds to the version of 11th April 1889.[35] **22.25**

---

31 Stephen Zürich Berti, *Swiss Debt Enforcement and Bankruptcy Law: English translation of the Amended Federal Statute on Debt Enforcement and Bankruptcy (SchKG): with an introduction to Swiss debt enforcement and bankruptcy law* (The Hague, Schulthess Polygraphischer Verlag / Kluwer Law international 1997), 75 (Original: 'Die Konkursverwaltung hat indessen das Recht, zweiseitige Verträge, die zur Zeit der Konkureröffnung nicht oder nur teilweise erfüllt sind, anstelle des Schuldners zu erfüllen. Der Vertragspartner kann verlangen, dass ihm die Erfüllung sichergestellt werde.').

32 Weydmann (Fn. 3) 28.

33 Swiss Federal Supreme Court, 26.10.1978, BGE 104 III 84, 89; Report of the Ministry of Justice, BBl. I 1994, 1316; Dieter Zobl, 'Das Eintrittsrecht der Konkursmasse in synallagmatische Verträge und die Vertragsfreiheit' in Isaak Meier, Hans Michael Riemer and Peter Weimar (eds), *Festschrift für Hans Ulrich Walder zum 65 Geburtstag -Recht und Rechtsdurchsetzung* (Schulthess Polygraphischer Verlag 1994) 537; Dieter Zobl and Thomas Werlen, *Rechtsprobleme des bilateralen Netting* (Schulthess Polygraphischer Verlag 1994) 78.

34 Martin Plenio, *Das Erfüllungsrecht der Konkursverwaltung und schuldrechtliche Verträge im Konkurs* (P. Haupt 2003) 8.

35 Report of the Ministry of Justice, BBl. I 1994, 1316; art. 211 para. 2 SchKG has only been modified slightly by the revision of 1994 (AS 1995 1227; BBl 1991 III 1). The proposition that all contracts not fulfilled in reality become terminated has been scrapped since it was considered as illegitimate interference with material

(II) Effects of insolvency proceedings on executory contracts

22.26 In principle, an insolvency proceeding has no direct effects on the validity of contracts.[36] The contractual relationship continues in insolvency. An insolvency administrator must take contracts exactly as they are.[37] Thus the administrator is in principle bound to the contractual content negotiated by the parties. In essence, contractual liabilities are to be paid to the insolvency estate, whereas the creditors are ultimately satisfied in the course of the procedure with a *pro rata* share.[38] If the contractual obligations are not completely performed, the solvent party benefits from a number of safeguards which act to protect the contractual synallagmatic[39] relation:[40]

22.27 The solvent party has the right to demand collaterals as a guarantee for payment upon performance of their obligation if the executory contract is continued during the insolvency proceeding (art. 83 OR).[41] Until the collateral is granted, the solvent party has the right to withhold performance. If the debtor fails to offer a suitable collateral, the creditor may resign from the contract (art. 83 para. 2 OR).[42]

---

law, cf. Daniel Staehelin, 'Vertragsklauseln für den Insolvenzfall' [2004] AJP/PJA 363 364; Pierre-Robert Gilliéron, *Commentaire de la loi fédérale sur la poursuite pour dettes et la faillite : loi du 11 avril 1889, texte en vigueur le 1er janvier 1997* (Payot 1999) art. 211, Rn. 4.

36 Swiss Federal Supreme Court, 6.2.2006, 4C.252/2005; Swiss Federal Supreme Court 24.10.1984, BGE 110 III 84, 85; Daniel Girsberger, *Grenzüberschreitendes Finanzierungsleasing : internationales Vertrags-, Sachen- und Insolvenzrecht : eine rechtsvergleichende Untersuchung* (Mohr; Schulthess Polygraphischer Verlag, 1997) 316; Report of the Ministry of Justice, BBl. 1994 I S. 1315, 1316; Jolanta Kren, *Konkurseröffnung und schuldrechtliche Verträge : eine dogmatische Analyse der Wirkungen der Konkurseröffnung auf die im Obligationenrecht geregelten schuldrechtlichen Verträge* (Stämpfli 1989) 9; Nicolas Jeandin, 'Les effets de la faillite sur le contrat de durée' in François Bellanger and others (eds), *Le contrat dans tous ses états: publication de la Société genevoise de droit et de législation à l'occasion du 125e anniversaire de la Semaine Judiciaire* (Stämpfli 2004) 72; Weydmann (Fn. 3) 9.

37 SchKG, art. 204, para. 1; Jeandin (Fn. 36) 92; Zobl (Fn. 33) 537; Hans Schoch, *Die juristische Natur der Pfändung und der Vermögensbeschlagnahme im Konkurs* (Buchdr. H. Schraner 1940) 63.

38 In detail: Sylvain Marchand, *Précis de droit des poursuites* (2. Aufl. edn, Schulthess 2013) 183 ff.; Jeandin (Fn. 36) 74; Plenio (Fn. 34) 29 f.; William W. McBryde and Axel Flessner, 'Principles of European Insolvency Law and General Commentary' in William W. McBryde, Axel Flessner and Sebastian Kortmann (eds), *Principles of European Insolvency Law* (Kluwer Legal Publishers 2003) § 6.

39 In civil law systems, a synallagmatic contract is a contract in which each party to the contract is bound to provide something to the other party.

40 Instead of many others, Report of the Ministry of Justice, BBl. 1994, 1317.

41 OR, art. 83, 266h, 316, 337a, 392 II. Renate Schwob, 'Art. 211' in Adrian Staehelin, Thomas Bauer and Daniel Steahelin (eds), *Basler Kommentar – Bundesgesetz über Schuldbetreibung und Konkurs II, Art 159 – 352 SchKG, Art 1 – 47 GSchG, Art 51 – 58 AVIG* (2. Aufl. edn, Helbing Lichtenhahn Verlag 2010) Rn. 9, 12.

42 In an extensive continental understanding collaterals are e.g., pledges, personal guarantees, deposition, cf. Wullschleger, 'Art. 83' in Andreas Furrer, Anton Schnyder (eds), *Handkommentar zur Schweizer Privatrecht, Art. 83 OR*, Rn. 5. Concerning the conditions for art. 83 OR cf. Franco Lorandi, 'Dauerschuldverhältnisse im Nachlassverfahren' (2004) AJP/PJA 1209, 1212; Marchand (Fn. 38) 37.

The most important instrument is the administrator's right to determine execution of the contract or to reject these obligations (art. 211 para. 2 SchKG). The option exists for contracts which are not, or which are partially, fulfilled.[43] The administrator's right of determination only exists if the contract is ongoing.[44] In this context it has to be pointed out that Swiss law provides a variety of explicit reasons for termination of contracts in the case of insolvency. The legislator balanced the interests for many types of contracts. These legal terminations are formally reserved in relation to the rights of the insolvency administrator, cf. art. 211 para. 3 SchKG.[45] In some cases there is automatic termination of the contract,[46] in others there are extraordinary dismissals.[47] Nevertheless, it should be clarified that insolvency itself is not in and of itself a good and valid reason to terminate a (continuing) contract.[48] **22.28**

Finally, the insolvency has no effect on executed contracts unless the rules on avoidance in insolvency are applicable.[49] **22.29**

(III) The exercise of the administrator's right in the liquidation procedure

1. Determination on whether the contract is executed

If the administrator opts for the execution of the contract, the liabilities become privileged obligations against the estate which have to be fulfilled before unsecured obligations. According to art. 211 para. 2 sent. 2 SchKG the **22.30**

43 Concerning the notion of contractual performance: Plenio (Fn. 34) 31 ff. Contracts where the performance is delivered personally are exempt from art. 211 para. 2 SchKG: Daniel Hunkeler, 'Wirkungen der Konkurseröffnung auf zweiseitige Verträge, insbesondere auf Werkverträge (ausgewählte Einzelfragen)' (2002) BR 5557; Plenio (Fn. 34) 36.
Moreover, unseizable property is also exempt: ibid. (Fn. 34) 35.

44 Zobl (Fn. 33) 533; Karl Spühler, 'Möglichkeiten eines Konkursverwalters bei zweiseitigen Verträgen' in Hans Caspar von der Crone, Rolf H. Weber, Roger Zäch, and Dieter Zobl (eds), *Neuere Tendenzen im Gesellschaftsrecht – Festschrift für Peter Forstmoser zum 60 Geburtstag* (Schulthess 2003) 674.

45 Cf. Ivan Cherpillod, *La fin des contrats de durée* (CEDIDAC 1988) 43 ff.; Hans Fritzsche and Hans Ulrich Walder-Bohner, *Schuldbetreibung und Konkurs nach schweizerischem Recht, Bd. II* (Schulthess Polygraphischer Verlag 1993) § 42, Fn. 32.

46 Insurance contracts (insolvency of the insurer, VVG, art. 37; insolvency of the insure, VVG, art. 55), donation contracts (insolvency of the donator, OR, art. 250, para. 2), leasehold (insolvency of the lessee, OR, art. 297a), proxies (OR, art. 35, para. 1), mandates (OR, art. 405), agency contract (OR, art. 418s), payment instructions (OR, art. 470, para. 3), company agreements (OR, art. 545, para. 1), ownership of undivided shares (ZGB, art. 343).

47 Lease contracts (insolvency of the lessee, OR, art. 266h), loans (OR, art. 316), work contracts (OR, art. 337a), publishing contracts (OR, art. 392, para. 3).

48 Staehelin (Fn. 35) 365; Swiss Federal Supreme Court, Urt v. 16.11.2006, 4C.280/2006; Marchand (Fn. 38) 38, 186; Lorandi, 'Dauerschuldverhältnisse im Nachlassverfahren' (Fn. 41) 1215.

49 Instead of many others Marchand (Fn. 38) 183.

solvent contractual partner may additionally demand collaterals for his privileged claim.[50] In this case the administrator has to provide collaterals in a reasonable time.[51]

22.31 The administrator may make this determination independently and without judicial supervision.[52] The administrator may exercise considerable discretion in the decision since uncertain factors with regard to economic utility have to be taken into account.[53] The administrator may, however, be instructed in some cases by the creditors' assembly.[54] If the administrator adopts the contract, the contract has to be accepted as it is.[55] In particular, the administrator has no additional termination rights resulting incidentally from the right to determine whether the contract is executed.

22.32 One peculiarity of Swiss insolvency law is the legal consequence if an executory contract is adopted. According to majority opinion, the complete claim of the solvent partner becomes a privileged liability of the estate – even if the performance is divisible.[56] Whether the claim is due or fulfilled before or after the opening of the insolvency procedure is irrelevant, but how these legal consequences affect continuing obligations has been debated.[57] Continuing obligations are considered as contracts which do not consist in a singular exchange of performance and counter-performance but, rather, are an enduring and repeated exchange of performances (e.g., work contracts, leases).[58] The legal situation was clarified in the 2014 reform with the new art. 211a

50 Weydmann (Fn. 3) 39; Schwob (Fn. 41) Rn. 11.

51 Schwob (Fn. 41) Rn. 9.

52 Marchand (Fn. 38) 185.

53 Plenio (Fn. 34) 40.

54 Ibid. (Fn. 34) 37 f.

55 Swiss Federal Supreme Court, 8.6.1916, BGE 42 III 279, 285; Kren (Fn. 36) 95; Weydmann (Fn. 3) 35; Girsberger (Fn. 36) 324.

56 Girsberger (Fn. 36) 338; Lorandi, 'Vorgeschlagene Änderungen zum Sanierungsrecht' (Fn. 14) 102; Jeandin (Fn. 36) 75, Fn. 19 with further proofs. Franco Lorandi, 'Arbeitsverträge im Konkurs des Arbeitgebers' [2000] 96 SJZ 150, 153; Thomas Pietruszak, 'Bemerkung zu BGE 127 III 273 ff.' (2001) AJP/PJA 1228 1230; opposite opinion Weydmann (Fn. 3) 37.

57 Cf. Franco Lorandi, 'Mietverträge im Konkurs des Mieters' (1998) mp 1 1, 16; Lorandi, 'Arbeitsverträge im Konkurs des Arbeitgebers' (Fn. 56) 153: Also obligations resulting from continuing obligations, established before opening of the insolvency procedure, are considered as privileged obligations against the estate. In this see Swiss Federal Supreme Court, 5.10.2006, 4C.239/2006 in regard to work contracts.

However, Swiss Federal Supreme Court, 6.2.2006, 4C.252/2005 determines an unjustified interference with the *conditio creditorum* and considers obligations resulting from leases, established before opening of the insolvency procedure, as *pro rata* claims, Girsberger (Fn. 36) 338; Weydmann (Fn. 3) 36 f.

58 Message to the parliament concerning the modification of Debt Enforcement and Bankruptcy Law, 8.9.2010, 10.077, BBl. 6455, 6472 with further proofs.

SchKG – which also put a stop to the non-uniform practice of the Federal Supreme Court.[59] Nowadays, art. 211a para. 2 SchKG provides that where a contract is adopted, only liabilities occurring after the opening of the insolvency procedure are privileged liabilities against the estate; earlier liabilities are *pro rata* claims.

2. Option to reject executory contracts

If the administrator does not adopt an executory contract, the contract is not terminated.[60] Instead, the creditor's claim is degraded to a *pro rata* claim.[61] The legal quality of this claim is disputed:[62] On the one hand, it is advocated that it is a claim for damages due to non-performance;[63] on the other hand, it is said that the original obligation is resumed and the creditor only gets a converted monetary *pro rata* claim.[64] **22.33**

The 2014 reform clarified the position of continuing obligations. If the administrator does not give notice about his or her determination, it shall be regarded on a par with an ordinary termination of contract.[65] According to the new art. 211a para. 1 SchKG, contractual claims which are not adopted may only be included in the insolvency procedure up to the next possible time for termination or to the end of the determined contractual duration. **22.34**

The administrator also has the possibility to use the ordinary legal method for termination of contracts. Moreover, the solvent contractual partner may resign from the contract in line with art. 83 para. 2 Code of Obligations (OR) for failure to provide sufficient collaterals to secure the performance of the **22.35**

59 Associated report concerning the draft, revision of the Debt Enforcement and Bankruptcy Law (SchKG): Reorganisation procedures (Bern, December 2008) 19; Daniel Staehelin, 'Dauerschuldverhältnisse in der Insolvenz' in Thomas Sprecher (ed), *Sanierung und Insolvenz von Unternehmen V: das neue Schweizer Sanierungsrecht* (Schulthess 2014) 108.

60 Instruction: Swiss Federal Supreme Court, 26.10.1978, BGE 104 III 84.

61 Swiss Federal Supreme Court, 26.10.1978, BGE 104 III 84, 91; Isaak Meier, 'Konkursrecht, Neuerungen des revidierten Rechts und aktuelle Fragen aus Lehre und Praxis' (1996) ZSR 277, 298.

62 In detail Schwob (Fn. 41) Rn. 12.

63 Swiss Federal Supreme Court, 9.6.1899, BGE 25 II 438; Swiss Federal Supreme Court, 8.6.1916, BGE 42 III 279, 284; Swiss Federal Supreme Court, 29.6.1938, BGE 64 II 220, 225 f.; Emile Taillens, *Des effets de la faillite sur les contrats du débiteur* (Klausfelder S.A. 1950) 149 f.

64 Swiss Federal Supreme Court, 26.10.1978, BGE 104 III 84, 91; Swiss Federal Supreme Court, 13.6.1989, BGE 115 III 67; Kren (Fn. 36) 100 ff.; Weydmann (Fn. 3) 59; Plenio (Fn. 34) 61 ff.

65 Message to the parliament concerning the modification of Debt Enforcement and Bankruptcy Law, 8.9.2010, 10.077, BBl. 6455, 6474.

executory contract.[66] If the contractual party resigns according to art. 83 para. 2 OR, he shall have no claim for damages for non-performance.[67]

3. *Deadline to accept or reject executory contracts*

22.36 Swiss insolvency law does not provide an explicit provision detailing how long the administrator's right of determination may be exercised. However, if the contract is not adopted, the claims have to be integrated into the distribution plan.[68] Therefore, by reading art. 232 para. 2 sent. 2 and art. 247 para. 1 SchKG together, we can deduce that there is a deadline of at least three months until the distribution plan may be established. In light of relevant German legal doctrine, any decision made in 'reasonable time' should be admissible[69] or indeed any timely exercise shall be an administrator's duty.[70] No specific means are provided for the solvent contractual partner to request a decision.

4. *Strict deadline obligations and financial contracts*

22.37 The Swiss legislator also recognised in the 1994 reform a need to provide for the execution of financial contracts in insolvency.[71] Therefore art. 211 para. 2bis SchKG was included into the law:

> The right of the bankruptcy administration pursuant to paragraph 2 is, however, excluded in the case of strict deadline obligations (article 108 number 3 Code of Obligations) and financial future, swap and option transactions, if the value of the contractual performance can be determined based on market or stock exchange prices at the time of the opening of the bankruptcy. The bankruptcy administration and the contractual partner are each entitled to claim the difference between the agreed value of the contractual performance and the market value at the time of the opening of bankruptcy proceedings.[72]

22.38 In strict deadline obligations (if the performance of the contract is fixed on a certain time) and some types of financial contract the administrator is not

---

66 The relationship between art. 211 para. 2 SchKG and art. 83 OR is disputed: *Weber* cf. Art. 83 OR N. 34 argues that the resignation according to art. 83 para. 2 SchKG is permissible in insolvency; in cases of adoption of the contract, the resignation is only valid if the estate is too small for privileged claims. However Kren (Fn. 36) 90 assumes that the resignation is only possible if the administrator rejected the executory contract; also Spühler (Fn. 44) 679.

67 Swiss Federal Supreme Court, 30.1.1979, BGE 105 II 28, 32; Schwob (Fn. 41) Rn. 9; Plenio (Fn. 34) 59; Cherpillod (Fn. 45) 42.

68 Plenio (Fn. 34) 44 f.

69 Ibid (Fn. 34) 45; refusing Taillens p. 73, Rn. 109.

70 Weydmann (Fn. 3) 31 f.

71 Report of the Ministry of Justice, BBl. 1994 I 1316, 1321 f.

72 Berti (Fn. 31) 76.

allowed to decide whether the contract is to be executed or not.[73] The aforementioned provision aims to protect netting clauses.[74] Despite netting provisions having always been preserved in business practice, the legislator wanted to exclude any risk of uncertainty in the law,[75] since close-out-netting was not clearly regulated and no jurisprudence existed.[76]

To sum up, even if the legislator has not provided a comprehensive, general rule on the treatment of *ipso facto* clauses in insolvency, it has introduced sufficiently certain rules for the financial sector.[77] This provision was inspired by the former German law as well as Belgium and U.S. law.[78] **22.39**

Concerning the strict deadline obligations, it is essential to comply with the fixed date since non-performance is very unfavourable.[79] The administrator shall be prohibited from speculating on possible market fluctuations.[80] A decision is required promptly from the law on whether such contracts are to be executed or not.[81] **22.40**

(IV) Executory contracts in the composition procedure

1. *In general*

There are even fewer explicit rules on executory contracts in composition procedures. Contractual obligations which are entered into with the consent of the administrator or have been performed (continuing obligations) during the moratorium are considered to be privileged obligations against the estate (art. 310 para. 2 SchKG). The privilege is only applicable during the moratorium. In case of a subsequent liquidation, the administrator has to determine once again whether the contract is to be executed.[82] Obligations entered into **22.41**

73 Concerning art. 211 para. 2bis SchKG in detail Plenio (Fn. 34) 77 ff.; Urs Bertschinger, 'Zur Neuregelung des Eintrittsrechtes der Konkursverwaltung in synallagmatische Verträge des Gemeinschuldners (Art. 211 Abs. 2bis SchKG) – Gleichzeitig ein Beitrag zum bilateralen Netting' (1995) AJP/PJA 889, 889.

74 Bertschinger (Fn. 73) 889. In detail concerning art. 211 para. 2bis SchKG, also in a comparative law perspective Jean-Claude Dubacher, *Close-out-Bestimmungen und das Eintrittsrecht der Konkursverwaltung: ein Rechtsvergleich zwischen der Schweiz, Deutschland und Österreich* (Schulthess Polygraphischer Verl. 1999) passim.

75 Bertschinger (Fn. 73) 891.

76 Martin Hess and Alexander Wyss, 'Die rechtlichen Grundlagen des Netting, unter besonderer Berücksichtigung des Close-out Netting (Art. 211 Abs. 2bis SchKG)' (1997) AJP/PJA 1219, 1224.

77 Concerning the genesis, ibid., 1224 f.

78 Ibid., 1225.

79 Plenio (Fn. 34) 77.

80 Ibid., 79.

81 Report of the Ministry of Justice, BBl. I 1994, 1316, 1325.

82 Staehelin, 'Dauerschuldverhältnisse in der Insolvenz' (Fn. 59) 119.

without the consent of the administrator are unprivileged *pro rata* claims; it is possible to provide collaterals according to art. 83 Code of Obligations.

2. *Continuing obligations*

22.42 Furthermore, the reform of 2014 also modified the rules for continuing obligations in composition agreements. During the reform it was accepted that an effective reorganisation law needs some (slight) interference with material law.[83] Therefore, the new art. 297a SchKG brought amendments in response to the situation whereby the administrator desires to reject the contract. During a composition procedure it is now possible to terminate the contract extraordinary if its performance appears contrary to the aims of the reorganisation. The solvent contractual partner is to be compensated; but only with a *pro rata* claim. Hence, reorganisation shall be facilitated if essential resources are tied up in burdensome continuing obligations.[84]

(V) Treatment of contractual remedies agreed by the parties in times of solvency

22.43 Swiss insolvency law represents a very liberal position concerning the permissibility of contractual remedies.[85]

1. *Termination clauses/*ipso facto *clauses*

22.44 There is no legal provision or clear jurisprudence prohibiting *ipso facto* clauses.[86] Swiss legal doctrine nearly unanimously recognises the validity of *ipso facto*/termination clauses.[87] The main argument is that art. 211 para. 2 SchKG, the administrator's right to determination whether the contract is to be executed, is a purely procedural provision without any interference with

83 Lorandi, 'Vorgeschlagene Änderungen zum Sanierungsrecht' (Fn. 14) 99.

84 Lorandi, 'Sanierung mittels Konkursaufschub oder Nachlassstundung: alte und neue Handlungsoptionen' (Fn. 2) 44.

85 Cf. for a comparative law perspective: Patrick Keinert, 'Vertragsbeendigung in der Insolvenz' (Mohr Siebeck 2018), passim; Fabrice Robert-Tissot, 'The Effects of a Reorganization on (Executory) Contracts: A Comparative Law and Policy Study [United States, France, Germany and Switzerland]' (2012) *IILR* 234, passim.

86 Cf. Zobl and Werlen (Fn. 33) 80.

87 Jeandin (Fn. 36) 93; Lorandi, 'Mietverträge im Konkurs des Mieters' (Fn. 57) 3; Plenio (Fn. 34) 119 f.; Taillens 60; Weydmann (Fn. 3) 35f.; Staehelin, 'Vertragsklauseln für den Insolvenzfall' (Fn. 35) 366; Zobl (Fn. 33) passim; Dieter Zobl and Thomas Werlen, *1992 ISDA-Master Agreement: unter besonderer Berücksichtigung der Swapgeschäfte* (Schulthess Polygraphischer Verl. 1995) passim; Schwob (Fn. 41) Rn. 13; David Borer and Thomas Müller, 'Vertragsauflösung in der Insolvenz: Besprechung des Urteils Az. IX ZR 169/11 des deutschen Bundesgerichtshofes (BGH) vom 15. November 2012' (2014) GesKR 77, 80 f.

material law[88] – although the insolvency provisions are mandatory.[89] As a result, freedom of contract precedes the provisions of insolvency law and permits *ipso facto* clauses in material law.[90] Insolvency law only permits exceptional interventions into material law.[91] If reorganisations are to be facilitated, it is said that material law has to be changed, not insolvency law.[92] Since an *ipso facto* clause prohibits the contract from being considered part of the estate, the principle of *par conditio creditorum* shall not be violated.[93] In some cases the rules for avoidance may restrict effects of *ipso facto* clauses.[94] Only a minority opinion regards *ipso facto* clauses as void because they may be used to terminate valuable contracts and the clauses would bind not the debtor but the totality of the creditors.[95]

2. *Exception in lease and employment contracts*

Exceptionally, *ipso facto* clauses are partially restricted in lease and employment contracts.[96] In case of the insolvency of the lessor, the lease continues without the possibility for the administrator to assume or reject the contract and the lease persists after the realisation of the object since the change of ownership has no effect on the lease (art. 261 para. 1 OR). Moreover, in the insolvency of an employee, the employment contract is to be continued if there is no extraordinary reason for termination according to art. 337 Code of obligations. **22.45**

3. *Other contractual remedies*

Other contractual clauses regulating the consequences of termination in an insolvency procedure are considered valid so long as the mandatory rules of material law are fulfilled.[97] Acceleration clauses are also valid since these **22.46**

---

88 Message to the parliament concerning the modification of Debt Enforcement and Bankruptcy Law, 8.5.1991, BBl. 1991 III, 284, 5; Report of the Ministry of Justice, BBl. 1994 I 1315, 1316; Spühler (Fn. 44) 677; Jeandin (Fn. 36) 92; Plenio (Fn. 34) 117.

89 Spühler (Fn. 44) 677; Staehelin, 'Vertragsklauseln für den Insolvenzfall' (Fn. 35) 366.

90 Zobl (Fn. 33) 533 and concerning the older doctrine Weydmann (Fn. 3): (1958), Taillens: (1950), Ernst Blumenstein, *Handbuch des Schweizerischen Schuldbetreibungsrechtes* (K. J. Wyss 1911) 654 ff.

91 Swiss Federal Supreme Court, 26.10.1978, BGE 104 III 84, 89.

92 Swiss Federal Supreme Court, 26.10.1978, BGE 104 III 84, 90 f.; Message to the parliament concerning the modification of Debt Enforcement and Bankruptcy Law, 8.5.1991, BBl. 1991 III, 284, 8, 9.

93 Zobl (Fn. 33) 545.

94 Schwob (Fn. 41) Rn. 13; Zobl and Werlen, *Rechtsprobleme des bilateralen Netting* (Fn. 33) 82.

95 Meier (Fn. 61) 303 f. Some doctrine argues against *ipso facto* clauses if they become effective after the opening of the insolvency procedure: Plenio (Fn. 34) 120, Borer and Müller (Fn. 87) 81. Moreover, it is argued that *ipso facto* clauses may be restricted on the balance of interests if the aim of the insolvency procedure is the reorganisation of the enterprise: Girsberger (Fn. 36) 327.

96 Indirectly, Swiss Federal Supreme Court, 21.3.2001, BGE 127 III 273, 276 f.; Jeandin (Fn. 36) 81; Staehelin, 'Vertragsklauseln für den Insolvenzfall' (Fn. 35) 366; Marchand (Fn. 38) 190; Fritzsche and Walder-Bohner (Fn. 45) § 42, Fn. 32.

97 Schwob (Fn. 41) Rn. 13a; Staehelin, 'Vertragsklauseln für den Insolvenzfall' (Fn. 35) 369.

clauses correspond to the legal provision of art. 208 SchKG.[98] The retention of title clause is not affected upon insolvency (art. 211 para. 3 SchKG). Set-off during insolvency procedures is in general admissible. It is excluded if the other party acquires its obligation or claim against the debtor after the opening of the insolvency procedure (art. 213 SchKG).

22.47 However, contractual clauses which stipulate an increase in insolvency claims, provide for a higher *pro rata* share than foreseen by the law, or fix a sum akin to donation to be paid in the event of insolvency, are considered void.[99] Moreover, contractual penalties in the event of insolvency shall be void.[100] Finally, it is disputed as to whether contractual clauses providing derogation from the damage account in financial contracts (art. 211 para. 2bis SchKG) are permissible.[101]

C. REFORMS

(I) SchKG reform 1994

22.48 During the elaboration of the proposed reform in 1994 an expert commission was appointed to review the regulations concerning executory contracts.[102] Four major deficits have been identified in this regards: (1) a lack of clarity if the administrator opts for the performance of the contract or not; (2) a lack of clarity concerning the relation between Article 83 OR (right of withdrawal in case of non-provision of collaterals) and art. 211 SchKG (administrator's right to demand performance); (3) an uncertainty of the legal consequences in the case when the administrator rejects an executory contract; (4) a legal uncertainty on the permissibility of *ipso facto* clauses.[103]

22.49 These inconveniences of the existing law only lead to the amendment of art. 211 para. 2bis SchKG which introduced a separate discipline for strict deadline obligations and financial contracts – without clarifying the four identified

98 Cf. Meier (Fn. 61) 305.

99 Court of Appeal Basel Stadt, BlSchK 16/1952, 88 ff.

100 Staehelin, 'Vertragsklauseln für den Insolvenzfall' (Fn. 35) 378.

101 Valid: Bertschinger (Fn. 73) 895; opposite opinion Hess and Wyss (Fn. 76) 1229. Void: With further references Staehelin, ibid., 375.

102 'Report of the Federal Ministry of Justice concerning the revision of the administrator's right to choose the performance of executory contracts under Art. 211 SchKG' (translation by the author of 'Neuregelung des Eintrittsrechts der Konkursverwaltung in zweiseitige Verträge nach Artikel 211 des Bundesgesetzes über Schuldbetreibung und Konkurs (SchKG)') from 1.9.1993, BBl. 1994 I 1315.

103 Ibid, BBl. 1994 I 1315, 1318 ff.

inconveniences. The sole purpose of the amendment was finally to assert that close-out netting provisions in financial contracts are considered valid.

Interestingly, four of the five members of the expert group elaborating these modifications had strong affiliations with the banking sector.[104] 22.50

(II) SchKG reform 2014

After the *Swissair* insolvency case in 2001, a number of parliamentary initiatives aimed to promote reorganisation in insolvency cases have been undertaken.[105] Legal scholars for instance stated: 22.51

> The Swiss reorganization law does not meet the demands of a modern reorganization law in many respects. [...] One of the main goals of a future reformation has therefore to be the maintenance of business operations.[106]

Two expert groups elaborated proposals to overhaul Swiss insolvency law in 2003 and 2006. Both groups suggested measures to promote reorganisation and reform the existing discipline on executory contracts. The expert groups consisted mainly of legal scholars and lawyers. These expert groups were, nevertheless, criticised for an apparent bias towards restructuring and for backing the interests of the involved law firms.[107] The interests of employees, in particular, and the courts may have degraded consequently. 22.52

A more far-reaching proposal affording the administrator the right to terminate contracts in the liquidation procedure was dismissed for excessive interference with material law. Such a right has therefore been limited to composition proceedings. 22.53

In the reform, it is explicitly noted that ideas have been borrowed from the Chapter 11 procedure in the U.S. Bankruptcy Code, as well as the UNCITRAL Legislative Guide on Insolvency Law.[108] In addition, a comparative law study was carried out on the jurisdictions of Austria, Belgium, Norway, Singapore and U.S.A.[109] These jurisdictions have been selected since 22.54

---

104 Ibid, BBl. 1994 I 1315.

105 For instance, the motion 09.3716 'Konjunkturprogramm im SchKG. Schaffung eines Sanierungsrechts' or the motion 01.3673 'Nach der Swissair-Krise. Änderung des Bundesgesetzes über Schuldbetreibung und Konkurs?'.

106 Caspar von der Crone, Kopta-Stutz and Pfister (Fn. 27).

107 Report on legislative process by consultation concerning the SchKG-reform (2009) 2.

108 Message to the parliament, 10.077, BBl. 2010, 6456, 6459.

109 Ibid., 6467 f.; Olivier Dunant and others, 'Grundlagen der Wirtschaftspolitik Nr. 19, Étude 1: Comparaison internationale du droit des faillites suisse' [2010] Staatssekretariat für Wirtschaft SECO 13, 33 f.

they were positively evaluated in a precedent legal study[110] on efficiency of different insolvency procedures. The result of the comparison between the five aforementioned jurisdictions has been a strong argument in favour of the recognition of a right to terminate continuing contracts in composition proceedings. The legislator concluded that the new provisions Articles 211a, 297a SchKG constitute modern restructuring law since the compared jurisdictions foresee similar rights.

(III) Current reform on the Law of Obligations (Law on Stock Companies)

22.55 It is discussed to modify the Law of Obligations, or more precisely, the Law on Stock Companies in the near future.[111] Subsequent to the SchKG-reform of 2014, a parliamentary initiative called upon the government to develop early restructuring in the law of obligations. The reform has no immediate effect on executory contracts in insolvency proceedings but may have an indirect influence on reorganisations. The current stay of insolvency proceedings (Konkursaufschub) shall hereby be integrated into the SchKG-composition procedure with a possible extended provisional moratorium. The proposed Articles 725–725c of the Code of Obligations shall permit restructuring at an early stage for quick notification of financial conditions – especially in the case of an imminent insolvency. The legislative process is still ongoing.

D. CONCLUDING REMARKS

22.56 Swiss insolvency law is strongly categorised as procedural law. For the large part, insolvency law dates back to 1889, including even the main provisions on executory contracts in the liquidation procedure. Only a handful of amendments concerning financial contracts (art. 211 para. 1bis SchKG) and the termination of continuing obligations (art. 211a, 297a SchKG) have been included in the meantime. Past reforms, especially the reform of Articles 211a, 297a SchKG, have revealed that legislator and scholar alike are reluctant to permit the interference of insolvency law into material law.

22.57 The main source of reform has been through parliamentary and governmental initiatives, notably coming about in the aftermath of the *Swissair* insolvency case in 2001. During this period, the national competitiveness of Swiss reorganisation law had been called into question. This was a period in which

---

110 Simeon Djankov and others, 'Debt Enforcement around the World' (2008) 116 *J Pol Econ* 1105.

111 Cf. Message to the parliament concerning the modification of the Law of Obligations (Law on Stock Companies) from 23.11.2016, 16.077, BBl. 2017, 399 ff.

legal scholars and insolvency experts punctually criticised the state of domestic insolvency law. Eventually, comparative law became a justification for some results of the reform.

The new reforms have regularly drawn parallels with the Chapter 11 procedure of U.S. law. To a lesser extent, the legislator cites the influence of the UNCITRAL Legislative Guide on Insolvency Law and various other jurisdictions. In regard to the 1994 reform of art. 211 para. 2bis SchKG, since the international financial markets have been affected the reform was considered as a necessity to comply with international standards.[112] **22.58**

Finally, it is difficult to establish the main trends surrounding executory contracts. Executory contracts were affected by the largest overhaul to date in the 2014 reform, which can be seen as a slight advance towards a stronger reorganisation environment. The importance of such a law is to give the administrator the possibility to terminate burdensome contracts – at least for executory contracts. Nevertheless, the legislator neglected to take into account that contracts such as essential utility contracts may also play an important role in a successful reorganisation. Thus, for the moment, contractual remedies like *ipso facto* clauses are basically permissible. For now, there is neither a legal prohibition of such clauses nor is there any ongoing discussion to restrict contractual remedies. Courts are likely to back the freedom of contract and to interpret the contractual clauses as valid. **22.59**

112 Cf. BBl. 1994 I, 1315, 1322 ff.

23

NATIONAL REPORT FOR THE NETHERLANDS

Marco Verdonk and Rolef de Weijs

A. INSOLVENCY PROCEDURES UNDER DUTCH LAW

23.01 Dutch insolvency law provides for two insolvency procedures that are available for corporate entity debtors and other businesses. These are the liquidation procedure[1] ('*faillissement*') and the suspension of payment procedure ('*surseance van betaling*'). Both procedures are to be found in the Dutch Insolvency Act ('*Faillissementswet*' hereinafter 'Fw'). The Insolvency Act entered into force in 1896. It contains most of the procedural as well as substantive rules on insolvency. Due to the Act's age however, many complementary rules of Dutch insolvency law are to be found in case law.

(1) Liquidation procedure (*faillissement*)

23.02 When a debtor is no longer able to fulfil its monetary obligations (art. 6 (3) Fw) and has more than one unpaid creditor, the court can upon request by the

1 The liquidation procedure is commonly translated as the bankruptcy procedure. Since the term bankruptcy under this project and in line with English law, is reserved for natural persons, the term bankruptcy will be avoided. The term liquidation procedure is, however, also an imperfect translation, since a company can still exit this liquidation procedure by offering a composition plan (reorganisation plan). Upon acceptance and court confirmation, the liquidation procedure ends and the company as a legal entity continues to exist.

debtor or its creditor open a liquidation procedure (art. 1 (1) Fw). The liquidation procedure is available for natural persons and business entities. It is a collective procedure aimed at the liquidation of the available assets of the debtor by a court-appointed trustee ('*curator*'). The task of the trustee is to collect and liquidate the debtor's assets and distribute the net proceeds to the creditors (art. 68 Fw). Also a supervisory judge ('*rechter-commissaris*') is appointed (art. 64 Fw). During the procedure, creditors are stayed from individual actions against the estate (art. 33 Fw). Secured creditors are unaffected by the opening of an insolvency procedure (art. 57 Fw), save for the possibility of a cooling-off period.

Creditors have to file their claim (art. 26 Fw) and are admitted by means of a **23.03** claim validation meeting (art. 108 Fw). Up until this claim validation meeting, the debtor can still offer a composition plan to his creditors (art. 138 Fw). If the composition plan is accepted by the required majority (art. 145 Fw) and confirmed by the court (art. 153 Fw), the liquidation procedure ends (art. 161 Fw) and the company as a legal entity continues to exist.

(2) Suspension of payment procedure (*surseance*)

The debtor that foresees the possibility that it can no longer pay its debts, may **23.04** request the court to apply for a temporal suspension of payment ('*surseance van betaling*'), see art. 214 (1) Fw. A request for a suspension of payment can be made by business entities and natural persons conducting a business (art. 214 (4) Fw).[2] During the suspension of payment procedure, individual claims of unsecured and non-preferred creditors are 'stayed' (art. 230 Fw). A suspension of payment procedure is a voluntary procedure, which is aimed at providing businesses with an effective tool to reorganise themselves. This emphasis on the reorganisation under this procedure of the business of the debtor is further expressed by the task of the court appointed administrator. Administration during suspension of payment is exercised by the administrator and the debtor together (art. 215 Fw).[3] Without consent of the administrator the debtor is

2 Not however to natural persons, a credit institution ex FW, art 212g (1)[a], or an insurance company as meant in Fw, art 213, see Fw, art 214 (4).

3 Unlike the trustee, the administrator is not authorised to unilaterally dispose of the assets of the estate. The debtor is the disposing actor during suspension of payment. It is for the administrator to decide whether consent is given or not.

not authorised to dispose of assets of the estate during the moratorium (art. 228 Fw).[4] Also a delegated judge in an advisory role can be appointed (art. 223a Fw).

23.05 The debtor can offer a composition plan to its creditors (art. 252 and 214 (3) Fw). If the plan is accepted by the required majority and confirmed by the court, the suspension of payment procedure ends (art. 276 Fw).[5] A weakness of this procedure is that it has no mechanisms to bind disagreeing shareholders and secured creditors. If the debtor fails to reach an agreement, suspension of payment is usually converted into a liquidation procedure.

B. TREATMENT OF EXECUTORY CONTRACTS

(1) Treatment of executory contracts[6] in insolvency

(a) Basic framework in the absence of a termination clause: art. 37 Fw and the counterparty's initiative

23.06 The legislative history of the Dutch Insolvency Act formulates as a starting point that the opening of a liquidation procedure in itself does not affect existing executory contracts to which the debtor is a party. An executory contract does not dissolve or end because of the commencement of the proceedings.[7] Rights and obligations deriving from the contract are upheld, as well as the general rules of contract law that govern the contract during insolvency. Thus debtor and counterparty remain bound by their obligations. The counterparty cannot invoke the sole opening of the insolvency procedure in itself as a ground for its non-performance. The principle of continuation of contract during insolvency has been reiterated many times by the Dutch Supreme Court.[8] This rule applies to all insolvency procedures under Dutch insolvency law. Thus the basic rule that the opening of insolvency procedures

---

4 Preliminary suspension of payment is upon request granted by the court with the appointment of one or more administrators (Fw, art 215 (2)). After hearing the creditors, mostly four months later, the court decides about final granting of suspension of payment (Fw, art 218 (1)). In the interim period the rule of 228 applies as well (Fw, art 217).

5 The plan of reorganisation is binding only to the creditors that are affected by the suspension. Those are the unsecured creditors (Fw, arts 273–232).

6 For the purpose of this study (and therefore this national report) *executory contracts* are defined as contracts that at the commencement of an insolvency proceeding have not yet been fully performed by both the insolvent debtor and its counterparty. This definition is applicable to Dutch law (comp. Dutch Civil Code, art 6:261 (1) and Fw, art 37 (1)) and is accurate for this report.

7 Parliamentary History of the Faillissementswet, MvT, Van der Feltz I, 409.

8 HR 14 January 2011, *JOR* 2011/101; *NJ* 2011, 114 (*Aukema q.q./Uni Invest*), HR 19 April 2013; *JOR* 2013, 224 (*Koot Beheer/Tideman q.q.*); HR 11 July 2014; *JOR* 2015/175; *NJ* 2014, 407 (*Berzona*).

does not affect existing contracts of the debtor, is a starting point for legal analyses. In practice however, since most insolvency procedures result in the liquidation of all assets, the opening will signal the end of contractual relations. Furthermore, upholding the continuation principle under all circumstances could lead to unreasonable consequences. Therefore the premise that the opening of insolvency procedures does not affect existing contracts may be qualified as highly symbolic.[9]

By means of art. 37 Fw, Dutch insolvency law provides for a basic framework for executory contracts, next to the applicable rules of general contract law.[10] Save for specific statutory rules, such as lease and labour contracts discussed in section B.(2) below, and save for specific contractual arrangements, the initiative to decide upon how to deal with existing executory contracts in insolvency is not left with the court-appointed trustee, but with the contractual counterparty.[11] The system provided by art. 37 Fw is as follows.[12] The solvent counterparty can give the trustee a reasonable period to declare whether the trustee will comply with the contract and perform the obligations (art. 37 (1) Fw).[13] If the trustee agrees to perform under the contract, the trustee must provide the counterparty adequate (art. 6:51 BW)[14] security (art. 37 (2) Fw). In practice though, the counterparty will agree with less due to the fact that it becomes creditor of the estate as a result of approval by the trustee. **23.07**

In cases where the trustee declines to continue the contract, or where the reasonable period given to the trustee expires without agreement to perform by the trustee, the counterparty is freed from its future obligations. At the same time, the trustee is no longer allowed to claim future specific performance **23.08**

9 See for this qualification F.M.J. Verstijlen, 'De betrekkelijke continuïteit van het contract binnen faillissement', in: *Materieel faillissementsrecht: de Peeters/Gatzen-vordering en de overeenkomst binnen faillissement* (Preadviezen uitgebracht voor de Vereniging voor Burgerlijk Recht, 2006), 95 (hereafter: Verstijlen 2006).

10 For instance the right for the solvent counterparty to an executory contract to suspend its performance if performance by the insolvent party is uncertain, see BW, art. 6:262 for the *exceptio non adimpleti contractus* and BW, art. 6:263. This however is only a temporary remedy which does not relieve the suspending party of its obligations under the contract.

11 As pointed out by D. Faber and N. Vermunt, 'National Report for the Netherlands', in D. Faber et al. (eds), *Treatment of Contracts in Insolvency* (Oxford University Press 2013), para 12.08, 'it does not follow from the continuity principle that executory contracts are deemed to be assumed by the insolvent estate' (hereafter: Faber and Vermunt 2013).

12 It should be noted here that the scope of Fw, art. 37 is limited, since it is based on the premise that the contract is governed by rules of general contract law that apply in insolvency as well, see Verstijlen 2006, 96. However, parties are free to deviate from these rules by way of contractual arrangements, making Fw, art. 37 a mere default rule, see Verstijlen 2006, 98.

13 The rationale being that insolvency brings about uncertainty for the counterparty of the debtor whether or not the trustee will continue the contract. As follows from its legal history Fw, art. 37 is intended to provide for a possibility for the counterparty to end this uncertainty, see Van der Feltz I, 409.

14 The abbreviation 'BW' stands for 'Burgerlijk Wetboek' (Dutch Civil Code).

(art. 37 (1) Fw). From this moment on, the counterparty can avail himself of all the statutory remedies he would normally have against a counterparty in default, except specific performance. In short, upon express or implied rejection by the trustee, the counterparty has the choice between full or partial repudiation of the contract (art. 6:265 BW) with additional compensation for damages (cfm. art. 6:277 BW) and/or compensation for breach of contract (art. 6:74 and 6:87 BW). The resulting monetary claim or reversal after rescission (art. 6:271 BW) can be filed as a non-preferential insolvency claim with the trustee (arts 37a and 26 Fw). The fact that the claim for damages formally comes into existence after the opening of the insolvency procedure does not by itself preclude admission in the procedure. This follows explicitly from art. 37a Fw and has been confirmed by the Supreme Court in *HR Credit Suisse/Jongepier q.q.*[15] The analyses provided here is the formal route for arriving at the legal basis for filing a claim for replacement or supplemental damages. In practice however, many creditors just stop making deliveries and submit their outstanding invoices to the court-appointed trustee (arts 26 and 110 Fw).

23.09 The rationale behind art. 37 Fw is to give the counterparty of the debtor in the insolvency proceedings a means to end its uncertainty about future performance under the executory contract by the insolvent estate. This is in addition to the general contract law remedies in case of an (anticipated) breach (especially art. 6:262 and 6:263 BW about temporary suspension of performance).[16] In that regard art. 37 Fw has a limited scope, which is even further limited by the fact that the uncertainty referred to cannot occur with passive obligations of the estate. This kind of obligation involves the use of goods belonging to the estate by the counterparty on a contractual basis (such as the right of use of the lessee or depository), or such obligations as arising out of an anti-competition clause. Since the counterparty in case of a passive obligation is not dependent upon the trustee to obtain specific performance by the estate, the Supreme Court in the landmark case *HR Credit Suisse/Jongepier q.q.* held that the trustee, save for statutory or contractual diversions, in general is not allowed to actively breach the performance of the passive obligations of the estate by way of cancellation of an IP right or give notice of eviction in relation to leased property belonging to estate. The – in our view undesirable – result is that the implied power of the trustee to choose if continuation of existing contractual obligations is in the interest of the estate on the basis of arts 37 and 26 Fw, is

15 HR 23 March 2018, ECLI:NL:HR:2018:424, *NJ* 2018, 290 (*Credit Suisse/Jongepier q.q.*).
16 Parl. Gesch. (Parliamentary History) Inv. Boek 3, 5 en 6 BW, MvT bij art. 37 Fw, p. 387.

restricted to contracts involving active obligations (to give or do) only.[17] It follows from the foregoing observation that the right of the counterparty to give the trustee a reasonable period for deciding on whether to continue an executory contract as provided for in art. 37 (1) Fw, has no relevance in case of passive obligations of the estate.

23.10 Another limitation of the scope of art. 37 Fw is that the system of the Insolvency Act (being the continuation of contract) and art. 37a Fw suggests that the counterparty will opt for termination of the contract if the trustee (implicitly) refuses continuation of the contract. However, this is not per se necessary. Art. 37 (1) is not compulsory. Instead of termination, the counterparty may wish to continue the contract in order to maintain an existing pre-insolvency claim for specific performance. For instance when the value of this claim is higher than that of a claim for damages resulting from the termination of the contract.[18] Both art. 26 Fw and the above mentioned ruling in *HR Credit Suisse/Jongepier q.q.* indicate also that a specific performance claim can be filed if this claim stems from before the proceedings. In contrast, it is uncertain if this may lead to the counterparty's continued performance during insolvency, thereby provoking an ex post specific performance claim or a higher claim for alternative compensation despite the fact that the trustee has expressed his unwillingness to continue the contract (art. 37 Fw).[19] Here one has to think of continued performance by the counterparty, for example providing services to the insolvent debtor.[20] Although this point used to be open for debate, in the aforementioned case of *Credit Suisse/Jongepier q.q.* the Supreme Court held that since, as a general rule, all passive obligations of the counterparty are upheld during insolvency, for instance as a lessor, the thereby periodically arising corresponding claims of the counterparty are admissible in the proceedings. The argument used here is that the corresponding claim stems from an obligation to which the counterparty had already committed

17 Thus infringing the fundamental principle of insolvency law that a creditor cannot exercise his contractual rights as if no formal insolvency occurred, since that would unacceptably contravene the *pari passu* principle. This is regardless of whether the claim concerned corresponds with an active or passive obligation, see HR 2 November 2006, *JOR* 2007/76; *NJ* 2007, 155 (*Nebula*). Idem. Faber and Vermunt 2013, par. 12.12; T.T. van Zanten, 'Geen Nebula, maar Berzona: de curator heeft toch geen recht op wanprestatie!', *TvI* 2014, 36, p. 191; F.M.J. Verstijlen, annotation of HR Berzona, *NJ* 2014, 407, sub 9–11; M.P. Verdonk, Over de herijking van het fixatiebeginsel voor faillissementsschulden. Een analyse van HR 23 maart 2018, ECLI: NL:HR:2018:424, *NTHR* 2018/4, par. 3.3.

18 See Verstijlen 2006, p. 109–111; T.T. van Zanten, De overeenkomst in het insolventierecht, Serie Recht en Praktijk, InsR2, Deventer: Wolters Kluwer 2012, par. 4.7.4.3 (hereafter: Van Zanten 2012).

19 See Van Zanten 2012, para 4.7.4.3, pp. 209–10, with references; Verstijlen 2006, p. 109, Van Andel and Van Zanten 2013, sub 5; G.A.J. Boekraad, annotation of HR Koot Beheer/Tideman q.q., *JOR* 2013/224, sub 17. Also Faber and Vermunt 2013, par. 12.21.

20 See Van Andel and Van Zanten 2013, sub 4, under 'vordering tot nakoming. Examples are insurance contracts or financial leases, see G.A.J. Boekraad, annotation of HR Koot Beheer/Tideman q.q., *JOR* 2013/224, sub 17.

itself before the proceedings.[21] Therefore, as long as the counterparty continues to comply with its obligation, the insolvent creditor will still owe the corresponding counterclaim. This does not mean that simply all claims resulting from the continuation of an executory contract by the counterparty are admissible. If an executory contract constitutes periodical obligations for either party, it has to be established if the counterparty, at the time of the opening of the proceedings, actually has a legal obligation to perform or only has the possibility to perform. In the latter case (only) the counterparty would increase its claims by way of performance while not being obliged to perform.[22] The criterion for the admissibility of claims arising after the opening of the proceedings used by the Supreme Court is that they originate from the legal position of the creditor at the time when the formal proceedings were opened. This is as a result of the principle of fixation.[23] It very much remains to be seen whether these new rules as formulated by the Supreme Court in its recent case *Credit Suisse/Jongepier* can be worked into a coherent and functioning framework. Here two arguments are submitted why the new approach by the Supreme Court cannot be held to form a consistent part of the larger framework for executory contracts in insolvency. First of all, the Supreme Court bypasses the key notion that creditors file a claim for damages and not for real performance.[24] As is always the case with damages, the party claiming damages is under the legal obligation to limit its own damage, which in the cases at hand would mean that the counterparty has to stop performing under the contract when due to insolvency its continuation has become illusory. Secondly, the distinction made by the Supreme Court between contracts under which the counterparty is actually obliged to perform or only has the possibility to perform, makes little sense from a general private law perspective and even less from an insolvency law perspective. Already from a private law perspective any obligation to perform can be suspended if there is sufficient ground to doubt whether the counterparty will also perform. Therefore, all obligations become more or less conditional from that perspective and as a consequence, the strict division between obligatory legal acts under a contract and more voluntary legal acts cannot be upheld in this context.

23.11 The trustee has, of course, the right to refuse to keep on actively performing under a pre-insolvency contract. As said, the initiative on how to deal with the contract is left with the counterparty (except for lease and labour contracts).

---

21 See under section 3.7.1 sub c and 3.7.4 of *HR Credit Suisse/Jongepier q.q.*

22 See under section 3.7.1 sub d and 3.7.5 of *HR Credit Suisse/Jongepier q.q.*

23 See under section 3.5.4 of *HR Credit Suisse/Jongepier q.q.*

24 As follows from art. 37a Fw and its parliamentary history, see already J.J. van Hees in his case note to the first instance of Mondial/Boddaert q.q., Rb Alkmaar, *JOR*, 2002/108.

An inconvenient consequence hereof, combined with the premise that contracts are not affected by the opening of an insolvency procedure, is that the trustee does not have the power himself to terminate executory contracts of the debtor. Such a right cannot be derived from art. 37 Fw (which gives the trustee the choice whether or not to continue the contract if requested by the counterparty). If the trustee does not comply with the request for specific performance, then the contract is not automatically terminated. It is still the counterparty that must act. Outside the rules on labour and lease contracts, only when the contract contains a stipulated right for the insolvent party to terminate the contract, or if there is a statutory ground for termination, the trustee is entitled to terminate the contract. See *HR Credit Suisse/Jongepier q.q.*

(b) Termination clauses in unspecified contracts

In the next paragraph, the rules for the special treatment of specified contracts such as lease and labour contracts will be discussed. Above the general system has been described as to the status of executory contracts in the absence of specific contractual clauses to that extent. There it was stated that art. 37 Fw is a mere default rule.[25] As to termination clauses in general, parties are free to stipulate in advance that the contract will be terminated in case of insolvency. This is common practice in commercial life, where many contracts include a right of termination for the solvent party upon the commencement of insolvency proceedings as to the other party. **23.12**

Under Dutch insolvency law, the approach taken by Supreme Court is that termination rights linked to the opening of insolvency procedures of one of the contractual parties can be invoked against the trustee and the insolvent estate by the counterparty. This is founded on the hailed principle of the continuation of contract in insolvency, see the Supreme Court's ruling in *HR BabyXL*.[26] Here we see as a starting point that contractual freedom prevails. As a consequence, parties are free to decide beforehand that their contract will end in the case of insolvency of one of them, whether automatically (*ipso facto*) or by a declaration of termination and regardless of any non-performance by the debtor. It is easy to see that this approach is problematic in cases where a contract is essential for the continuation of the business of the debtor and attempts to capture the going concern surplus are concerned.[27] **23.13**

25 *Supra* footnote 12.

26 HR 13 May 2005, *NJ* 2005, 406; *JOR* 2005/222; AA 2005, 938.

27 See for an example HR 2 December 2016, ECLI:NL:HR:2016:2744 (Ctac/Curatoren Free Record Shop) and the annotation of F.M.J. Verstijlen, *NJ* 2017, 21.

23.14 This does not mean that a termination clause cannot be curtailed. It is, as always, to be assumed that invoking such a clause may in exceptional cases constitute abuse of right (art. 3:13 BW).[28] Also, a termination based on a contractual clause in a case of insolvency may be held to be contrary to good faith and fair dealing (art. 6:248 (2) BW). See the Supreme Court cases *HR BabyXL*, *HR Van der Hel q.q./Edon*[29] and *HR Megapool*.[30] The yardstick of good faith and fair dealing requires a balance-of-interests-test. It seems that it must be assessed whether – as far as termination clauses go – the interest of the single creditor is outweighed by the interest of the estate with the continuation of the contract. In our view, the counterparty cannot invoke a termination clause if the contract is essential for the business as a going concern while at the same time the counterparty is given full compensation for all of its contractual expectations, past and present. See *HR BabyXL*.[31] It is in the legitimate interests of the non-debtor party that past defaults are cured and that adequate assurance of future performances is provided. If these conditions are met, contractual freedom can be overridden and the contract may be continued against the will of the counterparty and regardless of express contractual provisions to the contrary.[32] Overriding the contractual freedom of parties is then in the interest of all the creditors, since they get more than liquidation value for their claim, while conversely social interests (reorganisation) are served as well.[33]

(2) Some specified contracts: lease, labour, contracts for energy, future contracts and agency

(a) Lease contracts

23.15 Art. 37 Fw applies to all executory contracts. However, when a lessee becomes insolvent specific rules deviating from art. 37 Fw apply (art. 39 Fw).[34] In the view of the legislator, executory contracts as to leases bring about a conflict of interests. On the one hand the insolvent estate of the lessee must be protected

28 See E. Loesberg and J.L.M. Groenewegen, annotation of HR BabyXL, *TvI* 2005/36.

29 HR 16 October 1998, *LJN* ZC2741, *NJ* 1998, 896 (*Van der Hel q.q./Edon*).

30 HR 12 April 2013, *NJ* 2013/224; JOR 2013/193 (*Megapool*).

31 As the Supreme Court stated, a temporal measure for curtailing a termination clause during insolvency can be found in a cool-off period (Fw, arts 63 (a) and 241 (a)).

32 Note that this would be in line with assumption of a contract by the estate, thus leading to the application of Fw, art. 37 (2).

33 Comp. S.C.J.J. Kortmann and N.E.D. Faber (eds.), 'Geschiedenis van de Faillissementswet, Voorontwerp Insolventiewet met toelichting' (Serie Onderneming en Recht, deel 2-IV, Deventer Kluwer 2007), explanation to the proposed arts 3.4.1 (2) and 3.6.4 (4), 235 and 262.

34 In cases where the lessor becomes insolvent, in principle Fw, art. 37 must be applied. However, as decided in HR Berzona, in diversion of Fw, art. 37 and the *pari passu* rule, the insolvent estate of the lessor is not entitled to breach on a passive obligation to provide the use of the lease object. As stated, in our view this rule must be understood against the background of statutory protection of lessors.

against the costs for undesired lease, while the lessor needs to have certainty about payment of the lease terms on the other. The legislator has sought to balance these interests in an equitable and practical way in art. 39 Fw.[35] In case of the winding up of a lessee, both the trustee and the lessor can terminate the lease (*'opzegging'*) with a term of three months. The payment of lease terms over this three-month period becomes an obligation of the estate. A similar framework exists for the suspension of payment procedure (art. 238 Fw), except that the right to terminate the lease is given solely to the lessee (and its administrator). If a lease contract is terminated ex art. 39 Fw, the estate owes the lessor no compensation for other future lease terms other than the three months' period, see the Supreme Court case of *HR Aukema q.q./Uni Invest*.[36] Art. 39 Fw sought to strike a balance between the interests of the estate and the interest of the lessor. The result is, however, that the potential claim for damages by the lessor is largely capped by the working of art. 39 Fw to three months. In reality, if no subsequent lessee can be found, the damage incurred by the lessor by the non-performance of the lease contract, will often be much higher.

There have been several court cases on the question whether the lessor is still able to invoke a contractual right for termination outside art. 39 Fw and whether the lessor can thereby effectively circumvent the statutory cap on its damages. Under Dutch insolvency law, the possibility of a contractual right for the lessor to terminate a contract for lease upon insolvency of the lessee, becomes especially relevant in regard to the lessor's possible claim for damages resulting from an early termination of the lease. It is common practice that commercial lease contracts contain both a right of termination for the lessor in case of the lessee's insolvency and a subsequent claim for the remaining instalments. As to a *contractual* right of the lessor to terminate the lease, the Dutch Supreme Court in *HR BabyXL*[37] held that a contractual termination clause can still, regardless of the statutory regulation (art. 39 Fw), be invoked in insolvency. In the case leading to *HR BabyXL* this resulted in the possibility of the lessor filing as an insolvency claim a claim for damages in the insolvency procedure equal to all future installments under the contract (confirmed in *HR Aukema q.q./Uni Invest*). This leads to the rather undesirable outcome that depending on the ground on which the lease contract is terminated, completely different claims arise, both in nature (claim against the estate or insolvency claim) and in amount (claim against the estate for three months or the often nominally much higher insolvency claim for all future instalments **23.16**

35 Fw, arts 39 and 238 apply to the lease of both movables and immovables, see HR 9 January 2015, *NJ* 2015, 43 (*Doka/Kalmijn q.q.*).

36 HR 14 January 2011, *NJ* 2011/114; *JOR* 2011/101 (*Aukema q.q./Uni Invest*).

37 HR 13 mai 2005, *NJ* 2005, 406; *JOR* 2005/222; AA 2005, 938 (*BabyXL*).

under the contract). In case of a contractual termination by the lessor, the lessor can often claim a large amount of damages resulting from the prematurely ended contract. In case of statutory termination by the trustee, the claim is capped to three months, but is awarded the status of claim against the estate. Of course, from the perspective of the lessor, termination on the basis of the contract, resulting in a relatively high insolvency claim, is the preferable route if a significant pay out to unsecured insolvency creditors is to be expected. If the expected pay out on unsecured insolvency claims is low or zero, the route of art. 39 Fw, with a nominal smaller claim but a higher ranking (claim against the estate), is to be preferred by the lessor.

23.17 The plot keeps thickening however. The question still needs to be answered whether the lessor could still invoke the contractual claim if it is the trustee that has terminated a lease contract on the basis of art. 39 Fw (in the above it was assumed that it was the counterparty that terminated the contract on the basis of contractual clauses to that extent). In the case *HR Aukema q.q./Uni Invest*, the Dutch Supreme Court held that a statutory based termination of a lease contract ex art. 39 Fw is a regular manner of unilateral termination by the trustee, and that therefore the estate cannot be held liable for any further damages. A clause in the terminated lease contract that awards higher damages to the lessor as a result of a premature termination based on art. 39 Fw, therefore does not constitute an admissible claim if the trustee invoked art. 39 Fw. The reasoning is based on the fair balancing of interests of both lessor and lessee as embodied in art. 39 Fw, according to the Supreme Court in *HR Romania*.[38] So if the trustee is first, he can basically decide the route and nature of the claim. As a result, a contractual claim for damages, that is fixed to the sum of all payments that would have become due under the lease contract had it been properly performed, can only be recovered by the lessor against the estate, if the lease is terminated by the lessor on a contractual or statutory basis outside the application of art. 39 Fw.

23.18 There is yet another layer to the final plot of art. 39 Fw. In addition to the fact that that there is such a big difference in both nature and nominal amount of the claim depending on the ground of terminating the contract (thereby provoking possible strategic behaviour by both lessor and trustee as to the most beneficial outcome from their perspectives), as to leases of real estate the initiative has come to lie with the trustee. In the case of the lease of real estate and on the ground of breach of contract by the lessee (art. 6:265 BW), the

---

38 HR 15 November 2013, *JOR* 2014/27; *NJ* 2014, 68 (*Romania*). The same holds for stipulated rights to compensation for employees in case of the termination of a labour contract ex art. 40 Fw, see HR 12 January 1990, NJ 1990, 662; (*Van Gelder Papier*).

lessor, outside of art. 39 Fw, can only end a lease via the court, which of course takes time.[39] During this period the trustee can still invoke art. 39 Fw.

23.19 The regime of article 39 Fw can be deemed undesirable since it can trigger a strange battle as to who first terminates the lease contract on which ground. Equally undesirable is the effect that a lessor faced with significant losses because of non-performance under the contract by the lessee, sees its claim reduced to three months under the lease contract, be it as a claim against the estate. The regime of art. 39 Fw does not however render a clause for compensation for lost lease instalments in itself void, see Supreme Court cases *HR Romania* and *HR Hansteen/Verwiel q.q.*[40] The lessor therefore can still claim such damages from a *third party* that has guaranteed payment by the lessee, for instance under a guarantee in whatever shape or form from a parent company or under a bank guarantee.[41] If subsequently performance under the guarantee results in a claim by the guarantor under a counter-guarantee provided by the lessee, the resulting claim by the guarantor is inadmissible in case of a termination on the basis of art. 39 Fw, see the Supreme Court case of *HR Hansteen/Verwiel q.q.*

23.20 All in all, the system has grown overly complex. In our opinion, a good alternative would be to revoke art. 39 Fw altogether, only insofar that the trustee would like to use the goods leased, should there be a claim against the estate, instead of the current system of providing automatically a claim against the estate for three months. To the extent that the lessee does not perform under the contract, the lessor should be entitled to claim damages as an insolvency claim, provided that the lessor takes all measures to limit its damages, most notably by trying to find a new lessee.[42] Furthermore, the opening of insolvency procedures should not in itself, provide a ground for the lessor to terminate the lease contract.[43]

39 As follows from BW, art. 7:231 .

40 HR 17 February 2017, ECLI:NL:HR:2017:278 (*Hansteen/Verwiel q.q.*).

41 HR 15 November 2013, *JOR* 2014/27; *NJ* 2014, 68 (*Romania*); HR 17 February 2017, ECLI:NL:HR:2017:278 (*Hansteen/Verwiel q.q.*). In both cases the Supreme Courd held that if a third party has guaranteed the payment of such a claim, for instance by way of a bank or group guarantee, the third party is barred from having recourse to the insolvent estate for a subsequent contractual claim under a contra-guarantee provided by the lessee. In our view the rationale of this rule bars recourse by way of a security interest granted to the third party, or by way of set-off.

42 This is in conformity with HR 19 April 2013, *NJ* 2013/291 (*Koot Beheer/Tideman q.q.*), see para. 2.1.

43 See M.P. Verdonk, Een nieuw perspectief op beëindigingsclausules in huurovereenkomsten bij insolventie van de huurder, *NTHR* 2016/6, sub 3.2.1–3.2.2.

(b) Labour contracts

23.21 Another diversion from art. 37 Fw can be found for labour contracts in cases of insolvency of the employer (art. 40 Fw). Here we see a similar conflict of interests as identified under art. 39 Fw as to leases. In the first place, an employee will be placed in uncertainty about his job and his wages, including emoluments and the payment of social contributions. The estate however is confronted with the financial burden of prolonged labour contracts. For this reason, the legislator has tried to reconcile the interests of both parties. The estate trustee can terminate a labour contract on a short notice of six weeks in the interest of the estate ('*opzegging*'), while the employee's claim over this period is upgraded to a (preferred) claim against the estate (art. 3:288 BW and art. 40 Fw).[44]

(c) Utility contracts

23.22 A special rule in the insolvency context applies to contracts for energy and other utility contracts. A supplier of energy cannot suspend delivery on the ground that there is default of payment prior to the insolvency proceedings, if the delivery is in the interest of the business (art. 37b Fw). Also, a contract for energy supplies cannot be terminated by the supplier on the basis of a contractual clause that takes insolvency of the user as an event of default, unless the clause is invoked with approval of the trustee (art. 37b (3) Fw).

(d) Future contracts

23.23 The Insolvency Act provides in art. 38 Fw for a special rule for future contracts, that diverges from the system provided for by art. 37 Fw. It states that if, in the case of art. 37 Fw, it has been stipulated that goods, which are traded in the commodity market, are to be delivered at a fixed time or within a certain period, and if such time arises or such period expires after the opening of the insolvency procedure, the contract will be cancelled by the order opening the insolvency procedure, in which case the counterparty of the debtor may lodge a claim for damages as an unsecured creditor (cfm. art. 37a Fw).

44 Fw, art. 40 derogates from the general statutory rules of protection against dismissal for employees in the Dutch Civil Code. It also derogates from the possibility to file an additional contractual claim for severance pay in the insolvency proceedings of the employer if the trustee or employee terminates the employment contract using Fw, art. 40, see HR 12 January 1990, *NJ* 1990, 662 (*Van Gelder Papier*).

(e) Agency

23.24 Further examples of statutory deviations from the general principle in insolvency that contracts are made of steel,[45] are to be found in the Civil Code. For instance, in the case of agency, where the authority of the agent to represent the debtor and dispose over the insolvent estate ends by operation of law upon formal insolvency of the principal (art. 3:72 sub a BW). A similar provision is given in art. 7:422 (1), sub a BW for mandate.

(3) Insolvency clauses: divestment clauses and multiplier

23.25 Dutch insolvency law takes a liberal approach towards termination clauses, flowing from the principle that contractual freedom is as much as possible upheld in insolvency. This is also the case for stipulated claims for damages. This raises the question how far party autonomy within the context of insolvency goes.[46] This paragraph looks at clauses that are intended to use the opening of formal insolvency proceedings as a triggering event for the coming into existence of additional (monetary) obligations for the debtor (clauses for damages or a penalty), or the lapse of obligations towards the insolvent party (divestment clauses). These types of insolvency clauses may adequately be referred to as legal acts 'ruling from the grave'. Such acts are clearly detrimental to the joint creditors while at the same time they pose no burden on the debtor itself.[47] This observation calls for a conceptual distinction, for it should be noted that these types of insolvency clauses infringe different principles. Stipulations leading to new liabilities for the estate conflict with the *pari passu* principle embodied in art. 3:277 (1) BW. Stipulations leading to a decrease of the assets of the estate on the other hand, conflict with the principle that all the assets of debtor should be available for its creditors (art. 3:276 BW/art. 20 Fw).[48]

23.26 The question is on what grounds these types of clauses may be invalidated. Case law on this matter is scarce. As seen before, it follows from the relevant case law (*HR BabyXL* and *HR Van der Hel q.q./Edon*[49]) that insolvency clauses may be curtailed on the ground of good faith and fair dealing (art. 6:248 (2) BW). In the literature it has been suggested that transaction avoidance may also provide an instrument (art. 42 Fw). Also, abuse of right (art. 3:13 BW),

45 Taken from B. Wessels, 'Insolventierecht, 3e druk, Gevolgen van faillietverklaring (1)' (Deel II, Deventer' Kluwer 2012), par. 2491d, 327, sub (i).

46 See Verstijlen 2006, 129.

47 See ibid., 137.

48 See ibid., 137; Van Zanten 2012, 389–90.

49 HR 13 May 2005, *NJ* 2005, 406; *JOR* 2005/222; AA 2005, 938 (*BabyXL*) and HR 16 October 1998, *LJN* ZC2741, *NJ* 1998, 896 (*Van der Hel q.q./Edon*).

the principle of fixation, tort and the *pari passu* principle have been proposed.[50] The leading case in this respect is the Supreme Court case *HR Megapool*, which will be discussed below. Unfortunately, the scope of this case remains unclear.

(a) Divestment clauses

23.27 In *HR Megapool*,[51] the Supreme Court had to decide about a contract that first of all provided the right to terminate the contract in case of the opening of formal insolvency proceedings. The contract in addition provided that as a result of such a termination, existing claims of the insolvent party against the solvent counterparty would be extinguished. Here the interests of the joint creditors were clearly at stake. For that reason the clause may be deemed to form a 'ruling from the grave' legal act. The Supreme Court held that if, as a result of the clause, the counterparty is freed of its obligations only because of the insolvency of its counterparty while having received performance by the insolvent party, this would constitute an infringement on the interests of the estate (art. 20 Fw) and could therefore be void (art. 3:40 BW).[52] Art. 20 Fw refers to the principle that the insolvency procedure extends to all the available assets of the debtor.[53] In this case, the Supreme Court, however, held that the contract did not run afoul of such principles on the basis of three grounds. First of all, although the contract could be terminated in case of insolvency, there were also other grounds on the basis of which the contract could have been terminated. Secondly, the Supreme Court held that the solvent counterparty also incurred losses because of the insolvency procedure.[54] Thirdly, the Supreme Court deemed it relevant that both parties involved were professional parties.[55] It does, however, follow from this case that similar clauses, that purport to the loss of assets in cases of, or related to insolvency, could under the circumstances be declared void. This would for instance be the case if

---

50 See Verstijlen 2006, 136–42; Van Zanten 2012, par. 8.5.2–8.5.3; R.J. de Weijs, *Faillissementspauliana, Insolvenzanfechtung & Transaction Avoidance in Insolvencies* (Deventer, Kluwer 2010) 276 (hereafter: De Weijs 2010); R.M. Wibier, De geldigheid van vervalbedingen naar Nederlands recht, mede in het licht van HR 12 April 2013 (De Bruyn q.q. en Disberg q.q./Laser Nederland), *WPNR* 2013/6985, sub 2; R.M. Wibier, *Alternatieven voor zekerheid op bankrekeningen (diss. Tilburg)*, (Deventer: Kluwer 2007) 100.

51 HR 12 April 2013, *NJ* 2013/224, JOR 2013/193 (*Megapool*).

52 BW, art. 3:40 states that legal acts contrary to law, public morals or public order are void.

53 As follows from the Legislative History Insolvency Act, see: Kortmann/Faber, *Geschiedenis van de Faillissementswet* (Heruitgave Van der Feltz I), 339.

54 The Supreme Court seems to hold that since there are claims and counterclaims, such a divestment clause is an easy way to end the relationship without the need to calculate exactly the amount of both claims. The right way to approach the issue is of course to do exactly that, namely calculate the exact amount. If there are claims and counterclaims, the amount needs to be established and set-off can be applied to the extent of their common amount.

55 The argument could and should rather go the other way, since the ruling from the grave clauses dealt with here, are much more something inserted into contracts by professional parties at the expense of other non-professional creditors.

property is transferred under suspending or dissolutive condition of insolvency.[56] In *HR Megapool*, the Supreme Court also held it possible that the invocation of the clause concerned may be contrary to the principle of good faith and fair dealing (art. 6:248 (2) BW). This statutory provision requires a balancing of interests in the context of all circumstances, both at the moment of the conclusion of the contract and thereafter.[57] In the latter case of *HR Van Boekhold/Haveman*[58] the Supreme Court held that legal acts that are intended to be disadvantageous to creditors are contrary to public morals and therefore void (art. 3:40 BW). This signals the prohibition of legal acts with the sole[59] intention of prejudicing creditors as a subcategory of public morals.[60] It may be assumed that this provides for an instrument against 'ruling from the grave' clauses aimed at withholding assets from the estate in case of insolvency.[61]

(b) *Contractual increases (multipliers)*

Under Dutch insolvency law, the principle of fixation[62] may stand in the way of the admissibility of additional claims arising out of insolvency clauses that use the opening of formal insolvency procedures as an event of default. It is an aspect of this central principle of insolvency law, that the liabilities of the estate are frozen from the commencement of the proceeding. It follows from this aspect that in principle only pre-insolvency claims can be filed (arts 24 and 26 Fw).[63] The same applies if liquidation is preceded by suspension of payment. See Court of first instance Amsterdam, 25 January 2006, *JOR* 2006, 220 where an increase of a loan became due by invoking an Optional Redemption Notice after the opening of an insolvency proceedings (here a suspension of payment procedure). The increase in the due amount was held to be inadmissible. **23.28**

(c) *Penalty clauses*

Penalty clauses are defined in art. 6:91 BW as clauses that are aimed at the coming into existence of a monetary or other obligation in case of default of **23.29**

56 See J.J. van Hees, annotation of HR Megapool, *JOR* 2011/101, sub 8.

57 Asser/Hartkamp and Sieburgh 6-III* 2010, nr. 421 e.v.

58 HR 19 December 2014, *JOR* 2015/60 (*Van Boekhold/Haveman*).

59 S.C.J.J. Kortmann, annotation of HR Boekhold/Haveman, *JOR* 2015/60, sub 6 and HR 12 April 2013, *NJ* 2013/224, JOR 2013/193 (*Megapool*).

60 See B. Hoops, 'Het verbod van de opzettelijke en onevenredige benadeling van schuldeisers als een sub-norm van de goede zeden: lessen uit het arrest Van Boekhold/Haveman van de Hoge Raad', (2015) *WPNR* 7063.

61 Comp. K.P. Hoogenboezem, annotation to Gerechtshof Amsterdam, 26 July 2016, *JOR* 2017/47, sub 9.

62 The principle of fixation is the main principle of insolvency law, resulting in the fixation of the legal positions of the participants in the insolvency procedure from the moment of the opening thereof, see HR 31 December 1909, *W.* 8957 (*Op den Ende/De Haan*); HR 18 December 1987, *NJ* 1988, 340 (*OAR/ABN*); HR 17 February 1995, *NJ* 1996, 471 (*Mulder q.q./CLBN*); HR 26 June 1998, *NJ* 1998 745 (*Aerts q.q./ABN AMRO*).

63 See Verstijlen 2006, 138; De Weijs 2010, 276; Van Zanten 2012, 391.

the debtor, regardless of whether the clause is intended to compensate for damages or to urge the debtor to perform. It follows from this definition that there are two categories of penalty clauses. The first category is *fixed penalty* clauses that are intended to fixate beforehand the exact amount of damages to be awarded, thereby replacing statutory rules on compensation or specific performance. The second category is so called *pure penalty* clauses that are intended to induce the debtor to perform and where the penalty is often to be paid in addition to statutory rights for compensation or specific performance.[64]

Fixed penalty clauses ('schadefixerend boetebeding')

23.30 If the fixed penalty clause was intended to avoid discussions about compensation for damages in case of a breach of contract, there seems to be no problem with regard to its admissibility under Dutch insolvency law. Regardless of whether the penalty became due before the proceeding by the debtor or afterwards as a result of the refusal of the trustee to continue the contract, the resulting claim can be filed either on the ground that it is a pre-insolvency claim (art. 26 Fw) or because it qualifies as an art. 37a Fw claim.[65] See the aforementioned Supreme Court cases of *HR BabyXL* and *HR Aukema q.q./ Uni Invest*.

23.31 This outcome seems to be different if the fixed penalty clause is specifically linked to the opening of an insolvency procedure. In that case it might be that the penalty is intended solely to provide the counterparty with a higher claim in the proceedings. This could be in the counterparty's interest, for instance to provide the counterparty with a netting opportunity or if the counterparty is provided with a security interest for the penalty.[66] If so, the debtor is ruling 'from the grave' since he himself is unaffected by the clause outside of insolvency, whereas upon insolvency the other creditors are paid less out of the proceeds.[67] It is to be doubted if contractual freedom could validate such a *de facto* determination of third-party rights, since it would infringe upon the rules of distribution during a *concursus creditorum* (arts 3:276 and 3:277 BW).[68] For this reason it is assumed that the trustee may have ground to invoke transaction avoidance (art. 42 Fw).[69] The creation beforehand of a considerable monetary obligation for the insolvent party, lacks economic relevance if it

64 See Van Zanten 2012, par. 8.4.1. The distinction may not always be clear, see Parl. Gesch. Boek 6, 321 and Asser/Hartkamp and Sieburgh 6-I* 2012, nr. 414. By request of the debtor penalties can be limited by the courts (BW, art. 6:94).

65 Verstijlen 2006, 136.

66 See De Weijs 2010, 274.

67 Verstijlen 2006, 137.

68 Van Zanten 2012, par. 8.5.2.

69 Verstijlen 2006, 146; Van Zanten 2012, 390; De Weijs 2010, 275.

is intended only to give the counterparty a better position in insolvency.[70] This would then be to the detriment of the other creditors. As rightly pointed out in literature, if not on the ground of transaction avoidance, the resulting post-insolvency claim may be barred by the principle of fixation (arts 24 and 26 Fw).[71] Furthermore, as was seen before, legal acts purporting (solely) to unreasonably prejudice creditors can be contrary to public morals (art. 3:40 BW). It may be assumed that this will contribute to a more critical approach towards 'ruling from the grave' legal acts aimed at putting a penalty on insolvency of one of the contractual parties.[72]

Pure penalty clauses ('zuiver boetebeding')

Pure penalty clauses are aimed at inducing the debtor to perform. If the **23.32** penalty is forfeited after the proceedings the resulting claim would seem to be beyond meaning, since performance of the debtor itself is illusory. For penalties forfeited after insolvency admissibility is precluded on several grounds. First, the resulting claim comes into existence after the proceedings and its filing will therefore be barred by the principle of fixation (arts 24 and 26 Fw). Secondly, the fact that a pure penalty clause lacks the character of compensation for damages, means that the resulting claim cannot be filed by way of art. 37a Fw.[73]

C. LEGISLATIVE REFORMS

Although some revisions have been made, it is remarkable that the Insolvency **23.33** Act has been functioning for more than a century without any large modifications. Although remarkable, it is broadly felt that as a result of the contemporary economic climate, internationalisation, initiatives on the plane of the EU, and the development of more modern day views on the nature and purposes of insolvency law, a wider spectrum of insolvency measures has become necessary.

In November 2007 a preliminary draft of a new Insolvency Act was presented **23.34** by a committee.[74] In this preliminary draft the three currently existing procedures were combined into one insolvency procedure. The draft has,

70 Verstijlen 2006, 141; De Weijs 2010, 275.

71 Depending on whether the claim comes into existence on the sole ground of the commencement of proceedings, see Verstijlen 2006, 138; Van Zanten 2012, 391.

72 Comp. K.P. Hoogenboezem, annotation to Gerechtshof Amsterdam, 26 July 2016, *JOR* 2017/47, sub 9.

73 Verstijlen 2006, 142; Faber & Vermunt 2013, par. 12.111.

74 S.C.J.J. Kortmann and N.E.D. Faber (eds), 'Geschiedenis van de Faillissementswet. Voorontwerp Insolventiewet met toelichting' (Serie Onderneming en Recht, deel 2-IV, Deventer: Kluwer 2007).

however, formally been revoked.[75] Since then, the Dutch legislature has embarked on a project which does not provide for a complete overhaul of the Dutch Insolvency Act, but instead provides for a 'Recalibration of Insolvency Law'.[76] This programme consists of three pillars, each pillar providing for different legislative proposals. They are the fraud pillar, the reorganisation pillar, and the modernisation pillar.

23.35 As to the first pillar, dealing with fraud, three legislative acts have been adopted. First, one dealing with a civil law director's disqualification.[77] Secondly, a legislative act revising the criminal law provisions as to insolvency related fraud.[78] These first proposals are in force as of July 1, 2016. The third legislative proposal as to reinforcing the position of the trustee, entered into force on July 1, 2017.[79]

23.36 The second pillar of reorganisation, again consists of three legislative proposals. The first proposal referred to as the Act Continuity of Enterprises I (Wet Continuïteit Ondernemingen I) provides for the possibility of a pre-pack sale.[80] The second proposal, the Act on the Confirmation of a Private Restructuring Plan in order to Prevent Bankruptcy, provides for the possibility of a composition plan including a cram down outside a formal insolvency procedure.[81] The third proposal, the Act Continuity of Enterprises III, will provide for new tools for the trustee to deal with a liquidation procedure more efficiently.[82] Of these three proposals, only the first proposal on pre-packs has been accepted by the Second Chamber of Parliament.

---

75 *Kamerstukken II*, 2010/2011, Handelingen 1014.

76 *Kamerstukken II*, 2012/2013, 29 911, nr. 74.

77 Act Director's Disqualification under Civil Law, *Stb.* 2016, 153.

78 Act Revision Insolvency related Fraud, *Stb.* 2016, 154.

79 Act Reinforcement of the Position of the Trustee, *Stb.* 2017, 124.

80 See proposal *EK 34.218*, A, which was adopted by the Second Chamber of Parliament on 21 June 2016. For its current legislative status, see the letter of the Minister of 5 December 2017, *Kamerstukken I*, 2017–18, 34218, H.

81 Wet homologatie onderhands akkoord ter voorkoming van faillissement (WHOA). This draft proposal was formerly known as the Act Continuity of Enterprises II (WCO II), see *Kamerstukken II* 2013/14, 33 695, 5. It has recently been revised, introducing an Absolute Priority Rule, and was published for consultation between 5 September and 1 December 2017.

82 *Kamerstukken II* 2016/17, 33 695, nr. 14. This proposal contains new measures for the continuation of insolvent companies, including an obligation for essential suppliers to continue performing during a liquidation procedure, see *Kamerstukken II* 2013/14, 33 695, nr. 3.

The third pillar of modernisation produced a draft legislative proposal. Its measures are aimed at efficiency, knowledge concentration in the judiciary and simplification of the liquidation procedure.[83] 23.37

Given the current state of the proposals under the reorganisation pillar, it is uncertain if they will provide for a fundamental revision of the existing rules on non-specific executory contracts. 23.38

D. CONCLUDING REMARKS

Dutch insolvency law takes a liberal approach toward insolvency clauses in general. This is as a result of the principle of integral continuation of contracts during insolvency and the fact that the Dutch Insolvency Act lacks specific general rules on this point. Parties to long-term contracts are to a large extent free to decide beforehand what their positions will be if one of them becomes insolvent. Due to the continuation principle, insolvency clauses, save exceptions, can be invoked in insolvency proceedings. This ascertains that as a starting point under Dutch insolvency law party autonomy prevails within the context of insolvency. 23.39

The primacy of pre-insolvency party autonomy within the context of insolvency is, however, not absolute. From case law it follows that insolvency clauses may be curtailed, although this mainly depends on open norms such as equality of creditors, the principle of fixation, good faith and fair dealing and public moral rules, the latter being aimed at preserving the insolvent estate's assets and preventing against infringements on the *pari passu* rule. Transaction avoidance provides a substantive norm. It is however unclear to what extent these instruments invalidate insolvency clauses. 23.40

As to insolvency clauses, a more critical approach seems desirable. This would seem to be true not only for termination clauses when the counterparty is an essential participant for realising going-concern value. Especially with regard to the more suspicious 'ruling from the grave' clauses, being stipulations leading to either an increase of liabilities for the insolvent estate or a decrease of the estate's assets, such a critical approach seems desirable. These stipulations are clearly detrimental to the joint creditors. However, due to the absence of statutory rules, limited case law and the fact that there is little 23.41

83 *Kamerstukken II* 2015/16, 33 695, nr. 12; *Kamerstukken II* 2017/18, 33 695, nr. 15. Among other measures, this pillar introduces a bar date and allowing more electronic ways of communication and more tailor made solutions in individual cases.

academic debate on this point, at present a theoretical foundation for the approach on and admissibility of insolvency clauses, is largely absent under Dutch insolvency law.

24

NATIONAL REPORT FOR THE REPUBLIC OF TURKEY

Çağlar Kaçar

A. INTRODUCTION

Insolvency procedures in Turkey are mainly governed by the Enforcement and Bankruptcy Law No. 2004 ('EBL'). EBL was accepted by the Grand National Assembly of Turkey on June, 9th 1932 and entered into force on September, 4th 1932. Since then, EBL has been amended several times to remain in line with the needs of a growing economy. EBL is a set of rules governing debt recovery procedures, insolvency resolution and liquidation procedures. Insolvency procedures include formal restructuring mechanisms and insolvency liquidation. Out-of-court restructurings are not regulated under Turkish legislation.[1] **24.01**

1 But it should be noted that debtors frequently use negotiation techniques with their creditors to restructure the debt.

B. CORPORATE INSOLVENCY PROCEDURES

(1) Ordinary composition

24.02 Any debtor may prevent its insolvency by filing for an ordinary composition (insolvency preventive composition), which allows the debtor to restructure its debt by reaching an agreement with his/her creditors.

24.03 The debtor may apply for ordinary composition by producing its balance sheet and income statement and providing a restructuring plan before the enforcement court. If the court is convinced that the success of the restructuring plan is more likely than not, and that it will cause no loss on the part of the creditors, it will provide the debtor with a period of up to a three-month term to negotiate the composition, and it will appoint one to three commissioners to supervise the procedure.

24.04 Under Article 51/2 of EBL, no enforcement or bankruptcy proceeding can be made and the previously initiated proceedings will be stopped, except the foreclosure of pledged property for the receivables obtained through the pledge of movables and immovables, and the proceedings of seizure for the employees' receivables against the debtor during the term given for the composition. If the decision to affirm the composition is not issued within the term, the court may, with due regard to the report of the commissioner, suspend the proceedings previously initiated against the debtor or not initiate new proceedings for the period following the conclusion of the composition term.

24.05 During this period, the debtor may conduct its activity under the supervision of the commissioner. Thereafter, the commissioner will call the creditors and the creditors will decide whether to accept or reject the composition.

24.06 For the acceptance of the composition, both the majority of the creditors (i.e., a majority exceeding half of the informed and written creditors) and the receivable majority (i.e., the receivables of the informed and written creditors should exceed at least two-thirds of the total receivable amount) should be met and the requirement of depositing a security should be fulfilled. The privileged creditors and the pledgees are not included in this calculation.

24.07 If the creditors accept the proposed composition, it will be affirmed by the commercial court. The composition with creditors is compulsory for all non-privileged creditors including those who have cast a dissenting vote or who failed to have their claims registered in the composition of debts except the pledgees, public receivables and privileged receivables. The debtor will pay its debts pursuant to the affirmed composition.

(2) Post-insolvency composition

The insolvent debtor may also propose a composition during the liquidation which is also called insolvency removing composition. 24.08

The same majority in the ordinary composition is required for the acceptance of the post-insolvency composition. However, this time the proposal will be made during the bankruptcy administration; there is no time limit to submit this proposal, and no commissioner is appointed for the composition. The composition with creditors proposed during the liquidation will be examined in the second meeting of the creditors. A term of ten days is given for participation of the creditors. Upon expiration of this composition term, the insolvency administration will submit the composition project and its reasoned report to the commercial court competent for the insolvency procedure. The conditions required for approval of the composition are the same as those specified in the ordinary composition with creditors. The privileged creditors, including the creditors with public receivables and the pledgees are not included in this calculation. The encashment will be postponed until the commercial court takes a decision for affirmation. The court will affirm the composition if it determines the existence of the necessary requirements; its decision will then be communicated to the insolvent administrator. If the request for affirmation is rejected, the insolvency administration will continue the liquidation procedure following receipt of a notice in this respect. 24.09

(3) Postponement of insolvency/bankruptcy[2]

According to Article 179 of EBL[3] only over-indebted capital companies or cooperatives may request the postponement of bankruptcy (POB).[4] Creditors of those entities are also eligible to request POB. 24.10

2 As per Executive Order 669, issued in consequence of the coup attempt on July 15 2016, during the state of emergency, postponement of bankruptcy applications are prohibited.

3 EBL, art. 179. – If and when it is declared by the management and representative bodies or if the company or the cooperative society is in liquidation, by its liquidators or a creditor, or it is determined by the competent court that the liabilities of the capital company or the cooperative society are more than its assets, the capital company or the cooperative society will be adjudged bankrupt without a prior bankruptcy proceeding. Provided, however, that any one of the management and representative bodies or the creditors may demand adjournment of adjudication of bankruptcy by filing to the court a project of recovery proving that the company or the cooperative society may be recovered. If the project of recovery is found serious and persuasive, the court will adjourn adjudication of bankruptcy. Information and documents proving that the project of recovery is serious and persuasive must also be presented to the court. The court may, if deemed necessary, hear the management and representative bodies and the creditors. Demands for adjournment of adjudication of bankruptcy will be tried with priority and as a matter of urgency.

4 Supreme Court 19th Civil Chamber Decision dated 20.03.2008 (E. 2008/9249) – 'It is stated in the expert report that the assets of the Company are enough to cover its debts. Granting bankruptcy in such a case is against the law and the procedures. The first instance court should have rejected the requests of the claimant.'

24.11 The debtor or any creditor may request the postponement of the debtor's bankruptcy by providing the court with an improvement project indicating the objective and real sources, including investment of new cash capital.[5]

24.12 The information and documents (e.g., list indicating the payment terms and amounts of existing debts; addresses of creditors; inventories according to the features of the industry as well as their waiting period and amount; the latest balance sheet and income statement submitted to the tax office; trade registry certificate of the company or cooperative) proving that the improvement project is serious and persuasive should also be submitted to the court. In this respect, the debtor requesting the POB should have been over-indebted, the improvement project should be serious and persuasive,[6] there should be the hope of improvement and the debtor should not have made use of the extraordinary duration.[7]

24.13 The duration for the postponement of insolvency can be a maximum of one year. This duration may be extended for a year more where it is found appropriate by the court taking into consideration the reports given by the trustee.

24.14 Following the decision for postponement, no proceedings, including the proceedings related to the public receivables, can be commenced against the debtor and the previously initiated proceedings will be automatically stopped.[8]

24.15 During the postponement, a foreclosure proceeding against pledged property can be initiated by the creditors. However, protective measures cannot be taken and the sale of a pledged property cannot be realised due to such

---

5 Supreme Court 19th Civil Chamber Decision dated 01.05.2008 (E.2008/2268) – '… as a rule new financial resources should be found …'.

6 Supreme Court 19th Civil Chamber Decision dated 13.06.2002 (E. 2002/1267) – 'The Court shall decide on postponement in the event that it is convinced the measures to be taken are enough for the Company to recover. The Court may request a report from an expert team in order to decide whether or not the measures to be taken are sufficient.'

Supreme Court 19th Civil Chamber Decision dated 25.11.2010 (E. 2009/9027) – 'In the event that the recovery report has been found compelling and serious, the Court shall grant postponement to the Company. Compellingness and seriousness of the recovery report shall be determined on solid facts.'

7 Kuru, *Baki İcra ve İflas Hukuku El Kitabı* (2nd edn, 2013).

8 Supreme Court 23rd Civil Chamber Decision dated 06.05.2013 (E. 2013/3126) – In bankruptcy postponement cases the courts are empowered to take any precautions necessary to protect the applicant's assets if they find the reasons presented for it by the claimant compelling. When deciding for the measures, the Court should protect benefits of the creditors as well as the Company. However the Court should not eliminate legal ways enabling creditors to claim their receivables.

proceedings. In this case, the interest will accrue during the term of postponement and a security should be provided for the interests that cannot be met with the current pledge.

A proceeding through seizure may be conducted for the employee's receivables as provided by Article 206 of the EBL. **24.16**

This is a debtor-in-possession procedure: the debtor's bodies and representatives retain their powers, even if under the supervision of the trustee appointed by the court. The rights and obligations of the debtor arising from the agreements executed prior to the decision of postponement will continue to be valid. The opening of this procedure does not prevent the continuance of the previously initiated lawsuits or the initiation of new lawsuits, with the sole exception of bankruptcy petitions. **24.17**

Following rejection of the request for the postponement of insolvency or the determination of the impossibility of an improvement at the end of the duration for postponement, the court will decide whether the debtor should file for insolvency/liquidation. Even if the duration for postponement has not yet expired, if the court comes to the conclusion based on the reports delivered by the trustee that the improvement of the company's or the cooperative's financial position is not possible, it may withdraw the decision for postponement, and decide on the insolvency of the company or cooperative. If the improvement of the company is realised at the end of the duration for postponement, the decision of postponement will be removed and the company will continue to conduct its activities. **24.18**

(4) Restructuring of capital companies and cooperatives through mutual consent

Restructuring of capital companies and cooperatives through mutual consent is another insolvency resolution procedure introduced by the legislature to restructure the debts of large business entities. However, banks and insurance companies cannot file an application for this procedure. **24.19**

In order to benefit from this procedure, applications should be prepared in good faith. The debtor should be unable to pay its debts as they fall due, its current assets and receivables should not be sufficient to meet its debts or it should be on the verge of falling into such a situation. To file an application to the competent commercial court, the eligible capital company or cooperative should reach an agreement with the majority of the creditors that would be impaired by the procedure/agreement. **24.20**

24.21 The debtor is not obliged to reach an agreement with all its creditors. Nevertheless, the agreement shall include all the creditors affected by the project. It is also possible for the debtor to place similar creditors in different classes. In this case, each class should vote in favour of the project with the majority prescribed by the law. The necessary majority will be deemed to have been achieved if the restructuring project is approved by more than half of the creditors that are affected by the project which represent at least two-thirds of the creditors participating in the voting. If the project contains more than one class of creditors, each class should have voted in favour of the project with the majority prescribed by the law. The debtor should also prove in its application that the amount that each dissenting creditor would receive as a result of the plan/project will be no less than the amount that the same creditor would have likely acquired as a result of the liquidation in bankruptcy.

24.22 The court that receives the application will promptly take any measures it may deem necessary with regard to the activities of the debtor until the date in which the final decision regarding the application is taken. The court may suspend any executory or civil proceedings initiated against the debtor, and it may prohibit the commencement of new lawsuits.

24.23 The approved restructuring project and its conditions prevail over any other existing agreements with the creditors that are affected by the project.

Time extension in extraordinary cases

24.24 In extraordinary cases and especially during the periods of economic crisis, the government may extend the time limits imposed on the debtors. In cases where the debtor fails to execute the agreed plan through no fault of its own, the enforcement court may extend the time limit for a period not exceeding six months if it is proven to its satisfaction that the plan is still achievable.

24.25 Although a proceeding may be conducted against the debtor during the time extension given in extraordinary cases, these proceedings will not result in conservation, encashment or bankruptcy as long as the extension continues to be in effect.

(5) Liquidation through composition with creditors

24.26 In the liquidation through composition with creditors, the debtor transfers all its properties and assets to the creditors, who are in charge of liquidating them and distributing the proceeds among themselves.

The debtor provides the creditors with the power to perform any act of disposal on its property, or to transfer the whole or any part of its business to third parties. The creditors will exercise this power of performing any act of disposal through the liquidators appointed by the creditors. **24.27**

This method of liquidation is also in favour of the debtor since it protects the debtor against insolvency. Moreover, the debtor will get rid of its debts as a rule contrary to the debtor liquidated within the framework of the current insolvency liquidation procedure. **24.28**

(6) Insolvency liquidation

As a general rule, only merchants are subject to insolvency in the Turkish Law (art. 43 of the EBL, art. 20 of TCC). If the commercial court determines the existence of the debt and the reason for insolvency as a result of the investigation, it will directly decide for the bankruptcy of the debtor without rendering the depository injunction for the debtor. **24.29**

Insolvency decisions are rendered by the commercial courts. The commencement of liquidation is stipulated in the decision with the date and hour. The decision to open the proceeding is served to the bankruptcy office, which will automatically serve it to several bodies and authorities (the land registry, the trade registry, the customs and postal administrations, the Banks Association of Turkey, the local chambers of commerce, the chambers of industry, the stock exchange, the Capital Market Board and other necessary authorities). The bankruptcy office also publishes the decision in: **24.30**

- a national newspaper with circulation in excess of 50,000/day;
- a local newspaper at the debtor's centre of main interest; and
- a trade registry gazette.

Liquidation is ordinarily executed if the debtor's assets cover the liquidation costs. Ordinary liquidation is managed by the insolvency administration, which consists of three persons appointed by the enforcement court from the six nominees suggested by each creditor in the first creditors' meeting. The powers and responsibilities of the insolvency administration are limited to those stated in the EBL. **24.31**

In the ordinary liquidation (*adi tasfiye*), the creditors and those claiming progress payment are requested by the administration to file their claims and to produce the originals or certified copies of the supporting documents (share certificates and commercial book records, etc.). **24.32**

24.33 The administration will examine the claims. If it is possible to make available the insolvent debtor, the administration will ask its directors' statement and take a decision for the acceptance or rejection of the relevant claim registrations.

24.34 The opening of an insolvency procedure results in the following consequences, which cannot be averted even if the decision is appealed:

- all the debtor's sizeable assets, receivables and rights will be automatically entrusted in the bankruptcy estate;
- the right to initiate an avoidance action will pass to the bankruptcy estate;
- the debtor's power to perform any act over his/her properties will cease;
- as a rule, the proceedings initiated against the debtor prior to the initiation of the insolvency will be stopped and they will be terminated after the completion of the insolvency procedure. No new proceeding can be opened against the debtor during the liquidation without the leave of the court;
- the overdue receivables of the debtor except those which are secured under a mortgage will become due and payable concurrently with the opening of the liquidation;
- the non-pecuniary receivables will be converted into the pecuniary claims by the creditors thereof;
- interest will continue to accrue for the receivables included in the bankruptcy estate;
- set-off is permitted.

C. TREATMENT OF EXECUTORY CONTRACTS

(1) Effect of reorganisation applications

24.35 In Turkish law there is no provision regulating the termination of executory contracts upon the opening of a formal restructuring procedure.[9] Therefore herein we investigated the consequences arising in the case of the frequently used postponement of insolvency procedure.

24.36 Lacking any specific regulation in the EBL, the decision for postponement generally will not have any effect on the agreements previously signed by the company. That is to say, these agreements will be effective despite the decision

9 However it is important to note that in practice *ipso facto* clauses are generally observed in agreements and creditors are approached to terminate the ongoing contracts under these *ipso facto* clauses.

for postponement. However, in exceptional circumstances, if the agreement between the parties and the acts to be performed pursuant to this agreement conflict with the measures included in the improvement project submitted to the court by the company or cooperative, the court may decide to reject or terminate that agreement.

The law however prescribes that existing contracts can be terminated in cases of impossibility to perform pursuant to Article 136 of the TCO. The debtor can also ask the court to change the conditions of the contract if an extraordinary and unpredictable (at the time of the definition of the agreement) event occurs, and the performance of the contract would be contrary to the rules of honesty. **24.37**

As an alternative, if modification is not feasible, in the same circumstances the debtor is also entitled to withdraw from this agreement pursuant to Article 138 of the TCO. **24.38**

(2) Effect of the opening of a liquidation procedure

Agreements are not terminated automatically on the bankruptcy of one party. The law only states that the following exceptional agreements are deemed to be terminated on the bankruptcy of one party: **24.39**

Statutorily ceased agreements on the bankruptcy of one party:

- Deed of gift
  Deed of gift is a contract regulated under Article 285 of TCO by which a donor undertakes to give one of its own assets (either periodically or only on one occasion) to a beneficiary without receiving any consideration for it. According to Article 296 of TCO if a donor is declared bankrupt his obligations under a deed of gift will cease.
- Usufruct lease agreements
  The usufruct lease is a contract by which the lessor undertakes to give the lessee the use of a productive object or a right and the benefit of its fruits or proceeds in return for a rent. (TCO art. 357) Pursuant to Article 370 of the TCO if the lessee becomes bankrupt, the usufructuary lease agreement terminates *ipso facto* upon the commencement of the liquidation process. However if sufficient warranty is given for current year's lease and the inventory, the lessor is obliged to maintain the usufruct contract until the end of the lease year.

- Attorney agreements
  Attorney contract ends on the bankruptcy of the principal or the attorney, unless otherwise agreed or dictated by the nature of attorney business. (art. 513 of TCO)
- Commission agreements
  Commission agreements will terminate *ipso facto* upon the bankruptcy of the principal or the broker.
- Agency agreements
  Agency agreements will terminate on the bankruptcy of the principal or the agency, unless otherwise agreed or dictated by the nature of agency business. (art. 513 of TCO)
- Life annuity and lifelong support agreements
  Upon the bankruptcy of the debtor (annuity debtor or settlor) each contract will terminate.[10,11]
- Insurance contract
  According to Article 1418 of TCC in the case of the bankruptcy of the insurer the insurance contract will terminate.
- Ordinary partnership agreements
  Ordinary partnership agreements will be terminated on the bankruptcy of one of the partners unless otherwise stated in the agreement.
- Bank account agreements
  Pursuant to Article 98 of TCC, bank account agreements will be terminated upon the bankruptcy of one of the parties.
- Association of shipowners
  Association of shipowners is a kind of partnership which is regulated under Article 1064 of TCC where each partner has a joint ownership on the same ship. According to Article 1084 of the TCC, associations of shipowners will be automatically terminated upon the commencement of bankruptcy liquidation process against the association.
- Financial lease agreement
  Pursuant to Article 30 of FLL[12] unless otherwise specified in the contract, the contract shall be terminated automatically in case of the bankruptcy of the lessee. On the other hand, in case of the bankruptcy of the lessor the contract remains valid until the pre-agreed termination date. (art. 29 of FLL)

---

10 Kuru, *supra* note 7.

11 Atalay Pekcanıtez, *Sungurtekin Özkan, Özekes İcra ve İflas Hukuku Ders Kitabı* (3rd edn, 2016).

12 Financial Leasing Factoring, and Financing Companies Law No. 6361 Published in the Official Gazette dated December 13, 2012 No. 28496.

(3) Other agreements and general approach

The agreements generally will not be deemed rejected or terminated in the case of a bankruptcy of one party as stated above. In this case, the party which has not gone bankrupt may request execution of the agreement. However, the right of the other party to request the execution of the agreement is a bankruptcy claim.[13] If this right is pecuniary, the other party will have this claim registered as a bankruptcy claim in the bankruptcy estate. On the other hand, if the subject-matter of this right to claim is not money, the other party may have this amount converted into a pecuniary claim and have his claim registered as a pecuniary claim in the bankruptcy estate (art. 198/I). Herein, the pecuniary claim which may be requested by the other party in consideration of the right to claim execution is the positive damage of the other party (Code of Obligations, art. 96). That is to say, this is an amount of money which will ensure a situation equal to the situation which may have occurred in case of the specific performance of the obligation. If the subject-matter of the receivable is a product, the receivable of the creditor will be converted into the pecuniary claim equal to the value of the same as of the opening of bankruptcy. **24.40**

In Article 98 of the TCO, the following is stated: **24.41**

> In an agreement burdening mutual debts, if either party fails to fulfill its obligation and especially if it goes bankrupt or the transaction of attachment against the said party remains inconclusive and as a result, the right of the other party is endangered due to this reason, the said party may refrain from fulfilling its obligation until its performance is secured.
>
> The party whose right is endangered may withdraw from the agreement unless a guarantee is given within an appropriate duration.

As can be seen, in the case where either party fails to fulfil its obligation or goes bankrupt, the other (performing) party may request a guarantee for the payment of its own performance and it is entitled to refrain from fulfilling its obligation until such a guarantee is given. The party whose right is endangered may withdraw from the agreement unless a guarantee is given within an appropriate duration. **24.42**

With regard to the mutual agreements between the parties: **24.43**

(a) If, as of the commencement of bankruptcy liquidation, the other party has completely fulfilled its obligations and the bankrupt has failed to

---

13 Kuru, *supra* note 7, 1247.

completely fulfil its obligation, the other party will have its claim registered as a bankruptcy claim in the bankruptcy estate. If the subject-matter of the receivable is anything other than money, the other party may have its claim converted into a pecuniary claim and have the same written as a pecuniary claim in the bankruptcy estate (art. 198/I);

(b) If both parties have failed to completely fulfil their obligation as of the commencement of bankruptcy liquidation, the other party may refrain from fulfilling its obligation until the fulfilment of the obligation in its favour is secured. If, however, this security is not delivered within a time period to be found appropriate by the bankruptcy administration upon request of the other party, then the other party may terminate the agreement (TCO, art. 98). Following this termination, the other party cannot have its claim registered in the bankruptcy estate of the bankrupt and will get rid of fulfilling its obligation. If the other party has partly fulfilled its obligation at the moment when the agreement is terminated, it will register this claim as a bankruptcy claim in the bankruptcy estate pursuant to the provisions regarding unjust enrichment. Pursuant to Article 98 of the TCO, the other party terminating the agreement cannot demand any compensation from the bankruptcy estate of the bankrupt. In order for the other party to terminate the agreement pursuant to Article 98 of the TCO, it is not necessary for the bankrupt to be in default;

(c) If the other party does not terminate the agreement pursuant to Article 98 of the TCO, it will be obliged to fulfil its own obligation towards the bankruptcy estate. The other party will register its claim as a bankruptcy claim in the bankruptcy estate;

(d) the bankruptcy administration is authorized to proceed with the bilateral agreements. In cases where the specific performance is more profitable for the bankruptcy estate, the bankruptcy administration will prefer execution of an agreement, but it is not obliged to do the same.

24.44 Under Turkish law, the bankruptcy of an employer is not a valid reason to terminate an employment agreement. There are, however, exceptions, which have been analysed below.

24.45 As a matter of fact, there is no special regulation in the law stating that the bankruptcy will lead to the termination of the employment agreements as bankruptcy is not arranged as a reason that makes the fulfillment of the obligation impossible. The employers change as observed in the transfer of the workplace and the bankruptcy administration will have assumed the management of the business affairs. In this case, the bankruptcy administration may terminate the employment agreement complying with the notice period if the same is deemed to be necessary.

Although the fact of bankruptcy is not regulated as a reason leading to the termination of the employment agreement in the Turkish Labour Law, art. 98 of the TCO states that: 'If either party goes bankrupt and if the right of the other party is endangered in the agreements burdening both parties with debt, the said party may request a security within an appropriate duration or otherwise, it may withdraw from the agreement.' **24.46**

In case of the employer's bankruptcy, the employee's right to terminate the agreement will arise if a guarantee is not given within an appropriate duration although the employee requests the delivery of a security for his/her wage after the bankruptcy from the bankruptcy estate pursuant to Article 436 of the TCO. If a guarantee is given by the employer within an appropriate duration, the employee will be obliged to proceed with the employment contract towards the bankruptcy estate. **24.47**

(4) Effects of *ipso facto* clauses

There is no specific provision in Turkish law regulating the validity of *ipso facto* clauses upon the commencement of either a restructuring or liquidation process. For the purposes of this study, *ipso facto* clauses are any provisions in an agreement which permit its termination due to the bankruptcy, insolvency or financial condition of a party. **24.48**

In general, two approaches can be followed to assess the validity of *ipso facto* clauses. One is a debtor-friendly approach, by means of which the debtor would be entitled to enforce the contract despite the existence of this clause. The other one is the 'freedom of contract' approach, which preserves the validity and enforceability of *ipso facto* clauses in the insolvency context. **24.49**

To accept and to apply the second approach may sometimes be devastating for debtors, where a debtor provides a rehabilitation plan which depends on the agreements including *ipso facto* clauses. In this case upon determination of the importance of the relevant agreements which include *ipso facto* clauses, the court should take measures on the application of *ipso facto* clauses. **24.50**

D. REFORMS

24.51 There have been several amendments made to the EBL since its enactment in 1932. The aim of the reforms has not been consistent through time. Nonetheless, this chapter looks at the reforms introduced in the last decade to discuss the goals pursued by the legislature, and which interest groups have played an active role in shaping the regulatory agenda.

24.52 After the 2001 economic crisis, Turkey made several changes on a long-standing, but rarely used institution called postponement of insolvency influenced by the financial institutions in accordance with the economic programme designed by the same institutions. The duration of the automatic stay was extended, and the process was simplified to favour debtors. Ultimately the reform efforts aimed at protecting distressed yet viable corporations to give them enough time to improve their financial condition.

24.53 The first amendments focused on postponement of insolvency, and they were introduced by means of Law No. 4949 published in the official Gazette on 30/07/2003. The amendments had originally been prepared by the Amendment Committee but they were later revised by the Parliamentary Justice Committee. The revisions made by the Justice Committee without consulting the Amendment Committee have been criticised by legal scholars.[14]

24.54 Other amendments have been introduced by Law No. 5092 published in the Official Gazette on 21/02/2004. This new amendment has mainly stretched the postponement terms from one plus one years to one plus four years. As can be seen, just four months following the previous amendment, the legislator realised that the statutory duration of the procedure was too short, hence it extended it to up to five years. This amendment has equally been criticised by legal scholars for lacking rationale and justification.[15]

24.55 Postponement of insolvency has been the most frequently used restructuring mechanism in the last decade. The procedure itself is recognised as a supplementary tool rather than a sole restructuring mechanism.[16] The main aim of the postponement of insolvency is to support and make way for the composition and restructuring of capital companies and cooperatives through mutual consent proceedings. However, composition institution has been taken

---

14 Selçuk Öztek, 'İflasın Ertelenmes' (2006) (59 Bankacılar Dergisi) 39.

15 Ibid., 40.

16 Ibid., 39.

back by the amendments solely made by the justice committee.[17] Additionally, the Justice Committee has also introduced a new restructuring mechanism called 'restructuring of capital companies and cooperatives through mutual consent'.[18] As a result, companies preferred filing for the latter procedure, with the result that composition has been rarely used in the past years.[19]

In this context, postponement of insolvency remains the most widely used procedure. **24.56**

Between 2009 and 2014, 3,524 companies applied for postponement of insolvency in Turkey.[20] However among the applicants, which were ultimately granted a postponement, only 2 per cent were subsequently able to exit from insolvency. The remaining 98 per cent of postponement applicants were ultimately declared insolvent, despite the court's postponement decision. **24.57**

Accordingly, it is beyond doubt that the Turkish insolvency postponement route is failing to fulfil its intended goal and is vulnerable to abuse. Financial creditors and private investors also observed that many applications for postponement of insolvency are filed in bad faith. The most concerning point is that it is being observed that the debtors are creating fictitious debts and using the automatic stay terms to transfer assets to other corporations. This also affects the liquidation process, as most of the bankruptcy estates do not have any valuable assets which can be liquidated. **24.58**

In light of these criticisms, the legislature tried to address some of these shortcomings. In this vein, in June 2016 the Turkey's Ministry of Finance and the Ministry of Justice put forward a draft legislation mainly aimed to shorten the postponement term to one plus one again. The draft amendment had been accepted by the legislator and the Law No. 6728 has been published in the Official Gazette and became effective on 09/08/2016. **24.59**

E. CONCLUDING REMARKS

In the last decade reforms on insolvency proceedings have mainly be prompted by suggestions and recommendations from financial institutions. Scholars and practitioners have been less influential in the regulatory reform process. As a **24.60**

17 Ibid.

18 Ibid., 40.

19 Ibid.

20 According to main opposition party report dated 22 June 2016 submitted to parliament. See http://www2.tbmm.gov.tr/ d26/2/2-1267.pdf (only available in Turkish, last accessed 04.03.2017).

result, Turkish insolvency procedures appear inefficient, with an average duration of 13 years. As a way forward, the author suggests that any major amendments to the insolvency bills initially prepared by the committees organised by the scholars and practitioners should be approved only after a new consultation of these committees by the legislator.

24.61 Under Turkish insolvency law, the treatment of executory contracts is not duly regulated. There are grey areas that have yet to be addressed, such as the lack of clear guidance on the treatment of *ipso facto* clauses and their effects in restructuring proceedings. In the author's view, their treatment should be regulated according to the 'debtor-friendly' method described above, especially with reference to restructuring procedures. If implemented in the law, this reform would give the debtors the power to apply to the court to retain and execute contracts, which otherwise would be terminated by reason of the enforceability of *ipso facto* clauses. The opposite, 'freedom of contract' interpretation would negatively affect the chances to rescue distressed yet viable corporations which entered into a formal restructuring mechanism in good faith and to undertake a serious rehabilitation project.

PART II

COMMON LAW SYSTEMS

25

NATIONAL REPORT FOR AUSTRALIA

Elizabeth Streten

A. INTRODUCTION

25.01 This research forms part of a global study undertaking an international comparison of the treatment of executory contracts in the context of insolvency. This component of the study examines the treatment of such contracts in Australian corporate insolvency. It is written at a time of regulatory reconsideration and transformation in Australia; when the long-held tradition of upholding 'ipso facto' clauses is changing as part of the Australian Government's innovation and reform agenda. The change forms part of the current conservative government's policy to modernise, harmonise and strengthen Australia's insolvency and restructuring laws, and to improve Australian business growth and economic prosperity.[1] A proposal paper and model was released for public consultation with a submission deadline of 27 May 2016.[2] Subsequently, a draft exposure bill was released for consultation on 28 March 2017.[3] The resulting *Treasury Laws Amendment (2017 Enterprise Incentives*

---

1 Australian Government, 'National Innovation & Science Agenda' (*Australian Government*, 7 December 2015) <http://www.innovation.gov.au/system/files/case-study/National%20Innovation%20and%20Science%20Agenda%20-%20Report.pdf> accessed 20 January 2017; Australian Government, 'Options paper: a modernisation and harmonisation of the regulatory framework applying to insolvency practitioners in Australia' (*Treasury*, June 2011) <http://www.treasury.gov.au/~/media/Treasury/Consultations%20and%20Reviews/Consultations/2011/A%20Modernisation%20and%20Harmonisation%20of%20the%20Regulatory%20Framework/Key%20Documents/PDF/Options_Paper20110602.ashx> accessed 20 January 2017.

2 Australian Government, 'Improving bankruptcy and insolvency laws Proposal Paper' (*Treasury*, April 2016) <https://static.treasury.gov.au/uploads/sites/1/2017/06/C2016-017_pp_NIS_insolvency_measures.pdf> accessed 21 January 2017.

3 Exposure Draft, Treasury Laws Amendment (2017 Enterprise Incentives No. 2) Bill 2017 (Cth).

No. 2) Act 2017 (Cth) received Royal Assent on 18 September 2017. Part of the provisions, pertaining to a safe harbour carve out from director personal liability for insolvency trading, commenced in September 2018. However, provisions pertaining to the stay on ipso facto clauses did not commence until 1 July 2018.

Australian law and government are framed by Australia's constitution and colonial history: pursuant to the constitution, Federal Parliament is granted concurrent power with the six State governments to formulate laws pertaining to insolvency.[4] The primary legislation enacted to regulate Australian corporate insolvency is the *Corporations Act 2001* (Cth) ('CA'),[5] supported by various rules and regulations.[6] In addition to statute, Commonwealth general (or common) law principles are also adopted.[7] Personal bankruptcy law (relating to individuals) is in a separate regime which is subject to separate law and regulation and does not form part of this study.[8] **25.02**

Australian contract law is similarly subject to statute and general law, shaped by its English heritage.[9] A contract is a legally enforceable agreement between parties which involves three essential elements: contractual intention; agreement; and consideration.[10] It involves a 'concluded bargain' between persons involving an offer and acceptance and is entered into voluntarily with consideration provided.[11] The concept of consideration can be effectively described as the 'price' given for the other party's promise.[12] The terms 'executed' and 'executory' have specific meaning in the context of consideration – the contract being 'executed' when the agreement is completed and 'executory' when the obligation to perform a promise has not yet fallen due.[13] Throughout this research the definition applied to 'executory contract' is that of a contract which, at the commencement of an insolvency proceeding, has not yet been fully performed by either or both the insolvent company and the **25.03**

---

4 Rosalind Mason, 'Insolvency Academics Contributing to the Review of Insolvency Laws: An Australian Perspective' (2015) 3 *NIBLeJ* 263, 265; *Commonwealth of Australia Constitution* (Cth), s51(xvii).

5 *Corporations Act 2001* (Cth).

6 For example *Federal Court Rules 2011* (Cth); *Federal Circuit Court Rules 2001* (Cth); *Corporations Regulations 2001* (Cth); *Australian Securities and Investments Commission Act 2001* (Cth).

7 Lindy Willmot, Sharon Christensen, Des Butler, Bill Dixon, *Contract Law* (5th ed, Oxford University Press, 2018) 8.

8 *Bankruptcy Act* 1966 (Cth).

9 For a historical discussion see: Willmot, Christensen, Butler, Dixon, (n7), 9; A.W.B Simpson, *A History of the Common Law of Contract: The Rise of the Action of Assumpsit* (Clarendon Press, Oxford, 1975).

10 Vickneswaren Krishnan (ed.), *Obligations: Contract Law* (Old Bailey Press, 2000), 8.

11 *Commonwealth v Verwayen* (1990) 170 CLR 394, 501; Willmot, Christensen, Butler, Dixon, (n7), 3–4, 31, 140.

12 Willmot, Christensen, Butler, Dixon, (n7), 142–3; *Dunlop Pneumatic Tyre Company Ltd v Selfridge & Company Ltd* [1915] AC 847, 855.

13 Willmot, Christensen, Butler, Dixon, (n7), 145.

counterparty. This raises potential claims for non-performance or damages either in favour of the counterparty or of the liquidator/administrator on behalf of the company subject to external administration.

25.04 Pursuant to the CA, a company is solvent only if it is 'able to pay all … debts, as and when they become due and payable'.[14] If this is not the case, the company is insolvent.[15] In the event that a company becomes insolvent or financially distressed, the CA provides a number of formal insolvency proceedings for the restructuring or liquidation of that company. Liquidation involves the winding up of a company, its object being the division of proceeds among creditors in accordance with prescribed statutory priorities.[16] There are also formal procedures involving arrangements with creditors: being voluntary administration and schemes of arrangements. In addition, the CA provides for receivership, either court appointed or initiated by secured creditors.

25.05 Such processes are administered by insolvency professionals, being registered liquidators who are generally practising accountants and members of professional bodies. There are specific statutory requirements to become and remain registered as a liquidator.[17] Only natural persons can assume the role. It is possible for companies to enter into informal arrangements with creditors without the involvement of the court or insolvency practitioners. However, these informal arrangements are not legislated by the CA nor by associated regulation.

25.06 Contract law, property law and insolvency law in Australia are not without complexities. There is no overarching single principle which regulates the status of executory contracts to which an insolvent company is a party. When a company is placed into external administration, the rights of the company with respect to its property 'are not determined absolutely, nor do they pass in toto to the insolvency administrator'.[18] The effect of the external administration depends upon the type of administration to which the company is subject, the applicable statutory legislation and general common law, and the terms of relevant contracts themselves.[19] If an executory contract is rescinded or repudiated, the counterparty does have rights/recourses in response. For example, in a liquidation the counterparty may prove any claim for damages in

14 *Corporations Act 2001* (Cth) s95A(1).

15 Ibid., s95A(2).

16 Ibid., s556.

17 Ibid., Schedule 2—Insolvency Practice Schedule (Corporations), Part 2.

18 James O'Donovan and Celia Hammond, 'Insolvency Aspects of Property Law' (1993) 1 *APLJ* 211, 211.

19 Ibid., 211.

the same manner as the company's other unsecured creditors, by lodging a proof of debt.[20]

Historically, ipso facto (by the fact itself) clauses have been enforceable in executory contracts. These clauses have permitted a contract to be terminated by the counterparty solely due to the fact that the company has experienced an 'insolvency event' regardless of continued performance by the company under the contract terms. An 'insolvency event' is not restricted to liquidation and can include the appointment of a scheme administrator or voluntary administrator. However, these clauses have come under fierce criticism in Australia with a recent Productivity Commission Inquiry Report of 2015 recommending the CA be amended to render such clauses void, without contrary court order, if the relevant company is in voluntary administration or in the process of forming a scheme of arrangement.[21] This recommendation forms part of the standing government's 'innovation' agenda.[22] Legislation giving effect to change has been passed by both chambers of Australian Federal Parliament and commenced 1 July 2018.[23] **25.07**

This study deliberates on the reform in section C below. Prior to doing so, the framework of available insolvency procedures is examined in A (1–3) and the treatment of executory contracts is explored in section B. **25.08**

1. Liquidation

Some of the major effects of liquidation on creditors are a moratorium on enforcement of claims,[24] and a stay on the prosecution or commencement of legal proceedings, subject to court leave.[25] However, secured creditors retain their rights to their security, including the right to appoint a receiver subject to loan contract terms.[26] Since 2012, the introduction of the *Personal Property Securities Act 2009* (Cth) ('PPSA') has widened the scope of what constitutes a secured creditor to include both traditional security, such as mortgages, and less conventional security rights, such as retention of title arrangements.[27] **25.09**

20 *Corporations Act 2001* (Cth), s553.

21 Cth, Productivity Commission 2015, *Business Set-up, Transfer and Closure, Final Report 75*, (Mr Peter Harris AO, Chairperson) Canberra, 30 September 2015, Recommendation 14.5.

22 Australian Government, 'National Innovation & Science Agenda' (n1).

23 *Treasury Laws Amendment (2017 Enterprise Incentives No. 2) Act 2017* (Cth).

24 *Corporations Act 2001* (Cth), s468.

25 Ibid., ss471B, 500(2).

26 Ibid., s471C; *Smith & Judge v DCT & National Australia Bank* [1979] CLC 32, 425.

27 Michael Murray and Jason Harris, *Keay's Insolvency Personal and Corporate Law and Practice* (10th ed, Lawbook, 2018) 507–8; *Corporations Act 2001* (Cth), ss 51A, 51E, 471C; *Personal Property Securities Act*

25.10 Liquidation can be undertaken by way of court liquidation, creditors' voluntary liquidation or members' voluntary liquidation. Members' voluntary liquidation can be initiated with respect to a solvent company.[28] However, the insolvency of a company is the most common reason for liquidation,[29] which can be initiated by a creditor's voluntary winding up or by application requiring the company to be wound up by court order. A creditor's voluntary winding up is initiated by the company's members (rather than its creditors) resolving to liquidate the company.[30] Creditors then exercise some control over the liquidation process itself: for example by fixing the liquidator's remuneration.[31]

25.11 With respect to court liquidation, a creditor is one of the most common applicants,[32] but to be eligible the creditor must be owed a valid unpaid debt capable of legal enforcement.[33] Statutory presumptions of insolvency can be relied upon by the creditor applicant to avoid the need to prove the company's actual state of insolvency.[34] The court may presume a company insolvent if, during or after three months ending on the day of the application, a statutory prescribed action or inaction occurs.[35] The presumption most often relied upon is a company's failure to comply with a statutory demand.[36] This is a formal demand in a prescribed form requiring payment of the debt owing to the creditor within 21 days.[37] If, within that timeframe, the company debtor fails to either apply to court seeking to have the statutory demand set aside,[38] or fails to satisfy the creditor's demand, no extension of time can be granted without court leave.[39]

2009 (Cth). However, there is a requirement under the PPSA for the secured party to perfect its security interest. This is commonly achieved by registration of the interest on the Personal Property Register.

28 *Corporations Act 2001* (Cth), Part 5.5.

29 Murray and Harris, (n27), 383.

30 Ibid., 390; Australian Securities Investments Commission, Information Sheet 45 'Liquidation: A Guide for Creditors' (*Australian Securities Investments Commission*, 1 September 2017) <http://www.asic.gov.au/regulatory-resources/insolvency/insolvency-for-creditors/liquidation-a-guide-for-creditors/#purpose> accessed 29 November 2017.

31 Murray and Harris, (n27), 390–91; Jason Harris, Michael Gronow and Helen Anderson, *Insolvency Law Commentary and Materials* (Lawbook, 2015), 218; *Corporations Act 2001* (Cth) Schedule 2—Insolvency Practice Schedule (Corporations), Div 60.

32 A creditor, the company, a contributory, a director, a liquidator or provisional liquidator of the company, ASIC or a prescribed agency may apply for a court to wind up a company in insolvency: see *Corporations Act 2001* (Cth), ss459A, 459P. Note an application may be brought under ss461 and s462(2) and other sections also.

33 Murray and Harris, (n27), 445.

34 *Corporations Act 2001* (Cth) s459C.

35 Ibid., s459C.

36 Harris, Gronow and Anderson, (n31), 225; Murray and Harris, (n27), 447.

37 *Corporations Act 2001* (Cth) ss459E – 459G.

38 Ibid., ss459E, 459F.

39 Ibid., s459S.

2. Receivership

Receivership can be initiated by court appointment under a range of statutory powers or by private appointment. However, receivership by court appointment is very rare, for example in circumstances where there is sufficient risk to a company's assets and where remedies are unavailable other than the appointment of a receiver to take control of the company's business and assets.[40] In *National Australia Bank Ltd v Bond Brewing Holdings Ltd*[41] the court held that a judge must weigh risk against the danger of 'irreparable wrong' in dispossessing a company and must employ caution, given the significant effects such an order is likely to have upon a company. Private receivership is more common. In this scenario, a creditor holding a security interest relies upon the terms of a loan contract granting power to appoint an insolvency practitioner as receiver or receiver and manager. The receiver must abide by the terms of the contract, including any pre-conditions to appointment and security interests must be correctly registered.[42] **25.12**

3. Corporate rescue

Scheme of arrangement

A scheme of arrangement is a court-supervised process. It aims to produce a binding, court-approved agreement reorganising the rights and liabilities of creditors and members of a company.[43] These schemes involve a high degree of involvement from both the court and the Australian Securities and Investments Commission ('ASIC'), being the government regulator and enforcer in the corporate sphere.[44] To initiate a scheme, court hearings and meetings of creditors or members are involved.[45] The court cannot approve a scheme of arrangement unless, among other things, ASIC issues a statement voicing no objection.[46] Even if ASIC has no objection, it is not unusual for ASIC to wait **25.13**

40 Harris, Gronow and Anderson, (n31), 358; See for example *Corporations Act 2001* (Cth), s1323(1)(h); *Re Richstar Enterprises Pty Ltd; ASIC v Carey (No 3)* (2006) 57 ACSR 307.

41 [1991] 1 VR 386, [539].

42 Harris, Gronow and Anderson, (n31), 358.

43 *Corporations Act 2001* (Cth), Part 5.1; Australian Securities Investments Commission, 'Regulatory Guide 60 Schemes of Arrangement' (*Australian Securities Investments Commission*, September 2011) <http://download.asic.gov.au/media/1239045/rg60-published-22-september-2011.pdf> accessed 20 February 2017.

44 *Corporations Act 2001* (Cth), s411; Australian Securities & Investments Commission, 'Regulatory Guide 60 Schemes of Arrangement' (n43).

45 *Corporations Act 2001* (Cth), Part 5.1.

46 Ibid., s411.

until a second court hearing prior to issuing its certificate of no objection.[47] While often considered in a takeover context,[48] the process is rarely undertaken in corporate rescue,[49] due to the cost and time involved.

Voluntary administration

25.14 Upon appointment of a voluntary administrator,[50] there are various statutory provisions which protect the company's property during the administration process: including a stay of proceedings, suspension of enforcement processes and restrictions on the exercise of third-party property rights.[51] These facilitate achievement of the administration's statutory objections. These objectives are: (1) maximising the chances of the company, or as much as possible of its business, continuing in existence, or if that is not possible at the very least (2) resulting in a better return to creditors than an immediate winding up of the company.[52]

25.15 The administrator acts as the company's agent,[53] takes control of assets,[54] investigates affairs,[55] and forms a recommendation regarding the future of the company.[56] This recommendation must be one of three: a proposed deed of company arrangement ('DOCA'); placing the company into liquidation; or returning control of the company to the company directors.[57] The creditors consider the administrator's recommendation and determine the company's future at a meeting of creditors from those three options.[58] Voluntary administration may be an effective investigatory tool for creditors to consider their best course of action.[59] It is a temporary process which may result in a DOCA; a binding arrangement entered into in writing between the company

---

47 Alistair Jaque and Leila Golchin, 'Australia: Is A Scheme of Arrangement The Right Choice for Me?' (*Mondaq*, 19 May 2009) <http://www.mondaq.com/australia/x/79840/Directors+Officers/Is+A+Scheme+Of+Arrangement+The+Right+Choice+For+Me> accessed 20 February 2017.

48 Ibid.

49 Australian Securities & Investments Commission, 'Australian Insolvency statistics' (*Australian Securities & Investments Commission*, March 2016) <http://download.asic.gov.au/media/3558489/asic-insolvency-statistics-series-2-march-2016.pdf>, accessed 20 February 2017, Table 2.3.

50 Appointment may be made by a company, a secured creditor, a liquidator or provisional liquidator of a company that is insolvent or likely to become insolvent: see *Corporations Act 2001* (Cth), ss436A, 436B(1), 436C.

51 Ibid., ss440A–440JA.

52 Harris, Gronow and Anderson, (n31), 390–91; *Corporations Act 2001* (Cth), s435A.

53 *Corporations Act 2001* (Cth), s437B.

54 Ibid., s437A.

55 Ibid., s438A.

56 Ibid.

57 Ibid., ss 438A, 439C.

58 Ibid., ss439A–439C.

59 Cth, Productivity Commission 2015, (n21), 24.

and its creditors, which binds the deed administrator, binds the company and its officers and members, binds all creditors even if they voted against it, and binds owners of property.[60] The deed binds any secured creditors who voted in favour of the deed, those that did not vote in favour may realise or otherwise deal with their security.[61] DOCAs are currently utilised not only to enable a viable business to continue trading but, alternatively, to provide a better return to creditors in a 'quasi-liquidation process'.[62]

Informal arrangements

Informal alternatives to external administration include directly approaching creditors to request payment plans or to negotiate settlements. It is possible to enter into an arrangement with all or some of company's creditors without the involvement of the court, an insolvency practitioner or any adviser. These informal arrangements are not legislated nor government managed. While these negotiations might be undertaken with speed and efficiency, their success hinges upon all (or potentially most) creditors accepting the proposal.[63] This may prove difficult in complex matters where significant numbers of creditors are involved. **25.16**

B. TREATMENT OF EXECUTORY CONTRACTS

1. Liquidation

Liquidation itself does not automatically enable termination or repudiation of executory contracts.[64] A liquidator must consider the benefits of any executory contract weighed against the liabilities which would accrue to the company in either performing or terminating such contracts.[65] The liquidator may then decide to assume or reject each contract. A liquidator may assume contracts necessary to continue trading (e.g., to facilitate sale of the company's business as a going concern).[66] Alternatively, the liquidator may determine that the company is unready or unwilling to perform an executory contract and therefore reject or repudiate it giving the counterparty the right to terminate **25.17**

60 *Corporations Act 2001* (Cth), ss 444A, 444B, 444D, 444G.

61 Ibid., ss 444A, 444B, 444D, 444G.

62 Murray and Harris, (n27), 837.

63 Pearce & Heers, 'Informal Arrangements and Debt Settlements' (*Pearce & Heers Insolvency Accountants*, Undated), <http://pearceheers.com.au/informal-arrangements-settlements/> accessed 20 February 2017.

64 *Smith v DCT* (1996) 71 FCR 150; Murray and Harris, (n27), 510.

65 Christopher Symes and Jeffrey Fitzpatrick, 'National Report for Australia' in Dennis Faber, Niels Vermunt, Jason Kilborn, and Kathleen van der Linde (eds) *Treatment of Contracts in Insolvency* (Oxford University Press, 2013) 1, 4–5.

66 Murray and Harris, (n27), 510.

the contract.[67] An anticipatory breach may occur where a party, such as the liquidator as agent of the company, notifies the other that it is unable or unwilling to perform the contract terms.[68] In such circumstances, the innocent counterparty may claim damages and take steps to mitigate loss.[69]

25.18 Any act of repudiation can result in a claim of damages against the company, or damages against the counterparty in favour of the company, depending upon which party commits the repudiation.[70] However, the method of any counterparty pursuing a claim for damages is altered by the company's status in the liquidation. In order to permit the liquidator to carry out a pari passu distribution among unsecured creditors,[71] contracts cannot be enforced during the liquidation process,[72] and creditors are excluded from enforcing their claims through court proceedings against the company.[73] Instead, their rights 'in personam' against the company effectively become a right to prove along with other unsecured creditors in the liquidation.[74]

25.19 Secured creditors are in a different position and, as a general rule, may pursue action with respect to their security.[75] The policy justifications for this are entrenched in Australian law: the Australian Law Reform Commission's report of 1988 stating that as far as possible and practicable, insolvency law should harmonise with general law.[76] If Australian insolvency law were to abrogate freely negotiated contractual and property rights, it would undermine both Australian general contract and property law to the detriment of the Australian free market economy.[77]

25.20 An 'ipso facto' clause is a provision within a contract entitling the counterparty to terminate the contract solely due to the company experiencing an 'insolvency event', regardless of continued performance of the contract by the

---

67 Symes and Fitzpatrick, (n 65), 5.

68 Lee Atkin, 'Fundamental, and "anticipatory" Breach and the Impact of "rescission"' (2012) 36 *ABR* 18, 20.

69 Symes and Fitzpatrick, (n 65), 5.

70 Ibid.

71 Robert Langton and Lindsay Trotman, 'Sharing in the Proceeds of Business Failure: Competition Between Feudal and Democratic Principles in the Liquidation of Australian Companies' (1999) 11 *Corp & Bus LJ* 263, 265; Australian Law Reform Commission, *General Insolvency Inquiry Report*, Report No. 45 (1988) 16, 46; *Corporations Act 2001* (Cth), s555. See the exceptions to rateable distribution among all unsecured creditors in s566 of the *Corporations Act 2001* (Cth).

72 *Corporations Act 2001* (Cth), ss468, 471B, 500.

73 Ibid.

74 Thomson Reuters, *McPherson's Law of Company Liquidation* (1 October 2016) [3.100]; *Re Lines Bros Ltd (in liq)* [1982] 2 All ER.

75 *Corporations Act 2001* (Cth), Pt 5.6, Div 6C. See s554E specifically.

76 Australian Law Reform Commission, (n71), 2, 16–17.

77 Langton and Trotman, (n71), 269; Thomas Jackson, *The Logic and Limits of Bankruptcy Law* (Harvard University Press, 1986).

company.[78] There has been debate surrounding the ongoing application of such clauses.[79] However, there are no current plans to change the availability of ipso facto clauses triggered purely as a result of liquidation. Recent reforms offer protection against ipso facto clauses but only in relation to creditors' schemes of arrangements, receivership and voluntary administrations. In the context of a company that has transitioned from voluntary administration into a creditors' voluntary liquidation, a stay upon the operation of ipso facto clauses which applied in the voluntary administration will continue until the affairs of the company have been fully wound up.[80] However, the stay will only apply to the administrator's appointment and does not prevent reliance upon an ipso facto clause triggered simply by the commencement of voluntary liquidation.[81] Any contract containing an 'ipso facto' clause permits the other contracting party to terminate the contract in the event of liquidation, in accordance with the terms of such a clause.[82]

There are some specific rules that apply depending upon the nature of the contract involved and the type of winding up procedure. For instance, in the case of employment contracts, publication of a compulsory court winding up order operates as a notice of dismissal to all employees of the company.[83] These employees are left with a right to lodge a proof of debt with the liquidator for breach of contract.[84] However, the liquidator may either waive the notice of dismissal and continue the pre-existing employment contracts, or alternatively re-employ staff on the liquidator's own terms, should the liquidator consider it necessary, for example, to facilitate realisation of the company's assets.[85] This rule does not necessarily apply in the case of voluntary liquidation.[86] **25.21**

Another example of a specific rule is in respect to pre-existing lease contracts and unprofitable contracts. There is a specific statutory power entitling a liquidator to disclaim an unprofitable contract or a lease of land.[87] A liquidator cannot otherwise disclaim contracts, except with leave of the court which may **25.22**

---

78 Cth, Productivity Commission 2015, (n21), 25.

79 Ibid.

80 *Corporations Act 2001* (Cth), s451E(2).

81 Murray and Harris, (n27), 510

82 Ibid.

83 *Re General Rolling Stock Co* (1866) 1 Eq 346; Thomson Reuters, *McPherson's Law of Company Liquidation* (n74), [7.610]–[7.620]

84 *Re RS Newman Ltd* [1916] 2 Ch 309; Re Kanedale Pty Ltd (1987) 12 ACLR 449; Murray and Harris, (n27), 509.

85 *Re Associated Dominions Assurance Society Ltd* (1962) 109 CLR 516; Murray and Harris, (n27), 509.

86 See *McPherson's Law of Company Liquidation* (n74), [7.620]

87 *Corporations Act 2001* (Cth), s568; *Willmott Growers Group Inc v Willmott Forests Ltd (Receivers and Managers Appointed) (In Liquidation)* [2013] HCA 51.

be given subject to conditions and which may address matters arising under or relating to the contract as the court considers just and equitable.[88] From the date of effect,[89] the disclaimer terminates the company's rights, interest, liability and property in or in respect of the disclaimer property, but does not affect any other person's rights or liabilities except so far as necessary to release the company and its property from liability.[90] Any persons aggrieved by the disclaimer are then left to prove their loss as creditors in the winding up of the company.[91] In a 2013 High Court decision, it was held by a 4 to 1 majority that a liquidator can even disclaim a lease prior to the end of its term where the company is a landlord and the disclaimer is against a long-term lease tenant who has fully paid rent in advance.[92]

2. Receivership

25.23 As with liquidation, the appointment of a receiver or receiver and manager does not automatically terminate or rescind prior existing contracts.[93] The effect of receivership upon executory contracts is uncertain, often falling to decisions made on a case-by-case basis by each individual receiver.[94] In contrast to liquidation, there is no automatic stay preventing creditors from commencing or pursuing court action: unsecured creditors may pursue court proceedings seeking contractual remedies or apply for a court to wind up a company in insolvency.[95] However, proceedings are limited against the assets within the receiver's possession pursuant to the security interest under which the receiver has been appointed.[96]

25.24 Ipso facto clauses have been held valid and able to be relied upon by the counterparty to terminate a contract with the company placed into receivership.[97] However, this is subject to recent legislative reform which applies to new contracts entered into on or after 1 July 2018. A new section has been inserted into the *Corporations Act*[98] preventing the exercise of ipso facto clauses against companies in receivership, in certain circumstances. The section provides that such a clause cannot be enforced against a corporation for: (a) the

88 *Corporations Act 2001* (Cth), s568(1A)–(1B).
89 This date is determined by *Corporations Act 2001* (Cth), s568C.
90 Ibid., s568D(1).
91 Ibid., s568D(2).
92 *Willmott Growers Group Inc v Willmott Forests Ltd* (n87). For a discussion on this case see Susan Cirillo, 'When and how can a Liquidator "disclaim property of the company"'? (2014) Autumn *Bar News* 16.
93 *AGL Victoria Pty Ltd v Lockwood* (2003) 10 VR 596; *Parsons v Sovereign Bank of Canada* [1913] 1 AC 160.
94 Murray and Harris, (n27), 742.
95 Ibid.; *Corporations Act 2001* (Cth), ss459A, 459P.
96 Murray and Harris, (n27), 742.
97 *AGL Victoria Pty Ltd v Lockwood* (n93), [17].
98 *Corporations Act 2001* (Cth), s434J.

reason of the appointment or existence of a managing controller of the whole or substantially the whole of the corporation's property; or (b) the corporation's financial position, if there is a managing controller of the whole or substantially the whole of the corporation's property; or (c) a reason, prescribed by the regulations relating to (a) or (b); or (d) a reason that, in substance, is contrary to the section. This stay remains in effect until the managing controller's appointment ends or until the end of any extended period that the court orders.[99] The stay does not apply to contracts entered into after the managing controllership commences, nor where the managing controller consents to exercise of the right, nor does it apply to contracts, agreements or arrangements declared to be exceptions under prescribed regulations.[100] As at the date of writing (August 2018), most of these prescribed exceptions target finance arrangements.[101] Yet, these exclusions, for example rights of set off, may have a far-reaching impact upon other industries. The court retains the power to lift the stay.[102] The protection extends to self-executing clauses which can start to apply automatically.[103]

In the absence of an ipso facto clause, it is a matter for the appointed receiver to repudiate the contract, assume personal liability for the continuation of the contract, or allow the contract to continue.[104] If there is no ipso facto clause in the contract, and if it is not repudiated by the receiver, then the contract remains on foot.[105] The receiver may be required to make a commercial judgment as to whether the continuation of the contract is of financial benefit to the company in receivership.[106] In *Airlines Airspares Ltd v Handly Page Ltd*[107] it was noted that this decision might pertain to whether any repudiation would be detrimental to the company's trading prospects. Other relevant considerations may be loss of goodwill or harm to the sale of the company's assets.[108] **25.25**

If the contract is repudiated, the company and not the receiver is generally liable for damages incurred.[109] There are exceptions, for example where the **25.26**

99 Ibid., s434J(2),(3).
100 Ibid., s434J(5), (6), (7).
101 Corporations (Stay on Enforcing Certain Rights) Declaration 2018 (Cth); *Corporations Amendment (Stay on Enforcing Certain Rights) Regulations 2018* (Cth); *Corporations Amendment (Stay on Enforcing Certain Rights) Regulations (No. 2) 2018* (Cth).
102 *Corporations Act 2001* (Cth), s434K.
103 Ibid., s434LA.
104 *Re British Investments & Development Co Pty Ltd* (1979) CLC 40–522.
105 Murray and Harris, (n27), 743.
106 Ibid.
107 [1970] 1 Ch 193, 198–9.
108 Murray and Harris, (n27), 744.
109 Ibid.

receiver seeks to ignore a prior equity under a pre-existing contract between the company and a third party holding a lien over goods – in which case the court may award, among other things, damages against the receiver.[110]

25.27 Employee contracts are not automatically terminated upon the appointment of a receiver.[111] However, these contracts terminate if the receiver enters into fresh contracts with employees which are inconsistent with the terms of the prior contracts, if the continued employment is inconsistent with the role of the receiver, or if the appointment is accompanied by a sale of the company's business.[112] Should any employment contract be terminated by a receiver in a manner that constitutes breach of contract, a damages claim may arise.[113] This claim is generally against the company, as the receiver acts as agent of the company. Personal liability does not accrue to a receiver who simply retains an employee, as agent of the company, pursuant to a pre-existing contract.[114] Significantly, in the event that the receiver enters into a new contract, or in some way adopts a pre-existing contract, the receiver assumes personal liability under the contract.[115]

25.28 In contrast with a liquidator, a privately-appointed receiver does not have any statutory power to disclaim leases or other contracts. The receiver may disregard the contractual obligations under the lease unless this would prejudice the company's goodwill or future trading prospects or would create a 'prior equity'.[116] Yet, disclaimer of a lease is unlikely to do this.[117] In the event that a receiver adopts the pre-existing lease or re-negotiates a new lease, then the receiver assumes personal liability for the lease.[118] A receiver is given a grace period of seven days following appointment or entry into possession to decide whether to adopt an existing lease, negotiate new terms or vacate premises, after which time the receiver is personally liable for rent under a pre-appointment lease.[119] There are limited exceptions if the court grants an order.[120] The positive duty placed upon receivers within this time frame was introduced in response to the report of the Law Reform Commission in 1988 which recommended the reform in order to assist both a receiver and

110 Murray and Harris, (n27), 744; *Re Diesels & Components Pty Ltd* [1985] 2 Qd R 456.
111 *McEvoy v Incat Tasmania Pty Ltd* (2003) 130 FCR 503; Harris, Gronow and Anderson, (n31), 374.
112 *McEvoy v Incat Tasmania Pty Ltd*, ibid., [6]; Murray and Harris, (n27), 744.
113 Murray and Harris, (n27), 745.
114 *McEvoy v Incat Tasmania Pty Ltd* (n111).
115 *Corporations Act 2001* (Cth), s419; *McEvoy v Incat Tasmania Pty Ltd*, ibid.; Murray and Harris, (n27), 745.
116 O'Donovan and Hammond, (n18), 212.
117 Ibid.
118 *Corporations Act 2001* (Cth), s419.
119 Ibid., s419A; O'Donovan and Hammond, (n18), 214.
120 See *Corporations Act 2001* (Cth), s419A(7).

third party who are unaware of the existence, or the legal title, of relevant property.[121]

3. Corporate rescue

Voluntary administration does not automatically terminate executory contracts entered into by the company.[122] However, recent reform now provides protection for companies in administration against ipso facto clauses which are triggered merely because of, inter alia, the event of administration.[123] Again, the reform commenced on 1 July 2018. The stay against ipso facto clauses lasts until the administration ends, until the end of any extended period that the court orders, or until the company is fully wound up in liquidation (where liquidation ends the administration).[124] The right to terminate or vary the contract based on the administration is not re-engaged once the administration ends.[125] The provisions apply to self-executing clauses which can start to apply automatically.[126] The stay does not apply to contracts entered into after administration commences,[127] nor where the appointed administrator consents to exercise of the right.[128] Further exceptions can apply by ministerial declaration or under regulation.[129] As at the date of writing (August 2018), most of these prescribed exceptions target finance arrangements.[130] **25.29**

The reforms arose from severe criticism of the clauses, particularly in the context of voluntary administration where they 'can severely constrain the ability of a business to continue trading during restructure' and can 'reduce the scope for a successful restructure or prevent the sale of the business as a "going concern"'.[131] The motives behind the legislative amendments are discussed in detail in section C below. **25.30**

Upon the commencement of voluntary administration there is an automatic moratorium on the enforcement of any rights against the company and its **25.31**

---

121 Australian Law Reform Commission, (n71), 15.
122 *Smith v Deputy Commissioner of Taxation* (1997) 71 FCR 150.
123 *Treasury Laws Amendment (2017 Enterprise Incentives No 2) Act 2018* (Cth); *Corporations Act 2001* (Cth), ss451E–451H.
124 *Corporations Act 2001* (Cth), s451E(2).
125 Murray and Harris, (n27), 773.
126 *Corporations Act 2001* (Cth), s451GA.
127 Ibid., s451E(5).
128 Ibid., s451E(7).
129 Ibid., s451E(5), (6).
130 Corporations (Stay on Enforcing Certain Rights) Declaration 2018 (Cth); *Corporations Amendment (Stay on Enforcing Certain Rights) Regulations 2018* (Cth); *Corporations Amendment (Stay on Enforcing Certain Rights) Regulations (No. 2) 2018* (Cth).
131 Cth, Productivity Commission 2015, (n21), 25.

property, including the commencement of any winding up application.[132] Conversely, the court may permit the commencement of a winding up application if it is satisfied that it is in the best interests of creditors.[133] This stay facilitates the objects of the administrative process by giving the administrator an opportunity to develop a restructuring plan or time to plan the company's liquidation in a manner which will result in a better return to creditors.[134]

25.32 An administrator does not have a statutory right to disclaim contracts and the laws relating to repudiation (discussed above) apply – with any counterparty entitled to claim against the company as an unsecured creditor for any damages.[135] An administrator is liable for any new contracts entered into through the course of the voluntary administration.[136] However, as a general rule the administrator is not personally responsible for executory contracts.[137] An exception to this general rule, as with a receiver, is with respect to continuing leases. The CA imposes a statutory obligation upon the administrator – who is liable for such rent or other amounts payable by the company under the agreement which is attributable to a period beginning no more than five business days after the administration begins.[138] The administrator is given a grace period of five business days following appointment to decide whether to adopt an existing lease, negotiate new terms or vacate premises, after which time the administrator is personally liable for rent under pre-appointment leases.[139] During the five business day period, the administrator may give notice that the company does not intend to exercise rights with respect to the property.[140]

25.33 As discussed above, schemes of arrangement are rare in the insolvency context. Recent reform also introduces changes to the scheme provisions to provide protection against the operation of ipso facto clauses in pre-existing contracts

132 *Corporations Act 2001* (Cth), Pt 5.3A, Div 6. See in particular s440D.

133 *Creevey v Deputy Commissioner of Taxation* (1996) 19 ACSR 456; Harris, Gronow and Anderson, (n31), 407.

134 *Corporations Act 2001* (Cth), s435A.

135 Murray and Harris, (n27), 774.

136 *Corporations Act 2001* (Cth), s443A; Murray and Harris, (n27), 774.

137 As per s443C, the administrator is generally not liable for the debts of the company other than under ss443A–443BA of the *Corporations Act 2001* (Cth).

138 *Corporations Act 2001* (Cth), s443B; *Rapid Metal Developments (Aust) Pty Ltd v Rildean Pty Ltd (No 3)* [2010] NSWSC 7.

139 *Corporations Act 2001* (Cth), s443B(3).

140 Ibid., s443B(3).

that seek to terminate or vary contracts simply because the company is, amongst other things, forming a scheme of arrangement.[141]

C. REFORMS

A change to Australia's Federal law takes place with the authority of the Federal Parliament by way of an Act of Parliament.[142] A draft Act, in the form of a bill, is prepared by the Office of Parliamentary Counsel.[143] The impetus for the draft bill may arise from political reasons (at the suggestion of politicians and/or government departments), from community groups or lobbyists seeking change or in response to recommendations made in response to parliamentary reviews or committees.[144] An 'exposure draft' of the bill is usually released in order to ensure public consultation and stakeholder feedback. The bill is then considered by the House of Representatives and the Senate. To become law, the bill must be passed with a majority vote in both chambers in identical form, following which the Governor-General (as the Queen's representative) gives it Royal Assent.[145] Acts do not automatically come into effect immediately from the date of asset, and may specify a particular commencement date or provide for a date to be proclaimed at a later time by the Governor-General.[146] If no commencement date is specified in the Act itself, it will commence on the 28th day following assent.[147] 25.34

Over the past few decades various reviews have been undertaken into Australian insolvency laws.[148] Partly in response to recommendations made in these various reviews,[149] the following reforms have occurred: 25.35

141 *Treasury Laws Amendment (2017 Enterprise Incentives No 2) Act 2018* (Cth); *Corporations Act 2001* (Cth), ss415D–G.

142 Parliament of Australia, 'Infosheet 7 – Making Laws' (*Parliament of Australia*, Undated) <http://www.aph.gov.au/About_Parliament/House_of_Representatives/Powers_practice_and_procedure/00_-_Infosheets/Infosheet_7_-_Making_laws> accessed 20 January 2017.

143 Ibid.

144 Parliamentary Education Office, 'Bills and Laws' (*Parliamentary Education Office*, Undated), <http://www.peo.gov.au/learning/fact-sheets/bills-and-laws.html> accessed 20 January 2017.

145 Ibid.

146 Parliament of Australia, (n142).

147 Ibid.

148 Australian Law Reform Commission, (n71); Cth, *Review of the Regulation of Corporate Insolvency Practitioners: Report of the Working Party*, (Ms Veronique Ingram, Chairperson) Canberra, AGPS, Canberra, June 1997; Parliamentary Joint Committee on Corporations and Financial Service, Parliament of Australia, *Corporate Insolvency Laws: a Stocktake* (2004); Senate Economics References Committee, Parliament of Australia, *The regulation, registration and remuneration of insolvency practitioners in Australia: the case for a new framework* (2010).

149 Senate Economics References Committee, Parliament of Australia, (n148), [1.22]–[1.27].

(a) the *Corporate Law Reform Act* of 1992, which introduced Part 5.3A of the CA addressing voluntary administration;[150]
(b) the *Corporations Amendment (Insolvency) Act* of 2007, which introduced, inter alia, statutory priorities in favour of employees, greater powers to ASIC, changes to the insolvency practitioner registration process, and criteria for the court to determine the reasonableness of insolvency practitioner claims for remuneration;[151] and
(c) the *Insolvency Law Reform Act* of 2016 ('ILRA'), which introduced the most significant Australian insolvency reforms in over two decades.[152] The ILRA focuses on the conduct of insolvency administrations and practitioners and aims, amongst other things, to restore confidence in the insolvency profession.[153] The core provisions of the ILRA took effect in two stages, with parts commencing on 1 March 2017 and the remainder on 1 September 2017.[154]

25.36 While these reforms do not themselves focus on the law pertaining to executory contracts, the 2016 ILRA was intended as a first step in a general reform of insolvency law, including the treatment of executory contracts in insolvency. The current Australian Government has a National Innovation and Science Agenda, which incorporates the enhancement of insolvency laws.[155] This forms part of the Australian Government's policy to modernise, harmonise and strengthen Australia's insolvency and restructuring laws, and to improve Australian business growth and economic prosperity.[156] In a 2015/ 2016 interview, Christopher Pyne, the then Minister for Industry, Innovation and Science, discussed the government's motives for its agenda.[157] He cited the subsiding of the Australian mining investment boom and the need to create new businesses, jobs and exports as reasons why new sources of economic growth and innovation were needed to ensure Australia's long-term

---

150 *Corporate Law Reform Act 1992* (Cth).

151 *Corporations Amendment (Insolvency) Act 2007 (Cth);* Senate Economics References Committee, Parliament of Australia, (n148), [1.26].

152 John Winter, 'Law Reform: Biggest Changes in Over 20 Years ... and More to come' (2016) 28(1) *ARITA Journal* 4.

153 Department of Parliamentary Services (Cth), *Bills Digest*, No. 82 of 2015–2016, 22 February 2016, 5; Explanatory Memorandum, Insolvency Law Reform Bill 2015, 3.

154 Kelly O'Dwyer MP, 'Insolvency Law Reform Act' (Media Release, 23 August 2016) <http://kmo.ministers.treasury.gov.au/media-release/076–2016/> accessed 20 January 2017.

155 Australian Government, 'National Innovation & Science Agenda' (n1).

156 Ibid; Australian Government, 'Options paper: a modernisation and harmonisation of the regulatory framework applying to insolvency practitioners in Australia' (*Australian Government*, June 2011) <http://www.treasury.gov.au/~/media/Treasury/Consultations%20and%20Reviews/Consultations/2011/A%20Modernisation%20and%20Harmonisation%20of%20the%20Regulatory%20Framework/Key%20Documents/PDF/Options_Paper20110602.ashx> accessed 20 February 2017.

157 John Martin, 'Why the Government is Changing the Law' (2016) Summer Insolvency Reform Special Edition *Henry Davis York The Review* 1, 4.

productivity and business.[158] The Hon Christopher Pyne, MP also quoted the Australian Bureau of Statistics as empirical evidence of the value innovation has to Australian businesses.[159] Those statistics show, amongst other things, that in 2012–13 nine in ten innovating businesses benefited as a result of innovations, including reductions in cost, competitive advantages, increased revenue, and increased customer-service.[160]

The current government's insolvency reform strategies follow recent political campaigning, in particular by Senator John Williams, in response to public and creditor unease triggered by high profile misconduct of certain insolvency practitioners,[161] together with concerns regarding the reasonableness of insolvency practitioners' remuneration.[162] This political campaigning instigated a 2010 Senate Economic Reference Committee (Senate Committee) into the regulation and remuneration of insolvency practitioners.[163] What followed was a long gestation of draft legislation and consultation,[164] which culminated in the passage of the ILRA. **25.37**

As part of the government's agenda, in 2014 the then Federal Commonwealth Treasurer, Joseph Hockey, requested that the Productivity Commission[165] **25.38**

---

158 Ibid.

159 Ibid.

160 See Australian Bureau of Statistics, '8158.0 – Innovation in Australian Business', 2012–13 (*Australian Bureau of Statistics*, 20 July 2016) <http://www.abs.gov.au/AUSSTATS/abs@.nsf/Lookup/8158.0Main+Features12012–13?OpenDocument> accessed 20 February 2017.

161 In particular, Stuart Ariff who has been banned as an official and registered liquidator for life and who received a six-year jail sentence following conviction on 19 criminal charges: *Australian Securities and Investments Commission v Stuart Karim Ariff* [2009] NSWSC 829 (18 August 2009); Senate Economics References Committee, Parliament of Australia, (n148), [1.16]; Australian Securities & Investments Commission, '11–308Mr Stuart Ariff jailed on ASIC charges' (Media Release, 19 December 2011) <http://asic.gov.au/about-asic/media-centre/find-a-media-release/2011-releases/11–308mr-stuart-ariff-jailed-on-asic-charges/> accessed 20 February 2017.

162 Senate Economics References Committee, Parliament of Australia, (n148); Senator John Williams, 'Opinion Piece' (*Senator John Williams*, 9 March 2010) <http://www.senatorjohnwilliams.com/index.php/news-room/media-releases/144-opinion-piece> accessed 20 February 2017.

163 Senate Economics References Committee, Parliament of Australia, (n148); Senator John Williams, (n162).

164 The Insolvency Law Reform Bill was released as an exposure draft by the Attorney-General and Parliamentary Secretary to the Treasurer on 19 December 2012 seeking submissions by 8 March 2013; 16 submissions were received in response and no draft regulations were issued. Almost two years later, the Insolvency Law Reform Bill 2014 was released as an exposure draft on 7 November 2014 seeking submissions; 20 submissions were received in response. It then became the Insolvency Law Reform Bill 2015 before passing both chambers of the Houses of Parliament and receiving Royal Assent as the Insolvency Law Reform Act of 2016. For a summary of the progress of the 2015 bill see: Parliament of Australia, 'Insolvency Law Reform Bill 2015' (Parliament of Australia, Undated) <http://www.aph.gov.au/Parliamentary_Business/Bills_Legislation/Bills_Search_Results/Result?bId=r5587> accessed 20 February 2017.

165 The Productivity Commission is the Australian Government's independent research and advisory body which provides assistance 'on a range of economic, social and environmental issues affecting the welfare of Australians' see: Productivity Commission, 'About the Commission' (*Australian Government*, Undated) <http://www.pc.gov.au/about> accessed 20 February 2017.

undertake an inquiry 'into barriers to business entries and exits and identify options for reducing these barriers where appropriate, in order to drive efficiency and economic growth in the Australian economy'.[166] At this time Tony Abbott was Prime Minister of Australia. An issues paper was released on 19 December 2014 for initial public consideration.[167] The Productivity Commission then released its draft report on 21 May 2015 seeking submissions by 3 July 2015;[168] 38 initial submissions were made by academics, institutes and memberships pertaining to Australian property/company directors/banks, business interest groups (such as trucking associations and electrical associations), government departments, legal firms and associations, insolvency/accounting firms and associations, together with various other interested parties.[169] A further 37 submissions were received after the release of the draft report.[170]

25.39 One of the recommendations made in the draft report was the amendment of the CA so that ipso facto clauses that allow termination of contracts solely due to an insolvency event are unenforceable in certain circumstances.[171] The recommendation included recourse for 'suppliers' to apply to the court for an order to terminate the contract in circumstances of 'undue hardship'.[172] The Commission considered these reforms necessary due to the severe constraint ipso facto clauses can have on the success of restructuring processes.[173] In coming to this conclusion, the Commission gave regard to a submission by Australia's leading insolvency professional membership, the Australian Restructuring and Insolvency Turnaround Association ('ARITA'), which contended that such clauses have 'played a pivotal role in the shutdown of major organisations that were in financial distress' such as the carrier contracts of One.Tel.[174]

---

166 Joe Hockey, Treasurer, 'Productivity Commission Inquiry into Barriers to Business Entries and Exits' (Media Release, 19 November 2014) <http://jbh.ministers.treasury.gov.au/media-release/059–2014/> accessed 20 February 2017; Australian Government Productivity Commission, *Business Set-up, Transfer and Closure*, May 2015 (Draft Report) <http://apo.org.au/files/Resource/business-draft.pdf> accessed 20 February 2017, iv.

167 Productivity Commission, 'Business Set-up, Transfer and Closure Issues Paper' (*Australian Government*, Undated) <http://www.pc.gov.au/inquiries/completed/business/issues> accessed 20 February 2017.

168 Australian Government Productivity Commission, (n166) III.

169 Productivity Commission, 'Business Set-up, Transfer and Closure Submissions' (*Australian Government*, Undated) <http://www.pc.gov.au/inquiries/completed/business/submissions#initial> accessed 20 February 2017.

170 Ibid.

171 Australian Government Productivity Commission, (n166), Draft Recommendation 15.4.

172 Ibid.

173 Ibid. This appears on pp394–8 of the final report.

174 Ibid. This appears on p394 of the final report.

One.Tel spanned eight countries, employed 3,000 staff, was the fourth largest telecommunications company in Australia with more than two million customers and had annual sales close to $1 billion by 2001.[175] In the same year, it entered into voluntary administration as a result of poor corporate governance and limited cash flow.[176] Telstra and Optus provided One.Tel with essential telecommunication infrastructure but took advantage of ipso facto clauses in their contracts to terminate the services, which effectively brought down the business in a matter of hours.[177] It is a striking example of the destructive consequences ipso facto clauses can cause. **25.40**

In November 2015, the Australian Government issued an Innovation Report, which included a proposal to 'ban "ipso facto" contractual clauses that allow an agreement to be terminated solely due to an insolvency event, if a company is undertaking a restructure'.[178] The reason given for the proposed insolvency reforms was an overarching need to overcome the current 'focus on penalising and stigmatising business failure'.[179] Then, on 29 April 2016, a proposal paper was released as part of the National Innovation and Science Agenda setting forth the proposed model for the constraint of ipso facto clauses.[180] Submissions were sought in response to the model by 27 May 2016. **25.41**

Over 60 submissions were made by stakeholders, insolvency practitioner bodies, accountancy bodies, banks and various other interested parties in response to the proposal paper.[181] Of those publicly available, most addressed the proposed ipso facto amendments. The general response to the proposal was welcoming. This is unsurprising given long support for the reform from **25.42**

175 Reza Monem, 'The One.Tel Collapse: Lessons for Corporate Governance' (2011) 21(4) *AAR* 340, 340; Paul Barry, *Rich Kids: How the Murdochs and Packers Lost $950 million in One.Tel* (Bantam Books, Revised Edition, 2003).

176 Monem (n 175); Louise W. Floyd, 'Enron and One.Tel: Employee Entitlements After Employer Insolvency in the United States and Australia (Australian Renegades Championing the American Dream?)' (2003) 56 *SMULR* 975, 991.

177 James Eyers, 'ASIC Leniency for Business Failure', *The Australian Financial Review* (Sydney, 28 April 2009), 60.

178 Australian Government, 'National Innovation and Science Agenda Report' (*Australian Government*, November 2015) <https://www.industry.gov.au/data-and-publications/national-innovation-and-science-agenda-report> accessed 20 January 2017;

179 Ibid.

180 Australian Government, 'Improving bankruptcy and insolvency laws Proposal Paper' (n2).

181 Australian Government, 'Submissions', (*Australian Government*, Undated) <http://www.treasury.gov.au/ConsultationsandReviews/Consultations/2016/Improving-bankruptcy-and-insolvency-laws/Submissions> accessed 20 February 2017.

the Australian insolvency profession, ARITA and the general business community.[182] However, industry-specific concerns were raised by lenders/banks and various industries (such as the construction industry) regarding the impact the reform would have on Australian credit and Australian business.[183] Although, it is arguable that the company creditors from such industries could ultimately benefit from any increased returns resulting from 'more effective and meaningful restructuring processes'.[184]

25.43 There was contention about the proposed scope of the reform with respect to the inclusion of a moratorium on ipso facto clauses where a receiver is appointed, the exclusion of certain contracts, and any retrospective application of the reform. ARITA suggested that any statutory preclusion of ipso facto clauses in the context of receivership should be limited to situations where appointments are over the whole or substantially the whole of the company's assets, rather than simply to appointments involving the sale of an asset.[185] ARITA also endorsed retrospective application to clauses in existing contracts but opposed any retrospective application to insolvency administrations which commenced prior to any reform.[186] This is a valid and well-considered recommendation.

25.44 The government took heed of a number of the concerns and suggestions made throughout the submission process, many of which are reflected in the resulting reforms which have been incorporated into the CA.[187] Ipso facto clauses are now stayed during a formal restructure in relation to schemes of arrangement (where that scheme is for the purpose of avoiding insolvent liquidation), administration, or where a managing controller is appointed over all or substantially all of the property of the company.[188] This is subject to

---

182 Helen Anderson (ed), Anne O'Connell, Ian Ramsay, Michelle Welsh and Hannah Withers, *Corporate Insolvency The Productivity Commission, Corporate Insolvency and Phoenix Companies* (2015) 33 *CSLJ* 425, 426; Martin, (n157), 4.

183 See e.g.: Australian Bankers Association, Submission to Treasury, *National Innovation and Science Agenda – Improving Bankruptcy and Insolvency Laws*, 7 June 2016; Australian Finance Conference, Submission to Treasury, *National Innovation and Science Agenda – Improving Bankruptcy and Insolvency Laws*, 27 May 2016; Australian Financial Markets Association, Submission to Treasury, *National Innovation and Science Agenda – Improving Bankruptcy and Insolvency Laws*, 13 May 2016; Property Council of Australia, Submission to Treasury, *National Innovation and Science Agenda – Improving Bankruptcy and Insolvency Laws*, 2 June 2016.

184 Parliament of Australia, 'Report Treasury Laws Amendment (2017 Enterprise Incentives No. 2) Bill 2017 [Provisions]' (Australian Government, 8 August 2017) < http://www.aph.gov.au/Parliamentary_Business/Committees/Senate/Economics/EnterpriseIncentivesNo2/Report> accessed 21 August 2017.

185 Australian Restructuring Insolvency and Turnaround Association, Submission to Treasury, *National Innovation and Science Agenda – Improving Bankruptcy and Insolvency Laws*, 27 May 2016.

186 Ibid.

187 *Treasury Laws Amendment (2017 Enterprise Incentives No. 2) Act 2017* (Cth).

188 Explanatory Memoranda, Treasury Laws Amendment (2017 Enterprise Incentives No. 2) Bill 2017 (Cth), 2.24–2.26.

exceptions, including with consent from relevant appointed insolvency practitioners and with respect to contract types specified in regulation or ministerial declaration.[189] At the time of writing (August 2018), recent ministerial declarations have been forthcoming which pertain to, amongst other things, finance arrangements.[190] It is yet to be seen what unanticipated consequences the exceptions may have on wider industries. Once the stay is imposed it is permanent. However, the stay will only apply to rights arising under new contracts, agreements or arrangements entered into from the commencement of the reform, being 1 July 2018. It does not apply retrospectively. The court retains an overarching discretion including to override any stay and to grant interim orders.[191] It is yet to be seen how the court judicially interprets the reforms and applies its discretion.

In June 2017, the Australia House of Representatives passed the reform.[192] **25.45** On 15 June 2017, the Senate referred the matter to the Senate Economics Legislation Committee for inquiry and report.[193] The report released on 8 August 2017 concluded with a recommendation that it also be passed by the Senate.[194] This occurred on the evening of 11 September 2017, with some minor technical amendments incorporated. Both houses passed the reforms in their final form on 12 September 2017. The Act then received Assent on 18 September 2017 and the new laws pertaining to ipso facto provisions, commenced on 1 July 2018.

D. CONCLUDING REMARKS

Australia's treatment of executory contracts in insolvency is at a time of change **25.46** in line with the Australian Government's innovation and reform agenda. The reforms bring Australian insolvency laws one step closer to resembling international approaches – such as the approach under the United States' Chapter 11 Bankruptcy Code.[195] However, Australia has a different insolvency approach and culture, and care must be taken to ensure that reforms do

189 Ibid.

190 Corporations (Stay on Enforcing Certain Rights) Declaration 2018 (Cth).

191 Ibid.

192 Parliament of Australia, 'Treasury Laws Amendment (2017 Enterprise Incentives No. 2) Bill 2017' (Australian Government, Undated) <http://www.aph.gov.au/Parliamentary_Business/Bills_Legislation/Bills_Search_Results/Result?bId=r5886> accessed 21 August 2017.

193 Journals of the Senate, No. 44, 15 June 2017, 1433.

194 Parliament of Australia, 'Report Treasury Laws Amendment (2017 Enterprise Incentives No. 2) Bill 2017 [Provisions]' (Australian Government, 8 August 2017) < http://www.aph.gov.au/Parliamentary_Business/Committees/Senate/Economics/EnterpriseIncentivesNo2/Report> accessed 21 August 2017.

195 Martin, (n157), 5; Mark Schneider and Agnes Kang, 'The End of Ipso Facto: Distress is not a Death Sentence' (2016) Summer Insolvency Reform Special Edition *Henry Davis York The Review* 1, 8.

not have unforeseen detrimental consequences on Australian businesses and on the Australian economy.[196] The reform is intended to overcome the negative impact of ipso facto clauses on genuine work-out attempts and restructuring measures.[197] It is difficult to assess the full ramifications of the reform at this time. However, it is clear that ipso facto clauses will soon no longer have the same enforceability in Australian insolvency, and Australian businesses will need to re-evaluate their contractual agreements and how they approach doing business.

196 Martin, (n157), 5; Schneider and Kang, (n195), 8.

197 Cth, Productivity Commission 2015, (n21), 36–8.

26

NATIONAL REPORT FOR BANGLADESH

Morshed Mannan, Muhammad Mahbubur Rahman and Borhan Uddin Khan

A. INTRODUCTION

Bangladesh has a young market economy and correspondingly, the practice of corporate insolvency is still in its infancy. While the basic 'tools' for collective insolvency proceedings are in place, our consultations with corporate legal practitioners and judges of bankruptcy courts revealed that many issues pertinent to complex insolvency proceedings, such as the treatment of executory contracts, have yet to be fully appreciated in Bangladeshi courts. **26.01**

More generally, the topic of corporate insolvency law has also been under-theorised. With this chapter, the authors tentatively appraise Bangladesh's corporate insolvency regime and its treatment of executory contracts during insolvency proceedings, and thereby open a broader discussion on this central topic. **26.02**

To understand the genesis of Bangladesh's insolvency regime, and its particular treatment of executory contracts, it is necessary to connect the historical development of the legal framework of insolvency to the current regime. This aspect will be covered in this introductory section. Section B considers the various insolvency procedures available to a domestic company in financial distress, and the implications that entering into any such procedures have on **26.03** executory contracts. This is followed by considering certain types of contract and contractual provisions that are treated differently during insolvency proceedings. Section D, which contains a brief overview of recent and ongoing legislative reforms, provides further material for the concluding recommendations of this chapter.

(1) Commercial and creditor-debtor relations in Bengal in the colonial period

26.04 Before the 20th century, the variety of business entities operating in the Indian sub-continent consisted of *srenis* (an organisational entity that bears a resemblance to guilds, producers' cooperatives and early corporations) and eventually family firms and partnerships.[1] European companies and local intermediaries conducted their commercial transactions with contract farmers, skilled and unskilled labourers and other unincorporated businesses, such as partnerships. It was not common to incorporate businesses, hence distinct legal personality and limited liability[2] were largely unexplored principles. This may partially account for the well-documented and tragic history of debt in Bengal. One example will suffice by way of explanation.

26.05 In the early 19th century, the trade in salt presented a lucrative commercial venture for both local merchants and European companies active in Bengal. The salt was produced by a class of people known as *malangis* and in exchange for an advance payment, the *malangis* would agree to supply a set quantity of salt at a fixed price and date. Given the moral hazard inherent in such transactions, the penalties for failing to meet such conditions were severe.[3]

---

1 Khanna, Vikramaditya, 'Business organizations in India prior to the British East India Company', in Wells, Harwell (ed.), *Research Handbook on the History of Corporate and Company Law* (Edward Elgar, 2018), 33; Rungta, Radhe Shyam, *Rise of Business Corporations in India, 1851–1900* (Cambridge University Press, 1970) at Ch. 1.

2 Rungta makes an interesting observation that some partnerships were effectively structured as joint-stock companies, with the management of the company being conducted through a bespoke trust and an elected committee of directors. While this made it easier for a business to bring and defend suits, it was not sufficient to establish distinct legal personality. See Rungta, Radhe Shyam, 'Indian Company Law Problems in 1850' (1962) *American Journal of Legal History*, 6/298, 300–301. This ultimately led to creditors suing individual partners in the event of the partnership's liquidation. See Roy, Tirthankar and Swamy, Anand V., *Law and the Economy in Colonial India* (University of Chicago Press, 2016), 148. Khanna argues that the sreni entity form, that was used in India between 800 B.C.E. to 1000 C.E. enjoyed separate legal personality, however, this legal form experienced a slow decline over the last millennium. See Khanna, *supra* n. 1, 38, 41.

3 The possibility of non-performance, misappropriation of the advance payment, adulteration, selling the product to another party, etc. in the salt, as well as indigo and textile industries, was mitigated by criminalizing the non-fulfilment of contracts (e.g., Workman's Breach of Contract Act, 1859) and the deployment of *gomasthas* (local agents) to coercively enforce performance. See Swamy, Anand V., 'Law and Contract Enforcement in Colonial India' in Chaudhary, Latika *et al.* (eds) *A New Economic History of Colonial India* (Routledge, 2016), 221; Verelst, Harry, *A View of the Rise, Progress and Present State of the*

Often, due to unconducive weather or other *force majeure* events, a *malangi* would have to borrow additional funds and the exorbitant interest charged on the loan would invariably reduce him to an abject condition of bondage in the services of his creditor. A Salt Agent of Chittagong in 1821 remarked, '[s]uch is the wonderful state of bondage to which many of these unhappy men are reduced that death itself ...does not always relieve the molunghy [sic]', as the creditor could oblige future generations of the family to work off the debt.[4] Unlike the cities of Calcutta, Bombay and Madras, English law did not apply in rural areas and commercial disputes concerning debt rarely reached presidency courts.[5]

In contrast, in the pre-colonial era, it was not common for property or persons to be seized for debt. Village *panchayats* often adjudicated disputes between money-lenders and peasant-borrowers and their sympathies were more likely to lie with the latter than the former.[6] They were also not likely to 'take the shirt of the borrower's back'[7] and, within the Hindu community, applied the rule of *damdupat* whereby the absolute amount of interest could not exceed double the principal.[8] As the nature of commercial transactions radically transformed in the colonial period, the law did not keep pace. Lack of insolvency remedies[9] such as the discharge of debt forced the *malangis*, as with countless indigo farmers, weavers and labourers throughout South Asia, to be bonded to labour over successive generations.[10] **26.06**

English Government in Bengal (J. Nourse, Brotherton, Sewell, G. Robinson and T. Evans, 1772), 85. The inadequacy of the colonial civil court system to ensure contract enforcement is discussed in Roy, Tirthankar, *Company of Kinsmen: Enterprise and Community in South Asian History, 1700–1940* (Oxford University Press, 2010).

4 Serajuddin, A.M., 'The Salt Monopoly of the East India Company's Government in Bengal' (1978) *Journal of the Economic and Social History of the Orient*, 21/304, 320.

5 Roy, Tirthankar and Swamy, Anand V., *Law and the Economy in Colonial India* (University of Chicago Press, 2016), 128.

6 The influence of majority-opinion and majority-control over judicial institutions can be seen in Kumar's discussion about the adjudication of credit disputes by *panchayats* in Maharashtra. See Kumar, Ravinder, 'The Deccan Riots of 1875', *Journal of Asian Studies*, 24/613 (1965) at 614. However, it should be noted that there were differences in the practices between money lenders in Bengal and other parts of India. See Letter 3565 L.R. dated 16 July 1894, from C.E. Buckland, secretary to the government of Bengal to secretary of the government of India, Revenue and Agricultural Department, in India, *Selection of Papers on Agricultural Indebtedness*, 1: 284.

7 Roy and Swamy, *supra* note 5, 57.

8 This was partially codified in certain State legislation in India, also encompassing the city of Calcutta. It is an equitable principle that is still applicable in Hindu law in certain states of India. See Roy and Swamy, ibid., 60. This principle is also embodied in s 30 of Bangladesh's Money Lenders Act, 1940.

9 In the early legislation of British India, the term insolvency was applied to natural persons and unincorporated businesses. Following the passage of the Bankruptcy Act, 1997 in modern Bangladesh, which applies to both natural and legal persons, all references to 'insolvent' are construed as being 'bankrupt' (s 116).

10 See, e.g., Campbell, Gwyn and Stanziani, Alessandro, *Bonded Labour and Debt in the Indian Ocean World* (Routledge, 2015); Swamy, Anand V., 'Law and Contract Enforcement in Colonial India' in Chaudhary, Latika *et al.* (eds) *A New Economic History of Colonial India*, (Routledge, 2016) at 220ff.

26.07 The dearth of regulation of creditors, in general, exposed the populace to predatory lending practices,[11] particularly in the rural, agrarian sector. The repercussions of this violently manifested in 1875 in the Deccan region of India where riots erupted, money-lenders were attacked and bonds were destroyed. This conflagration prompted the passage of the Deccan Agriculturist's Relief Act ('DARA'), 1879 to stem the accumulation of debt and the transfer of property to money-lenders. DARA permitted judges to amend the terms of a loan agreement and reduce or delay payment to the lender.[12] More generally, Chapter 20 of the Code of Civil Procedure, 1882 and the Provincial Insolvency Act, 1907 made rudimentary bankruptcy protections available for debtors in provincial areas and introduced the concept of receivership into the law to conduct trade on behalf of businesses.

26.08 Thus, it appears that in the absence of adequate insolvency laws prior to the 20th century, unincorporated businesses and tradesmen could not seek discharge from debts and were thus often bonded to labour. Moreover, in the absence of receivership system, the debtor had little option but to honour the contracts they had made prior to insolvency.

(2) Early insolvency legislation

26.09 It was only in 1828 that the first special insolvency legislation was enacted in colonial India,[13] providing for the relief of insolvent personal debtors, but its jurisdiction was exclusively over the presidency towns of Calcutta, Bombay and Madras.[14] This legislation did not ease the volatility of metropolitan India's inchoate business sector, with Calcutta experiencing a series of business and bank failures in 1846.[15] Subsequent reforms of insolvency legislation, in 1848[16] and 1909,[17] continued to focus on the metropolises of colonial India, rather than the *mofussil* regions, as there was a purported 'absence of any flourishing trade and commerce'[18] in those localities. While India's first

11 Rungta, *supra* note 2, 302.

12 Chaudhary, Latika and Swamy, Anand V., 'Protecting the Borrower: An Experiment in Colonial India' *Explorations in Economic History*, 65/36 (2017) at 37.

13 Statute 9 (Geo IV c. 73). It was described as a 'human and wise statute' at the time of its enactment. See *Asiatic Journal and Modern Register for British India and its Dependencies*, vol. 26, July–December 1828 (Parbury, Allen & Co 1828), 267–8.

14 Before the enactment of this law, ss 23 and 24 of the Government of India Act, 1800 conferred limited insolvency jurisdiction on the Supreme Court at Calcutta and Madras and the Recorder's Court at Bombay. See Sirohi, J.P.S., *Law of Insolvency in India* (Allahabad Law Agency, 1999) at 1.

15 Roy and Swamy, *supra* note 5, 147.

16 The Indian Insolvency Act, 1848.

17 The Presidency Towns Insolvency Act, 1909.

18 The Law Commission of India, *Twenty-Sixth Report on Insolvency Laws* (February 1964), para 3.

companies' legislation came into force in 1850,[19] and was subsequently reformed in 1866[20] and 1882,[21] its application was relatively limited and inadequate for collective insolvency proceedings. One study indicates that during the period of 1851–1900, only 3,732 companies were registered in all of India, with only 1,364 continuing operation beyond 1900.[22] The legislation did provide for court-ordered and voluntary winding-up proceedings commenced by the debtor but the fact that these companies were unincorporated meant that these proceedings did not shield shareholders from debt-collection suits following the dissolution of the company.[23]

During the first half of the 20th century, two insolvency laws were enacted, one having jurisdiction over metropolitan areas and the other over provinces. The ostensible reason for two separate insolvency regimes was the disparity in conditions between urban and rural areas.[24] These laws continued to be in force following Partition and Bangladesh's independence from Pakistan on 26 March 1971. The Insolvency Act ('DACCA'), 1909[25] and the Provincial Insolvency Act, 1920,[26] as with earlier 20th century legislation, regulated personal rather than corporate insolvencies,[27] but included unincorporated business entities such as partnerships within their ambit.[28] **26.10**

An insolvency petition could be filed under these laws by a creditor or the debtor.[29] After conducting a hearing on the petition, the court could make an order of adjudication rendering the debtor insolvent.[30] The effect of the order is that the property of the insolvent be vested in the court or in a receiver, under the Provincial Insolvency Act, 1920, or in the official assignee, under the Insolvency Act (Dacca), 1909 for division among the creditors. This **26.11**

---

19 The Indian Companies Act, 1850.

20 The Indian Companies Act, 1866 (10 of 1866).

21 The Indian Companies Act, 1882 (6 of 1882).

22 Rungta, Radhe Shyam, *Rise of Business Corporations in India, 1851–1900* (Cambridge University Press, 1970) at 256.

23 Rungta, *supra* note 2, 307.

24 Quotation of the Hon'ble Sir H. Erle Richards who moved the Bill for the Presidency-towns Insolvency Act, 1909, cited in Law Commission of India, *Twenty-Sixth Report on Insolvency Laws* (February 1964), para 4.

25 This was facsimile to the Presidency Towns Insolvency Act, 1909 (Act No. 3 of 1909), which extended its jurisdiction to key cities in British India-Calcutta, Madras and Bombay. This Act concerned the leading cities of Pakistan – Karachi and Dacca respectively.

26 The Provincial Insolvency Act, 1920 encompassed the area outside of the Presidency Towns: Karachi and Dacca.

27 The Insolvency Act (Dacca), 1909, s 107; The Provincial Insolvency Act, 1920, s 8.

28 See, e.g., The Insolvency Act (Dacca), 1909, s 49 (4) regarding priority of debts when the insolvent business is a partnership and ss 97–99 concerning insolvency petitions against partners.

29 The Provincial Insolvency Act, 1920, s 7; The Insolvency Act (Dacca), 1909, s 10.

30 The Insolvency Act (Dacca), 1909, ss 13(5) and 15(3); The Provincial Insolvency Act, 1920, s 27.

barred creditors from seeking individual remedies or filing parallel legal actions against the estate of the insolvent, except for secured creditors[31] who could realize their security as if the order of adjudication had not been made.[32] One option for the court or the intermediary to satisfy the creditors' claims is to proceed to sell and distribute the debtor's property.[33]

26.12 As private companies were not covered by the insolvency legislation of the time, financially distressed or bankrupt companies had to look to the companies' legislation[34] for formal and hybrid mechanisms to distribute assets to creditors and protect corporate debtors in the event that it was no longer able to pay its debts. An important exception to this was introduced after the independence of Bangladesh in 1971. The state-owned Jute, Textile, Sugar, Steel and Engineering and Chemical Industries corporations, and the private industrial enterprises placed under their control were placed outside the operation of the companies' legislation.[35] In this newly introduced system, the winding-up of such corporations and enterprises were to be conducted in the manner directed by the government.[36] As such, a large number of companies were excluded from the Companies Act, 1913 and could not benefit from its protection when they needed to be wound-up.[37]

26.13 For those companies subject to the Companies Act, 1913, following a petition by creditors, shareholders, the companies' registrar or the company itself, the court was empowered to wind up any other private company if it was no longer

31 In the Provincial Insolvency Act, 1920, secured creditor is defined as 'a person holding a mortgage, charge or lien on the property debtor or any part thereof as a security for a debt due to him from the debtor' (s 2(e)). In contrast, the Insolvency Act (Dacca), 1909, has a more open definition, with it including 'a landlord who under any enactment for the time being in force has a charge on land for the rent of that land' (s 2(g)).

32 The Insolvency Act (Dacca), 1909, s 17; The Provincial Insolvency Act, 1920, s 28(6).

33 The debtor's property is defined in The Insolvency Act (Dacca), 1909 s 52 (2); The Provincial Insolvency Act, 1920, s 28(3).

34 The Companies Act, 1913 (No. 7 of 1913). This Act applied to companies limited by shares, companies limited by guarantee and unlimited companies (s 5).

35 The Bangladesh Industrial Enterprises (Nationalisation) Order, 1972 (P.O. No. 27 of 1972).

36 The Bangladesh Industrial Enterprises (Nationalisation) Order, 1972, s 23, as amended by the Bangladesh Industrial Enterprises (Nationalisation) (Amendment) Order, 1972 (P.O. No. 37 of 1972) and Bangladesh Industrial Enterprises (Nationalisation) (Amendment) Ordinance, 1984 (Ordinance No. LXXIII of 1984). The three schedules to the Order indicate 169 nationalized industrial enterprises, with others being added subsequently through the Official Gazette. Note that the Bangladesh Industries Enterprises (Nationalization) Order, 1972 has been repealed by the Bangladesh Industries Enterprises (Nationalization) Act, 2018. The provision for terminating these enterprises are preserved in s 22. The updated schedule to the Act indicates 219 industrial enterprises that operate under this Act.

37 When an order for winding up of Dhakeshwari Cotton Mills Ltd, one of the largest privately owned mills in Bengal in terms of workforce, was made in 1982, it could not benefit from bankruptcy protection under s 171 of the Companies Act, 1913, thereby allowing creditors and other parties to file suits and other legal proceedings against the Mill during the winding up process. See Iftikhar-ul-Awal, A.Z.M., *The Industrial Development of Bengal, 1900–1939* (Vikas Publishing, 1982), 151–2 and *Abdul Hamid vs. Dhakeshwari Cotton Mills Ltd and ors* 36 DLR (1984) 257, para 17.

able to satisfy its debts.[38] The case law from the period indicates a general disinclination towards granting such orders as it amounted to the 'killing of a company'.[39] The court generally looked towards whether the company was commercially insolvent. However, there is some debate over what constituted 'commercial insolvency'.

Unlike the UK, where courts are able to consider either the cash flow test or balance sheet test under the Insolvency Act,[40] Bangladeshi legislation was silent on this issue, leaving it for the court to interpret. In some decisions, it appeared that the court favoured the cash flow test, strictly looking towards whether the company could meet debts as they fell due. For instance, in *Nizamul Haque vs. Singa Bangla Garment*,[41] the High Court Division of the Supreme Court of Bangladesh granted a landlord's petition for the winding up of a company for a debt of some 700,000 BDT, despite the company having total assets valued at 30,000,000 BDT. In *Rehana Ahmed and ors vs. Nahar Shipping Lines Ltd*[42] the High Court Division stated that the question that confronted a court was not whether a company has more liabilities than assets, but whether it was able to pay its debts.[43] This would be satisfied where the company is able to carry on its business and is repaying its debts, regardless of the long-term liabilities and illiquid assets it might have. In contrast, the Appellate Division of the Supreme Court of Bangladesh seems to fuse both tests. In *Agrani Bank vs. Bangladesh Tyres Ltd*,[44] it was held that a company was commercially insolvent and could be wound up when 'its existing and possible assets are insufficient to meet the existing liabilities, it is heavily indebted to various creditors, all its assets being in mortgage or in pledge and there is no possible chance of profit being made or its business carried out'.[45] **26.14**

38 The Companies Act, 1913, ss 162(v), 163 and 166.

39 *Mohiul Islam vs. Century Properties Development Ltd and others* 7 BLC [2002] 248 (HCD). The High Court Division of the Supreme Court of Bangladesh held that winding up by a court is a 'very serious matter and it amounts to killing of a company'. Consequently, petitions for winding-up would have to meet a high threshold to be granted. See Zahir, M., *Company and Securities Laws* (University Press Limited, 2015) 231.

40 The Insolvency Act, 1986, s 123 (2).

41 *Nizamul Haque vs. Singa Bangla Garment Manufacturing Company (Pvt.) Ltd* 43 DLR [1991] 603.

42 44 DLR [1992] 256.

43 *Rehana Ahmed and ors vs. Nahar Shipping Lines Ltd* 44 DLR [1992] 256, para 20.

44 43 DLR (AD) [1991] 164.

45 *Agrani Bank vs. Bangladesh Tyres Ltd.* 43 DLR (AD) [1991] 164, para 21. While the case is not cited by the Appellate Division, the wording used by the court is similar to that in *In Re European Life Assurance Society* [1869] LR 9 Eq 122, where Sir William James V-C said on p 128 that a company is commercially insolvent if 'its assets are such, and its existing liabilities are such, as to make it reasonably certain – as to make the court feel satisfied – that the existing and probable assets would be insufficient to meet the existing liabilities'. This adoption of the balance sheet test for existing liabilities was not accepted with much enthusiasm by Lord Walker in *BNY Corporate Trustee Services Ltd and others v Eurosail*-UK 2007–3BL PLC [2013] UKSC 28 where on p 14 he commented that '[i]t may be regarded as unfortunate that his judgment has come to be regarded as a leading case'.

26.15 Along with granting winding-up orders in only limited circumstances, the courts generally encouraged the revival and rehabilitation of companies where possible.[46] Two hybrid procedures were available for this under the companies' legislation that was analogous to the procedures available under the insolvency laws. The debtor or a liquidator[47] could propose submission of a property for a composition or compromise to satisfy his debts or a scheme of arrangement of his affairs.[48] One interesting early example of a scheme of arrangement was a worker buyout of a cotton mill in early 1972, after the High Court Division stayed an earlier winding up order and the workers paid for the buyout.[49] In the companies' legislation, this could be pre- and post-winding-up proceedings while under the (personal) insolvency law, it would be after the order of adjudication was made. If this proposal was approved by a majority of the creditors, amounting to three-fourths of the value of the estate, it would cram-down on the creditors as a class.[50] In the companies legislation the scheme or compromise once approved by the court would bind all of the creditors, as well as the liquidator and contributories in the case of insolvency. The insolvency laws permitted the (personal) debtor to amend the proposal during the meeting to garner greater creditor support and included extensive guidelines on how the court should assess the proposal for approval. The proposal would be scrutinized by the court as to its reasonableness, its benefit to the general body of creditors, its adherence to the priority ranking that governs the distribution of property[51] and its security for payment of at least 37.5 per cent[52] or 25 per cent[53] of all unsecured debts. The court would also consider the objections of any of the minority creditors and the reports made by the receiver or official assignee. After such an assessment, the court could

46 See, e.g., *Nazrul Islam Khan Badol vs. Al Baraka Bank Bangladesh*, Company Matter No. 40 of 1991, decided on 15.03.1992 [unreported].

47 The Companies Act, 1913, s 234.

48 The Companies Act, 1913, s 153 (1); The Insolvency Act (Dacca), 1909, s 28; The Provincial Insolvency Act, 1920, s 38.

49 Unreported case discussed in Zahir, *supra* note 39, 246–7. However, as the cotton mills were soon nationalised, this worker buyout eventually came to nought.

50 The Companies Act, 1913, s 153(2); The Insolvency Act (Dacca), 1909, s 28 (2); The Provincial Insolvency Act, 1920, s 38 (2).

51 The Provincial Insolvency Act, 1920, s 61 specifies that all debts due to the Government or local authorities and wages owed to clerks, servants or labourers up to a fixed amount will have priority over all other debts. The remaining debts entered in the schedule of creditors were to be paid pro rata and without any preference. The only difference in the Insolvency Act (Dacca), 1909 was that it added a third priority rank: up to one month's rent due to a landlord by the insolvent debtor (section 49).

52 The Provincial Insolvency Act, 1920, s 38 (5). The section specifically says payment of 'six annas to the taka'. A taka is composed of 16 annas, which amounts to 37.5 per cent of each taka.

53 Insolvency Act (Dacca), 1909, s 29 (5). The section specifically says payment of 'four annas to the taka'. This amounts to 25 per cent of each taka.

approve the proposal through a fresh order, thereby binding all the creditors and annulling the order of adjudication.[54]

B. CURRENT FRAMEWORK AND AVAILABLE INSOLVENCY PROCEDURES

A limited array of formal and hybrid insolvency proceedings were available in Bangladesh since the time of its independence. However, this framework did not cover several key industries and proved inadequate in recouping loans, thus precipitating a spiralling number of wilful defaulters and non-performing loans.[55] In practice, collective insolvency proceedings and debt restructuring in Bangladesh were cumbersome, with weak supervision and enforcement perpetuating unduly lengthy procedures and low recovery rates. **26.16**

Since the 1990s, the government has initiated multi-pronged legislative efforts to reduce the proportion of non-performing loans and more generally bolster the private sector. The first was the *Artha Rin Adalat Ain*, 1990 (Money Loans Court Act, 1990), subsequently replaced by the *Artha Rin Adalat Ain*, 2003 (Money Loans Court Act, 2003). The second was the promulgation of a new Companies Act[56] and the third was the introduction of a Bankruptcy Act[57] repealing and consolidating the earlier insolvency legislation. **26.17**

The Money Loans Court Act, 2003 is a special law to facilitate the recovery of loans by banks and other financial institutions.[58] As with the 1913 Act, the newer companies' legislation includes facsimile provisions for compromises, compositions and schemes of arrangement prior to or pursuant to insolvency,[59] as well as involuntary winding-up by a court[60] and creditors' voluntary **26.18**

54 The Insolvency Act (Dacca), 1909, s 30; The Provincial Insolvency Act, 1920, s 39. Under s 32 read with s 45 of the Act of 1909, there are exceptions to the universal binding effect of a composition or scheme of arrangement. Among other things, any debt due to the government or debts or liabilities incurred by means of fraud or fraudulent breach of trust can still be provable by a creditor, regardless of the composition or scheme of arrangement, unless they explicitly assent to it.

55 See, e.g., Adhikary, Bishnu Kumar, 'Nonperforming Loans in the Banking Sector of Bangladesh: Realities and Challenges' (2006) *Ritsumeikan Journal of Asia Pacific Studies*, 21/75,77.

56 The Companies Act, 1994 (Act No. 18 of 1994).

57 The Bankruptcy Act, 1997 (Act No. 10 of 1997).

58 Money Loans Court Act, 2003, s 5 sets out the jurisdiction of the Money Loans Court.

59 The Companies Act, 1994, s 228. A liquidator is empowered to enter into compromises or arrangements with creditors regarding any claim, past or future, that may become liable, see The Companies Act, 1994, s 330 (1) (ii). Conversely, with regard to compromises or arrangements with any person indebted to the company under liquidation, the liquidator can only abandon them upon sworn affidavit by the liquidator that it will be beneficial to the company. See Rule 164, The Companies Rules, 2000.

60 The Companies Act, 1994, s 241.

winding-up.[61] Judgments under this law indicate a reluctance to admit applications for court-ordered winding-up, out of concern for the goodwill of the company and the interest of shareholders and creditors.[62] If a scheme or composition is proposed and accepted, the court can stay ongoing winding-up proceedings if required.[63]

26.19 While the Money Loans Court Act furnishes a new mechanism for realizing non-performing loans within a short timeframe, the Bankruptcy Act of 1997 creates further avenues for debtors to satisfy their debts short of liquidation. The Bankruptcy Act extends to both natural and legal persons.[64] Unlike earlier insolvency legislation, a definition of 'bankrupt' is attempted. Section 2(18) states that bankrupt is a debtor who is adjudged bankrupt: after an order of adjudication following an act of bankruptcy;[65] for failing to pay instalments under a scheme or composition; for obtaining approval of a scheme or composition through fraud; and if implementing the scheme, composition or reorganization will cause injustice or undue delay for the creditors.[66]

26.20 As a result, both creditors and debtors can file a plaint for an order of adjudication that the debtor is bankrupt. When fixing a date for hearing the plaint, the court may appoint an (interim) receiver to take possession of the debtor's property, but must do so after an order of adjudication is made.[67] Receivers have extensive powers under the Bankruptcy Act and the Bankruptcy Rules, 1997 (as do liquidators if they are appointed under the Companies Act, 1994 and the Code of Civil Procedure, 1908). This includes, but is not limited to, managing, protecting and improving the property, examining the conduct of the representative officers of the debtor estate, convening creditors' committee meetings, assessing debtor proposals for compositions and schemes of arrangement, collecting rent and profits accrued by the estate, executing documents and entering contracts on behalf of the estate and

---

61 The Companies Act, 1994, s 286 (1) (c) states that a company can be voluntarily wound-up through an extraordinary resolution when its liabilities indicate that it cannot continue its business. The Companies Act, 1994, s 290 (3) imputes that a voluntary winding-up proceeding becomes a creditors' voluntary winding-up proceeding when a company is unable to furnish a declaration of solvency as specified in The Companies Act, 1994, s 290 (1)–(2). A voluntary winding-up proceeding can be subjected to court supervision pursuant to ss. 316ff. This distinction between members' voluntary winding-up proceedings and creditors' voluntary winding-up proceedings is likely to be erased if the Draft Companies Act, 2013 is passed into law in its current form. A voluntary winding-up proceeding will not be classified as being a creditors' voluntary winding-up proceeding if a declaration of solvency is not furnished (ss 455–456).

62 *Amin (Md.) vs. Bengal Shipping Line*, 60 DLR [2008] 444. The Companies Act, 1994, s 254.

63 The Companies Act, 1994, s 253.

64 The Bankruptcy Act, 1997, s 2(36).

65 ibid., s 10.

66 ibid., ss 45 and 46(13).

67 ibid., ss 23 and 31.

referring disputes concerning the estate to arbitration.[68] The receiver has the discretion to continue or discontinue a suit filed by the now insolvent party if it may be of benefit to creditors,[69] as well as sue and be sued on behalf of the estate.[70] They can also give notice to any debtor of the insolvent party to realize a debt, with the support of a court order if necessary.[71]

As part of the bankruptcy proceedings, all debts and liabilities, present or future, certain or contingent, to which the company was subject prior to bankruptcy shall be provable.[72] While the receiver can ultimately distribute the assets of the estate to meet these debts, the debtor can propose a reorganization prior to the order of adjudication or a composition and scheme of arrangement after the order of adjudication. In contrast to the three-fourths requirement under the earlier personal insolvency legislation, the reorganization or composition of debts or scheme of arrangement of affairs have to be approved by creditors constituting two-thirds of the provable debts in person or by proxy to be deemed to be crammed-down on all the creditors.[73] **26.21**

As a consequence, the formal, court-supervised[74] insolvency procedures available to a debtor are: **26.22**

(1) Compromises, Compositions and Schemes of Arrangement under the Companies Act, 1994;
(2) Reorganization prior to an order of adjudication of bankruptcy under the Bankruptcy Act, 1997;
(3) Composition/Scheme of Arrangement after an order of adjudication of bankruptcy under the Bankruptcy Act, 1997;
(4) Liquidation pursuant to a creditors' voluntary winding-up or involuntary winding-up by a court under the Companies Act, 1994.

With regard to a reorganization proposal, the court will note if it protects the interests of dissenting creditors, the various classes of creditors and the general body of creditors, as any order made will be binding on the debtor and all **26.23**

---

68 ibid., ss 65, 67, 68(3) and 71; Bankruptcy Rules, 1997, rule 48; Order 40, Rule 1(1)(d), The Code of Civil Procedure, 1908 (with respect to receivers appointed following the application of e.g. a secured creditor or by order of the Court prior to appointment of a liquidator). While a liquidator enjoys wide-ranging powers under the Companies Act, 1994, s 262 it is unlikely that they can 'improve' the property beyond what is necessary to ensure a beneficial winding up. They also cannot refer a dispute to arbitration. See Soiloor, S.L.R. (ed.), *Company Law and Practice*, Vol. 2 (New Warsi Book Corporation, 2007), 1158.

69 Order 22, Rule 8(1), The Code of Civil Procedure, 1908

70 The Bankruptcy Act, 1997, s 65; Order 40, Rule 1(1)(d), The Code of Civil Procedure, 1908.

71 ibid., s 69.

72 ibid., s 39(2).

73 ibid, ss 43(2), 46(5).

74 Thus excluding purely contractual work-outs.

creditors. If satisfied, the court will vest the debtor's property in a receiver but notably, may allow the debtor to be the 'special manager' of the estate, including the business, under the receiver's supervision.[75]

C. TREATMENT OF EXECUTORY CONTRACTS

26.24 As indicated above, corporate insolvency is a nebulous field in Bangladesh. There is an absence of Bangladeshi case law specifically dealing with the treatment of executory contracts during insolvency proceedings and from our discussions with corporate lawyers and judges of bankruptcy courts, it appears that there is a lack of experience with such matters. As such, there is also a dearth of authoritative, academic work on the subject.[76] In light of this, the following section reviews primary legislation to ascertain the extent to which executory contracts are honoured in Bangladesh during insolvency proceedings.

(1) Executory contracts are deemed to be assumed

26.25 In relation to executory contracts, the Bankruptcy Act, 1997 generally follows the provisions of sections 46(3) and 34 of the Acts of 1909 and 1934 respectively. It provides that:

> all debts and liabilities, present or future, certain or contingent, to which a debtor, other than an individual debtor, is subject at any time before he is adjudged bankrupt, or in the case of an individual debtor, to which he may become subject before his discharge by reason of any obligation incurred before the date of such adjudication, shall be deemed to be debts provable under this Act unless otherwise determined by the Court.[77]

---

75 The Bankruptcy Act, 1997, s 46(8).

76 There is, however, research on the treatment of contracts in colonial India conducted by economic historians. From the perspective of the colonial authorities, there was a considerable risk that peasants and indigenous businesses would not uphold their side of a bargain. These fears were not unfounded, as most explicitly shown by the Indigo Mutiny in 1859 where Bengali indigo farmers refused to sell indigo to the European owners of indigo factories thereby breaching written sales contracts. Incidents such as this sparked regulatory activity, including the passage of the (still extant) Contract Act, 1872, as well as severe punishments for breach of contract, including imprisonment. Penal contracting was only abolished in India in 1926. See Anderson, David, 'India, 1850–1930: The Illusion of Free Labor', in Hay, Douglas and Craven, Paul (eds), *Masters, Servants and Magistrates in Britain and Empire, 1562–1955* (University of North Carolina Press, 2014) 422–54; Roy and Swamy, *supra* note 5, 123, 134; British Parliamentary Papers, *Copy of the Legislative Despatch on the Breach of Contracts (East India) Bill, together with a Copy of the Bill* (HMSO, 1862) 1.

77 The Bankruptcy Act, 1997, s 39(2).

Accordingly, contractual liabilities of the insolvent party may be provable by creditors as part of insolvency proceedings. The Act of 1997 also stipulates that any contract for valuable consideration[78] with the debtor will not be invalidated by the event of insolvency,[79] as long as there was no fraudulent preference or fraudulent transfer made.[80] In interpreting a similar provision of the Act of 1920,[81] the Madras High Court observed that the official receiver appointed by the government: 26.26

> merely steps into shoes of the insolvent and can claim no higher rights than the insolvent. If the contract to adjust was binding on the insolvents it was equally binding on the Official Receiver who is merely their representative in law.[82]

Certain contracts will have to be assumed if the insolvency office holder wishes to carry on the debtor's business. A notable example of this are utility contracts. If a debtor or a debtor's estate fails to pay, e.g. an electricity bill, then the electricity provider can eventually disconnect the debtor and a court cannot order a reconnection.[83] At the same time, the law allows for the debtor's estate to retain the apparatuses needed for essential services, so as to facilitate activities that are necessary during bankruptcy. The Electricity Act, 2018, for instance, provides that electricity supply-lines, meters, fittings or other machinery used for the supply of electricity cannot be seized from property the debtor owns, due to their bankruptcy or due to a civil suit judgment being made against them.[84] The insolvency office holder can thereby re-establish an electricity connection if needed, pursuant to certain 26.27

78 The Contract Act, 1872, s 2(d) defines consideration as: 'When, at the desire of the promisor, the promisee or any other person has done or abstained from doing, or does or abstains from doing, or promises to do or to abstain from doing, something, such act or abstinence or promise is called a consideration for the promise.' As such, there is no general requirement as to adequacy or form of consideration. However, in determining whether said consideration is valuable, the interpretation of Lush J in *Curre vs. Misa* [1875] LR 10 Ex 153, 162 is widely referred to: 'A valuable consideration in the sense of the law, may consist either in some right, interest, profit or benefit accruing to one party, or some forbearance, detriment, loss or responsibility given, suffered, or undertaken by the other.' Qualifications as to the value or adequacy of consideration turn on the facts, circumstances and necessities of individual cases. In India, see e.g., *Sonia Bhatia vs. State of U.P. & Others* [1981] SCR (3) 239 (Supreme Court of India), *M.M. Hussain and Others vs. Laminated Package (P) Ltd* [1999] (6) ALD 248 (Andhra High Court), the unreported decision in *M/S Sumer Corporation vs. The State of Maharashtra and Another*, Writ Petition No. 2119 of 2016 in the Bombay High Court, decided on 25 April 2017.

79 Bankruptcy Act, 1997, s 63(d).

80 ibid., ss 50, 59–62. The Companies Act, 1994, ss 322 and 327 also contain a transfer avoidance and fraudulent preference provision.

81 The Provincial Insolvency Act, 1920, s 55(d). The Insolvency Act (Dacca), 1909, s 57(d) also contained similar provision.

82 *A.R. Ghazani Mohammed Sahib vs. The Official Receiver* [1958] 1 MLJ 424.

83 The Electricity Act, 2018, s 18(1)–(2). Outstanding electricity invoices may be recovered by the Government of Bangladesh under the Public Demands Recovery Act, 1913. See The Electricity Act, 2018, s 54.

84 ibid, s 24.

conditions being met.[85] In contrast, it is apparent from the wording of commercial legislation, such as the Sale of Goods Act,[86] that in the event of a party's insolvency, other counterparties can withhold performance. For example, an unpaid seller may retain possession, or stop in transit, goods that it is in the process of delivering to a buyer when the latter becomes insolvent, irrespective of a retention of title clause being included in the sales contract.[87]

26.28 It is therefore arguable that an *ipso facto* clause (i.e., a clause stipulating that a contract is automatically terminated or performance is accelerated if a counterparty enters into receivership) in a bona fide contract is potentially enforceable, especially as there is no explicit prohibition of them in the Bankruptcy Act, 1997 or the Contract Act, 1872. Our consultations with three corporate law firms reveal that the use of *ipso facto* clauses is quite common in corporate contracts. The validity of such a clause however is yet to be tested before a court of law.[88]

26.29 Similarly, we have been informed through these consultations that banks in Bangladesh often include flip clauses in syndicated loan agreements. The liability that is incurred under such executory contracts is an ordinary debt that ranks for claim along with other unsecured creditors and is paid *pro rata*, unless it is a debt that can be described as part of the costs and expenses of winding up when it will receive preferential treatment.[89]

26.30 The Bankruptcy Act, 1997 also provides that 'the Receiver, if he deems it necessary in the best interest of creditors, *may carry on the business of the debtor* so far as is necessary for the beneficial winding up of the same'.[90] This provision also allows the receiver to assume executory contracts for the purpose of beneficial winding up. The receiver may also appoint the individual

---

85 ibid, s 20.

86 Sale of Goods Act, 1930. It should be noted that the Sale of Goods Act is only applicable to sales transactions within Bangladesh, unless the law of Bangladesh is the governing law of an international sales contract. Retention of title clauses may be included in international sales contracts, but they do not need to be registered in Bangladesh.

87 Sale of Goods Act, 1930, ss 47 and 50.

88 It should be noted that the Insolvency and Creditor/Debtor Regimes United Standard (ICR Standard), comprised of the World Bank's Principles for Effective Insolvency and Creditor/Debtor Regimes (2016) read with the UNCITRAL Legislative Guide on Insolvency Law (2005), recommends that *ipso facto* clauses – including acceleration clauses – should be rendered unenforceable. See UNCITRAL Legislative Guide on Insolvency Law (2005), Recommendation 70.

89 In *Official Liquidator, U.P. Union Bank Ltd vs. Rameshwar Nath Agarwal* [1960] 30 Comp Cas 114, p. 117. See *The Liquidator, Economic Aid Corporation vs. The Chandpur Mills Ltd* 8 P.L.R. (Dac) 409 D.B. as an example of a Dhaka court ordering that the retention of a lease for the benefit of a company in liquidation was an administrative expense of the liquidator that should be satisfied fully.

90 The Bankruptcy Act, 1997, s 71(2). The Insolvency Act (Dacca), 1909, s 68(1)(c) and The Provincial Insolvency Act, 1920, s 59(c) also contained similar provisions.

bankrupt to carry on the existing trade during the insolvency proceedings if it would be beneficial to the creditors.[91]

With respect to winding-up under company law, the liquidator may 'carry on the business of the company so far as may be necessary, for the beneficial winding-up of the same'.[92] While carrying out business activities, it has long been settled that during winding-up proceedings, 'outstanding contracts of the company do not become *ipso facto* inoperative'.[93] **26.31**

(2) Executory contracts may be rejected by disclaimer

In lieu of an *ipso facto* clause, in case of winding-up of an insolvent company, the liquidator may, with the leave of the court, disclaim 'onerous' executory contracts.[94] This may be, for instance, a requirement to hand over real estate property at a contractually agreed deadline.[95] Such disclaimers amounting to rejection of executory contracts, however, do not *ipso facto* affect the rights or liabilities of the counterparties of the contracts,[96] unless the contracts were fraudulent in the first place.[97] The affected parties therefore can apply to the court for damages arising out of non-performance of executory contracts. Any order of damages in such cases may be proved by the affected parties as debt in **26.32**

91 The Bankruptcy Act, 1997, s 81(1). The Insolvency Act (Dacca), 1909, s 75(1) also contained a similar provision.

92 The Companies Act, 1994, s 262(b). This provision only applies to court-ordered involuntary winding-up proceedings, not creditors' voluntary winding-up. See The Companies Act 1994, s 308(1).

93 See, *In Official Liquidator, U.P. Union Bank Ltd vs. Rameshwar Nath Agarwal* [1960] 30 Comp Cas 114, p. 117, affirmed in *Smt. Kaushalya Aggarwal vs Punwire Paging Services Ltd (In Liquidation)* [2004] 121 Comp Cas. 431 (PHC), para 25. The Supreme Court of India also held that surety agreements/guarantees are also not discharged by the fact of the debtor's liquidation. This is an exception to the general rule in Contract Act, 1872, s 134 and Companies Act 1994, s 160 and was discussed approvingly in the Bangladesh context in Zahir, *supra* note 39, 252.

94 The Companies Act, 1994, s 326(1) provides that:

> where any part of the property of company which is being wound up consists of land of any tenure burdened with onerous covenants, of shares, or stock in other companies, of unprofitable contracts or of any other property that is unsalable, or not readily saleable, by reason of its binding the possessor thereof to the performance of any onerous act, or to the payment of any sum of money, the liquidator of the company, notwithstanding that he had endeavoured to sell or has taken possession of the property, or had exercised any act of ownership in relation thereto, may with the leave of the Court and subject to the provisions of this section, by writing signed by him at any time within twelve months after the commencement of the winding up or such extended period as may be allowed by the Court disclaim the property.

95 In normal circumstances, if real estate property is not handed over to a buyer within six months of a contractually agreed deadline, compensation must be paid to the buyer. See Real Estate Development and Management Act, 2010, s 15.

96 The Companies Act, 1994, s 326(2). The Insolvency Act (Dacca), 1909, s 62 also contained similar provision.

97 The Companies Act, 1994, s 327.

the winding-up.[98] The court can of its own motion also order rescission of executory contracts in the general interest of creditors.[99]

26.33 When a party interested in an executory contract submits an application to the liquidator to make a decision on disclaimer of contract, the liquidator must notify, within a period of 30 days or such further time as may be allowed by the court, the interested party that s/he intends to apply to the court for leave to disclaim. Otherwise, the contract shall be deemed to be assumed.[100]

26.34 In the event that there have been mutual transactions between a debtor and a creditor, set-offs are possible and will have priority over all other debts.[101]

(3) Role of the creditors

26.35 In deciding to disclaim a contract, the receiver or liquidator has to consider the interests of creditors as a class, bearing in mind the preferential payments that need to be made to tax authorities and to workers to offset unpaid wages.[102] During bankruptcy proceedings, where the number of eligible creditors is more than ten, the Bankruptcy Act, 1997 empowers the court to order the formation a creditors' committee.[103] This committee consisting of not more than five members may pass necessary resolutions to advise the receiver in the discharge of his functions.[104] Such advice is generally binding on the receiver.[105] In the absence of the creditors' committee, the receiver should convene meetings of creditors holding at least 50 per cent of the total debts and act according to the desires of the creditors as far as practicable.[106]

26.36 During court-ordered involuntary winding-up proceedings, the Companies Act, 1994 requires the liquidator to convene a meeting of creditors and

98 ibid, s 326(5) and (7). The Insolvency Act (Dacca), 1909, s 67 also contained a similar provision. Section 326(7) does not specify whether the creditor would have a secured or unsecured claim when proving their debts for a disclaimed executory contract, which means that the nature of the claim would turn on the type of contract in question.

99 See, e.g., *Smt. Kaushalya Aggarwal vs. Punwire Paging Services Ltd (In Liquidation)* [2004] 121 Comp Cas 431 (PHC), para 29.

100 The Companies Act, 1994, s 326(4).

101 Contract Act, 1872, s 50(b); see also The Bankruptcy Act, 1997, s 53.

102 The Bankruptcy Act, 1997, s 75(1); Section 325(1) of The Companies Act, 1994 sets out the preferential payments that need to be made during court-ordered involuntary winding-up proceedings and creditors' voluntary winding-up proceedings. In addition to workers, payments need to be made to clerks and other servants who provide a service to the company, compensation for the death or disablement of any officer or employee of the company and the expenses of any investigation conducted into the affairs of the company.

103 The Bankruptcy Act, 1997, s 36(1).

104 The Bankruptcy Rules, 1997, rule 36.

105 The Bankruptcy Act, 1997, s 36(2).

106 ibid., s 68(3).

subsequently, contributories of the company, so as to determine whether a Committee of Inspection, composed of both creditors and contributories representatives should be appointed.[107] The creditors' general meeting or the delegated Committee of Inspection may give directions to the liquidator on how to discharge his functions.[108] Similarly, in the event of a creditors' voluntary winding-up proceedings following the insolvency of a debtor company, the creditors' general meeting will at its discretion form a Committee of Inspection. Either body may exercise control over the powers exercised by the company's liquidator.[109]

(4) Special contracts and contractual provisions

To conclude this section, it is worth considering special contractual provisions that would be 'activated' in the event of contractual default (due to insolvency or otherwise). In contrast with *ipso facto* clauses discussed above, penalty clauses requiring a certain sum to be payable when a counterparty terminates a contract, is prima facie permissible.[110] As with damages for rescinded or disclaimed contracts, it can be proven as a debt in insolvency proceedings. By reason of this, acceleration clauses are also permissible under Bangladesh contract law whereby the whole sum of a debt may become due for failure to meet an instalment.[111] **26.37**

It is also notable that there is a possibility of a court re-opening loan agreements if the interest charged is seen to be 'excessive' or the transaction is deemed to be 'substantially unfair' under the Usurious Loans Act.[112] This not only extends to suits filed for recovery of loans or enforcement of security but also to loans that have been admitted as part of insolvency proceedings.[113] **26.38**

The Act confers wide-ranging discretionary powers on the court, from setting aside excess interest payments to ordering creditors to indemnify debtors of any excess interest or security paid at the time of the suit.[114] Similar relief can also be sought under the Money Lenders Act, 1940 in the context of insolvency proceedings if excessive interest rates are charged or a court **26.39**

107 The Companies Act, 1994, s 261.
108 ibid., s 266(1)–(2).
109 ibid, s 308(1).
110 Contract Act, 1872, s 74.
111 ibid., s 74 illustration (g) in particular.
112 The Usurious Loans Act, 1918, s 3(1)(a)–(b). Roy and Anand, *supra* note 5, 75, report that this Act was 'viewed as necessary because judges were taking a narrow view of provision in the Indian Contract Act pertaining to unconscionable bargains and undue influence'.
113 The Usurious Loans Act, 1918, ss 2(3) and 4.
114 ibid., s 3(1)(b)(i)–(iii).

considers the reopening of the transaction necessary to grant relief against loans furnished by licensed individual money lenders and state, commercial and cooperative banks.[115] Of course, these Acts apply to unincorporated businesses and individuals rather than incorporated firms.

26.40 Furthermore, certain rules apply depending on the subject-matter of the contract. With regard to employment contracts,[116] in the event that workers are owed compensation payments and their employer enters into an insolvency proceeding or a scheme of arrangement, the right to claim for liability against the employer's insurer (if any) will vest in the workers and they will be paid in priority over all other debts.[117] The same priority rule applies to the employer's payment of subscriptions to provident funds.[118] If the insolvency office holder decides to continue the business of a company for the beneficial winding up of the same, the presumption that the servants of the company have been given notice of discharge due to the filing of a winding up order, is rebutted.[119] In the mortgage of merchant shipping vessels, it is clear that a mortgagor cannot set aside a mortgage over a ship on the basis of insolvency, with the outstanding mortgage payments having preference over the rights, claims and interests of other creditors.[120] In such cases, mortgagees can lawfully assign their interest to another party if they themselves become insolvent.[121]

D. REFORMS

26.41 As said earlier, there have been significant legislative reforms between 1990 and 1997. These included the enactment of the Money Loans Court Act of 1990, the Companies Act of 1994 and the Bankruptcy Act of 1997. However, the only relevant legislative reform since 2000 appears to the replacement of the Money Loans Court Act of 1990 by the Money Loans Court Act of 2003. The financial sector in Bangladesh was faced with an acute bank loan default problem and this was the major driver of reform behind this special law. This

115 The Money Lenders Act, 1940, ss 36(1),(3) and 30(1). This particular Act has its origins in a series of measures taken by the government of A.K. Fazlul Huq, Chief Minister of Bengal, to ameliorate the predatory informal credit market of the region. See Rutherford, Stuart, *The Pledge: ASA, Peasant Politics, and Microfinance in the Development of Bangladesh* (eBook edn, Oxford University Press, 2009), Ch. 2, text above fn. 2.

116 Employment contracts can be written or oral, express or implied. However, there are ancillary formalization requirements such as employers issuing workers appointment letters, identity cards, service books, etc. See The Labour Act 2006, ss 5–8.

117 ibid., s 162.

118 ibid., s 271.

119 Companies Act, 1994, s 252(3).

120 The Bangladesh Merchant Shipping Ordinance, 1983, s 44.

121 ibid., s 46.

new law aimed at the speedy recovery of loans by financial institutions does not, however, directly deal with the treatment of executory contracts.

Arguably, there is a conflict over the jurisdiction of the Bankruptcy Courts and the Money Loans Court. One judge of the latter court has already observed that the overlapping jurisdiction of the two courts may cause problems in practice. For example, section 33 of the Bankruptcy Act provides that pending proceedings in other courts concerning money or property claims should be transferred to the Bankruptcy Court, yet the Money Loans Court Art provides for its primacy over any other law.[122] This is in need of judicial scrutiny and/or legislative review. 26.42

E. CONCLUDING REMARKS

As the appraisal above indicates, corporate insolvency is a relatively new phenomenon in Bangladesh, corresponding to the growth of the country's private sector. Under the current regime, it is possible for executory contracts to be assumed or disclaimed by receivers or liquidators in the event of a business's insolvency. Certain contractual clauses, such as flip clauses, that are common in jurisdictions with mature corporate debt markets are used in international creditor loan agreements but whose validity has yet to be tested against Bangladeshi statutory law. Other clauses, such as penalty clauses, acceleration clauses and set-off, are permissible under the Contract Act. 26.43

That being said, the legal framework of Bangladesh relating to insolvency falls well short of the UNCITRAL Legislative Guide.[123] The need for urgent reform is apparent from the country's year-on-year performance in the World Bank's Doing Business rankings, which among other metrics, assesses the robustness of a state's domestic insolvency framework. Between 2014 and 2018, Bangladesh's 'rank' for resolving insolvency hovered between 147 and 153 out of 189 countries. In the latest edition of the Doing Business ranking, it was reported that insolvency proceedings in Dhaka took, on average, four years and the recovery rate was 29.2 cents on the dollar.[124] As of writing, there 26.44

122 Monsur, Syed Jahed, 'The Artha Rin Adalat Ain/2003: A Review' (*The Daily Star*, 01 July 2006) <http://archive.thedailystar.net/law/2006/07/01/analysis.htm> accessed 12 February 2017.

123 Mannan, Morshed, 'Are Bangladesh, India and Pakistan Ready to Adopt the UNCITRAL Model Law on Cross-Border Insolvency?', *International Insolvency Review*, 25/195 (2016).

124 <http://www.doingbusiness.org/data/exploreeconomies/bangladesh#resolving-insolvency> accessed on 2 January 2019.

is a proposal for amending and updating the Companies Act, 1994,[125] for transposing Bangladesh's accession to the Cape Town Convention and Aircraft Protocol (including its insolvency provisions)[126] and for developing a personal property security regime, but it remains to be seen whether, like in India, this reform process will have a salutary impact on the country's corporate insolvency regime.

125 The [Bangladesh] Companies Act, 2013 [on file with the authors]. Information about this early-stage legislation was obtained by the authors from discussions with lawyers involved in the drafting process.

126 Cape Town Convention on International Interests in Mobile Equipment, 2001 and Protocol to the Convention on International Interests in Mobile Equipment on matters specific to aircraft equipment, to which Bangladesh acceded on 15 December 2008 and entered into force on 01 April 2009.

27

NATIONAL REPORT FOR ENGLAND AND WALES

Eugenio Vaccari

A. INTRODUCTION

27.01 This report forms part of a global study undertaking an international comparison of the treatment of executory contracts in the context of insolvency. The introduction covers the history of insolvency law in England and Wales, while section B outlines the procedures available to distressed companies to liquidate their assets or restructure their activities. Section C describes the treatment of executory contracts under the law. It explores if and to what extent it has changed over time and whether their treatment is consistent with the pivotal principles of the common law of contract: party autonomy, freedom of contract and legal predictability. These principles also underpin the English corporate insolvency framework.

27.02 Section D extends this consistency exercise to recent reforms on the treatment of these clauses. The final section concludes by observing that the proposed changes to the treatment of executory contracts and termination clauses do not go as far as to reverse the long-established principles that underpin the English corporate and insolvency framework.

B. INSOLVENCY PROCEDURES

27.03 In England, the idea that creditors might act collectively was first introduced by the *Bankruptcy Act 1542*. The recognition of the limited liability concept, both under the law (*Limited Liability Act 1855*) and by the judiciary (*Salomon's* case),[1] represented a turning point for the development of early insolvency law.

27.04 The stratified and uncoordinated development of rules resulted in a 'confused tangle of insolvency laws that was both difficult to operate and prone to manipulation by the unscrupulous'.[2] This situation and the UK's accession to membership of the European Economic Community (EEC) rendered a comprehensive review of the UK insolvency system no longer escapable.[3]

27.05 A Review Committee on Insolvency Law and Practice was appointed in January 1977. Its final report ('Cork Report')[4] marked the beginning of a movement towards stricter penalties against errant directors and increasing emphasis on the rehabilitation of the company. Large parts of its recommendations were transposed into a unified code of insolvency law, the *Insolvency Act 1986* (IA 1986 or the Act).

27.06 Due to the general dissatisfaction towards the newly introduced procedures and the low returns for unsecured creditors, the government further amended the law by means of the *Enterprise Act 2002* (EA 2002) and the *Companies Act 2006* (CA 2006). The first Act substantially replaced the administrative receivership with the administration procedure, removed the Crown's status as preferential creditor and introduced the 'prescribed part' for unsecured creditors.[5] The second statute codified and expanded the directors' duties towards the company, and reversed the *Leyland DAF* ruling[6] on the priority of liquidation expenses by introducing s.176ZA to the IA 1986.

27.07 This section provides an outline of the main procedures available under the law.

1 *Salomon v. A. Salomon & Co Ltd* [1897] AC 22.

2 V Finch and D Milman, *Corporate Insolvency Law: Perspectives and Principles* (3rd edn, CUP: Cambridge, 2017) 12.

3 Report of the Cork Advisory Committee (Cmnd 6602, 1976).

4 Report of the Review Committee in Insolvency Law and Practice (Cmnd 8558, 1982).

5 Under s.176A of the Act and the *Insolvency Act 1986 (Prescribed Part) Order* 2003, the 'prescribed part' is the part of the proceeds from realising the assets covered by a floating charge which must be set aside and made available to satisfy unsecured debts in liquidation and administration procedures. The rationale for the creation of the prescribed part was to redistribute the funds that would have been allocated to the Crown by reason to its preferential status to all unsecured creditors.

6 *Buchler v. Talbot* (aka Leyland DAF) [2004] UKHL 9, [2004] 2 AC 298.

(1) Liquidation proceedings

Liquidation is a procedure of last resort, aimed at collecting, realising and distributing the assets and proceeds of the company to its creditors. Liquidation cases still represent the bulk work of insolvency proceedings.[7] Under the current law, companies can be liquidated in three ways.[8] **27.08**

A *Members' Voluntary Liquidation (MVL)*[9] can be activated only by the company itself if its directors can issue a statutory declaration that the company is solvent. **27.09**

A *Creditors' Voluntary liquidation (CVL)*[10] can be triggered only by the company itself whenever it is insolvent and after a resolution of its shareholders (75 per cent majority). There is no moratorium, but parties may apply to the court for a stay of the proceedings. **27.10**

Finally, an *Involuntary Liquidation (IL)*[11] may be triggered by the creditors, the directors, the company shareholders and, under certain circumstances, the Department of Trade and Industry (DTI), usually upon proof that the company is unable to pay its debts.[12] Once the winding up order is made, no action may be started or proceeded against the company without the permission of the court. **27.11**

(2) Rescue proceedings

Company Voluntary Arrangements (CVAs)[13] were first introduced by IA 1986. These are agreements between a registered company (not necessarily insolvent), its shareholders and its creditors. The reorganisation plan usually involves delayed or reduced debt payment or capital restructuring. However it cannot modify the rights of secured creditors except with the concurrence of the concerned creditor. **27.12**

---

7 Of the 17,243 companies that entered insolvency in 2017, there were 12,861 creditor voluntary liquidations (74.6 per cent of total insolvencies) and 2,799 compulsory liquidations (16.2 per cent) – The Insolvency Service, *Insolvency Statistics – October to December 2017 (Q4 2017)* 5 <https://assets.publishing.service.gov.uk/government/uploads/system/uploads/attachment_data/file/675931/Insolvency_Statistics_-_web.pdf> accessed 8 September 2018.

8 Companies may also be wound up by the Department of Business, Enterprise and Regulatory Reform (BERR) or the Financial Services Authority (FSA) if this is in the public interest.

9 Part IV, Chapter III IA 1986.

10 Part IV, Chapter IV IA 1986.

11 Part IV, Chapter VI IA 1986.

12 The specific grounds to petition the court are listed in s.122 IA 1986.

13 Part I, ss.1–7B IA 1986 and rules 2.1–2.45, Part II, IR 2016.

27.13 No statutory moratorium is granted, except for small enterprises,[14] which are given a 28-day stay.[15] Numerous proposals have been advanced in recent years to extend the moratorium to *all* companies that file for a CVA.[16] One of the proposals was to create a new restructuring moratorium for companies considering restructuring their business,[17] another to introduce a new flexible restructuring procedure alongside CVAs.[18] While CVAs can be used as autonomous procedures, they are frequently complemented with administrations, winding ups or schemes of arrangement.

27.14 *Administration*[19] was first introduced by IA 1986 as an alternative to liquidation. It allows an ailing but not necessarily insolvent company, partnership or other entity to conceive a rescue plan while trading. During this period, the company is protected by a moratorium against creditors' actions.

27.15 Any administration has to pursue one of the following three objectives, listed in order of priority in s.3(1), Sch. B1 IA 1986:

1. rescue the company as a going concern;
2. achieve a better result for the company's creditors as a whole than would be likely if the company were wound up;
3. realise the property and distribute the proceeds.

27.16 To make the order, the court has to be satisfied that the company is, or is likely to become, unable to pay its debts[20] and that an administration order is

---

14 A company is eligible for a moratorium if it meets two or more of the three conditions specified in s.382(3) CA 2006 and it is not excluded from eligibility by s.2(1) and s.3, Sch. A1 IA 1986.

15 The moratorium is regulated by Sch. A1 IA 1986 and was introduced by the Insolvency Act 2000.

16 The Insolvency Service, *Encouraging Company Rescue* (June 2009) 14–16 <http://webarchive.nationalarchives.gov.uk/20140311023846/http:/www.insolvencydirect.bis.gov.uk/insolvencyprofessionandlegislation/con_doc_register/compresc/compresc09.pdf> accessed 8 September 2018.

17 The Insolvency Service, *Encouraging Company Rescue* (June 2009) 16–19 <http://webarchive.nationalarchives.gov.uk/20140311023846/http:/www.insolvencydirect.bis.gov.uk/insolvencyprofessionandlegislation/con_doc_register/compresc/compresc09.pdf> accessed 8 September 2018; The Insolvency Service, *A Review of the Corporate Insolvency Framework* (May 2016) 10–18 <https://www.gov.uk/government/uploads/system/uploads/attachment_data/file/525523/A_Review_of_the_Corporate_Insolvency_Framework.pdf> accessed 8 September 2018.

18 The Insolvency Service, *A Review of the Corporate Insolvency Framework* (May 2016) 22–27 <https://www.gov.uk/government/uploads/system/uploads/attachment_data/file/525523/A_Review_of_the_Corporate_Insolvency_Framework.pdf> accessed 8 September 2018.

19 Sch. B1, IA 1986.

20 The 'inability to pay its debts' is defined by s.123 IA 1986 as both want of liquidity (i.e. cash flow insolvency) and balance sheet insolvency. In assessing the latter, the court is required to have regard to prospective and contingent liabilities (*BNY Corporate Trustee Services Ltd v. Eurosail UK 2007–3BL Plc* [2013] UKSC 28, [2013] 1 WLR 1408).

reasonably likely to achieve the stated purpose. The applicant has to prove on the balance of probabilities test that these thresholds are met.[21]

Since the admission to the procedure, the company is controlled by an administrator, who is chosen among the licensed insolvency practitioners ('IPs'). Admission may be granted via a court-based procedure (application by the company's creditors to the court) or via an out-of-court route (by the holder of a qualifying floating charge, the company itself or its creditors). **27.17**

A *sui generis* form of administration which continues to gain increasing popularity in recent years[22] is the pre-pack procedure. These are arrangements for the sale of the debtor's business negotiated with the prospective purchasers and agreed by major creditors prior to the formal commencement of the statutory procedure. The sale is completed shortly after the administration order is made. **27.18**

(Administrative) Receivership[23] have been the most widely used formal insolvency proceeding in the UK. In a receivership, the receiver is demanded to administer the whole, or substantially the whole, of the company's property for the satisfaction of its creditors. **27.19**

The importance of this procedure greatly diminished since the amendments introduced by EA 2002, which prevented the holders of qualifying floating charges created on or after 15 September 2003 from appointing an administrative receiver. According to the Insolvency Service,[24] in 2017 only two receiverships took place in the UK (less than 0.1 per cent of all corporate insolvencies). **27.20**

(3) Schemes of arrangement

Schemes of arrangement (SoA)[25] present an alternative to formal insolvency proceedings and are regulated under general, company law. SoAs facilitate **27.21**

21 *Re AA Mutual International Insurance Co Ltd* [2004] EWHC 2430 (Ch), [2005] 2 BCLC 8.

22 J Armour, 'The Rise of the 'Pre-Pack': Corporate Restructuring in the UK and Proposals for Reform' in RP Austin, Fady JG Aoun (eds), *Restructuring Companies in Troubled Times: Director and Creditor Perspectives* (Law Publishing Unit: Sydney, 2012). See also the introductory analysis in Teresa Graham CBE, *Graham Review into Pre-pack Administration* (The Insolvency Service, 2014), <https://www.gov.uk/government/publications/graham-review-into-pre-pack-administration> accessed 8 September 2018.

23 Part III, IA 1986.

24 The Insolvency Service, *Insolvency Statistics – October to December 2017 (Q4 2017)* 5 <https://assets.publishing.service.gov.uk/government/uploads/system/uploads/attachment_data/file/675931/Insolvency_Statistics_-_web.pdf> accessed 8 September 2018.

25 Part 26, CA 2006.

entrance of a company into a compromise or arrangement with its creditors (including secured ones).

27.22 Under English law, a company is entitled to enter into a scheme if it is capable of being wound up in England and Wales. This is possible if the company has 'sufficient connection' with those territories, a concept that courts have construed in a very broad manner.[26]

C. TREATMENT OF EXECUTORY CONTRACTS

27.23 This section describes the rules applicable to executory contracts[27] when the debtor enters into any type of formal insolvency proceedings.[28] It reports on the special precepts applicable to contracts considered worthy of peculiar consideration by the legislator and on the validity of contractual remedies negotiated by the parties in solvent times.

27.24 The focus of this chapter is on the evolutionary aspect of the law, to evaluate if insolvency rules have been applied in a manner consistent with the principles of party autonomy,[29] freedom of contract[30] and legal predictability of judicial

26 In *Re Van Gansewinkel Groep BV* [2015] EWHC 2151 (Ch), [2015] Bus LR 1046 the court was required to determine if it had jurisdiction to sanction schemes of arrangement in respect of Dutch and Belgian companies with no establishment in England. It held that a sufficient connection had been shown in that the governing law of all the finance documents was English. Also: *Re Hibu Group Ltd* [2016] EWHC 1921 (Ch).

27 For the purposes of this chapter, executory contracts are onerous contracts under which neither party has performed any of its obligations, or both parties have partially performed their obligations to an equal extent – See International Accounting Standards (IAS) 37, *Provisions, Contingent Liabilities and Contingent Assets* (16 September 2009) <http://ec.europa.eu/internal_market/accounting/docs/consolidated/ias37_en.pdf> accessed 8 September 2018.

28 With reference to SoAs, since they are *de facto* contracts sanctioned by the court, parties are free to determine their content; no special statutory rule applies to them.

29 The cardinal importance of the principle of autonomy of the parties in common law is often presumed: see JN Adams and R Brownsword, 'The Ideologies of Contract' (1987) 7 *Leg. Stud.* 205, 208–10. Autonomy was clearly placed to the fore by Diplock LJ in *Photo Production Ltd v. Securicor Transport Ltd* [1980] AC 827 (HL), at 848: 'A basic principle of the common law of contract [...] is that parties to a contract are free to determine for themselves what primary obligations they will accept.' It is also reinstated in art 3 of the Regulation (EC) No. 593/2008 of the European Parliament and of the Council of 17 June 2008 on the law applicable to contractual obligations (Rome I) [2008] OJ L 177/6, which applies to contracts concluded on or after 17 December 2009 all over Europe (with the exception of Denmark). For a detailed analysis of the scope of this principle, see S Worthington, 'Common Law Values: The Role of Party Autonomy in Private Law' (June 1, 2015) University of Cambridge Faculty of Law Research Paper No. 33/2015 <https://ssrn.com/abstract=2620191> accessed 8 September 2018.

30 The pivotal significance of the principle of freedom of contract emerges from different sources. One of the most often cited is the decision in *Printing and Numerical Registering Co v. Sampson* (1874–75) LR 19 Eq. 462, 465 Ct of Chancery. On that occasion, Sir George Jessel, the Master of the Rolls, stated that:

decisions.[31] These principles represent the backbone of the entire English legal system.

(1) The effects of insolvency proceedings on executory contracts

27.25 The opening of formal insolvency proceedings does not in itself affect the validity of ongoing contracts.[32] It is, however, unlikely that official receivers and liquidators will *continue to perform* all of the debtor's duties, especially when the company has no prospects of revival. In some large cases, such as the collapse of *Carillion*, third parties and the government may step in and use their funds to ensure that the executory agreements (in this case, public procurement contracts) continue to be performed.[33]

27.26 If contracts continue to be performed, payments for obligations performed *after* the company entered into liquidation or administration are ranked as an expense of the procedure. They are paid in priority over other creditors, despite the fact that they arose out of contracts signed before the filing of the insolvency petition.[34]

27.27 *Game Station*[35] adds a layer of complexity to this narrative.[36] In this case, it was held that, where property leased by a company was retained during the administration procedure, the creditor was entitled to full payment of the

[...] if there is one thing more than another public policy requires it is that men of full age and competent understanding shall have the utmost liberty of contracting, that their contracts when entered into freely and voluntarily shall be held sacred and shall be enforced by Courts of Justice. Therefore, you have this paramount public policy to consider – that you are not likely to interfere with this freedom of contract.

31 The terms 'predictability' and 'certainty' are frequently used as synonyms, but this chapter prefers to rely on the less assertive term, as it has already been observed that 'in this world nothing can be said to be certain, except death and taxes'. For the value of predictability in the law, see R Goode, 'The Codification of Commercial Law' (1988) 14 *Monash U. L. Rev.* 135, 150.

32 It is possible, however, to seek a declaration that a contract has been terminated by frustration, a circumstance, which occurs only if the commencement of an insolvency proceeding by one of the contracting parties determines a significant modification of the rights and obligations contemplated at the time of its execution. See *National Carriers Ltd v. Panalpina (Northern) Ltd* [1981] AC 675 (HL) and *Tradigrain Do Brasil v. Ace Insurance SA-NV* [2002] EWHC 2110 (Comm).

33 O Gill, 'The Government is Paying Millions of Pounds a ay to keep Carillion Public Sector Projects going' *City A.M.* (23 January 2018) <http://www.cityam.com/279297/carillions-collapse-costing-taxpayer-gbp54m-day> accessed 7 March 2018.

34 *Re Lundy Granite Co* [1870–1871] LR 6 Ch App 462 (CA). This exception has been encapsulated in rule 4.218(3)(a)(ii) of the Insolvency Rules 1986, now replaced by rule 6.42(4)(a) for creditors' winding up and rule 7.108(4)(a)(ii) for winding up by courts in the Insolvency Rules 2016. With reference to administration proceedings, the same principle applies by virtue of rule 3.51(1) of the Insolvency Rules 2016, which replaces rule 2.67(1) of the Insolvency Rules 1986.

35 Sub nomine *Jervis v. Pillar Denton Ltd* [2014] EWCA Civ 180, [2015] Ch. 87.

36 *Goldacre (Offices) Ltd v. Nortel Networks UK Ltd (In Administration)* [2009] EWHC 3389 (Ch), [2010] Ch. 455; and *Leisure (Norwich) II Ltd v. Luminar Lava Ignite Ltd (In Administration)* [2012] EWHC 951 (Ch), [2014] Ch. 165.

outstanding rent as an expense of the administration even if the expenses became due *before* the company entered into administration.

27.28 The relevance of this decision, however, should not be overstated. In *Game*, it is conceded that the debtor entered into insolvency *after* the contractual rent had fallen due. However, that instalment would have covered the quarter *after* the appointment of the administrators. Therefore, the Court of Appeal relied on equitable principles to hold that the portion of the rent that covers the post-appointment occupation of the property should be considered as an expense of the administration.

27.29 This apportionment put an end to an established practice of game playing.[37] It has been highly praised by commentators[38] as it prevents both the proprietor and the insolvent estate from being disproportionately burdened by liabilities.[39] While the legislature omitted to codify the decision in *Game* in the Insolvency Rules 2016 (thus not making life easier for practitioners),[40] it is unlikely that this approach will soon be overturned.[41] At the same time, it is equally likely that courts will continue to adopt a restrictive interpretation of the use of their equitable powers in similar circumstances.[42]

27.30 The assumption of existing liabilities or continuation of contractual duties cannot be inferred in the following circumstances:

1. where the creditor or the debtor can expressly or implicitly repudiate the contract or decline the performance offered by the counter-party;
2. where the parties have negotiated a provision to terminate the contract in the event of insolvency;
3. where contracts can be disclaimed as onerous.[43]

---

37 Finch and Milman, *supra* note 2, 345.

38 A Sharp and others, 'Game Over: Rent as an Administration Expense on a Pay As You Go Basis' (2014) 7 *C.R. & I.* 57; J Verrill and P Pal, 'Cherry Picking, Break Dancing and Gaming' (2014) 4 *JIBFL* 227; J Bannister and J Dabbs, 'Game: A Victory for Common Sense?' (2014) 27(5) *Insolv. Int.* 74.

39 It is still debatable whether the *Game* case allows rents to be apportioned not only by time but also by space. The author is sceptical about the latter, as it would result in a unilateral *ex post* amendment of a contract freely entered into by the parties, while English judges have always tried to preserve party autonomy to the highest possible extent: G Fetherstonhaugh, 'An Adventure in Time and Space' (2017) 1716 *E.G.* 63.

40 J Kaffash, 'Where Next for IPs?' (2014) 152(1449) *Accountancy* 8; C Shuttleworth and S Lynch, 'Game On: Tackling the Impact of *Game* – A Look at the *Clinton Cards* Liquidation' (2016) 9(4) *C.R. & I.* 137.

41 S Gray and T Cox, 'The Insolvency Merry-Go-Round' (2017) 1705 *E.G.* 63, 64.

42 *Laverty v. British Gas Trading Ltd* [2014] EWHC 2721 (Ch), [2015] 2 All ER 430; *Re Birchall (A Bankrupt)* [2015] EWHC 1541 (Ch), [2017] 1 WLR 667.

43 IA 1986, ss.178–182. See generally IF Fletcher, *The Law of Insolvency* (5th edn, Sweet & Maxwell: London, 2017) [24-003]-[24-013].

Absent any statutory obligations to perform, *creditors and suppliers* may lawfully withdraw their performance unless the debtor pays for the outstanding invoices.[44] This outcome is particularly taxing for the office-holder, since paying for the outstanding invoices usually requires the approval of the creditors' committee. It also requires breaching the *pari passu* principle of distribution among unsecured creditors.[45] **27.31**

However, courts have restricted the creditors' power to withdraw performance. In *HMRC v. Wimbledon FC*,[46] the Court of Appeal held that such a course of action could be taken only '*in the most exceptional circumstances*'. **27.32**

Conversely, *office-holders* may equally decline to procure performance if the buyer has no proprietary rights on the goods manufactured or services offered by the debtor. However, creditors may challenge the office-holder's rejection, thus further reducing the power of the insolvent estate to discontinue executory contracts even if they traded the contract at a loss.[47] **27.33**

Additionally, para 74, Sch. B1 of the Act gives the creditors the power to challenge an administration's decision if conspicuously unfair to a particular contractor or creditor. Nevertheless, courts are reluctant to use these equitable powers if performance of the contract would be to the detriment of the creditors as a whole *and* unsecured creditors would be treated according to their legal rights in insolvency.[48] **27.34**

Similarly, liquidators (but not administrators)[49] in England and Wales can unilaterally (i.e., without the need for a court sanction)[50] *disclaim onerous property* pursuant to s.178 IA 1986.[51] The notion of 'onerous property' includes any: **27.35**

44 *Leyland DAF Limited v. Automotive Products Plc* [1993] B.C.C. 389 (CA): an unpaid seller who refuses to supply further goods to the company until the company meets its debts was not abusing a dominant position.

45 Suppliers are usually unsecured creditors. However, their strong bargaining position may allow them to obtain a higher return for their claims.

46 *Inland Revenue Commissioners v. Wimbledon Football Club Ltd* [2004] EWCA Civ 655, [2004] BCC 638: a proposed CVA did not infringe insolvency rules even if certain unsecured creditors were to be paid in full whereas the Inland Revenue as a preferential creditor was only to receive a dividend of 30 pence in the pound when the proceeds of sale were distributed under the arrangement.

47 *Land Rover Group Ltd v. UPF (Uk) Ltd (in Administrative Receivership)* [2002] EWHC 2128 (QB), [2003] 2 BCLC 222.

48 *Joint Administrators of Rangers Football Club Plc, Noters* [2012] CSOH 55.

49 IA 1986, s.178(2) and *Re P&C and R&T (Stockport) Ltd* [1991] BCC 98 (Ch).

50 *Firmin v Aardvark Tmc Ltd* [2013] EWHC 1774 (Ch).

51 For an exhaustive analysis: IF Fletcher, *The Law of Insolvency* (5th edn, Sweet & Maxwell: London, 2017) 742–7.

a) unprofitable contract;
b) other unsaleable or not readily saleable property; and
c) property that may give rise to a liability to pay money, or perform an onerous act on the debtor.[52]

27.36 There is no time limit on the liquidator to exercise the right of a disclaimer, but the other contracting party may solicit a decision by asking for a clear determination within a 28-day period. If the liquidator does not exercise this right within the statutory period, he/she loses the right to terminate (i.e., repudiate) the contract unilaterally by notice, thus enabling the counter-party to elect to hold the contract open for future performance.[53]

27.37 Where the contract is repudiated, the non-breaching party has the right to ask for damages for non-performance. These claims rank as unsecured entitlements against the insolvent estate.[54]

27.38 The power to disclaim onerous contracts has been interpreted restrictively where the decision to divest could have potentially negative consequences for the environment.[55] However courts have established that liquidators can disclaim environmental costs and waste management licences.[56] Despite the existence of the 'polluter pays' principle,[57] there is no statutory or equitable rule that can force the liquidator/polluter to pay where there is no money to meet environmental liabilities.[58] These disclaimer powers can be used in conjunction with administration proceedings to facilitate the sale of profitable

52 IA 1986, s.178(3).

53 Ibid., s.178(5) and *Stead, Hazel & Co v. Cooper* [1933] 1 KB 840.

54 Ibid., s.186.

55 *Re Mineral Resources Ltd* [1999] 1 All ER 746, where Neuberger LJ held that the broad scope of the powers conferred by s.178 IA 1986 could not prevail over special provisions in the law, such as s.35(11) of the *Environmental Protection Act 1990.*

56 *Re Celtic Extraction Ltd (in liq.)* [2001] Ch. 475 (CA) (which was effectively an appeal from *Re Mineral Resources*); *Environment Agency v. Hillridge Ltd* [2003] EWHC 3023 (Ch), [2004] 2 BCLC 358.

57 Environmental Protection Act 1990 enacted to give effect to Council Directive 72/442/EEC of 15 July 1975 on Waste [1975] (OJ L 194).

58 *Re Celtic Extraction Ltd (in liq.) supra* note 56, [39]. On this topic, see generally: H Hill, 'Bankruptcy vs Environmental Protection: A Case Study in Normative Conflict' (1998) 11 *C.J.L.J.* 245; C Shelbourn, 'Waste Management and the Insolvent Company' (2000) *J.P.L.* 134; J Armour, 'Who Pays When Polluters Go Bust?' (2000) 11 *L.Q.R.* 200; A Keay and P de Prez, 'Insolvency and Environmental Principles: A Case Study in a Conflict of Public Interests' (2001) 3(2) *Env. L. Rev.* 90; A Keay and P de Prez, 'Should Insolvent Companies Pay? The Search for Environmental Principle' (2001) 9(1) *Env. Liability* 11; B Mamutse and V Fogleman, 'Improving the Treatment of Environmental Claims in Insolvency' (2013) 5 *J.B.L.* 486; B Mamutse, 'Environmental Liabilities in Insolvency – An Area Ripe for Reform?' (2016) 8(3) *International Journal of the Law in the Built Environment* 243; IL Fannon, 'Managing Waste: The Gap Between the EU Directives and Corporate Law in Member States – A Mess of Case Law Needing Clean-up' (2016) 24(6) *Env. Liability* 203.

parts of a distressed company,[59] thus giving rise to dubious rescue practices for their potential implications for public health and unfair competition.

Finally, courts held that the liquidator's power to disclaim a lease (s.179 IA 1986) could only be challenged if the liquidator acted with *mala fide* or the decision was perverse.[60] A liquidator cannot disclaim a contract merely because the company could have made, or could make a better bargain.[61] **27.39**

Liquidators do not have similar powers in Scotland. In *Joint Liquidators of the Scottish Coal Co Ltd, Noters*[62] the Scottish Court of Session held that a debtor could not divest the company of a real right in land by unilateral disclaimer whereby the land would become *bona vacantia* and fall to be administered by the Crown because of the monthly costs of complying with the environmental statutory obligations. **27.40**

Overall, it appears that deviations from the 'continuation' rule do not seriously infringe the general principles mentioned above. The most problematic deviation is the right to disclaim onerous contracts. Despite its potentially wide scope, courts have consistently checked that these powers are not used in an inequitable manner. Nevertheless, their existence represents a serious breach to the principles of party autonomy and freedom of contract. Creditors are not without remedies, both procedural and substantial in nature, which ensure a certain degree of protection to their interests. **27.41**

(2) Special precepts applicable to specific contracts

Beside the above-mentioned general rules, the English legislator has over the years introduced special precepts for nominated contracts. These may result in significant exceptions from the established rule that contracts and their clauses are unaffected by the opening of an insolvency procedure. **27.42**

This sub-section covers these statutory exceptions to investigate if and to what extent they represent a deviation from an established tradition of reliance on legal predictability, party autonomy and freedom of contract. **27.43**

---

59 See the case of *Re UK Coal Operations Ltd* [2013] EWHC 1774 (Ch), [2014] 1 BCLC 471, as described by B Mamutse, 'Environmental Liabilities in Insolvency – An Area Ripe for Reform?' (2016) 8(3) International Journal of the Law in the Built Environment 243, 245.

60 *Re Hans Place Ltd* [1992] BCC 737 (Ch); *Mahomed v. Morris (No. 2)* [2001] BCC 233 (CA).

61 *Re SSSL Realisations (2002) Ltd* [2006] EWCA Civ 7, [2006] Ch. 610. See in particular [36]–[54] for the principled approach to disclaiming unprofitable properties.

62 *Joint Liquidators of the Scottish Coal Co Ltd, Noters* [2013] CSIH 108.

27.44 With reference to *sale contracts*, the law recognises that the buyer or seller has a right to specific performance against the insolvent estate when the applicant has a proprietary right over the good(s). This is the case, for instance, of a contract of sale of land concluded before the opening of insolvency proceedings, as the property in this case passes in equity when contracts are exchanged, subject to the payment of the purchase price.[63]

27.45 In all other sale contracts, it is essential to look at the objective intention of the parties[64] to determine on one hand if the insolvent debtor has the right to decline to procure performance and, on the other, if the creditor can demand specific performance. If the sale or the executory contract between the parties has been conducted under an agreement incorporating a retention of title clause,[65] the debtor is not free to dispose of the goods,[66] as this would give the insolvent administrators the power to override third parties' proprietary rights.

27.46 The same rule applies also when parties place money or assets in a trust,[67] or when they agree on money being used for a specific purpose (e.g., 'purpose trust' or 'project bank accounts').[68] However, the intention of the parties shall result in a declaration that brings certainty not only to the existence of, but also the scope and the assets subject to the trust.[69] Additionally, any trust can be challenged if its creation offended the anti-deprivation rule or in circumstances where transaction avoidance rules apply.[70]

27.47 Section 43(3), Sch. B1 of the Act entitles the insolvent estate in an administration procedure to reject the request submitted by the buyer for repossession of the goods sold under a hire-purchase agreement. For the purposes of the

---

63 *Law of Property (Miscellaneous Provisions) Act 1989* and *Pearce v Bastable's Trustee In Bankruptcy* [1901] 2 Ch. 122, applied by *Capital Prime Properties plc v. Worthgate Ltd (in Liq)* [2000] BCC 525 (Ch), where the court held that the disclaimer offered by s.178 IA 1986 could operate only to release from onerous contractual obligations, but not from recovering the ownership of a real estate property.

64 *Smith v. Hughes* [1870–71] L.R. 6 QB 597; *Destiny 1 Ltd v. Lloyds TSB Bank plc* [2011] EWCA Civ 831.

65 *Aluminium Industrie Vaassen BV v. Romalpa Aluminium Ltd* [1976] 2 All ER 552. For an illuminating analysis of these clauses: RM Goode, *Proprietary Rights and Insolvency in Sales Transactions* (3rd edn, Sweet & Maxwell: London, 2009), Ch. 5; and IF Fletcher, *The Law of Insolvency* (5th edn, Sweet & Maxwell: London, 2017) 800–802.

66 *Hachette UK Ltd v. Borders (UK) Ltd* [2009] EWHC 3487 (Ch).

67 *Re Kayford Ltd* [1975] 1 All ER 604; *Re Fleet Disposals Ltd* [1995] BCLC 345.

68 Project Bank Accounts (PBAs) are ring-fenced accounts that have trust status where payments are made directly and simultaneously by a client to members of its supply chain down to second tier suppliers.

69 *Re Goldcorp Exchange* [1995] 1 AC 74 (PC).

70 English law applies even to cases where the beneficiaries of the trust are incorporated in a jurisdiction that did not recognise the institution of a trust or a division between legal and equitable property interests, such as Saudi Arabia: *Akers v. Samba Financial Group* [2017] UKSC 6, [2017] AC 424.

section, the notion of 'hire purchase agreement' includes conditional sale, chattel leasing and retention of title agreements.[71]

Courts have imposed limits on the right of the administrator to reject a request of repossession of goods,[72] particularly when the procedure appears as a delaying tactic, a '*bogus*'.[73] **27.48**

Accordingly, the author submits that this statutory trade-off between the interests of all of the affected parties respects the principles underpinning the general law of contract and the corporate insolvency framework. The limited equitable exceptions recognised following *Berkeley Applegate* do not change the overall valuation of the institute, as these deviations apply only when it appears manifestly unfair and unjust to leave the claimant without remedies.[74] **27.49**

In the author's view, the same rationale can be found also with reference to other statutory deviations from the established rule on the treatment of executory contracts. **27.50**

This is the case, among others, of the treatment of *insurance contracts.* Originally, if a person obtained a judgment for damages against a company and that company – despite carrying an insurance against the type of damage – went into liquidation, the claimant could not recover directly from the insurer. The claimant could only place a claim as an unsecured creditor against the insolvent estate, with no special interest in the insurance monies.[75] **27.51**

This rule has been reversed by means of the *Third Party (Rights Against Insurers) Act 1930*, which gave the power to creditors to claim the indemnity directly from the insurer.[76] The *Third Party (Rights Against Insurers) Act 2010*, which entered into force only in 2016 after further amendments made by the Insurance Act 2015 (SI 2016/550), addressed some of the shortcomings of the 1930 Act. However, it retained possibility for the claimant to demonstrate its **27.52**

71 IA 1986, s.111(1), Sch. B1.

72 *Re Atlantic Computer Systems plc (No. 1)* [1992] Ch 505 (CA).

73 *Bernard Sport Surfaces Ltd v. Astrosoccer4U Ltd* [2017] EWHC 2425 (TCC); [2018] BCC 147 [15].

74 *Re Berkeley Applegate (Investment Consultants) Ltd (No. 2)* [1989] 1 Ch 32: office-holders who have carried out substantial works for assets that in the end did not belong to the company were entitled to remuneration over the concerned assets. Also, *Gillan v. HEC Enterprises Ltd* [2016] EWHC 3179 (Ch); [2017] 1 BCLC 340.

75 *Re Harrington Motor Co Ltd* [1928] 1 Ch 105.

76 Additionally, courts have found that any clause in an insurance contract, which provides that an indemnity would cease on a company's insolvency, represents a breach of the anti-deprivation principle, as it deprives the administrator (and, potentially, third parties) of an asset of the company: *Mayhew v. King* [2011] EWCA Civ 328, [2011] Bus LR 1327.

rights and obtain the distribution directly from the insurer in a single proceeding,[77] thus circumventing insolvency rules on the distribution of proceeds.

27.53 This statutory choice is not in conflict with the principles mentioned above. On the contrary, the opposite solution suggested by the judiciary in *Harrington* would have resulted in an unpredictable and unjust windfall to the advantage of the insolvent estate.

27.54 The same considerations apply in regards to the protection afforded to *pension contracts*. The legislator has protected employees' entitlements to their wages with a system of statutory liabilities, protected funds[78] and independent authorities.[79] As these are monies of the company administered for the benefit of third parties, it is only appropriate that these third parties should be entitled to exercise their contractual rights even in insolvency scenarios.

27.55 For other contracts such as *building or construction contracts*[80] and *IP, domain name and licensing contracts*, the law does not prescribe fixed solutions. In these cases, courts adopt a case-by-case approach to determine if the provisions negotiated by the parties in solvent times result in a breach of equitable principles.[81]

27.56 There are cases, however, where the balance struck by the legislation can prove more problematic to justify in conceptual terms.

27.57 One of them is the matter of '*utility*' *and essential contracts*. Under s.233 IA 1986, as amended by the *Insolvency (Protection of Essential Supplies) Order 2015*, private utility suppliers (including landlords) and statutory undertakers of gas, electricity, water and communication services cannot compel future performance to the payment of debts incurred before the commencement of insolvency proceedings.[82]

---

77 *BAE Systems Pension Funds Trustee Ltd v. Bowmer and Kirkland Ltd* [2017] EWHC 1200 (TCC).

78 Pension Protection Fund (PPF), which became operational on 6 April 2005 and is regulated by the *Pensions Act 2004*, Part 2. D Pollard, 'Pensions and TUPE' (2005) 34(2) *ILJ* 127; D McCarthy and A Neuberger, 'The Pension Protection Fund' (2005) 26(2) *Fiscal Studies* 139.

79 Pension Regulator (PR), which equally became operation on 6 April 2005 and is regulated by the *Pensions Act 2004*, Part 1.

80 Other jurisdictions such as Argentina, on the other hand, have introduced measures to protect buyers.

81 C Cooke and others, 'National Report for England' in D Faber and others (eds), *Treatment of Contracts in Insolvency* (OUP: Oxford, 2013) 161.

82 IA 1986, ss.372 and 372(A) extend this framework to individual voluntary arrangements (IVAs). The 2015 amendments apply only to contracts entered into on or after 1 October 2015.

This restriction, whose introduction was recommended in the Cork Report,[83] can potentially promote rescue activities. However, this is only made possible at the expense of one of the pillars of contract law, i.e. the principle of party autonomy. Still, the changes may be less radical than they appear. **27.58**

In fact, despite the inclusion of private utility providers and the use of a wide notion for 'communication services',[84] the government deliberately rejected the calls (in particular, from rescue professionals and practitioners) to extend the protection to *all* those contracts that the debtors claimed to be essential to the continuation of their business. In fact, no obligations of such kind have been extended to card payment providers and the list of 'essential suppliers' has been made exhaustive.[85] **27.59**

However, the complexities of market relations may render this list inadequate for some businesses, which may alternatively only rely on the discretionary and equitable powers of the courts to obtain protection in the cases not mentioned in the law. English courts have insofar proven willing to comply, for instance in extending the effect of the s.233 order to cross-border disputes.[86] Even when they dismissed the request to compel a supplier to provide essential goods unless pre-insolvency debts were paid, they hinted at reaching a different conclusion should the supplier's actions prove unfair or unreasonable, or amount to an abuse of a dominant position.[87] **27.60**

Creditors still benefit from significant protections, as suppliers can still make it a condition of the supply process that office-holders personally guarantee future (but not pre-petition) payments.[88] However, if the contract is terminated (e.g., by mutual agreement) but the supply continues under a 'deemed contract', the office-holder is not personally liable for the payments and the mere fact of continuing supply does not entitle the supplier to priority of payment over secured creditors.[89] **27.61**

---

83 Report of the Review Committee on Insolvency Law and Practice (Cmnd 8558, 1982) Ch. 33, esp. paras 1451–1462.

84 IA 1986, s.233(3)(d) and (5)(d).

85 This solution sits at odds with the recommendation in the Cork Report, where it is possible to read that 'the situation [that justifies the introduction of the law] is not confined to public utilities. It may arise whenever there is an outstanding account with a private supplier': Report of the Review Committee on Insolvency Law and Practice (Cmnd 8558, 1982) Ch. 33, para 1453.

86 *Official Receiver v. Sahavitiya Steel Industries plc* [2015] EWHC 2877 (Ch), [2016] BCC 456. This outcome is even more striking when it is considered that the application was heard in private and the order made without notice.

87 *Leyland DAF Ltd v. Automotive Products plc* [1993] BCC 389 (CA).

88 IA 1986, s.233(2).

89 *Laverty v. British Gas Trading Ltd* [2014] EWHC 2721 (Ch), [2015] 2 All ER 430.

27.62 A further restriction applicable to essential suppliers has been introduced by s.233A of the Act. According to this provision, any insolvency-related term of a contract for the supply of essential goods and services that seeks to either terminate or vary the terms of the contract where the customer entered into a CVA or administration procedure is automatically rendered void.

27.63 Nevertheless, while courts could void insolvency-related contractual terms to charge higher prices or terminate the contract by reason of the debtor's insolvency filing, the supplier can still rely on:

a) non-insolvency-related contractual terms for the purpose of terminating the contract, such as changes in consumption, or downgraded credit ratings; and
b) insolvency-related terms insofar as they relate to other insolvency (such as bankruptcy or liquidation) and restructuring (e.g. currently schemes of arrangements) procedures.

27.64 Moreover, termination is still possible:

1) if the cause of the termination is an event that occurred after the commencement of the insolvency procedure;
2) if charges incurred after the company entered into administration or CVA are not paid for a period exceeding 28 days when the first payment was due;
3) if the office-holder does not provide a personal guarantee for the payment of essential supplies received after the commencement of the procedure;[90] or
4) when the office-holder or the court consent to the termination.[91] Courts usually authorize termination when they are satisfied that the continuation of the contract would cause undue hardship to the supplier.

27.65 While it is extremely challenging for a supplier to prove the existence of a relevant level of undue hardship, creditors can rely on a variety of mechanisms to protect their interests. Additionally, it is unlikely that the debtor will default on a payment for the supply of products if the company really deems that the contract is valuable and essential for the turnaround of the insolvent estate.[92]

---

90 IA 986, s.233A(5).
91 Ibid., s.233A(4).
92 As it happened before the enactment of IA 1986: *Wellworth Cash & Carry (North Shields Ltd) v. North Eastern Electricity Board* [1986] 2 BCC 99 (Ch).

In this context, the outright exclusion of the voidability of insolvency-related clauses in liquidation procedures is troublesome to justify in conceptual terms, as there may be liquidation procedures where continuation of the business for a limited time is required for the orderly sale of its assets. **27.66**

Similar problematic considerations might also be found in *leasing or rental contracts*. Upon the opening of formal proceedings, the insolvent lessee can disclaim a lease where the property is not necessary for the company to continue its business,[93] except when the lessee's use of land is governed by statutory permits.[94] Conversely, the lessor may not force re-possession, except with the permission of the court.[95] The insolvency of the lessor does not affect the enforceability of the leasing or rental contract. **27.67**

It is undeniable that the autonomy of the solvent lessor is significantly curtailed. However, their substantive rights (and, primarily, the right to remuneration) are protected and the compression of their autonomy is justified in light of opposing principles (legal predictability and promotion of rescue of viable businesses). **27.68**

Autonomous considerations deserve those contracts, whose special regulation is justified on one hand by their particular content and, on the other, by the interference with European binding provisions. This is the case of employment and financial contracts. **27.69**

Following the general rule on the treatment of executory contracts, the opening of an insolvency procedure does not cause the termination of *employment contracts*. Exceptions include liquidations aimed at terminating the activity of the company[96] and cases where there are enforceable termination clauses in the employment contract. **27.70**

Employment contracts are potentially affected by the EU Business Transfers Directive ('2001 Transfer Directive'),[97] enforced in the UK by means of the *Transfer of Undertakings (Protection of Employment) Regulations 2006* **27.71**

---

93 *Schroder Exempt Property Unit Trust v. Birmingham City Council* [2014] EWHC 2207 (Admin), [2014] BCC 690.

94 *Joint Liquidators of the Scottish Coal Co Ltd, Noters* [2013] CSOH 124.

95 *Metro Nominees (Wandsworth) (No. 1) Ltd v. Rayment* [2008] BCC 40.

96 *Reigate v. Union Manufacturing Co (Ramsbottom) Ltd* [1918] 1 K.B. 592; *Gerard, Fowler v. Commercial Timber Co* [1930] 2 KB 1.

97 Council Directive 2001/23/EC of 12 March 2001 on the approximation of the laws of the Member States relating to the safeguarding of employees' rights in the event of transfers of undertakings, businesses or parts of undertakings or businesses [2001] OJ L 82.

(SI 2006/246) ('TUPE Regulations')[98] as amended by the *Collective Redundancies and Transfer of Undertakings (Protection of Employment) (Amendment) Regulations 2014* (SI 2014/16).

27.72 The European and British statutes preserve the validity of employment contracts when a business or undertaking, or one of their units, is transferred to a new employer. The original directive and the pre-2006 TUPE affected transfers both in non-rescue insolvency and in non-insolvency cases, an interpretation confirmed by the ECJ.[99] The established common law approach that a business transfer terminated all employment contracts[100] was subverted. However, the most recent 2001 Transfer Directive (art. 5) and TUPE Regulations (reg. 8) clarified that the protective measures do not apply to certain insolvency proceedings. Autonomy of the parties has been restored.

27.73 Under the current version of TUPE Regulations, whenever insolvency proceedings are not opened with a view to liquidation of the assets of the transferor, employment contracts are still transferred, but certain of the transferor's debts do not pass over to the transferee (regs 8(1)–(6)).

27.74 Despite having been criticised by the doctrine,[101] the author considers that TUPE Regulations strike an appropriate balance between conflicting interests.[102] Autonomy of the parties is somehow preserved, as insolvency officers can always dismiss employees if the dismissal is justified by economic, technical or organisational reasons,[103] but not if the main justification is to make the business more attractive to would be purchasers[104] (reg. 7(2–4)). Additionally, the buyer can vary the contractual terms of the transferring

98 The TUPE Regulations replaced the *Transfer of Undertakings (Protection of Employment) Regulations 1981* (SI 1981/1794) ('old TUPE'), which implemented the European Acquired Rights Directive 77/1987. The adoption of the old TUPE had been highly controversial: see David Waddington MP, Under-Secretary of State for Employment, HC Debates, vol. 14, col. 680; R Eldridge, 'TUPE Operated to Damage Rescue Culture' (2001) Sept. Recovery 21; S Frisby, 'TUPE or not TUPE? Employee Protection, Corporate Rescue and 'One Unholy Mess" (2000) 3 *CFiLR* 249.

99 C-135/83 *Abels* [1985] ECR 469.

100 *Nokes v. Doncaster Amalgamated Collieries* [1940] AC 1014 (HL).

101 The criticism was particularly directed to the pre-2006 version of the TUPE Regulations: D Pollard, 'Insolvent Companies and TUPE' (1996) 25(3) *Industrial L.J.* 191.

102 On the same vein: C Villiers, 'Employees as Creditors: A Challenge for Justice in Insolvency Law' (1999) 20(7) *Comp. Law.* 222 (with reference to the pre-2006 version); and C Nyombi, 'Employees' Rights During Insolvency' (11/2013) 55(6) *Intl. J. Law & Management* 417 (with reference to the amended version).

103 *Kavanagh v. Crystal Palace FC 2000 Ltd* [2013] EWCA Civ 1410, [2014] 1 All ER 1033 commented among others by R Mundy, 'TUPE and Mental Gymnastics' (2014) 7(1) *C.R. & I.* 31; S Brookes and C Davies, 'TUPE Restrictions in Administrations' (2014) 152(1445) *Accountancy* 48. In fact, pursuant to IA 1986, s.99, Sch. B1, the administrator has a short, 14-day window from the appointment to dismiss employees.

104 *Spaceright Europe Ltd v. Baillavoine* [2011] EWCA Civ 1565, [2012] 2 All ER 812.

employees if these changes are designed to safeguard employment opportunities and are approved by appointed representatives of the affected workers (reg. 9). Statutory provisions prescribe a compulsory outcome (transfer of the employees) only when there is a high likelihood that dismissal would be unfair or unjust. Even in this case, parties are free to rebut this presumption.

The main issues arise over the interpretation given by the courts of the statutory text. In particular, the author believes that cases like *OTG v. Barke*,[105] *Key2Law (Surrey) LLP*[106] and *Crossroads Caring Scotland Ltd v. McGuire*[107] have been wrongly decided[108] as they assumed that administration procedures always fall in the category of formal insolvency procedures not aimed at the liquidation of the debtor. **27.75**

In the author's view, the interpretation given in previous cases,[109] which stressed the need to adopt an approach that was in tune with the 'rescue' spirit of insolvency legislation, would better preserve the established principles of party autonomy. **27.76**

With reference to *financial collaterals* and the payment and securities settlement systems, rules have been imposed by the European institutions[110] and implemented by means of the *Financial Collateral (No. 2) Regulations 2003* (SI 2003/3226). This law invalidates some insolvency law provisions (including those on moratorium and the administrator's disclaimer powers) with reference to these specific contracts. **27.77**

As a result, netting and close-out arrangements are always admissible, if the lender demonstrates the existence of the collateral. This is because both the domestic and the European legislator shared the view that the integrity of **27.78**

105 According to *OTG Ltd v. Barke* [2011] IRLR 272 (EAT), which overruled a previous judgment in *Oakland v. Wellswood (Yorkshire) Ltd* [2009] ILRL 250 (EAT), the absolute approach has to be preferred over the fact-specific approach because it promotes legal predictability and it is the preferable construction to achieve the purpose of the EU directive to protect employees in the event of a transfer.

106 *Key2Law (Surrey) LLP v. De'Antiquis* [2011] EWCA Civ 1567, [2012] BCC 375.

107 *Crossroads Caring Scotland Ltd v. McGuire* EAT(SC) 2014 WL 10653819.

108 Against: L Robertson, 'To TUPE or not to TUPE' (2011) 3 *C.R. & I.* 97.

109 See *Re Allders Department Stores Ltd (in Admin.)* [2005] EWHC 172 (Ch), [2005] 2 All ER 122 and *Re Huddersfield Fine Worsteds Ltd* [2005] EWCA Civ 1072, [2005] 4 All ER 886 commented by A Walters, 'The Impact of Employee Liabilities on the Administrator's Decision to Continue Trading' (2005) 26(11) *Comp. Law.* 321.

110 Recital 5 of the Directive 2002/47/EC of the European Parliament and of the Council of 6 June 2002 on financial collateral arrangements [2002] OJ L 168/43 (FC Directive), and Directive 98/26/EC of the European Parliament and of the Council of 19 May 1998 on settlement finality in payment and securities settlement systems [1998] OJ L 166/45.

the financial system is more important than the individual interests of the creditors in the insolvency procedure.

27.79 While it is debatable whether the directives achieved the intended, original purpose (i.e., to limit systemic risk and promote integration and cost-efficiency of the financial market),[111] what cannot be questioned is that party autonomy is protected. This legislative choice is perfectly consistent with the general rule on the treatment of executory contracts and it is likely to remain unaffected in the process of withdrawal of the UK from the European Union ('Brexit').

(3) Contractual remedies negotiated by the parties in solvent times

27.80 If parties were always free to determine the outcome of their contractual relations in insolvency, this free-for-all approach would lead to abusive commercial practices by strong or institutional creditors at the expense of general suppliers and consumers.

27.81 This sub-section investigates the matter of termination clauses, also known as *ipso facto* clauses. These are contractually negotiated provisions which permit the termination of a contract due to the insolvency of one of the contracting parties. This section also investigates the treatment of non-assignment clauses to determine their compatibility with the general principles of party autonomy, freedom of contract and legal predictability.

Ipso facto clauses

27.82 Under English law, these arrangements are upheld upon insolvency, provided that the negotiated clauses do not breach the 'anti-deprivation principle'.[112] The interaction between this principle and the general enforceability of *ipso facto* clauses results in a significant limitation to the right of the parties to make abusive use of their pre-insolvency rights.

---

111 Recitals 1 and 3, FC Directive.

112 The anti-deprivation principle is a common law rule which renders an arrangement void if it has the effect of removing an asset from an insolvent entity that would otherwise be capable of realisation for the benefit of the entity's creditors. See *Belmont Park Investments Pty Ltd v. BNY Corporate Trustee Services Ltd & Anor* [2011] UKSC 38, [2012] 1 AC 383 and IF Fletcher, *The Law of Insolvency* (5th edn, Sweet & Maxwell: London, 2017) 771–7.

Beside these cases, courts are generally willing to uphold the validity and enforceability of '*ipso facto*'[113] and flip clauses.[114] Close-out nettings[115] (outside financial contracts) however, may come under scrutiny if they occur after the debtor has filed for insolvency. **27.83**

The afore-mentioned *Insolvency (Protection of Essential Supplies) Order 2015* represents a significant departure from this established approach. However, as discussed before, a more accurate analysis proves that such a departure is less radical than it appears at first sight. **27.84**

The English understanding of *ipso facto* and similar clauses has cross-border implications. As shown in *Pan Ocean*, despite the recognition of the Korean rehabilitation proceedings as foreign main proceedings pursuant to the *Cross-Border Insolvency Regulations 2006*, the English court refrained from issuing an injunction restraining *Fibra* from terminating the contract when the English court could not itself have made such an order (i.e., invalidating the *ipso facto* clause) in its own domestic proceedings.[116] In other words, the fact that the relevant termination provisions were invalid 'as a matter of Korean law' was irrelevant: it was the English anti-deprivation principle, not any Korean law rule, which should have governed the validity of the termination provisions.[117] **27.85**

Non-assignment clauses

Should the law impose limits on the abilities of the contracting parties to prevent the assignment of receivables arising from a contract to a third party? **27.86**

At first glance, the answer should be in the negative, as the ability to negotiate such clauses is a clear expression of the principle of party autonomy. However, there are some concerns that this freedom, if unregulated, may result in abusive practices and unfair competitive advantages for large retailers and distributors against smaller companies in the supply chain. In fact, by inserting **27.87**

113 *Revenue and Customs Commissioners v. Football League Ltd* [2012] EWHC 1372 (Ch), [2012] Bus LR 1539.

114 Flip clauses are contractually negotiated provisions which alter the right to a priority of payment among the contracting parties by reason of an insolvency event.

115 Close-out nettings are risk-mitigation tools used by financial institutions to offset mutual obligations whenever a termination event occurs. *Lomas v. Firth Rixson Inc* [2012] EWCA Civ 419, [2012] 2 All ER (Comm) 1076.

116 *Re Pan Ocean Co Ltd* [2014] EWHC 2124 (Ch), [2014] Bus LR 1041. The applicant, the administrator of a company which has filed for insolvency relief in South Korea, sought an order to refrain the counter-party from terminating a contract which included an *ipso facto* clause and was subject to English law. Such a clause would have been voided under Korean law and the relief granted. Distancing themselves from the US approach in *Re Condor Insurance Co Ltd* (2010) 601 F 3d 319, the court refused to issue such an order.

117 R Matthews, 'Tough Choices: *Ipso Facto*, the Anti-Deprivation Principle and Choice of Laws' (2015) 30(2) *JIBLR* 62, 63.

non-assignment clauses in their contracts, large companies restrict the suppliers' ability to raise finance by using their receivables as collaterals and fencing themselves from aggressive credit recovery practices by any potential assignees.

27.88 Section 1 of the *Small Business, Enterprise and Employment Act 2015* allowed regulations to be used to invalidate clauses that prevent the assignment of receivables. In the legislature's mind, these regulations would have applied only to selected contracts where one of the parties was a SME. However, the proposed *Business Contract Terms (Assignment of Receivables) Regulations 2017*[118] went far beyond that, as it proposed a general ban on non-assignment clauses that would apply to all but the excluded contracts and irrespective of the nature and size of the businesses involved in the transaction.

27.89 The consultation that followed was marked from the widespread criticism by the industry. The government was cautioned about the potential consequences for several sectors of the economy (in particular, construction and cross-border contracts) caused by the introduction of a general ban on non-assignment clauses. Respondents contested the lack of consideration for the long-standing English principle of freedom of contract and highlighted the risks for insolvency practice, as the rights of set-off for creditors and the insolvent debtor would then be significantly restricted.[119]

27.90 Following a persuasive paper written by the City of London Law Society,[120] the government withdrew the bill from Parliament, but it still seems that it intended to present a new proposal in the near future.[121] The industry does not seem persuaded that the new proposal would properly consider the observations, which have emerged in the course of the 2017 consultation.[122]

(4) Concluding remarks

27.91 This cursory analysis of the most significant exceptions to the general continuation rule in the treatment of executory contracts has proven that –

118 Available at <https://www.legislation.gov.uk/ukdsi/2017/9780111160305/pdfs/ukdsi_9780111160305_en.pdf> accessed 8 September 2018.

119 R Calnan, 'Ban the Ban: Prohibiting Restrictions on Assignment of Receivables' (March 2015) *JIBFL* 136.

120 Available at: <http://www.citysolicitors.org.uk/attachments/category/117/CLLS%20-%20Note%20to%20BEIS%20on%20Business%20Receivables%20legislation%20-%2020%2011%2017.pdf> accessed 8 September 2018.

121 Herbert, Smith, Freehills LLP, *England and Wales. Preview of 2018* (January 2018) 15.

122 Allen & Overy, 'Why the Proposed UK Regulation Prohibiting Non-Assignment Clauses is Bad' (16 January 2018) <http://www.allenovery.com/SiteCollectionDocuments/Why%20the%20proposed%20UK%20regulation%20prohibiting%20non-assignment%20clauses%20is%20bad.pdf> accessed 8 September 2018.

with the sole, remarkable exceptions of the judicial interpretation of employment provisions and the proposed legislation on non-assignment clauses – English insolvency law is consistent with the principles of party autonomy, freedom of contract and legal predictability.

In their attempt to strike a balance between opposing interests, the highly skilled English judiciary produced a significant number of judicial precedents. Navigating through them may be extremely challenging for experienced practitioners and academics, let alone for anybody else. It might therefore be questioned if the current system really preserves these values. However, this is a question for further studies. **27.92**

D. REFORMS

Three aspects have to be considered to understand the existing law and its evolution: **27.93**

1. the long-established pro-creditor[123] approach to insolvency cases, rooted in the centrality of the principles of party autonomy, sanctity of contracts and promotion of legal predictability;
2. the eagerness shared by all recent governments to have the country ranking at the top of the World Bank's annual *Doing Business* Reports;[124] and
3. 'Brexit' and the resulting aspiration to promote the country as a global hub for rescue proceedings.

While the second and third aspects justify the recent attempts to promote a pro-rescue, pro-debtor culture in the country, they invariably collide with the first axiom. This explains to a certain extent why some proposals for reform – **27.94**

123 The distinction between pro-debtor and pro-creditor jurisdictions comes from PR Wood, *Principles of International Solvency* (Sweet and Maxwell: London, 1995). It is acknowledged that these labels tend to over-simplify an otherwise very complex classification problem. As a general rule, pro-creditor systems tend not to infringe significantly on the rights bargained by creditors in solvent times. At the opposite end of the spectrum, pro-debtor systems erode those rights whenever it appears to be appropriate to achieve the rehabilitation of the distressed business. Among others: M Pomerleano and W Shaw, *Corporate Restructuring. Lessons from Experience* (The World Bank: Washington D.C., 2005) 308. For a challenge to the standard characterization as US law being 'pro-debtor' and UK law being 'pro-creditor', see: G McCormack, 'Apples and Oranges? Corporate Rescue and Functional Convergence in the US and UK' (2009) 18 *Int. Insolv. Rev.* 109.

124 In all recent consultations, the proposed reforms were designed to make England the best place in the world to start and grow a business, while the Conservative Party 2015 manifesto included the promise to achieve the highest ranking in Europe and a place in the top five countries in the world in the World Bank's annual *Doing Business* Report.

such as those to extend an automatic moratorium in CVAs to medium- and large-sized companies – have not fallen on fertile ground.

27.95 First suggested in 2009,[125] the proposal to extend the moratorium to medium and large enterprises entering into a CVA failed to result in a bill due to the termination of the Labour legislature and the disapproving replies from the industry. Less than one year passed before the newly appointed government issued a new consultation,[126] which did not significantly differ from the previous paper in terms of the content. Unsurprisingly, in analysing the responses received from the industry, the then Under-Secretary of State for BIS had to admit 'that, while the refinancing and restructuring of company debt remains a valid concern, the urgency of the case for introducing such a moratorium is not as great as previously thought'.[127]

27.96 The government's eagerness to promote corporate rescue has been successful in other, more limited and less controversial initiatives. Following the enactment of the *Enterprise and Regulatory Reform ('ERR') Act 2013*, the government succeeded in preventing essential utility and IT suppliers[128] from withdrawing their supplies to businesses admitted to CVAs or administration.

27.97 However, the mixed replies from the industry in the ensuing consultation,[129] as well as the awareness that '[t]he freezing or stay on self-help termination is unquestionably one of the most draconian and controversial of all stays, because of its massive impact on transactions',[130] pushed the government to adopt a more cautious approach than it had previously envisaged.

27.98 On one hand, no obligations of such a kind have been extended to card payment providers and the list of 'essential suppliers' has been made exhaustive. On the other, suppliers were granted the right to ask for additional safeguards – even of personal nature – from the debtor to continue their business.

---

125 The Insolvency Service, *Encouraging Company Rescue* (June 2009), <http://webarchive.nationalarchives.gov.uk/20140311023846/http:/www.insolvencydirect.bis.gov.uk/insolvencyprofessionandlegislation/con_doc_register/compresc/compresc09.pdf> accessed 8 September 2018.

126 The Insolvency Service, *Proposals for a Restructuring Moratorium: A Consultation* (June 2010) <http://webarchive.nationalarchives.gov.uk/+/http:/www.insolvency.gov.uk/insolvencyprofessionandlegislation/con_doc_register/RestructuringMoratoriumConsultationDocument.pdf> accessed 8 September 2018.

127 Written Ministerial Statement, 11 May 2011.

128 Even though supplier of communications services by a provider of a public electronic communications service were already prevented from discontinuing their services by virtue of the *Communications Act 2003*.

129 <https://www.gov.uk/government/uploads/system/uploads/attachment_data/file/402336/responses-merged.pdf> accessed 8 September 2018.

130 Wood, *supra* note 123; R Suchak, 'Corporate Rescue Proceedings and the Enforcement of Ipso Facto Termination Clauses: A Comparison of the English and US Approaches' (2011) 8(2) *Int. C.R.*

More remarkable results have been achieved in the reform of the new 27.99
Insolvency Rules 2016 published on 25 October 2016, which entered into force on 6 April 2017. Significant proposals for the purposes of this study have been included in the 2016 consultation *A Review of the Corporate Insolvency Framework*.[131] A more recent consultation focused on improving corporate governance aspects in insolvency and rescue cases[132] and elusive fiscal practices in insolvency.[133] They are, therefore, less relevant for the purposes of this work.

The 2016 paper proposed to enhance the protection of essential agreements by 27.100
giving the company the right to designate some contracts as essential. The enhanced protection would last for the duration of the restructuring moratorium (proposed in the same consultation), the subsequent CVA or administration procedure, and would be available to businesses entering into an alternative restructuring plan (equally proposed for the first time in the same paper).

The government was aware that these provisions would significantly impair 27.101
the autonomy of the parties. Therefore, it envisaged specific protections for the suppliers and the opportunity for courts to reject the debtor's designation if the provision was not essential and alternative arrangements could be made at a reasonable cost and within short notice.

Following the analysis of the responses to the consultation, the government 27.102
decided to abandon the original proposal and, instead, legislate to prohibit the enforcement of termination clauses on the ground that one of the parties has entered into a formal insolvency procedure.[134]

This would seem to be a significant shift towards a pro-debtor, US-informed 27.103
approach to the treatment of termination clauses, similar to regulatory changes

131 The Insolvency Service, *A Review of the Corporate Insolvency Framework* (May 2016) <https://www.gov.uk/government/uploads/system/uploads/attachment_data/file/525523/A_Review_of_the_Corporate_Insolvency_Framework.pdf> accessed 8 September 2018.

132 The Insolvency Service, *Insolvency and Corporate Governance* (20 March 2018) <https://assets.publishing.service.gov.uk/government/uploads/system/uploads/attachment_data/file/691857/Condoc_-_Insolvency_and_Corporate_Governance_FINAL_.pdf> accessed 8 September 2018.

133 HM Revenue & Customs, *Tax Abuse and Insolvency: A Discussion Document* (11 April 2018) <https://assets.publishing.service.gov.uk/government/uploads/system/uploads/attachment_data/file/698173/Tax_Abuse_and_Insolvency_A_Discussion_Document.pdf> accessed 8 September 2018.

134 Department for Business, Energy & Industrial Strategy, *Insolvency and Corporate Governance: Government Response* (26 August 2018) 59–63 <https://assets.publishing.service.gov.uk/government/uploads/system/uploads/attachment_data/file/736207/ICG_-_Government_response_doc_-_24_Aug_clean_version__with_Minister_s_photo_and_signature__AC_final.pdf> accessed 8 September 2018.

recently introduced in Australia.[135] However, the government recognised that suppliers would still be able to terminate their contracts on other grounds (such as delays in the payment of outstanding invoices). This ban would not be applicable to financial products and services. With reference to licenses, it would apply only to contractual licenses but not to those granted by public authorities, as there may be legitimate public policy grounds to remove these licenses on the insolvency of a company.

27.104 It follows therefore that, even if enacted in the form envisaged in the government's response to the 2016 consultation, the proposed changes to the treatment of executory contracts and termination clauses would not in themselves determine the reversal of the established creditor-centred policy that has insofar characterised English insolvency law.

E. CONCLUDING REMARKS

27.105 The treatment of executory contracts in insolvency during the last two decades has been extremely unstable. Furthermore, as suggested by some commentators,[136] the decision to withdraw from the EU and the regulatory reforms undertaken in other countries[137] risk compromising the country's reputation of being at the forefront of international corporate restructurings.

27.106 Some of the apparent confusion arises from an inadequate understanding and study of the principles that undergird the current insolvency law. Legal provisions appear more as a reaction to circumstances and high-profile cases rather than as a result of principled planning.

27.107 This perception is misleading. Less recent reforms, consultations and proposals – including the 'Graham Report'[138] – have favoured the implementation of changes aimed at preserving the generally accepted principles of party autonomy (both before and after the commencement of a formal insolvency procedure), freedom of contract and legal predictability. These principles

---

135 E Streten, 'National Report for Australia', in J Chuah and E Vaccari (eds). *Treatment of Executory Contracts in Insolvency Law: A Transnational Study* (EE Publishing: Cheltenham, 2019).

136 R Paterson, 'Winds of Change: Corporate Insolvency and Proposed Reform' (2018) 11(1) *C.R. & I.* 17.

137 Such as Singapore. See, among others: G McCormack G and W Yee Wan, 'Transplanting Chapter 11 of the U.S. Bankruptcy Code into Singapore's Restructuring and Insolvency Laws: Opportunities and Challenges' (2018) *J. Corp. L. Stud.* (1473–5970) 1.

138 Teresa Graham CBE, *Graham Review into Pre-pack Administration* (The Insolvency Service, 2014), <https://www.gov.uk/government/publications/graham-review-into-pre-pack-administration> accessed 8 September 2018.

informed what is commonly known as the English creditor-friendly approach to the management of insolvency cases.

More recent consultations[139] and the government's response to these exercises[140] seem to mark a significant shift towards the adoption of a more debtor-friendly approach. This chapter has argued that – at least with reference to termination clauses – party autonomy, freedom of contract and legal predictability are preserved. Nevertheless, if enacted in conjunction with other measures, such as the proposed restructuring moratorium and the flexible restructuring plan, they may have the potential to significantly alter this fragile equilibrium. **27.108**

139 The Insolvency Service, *A Review of the Corporate Insolvency Framework* (May 2016) <https://www.gov.uk/government/uploads/system/uploads/attachment_data/file/525523/A_Review_of_the_Corporate_Insolvency_Framework.pdf> accessed 7 March 2018; The Insolvency Service, *Insolvency and Corporate Governance* (20 March 2018) <https://assets.publishing.service.gov.uk/government/uploads/system/uploads/attachment_data/file/691857/Condoc_-_Insolvency_and_Corporate_Governance_FINAL_.pdf> accessed 8 September 2018.

140 Department for Business, Energy & Industrial Strategy, *Insolvency and Corporate Governance: Government Response* (26 August 2018) <https://assets.publishing.service.gov.uk/government/uploads/system/uploads/attachment_data/file/736207/ICG_-_Government_response_doc_-_24_Aug_clean_version__with_Minister_s_photo_and_signature__AC_final.pdf> accessed 8 September 2018.

28

NATIONAL REPORT FOR NEW ZEALAND

Scott Abel

A. INTRODUCTION AND INSOLVENCY PROCEDURES

28.01 There are a number of insolvency procedures which are available in New Zealand to a company that is in financial and/or economic distress, as summarised below.

(1) Receivership

28.02 Private receivership involves the appointment, by a secured creditor, of a person to take control of the debtor's secured assets for the purpose of enforcing the secured creditor's security interest in those assets, in order to recover the debt that it is owed. It is an enforcement process primarily governed by the terms of the security agreement (with the rights, powers and obligations of receivers subject also to common law and statutory duties) rather than a formal winding up procedure.

28.03 Receivers are invariably appointed by secured creditors pursuant to a contractual right to do so in a security agreement (typically over all present and after acquired property).[1] While it is not necessary for a debtor to be insolvent for a

1 There are limited circumstances in which the High Court may also appoint a receiver.

receiver to be appointed, the appointment of a receiver will itself be evidence that the debtor is unable to pay its debts as they fall due (and is therefore cash flow insolvent).[2]

Upon appointment of a receiver to a debtor which is a company, the company's directors remain in office but cease to have the power to manage and control the company's assets.[3] A receiver is the agent of the company (unless provided otherwise in the security agreement) and can contract on the debtor's behalf.[4] A receiver's powers are prescribed by the Receiverships Act 1993 and the terms of the instrument under which a receiver is appointed. A receiver may also apply to the Court for directions in connection with the performance of his or her functions.[5] **28.04**

(2) Voluntary administration

Voluntary administration allows companies that are under financial distress a chance to rehabilitate, by imposing a moratorium on claims while an independent administrator is appointed to investigate the company's affairs and chances of survival. The moratorium is similar to that which occurs in liquidation as it precludes any:[6] court proceedings being taken against the company; creditors taking possession of company property; and any beneficiaries enforcing demands under any third party guarantees. Secured creditors (except those with a general security interest) are precluded from enforcing their charges over secured property.[7] **28.05**

Once the administrator has investigated the company's affairs, he or she provides a report to creditors with a recommendation as to whether the company:[8] be liquidated; enter into a deed or company arrangement, or has its control returned to its directors. **28.06**

(3) Liquidation (company, creditor, or court-initiated)

The most common corporate insolvency procedure in New Zealand is liquidation,[9] and involves the appointment of an independent liquidator for the **28.07**

2 Companies Act 1993, s 287(c).
3 See P Blanchard and M Gedye, *Private Receivers of Companies in New Zealand* (LexisNexis 2008) at [10.02].
4 Receiverships Act 1993, s 6(3).
5 Ibid., s 34(1)(a).
6 Companies Act 1993, ss 239ABC–239ABJ.
7 Ibid., ss 239ABL–239ABM.
8 Ibid., s 239AE.
9 In 2013–2014 'only 13 companies entered voluntary administration, while 4,089 were placed in liquidation': L Taylor and G Slevin *The Law of Insolvency in New Zealand* (Thomson Reuters 2016) at [32.1].

purpose of collecting and distributing a company's unsecured assets among unsecured creditors, following payment of preferential debts. A liquidator can be appointed by:[10] special resolution of the company's shareholders, the company's board, or by the Court. Court-appointed liquidators are usually appointed following an application by a creditor, after the company has failed to pay that creditor a debt owed, or by a shareholder.

28.08 With the exception of secured creditors,[11] when a company enters liquidation, a moratorium is imposed that prevents third parties from exercising any rights over the company's property and commencing or continuing any legal proceedings against the company. It is possible for certain parties to be exempted from the moratorium, if leave of either the liquidator or the Court is obtained.[12]

28.09 A liquidator, in addition to the ability to realise the company's assets, has broad powers to (among other matters) avoid certain insolvent transactions entered into by the company within two years prior to liquidation.[13] A liquidator also has the ability to pursue claims against the company's director(s) for breach of statutory or common law duties owed to the company.[14]

(4) Creditors' compromise

28.10 A creditors' compromise allows for a distressed company to cancel or vary certain debts that it owes to its creditors. A creditors' compromise can be initiated by:[15] a company's board of directors, a receiver or a liquidator. In limited circumstances, a compromise can also be proposed by a company's creditors or shareholders (subject to having first received leave of the High Court to do so).[16]

28.11 While there is no requirement that a company be insolvent before a creditors' compromise is proposed, the proponent must have a genuine reason to believe that the company is (or will be) unable to pay its debts.[17]

10 Companies Act 1993, s 241(2).
11 And parties with a beneficial interest in property held by the company as trustee, as explained in footnote 27.
12 Companies Act 1993, s 248(1)(c).
13 Ibid., s 292.
14 Ibid., s 301.
15 Ibid., s 228(1)(a)–(c).
16 Ibid., s 228(1)(d).
17 Ibid., ss 227 and 228(1).

Ordinarily, the terms of a compromise stipulate that each creditor subject to it is to receive an amount less than that which they are owed, in satisfaction of the creditor's entire debt. Provided that the terms of a compromise are accepted by a requisite majority of creditors, it is binding on all creditors that are subject to it.[18] 28.12

(5) Scheme of arrangement

Schemes of arrangement allow for a company, or its shareholders or creditors, to put forward a proposal (in the form of an arrangement, amalgamation, or compromise) that the Court can impose on the company and any other person(s) that it thinks fit. The Court may make a wide-ranging set of procedural orders, including ordering that:[19] a meeting of creditors be held for the purposes of approving the arrangement; notice of the application be given to certain persons, or a report on the arrangement be produced for the Court's consideration. 28.13

The Court has far-reaching powers that it may exercise for the purpose of giving effect to the arrangement. Those powers include the ability to:[20] transfer property, issue shares, continue legal proceedings, liquidate a company, and to make such other orders that are necessary for the purpose of giving effect to the arrangement. While it is not necessary for the company to be insolvent, creditors' schemes are often utilised (as in other common law jurisdictions) to effect a re-organisation of creditors' rights when a company is in financial and/or economic distress. 28.14

(6) Statutory management

Statutory management is a rarely used insolvency procedure, unique to New Zealand. It is only used in limited circumstances either where a corporation has been operating fraudulently or recklessly, or has problems of such particular significance or public interest that no other insolvency procedure is apt to deal with them.[21] 28.15

18 Ibid., s 230(2).
19 Ibid., s 236.
20 Ibid., s 237.
21 *Ararimu Farms and Investments Ltd v Stotter* [1993] MCLR 1 (CA) at 7.

B. TREATMENT OF EXECUTORY CONTRACTS

28.16 In New Zealand, the treatment of executory contracts in the event of corporate insolvency depends upon the insolvency procedure the debtor company is subject to, and the subject-nature of the particular contract(s) in question.

28.17 As to *ipso facto* clauses in general, it is settled law in New Zealand that there is no prohibition on parties including or relying upon clauses in contracts which provide for a party to terminate the contract upon the counterparty being insolvent or subject to a formal insolvency procedure.[22] However, there are limited circumstances referred to below where, notwithstanding a counterparty's desire to terminate a particular executory contract, it may be compelled to perform its contractual obligations.

(1) Receivership

28.18 Unless there is a specific provision providing otherwise, contracts that existed prior to appointment of a receiver are not automatically brought to an end by the occurrence of receivership.[23] Subject to available funding, a receiver may elect to allow the company to continue to perform many of the contracts that the debtor company entered into pre-receivership and those contracts would continue to subsist on the same contractual terms as agreed prior to the receiver's appointment.[24] Otherwise, a receiver, as the debtor company's agent,[25] may choose to cause the company to repudiate those contracts, leaving the counterparties having to claim against the debtor company as unsecured creditors.[26] Claims by unsecured creditors in this context are often not worth pursuing, both because their claims are subordinate to that of the secured creditor that appointed the receiver, and because (subject to the exceptions described below) a receiver is not personally liable for pre-receivership contracts in his or her personal capacity, unless the receiver expressly adopts or assumes personal liability for those contracts (or holds itself out in a manner

22 *Re Premier Products Limited (in liquidation)* [1963] NZLR 368 at 373 and 375. See also L Taylor and G Slevin, above note 9, at [22.6].

23 See P Blanchard and M Gedye, above note 3, at [10.16]. It is a common misconception that once a receiver is appointed, the debtor company itself is 'in receivership'. Strictly speaking that is incorrect as it is the company's assets, which are the subject of the security interest that led to the appointment of a receiver, that are in receivership.

24 P Heath and M Whale *Heath & Whale on Insolvency* (online looseleaf ed, LexisNexis) at [14.39].

25 Receiverships Act 1993, s 6(3). In doing so, a receiver will not be liable for inducing a breach of contract unless it is acting in bad faith or outside the scope of its authority as agent of the company: see P Blanchard and M Gedye, above note 3, at [11.33].

26 Unless counterparties have a security interest (such as a purchase money security interest, which has priority over a general security agreement) or a beneficial interest (which would allow a counterparty the ability to seek equitable protection such as an order for specific performance) in property held by the debtor company.

which prevents the receiver from denying personal liability).[27] A receiver is, in general, personally liable for any contracts entered into by the receiver on behalf of the company, but the receiver may expressly limit or exclude personal liability by contract.[28]

There are two statutory exceptions to the rule that a receiver is not personally liable for contracts that the debtor company entered into prior to the receiver's appointment, namely:[29] employment contracts and those relating to property that was leased before, and continues to be leased after, the appointment of a receiver. **28.19**

The Receiverships Act provides that if a receiver does not give lawful notice terminating an existing contract of employment within 14 days of the receiver's appointment, he or she becomes personally liable for the payment of wages or salary which accrue to the employee from the date of receivership.[30] In complex cases where a receiver is unable to determine within 14 days whether certain employees should be retained or dismissed, he or she is able to apply to the Court for an extension of the 14-day time period.[31] **28.20**

Similarly, the Act also stipulates that a receiver is personally liable for rent and other payments accruing during the receivership that relate to property leased or rented by the company pursuant to a pre-receivership contract. The receiver's personal liability in relation to such payments begins 14 days after the receiver's appointment and continues until such time as the debtor company no longer uses or occupies the property, or until the receivership ends.[32] **28.21**

The Receiverships Act 1993 also imposes a restriction on suppliers of 'essential services' from refusing supply of those services to a company whose assets are in receivership. Essential services are defined in the Receiverships Act as being:[33] the supply of water, the supply of retail gas and electricity, and the provision of telecommunications services. Suppliers of those services must not refuse supply to a company that has had a receiver appointed on the basis that the company is in default of charges due prior to the receiver's appointment.[34] **28.22**

27 P Heath and M Whale, above n 24, at [14.39], and P Blanchard and M Gedye, above n 3, at [10.10].
28 Receiverships Act 1993, s 32(1)(a) and s 32(2).
29 Ibid., ss 32(1)(b) and 32(5).
30 Ibid., s 32(1)(b) and s 32(5).
31 Ibid., s 32(3).
32 Ibid., s 32(6).
33 Ibid., s 40(1).
34 Ibid., s 40(3).

The restriction is very similar to that which exists when a company is in liquidation (as discussed below).

(2) Voluntary administration

28.23 In addition to the moratorium that is imposed upon the appointment of an administrator (as discussed above), there is a further restriction in relation to transactions affecting the property of a company in administration. Any transaction entered into, or dealing made by a company in relation to its property is void unless personally authorised by the administrator or an order of the Court.[35]

28.24 As to the effect on executory contracts, if a company enters administration, it is sometimes the case that the appointment of an administrator does not amount to a breach or repudiation of an executory contract (which contains an *ipso facto* clause) that was entered into prior to the administrator's appointment.[36] As an agent of the company, provided that the administrator acts in good faith it will not be liable in tort if it procures or allows the company to breach an existing contract.[37] Administrators are however liable for debts incurred in the performance or exercise, or purported performance or exercise, of any of his or her functions or powers as administrator for the purposes of funding the company; any services rendered; any goods bought; or any property hired, leased or occupied.[38] This would extend to, for example, orders made by the administrator for the supply of goods or services under an existing contract.

28.25 Similar to a receiver, an administrator is also liable for rent and other payments due under an existing lease agreement that accrue within the period commencing seven days after the date of administration until such time as the administration ends, and during which the company continues to use, occupy or possess the relevant property.[39]

35 Companies Act 1993, s 239Z. See L Taylor and G Slevin, above n 3, at [32.6.9].

36 See, e.g., *Smith v DCT* [1996] FCA 1022, (1996) 22 ACSR 331; 15 ACLC 3. However, many contracting parties (since the introduction of voluntary administration) have included the appointment of an administrator as an 'insolvency event' entitling the solvent party to terminate the contract.

37 *Lictor Anstalt v MIR Steel UK Ltd* [2011] EWHC 3310 (Ch).

38 Companies Act 1993, s 239ADH.

39 Ibid., s 239ADI. The administrator can avoid that liability by issuing a 'non-use notice' in relation to that property, prior to the expiry of the seven-day period: Companies Act 1993, s 239ADJ.

Further, unlike a liquidator or statutory manager, an administrator does not have the ability to disclaim contracts entered into by the company in administration prior to his or her appointment.[40] An administrator also does not enjoy the same ability as a liquidator to demand the continued provision of essential services. However, section 239ADO of the Companies Act 1993 confers a broad discretion on the Court to make *any* order that it deems appropriate for the conduct of any given voluntary administration. Accordingly, in the event of essential services being refused to a company in administration, an administrator may arguably seek an order from the Court requiring the provision of such services as is necessary for the efficient conduct of the administration.[41] **28.26**

As to employment contracts, a regime similar to that of receivership exists in the case of voluntary administration. While the appointment of an administrator does not automatically terminate any employment contract(s),[42] there exists a 14-day window in which an administrator may give lawful notice of termination to any given employee(s) so as to avoid being personally liable for any obligation of the company under those contracts.[43] **28.27**

There are special rules which apply in relation to bilateral and certain multilateral netting agreements, which generally operate to ensure that such netting agreements are enforceable if one of the parties to the agreement is in administration.[44] In particular, any netted balance payable by or to the company must be calculated in accordance with the netting agreement,[45] and statutory insolvency set-off which would otherwise apply does not apply to the transactions subject to the netting agreement.[46] In addition, the stay on dealing with company property that otherwise applies in administration does not affect the ability to exercise any termination rights in respect of events occurring not later than the commencement of the administration, or any right to take an account of all money due between the parties in accordance with (and in respect of transactions under) the netting agreement.[47] **28.28**

---

40 Meaning that termination or non-performance of such contracts by the company (at the administrator's direction) may amount to a breach: *Osborne Computer v Air Road Distribution* [1995] 37 NSWLR 382 at 390; *Hyatt of Australia Ltd v Coolum Resort Pty Ltd* [2012] QSC 49.

41 P Heath and M Whale, above n 24, at [17.38].

42 Companies Act 1993, s 239Y(1).

43 Ibid., s 239Y(3). The 14-day timeframe can be extended by the Court on the application of an administrator. See, e.g., *WGL Retail Holdings Ltd* [2011] BCL 340, [2011] NZCCLR 22; *Re Pumpkin Patch Limited* [2016] NZHC 2771; *Re Bridgman* [2016] NZHC 1050; *Re Grenfell* [2016] NZHC 36; *Re Postie Plus Group Ltd* [2014] NZHC 1337; *Re Gourmet Food Holdings New Zealand Ltd* [2012] NZHC 3606.

44 Companies Act 1993, ss 239AEH–239AEP.

45 Ibid., s 239AEI.

46 Ibid., s 239AEL.

47 Ibid., s 239AEN.

(3) Liquidation

28.29 As to contracts that an insolvent company became party to pre-liquidation, the Companies Act 1993 does not specifically provide that those contracts come to an end solely by virtue of a company entering liquidation.[48] However, as referred to previously, if a contract contains an *ipso facto* clause which allows a party to terminate in the event of the other party entering liquidation, there is generally no restriction on the operation of that clause. Even in cases where there is no *ipso facto* clause in a given contract, it is possible, albeit in very rare circumstances, for a Court to imply a term that the duration of the contract was intended by the parties to only last while the (now insolvent) company was trading, meaning that the contract becomes frustrated upon one of the parties entering liquidation.[49]

28.30 Another means by which executory contracts can come to an end by virtue of a company entering liquidation is pursuant to a liquidator's ability to disclaim onerous property,[50] the definition of which includes an unprofitable contract.[51] Contracts are considered unprofitable where, inter alia, they impose continuing financial obligations that are detrimental to the creditors of the company as a whole, and where they are likely to delay the liquidation of the company's affairs.[52] An aggrieved contract counterparty is able to claim as a creditor for the amount of loss or damage arising as a result of the liquidator's disclaimer.[53] However, the amount of loss that the counterparty is entitled to claim for is the amount of loss suffered as a result of the disclaimer, not the loss suffered under the contract disclaimed.[54]

28.31 As with administrations, there are special rules which apply in relation to bilateral and certain multilateral netting agreements, which generally operate to ensure that such netting agreements are enforceable if one of the parties to

48 *Laws of New Zealand* Liquidation: Effect of commencement of liquidation (online ed) at [397].

49 *Re Arawa Dairy Co Ltd* [1938] NZLR 411 (SC); *Re Premier Products Ltd* [1963] NZLR 368 (SC) at 377–379.

50 Companies Act 1993, s 269.

51 Ibid., s 269(2)(a)(i).

52 *Trinity Foundation (Services No 1) Ltd v Downey* (2005) 9 NZCLC 263,917 at [49]–[50]; *Re SSSL Realisations (2002) Ltd* [2004] EWHC Ch 1760.

53 Companies Act 1993, s 269(5).

54 Therefore, the measure takes into account any loss mitigation on part of the contract counterparty. See, e.g., *Re Tasman Logistics Ltd (in liquidation)* [2004] 3 NZLR 23 (HC) where it was held that a company which had leased property to the liquidated lessee company could claim for loss that was to be quantified as the difference between the amount of rent outstanding under the disclaimed lease and the amount of rent the lessor was entitled to receive under a new lease agreement it had entered into with a third party.

the agreement is in liquidation.[55] A netting agreement, and the transactions under any such agreement, are not capable of being disclaimed as onerous property.[56]

A supplier of certain 'essential services' to a company in liquidation is restricted in its ability to refuse to supply the service to a company in liquidation by reason of the company's default in paying charges for the period prior to liquidation.[57] The services that are regarded as essential for the purposes of a liquidation are the same as those outlined above in relation to a receivership.[58] The restriction under section 275 of the Companies Act is of limited utility in that it does not however prevent a supplier from relying on rights to terminate a contract or refuse to supply by reason of the company's insolvency or liquidation. The Court has previously held that the list of essential services prescribed by the Act is exhaustive, and that suppliers of services other than those referred to in the Act are entitled to rely on their contractual rights to refuse supply.[59] Furthermore, providers of essential services are unable to demand payment of arrears for services rendered prior to liquidation as a condition of supplying services post-appointment of a liquidator.[60] Essential service providers are also restricted from requiring a liquidator to personally guarantee payment of charges to be incurred as a result of the supply of the service(s).[61] The Act does not prescribe the provision of premises leased by the debtor company up until the appointment of a liquidator, as an essential service. The determination of a lease by the lessor upon the liquidation of the lessee has the potential to greatly inhibit a liquidator's ability to realise the insolvent company's assets for the benefit of unsecured creditors. **28.32**

An example of this was seen in the High Court decision of *Hartley v Fatupaito and Mccloy*.[62] In that case, the liquidators sought to sell the debtor company's restaurant business. However, the sale was conditional on receiving the landlord's consent to assign the lease of the premises upon which the restaurant business was based. The landlord refused to provide the consent required to assign the lease until $24,431.27 of unpaid rent that was due and owing by the debtor company was first paid. The liquidators argued that the landlord's refusal to permit assignment of the lease amounted to a breach of **28.33**

55 Companies Act 1993, ss 310A–310O.

56 Ibid., s 269(2).

57 Ibid., s 275.

58 Ibid., s 275(1).

59 *Hardley v Fatupaito and Mccloy (as liquidators of Normanby Project Ltd) (in liq)* HC Auckland CIV-2008-404-8585, 30 June 2009, at [73].

60 Companies Act 1993, s 275(3)(b).

61 Ibid., s 275(3)(c).

62 *Hardley v Fatupaito and Mccloy*, above n 59.

section 227(1)(a) of the Property Law Act 2007, which prohibits a lessor from refusing to permit an assignment pending payment of any amount or consideration when the lessee seeks the consent of the lessor for the purposes of an assignment. The liquidators' argument was rejected as the Court did not consider that rent payable that was due for a period before the company entered liquidation constituted an 'amount or other consideration' for the purposes of section 227(1)(a).[63] Accordingly, liquidators are not afforded the same latitude to demand the continued provision of leased premises when the lessee company is liquidated, as they are the essential services prescribed by the Act. It remains to be seen in New Zealand whether a landlord's refusal to permit an assignment that is necessary to allow a liquidator to perform his or her statutorily prescribed functions in situations where there are not significant rent arrears, would amount to an unreasonable withholding of consent.

(4) Creditors' compromises and schemes of arrangement

28.34 The terms of any given creditors' compromise or scheme of arrangement differ significantly from one another. Furthermore, given the private nature of creditors' compromises,[64] it is not possible to exhaustively describe the manner in which executory contracts are treated in the event of a compromise being adopted by a debtor company's creditors.

28.35 In practice, a creditors compromise or scheme will provide that each creditor subject to the compromise or scheme receives a partial payment from the debtor company in full satisfaction of the debt that the creditor was owed.[65] In consideration of receiving a compromise payment, creditors are usually subject under the terms of the compromise to a continuing moratorium preventing them from making any claim, or initiating any proceeding, against the debtor company for services rendered or goods provided prior to the date of the compromise. In such circumstances, disaffected creditors may nevertheless elect to terminate any executory contracts in relation to ongoing supply with the debtor company following the compromise being effected, if the terms of the contract permit termination.[66] Ordinarily, in the event of a compromise,

---

63 Ibid., at [15]–[43].

64 Unlike receivership and liquidation, there is no requirement that a company provide public notice of the fact that a class of its creditors are the subject of a compromise.

65 See, e.g., *Advicewise & Ors v Trends Publishing International Ltd* [2017] NZCA 365, *Morris Contractors Ltd (in rec) v Matai Mining Ltd HC Christchurch* [2011] CIV 2010–409–000724 ; and *CIR v Atlas Food and Beverage Ltd* [2011] 25 NZTC 25,005; 10 NZCLC 264,777 (HC).

66 Noting however that, as the effect of a compromise or scheme will typically be to restore the company to a solvent position, termination would ordinarily need to be for grounds other than ongoing insolvency. For that reason, termination events in a contract may separately include reference to the company being subject to a compromise or scheme (or to one being proposed), as a distinct termination event from insolvency.

there are no special rules that apply to certain creditors based on the nature of the contract(s) between the debtor company and the compromised creditors. There is, however, an overarching principle relating to all creditors' compromises, which is that only creditors whose economic and legal interests are aligned, can be grouped together and made subject to the same compromise terms.[67] For example, creditors whose contracts involve the debtor granting a charge over its property could not be grouped together with unsecured creditors for the purpose of a compromise.

In relation to the enforceability of *ipso facto* clauses in the event of a compromise, the enforceability of those clauses is case-specific to each creditor and is likely to depend heavily on whether the counterparty is subject to the compromise. For example, if the debtor company was in breach of its contractual obligation(s) to a creditor subject to a compromise, and there was a clause in the contract between the debtor company and that creditor, which required that the debtor company pay the creditor a sum of liquidated damages in the event of breach, the clause would likely be overridden by the terms of the creditors' compromise (which would have statutory effect). **28.36**

Other than contract counterparties that are subject to a creditors' compromise or scheme of arrangement, and contracts terminated for convenience or because of an *ipso facto* termination clause being engaged by a solvent party, all other executory contracts generally survive the imposition of a creditors' compromise. **28.37**

(5) Statutory Management

When a corporation enters statutory management, many of the rights that contracting counterparties would have otherwise been able to exercise are subject to a comprehensive moratorium which both restricts creditors from exercising rights against the corporation and allows the statutory manager to suspend obligations and terminate certain contracts to which the corporation is party.[68] There are only very limited exceptions to the moratorium that is imposed following a corporation entering statutory management. Those exceptions include certain rights of set-off and the commencement or continuation of proceedings for the purpose of determining whether any right or liability exists (provided that leave of either the statutory manager or the Court is first obtained). Additionally, a statutory manager also has the ability to **28.38**

67 *Advicewise People Ltd & Ors v Trends Publishing International Ltd*, above n 65 at [53].
68 CIMA, s 42(1). See L Taylor and G Slevin, above note 9, at [34.2].

suspend the:[69] repayment of any deposit, payment of any debt, or the discharge of any obligation. Critically, the Corporations (Investigation and Management) Act 1989 ('CIMA') also provides that when this power is exercised by the statutory manager, it does not amount to either a breach or a repudiation of the contract on part of the corporation being managed.[70] The restrictions which apply to the ability of a supplier of certain 'essential services' to a company in liquidation to refuse to supply the service, similarly apply in statutory management.[71]

28.39 Whether many executory contracts survive statutory management depends largely on the actions of the statutory manager. The CIMA confers a discretion on a statutory manager that allows him or her to terminate, at any time, any contract of service or agency that the corporation being managed is party to.[72] The discretion may be exercised even in circumstances where, but for the appointment of a statutory manager, the contract could not have been terminated until a later date or without cause. Termination of contracts by the statutory manager both discharges the corporation from future performance and all liability for subsequent non-performance.[73] Like contract counterparties that have had their contracts disclaimed by a liquidator, those that have been terminated pursuant to a statutory manager's discretion to do so are entitled to apply to the Court for compensation within six months of receiving notice of their contract being terminated. In making a determination as to whether a contract counterparty is entitled to compensation, the Court is to have regard to: the value of the consideration provided by the counterparty, all amounts and benefits that the counterparty has received under the contract, and the conduct of the parties.[74]

28.40 As with liquidations, there are special rules which apply in relation to bilateral and certain multilateral netting agreements, which generally operate to ensure that such netting agreements are enforceable notwithstanding the moratorium referred to above if one of the parties to the agreement is in statutory management.[75]

69 Ibid., s 44(1).
70 Ibid., s 44(2).
71 Ibid., s 55(1).
72 Ibid., s 49(1).
73 P Heath and M Whale, above n 24, at [36.32].
74 CIMA, s 49(2).
75 Ibid., s 42(7).

C. MAJOR REFORMS

There have been a number of reforms relating to corporate insolvency in New Zealand in recent years. The majority of these reforms were enacted pursuant to the 2006 amendments to the Companies Act 1993 (the principal statute regulating companies and corporate insolvency in New Zealand). These reforms included: the ability for a liquidator to assign statutory rights to sue;[76] prohibitions on directors of failed companies from being directors of companies with substantially similar trading names (phoenix companies);[77] and a new offence for directors that intentionally cause material loss to company creditors.[78] The Insolvency (Cross-border) Act 2006 was also enacted to implement the UNCITRAL Model Law on Cross Border Insolvency in New Zealand,[79] and to promote international cooperation in relation to cross-border insolvencies.[80] **28.41**

Despite the various changes that have been effected to corporate insolvency in New Zealand in recent times, there remains no general prohibition on *ipso facto* clauses other than the limited exceptions discussed above. Accordingly, parties to executory contracts that contain *ipso facto* clauses permitting termination in the event of the other's insolvency often exercise their right to do so, meaning that such contracts come to an end. **28.42**

Currently there is no indication that any change will be made in New Zealand as to the treatment of executory contracts or how *ipso facto* clauses operate in the event of corporate insolvency at any point in the foreseeable future. Although an insolvency law working group was established in November 2015 for the purpose of reviewing various aspects of corporate insolvency in New Zealand, the group's attention was largely focussed on addressing other issues that have been topical in New Zealand recently, such as the treatment of defrauded investors in Ponzi schemes,[81] and the extent of regulation of insolvency practitioners. Law reform in New Zealand, particularly in relation to corporate insolvency, is often informed by changes made in Australia. In that regard, it is worth noting that prohibitions on the enforcement of *ipso facto* clauses are contained in the Treasury Laws Amendment (2017 Enterprise Incentives No. 2) Bill 2017, which passed the Australian House of Representatives on 22 June 2017, and has now been passed into law. The insolvency **28.43**

76 Companies Act 1993, s 260A.
77 Ibid., ss 386A–386F.
78 Ibid., s 380(3).
79 Insolvency (Cross-border) Act 2006, s (3)(a).
80 (26 October 2006) 634 NZPD 6171 Hon Lianne Dalziel MP.
81 *McIntosh v Fisk* [2017] NZSC 78, [2017] 1 NZLR 863.

law working group, in its second report, noted the Australian changes but expressed the view that those reforms are not needed in New Zealand at present, but should be kept under review:

> We are not aware of ipso facto clauses being an issue in New Zealand ... We do not see any need to make any ipso facto clause-related changes in New Zealand at this time. However, further consideration could be given to this issue once the Australian government releases the details of this change.[82]

D. CONCLUDING REMARKS

28.44 Insolvency law reform throughout the last decade in New Zealand has been largely ad hoc and the trend as to upcoming reform appears to be no different. The main drivers of reform in this area have been to both achieve conformity with other countries (particularly Australia) and to both achieve efficiency and provide a greater level of certainty to a company's creditors. Advocates of the reforms that have been effected in the last decade have included national government, insolvency professionals, lawyers and many other interested parties. Despite a number of wide-ranging reforms, other than the very few exceptions described above, there is currently no prohibition on the operation of *ipso facto* clauses in New Zealand, the result of which is that executory contracts are often terminated in the event of a party entering insolvency. It is unlikely that there will be any forthcoming changes to New Zealand law in relation to the treatment of executory contracts in the future.

82 Review of Corporate Insolvency Law – Report No. 2 of the Insolvency Working Group, on voidable transactions, Ponzi schemes and other corporate insolvency matters (May 2017) at 57.

29

NATIONAL REPORT FOR SINGAPORE

Bingdao Wang

A. INTRODUCTION

Singapore has become an important restructuring hub within the Asian-Pacific area for several reasons, including the fact that it is one of the few countries in the area to have an efficient and effective legal system.[1] Since the financial crisis of 2008, cross-border insolvency cases have significantly increased in number, and regional firms and courts have had to cope with a heavier workload. Facing the global challenges, the Singapore government has been active to review and reform the corporate insolvency system. The recent recommendations of reform from the Insolvency Law Review Committee ('ILRC') in 2013 and from the Committee to Strengthen Singapore as an International Centre for Debt Restructuring in 2016 led to the introduction of The Companies (Amendment) Act 2017.[2] In October 2018, further reforms were passed by the Singapore Parliament in the Insolvency, Restructuring and Dissolution Act 2018, which is an omnibus legislation consolidating the personal and corporate insolvency and debt restructuring laws. **29.01**

This chapter specifically considers the issues relating to the treatment of executory contract according to Singapore corporate insolvency framework. The general and specific rules applicable to these contracts, and the over-arching need not to unduly prejudice the autonomy of the parties are evaluated **29.02**

1 Ministry of Law, Report of the Committee to Strengthen Singapore as an International Centre for Debt Restructuring (Singapore, 2016).

2 The Companies (Amendment) Act 2017.

against the insolvency law policy goals, i.e., to maximise the insolvent's assets for the satisfaction of their creditors and to promote the rescue of distressed yet viable businesses.

29.03 In order to examine the current legal position on this issue, Singapore's corporate insolvency framework and its latest reform will be reviewed in Part B. Then, Part C will discuss the treatment of executory contracts in insolvency, which is based on three established legal principles. The first is the insolvency office-holders' right of disclaimer. While it is necessary in the case of insolvency, such rights may be more useful and essential in restructuring proceedings. The second is the common law principle on the enforceability of *ipso facto* clauses. Currently, Singaporean courts, following the UK's lead, generally withhold the validity of such self-help termination right, thus prompting a critical debate on whether the enforceability of such clauses should be restricted. Lastly, the relationship between insolvency and the claim of anticipatory breach will be examined by making reference to a leading case, *STX Mumbai*.[3] This judgment introduced a fresh approach to the treatment of these clauses, as it established that insolvency cannot be a ground to claim anticipatory breach of contract. General conclusions will be provided in Part D.

B. OVERVIEW OF SINGAPORE LEGAL FRAMEWORK ON CORPORATE INSOLVENCY, AND RECENT REFORMS

29.04 The corporate insolvency system in Singapore has two pillars. The primary source for solving insolvency issues is the Companies Act ('the Act'). The Act was enacted in 1967 and it used the UK's then enforceable corporate law as a blueprint. The Act includes provisions relating to the whole life-cycle of companies, and the insolvency provisions are supplemented by the Companies (Winding-Up) rules and the Companies Regulations. Relevant principles from personal bankruptcy regime are also applicable to corporate insolvency.

29.05 Another important source is represented by the common law, which is built upon judicial precedents and insolvency case law from the UK and other Commonwealth jurisdictions. Although Singapore's common law is heavily influenced by English cases, rulings from this and other Commonwealth jurisdictions are not binding in Singapore. In order to decide whether to follow the decisions from other common law jurisdictions, Singapore courts

3 *The 'STX Mumbai' and Another Matter* [2015] SGCA 35.

will examine the legal reasoning underlying the precedents and its adaptability to local circumstances.

When it comes to the formal procedures for companies in financial difficulties, the Act provides a wide range of options, including winding-up, receivership, judicial management and arrangements or compromises reached between the company and its creditors and shareholders, such as schemes of arrangement. **29.06**

The most common procedure is winding-up, which can either be voluntary or court ordered. To obtain such an order from the competent court, the claimant shall prove that the debtor is unable to pay its debts as they fall due or that it is just and equitable that the company is wound up. A liquidator will be appointed following the winding-up order to carry on the business (when this is in the best interest of creditors) and to manage the liquidation proceeding. **29.07**

Receivership is also available under the Act. This procedure is mainly triggered to enforce security rights. The receiver's main task is to administer and realise assets for discharging secured debts. Courts do not recognise the existence of contractual duties to promote the interests of the creditors as a whole.[4] The discipline of receivership is the result of a legal transplant from the Australian tradition, namely the Australian Companies Act 1961. **29.08**

The emergence of a corporate rescue culture first within the business and legal/academic community and then in the legislative context determined the introduction in the Act of several procedures to promote effective corporate restructuring and rescue. Scheme of Agreement is one option that can be utilised for such purpose. The aim of the mechanism is to achieve a compromise or agreement between the company and its creditors, which would provide the creditors with better financial returns than the winding-up proceeding. One advantage is that such an agreement becomes binding on all creditors once it has been approved by the majority of creditors holding 75 per cent in value of the company's debts. **29.09**

Another alternative procedure is called 'judicial management', which is similar to the administration regime under the UK insolvency system.[5] Both the company and its creditors have the right to apply for a judicial management order when the company is insolvent and they believe certain purposes could **29.10**

4 Lee Eng Beng, 'Recent Developments in Insolvency Laws and Business Rehabilitations-National and Cross-Border Issues' (2003) Asean Law Association General Assembly, at 323.

5 Ministry of Law, *Report of the Insolvency Law Review Committee: Final Report* (Singapore 2013), Ch 6 Judicial Management, para 1.

be achieved, including business rehabilitation, better financial returns than winding-up and the success in rescuing the company as a going concern.[6] Petitioning for the commencement of a judicial management procedure is advantageous for the debtor, as it results in the automatic stay against all executory actions and winding-up petitions against the company.[7]

29.11 However, data shows that the legislature's expectations have been largely over-estimated, as judicial managements have had limited impact in promoting the rescue of insolvent companies in Singapore.[8] One of the reasons most commonly mentioned to explain this failure is that under the procedure, the company's management would be replaced by the judicial manager approved by the court. Accordingly, the company directors have little incentive to timely commence this procedure[9] and, following the appointment of the judicial manager, they are reluctant to co-operate with him/her.[10]

29.12 Additionally, the Act fails to provide a comprehensive system to support the rescue objective.[11] For example, the statutory moratorium on creditor actions does not prevent the enforceability of self-help remedies, such as contractual (i.e., *ipso facto*) termination clauses. Finally, insolvency practitioners in Singapore do not enjoy a good reputation.

29.13 Unsurprisingly, according to an empirical research conducted by the Companies Legislative and Regulatory Framework Committee (CLRFC), the majority of judicial management cases have resulted in a sale of assets or in a winding-up order. The same report found no evidence of cases where insolvent companies used judicial management as an opportunity to trade out of their financial troubles.[12] It is quite often the judicial managers who focus on the negotiation of shares taking over or asset acquisitions by potential investors rather than the rehabilitation of old businesses.[13]

---

6 The Companies Act 1967, s 227 B (1) (b).

7 Ibid., s 227C.

8 CLRFC Working Group 4, *Interim Report on the Corporate Regime in Singapore* (2011), Annex B – Review of JM Cases.

9 The applicant should nominate a public account, who is not the auditor of the company, to act as judicial manger. The court has the discretion to reject the nomination and appoint another person as judicial manager if there is objection to the applicant's nomination. The Companies Act, s 227 B (3).

10 Lee Eng Beng, see above note 4, at 335.

11 Ibid.

12 CLRFC Working Group 4, *Interim Report on the Corporate Regime in Singapore* (August 2011) Annex B – Review of JM Cases.

13 Lee Eng Beng, see above note 4, at 336–7.

Compared to judicial management, the use of schemes of arrangement has been much more successful.[14] One of the main reasons is that the procedure is supported by an interim moratorium under section 210 of the Act. The absence of such a moratorium has been argued as the main reason for the unpopularity of the scheme of arrangement in other jurisdictions, such as Hong Kong.[15] Another advantage over judicial management is the absence of any provision which displaces the existing management of the debtor, thus allowing the company to make use of the procedure to promote a timely overhaul. Furthermore, while public companies are reluctant to use judicial management procedures due to the stigma attached to it, and the requirement to suspend the trading of their shares in the stock exchange market, they found a welcome alternative in the schemes. Since there is no such suspension under the scheme of arrangement, the company would mitigate the negative influences in the commercial community when the company is dealing with financial difficulties.[16] **29.14**

(1) New Companies (Amendment) Act 2017[17]

In early 2017, as the result of the recent round of insolvency system reform, the Companies (Amendment) Act was passed by the Parliament. This Act introduced major changes to Singapore's restructuring and insolvency framework. **29.15**

The main purpose of this reform is to promote Singapore as an international centre for debt restructuring.[18] In fact, the Singapore government has strongly advocated for a reform of the insolvency system since the 2008 global financial crisis. The Insolvency Law Review Committee, which was appointed in 2010, published its final report with detailed recommendations;[19] shortly afterwards, following these recommendations, the Committee to Strengthen Singapore as an International Centre for Debt Restructuring was appointed by the Ministry of Law. Its final report was published in 2016.[20] **29.16**

The Amendment Act was drafted mainly on the basis of the recommendations of these reports. The introduction of this supplement document has been **29.17**

---

14 John Kong Shan Ho and Raymond Siu Yeung Chan, 'Debtor-in-possession: Not Appropriate for Hong Kong and Singapore' (2011) 32(1) *Company Lawyers* 304.

15 Ibid.

16 Ibid.

17 The Companies (Amendment) Act 2017.

18 See above note 1.

19 Ministry of Law, Report of the Insolvency Law Review Committee: Final Report (Singapore 2013).

20 Ministry of Law, Report of the Committee to Strengthen Singapore as an International Centre for Debt Restructuring (Singapore 2016).

treated as a ground-breaking development for enhancing the country's debt restructuring framework.[21]

29.18 The major changes focus mainly on three aspects. The first part is to improve the attractiveness of the scheme of arrangement as corporate rescue device. The new law includes further clarifications and guidance on the moratorium under section 210 for the purpose of providing greater protection to creditors. For example, it requires that certain eligibility conditions are satisfied when filing the application to prevent an abusive use of this mechanism. It also provides that the automatic 30-day interim moratorium can be granted to the same applicant only once every 12 months, to prevent repeated filings.[22] Furthermore, the new law also incorporates new concepts from the US Chapter 11 process to encourage the use of schemes of arrangement. These include the 'cram-down' provisions in section 1129(b) of the Bankruptcy Code, which gives Singapore courts the right to approve a scheme over the objection of a class of creditors; and the 'debtor-in-possession' financing, which means the court may authorise the debtor to incur priority financing under certain conditions. Generally, the new provisions have broadened the flexibility and scope of the scheme of arrangement procedure.[23]

29.19 The second part of the reform deals with the modernisation of judicial management. First, the law makes it easier for the company or its creditors to obtain the judicial management order. In the past, a company could apply for such order if 'it is or will be unable to pay its debts'. This requirement has been made more flexible, as the new version prescribes that a company can file for judicial management if 'it is or is likely to become unable to pay its debts'.[24] Additionally, the new law also gives the courts the power to issue a judicial management order even where one of the company's creditors would have the power to appoint a receiver. In order to prevent the appointment of a judicial manager, a creditor needs to prove the order would cause him/her disproportionately greater prejudice.[25]

---

21 Ibid.

22 Companies (Amendment) Act 2017, s 211B (2).

23 Meng Seng Wee, 'Reforms to Strengthen Singapore as an International Centre for Debt Restructuring' (Faculty of Law University of Oxford, 2016) <https://www.law.ox.ac.uk/business-law-blog/blog/2016/11/reforms-strengthen-singapore-international-centre-debt-restructuring> accessed 20 August 2017.

24 Companies (Amendment) Act 2017, Amendment to Section 227B (a).

25 Ibid., Amendment to s 227B (d).

The new changes may encourage companies to consider initiating the rescue procedure at early stages. However, it seems that the new law does not comprehensively address the shortcomings of the previous version of judicial management, as highlighted above. As a result, it is open to debate whether the new law will result in a meaningful change in the popularity and perception of judicial management across the commercial community. **29.20**

The third main change under the Amendment is concerned with the solutions of cross-border insolvencies. Judicial management has now been made available to 'any corporation liable to be wound up under this Act'. This has granted foreign companies with substantial connection to Singapore the right to use this procedure.[26] More significantly, the UNCITRAL Model Law on Cross-Border Insolvency has been formally enacted with this new law. This made Singapore the 45th jurisdiction in the world to incorporate the international resolution regime into domestic law. The adoption of the UNCITRAL Model Law is expected to facilitate cross-border insolvencies and encourage judicial assistance and cooperation between Singapore and foreign jurisdictions. With a more efficient recognition system in place, multinational companies would be encouraged to restructure their business in Singapore. As these companies will have to move their centre of main interests (COMI) to Singapore before applying, the government expect an increase in overall, direct and indirect foreign investments. **29.21**

C. TREATMENT OF EXECUTORY CONTRACTS

Executory contacts have been defined as 'a contract under which the obligations of the debtor and the other party are so far unperformed that the failure of either to perform would constitute a material breach of excusing the performance of the other'.[27] In some jurisdictions, these kind of contracts are referred to merely as uncompleted contracts or unperformed contracts. Treatment of such contracts in insolvency is widely recognised as a challenging area.[28] **29.22**

26 Ibid., s 211A (3).

27 Vern Countryman, 'Executory Contracts in Bankruptcy: Part 1' (1973) 57 *Minnesota Law Review* 439, 460; see also Jay L Westbrook, 'A Functional Analysis of Executory Contracts' (1989) 74 *Minnesota Law Review* 227.

28 Michael Andrew, 'Executory Contracts in Bankruptcy: Understanding 'Rejection' [1988] 59 *University of Colorado Law Review* 845.

29.23 As a way of example, UNCITRAL identified at least two basic difficulties when dealing with contract-related issues in insolvency.[29] The first is that any decision in formal insolvency procedures should aim at maximising assets' value and reducing debtor's liabilities, thus questioning whether freely assumed obligations should be respected in insolvency. The second one is that, due to the different nature, scope and characteristics of existing contracts, it is extremely difficult to conceive a one-fits-all solution.[30] From the perspective of contract law, the essential issue is the conflict of interests between the insolvent company and the other contracting party, and the question that needs to be answered is 'whether the solvent party is entitled to withhold performance or to terminate the contract on account of the other party's breach, whether actual or prospective'.[31] Since contract is the basic commercial form in modern community, the treatment of contract is vital to insolvency proceedings.

(1) Disclaimer

Liquidation

29.24 Generally, the fact of a company entering into insolvency proceeding does not put an end to contracts that the company made prior to insolvency.[32] Nevertheless, the Singaporean Act allows a company in insolvency to assume or reject executory contracts, and in the case of rejection, the damage claim will be treated as an unsecured claim. Under the insolvency system in Singapore, insolvency office-holders have statutory power to disclaim property and contractual obligations. Section 332 of the Act states that onerous property may be disclaimed, including estate in land imposing onerous burdens, shares in corporations, unprofitable contracts and readily unsaleable property. In winding-up proceedings, the liquidator has to apply to the court or the committee of inspection to obtain a leave to disclaim any property, which can be done at any time within 12 months after the commencement of the winding-up (subject to extensions by the court).[33] Any parties who suffer

---

29 UNCITRAL, *UNCITRAL Legislative Guide on Insolvency Law* (2004) Part 2. II, E Treatment of Contracts.

30 They include simple contracts for the sale of goods; short-term or long-term leases of land or of personal property; and immensely complicated contracts for franchises or for the construction and operation of major facilities, among many others. Additionally, the debtor could be involved in the contract as buyer or seller, lessor or lessee, licensor or licensee, provider or receiver and the problems presented in insolvency may be very different when viewed from different sides.

UNCITRAL, *UNCITRAL Legislative Guide on Insolvency Law* (2004), at 120.

31 Meng Seng Wee, 'Insolvency and the Survival of Contracts' (2005) *Journal of Business Law* 494, 496.

32 *Morgan v Bain* [1874] LR 10 CP 15, para 24.

33 The Companies Act 1967, s 332 (1).

loss as the result of the disclaimer action shall be a creditor of the company for the equivalent of the damages suffered by reason of the disclaimer.[34]

Courts have held that a contract is unprofitable if it has resulted in further liabilities for the debtor, or if it requires monetary disbursements from the insolvent estate. Additionally, the inability to adequately perform the contract is also considered a valid reason to disclaim it.[35] **29.25**

Despite this flexibility, courts have consistently held that a contract cannot be rejected simply because it is a 'bad bargain' and the office holder would be able to negotiate better conditions on the market.[36] **29.26**

The disclaimer powers are still very much like the provisions of the pre-1986 UK insolvency law. This is despite the ILRC recommending a comprehensive overhaul of those provisions. **29.27**

Under the current UK's Insolvency Act, the liquidator does not need a preliminary leave from the court to disclaim a property despite his occupation of the property or exercised rights of ownership over it.[37] Regarding the categories of property that can be disclaimed, the UK system adopted a more liberal approach, which includes two main types: **29.28**

(a) Any unprofitable contract; and
(b) Any other property of the company which is unsaleable or not readily saleable *or* is such that it may give rise to a liability to pay money or perform any other onerous act.[38]

The main difference between Singapore and the UK law is about the second category. Under current Singapore law, unsaleable property cannot be disclaimed if the unsaleability is not caused 'by reason of the property binding the possessor thereof to any onerous act, or to the payment of any sum of money'.[39] The committee pointed out that since the main objective of the disclaimer powers is to assist the liquidator in getting rid of continuing obligations under unprofitable contracts or ownership of assets that have no **29.29**

34 Ibid., s 332 (8); Creditors have the right to request appointment of the committee of inspection, and the committee represents the interests and rights of creditors and oversees the liquidator's decisions. The process of appointment is regulated under Subsection (3) Committees of Inspection, The Companies Act.
35 Giselle McGowan, 'The Law of Disclaimer' (2016) 11 *International Corporate Rescue* 234.
36 Ibid.
37 The Insolvency Act (UK), s 178 (2).
38 Ibid., s 178 (3).
39 The Companies Act, s 332 (1) (D).

value to the debtor, there is no reason to limit the disclaimer powers to unsaleable property only.[40]

29.30 The committee however criticised a particular aspect of the UK law, i.e., the standard of proof to reject a proposed disclaimer. The UK courts would not approve the disclaimer if the liquidator exercised his power in bad faith or acted in a certain way that no reasonable liquidator would act in.[41] The Singapore committee considered that this may lead to unfair consequences for the interested parties, since their interests could still be prejudiced even if the liquidator acted in good faith.[42] Therefore, it was suggested that the traditional standard of proof should be applied, with the result that any disclaimer should be disallowed if 'the injury caused to the person affected by the disclaimer outweighs any advantage likely to be gained by the liquidator in administering the assets'.[43] The innocent party injured by the operation of the disclaimer would be treated as a creditor of the insolvent company and can claim the amount of the injury in winding up.[44]

Judicial management

29.31 As mentioned above, judicial management in Singapore was based on the administration procedure under the UK insolvency system. In the UK, although the administrator is treated as the agent of the insolvent company as for liquidation, he does not have the right to disclaim property. In *Re P&C and R&T*, Scott J. made it clear that 'an administration order does not constitute an authority for the administrators to break the company's contracts. There is no power of disclaimer such as is available to liquidators'.[45]

29.32 Following the UK approach, the power of disclaiming onerous contracts is not available to judicial manager. However, the ILRC pointed out that if insolvent companies end up entering into winding-up proceedings, it may in some cases be inappropriate to wait until the opening of a formal liquidation procedure to disclaim onerous contracts. Accordingly, the committee has recommended the extension of disclaimer powers to the judicial management, as this would assist judicial managers to accomplish the three main objectives set out under section 227B (1).

40 See above note 5, Ch 8 Avoidance Provisions, para 48.
41 *Re Hans Place Ltd* [1992] BCC 737.
42 See above note 5, Ch 8 Avoidance Provisions, para 45.
43 Ibid.
44 The Companies Act, s 332 (8).
45 *Re P&C and R&T (Stockport)* [1991] BCLC 366, 374.

(2) Special executory contracts

Employment contract

The effect on employment contracts after the debtor enters insolvency proceedings differs between the various types of procedures. Under compulsory liquidation, the traditional common law position is that the liquidation order automatically terminates the employment contracts of the company.[46] However, such a position has been heavily criticised over the years. It has been argued the rationale behind the rule was not clear and it was a rule of convenience developed to help liquidators.[47] Nowadays, the liquidation order is treated as notice to the employees that the debtor is unable to perform its contractual obligations as an employer, but there is no direct effect between granting a liquidation order and the termination of employment contracts.[48] Singapore legislation adopted a similar position and employment termination is based on breach of terms. Under the Employment Act, an employee could terminate his contract without notice if his employer failed to pay salary within seven days after it being due.[49] This approach means that there is no fundamental difference between employment contracts and other types of contracts in terms of their treatment in insolvency. However, employees are entitled to have better protection because, compared to normal creditors, they are more vulnerable in the event of employer's insolvency, and thus protection is provided under the rule of distribution priorities.[50] The Companies Act states the outstanding salary claims and other payments owed to employees are ranked the second among unsecured creditors.[51] **29.33**

Under company rescue proceedings, existing contracts of employment are usually not terminated by the start of proceedings, and whether to adopt those contracts will be decided by the appointed insolvency practitioner. Regarding the adoption of contract, section 227I(1)(b) states that the judicial manager is personally liable for the contracts entered into or adopted by him (unless he/she disclaims liability). In practice, the judicial manager may have the right to decide whether to adopt certain ongoing contacts. For instance, the judicial manager would face the issue of whether to adopt existing employment contracts or to terminate them. By adopting the existing contracts, the **29.34**

46 *Re General Rolling Stock Co, Chapman's Case* [1866] LR 1 Eq 346.

47 Meng Seng Wee, see above note 23; see also David Pollard, *Corporate Insolvency: Employment Rights* (Bloomsbury 2016) 145.

48 Ibid.

49 Employment Act 1968, s 11.

50 See above note 47, David Pollard.

51 The Companies Act 1967, s 328 (1) (b) (c).

manager would be personally liable in case of non-performance. Consequently, liabilities owed to the employees during the period of judicial management would enjoy priority over other creditors. Those liabilities would include both wages and other payments they are entitled to under existing contracts.

29.35 In the author's view, the current situation is unsatisfactory. The judicial manager's main task is to rescue the insolvent company. As a result, continuation of employment contracts should represent an essential part of the rescue plan. Although the judicial manger is entitled to be indemnified in respect of such extra liabilities, the existing framework places an unduly high burden on him/her, thus potentially afflicting the outcome of the corporate rescue process.

Chattel agreements

29.36 Chattel agreements refers to conditional sale agreement, chattels leading agreement and retention of title agreement.[52] In order to protect all creditors' interests and maximise the assets of the debtors' assets, there are certain rules to stay contractual rights under those contracts after the commencement of insolvency proceedings.

29.37 For court-ordered liquidation, there is a stay on all actions relating to those contracts against the debtor at any time after the making of liquidation petition and before such order has been made, and all the legal actions against the debtor need to get court permission after the order has been made.[53] Furthermore, the liquidator also has the right to disclaim those contracts if he/she thinks it is onerous to the debtor, and the party injured by the disclaimer needs to claim damage as creditor.[54]

29.38 Under rescuing proceedings, the protection of assets is more specific. For example, for judicial management, there is a statutory moratorium from the date of the submission of the application.[55] It means that those secured creditors under those chattel agreements, without court approval, cannot commence any legal proceedings against the debtor or enforce any security over the debtors' assets. Additionally, the recent reform has given the judicial manager the right to get rescuing finance, which could be secured by a security that is subject to a pre-existing security interest, provided that there is

52 Ibid., sch 10, art 2 (b).
53 Ibid., s 258, 262 (3).
54 Ibid., s 332 (8).
55 Ibid., s 227C, 227D (4).

adequate protection for the existing security.[56] A similar moratorium is also available when the debtor company is trying to reach agreement with its creditors. When there is intention for an agreement, an automatic interim 30-day moratorium can be applied.[57]

Set-off and netting arrangements

29.39 Under Singapore law, contractual set-off and insolvency set-off under liquidation are available. The ILRC clearly stated that self-help remedies, such as termination of contract and set-off, will not be affected by a moratorium under rescuing proceedings, and the restrictions on set-off or netting in corporate rescue should not be introduced.[58] Although sett-off and netting arrangements may remove cash and reduce the assets of the debtor, financial exposure and transaction costs can be reduced.[59] The Singapore law makers believed that super priority financing would be a better way to support rescue plans.[60] However, it should be noticed that the court may be very cautious about granting super priority financing. In their first super priority case, the High Court decided super priority financing is available, but the priority status needs to be granted only when it is strictly necessary.[61]

(3) *Ipso facto* clauses

29.40 *Ipso facto* clauses have been widely included in modern commercial contracts. They confer on the performing party the right to terminate a contract and/or exercise certain remedies when the counterparty enters into an insolvency proceeding.[62] As a matter of fact, the validity and scope of such self-help termination have always proven controversial topic in both commercial and legal communities around the globe, with the result that some jurisdictions do not recognise their enforceability.

29.41 In the common law world, for example, *ipso facto* clauses are valid in the UK, as opposed to the US approach where those clauses are unenforceable. Regarding the position of Singapore law, as an extension of the English law, the courts generally choose to respect the intention of contracting parties, so

56 Ibid., s 227HA (1)(d).
57 Ibid., s 211B (1) (e), (13).
58 Ministry of Law, Report of the Insolvency Law Review Committee: Final Report (Singapore 2013), Ch 6 Judicial Management, para 10.
59 Ibid., paras 79–80.
60 Ibid.
61 *Re Attilan Group Ltd* [2017] SGHC 283.
62 Ravi Suchak, 'Corporate Rescue Proceedings and the Enforcement of Ipso Facto Termination Clauses: A Comparison of the English and US Approaches' (2016) 8 *International Corporate Rescue* 131.

an innocent party is usually not precluded from relying on *ipso facto* clauses when the counterparty enters into insolvency-related proceedings.

29.42 The English law is famous for respecting the autonomy of the parties to a high extent and for withholding their freedom to decide the contractual terms of their obligations.[63] Inserting *ipso facto* clauses into contracts reflects such autonomy and freedom. Additionally, both suppliers and customers rely on their validity during the commercial negotiations, as they see these clauses as a mechanism to secure an exit strategy when their counterparty is in financial difficulties.

29.43 Commentators who argue for retaining the *status quo* claim that it does make little sense to restrict the parties' bargaining rights to foster commercial predictability. Additionally, even if the application of *ipso facto* clauses was precluded, in the vast majority of cases the insolvent companies would not be able to perform the contracts; therefore, restricting the *ipso facto* clauses is not justified in the majority of situations.

29.44 The development of corporate rescue proceedings has put the English approach on *ipso facto* clauses under increasing pressure, because the success of a rescue plan may depend on the continuation of contracts between the insolvent company and its suppliers and customers.[64] Acknowledging this fact, section 365 of the 11 US Code bans the enforceability of *ipso facto* clauses in executory contracts after the commencement of the bankruptcy case. Section 541(c) further provides that the interest of the debtor in the property becomes property of the estate notwithstanding any types of *ipso facto* contractual terms.

29.45 The ILRC of Singapore noted the different approach adopted in the US, and considered the arguments for restricting the enforcement of *ipso facto* clauses.[65] It concluded that termination rights should be restricted to ensure the effectiveness of judicial management or schemes of arrangement. Another concern is that, without the restrictions on the right of termination, the creditors may have considerable bargaining power over the judicial manager or the company, with the result that they could be able to demand advance payments in exchange for continued performance (in blatant breach of general distribution rules). It also has been suggested that one of the main reasons why many rescue proceedings fail in Singapore is the lack of incentives for

63 See above note 5, Ch 6 Judicial Management, para 88.

64 See above note 62.

65 See above note 5, Ch 6 Judicial Management, para 87 (1).

company directors to attempt formal proceedings until the 11th hour.[66] The ILRC therefore argued that, should *ipso facto* clauses be banned, key contracts could not be terminated by counterparties, 'ransom' negotiations would not take place and distressed companies would be more willing to initiate rescue proceedings at an early stage.

Under the current law, however, not all clauses are valid and enforceable. Similarly to the English common law, Singaporean courts might restrict the application of *ipso facto* clauses when their application would breach the anti-deprivation principle. The purpose of this principle is to avoid any unjust withdrawal of assets from the insolvent company.[67] However, the scope of this principle is very limited and narrow. The UK Supreme Court has emphasised that the intention of the contracting parties should be respected, so a contractual provision entered in good faith should not be readily held to infringe the anti-deprivation rule.[68] Therefore, the contractual right of termination would not be in breach of this rule, unless it results in the transfer of assets that belong to the insolvent estate to third parties or creditors, in breach of the general distribution rules. **29.46**

Nevertheless, although the Singapore government was eager to promote the country as international restructuring centre, both the Insolvency Law Review Committee and the Committee to Strengthen Singapore as an International Centre for Debt Restructuring did not recommend any changes on the treatment of *ipso facto* clauses. **29.47**

The principal advocate for maintaining the current treatment of *ipso facto* clauses has been the law review committee. They argued that the different solution would have placed Singapore among the few countries (albeit including the US and Canada) where such clauses would have not been enforceable. Even if, since 2010, other countries such as Australia[69] have recently introduced bans on these clauses, some of other major economies (including the UK, Germany, China and Japan) still do not impose limitations on their use. **29.48**

66 John Kong Shan Ho and Raymond Siu Yeung Chan, see above note 14.

67 *Perpetual Trustee Co Ltd v BNY Ltd* [2011] 3 WLR 521.

68 Ibid.

69 Treasury Laws Amendment (2017 Enterprise Incentives No. 2) Act 2017 (Australia). New provisions on *ipso facto* clauses will come into effect on 1 July 2018 (or earlier by proclamation). The new provisions would, subject to exceptions, prohibit the application of contractual rights imposed by *ipso facto* clauses upon the commencement of certain corporate rescue or insolvency-related proceedings.

29.49 As another major common law jurisdiction, Australian experiences on *ipso facto* clauses has been carefully observed by Singaporean law makers. Nevertheless, the committee is concerned with some practical issues that would arise from the introduction of such restrictions. For instance, supplementary provisions that would allow parties to challenge an *ipso facto* clause in front of a court wold have to be introduced. They believe that this would cause an additional burden on courts, and would negatively affect the commercial judgment of insolvency practitioners.

29.50 More importantly, the committee thought that the treatment of these contractual clauses is best determined by the market, rather than by statutory clauses. Different types of contracts may carry different risks, and nobody is better placed than the contractual parties themselves to assess these risks.[70] Therefore, the law review committee concluded, and the legislature agreed, that the determination of the fate of these clauses should be left to the parties.

However, based on the industry feedback on recent insolvency system reforms, the Singapore law makers have changed their opinion about the operation of *ipso facto* clauses in the past year and introduced new restrictions in the Insolvency, Restructuring and Dissolution Act 2018.[71] Section 440, which was based on the corresponding sections in the Canadian insolvency law, provides that the restrictions on *ipso facto* clauses will be triggered upon the commencement of restructuring proceedings.[72] The legislators believe that such new provision would further boost companies' chance of being rescued or restructured.[73] This provision reflects the government's determination to build an international restructuring centre, and it would be interesting to observe whether it will bring significant changes in the next few years.

Anticipatory breach

29.51 A further argument against restricting the enforcement of *ipso facto* clauses is that if the innocent parties do not have any corresponding right to terminate, the performing party could only rely on the doctrine of anticipatory breach to terminate the contract, which could lead to an increase in litigation and legal complexity.[74] It has been recognised that establishing the claim of anticipatory

70 See above note 5, Ch 6 Judicial Management, 88 (4) (b).

71 Section 440, the Insolvency, Restructuring and Dissolution Act 2018.

72 Ministry of Law, Second Reading Speech by Senior Minister of State for Law, Mr Edwin Tong, on the Insolvency, Restructuring and Dissolution Bill (Singapore 2018).

73 ibid

74 Anton Trichardt, 'Breach by Anticipatory Repudiation' (2015) 29 *Commercial Law Quarterly: the Journal of the Commercial Law Association of Australia* 3; see also above note 5, Ch 6 Judicial Management, para 88 (6).

breach can be far from straightforward.[75] Singapore's position regarding the doctrine of anticipatory breach and corporate insolvency has been recently discussed and clarified in a landmark admiralty judgment delivered by the Singapore Court of Appeal.

The significant case, *the STX Mumbai*,[76] is briefly summarised: **29.52**

Transocean Oil Pte Ltd (supplier) supplied bunkers to POS Maritime (vessel owner), the registered owner of the vessel 'STX Mumbai', on the instructions of the agent of vessel owner, STX Corporation, with payment due on 16 June 2013. The supplier duly performed its obligations in mid-May. During the same period, the supplier was also dealing with four other vessels with STX Corporation. POS Maritime was the owner of one of the four vessels too and formed part of the STX Pan Ocean group (parent company). The supplier assumed that all five vessels were part of the STX Pan Ocean group. After learning from the newspapers that one vessel owned by STX Pan Ocean had been arrested for unpaid bunkers, and that the group had filed for bankruptcy protection in South Korea (date), Transocean emailed STX Corporation and the vessel owner requiring immediate payment for the sum relating to all five vessels. On 14 June, Transocean arrested the STX Mumbai when the payment was not received, based on the claim of the ship owners' anticipatory breach of contract. To support the claim, Transocean argued that the ship owner would have not been able to honour the payment on the established date due to the financial difficulties of its parent company. **29.53**

The Court of Appeal considered two main issues related to this discussion: (i) whether the doctrine of anticipatory breach applies to an executed contract and (ii) whether insolvency could be a ground for invoking the doctrine of anticipatory breach.[77] **29.54**

With reference to the first legal issue, the court held that the doctrine could be applied to both executed and executory contracts, as well as to unilateral contracts. As for the latter, the court clarified that the mere commencement of an insolvency proceeding does not represent an 'anticipatory breach'. In the Court of Appeal's view, it is necessary to look at the specific facts of the case to determine whether the breaching party has demonstrated by its words or actions that the contractual obligations will not be performed. **29.55**

---

75 See above note 62.
76 See above note 3.
77 Ibid., para 39.

29.56 The doctrine of anticipatory breach means that, before the contractual time for performance has arisen, a party declares the intention not to fulfil his future obligations.[78] Such a breach will lead to serious consequences, such as the right to terminate a contract.[79] The application of this doctrine has proven to be extremely troublesome, and the Singapore Court of Appeal acknowledged that 'its problems continue to trouble the courts in various jurisdictions'.[80] Traditionally, the doctrine is only applicable to executory contracts, and not executed contracts, which refer to those contracts where the innocent party has performed all the contractual obligations.[81] The reason behind this traditional approach is that it would be unfair for the breaching party to be punished even though the actual date of performance had not yet expired.[82] Accordingly, the innocent party under executed contract would have to wait until the agreed date has passed to claim a breach (and commence an action for damages) against the non-performing party.

29.57 The Court of Appeal considered the traditional narrative to be too 'strained and artificial'.[83] Since there is no clear English authority on the matter of the application of anticipatory breach in an executed contract, the Singaporean judges were ready to challenge the established wisdom, as they in fact held that the doctrine of anticipatory breach can be invoked with reference to both executory *and* executed contracts.[84]

29.58 First, the court considered that the innocent party's right to sue for anticipatory breach of contract is based on:

> [T]he actual breach by the defendant of an implied promise that the defendant party would not prevent the plaintiff from performing its contractual obligations which simultaneously constitute the conditions precedent to the plaintiff's entitlement to the performance of the defendant's obligations pursuant to the same contract.[85]

29.59 Accordingly, the purpose of adopting the implied promise is to make sure the contract is not 'rendered an exercise in futility'.[86] However, the Court of Appeal felt this implied promise would be difficult to explain in the case of

---

78 Ewan McKendrick, *Contract Law* (11th edn, Palgrave, 2015) 336.

79 Ibid.

80 See above note 3, para 40.

81 Henry Winthrop Ballantine, 'Anticipatory Breach and the Enforcement of Contractual Duties' (1924) 22 *Michigan Law Review* 329.

82 See above note 3, para 41.

83 Ibid., para 48.

84 Ibid,. para 40.

85 Ibid., para 42.

86 Ibid., para 42.

executed contracts, since if one party has already performed his obligations, there is nothing the other party would prevent from performing.[87] Therefore, the implied promise became redundant. The court's view was that if the defendant announced, in advance, that the contractual obligations would not be performed when the date of actual performance arrived, it would have rendered the innocent party's performance an exercise in futility. Accordingly, the court concluded that there is really no difference between the executed and executory contracts for the purpose of applying the doctrine of anticipatory breach.[88] The court thus proposed a modern view on this matter, provided that anticipatory breach could be invoked if 'the defendant has evinced a clear intention that it will not perform its obligations under the contract'.[89] The intention would be the basis of actual breach even though the time agreed for performance had not yet expired.

The court also considered that the equitable principles of justice and fairness would be unjustly disregarded if the innocent parties under executed contracts were not able to invoke the doctrine of anticipatory breach. The opposite conclusion would put the innocent party who has duly performed their obligations in a worse position than those who have not yet performed their portion of the contract but nevertheless are willing to do so.[90] **29.60**

Anticipatory breach and insolvency

For the second issue, the Court of Appeal made it clear that – in line with the general rules on executory contracts – a company entering into insolvency proceeding should not be automatically considered in breach of a contract. The court stated that: **29.61**

> [I]t is one thing to say that a party is insolvent, but it is quite another to say the insolvent party does not intend to be bound by the contract ... the former goes to the ability of the party to complete its performance due, while the latter goes towards its willingness to carry out its obligations ... they are two separate concepts and should not be conflated.[91]

In order to distinguish those two concepts, the court emphasised the importance of examining all the relevant facts of each case. In some situations, the financially distressed company may be able to trade out of its difficulties by **29.62**

87 Ibid., para 45.
88 Ibid., para 51.
89 Ibid., para 50.
90 Ibid., para 47; see also, Michael Davey QC, 'Insolvency and Anticipatory Breach of Bunker Supply Contract: The "STX Mumbai"' (2016) 12 *International Corporate Rescue* 140.
91 See above note 3, para 83.

means of formal rescue proceedings, which encourage the continuation of contracts rather than their termination.[92] It means, in certain situations, insolvency could amount to anticipatory breach of contracts; but such a conclusion cannot be reached upon a consideration of the insolvency alone, as all the relevant facts relating to the company's ability to perform and arguments raised by the innocent party should be taken into account.

29.63 The further issue is what types of facts or information would be sufficient to establish the anticipatory breach in the event of insolvency. It has been argued that to prove the breach, evidence shall be given to the court that the insolvent entity has either renounced their liability or has disabled themselves from performing it.[93]

29.64 The burden of proving the 'disability to perform' is on the innocent party.[94] The inability must be actually proved, so the innocent party only proving that he reasonably believed the other party's inability would not be sufficient.[95]

29.65 Based on this reason, the court referred the case back to the lower court to decide whether the insolvency at group level had determined the vessel owner's inability to perform the contract at the agreed date.[96] Hence, it would be risky for a party to terminate a contract on this ground, as wrongful termination of a contract may lead to breach of contract and liability for damages.

29.66 The argument built on 'renunciation' may be relatively easier.[97] The intention of renunciation could be communicated by words or conducts. '[W]hether an intention is sufficiently evinced by conduct is whether the party renunciating has acted in such a way as to lead a reasonable person to the conclusion that he does not intend to fulfil his part of the contact'.[98] To establish renunciation in the event of insolvency, a contracting party could treat the conduct of the insolvency office-holder as evincing a clear intention that it will not perform its obligations under the contract. At the moment, the Companies Act prescribes some time limits to determine the fate of these contracts. As a result, this type of conduct can be ascertained to establish anticipatory breach of contract.

92 David Hahn, 'The Internal Logic of Assumption of Executory Contracts' (2011) *Journal of Business Law* 723.

93 *Universal Cargo Carriers Corp v Citati* [1957] 2 QB 401, paras 436–438.

94 Ibid., para 437.

95 Ibid.

96 See above note 3, para 95.

97 Ibid.; see also Meng Seng Wee, above note 31.

98 See above note 74, paras 436–437.

Another factor to consider is the difference between executory and executed contracts. It has been argued that the mere fact of insolvency cannot be used as a basis for establishing the impossibility of performance, since it does not necessarily mean that the company has reached the point of no return. Even if the insolvent company is going to be liquidated, it is possible that the insolvency representative would decide to adopt the company's contracts, provided such contracts are beneficial to the company's estate.[99] In the judgment, the Singapore Court of Appeal noted that the High Court judge had relied upon a series of English authorities in which beneficial executory contracts were eventually adopted by the insolvency representatives. However, the learned judges objected that this reasoning is only applicable to executory, not executed contracts.[100] For executed cases, the insolvent company may have already enjoyed benefits since the other party has performed contractual obligations and only outstanding obligations are left for it to fulfil. Following the rationale of dealing with executory contracts, those detrimental contracts are not likely to be adopted in insolvency. Therefore, the Court of Appeal was in the opinion 'the line of authority does not provide any blanket rule to the effect that insolvency per se can never amount to an anticipatory breach'.[101] The ultimate decision has to be made based on the specific facts that whether the insolvency would actually make the contracts became impossible to perform.[102] This opinion is consistent with the judgment on the first issue, which emphasises there is no difference between executory and executed contracts in terms of deciding anticipatory breach of contract in insolvency. **29.67**

D. CONCLUDING REMARKS

The latest insolvency framework reform led by the Committee to Strengthen Singapore as an International Centre for Debt Restructuring introduced significant improvements to the restructuring and insolvency landscape in Singapore. The new changes which focused on the easier access and efficiency of corporate rescue proceedings would no doubt encourage its application among companies with financial difficulties. More importantly, the major steps of adopting the UNCITRAL cross-border regime and debtor-friendly approaches from the US insolvency system would make Singapore more attractive as an international restructuring hub. **29.68**

99 Meng Seng Wee, see above note 31.
100 See above note 3, para 88.
101 Idem.
102 Idem.

29.69 This reform has come at an important time due to the increasing number of global corporate defaults in recent years.[103] However, the treatment of contracts in insolvency has not received appropriate legislative attention. Specifically, the right to disclaim an unprofitable contract is directly related to the fate of uncompleted obligations, but this chapter has demonstrated that the provisions in the current legislation are outdated.

29.70 According to the UNCITRAL Legislative Guide on Insolvency Law ('legislative guide'),[104] an efficient set of rules on the treatment of (executory) contracts is important to maximise the value and reduce the liabilities of the insolvency estate.[105] The fact that the right to disclaim unprofitable contracts is not available under restructuring proceedings is not consistent with such objectives, and with the intention to promote corporate rescue in the legal and business community.

29.71 The enforceability of *ipso facto* clauses may have negative consequences on corporate rescue proceedings too. The UNCITRAL legislative guide and the U.S. law adopt the same approach on this issue, as they prescribe that any contractual clauses imposing automatic termination or acceleration of a contract in the event of insolvency should be unenforceable, subject to certain exceptions.[106]

29.72 As the current position under Singaporean law is too much imbalanced to favour the interests of the creditors, the author believes that reforms should be taken to regulate *ipso facto* clauses with the intention to find a more appropriate balance between the rights and interests of both creditors and debtors. The newly passed provision on limiting *ipso facto* clauses within restructuring proceedings was a positive step and the ability to rescue or restructure insolvent companies would be significantly improved. The pro-creditor common law position emerges also from the *STX Mumbai* case. This decision will obviously be welcomed by the sellers of goods or suppliers of services that operate on deferred payment contracts, because it offers them a basis for taking early steps to protect their rights.[107] While the approach the Court of

103 Shaun Langhorne and Carol Hartopp, '2017 Singapore Insolvency and Restructuring Reforms' (2017) Hogan Lovells.

104 UNCITRAL, UNCITRAL Legislative Guide on Insolvency Law (2004).

105 Ibid., Recommendation 1 (c).

106 Ibid., Recommendation 70; see also Gerard McCormack, *Secured Credit and the Harmonisation of Law: The UNCITRAL Experience* (Edward Elgar, 2011).

107 Yihan Goh and Man Yip, 'Rationalising Anticipatory Breach in Executed Contracts' (2016) 75 Cambridge Law Journal 18 <https://www.cambridge.org/core/journals/cambridge-law-journal/article/rationalising-anticipatory-breach-in-executed-contracts/9EED990A3BADFD17A715174B9E2C448C> accessed 17 August 2017.

Appeal applied was commercially practical, it is important to remember, especially for contracts in insolvency cases, that decisions on anticipatory breach should keep in high consideration the facts of the case.

From publishing the Insolvency Law Review Committee Report in 2013 to passing the omnibus legislation, Insolvency, Restructuring and Dissolution Act, in 2018, Singapore's insolvency system has experienced remarkable reforms in the last few years. As the government's efficiency in implementing reforms has shown its strong determination to develop a global restructuring hub, it could be expected those latest changes would not be the final step. **29.73**

30

NATIONAL REPORT FOR THE UNITED STATES

Roberta Righi and Jessica J. Winters

A. INTRODUCTION AND AVAILABLE PROCEDURES

30.01 In the United States, the Bankruptcy Code regulates the insolvency procedures. All bankruptcy cases are handled in federal courts. Out of court agreement with the creditors or debt counseling services, are alternative to bankruptcy filing, yet are not specifically regulated by the legislator.

30.02 The different types of bankruptcies are usually referred to by their chapter in the U.S. Bankruptcy Code. Chapters, 1, 3 and 5, the first three chapters, contain general provisions that apply, with some exceptions, to all the other chapters of the Code. Chapters 7, 9, 11, 12, 13 and 15 are the chapters that offer relief under the Code, and are the chapters under which cases are actually filed.

- Individuals may file Chapter 7 or Chapter 13 bankruptcy, depending on the specifics of their situation.
- Municipalities—cities, towns, villages, taxing districts, municipal utilities, and school districts may file under Chapter 9 to reorganize.
- Chapter 12 provides debt relief to family farmers and fishermen.

- Bankruptcy filings that involve parties from more than one country are filed under Chapter 15.[1]

As far as the businesses are concerned, they may file bankruptcy under Chapter 7 to liquidate or Chapter 11 to reorganize. 30.03

Statistics data about business and non-business cases filed, by Chapter of the Code, and other data about cases commenced, terminated and pending can be found at http://www.uscourts.gov/statistics-reports/caseload-statistics-data-tables.[2] 30.04

(1) The chapter 7 procedure

A chapter 7 bankruptcy case does not involve the filing of a plan of repayment as in chapter 13. Instead, the bankruptcy trustee gathers and sells the debtor's nonexempt assets and uses the proceeds of such assets to pay creditors in accordance with the provisions of the Bankruptcy Code. 30.05

To qualify for relief under chapter 7 of the Bankruptcy Code, the debtor may be an individual, a partnership, or a corporation or other business entity; the relief is available irrespective of the amount of the debts or whether the debtor is solvent or insolvent. The debtor shall however pass the so-called 'means test' which is used to determine whether the chapter 7 filing is presumptively abusive.[3] Unless the debtor overcomes the presumption of abuse, the case will generally be converted to chapter 13 (with the debtor's consent) or will be dismissed. 30.06

One of the primary purposes of bankruptcy is to discharge certain debts to give an honest individual debtor a 'fresh start.' In a chapter 7 case, however, a 30.07

1 While the author was unable to locate any case law directly on-point, it appears that the definition of a 'foreign country' or 'foreign proceeding' under the United States Bankruptcy Code would include proceedings or countries not officially recognized as such. The focus under the code is the 'foreign,' nature of the party or proceeding. *See* 11 U.S.C. §101(23) (defining 'foreign proceeding' as 'a collective judicial or administrative proceeding in a foreign country, including an interim proceeding, under a law relating to insolvency or adjustment of debt in which proceeding the assets and affairs of the debtor are subject to control or supervision by a foreign court, for the purpose of reorganization or liquidation.').

2 28 U.S. Code § 159, titled 'Bankruptcy statistics' provides for the clerk of the district court, or the clerk of the bankruptcy court to collect statistics regarding debtors who are individuals with primarily consumer debts seeking relief under chapters 7, 11, and 13 of title 11 and other kind of data.

3 If a debtor's income is in excess of certain thresholds, the debtor may not be eligible for chapter 7 relief. Abuse is presumed if the debtor's aggregate current monthly income over five years, net of certain statutorily allowed expenses, is more than (i) $11,725, or (ii) 25 percent of the debtor's nonpriority unsecured debt, as long as that amount is at least $7,025.

discharge is only available to individual debtors, not to partnerships or corporations.

30.08 A chapter 7 case begins with the debtor filing a petition with the bankruptcy court serving the area where the individual lives or where the business debtor is organized or has its principal place of business or principal assets.

30.09 Commencement of a bankruptcy case creates an 'estate.' The estate technically becomes the temporary legal owner of the entire debtor's property.

30.10 Filing a petition under chapter 7 'automatically stays' most collection actions against the debtor or the debtor's property. The stay arises by operation of law and requires no judicial action.

30.11 When a chapter 7 petition is filed, the U.S. trustee (or the bankruptcy court in Alabama and North Carolina) appoints an impartial case trustee to administer the case and liquidate the debtor's nonexempt assets in a manner that maximizes the return to the debtor's unsecured creditors. In addition, if the debtor is a business, the bankruptcy court may authorize the trustee to operate the business for a limited period, if such operation will benefit creditors and enhance the liquidation of the estate.

30.12 The trustee may also attempt to recover money or property under the trustee's 'avoiding powers.' The trustee's avoiding powers include the power to: set aside preferential transfers made to creditors within 90 days before the petition; undo security interests and other prepetition transfers of property that were not properly perfected under no bankruptcy law at the time of the petition; and pursue no bankruptcy claims such as fraudulent conveyance and bulk transfer remedies available under state law.

(2) The chapter 11 procedure

30.13 Cases filed under chapter 11 of the United States Bankruptcy Code is also referred to as a 'reorganization' bankruptcy that may be filed by businesses (corporations, sole proprietorships and partnerships).

30.14 A chapter 11 case begins with the filing of a petition with the bankruptcy court serving the area where the debtor has a domicile or residence. A petition may be a voluntary petition, which is filed by the debtor, or it may be an involuntary petition, which is filed by creditors that meet certain requirements.

Upon filing a voluntary petition for relief under chapter 11 or, in an involuntary case, the entry of an order for relief, the debtor automatically assumes an additional identity as the 'debtor in possession', meaning a debtor that keeps possession and control of its assets while undergoing a reorganization under chapter 11, without the appointment of a case trustee. A debtor will remain a debtor in possession until the debtor's plan of reorganization is confirmed, the debtor's case is dismissed or converted to chapter 7, or a chapter 11 trustee is appointed. **30.15**

Section 1107 of the Bankruptcy Code places the debtor in possession in the position of a fiduciary, with the rights and powers of a chapter 11 trustee. **30.16**

The U.S. trustee is responsible for monitoring the debtor in possession's operation of the business and the submission of operating reports and fees. **30.17**

Creditors' committees, is appointed by the U.S. trustee and ordinarily consists of unsecured creditors who hold the seven largest unsecured claims against the debtor. The committee: consults with the debtor in possession on administration of the case; investigates the debtor's conduct and operation of the business; and participates in formulating a plan. **30.18**

Also, in the chapter 11 case, a stay of creditor actions against the debtor automatically goes into effect when the bankruptcy petition is filed. The automatic stay provides a period of time in which all judgments, collection activities, foreclosures, and repossessions of property are suspended and may not be pursued by the creditors on any debt or claim that arose before the filing of the bankruptcy petition. **30.19**

The debtor in possession or the trustee, as the case may be, also has 'avoiding' powers. These powers may be used to undo a transfer of money or property made during a certain period of time before the filing of the bankruptcy petition. By avoiding a particular transfer of property, the debtor in possession can cancel the transaction and force the return of the payments or property, which then are available to pay all creditors. Generally, the power to avoid transfers is effective against transfers made by the debtor within 90 days before filing the petition, while it is effective against transfers to 'insiders' (i.e., relatives, general partners, and directors or officers of the debtor) made up to a year before filing. **30.20**

The debtor (unless a 'small business debtor') has a 120-day period during which it has an exclusive right to file a plan. Section 1141(d)(1) generally provides that confirmation of a plan discharges a debtor from any debt that **30.21** arose before the date of confirmation. After the plan is confirmed, the debtor is required to make plan payments and is bound by the provisions of the plan of reorganization. The confirmed plan creates new contractual rights, replacing or superseding pre-bankruptcy contracts.

(3) The insolvency procedures versus out of court agreements

30.22 As discussed *supra*, chapter 7 is aimed at a liquidation of the debtor's assets and the distribution of the proceeds obtained to creditors and, if the debtor is an individual, the discharge of certain debts. Chapter 13 is designed for an individual debtor who has a regular source of income. It is often preferable to chapter 7 because it enables the debtor to keep a valuable asset, such as a house, and because it allows the debtor to propose a 'plan' to repay creditors over time – usually three to five years.

30.23 Chapter 11, is used by commercial enterprises that desire to continue operating a business and repay creditors concurrently through a court-approved plan of reorganization. Under the confirmed plan, the debtor can reduce its debts by repaying a portion of its obligations and discharging others. The debtor can also terminate burdensome contracts and leases, recover assets, and rescale its operations in order to return to profitability.

30.24 Restructuring debts outside a bankruptcy case, it is a much more flexible process that allows the parties to define the conditions and parameters of the negotiation with the debtor. On the other hand, out of court agreements require coordinating and motivating disparate groups of creditors, creditors' voluntary forbearance from exercising default remedies, governance structures, confidentiality, and generally keeping parties engaged in a restructuring process when they are not forced to by rules of law. Furthermore the restructuring process is often challenged by creditors that are in a position to block a restructuring and use that advantage to get additional value for themselves.

30.25 In bankruptcy cases, instead, a restructuring plan can be confirmed and become binding on all creditors, by the consent of a sufficiently large number of creditors, according to specific class voting rights, binding even those who object to the plan and those who did not vote on it.

B. TREATMENT OF EXECUTORY CONTRACTS IN THE US LAW

Under the Bankruptcy Code, debtors and bankruptcy trustees are authorized to assume or reject executory contracts (and unexpired leases) in bankruptcy. This reflects the underlying bankruptcy policy that debtors should have the ability to abandon burdensome contracts and retain beneficial contracts. **30.26**

The 11 USCS § 365 is titled 'Executory contracts and unexpired leases' and its subsection (a) recites as follows: **30.27**

> (a) Except as provided in sections 765 and 766 of this title [11 USCS §§ 765 and 766] and in subsections (b), (c), and (d) of this section, the trustee, subject to the court's approval, may assume or reject any executory contract or unexpired lease of the debtor.

The Bankruptcy Code does not define 'executory contract' and leaves it to the courts to decide when a contract achieves the classification of executory. **30.28**

As a result, the courts have adopted two opposing tests for the identification of executory contracts in bankruptcy: the Countryman Test also called 'material breach' test and the Functional Test. **30.29**

Most courts adopt the Countryman definition of an executory contract as an agreement where 'the obligations of both the bankruptcy and the other party are so far unperformed that the failure of either to complete performance would constitute a material breach excusing performance of the other.'[4] Courts of Appeal in the Third, Fourth, Seventh, Eighth and Ninth Circuits use this 'material breach' test. **30.30**

Some courts in the First, Sixth and Eleventh Circuits instead use the 'Functional test', which works 'backward from an examination of the purposes to be accomplished by rejection, and if they have already been accomplished then the contract cannot be executory.'[5] **30.31**

---

4 Countryman, 'Executory License Agreements in Bankruptcy' (1973) 57 *Minn. L. Rev.* 439, 460.

5 See, e.g., *In re Magness*, 972 F.2d 689, 693 (6th Cir. 1992); *In re Cardinal Indus., Inc.*, 146 B.R. 720 (Bankr. S.D. Ohio 1992) (discusses how 6th Circuit has adopted both Countryman definition and functional approach); *In re General Dev. Corp.*, 177 B.R. 1000, 1013 (S.D. Fla. 1995); *In re Drexel Burnham Lambert Group, Inc.*, 138 B.R. 703, 708 n.24 (Bankr. S.D.N.Y. 1992). *Chattanooga Memorial Park v. Still (In re Jolly)*, 574 F.2d 349, 351 (6th Cir.) (proper approach 'to deciphering the meaning of the executory contract rejection provisions, is to work backward, proceeding from an examination of the purposes rejection is expected to accomplish'), *cert. denied*, 439 U.S. 929 (1978); *Camp v. National Union Fire Ins. Co. (In re Government Secs. Corp.)*, 101 B.R. 343, 348 n.2, 348–9 (Bankr. S.D. Fla. 1989) (same), *aff'd*, 111 B.R. 1007 (S.D. Fla. 1990); *In re G-N Partners*, 48 B.R. 462, 465–6 (Bankr. D. Minn. 1985) (contract was not executory if 'a rejection by the trustee would neither add to nor detract from the estate's benefits or liabilities') (quoting *Jenson v. Continental Fin. Corp.*, 591 F.2d 477, 481 n.5 (8th Cir. 1979)). For a brief discussion of this definition and

30.32 In general, any ongoing obligations on both sides, if material, are examined as part of the analysis of whether it is an executory contract or not.

30.33 Contracts where performance remains due on both sides are executory.[6] Contracts in which one party has no post-petition obligation or no obligation other than the payment of money are not executory.[7]

30.34 A contract substantially performed is not executory.[8]

30.35 A contract where only 'mere formality' is required for performance is not an executory contract (Compare in *re Heartline Farms v. Daly*, 128 B.R. 246, 250 (D. Neb. 1990) – 'mere formality' remaining for performance 'does not represent the kind of significant legal obligation that would render a contract executory').

30.36 A contract or lease no longer in existence is not executory and cannot be assumed.[9] Executory contracts that are terminated prior to the filing of the bankruptcy petition do not become property of the estate.[10] But the termination 'must be complete and not subject to reversal, either under the terms of the contract or under state law.' Thus, in situations where the non-debtor party to the contract has given its termination notice for the contract, and the debtor subsequently files for bankruptcy protection but before the cure or

examples of other cases that have employed this test, see Lawrence J. La Sala, Note, 'Partner Bankruptcy and Partnership Dissolution: Protecting the Terms of the Contract and Ensuring Predictability' (1991)59 *Fordham L. Rev.* 619, 624–5 n.30.

6 See, e.g., *In re Columbia Gas Sys., Inc.*, 50 F.3d 233 (3d Cir. 1995) (settlement agreement may be an executory contract); *In re Hooker Investments*, 145 B.R. 138, 144 (Bankr. S.D.N.Y. 1992) (employment contracts are executory contracts).

7 See *In re Chesapeake Fiber Pkg. v. Sebro Packaging Corp.*, 143 B.R. 360 (D. Md. 1992) (agreements conveying patent rights are not executory contracts); *In re Spectrum Information Technologies, Inc.*, 190 B.R. 741, 748 (Bankr. E.D.N.Y. 1996) ('where the only performance that remains is the payment of money, the contract will not be found to be executory'); *In re F.B.F. Indus., Inc.*, 165 B.R. 544, 549 (Bankr. E.D. Pa. 1994) (promissory notes are not executory contracts); *In re U.S. Metalsource Corp.*, 163 B.R. 260, 269 (Bankr. W.D. Pa. 1993) (terminable-at-will employment contracts are not executory contracts because debtor's only legal obligation is to pay severance pay).

8 *In re Pacific Exp. Inc.*, 780 F.2d 1482, 1487 (9th Cir. 1986); *In re Sundial Asphalt Co.*, 147 B.R. 72, 80 (E.D.N.Y. 1992) (contract for sale of land ceases to be executory when court issues decree of specific performance); *In re Norwood Chevrolet Co.*, 143 B.R. 804 (Bankr. D.R.I. 1992) (substantial performance by both parties precludes rejection of contract).

9 See *In re Thompson*, 186 B.R. 301, 307 (Bankr. N.D. Ga. 1995) (contract terminated prepetition 'cannot be revived solely by virtue of a bankruptcy petition. Filing for bankruptcy relief does not confer new rights on a debtor in regard to [] terminated agreements and a debtor is not permitted to cure his defaults and/or assume such agreements.')

10 *In re Moody v. Amoco Oil Co.*, 734 F.2d 1200 (7th Cir. 1984)

termination period has expired, courts may treat the underlying contract as an executory contract.[11]

A single document may contain more than one contract for § 365 assumption-rejection purposes. State law determines if the contract is divisible for assumption-rejection purposes. The assessment to determine if one part of a single contract is severable and enforceable on its own is based on whether there was separate and distinct consideration and performance under each 'contract'.[12] **30.37**

A prepetition termination of an executory contract is not an avoidable transfer of an interest in property under §§ 547; 548 of the Bankruptcy Code.[13] **30.38**

A long-term supply agreement, a franchise agreement, or most intellectual property licenses would usually be considered an executory contract. A promissory note, a completed sale or assignment, an expired agreement, an agreement effectively and completely terminated prior to the bankruptcy filing, or a single purchase order would typically not be an executory contract. Exclusive and perpetual licenses are sometimes argued to be more like a completed assignment for the rights and/or territory covered than an executory contract. **30.39**

(1) Assumption, assignment and/or rejection of an executory contract

Upon a bankruptcy filing, an executory contract becomes property of the bankruptcy estate. As such, the 'automatic stay' protects it. The stay also prevents the non-debtor party from unilaterally terminating an executory contract with the debtor or exercising any other contract remedy or right against the debtor. Therefore 'ipso facto' clauses are generally unenforceable. A debtor cannot in prepetition agreement, unilaterally waive its authority to assume or reject an executory contract, as such violates public policy.[14] **30.40**

Section 365 may be used by the debtor or the trustee to assume, reject or assign any type of contract. Exceptions are for contracts with respect to which applicable law excuses the non-debtor party from accepting performance from, or rendering performance to, a third party, such as certain personal services **30.41**

11 *In re Masterworks, Inc.*, 100 B.R. 149 (Bankr.D.Conn. 1989); In re C.W. Mining Co., 422 B.R. 746 (10th Cir. BAP 2010).

12 *In re Leslie Fay Co., Inc.*, 168 B.R. 294, 301 n.7 (Bankr. S.D.N.Y. 1994).

13 *In re Egyptian Brothers Donut, Inc.*, 190 B.R. 26, 28–30 (Bankr. D.N.J. 1995).

14 *In re TWA* (2001, BC DC Del) 261 BR 103.

contracts, certain non-assignable governmental contracts and certain intellectual property licenses.

30.42 The trustee or the debtor in possession has a 'reasonable time' to decide whether to assume or reject. In a chapter 7 liquidation, executory contracts are generally rejected 60 days into the bankruptcy case absent special relief from the bankruptcy court. In a chapter 11 case, there is no set time to make the decision to reject or assume a general executory contract. Instead, absent an earlier rejection of an executory contract, decisions on whether to assume or reject typically do not occur until a chapter 11 plan is confirmed or until the division, assets or entity, which the contract relates to, is sold or liquidated.[15]

30.43 What is however not clear is the status of an executory contract between filing of petition and the decision of the trustee or the debtor to assume or reject[16] and the relevant duties and obligations of the debtor. However, the contract is generally considered to remain 'in effect'[17] while the non-debtor parties are bound to honor it and perform.[18]

30.44 A counterparty can file a motion to seek to compel an assumption or rejection of the contract but such relief is extremely difficult to obtain. 11 U.S.C. § 365(d)(2); *In re Physicians Health Corp.*, 262 B.R. 290 (Bankr.D.Del. 2001). Moreover, the counterparty's desire for certainty or for payment of unpaid prepetition amounts as a 'cure cost' is generally not compelling to a bankruptcy court, which is typically more focused on the bankruptcy estate's attempt to reorganize or sell its assets. Bankruptcy courts reviewing the trustee or the debtor in possession's decision to assume or reject an executory contract will examine the contract and surrounding circumstances and apply the 'business judgment' standard to determine if it would be beneficial or burdensome to the estate, without consideration to the non-debtor counterparty to the contract.

---

15 In Chapter 11, debtor may assume or reject lease at any time before confirmation of plan but court may, on request of the non-debtor party, order debtor to determine within specified period of time whether to assume or reject the contract. *In re Lionel Corp.* (1983, BC SD NY) 29 BR 694, 10 BCD 611.

16 'Exactly how and when executory contracts come into the estate has been the source of continuing controversy and progressive development. One view, the exclusionary analysis, holds that executory contracts remain outside the estate prior to assumption. The competing view is that they enter the estate initially, but are thereafter subject to abandonment via rejection.' *In re Drexel Burnham Lambert Group, Inc.*, 138 B.R. 687, 701 (Bankr. S.D.N.Y. 1992).

17 See *In re Modern Textile, Inc.*, 900 F.2d 1184, 1191 (8th Cir. 1990) (executory contracts are 'an existing and continuing legal obligation of the debtor' subject to rejection); *In re Thomas Co., Inc.*, 166 B.R. 677 (Bankr. C.D. Ill. 1994) (executory contract remains in existence until rejected).

18 The non-debtor counterparty to an executory contract is obligated to perform its obligations under the contract pending assumption, assignment, or rejection of that contract by the debtor. *In re Leslie Fay Companies, Inc.*, 166 B.R. 802 (Bankr.S.D.N.Y. 1994).

Claims for damages based on the unassumed and unrejected contract may be entitled to an administrative expense priority.[19] 30.45

An executory contract which is not assumed or rejected during the bankruptcy will be unaffected by the bankruptcy filing, will pass through to, and be binding upon, the reorganized debtor.[20] 30.46

Assumption

A debtor may assume an executory contract by: 30.47

- Obtaining an order from the bankruptcy court permitting assumption of such contract after notice and an opportunity for the non-debtor counterparty to be heard in the bankruptcy court, or
- Confirming a plan of reorganization, which provides for assumption of such contract upon the effective date of the confirmed plan.[21]

If a contract is assumed, the debtor reaffirms its obligations under the agreement and must then continue to perform the contract as written. The contract is assumed in its entire entirety and with all the relevant burdens. If an executory contract is in default at the time the debtor seeks to assume the contract, assumption will not be permitted unless all monetary defaults are promptly cured, and adequate assurance of future performance of the debtor's obligations under the contract is provided. 30.48

Any breach of or liability under the assumed contract constitutes an administrative expense claim which is generally entitled to be paid in full. 30.49

---

19 *In re Bridgeport Plumbing Prods., Inc.*, 178 B.R. 563 (Bankr. M.D. Ga. 1994) (creditor may file an administrative expense claim for the 'reasonable value of the use' of the creditor's property during the gap period); *In re Sharon Steel Corp.*, 161 B.R. 934, 937 (Bankr. W. D. Pa. 1994).

20 *In re Polysat, Inc.*, 152 B.R. 886, 890 (Bankr. E.D. Pa. 1993); *International Union v. Miles Mach. Co.*, 34 B.R. 683, 687 (E.D. Mich. 1982) (collective bargaining agreement which is ignored during bankruptcy survives confirmation and is binding upon the debtor); *Matter of Central Watch, Inc.*, 22 B.R. 561, 565 (Bankr. E.D. Wis. 1982.

21 In bankructy proceedings, a plan of reorganization must be confirmed by the court. See *Board of County Comm'rs v. Coleman Am. Properties, Inc.* (*In re American Properties, Inc.*), 30 B.R. 239, 246 (Bankr. D. Kan. 1983) ('After confirmation of a chapter 11 plan, a creditor's lien rights are only those granted in the confirmed plan.'); 1 David G. Epstein et al., Bankruptcy 151 (1993) ('In a reorganization case, any of the preexisting liens that still survive will eventually die upon confirmation.'); 5 Collier on Bankruptcy, supra note 35, at 1141–11, 1141–12; David A. Lander and David A. Warfield, 'A Review and Analysis of Selected Post-Confirmation Activities in Chapter 11 Reorganizations', 62 *Am. Bankr. L.J.* 203, 205 (1988) ('If the plan makes no provision for any, ... lien, then the lien is cancelled. If the debt underlying any lien is discharged or cancelled, then that lien is automatically cancelled.'); cf. *Brady v. Andrew (In re Commercial W. Fin. Corp.)*, 761 F.2d 1329, 1334–8 (9th Cir. 1985) (confirmation order purporting to invalidate security interests of investors in debtor reversed for failure to accord investors procedural rights provided in Bankruptcy Rules).

Assignment

30.50 Upon assumption, the debtor may assign an executory contract to a third party provided there is adequate assurance of future performance by the assignee of the executory contract. It is the bankruptcy court that ultimately determines whether the proposed assignee meets the standards. Contractual limitations on the assignment of an executory contract are generally not enforceable in bankruptcy, with some exceptions. One such exception arises in contracts that are not assignable to third parties under applicable law and the party does not consent to such assumption or assignment.

Rejection

30.51 Rejection of an executory contract is essentially the debtor's declaration that it will not perform its remaining obligations under a contract under which performance remains due from each party. Upon rejection, the debtor is no longer bound to perform the remaining obligations of the contract, leaving the counterparty with the sole remedy of a breach of contract damage claim against the bankruptcy estate, which ordinarily will constitute a general prepetition unsecured claim, which often is paid only cents on the dollar. In addition, an executory contract cannot be rejected in parts and assumed in parts. In situations where the executory contract is found to form a part of a series of related agreements (which may be difficult to prove), all the agreements will be deemed to constitute a single integrated transaction, requiring that all of such agreements either be assumed or rejected as a group.[22]

C. REFORM PROPOSALS[23]

30.52 In light of the expansion of the use of unsecured credit, the growth of distressed-debt markets, and other externalities that have affected the effectiveness of the Bankruptcy Code, in 2012, the American Bankruptcy Institute formed a Commission (the 'Commission') to examine and propose reforms to chapter 11.[24] In 2014, the Commission released a 400-page report (the

22 *In re Atlantic Computer Systems, Inc.*, 173 B.R. 844 (S.D.N.Y. 1994); *In re Grede Foundries, Inc.*, 440 B.R. 497 (Bankr.W.D.Wis. 2010).

23 In 2017, In 2017, the Judicial Conference Committee on Rules of Practice and Procedure approved publication of proposed amendments to Bankruptcy Rules 2002, 4001, 6007, 9036, 9037, and Official Form 410. The comment period opened in August 2017, and closes February 15, 2018.

24 Founded on Capitol Hill in 1982, the American Bankruptcy Institute ('ABI') is the only multidisciplinary, nonpartisan organization devoted to the advancement of jurisprudence related to problems of insolvency. The ABI membership includes more than 13,000 attorneys, bankers, judges, accountants, professors, turnaround specialists and other bankruptcy professionals, providing a forum for the exchange of ideas and information.

'Report') that included over 200 distinct proposals. The Commission's stated purpose was to propose recommendations that would better balance the goals of effectuating the effective reorganization of business debtors – with the attendant preservation and expansion of jobs – and the maximization and realization of asset values for all creditors and stakeholders.

As discussed, supra, courts traditionally have used what is commonly referred to as the 'Countryman' definition of executory contracts.[25] This test was developed by Professor Vern Countryman, and defines an executory contract for bankruptcy purposes as 'a contract under which the obligation of both the bankrupt and the other party to the contract are so far unperformed that the failure of either to complete performance would constitute a material breach excusing the performance of the other.'[26] Although widely used, courts have recognized limitations and potential inconsistencies in the application of the Countryman test.[27] In addition, the test may not be a good fit for certain kinds of contracts, such as options and rights of first refusal; restrictive covenants (covenants not to compete; restrictive covenants on land); oil and gas agreements (e.g., the oil and gas leases themselves and variations thereof, like farmout agreements; and related agreements, like surface use agreements and joint operating agreements); licenses, distributor agreements, and trademark agreements; warranties; rights of first refusal; employment contracts; and severance agreements; arbitration clauses; forum selection clauses; distributor agreements; trademark agreements; and indemnity clauses; and settlement agreements.[28] 30.53

ABI was founded to provide Congress with unbiased testimony and research on insolvency issues. *See* http://commision.abi.org.

25 See, e.g., *In re Baird*, 567 F.3d 1207, 1211 (10th Cir. 2009); *In re Columbia Gas Sys., Inc.*, 50 F.3d 233, 239 (3d Cir. 1995); *In re Streets & Beard Farm P'ship*, 882 F.2d 233, 235 (7th Cir. 1989); *Lubrizol Enters., Inc. v. Richmond Metal Finishers, Inc.*, 756 F.2d 1043, 1045 (4th Cir. 1985); *In re Select-A-Seat Corp.*, 625 F.2d 290, 292 (9th Cir. 1980).

26 Vern Countryman, 'Executory Contracts in Bankruptcy: Part I' (1973) 57 *Minn. L. Rev.* 439, 460.

27 See, e.g., *In re Gen. Dev. Corp.*, 84 F.3d 1364, 1374 (11th Cir. 1996); *In re RoomStore Inc.*, 473 B.R. 107, 111–12 (Bankr. E.D. Va. 2012).

28 See, e.g., *Water Ski Mania Estates Homeowners Ass'n v. Hayes (In re Hayes)* (2008) Bankr. LEXIS 4668, at *31–32 (B.A.P. 9th Cir. Mar. 31, 2008) ('[A] lthough restrictive covenants contain the characteristics of both a contract and an interest in land, the primary nature of such covenants is preservation of a land interest, not future duties in contract. Although there will almost always be some incidental continuing obligations under a restrictive covenant, those duties were not the kind of obligations Congress intended to impact in enacting § 365.') (citation omitted); *Frontier Energy, LLC v. Aurora Energy, Ltd. (In re Aurora Oil & Gas Corp.)*, 439 B.R. 674, 680 (Bankr. W.D. Mich. 2010) ('The court's conclusion that the [oil and gas leases] qualify as "leases" within the meaning of Section 365 makes it unnecessary to consider whether the [oil and gas leases] meet either the functional test or Countryman definition for executory contracts. Given the confusion in the case law, it is also improvident to opine on the question.') (citations omitted); *In re Bergt*, 241 B.R. 17, 29–31 (Bankr. D. Alaska 1999) (discussing the application of the Countryman test in recent case law to options); *Bronner v. Chenoweth-Massie, P'ship (In re Nat'l Fin. Realty Trust)*, 226 B.R. 586, 589 (Bankr. W.D. Ky. 1998) ('The contingent nature of the obligations arising from an option agreement make them quite

30.54 Given the noted flaws in the Countryman test, courts have developed alternative approaches to assess executoriness, such as the 'functional approach' and 'exclusionary approach,' discussed supra. The Commission conducted an in-depth review of the literature and case law on executoriness under the Bankruptcy Code. The Report, released in 2014, notes the experience of the Commissioners with litigation concerning the executoriness issue and the attendant uncertainty and expense.[29] The focus of the executoriness inquiry is whether each party has significantly unperformed obligations under the contract. The Commissioners discussed examples of contracts when this issue may be of particular concern, such as options, covenants not to compete, and oil and gas leases. Although executoriness is not necessarily a bright-line determination, the Commissioners generally agreed that courts typically resolve this issue fairly or that parties have historically been able to negotiate a resolution.

30.55 The Report further notes that the Commission also considered the possibility of eliminating the concept of executoriness from the Bankruptcy Code. Both the advisory committee and the 1997 NBRC endorsed this position.[30] The Commissioners debated at length the potential utility to this approach. They discussed the meaningful benefits to refocusing contract disputes on the merits of the proposed assumption or rejection rather than extensive litigation on executoriness. The Commissioners supporting this approach emphasized the value to such a clean solution: with the distraction of executoriness off the table, parties could devote more attention on their rights, obligations, and remedies under the contract. Many Commissioners found the simplicity of this approach attractive.

30.56 The Report goes on to note, however, that further deliberations about the elimination proposal revealed the potential of unintended consequences of such a dramatic shift in a fundamental bankruptcy principle. The Commissioners noted the common law origins of the executoriness requirement of section 365, and they perceived value in maintaining some type of gating feature to vet those contracts that a debtor in possession could assume, assign, or reject in the chapter 11 case. Thus, the Commission concluded that

---

distinguishable from the typical contract. This distinction has puzzled many courts, resulting in two distinct lines of cases. The first line of cases, while recognizing the contingent nature of the obligations arising under option agreements, and while also expressly acknowledging that they are unilateral contracts until exercised, have nevertheless engaged in what could be described as analytical gymnasts to arrive at a finding that they are nonetheless executory contracts.') (citations omitted).

29 The full report is available at www.abi.commission.org.

30 See NBRC Report, supra note 37, at 21 ('Title 11 should be amended to delete all references to 'executory' in section 365 and related provisions, and 'executoriness' should be eliminated as a prerequisite to the trustee's election to assume or breach a contract.').

elimination of the executoriness concept could simply shift, rather than reduce, the amount of litigation or uncertainty in the first instance under section 365. Moreover, many Commissioners believed that the assumption or rejection decision was largely irrelevant to contracts that have already been fully performed by at least one of the parties.

The Commissioners also discussed the functional approach to determining executoriness, but most perceived the test to be unfair toward counterparties and too heavily weighted in favor of the interests of the debtor and the estate. The Commissioners acknowledged the potential value of allowing a debtor in possession to assume or reject any contract that would provide a benefit to the estate. As with the elimination proposal, however, the Report notes that the Commissioners were concerned about diminishing the rights of the non-debtor counterparties under the contracts. The Commission found that subjecting any contract to section 365 primarily, if not solely, for the benefit of the estate imposed a greater burden on non-debtor parties than necessary to achieve a fair result for the estate in a chapter 11 case. **30.57**

Given the foregoing considerations, the Commission voted to adopt the Countryman test and to recommend its express incorporation into the Bankruptcy Code. The Commission found that, although imperfect, the Countryman test strikes an appropriate balance between the rights of debtors in possession and non-debtor counterparties to a contract. If the parties have material unperformed obligations, it is fair and reasonable to allow a debtor to choose to assume, assign, or reject such an agreement under section 365. The Commission also determined that many of the potentially challenging issues under the Countryman test have been resolved by the courts and that this case law is a valuable resource that would guide the implementation of the codified standard. **30.58**

Critics of the Report argued that it is based on anecdote unsupported by data or rigorous academic work. In response, at least one special interest organization – the Loan Syndications and Trading Association (LSTA) – released a contrary report (the 'LTSA Report') with a different set of recommendations.[31] The LSTA Report asserts that the consensus of modern empirical studies is that the United States' bankruptcy system is functioning well and there is no basis for extensive reform. In the view of the LTSA, many of the reforms proposed by the Commission that narrow secured creditors' rights would do more harm than good, to both the bankruptcy process and the **30.59**

31 Realsed in October of 2015, available at http://www.lsta.org/uploads/DocumentModel/1860/file/lsta-abi-10615-final.pdf.

broader credit markets and would result in reduced availability and higher costs for corporate credit. The LSTA Report argues that the reforms will increase the costs of secured credit, while reducing the availability thereof. It also contends that chapter 11 cases will last longer and will be more complicated and expensive, thereby reducing recoveries to all creditors. The LSTA Response further argues that the ABI Commission Report, by proposing to scale back chapter 11's existing protections for secured creditors, undermines one of the conceptual foundations of the Bankruptcy Code – namely, that of maximizing the value of enterprises and the distribution of that value in accordance with no bankruptcy priorities. The LSTA was particularly concerned that, without a response, the Report might be used to change bankruptcy practice in ways that could undermine the position of secured lenders to the detriment of the loan markets generally.

30.60 LTSA's concerns appear to be largely unfounded, however, as no legislative action has been taken regarding the Report's proposals in the two years since its release. In fact, while the Commission proposals were structured to be adopted as amendments to the current Bankruptcy Code, there appears to be no appetite on Capitol Hill for corporate bankruptcy reform. Indeed, the Judiciary Committees of both the House and Senate have largely ignored the Report; no hearings have been scheduled since the publication of the Report to discuss its findings and none have been scheduled. In light of the lack of response, the Commission appears to have pivoted to a different strategy, urging that its proposals should, where possible, be adopted unilaterally by bankruptcy judges in individual cases without legislation and that others be adopted by courts as best practices applicable more broadly.

30.61 Courts have also been slow to respond, however. Just eight cases in the past two years have directly cited the Report, and the author was unable to locate any decision discussing in detail the Report's recommendation regarding the codification of the Countryman test. There also seems to be little new academic support for the Commission's view of the role of secured creditor in recent empirical studies. While companies are entering bankruptcy more levered than they were decades ago, and fewer companies go through a traditional restructuring, recent studies suggest that these changes may be less the product of overbearing secured creditors than the unintended side-effects of the 2005 amendments to the code. A recent study by Kandarp Srinivasan, Did Bankruptcy Reform Contribute to the Rise in Structured Finance? shows how BAPCPA's expansion of the safe harbors led to a flash flood of securitization, which in turn created many of the assets that proved most toxic in the Great Recession.[32] Also looking at the impact of BAPCPA, Ken Ayotte has found that the changes to Section 365(d)(4), which shortened the amount of time that debtors have to accept or reject leases, significantly lower[s the] probability of reorganization for the most lease-intensive firms.[33] Both studies suggest that any changes to the Bankruptcy Code can have profound and swift consequences for our economy. Only time will tell what, if any, effect the Commission recommendations will have on Chapter 11.

D. CONCLUDING REMARKS

The Bankruptcy Code attempts to empower the trustee or the debtor in possession to take advantage of the rights and assets of the bankruptcy estate. The power to assume or reject executory contracts constitutes a pivotal power in restructuring insolvency procedures. Thus, Section § 365, as construed and interpreted by the Federal Courts, provides more protection to the bankruptcy estate than to the non-debtor party which has limited protection. **30.62**

32 Available at, https://papers.ssrn.com/sol3/papers.cfm?abstract_id=2814717&download=yes.

33 Ken Ayotte, 'Leases and Executory Contracts in Chapter 11' (2015) 12 *Journal of Empirical Legal* Studies 637, 640.

PART III

HYBRID LEGAL SYSTEMS

31

NATIONAL REPORT FOR CANADA

Alfonso Nocilla

A. INTRODUCTION

Canada possesses a bifurcated commercial insolvency system. Insolvent corporations with over $5 million in debt may file for protection under the Companies' Creditors Arrangement Act[1] (CCAA). In addition, Part III of the Bankruptcy and Insolvency Act[2] (BIA) permits insolvent debtors to reorganize themselves by making a proposal to their creditors. Both regimes are court-supervised in varying degrees and permit the debtor to remain in possession of its assets and affairs while carrying out the reorganization. The below discussion briefly summarizes the evolution and key features of each regime. **31.01**

(1) Overview of CCAA restructuring

Parliament enacted the CCAA in 1933 as a response to the many business failures during the Great Depression. At that time, no formal method existed for insolvent companies to reorganize themselves and avoid bankruptcy. Although the Bankruptcy Act of 1919[3] permitted reorganization, the process was only available to bankrupt companies. In addition, the trust deeds of many Canadian companies did not contain clauses permitting reorganization with **31.02**

1 RSC 1985, c C-36.
2 RSC 1985, c B-3.
3 9–10 Geo V, Can S 1919, C 36.

the consent of the debenture holders. As a result, many insolvent companies had no formal or informal methods of reorganizing themselves prior to entering bankruptcy proceedings, at which point it was often too late to effect a successful reorganization.[4] Accordingly, as stated in the CCAA's purpose clause, the Act was designed to 'facilitate compromises and arrangements between companies and their creditors.' The structure of the Act reflects this purpose – the provisions of the Act contemplate that the debtor will negotiate and develop 'a plan of arrangement', i.e., a reorganization plan, which the debtor will ultimately present to its creditors for their approval.

31.03 A debtor seeking CCAA protection must meet several threshold requirements. First, the debtor must be a 'company' within the meaning of the Act. That is, it must be a Canadian or foreign incorporated company or income trust having assets or doing business in Canada, other than a bank, railway, telegraph or insurance company, or a company to which the Trust and Loan Companies Act applies.[5] Notably, although the language of the Act limits its application to corporations, courts have extended 'CCAA' protection to partnerships in certain cases as well.[6] Secondly, the debtor must be a 'debtor company', meaning a company that (a) is bankrupt or insolvent, (b) has committed an act of bankruptcy within the meaning of the 'BIA' or is deemed insolvent under the Winding-Up and Restructuring Act[7] ('WURA'), (c) has made an assignment or been subject to a bankruptcy order under the BIA, or (d) is being wound up under the WURA.[8] Thirdly, the debtor and its affiliates, if any, must have aggregate debts of more than $5 million.[9]

31.04 With respect to the requirement that the debtor be insolvent, it is important to note that the CCAA does not contain a definition of 'insolvency'. The definition of 'debtor company' under the CCAA refers to the test under the BIA. Accordingly, a debtor will be deemed insolvent if it meets the definition in the BIA, namely, that it is insolvent according to either a cash flow or balance sheet test. Even if a debtor is not deemed to be insolvent within the meaning of the BIA, however, it may still qualify for CCAA protection if the

4 House of Commons, Study Committee on Bankruptcy and Insolvency Legislation, *Report of the Study Committee on Bankruptcy and Insolvency Legislation* (June 1970, Chair: Roger Tassé), 1.2.19. See also Alfonso Nocilla, 'The History of the Companies' Creditors Arrangement Act and the Future of Restructuring Law in Canada' (2014) 56 *CBLJ* 73, 74.

5 CCAA (n 1) s 2(1); Trust and Loan Companies Act, SC 1991, c 45.

6 A partnership cannot apply for a CCAA order but the court can extend protection to a partnership that is affiliated with a CCAA corporation, see *Lehndorff General Partner Ltd (Re)* [1993], 17 CBR (3d) 24 (Ont Gen Div [Commercial List]).

7 RSC 1985, c W-11.

8 CCAA, s 2(1).

9 CCAA, s 3(1).

court determines that the debtor is insolvent based on a 'contextual and purposive interpretation' of the definition.[10] Specifically, CCAA courts will consider factors such as whether the debtor is facing a liquidity crisis which would cause it to run out of money if the CCAA order were not granted. While this would not permit the debtor to file under the BIA, it would permit the debtor to pursue a restructuring under the CCAA. The rationale for this approach is straightforward: a debtor should not be forced to wait until it is in its financial 'death throe[s]', that is, when bankruptcy is imminent, before filing for CCAA protection because the CCAA is remedial legislation designed to prevent bankruptcy.[11]

The CCAA process is initiated when an insolvent debtor, its trustee in **31.05**
bankruptcy, liquidator or creditors file an initial application for protection with the court.[12] In practice, the court will typically grant the protection order, which will include a stay of proceedings not to exceed 30 days, during which time a 'comeback hearing' will be held for any objecting creditors. The primary purpose of the stay is to maintain the status quo among the creditors and provide the debtor with breathing space to reorganize.[13] To that end, the initial order will also authorize the debtor to appoint a monitor, that is, a licensed insolvency professional who will supervise and assist the debtor in preparing the reorganization plan.[14] Notably, the debtor remains in control of its assets and affairs during this process, provided however that the monitor files regular reports on the debtor's progress toward developing and implementing a plan. The debtor may apply for one or more extensions of the CCAA stay while it negotiates with its creditors and develops the plan. The court will typically grant such extension requests provided that the debtor has made progress in developing its plan and the creditors do not object.[15] Having developed a plan, the debtor must then present it to the creditors for their approval. The threshold for creditor approval is a majority in number representing two-thirds of the value of debt held by each class, calculated based on the voting creditors.[16] If the creditors approve the plan, the debtor must then apply to the court for final sanction before implementing it. In particular, the

---

10 *Stelco Inc, (Re)* [2004] 48 CBR (4th) 299 para 40.

11 Ibid., paras 13 and 14, citing *Cumberland Trading Inc (Re)* [1994] 23 CBR (3d) 225 (Ont Gen Div), 228.

12 CCAA (n 1) ss 4–5. The application must include a projected cash-flow statement and copies of financial statements prepared in the past year.

13 See *Century Services Inc v Canada (Attorney General)* [2010] SCC 60 para 14.

14 The role of the monitor is unique to the CCAA and has evolved considerably over time. Legally, the monitor is an officer of the court and is responsible for reporting to the court on the debtor's progress in preparing and implementing a reorganization plan.

15 CCAA (n 1) s 11.02. See also Anthony Duggan and others, *Canadian Bankruptcy and Insolvency Law: Cases, Text and Materials* (3rd edn, Emond Montgomery 2015) 631–5.

16 CCAA (n 1) ss 4–6. The provisions dealing with the classification of creditors for the purposes of voting are contained in s 22.

court must be satisfied that the following requirements are met before the court exercises its discretion to sanction the plan:[17]

1) there must be strict compliance with all statutory requirements and adherence to the previous orders of the court;
2) all materials filed and procedures carried out must be examined to determine if anything has been done or purported to be done which is not authorized by the CCAA; and
3) the plan must be fair and reasonable.

31.06 With respect to the third requirement, Canadian courts have long recognized that a reorganization plan is a compromise among the various creditors of the insolvent debtor and that this necessarily means that certain of the creditors' claims will be compromised under the plan:[18]

> In insolvency restructuring proceedings, almost everyone loses something. To the extent that creditors are required to compromise their claims, it can always be proclaimed that their rights are being unfairly confiscated and that they are being called upon to make the equivalent of a further financial contribution to the compromise or arrangement. Judges have observed on a number of occasions that CCAA proceedings involve 'a balancing of prejudices', inasmuch as everyone is adversely affected in some fashion.

31.07 The question for the CCAA judge, therefore, is whether the plan treats all creditors fairly, equitably and reasonably. Importantly, in conducting this analysis, the CCAA judge will not second guess the business judgment of the parties with respect to the business aspects of the plan. Rather, the role of the CCAA judge is to 'look at the creditors as a whole (i.e. generally) and to the objecting creditors (specifically) and see if rights are compromised in an attempt to balance interests … as opposed to a confiscation of rights'.[19]

31.08 The foregoing summary illustrates the heavily court-driven nature of the CCAA process. The CCAA is often praised as a highly sophisticated tool for resolving complex insolvencies because of the Act's flexibility. However, this flexibility also imposes costs on the parties in terms of the uncertainty generated by the process and the need for frequent court appearances. At times, these costs can be prohibitive, particularly for small and mid-sized

---

17 *Sammi Atlas Inc, Re* [1998] 3 CBR (4th) 171 (Ont Gen Div) para 2.

18 *Metcalfe v Mansfield Alternative Investments II Corp, (Re)* [2008] ONCA 587 para 117.

19 Ibid., para 4.

debtors.[20] As discussed immediately below, the BIA commercial reorganization process, though less flexible than the CCAA, is also a more streamlined and cost-effective process.

(2) Overview of BIA commercial proposals

Part III, Division I of the BIA permits an insolvent debtor, liquidator, trustee or receiver to file a proposal with the court. Like a CCAA plan, the proposal is an agreement between the debtor and its creditors to compromise certain of the debtor's financial obligations. In practice, the BIA reorganization process typically is initiated when a debtor files a notice of intention to make a proposal (NOI). Whether an NOI or a proposal is filed, the filing triggers an automatic 30-day stay of proceedings effective against all secured and unsecured creditors, with some exceptions.[21] At the same time, a trustee must be appointed to serve as a monitor of the debtor's business and financial affairs for the benefit of the creditors. Within ten days of filing the NOI, the debtor must file a cash flow statement showing its projected cash flow on at least a monthly basis and which the trustee has reviewed for reasonableness.[22] The debtor has 30 days from filing the NOI to file its proposal, failing which the debtor is automatically assigned into bankruptcy. Alternatively, the debtor can apply to the court for one or more extensions of time not to exceed 45 days each, up to a maximum of six months following the filing of the NOI.[23] Once the proposal is filed, the creditors vote on it.[24] In order for the proposal to succeed, it must be approved by a majority of the creditors in each class present and voting at the creditors' meeting and representing at least two-thirds of the value of the claims in each class.[25] **31.09**

The BIA commercial proposal process is more rigid than the CCAA process in several ways. First, as noted above, whereas in principle the CCAA process can be extended indefinitely, BIA reorganizations end automatically after six months. Secondly, the requirements for granting an extension in a BIA reorganization are somewhat stricter than under the CCAA. Specifically, **31.10**

20 See generally Paul Goodman and Anna Lund, 'Concerns of Insolvency Professionals – Small and Medium Size Enterprises' in Janis Sarra (ed) *Annual Review of Insolvency Law 2011* (Carswell 2012).

21 BIA (n 2) s 69. Certain Crown claims are exempt under s 69.1. Furthermore, the stay will not apply to secured creditors who exercised their right to seize collateral prior to the filing or who served an enforcement notice under s 244 more than ten days before the NOI or proposal was filed.

22 Ibid., s 50.4(1).

23 Ibid., s 50.4(9).

24 Pursuant to s 54(2), creditors are entitled to vote if they have proven claims and, in the case of secured creditors, only if the proposal affects their secured claims. Crown claims under the *Income Tax Act*, *Canada Pension Plan* and *Employment Insurance Act* can be voted, but pursuant to s 54(2.1), rank as unsecured claims.

25 Ibid., s 54(2)(d).

the court must be satisfied that the debtor: (a) has acted and is acting in good faith and with due diligence, (b) would likely be able to make a viable proposal if the extension were granted, and (c) no creditor would be materially prejudiced if the extension were granted.[26] Thirdly, if the creditors reject the proposal, the debtor is automatically assigned into bankruptcy.[27] In contrast, if the creditors reject a CCAA plan, the court is permitted to extend the stay upon request so that the debtor can negotiate and prepare a new plan. Accordingly, although the BIA process provides a more streamlined approach to reorganization, and the costs of the process are correspondingly lower than CCAA restructuring, the BIA process is stricter and less suited to very large, complex insolvencies.

(3) Receivership, liquidation and out-of-court procedures

31.11 Although the CCAA and the BIA proposal process are the most commonly used procedures for commercial insolvency reorganization, additional procedures are available. One or more receiver can be appointed to take possession of an insolvent debtor's assets and affairs, both privately and by court order under the BIA upon the request of a secured creditor.[28] In principle, receivership can be used to effect a reorganization of the debtor, but in practice receivership tends to result in the liquidation of the insolvent debtor. In such cases, or where a reorganization fails, the BIA contains detailed provisions for the liquidation of the debtor's assets and distribution of the proceeds to the creditors. Informal restructurings are also possible and can take many forms, ranging from entirely private negotiations to private negotiations coupled with simultaneous receivership, CCAA and BIA proceedings. Lastly, the WURA also permits reorganization, however it is important to note that the WURA's application is restricted to certain types of financial institutions and has been used very rarely.

B. TREATMENT OF EXECUTORY CONTRACTS

(1) Disclaimer and assignment in BIA commercial reorganizations

31.12 Section 65.1 of the BIA provides that no person may terminate or amend any agreement with an insolvent debtor by reason only that the debtor is insolvent or that a NOI or proposal has been filed in respect of that debtor. This

26 Ibid., s 50.4(9).
27 Ibid., s 61(2)(b).
28 Ibid., s 243.

provision nullifies 'ipso facto' clauses in contracts with the insolvent debtor. In addition, section 65.11 permits the debtor, on notice to the other parties and with the trustee's approval, to disclaim or resiliate any agreement to which the debtor was a party on the date that the NOI or proposal was filed.[29]

There are limits on a debtor's ability to disclaim or resiliate contracts. First, objecting counterparties may, within 15 days after the debtor gives notice, apply to the court for an order prohibiting the disclaimer or resiliation.[30] In deciding whether to make the order, the court will consider the following non-exhaustive list of factors:[31] **31.13**

1) Whether the trustee approved the proposed disclaimer or resiliation;
2) Whether the disclaimer or resiliation would enhance the prospects of a viable proposal being made in respect of the debtor; and
3) Whether the disclaimer or resiliation would likely cause significant financial hardship to a party to the agreement.

Section 65.11(8) provides that if an agreement is disclaimed, a party to the agreement who suffers a loss has a provable claim against the debtor.[32] **31.14**

Secondly, certain types of contracts are excluded entirely. Specifically, a debtor cannot disclaim or resiliate: (1) intellectual property licenses, where the debtor is the licensor and so long as the licensees continue to perform their obligations; (2) collective bargaining agreements; (3) real property leases where the debtor is the lessor; (4) financing agreements if the debtor is the borrower; or (5) eligible financial contracts ('EFCs').[33] In addition, where the debtor is a commercial lessee of real property, section 65.2 provides that the debtor must give 30 days' notice before disclaiming, and the lessor may challenge the disclaimer within 15 days of receiving notice.[34] Among other **31.15**

29 Significantly, s 65.11 is limited to BIA commercial proposals. A trustee's ability to disclaim agreements in bankruptcy proceedings is subject to the common law and, in the case of leases, provincial landlord and tenant law.

30 Ibid., s 65.11(3).

31 Ibid., 65.11(5). There are no reported cases, as yet, applying these factors. However, it is reasonable to expect that courts will interpret and apply s 65.11(5) in much the same way as they have s 32(4) of the CCAA because these sections mirror each other. For an analysis in the CCAA context, see *Target Canada Co (Re)* [2015] ONSC 1028.

32 As with s 65.11(5), there are no reported cases applying this section yet. However, it should be noted that any claim for damages against the debtor, including pursuant to s 65.11(7), would rank as unsecured.

33 Ibid., ss 65.11(7) and 65.11(10). EFCs are defined in the Regulations as derivatives agreements, agreements to borrow, lend, clear, settle, or repurchase securities or commodities, margin loans, or any combination thereof, including master agreements, collateral agreements and guarantees or indemnities in relation to the foregoing types of agreements.

34 Ibid., ss 65.2(1) and (2).

things, the effect of the disclaimer is to nullify any accelerated rent clauses in the lease.[35] These provisions reflect the rights of landlords under provincial landlord and tenant legislation.[36]

31.16 Following amendments to the BIA in 2009, the Act also permits the assignment of contracts to which the debtor is a party.[37] Section 84.1 provides that on application by the trustee and on notice to the counterparties, the court 'may make an order assigning the rights and obligations of a bankrupt under the agreement to any person who is specified by the court and agrees to the assignment'. Again, EFCs and collective agreements cannot be assigned, nor can rights and obligations that are not assignable by their nature (i.e., contracts that are personal in nature) or contracts entered into on or after the date of bankruptcy.[38] Section 84.1(4) states that in deciding whether to make the order, the court must consider, among other things, whether the assignee is able to perform the obligations and whether it is 'appropriate to assign the rights and obligations to that person'.[39] The underlying purpose of section 84.1 is straightforward: the provision is aimed at preserving the value of the estate by allowing the assignment of contracts to third parties even where doing so would adversely affect the solvent counterparties.[40]

(2) Disclaimer and assignment under the CCAA

31.17 As under the BIA, ipso facto clauses in agreements to which the debtor is a party are nullified. But whereas the BIA explicitly nullified such clauses in section 65.1, the CCAA contained no such language prior to the 2009 amendments to the Act. Instead, courts typically included prohibitions on ipso facto clauses in the initial CCAA order.[41] This approach was codified in the new section 34 which, like section 65.1 of the BIA, prohibits the termination or amendment of agreements, including claims for accelerated payments or forfeiture of the term, by reason only of the debtor's insolvency or the commencement of proceedings. Accordingly, contracts that the debtor entered into prior to filing for CCAA protection typically remain in force unless the debtor disclaims them.

---

35 Ibid., s 65.2(4).

36 In Ontario, the relevant legislation is the Commercial Tenancies Act, RSO 1990, c L.7. In particular, ss 38 and 39 set out the right of a trustee to surrender or disclaim a lease.

37 The right to assign commercial leases existed prior to the 2009 amendments in virtue of ss 30(1)(k) and 146; the 2009 amendments created a statutory right in respect of all contracts.

38 Ibid., s 84.1(3).

39 The question of appropriateness must be considered from the perspective of the counterparties to the agreement, see *Ford Motor Company of Canada, Ltd v Welcome Ford Sales* [2011] ABCA 158.

40 Ibid., para 30.

41 See Duggan and others (n 15) 685.

Historically, CCAA courts exercised their broad discretion under section 11 of the Act (now section 11.02) to permit insolvent debtors to disclaim onerous contracts as part of the restructuring plan.[42] This approach was codified in the 2009 amendments that added section 32, which provides that an insolvent debtor may, on notice to its counterparties and with the monitor's approval, disclaim or resiliate any agreement to which the debtor is a party at the time of commencements of the CCAA proceedings. Section 32(2) provides that within 15 days after the debtor gives notice, an objecting counterparty may apply for a court order prohibiting any such disclaimer or resiliation. In addition, section 32(3) provides that if the monitor does not approve the proposed disclaimer or resiliation, the debtor may apply to the court for an order to disclaim or resiliate. Section 32(4) sets out a non-exhaustive list of factors that the court must consider in deciding whether to grant the order, which mirror the factors in section 65.11(5) of the BIA.[43] Section 32(7) provides that if an agreement is disclaimed, a party to the agreement who suffers a loss as a result of the disclaimer has a provable claim against the debtor.[44] **31.18**

Certain types of agreements are excluded from these disclaimer provisions. First, the disclaimer of intellectual property licenses in which the debtor is the licensor does not affect the licensee's right to continue using the intellectual property during the term of the agreement, so long as the licensee continues to perform its obligations under the agreement.[45] Secondly, EFCs, real property leases in which the debtor is the lessor, and financing agreements in which the debtor is the borrower are excluded entirely.[46] Section 34(8) permits certain actions with respect to EFCs, such as netting and setting off, provided that such actions are in accordance with the terms of the EFC. Thirdly, collective agreements are also excluded under section 32(9), and the new section 33 sets out the process by which a debtor may alter a collective agreement in CCAA proceedings. In particular, a court may only issue an order authorizing the debtor to serve a notice to bargain if the court is satisfied that:[47] **31.19**

(a) a viable compromise or arrangement could not be made in respect of the company, taking into account the terms of the collective agreement;

42 See *Dylex Ltd, Re* [1995] 31 CBR (3d) 106 (Ont Ct Gen Div).

43 For an example of how CCAA courts have interpreted and applied s 32(4), see *Target Canada Co* (n 31).

44 The amount of the claim need not be determined at the time of disclaimer, as the court will determine it later if necessary. However, the claim will rank as unsecured and the creditor is therefore unlikely to recover much, if at all. See *Aveos Fleet Performance Inc / Aveos Fleet performance aéronautique inc (Arrangement relatif à)* [2012] QCCS 6796 para 65.

45 CCAA (n 1) s 32(6).

46 Ibid., s 32(9).

47 Ibid., s 33(3). See also *White Birch Paper Holding Company (Arrangement relatif à)* (2010) QCCS 2590.

(b) the company has made good faith efforts to renegotiate the provisions of the collective agreement; and
(c) a failure to issue the order is likely to result in irreparable damage to the company.

31.20 With respect to commercial tenancy agreements, a notable difference between the CCAA and BIA regimes is that the CCAA does not impose limits on the amount a landlord may claim when a debtor disclaims a lease. Under both the BIA and CCAA, the disclaimer has the effect of giving the landlord a provable claim against the debtor. Section 65.2 of the BIA limits any such claims by nullifying accelerated rent clauses in leases. However, the CCAA contains no such provision and courts have held that section 65.2 of the BIA should not be read into the CCAA.[48] Accordingly, unlike under the BIA, there are no statutory provisions governing the valuation of landlords' claims in CCAA proceedings.[49]

31.21 In addition, the new section 11.3 also permits debtors to assign most types of agreements with court approval.[50] In deciding whether to permit the assignment, the court must consider the following non-exhaustive list of factors:[51]

(a) whether the monitor approved the proposed assignment;
(b) whether the person to whom the rights and obligations are to be assigned would be able to perform the obligations; and
(c) whether it would be appropriate to assign the rights and obligations to that person.

31.22 With the exception of (a), these factors mirror section 84.1(4) of the BIA.[52] Again, EFCs and collective agreements are excluded. As with section 84.1, the underlying purposes of section 11.3 of the CCAA are straightforward: the power to assign agreements for value is intended to assist the debtor with the restructuring while treating counterparties fairly and equitably.[53]

48 See *Alternative Fuel Systems Inc v Remington Development Corp* [2004] ABCA 31.
49 See Duggan and others (n 15) 677.
50 As with the power to disclaim, the power to assign does not apply to EFCs and collective agreements.
51 CCAA (n 1), s 11.3(3).
52 Under s 84.1, the trustee must apply directly to the court for the assignment, so there is no need to consider whether the trustee approved the proposed assignment.
53 See *Veris Gold Corp (Re)* [2015] BCSC 1204 para 58; *TBS Acquireco Inc. (Re)* [2013] ONSC 4663.

C. RECENT REFORMS

The current statutory framework is the result of two major reform efforts in 2005 and 2009. As part of amendments to the BIA and CCAA in 1998, Parliament included a requirement to review the legislation again within five years. That review culminated in the 2003 report of the Senate Committee on Banking, Trade and Commerce entitled *Debtors and Creditors Sharing the Burden* (Senate Report).[54] The Senate Report made wide-ranging recommendations for the reform of both the BIA and CCAA. The government proposed to adopt most of those recommendations in Bill C-55, which was given first reading in June of 2005.[55] With the upcoming election in October of that year, the government sought to rush the bill through Parliament without debate. The end result, as the Senate Committee acknowledged, was hastily drafted legislation that received inadequate review and commentary in the House and Senate.[56] The Senate agreed to pass Bill C-55 on the condition that revisions would be made as soon as possible. The election of a new government in October delayed the tabling of those revisions until June of 2007, with Bill C-62.[57] Subsequently, Parliament was prorogued and Bill C-62 died on the Order Paper. It was reintroduced as Bill C-12, which became Chapter 36 upon enactment, and came into force on September 18, 2009.[58] 31.23

The 2005 and 2009 reforms made wide-ranging and significant amendments to the BIA and CCAA. The key changes with respect to executory contracts were the additions of sections 65.11 and 84.1 of the BIA – the debtor's powers to disclaim and assign agreements, respectively – and corresponding provisions in sections 11.3 and 32 of the CCAA. As noted above, the amendments to the 31.24

---

54 Senate, Standing Committee on Banking, Trade and Commerce, Debtors and Creditors Sharing the Burden: A Review of the Bankruptcy and Insolvency Act and the Companies' Creditors Arrangement Act (November 2003, Chair: Richard H. Kroft).

55 An Act to establish the Wage Earner Protection Program Act, to amend the Bankruptcy and Insolvency Act and the Companies' Creditors Arrangement Act and to make consequential amendments to other Acts, 3 June 2005.

56 Senate Standing Committee on Banking, Trade and Commerce, 'Seventeenth Report' in *Official Report of Debates (Hansard)*, (24 November 2005) (noting the Senate 'had an inadequate opportunity to review comprehensively such an important piece of framework legislation'). See also Stephanie Ben-Ishai and Anthony Duggan, *Canadian Bankruptcy and Insolvency Law: Bill C-55, Statute c. 47 and Beyond, (LexisNexis 2007) 5.*

57 An Act to amend the Bankruptcy and Insolvency Act, the Companies' Creditors Arrangement Act, the Wage Earner Protection Program Act and chapter 47 of the Statutes of Canada, 2005, 13 June 2007.

58 An Act to amend the Bankruptcy and Insolvency Act, the Companies' Creditors Arrangement Act, the Wage Earner Protection Program Act and chapter 47 of the Statutes of Canada, 2005, 39th Parl, 1st Sess (27 October 2007).

CCAA largely codified existing practice by giving debtors the express statutory authority to disclaim and assign agreements that was previously contained in initial CCAA orders.

31.25 As noted, the amendments created exclusions for several types of agreements. Specifically, intellectual property licenses in which the debtor is a licensor, real property leases where the debtor is the lessor, collective bargaining agreements, and EFCs cannot be disclaimed or assigned. The Senate Report acknowledged that the exclusion of these types of agreements is an exception to the general principle that debtors should be permitted to disclaim and assign agreements where doing so would preserve value and enhance the prospects of a successful restructuring. In each case, the exclusion from the general rule reflects intense lobbying efforts by various groups. For example, both the Canadian Auto Workers and United Steelworkers of America argued that courts should not be permitted to use the broad authority afforded to them under the CCAA to disclaim collective agreements, as doing so 'would eliminate workers (sic) rights with the stroke of a pen and subvert the primacy of collective bargaining'.[59] The Canadian Labour Congress agreed, stating that employees are different from other types of creditors in that they 'are not in a position to assess the risks that they are required to bear ... [or] to guarantee their employer's obligation by way of a secured charge'.[60]

31.26 With respect to intellectual property licenses, the Intellectual Property Institute of Canada (IPIC) recommended, among other things, a time limit of three months on the exercise of the right of disclaimer where the debtor is the licensor and a right for licensees to elect to retain the licence despite the disclaimer.[61] In addition, the Writers' Union of Canada pointed out that the CCAA did not address copyright issues at all and that the BIA provided writers 'with very limited protection and often too late'.[62] The Writers' Union recommended that debtors not be permitted to assign copyright interests on the basis that 'the relationship between a writer and his or her publisher is personal; the writer would be permitted to make any alternative arrangements in the event of his or her publisher's insolvency'.[63]

31.27 The opinions of the leading professional associations, the Insolvency Institute of Canada and the Canadian Association of Insolvency and Restructuring

59 Senate Report (n 54) 134.
60 Ibid.
61 Ibid., 135.
62 Ibid., 136.
63 Ibid.

Professionals, were set out in the report of the Joint Task Force (JTF).[64] Although the JTF argued for a general right to disclaim all types of executory contracts in all bankruptcy and reorganization proceedings without the need for court approval, it also recommended the foregoing exclusions. With respect to EFCs, intellectual property licenses and real or personal property leases, the JTF recommended that where an insolvent debtor is the lessor of real or personal property or the licensor of intellectual property, the disclaimer should not affect the solvent counterparty's rights to maintain possession and use the leased or licensed property. The JTF reasoned that these exclusions would 'protect property entitlements that vest in [the counterparty] before the contract is disclaimed'.[65] For all other types of contracts, the JTF proposed that disclaimer should give counterparties an unsecured provable claim for damages against the debtor.[66]

The Senate Report said little about the foregoing recommendations. With respect to IPIC's recommendations, the Senate Report commented simply that 'there are a variety of unresolved issues related to the insolvency of a licensor or licensee in the context of an intellectual property licence' and urged further discussion among the relevant parties to resolve the issues raised by IPIC.[67] 31.28

Ultimately, the Senate Report recommended amendments permitting the disclaimer and assignment of all types of executory contracts subject to certain conditions. Specifically, with respect to disclaimers, the Senate Report recommended that the debtor should be required to establish 'inability or serious hardship in restructuring the enterprise without the disclaimer' and the counterparty should be permitted to file a claim for damages.[68] In addition, the Senate Report recommended that disclaimers of collective agreements should only be permitted where the debtor demonstrates that post-filing negotiations have been carried on in good faith and that 'the disclaimer is necessary in order to allow for a viable restructuring'.[69] As noted above, section 33 contains robust provisions dealing with the alteration of collective agreements which substantively adopt the Senate Report's recommendations. 31.29

64 *Report to Industry* Canada, Joint Task Force on Business Insolvency Law Reform (March 15, 2002). Online: <https://www.insolvency.ca/en/iicresources/resources/JTF_Report_ReformProposals_2002.pdf> (accessed September 8, 2017).

65 Ibid., 47.

66 Ibid.

67 Senate Report (n 54) 136.

68 Ibid., 137.

69 Ibid.

31.30 Regarding assignments, the Senate Report recommended permitting them only where 'the proposed assignee is at least as credit worthy as the debtor was at the time the contract was entered into; and the proposed assignee agrees to compensate the other party for pecuniary loss resulting from the default by the debtor or give adequate assurance of prompt compensation'.[70] Notably, the final versions of sections 11.3(3) of the CCAA and 84.1 of the BIA contained no such requirements, focusing instead on the broader questions of whether the assignee is able to perform the obligations under the contract and whether it is appropriate to assign the contract to them. The existing versions of sections 11.3 of the CCAA and 84.1 of the BIA, therefore, may well reflect the concerns of the Canadian Bankers Association that placing additional constraints on the debtor's ability to disclaim or assign contracts in insolvency 'can affect pre-insolvency contracting behaviour and may reduce credit availability'.[71] Accordingly, the current statutory provisions favour the goals 'of assisting the reorganization process ... while also treating a counterparty fairly and equitably'.[72]

31.31 The Senate Report summarized the underlying policy of the recommended amendments as follows:[73]

> More generally, the Committee supports the concept of permitting disclaimer of all executory contracts, since we believe that the flexibility to take this action increases the probability of successful reorganization and thereby – in some sense – a fresher, if not fresh, start for the business ... Nevertheless, disclaimer should only be allowed where certain conditions are met, including good faith attempts to negotiate mutually acceptable changes to the contract and serious hardship in restructuring without the disclaimer.
>
> [...]
>
> Moreover, the Committee is of the view that trustees, Court-appointed receivers and monitors should be able to assign executory contracts where doing so would enhance the value of the assets and, thereby, moneys available for distribution to creditors. We recognize that while this circumstance would not permit the co-contracting party to choose its commercial partner, we feel that if the co-contracting party is no worse off financially, it would suffer no prejudice.

70 Ibid., 138.
71 Ibid., 133.
72 *Veris Gold* (n 53) para 58.
73 Senate Report (n 54) 137–8.

The Senate Report further stated that permitting the assignment of agreements, in particular, would enhance the efficiency and effectiveness of the insolvency system.[74] 31.32

More recently, royal assent was given to Bill C-86,[75] which amends the CCAA and BIA so as to provide additional protection for licensees of intellectual property in various circumstances. In particular, the amendments provide that where an insolvent debtor sells intellectual property under the CCAA or in a BIA proposal, the sale will not affect the rights of third party licensees to continue using the intellectual property so long as the licensees continue to perform their obligations. 31.33

D. CONCLUDING REMARKS

Despite some asymmetries between CCAA restructurings and BIA commercial proposals, notably with respect to the valuation of landlords' claims when leases are disclaimed, the two procedures pursue the same underlying goals with respect to the disclaimer and assignment of executory contracts. Namely, both procedures aim to preserve value and enhance the chances of a successful reorganization by prohibiting ipso facto clauses and permitting debtors to disclaim and assign contracts while treating counterparties fairly and equitably. In these regards, the existing statutory framework is unremarkable insofar as it largely codifies longstanding practices in Canadian restructuring law. 31.34

74 Ibid.

75 A second Act to implement certain provisions of the budget tabled in Parliament on February 27, 2018 and other measures, 42nd Parl, 1st Sess (13 December 2018).

32

NATIONAL REPORT FOR CYPRUS

Anna Plevri

A. INTRODUCTION

32.01 The law governing the liquidation of companies is the Companies Law, Chapter 113,[1] which is almost a copy of the English Companies Law of 1948 and the Companies Regulations (Liquidations).[2] According to the fifth part of Chapter 113, which is relevant to the liquidation of companies, the liquidation can be executed, as provided in article 203, either by the court (compulsory liquidation)[3] or as a voluntary liquidation[4] or as a liquidation under the supervision of the court.[5,6]

32.02 The fifth part of Chapter 113 has recently been modified by law 63(I)/2015. Furthermore, Chapter 113 was also modified by law 62(I)/2015, which added the IVA part. This part, refers to the appointment of an examiner in companies. The procedure of liquidation of insolvent companies and of the appointment of the examiner, are discussed below.

1 Chapter 113 from now on.

2 For individuals, (but not for legal entities) who go bankrupt, the Bankruptcy Law, Chapter 5, applies and the Bankruptcy Regulations.

3 See A. Poiiti, *Companies Liquidation* (Larnaka, 2013) 14–35 (in Greek).

4 When, among other reasons, the court votes with an extraordinary resolution that the company cannot continue with its activities because of its liabilities, and therefore it must be liquidated.

5 When a resolution for the voluntary liquidation of the company has already been approved and the court decides that the voluntary liquidation will be continued but only under its supervision.

6 See Poiiti, (n 3), 8–9.

B. INSOLVENCY PROCEDURES

(1) Compulsory liquidation

According to article 211 case fifth of Chapter 113, a company may be liquidated by the court, among other reasons, if it is unable to pay its debts. It is noted that the word 'may', which existed in the English text, means that the court has the right and not the obligation to exercise the powers conferred upon by law. **32.03**

The notion of 'debt' includes any outstanding liability which is already overdue and remains to be paid. Article 212 (c) of Chapter 113 gives the courts discretion to take into account the potential and future liabilities of the company. Under this test, a company is thought to be unable to pay its debts when it is determined that the value of the company's assets is less than the sum of its liabilities, taking into account its potential and the future liabilities.[7] Under the company's liquidation, the actions taken by the liquidator, are designed to collect the owed sums, the payment of the debts and the receipt of any property to the beneficiaries. **32.04**

To be more specific, according to article 212 of Chapter 113,[8] a company is considered unable to pay its debts when: **32.05**

(1) A creditor, by assignment or otherwise, to whom the company owes an amount of money that exceeds € 5,000,[9] has legally serviced to the registered office of the company a notice demanding the payment of the amount owed and the company, for the following three weeks,[10] has failed to pay the sum, to secure it or to settle the dispute to the reasonable satisfaction of the creditor. The term 'creditor' does not include a person whose debt is under substantial controversy, even if the company is actually insolvent. Also, the term 'creditor' does not include a person who has an illiquid or otherwise not yet enforceable claim. Thus, if there is a substantial controversy on the existence of the debt, the liquidation petition must be rejected because the existence of the debt is uncertain. It is prudent for a lawsuit to be registered first in order to be determined whether there is real debt or not. In this context, the good-faith

7 This case was added by the modification of law 63(I)/2015.

8 As modified by law 63(I)/2015.

9 Before the modification of Chapter 113 with law 63(I)/2015, the amount of money which the company should owe would be over € 854.30.

10 Days are counted whole and the period starts from the next day of the delivering.

controversy of the existence of debt,[11] as well as the existence of a counterclaim from the company's side, is a defence for the company, in request for its liquidation.

(2) If an enforcement measure or another procedure taken by judicial decision, order or decree of any court for the benefit of a company's creditor, is returned wholly or partly unsatisfied. This failure to enforce a judicial order determines a rebuttable presumption of 'default'. As for the other cases falling within the scope of article 212, parties retain the right to submit any other evidence that reinstates or rebuts the default presumption.[12]

(3) If it is proven in court that the company is unable to pay its debts at the time when they are payable. In this case, a mere reference to the request for liquidation on the company's failure to pay its debts is not enough. In the context of weighting its general solvency, the parties have to produce a report on the overall situation of the company, taking into account all of its liabilities, including potential and future ones.

(4) If it is proven in court that the value of the company's assets is less than the amount of its liabilities, taking into account its potential and future liabilities.

32.06 As stated before, a company can be liquidated by the court, according to article 211, case fifth of Chapter 113. In compulsory liquidations, which are covered in this chapter, the territorially competent court is the district court located in the company's registered office[13] and either the chairman of the court or any senior provincial judge or provincial judge is responsible. Competence is allocated on the basis of the value of the company. The law grants the competence to wind up a company to the territorially competent court in the province (territory) where the company has a registered office, regardless of the fact that the company is free to carry on business activities through Cyprus.

Who can file for the winding up (liquidation) procedure?

32.07 Article 213 of Chapter 113 provides information about who may apply (together or separately) for liquidation of the company by the court.[14] In brief, an application may be submitted by:

---

11 *[2010] 1 Supreme Court of Cyprus Decisions 991 Antreas Chatzigiannis v. C. &J. Kyprianou Promotions Ltd.*

12 *[2009] 1 Supreme Court of Cyprus Decisions 1457 C. Phasarias (Automotive Centre) Ltd v. Leonik Company Ltd.*

13 According to Chapter 113, article 209 (1). In the frames of article 209 (2), the term 'registered office', refers to the place (locus) where the office of the company was registered for a period of six months before the submission of an application for liquidation.

14 See Poiiti (n 3) 36–53.

a) The company itself. For an application to be submitted by the company's consultants, it is required to be authorized by the general meeting of shareholders, before the registration of the application or decision of the general meeting which will act retroactively;
b) Any creditor, including potential or prospective claimants. The creditor of a company is the person who, due to legal transaction or tort, is entitled to receive any amount from the company. An application can also be submitted by the secured and the unsecured creditor. The secured creditor should also prove that without issuing a decree for liquidation, he will not be able to collect all or even part of his claim;
c) The contributor, under the conditions defined by the law. A 'contributor' is any person liable to contribute to the assets of the company in case of its liquidation;[15]
d) The official recipient,[16] whether it is a voluntary liquidation or a liquidation under court supervision;
e) The Administrator of another Member State, as defined in article 2 § b of the Council regulation (EC) No 1346/2000 on insolvency proceedings or a temporary administrator, who is appointed by the court of another Member State, according to article 38 of the aforementioned Regulation;
f) The examiner.

In practice, winding up applications are usually submitted by the company's creditors, most frequently by a bank. What can be noted as a disadvantage of the overall procedure, is its lengthy duration. It is also noted that in the Cypriot legislation there is no provision that assists extrajudicial direct negotiations or other out of court proceedings between the debtor and its creditors. **32.08**

The application for the liquidation of the company by the court is made by the registration of a certain type of application, which has a specific content.[17] In it, all facts and legal grounds which entitle the applicant to submit the application for the liquidation of the company must be reported and, among others, reference shall be made to the specific ground of Chapter 113 upon which the application is based. **32.09**

The notification of the application, stating the date of the hearing that is set, is issued as many times and in as many newspapers as the court orders; otherwise the application is rejected. This issuance is a prerequisite not provided for by law, but it has been established in the practice of the courts. The above **32.10**

15 The term 'contributor' is included in Chapter 113, article 204.
16 According to Chapter 113, article 222 subpara 1.
17 See Poiiti (n 3) 54–6.

issuance must not be misleading or confusing because in that case, the application will be rejected. The application for liquidation must necessarily be accompanied by an 'affidavit' of the applicant or by its lawyer or by the applicant's representative and must have a date prior to the date of the registration of the application.

32.11 In accordance with article 214 of Chapter 113 the court, during the hearing of a request for liquidation, can reject or postpone it. In any case, it will issue any interim order which it considers appropriate. The surcharge or mortgaging of the company's assets for amounts equal to their value, as well as when the company has no assets, are reasons for issuing a liquidation order. The court has the power to not issue a liquidation order, if it considers that there is another possible treatment and that the applicants are acting unjustifiably with their request for the dissolution of the company.

32.12 Upon registration of the application for liquidation and before the issuing of the liquidation order, the court may appoint a provisional liquidator to protect the company's assets and to maintain the company's status. The court may also appoint a solvency consultant as a provisional liquidator, according to article 227 of Chapter 113. The provisional liquidator shall exercise the powers which the court assigns.

Results of the company's liquidation and influence of the liquidation procedure on the company's property

32.13 The liquidation of the company by the court is considered to commence from the time of submission of the application for liquidation.[18] From this time, any seizure by a third party, escrowing, seizure or implementation against the property or objects of the company commenced after the beginning of the liquidation is invalid.[19] Furthermore, after the issuance of the decree of liquidation, which acts in the interests of all creditors and all the company's contributories, that is, as if it was issued after a joint application of creditor and contributor,[20] the following effects occur:

1) Any lawsuit that had already started against the company, before it entered into liquidation cannot continue, because this would result in

18 According to Chapter 113, article 218 (2). See Poiiti, ibid., 72.

19 Chapter 113, article 217.

20 Chapter 113, article 221.

providing privileged satisfaction to the creditor who started the procedure. Therefore, the lawsuit is suspended and the applicant may proceed to verify his claim to the liquidator.[21]

2) The commencement of new judicial procedures against the company is not allowed, absent any permission of the court.[22]
3) Any available property or company requirements, including conductive rights and any transfer of shares or change in the status of shares is invalid, unless the court orders something different.[23]
4) The employment of all employees of the company and the services of its directors is terminated immediately.

The liquidation order does not mean the liquidation of the company at the same time and it does not result on its own in the dissolution of the company, as a legal person, nor transfers the company's assets to the liquidator. **32.14**

After the issuing of a liquidation order,[24] which enters into effect retroactively (*ex tunc*) from the date of registration of the relevant application, a procedure begins by which the rights and the obligations of the company are settled, as the law requires. For the conduct of the liquidation, the court appoints a liquidator or liquidators, who must execute the duties imposed by the court. By issuing a liquidation order, the official receiver becomes a liquidator and not a provisional liquidator, as applied in the past. The official receiver remains the liquidator, unless another person is appointed as such.[25] The first duty of the official receiver is to hold separate meetings of creditors and contributories of the company so as to decide if any application will be submitted to the court for the appointment of another liquidator in the position of the official receiver. The creditors and the contributories may designate a person as liquidator in their respective meetings. The liquidator has a duty to ensure that the fact that the company is under liquidation appears in each and every invoice, order or letterhead issued by or on behalf of the company, so as to protect the people who deal with the company. **32.15**

Upon issuance of the liquidation order, the liquidator or the provisional liquidator, depending on the case, takes into his control or into his custody the whole property and enforceable rights that the company is or appears to be entitled to.[26] **32.16**

---

21 Chapter 113, article 220.
22 See Poiiti (n 3) 72–5.
23 Chapter 113, article 216.
24 See Poiiti (n 3)79–97.
25 Chapter 113, articles 222 and 228.
26 Chapter 113, article 231.

32.17 The creditors can verify their claims within the deadline specified by the court. The law itself does not actually provide guidance on the determination of this deadline, which is therefore very much in the discretion of the court. Despite that, article 251 (2a), (6) and (7) prescribes detailed intervals of time with reference to certain, necessary actions on behalf of the creditors.

32.18 The verification of the claims should be done in accordance with the Regulations on Liquidation of the Companies.[27] Of the company's assets, the secured creditors must be satisfied first, by the guarantee that has been allotted to them, provided that their rights are unaffected by the law.

32.19 Article 300 of Chapter 113 lists the privileged payments that have to be made by the bankruptcy estate. These payments mainly relate to local and government taxes. Taxes do not have priority over the secured creditors. Other priority claimants include employees for the arrears in their salaries and for contractual benefits. The employees' priority also extends to any amount due as a compensation for damages and to any amount owed to the employee as a day off from his employment by the company. These priority claimants (i.e., revenue collectors and employees) rank equally among themselves and shall be paid in full before any other debt is paid. If the company's assets are not enough to satisfy them, these debts are reduced in equal proportions.

32.20 As defined in article 239 A of Chapter 113, the forced (compulsory) liquidation should be completed within 18 months from its commencement. If the official receiver or the liquidator decides that the compulsory liquidation of the company cannot be completed within the statutory timeframe, he may request from the court an extension of the period of time.[28] In practice liquidation proceedings generally take several years to complete.[29] Furthermore, the official receiver, as the company's liquidator, may request from the court the early dissolution of the company, if the liquid assets of the company are insufficient to cover the liquidation costs, and the affairs of the company do not require further investigation.

27 Chapter 113, article 251.

28 According to Chapter 113, article 243 the court may, at any time upon issuance of the decree of liquidation, upon a relevant request and since it has been proven that any procedure relevant to the liquidation should be suspended or discontinued, issue a suspension order or shutdown of the procedure, either entirely or for a limited time under terms and conditions.

29 When it comes to voluntary liquidation, if it lasts longer than a year, separate annual meetings of members and creditors must be held within three months of each anniversary to consider the conduct of the liquidation and the liquidator's receipts and payments account, according to section 282 of Companies Law.

When all affairs of the company have been wound down, the court may, if the liquidator applies for this, issue an order for the dissolution of the company.[30] The order does not have retroactive effects, as it applies *ex nunc* (i.e., for the future). After the issuance of a dissolution decree, the company ceases to exist as a legal person and the duties of the liquidator cease, too. **32.21**

(2) Examinership

The mechanism provided in the law of examining companies ('examinership') aims at rescuing and restoring a company's business activity, maintaining in operation sustainable enterprises, and promoting both economic growth and job preservation. **32.22**

This mechanism was established by the recent law 62(I)/2015. According to this Act, the court has the power to appoint an examiner for the purposes of assessing the conditions of the company's affairs, where it judges that cumulatively: **32.23**

a) the company is most probably unable to pay its debts;[31]
b) there has been no approval and publication of any order on the company's liquidation on the Official Government Gazette of the Republic of Cyprus; and
c) no order has been issued for the liquidation of the company while there is a plausible perspective for its survival either as a whole, or for some of its financial/operative units.

No examiner can be appointed for credit institutions and insurance companies, whereas an associated company (i.e., a company part of the same group) can be designated as examiner. Courts have the discretion to appoint an examiner in cases where the company has been negotiating with its creditors for a renegotiation of its debt, or it has used the restructuring process provided for in the guidelines of the Central Bank. **32.24**

30 Chapter 113, article 260.

31 A company cannot pay its debts if: a) it cannot pay its debts within the time these become payable or the value of the assets of the undertaking are smaller than the amount of its liabilities, taking into consideration its possible and future liabilities or, b) if the creditor to whom the company owes more than € 5,000 has delivered a notice of demand in the registered office of the company, and the company for the following three weeks has neglected to pay the amount or to rectify it to the reasonable satisfaction of the creditor or, c) if an enforcement or any other process by court decision, order or decree by any court in the interest of a creditor of the company is returned wholly or partially unmet.

32.25 The application concerning the appointment of an examiner can be submitted, together or separately, by the company, by a certain possible or future creditor, or by any employee of the company. Members who own at least one-tenth of the paid-in capital conferring the right to vote at general meetings of the company and appointed guarantors for the obligations of the company also feature among the potential applicants. The application shall propose the appointment of a specific examiner,[32] and it should be backed by an expert witness, to prove that the statutory requirements are met.

32.26 The application shall cover specific aspects highlighted by the law, and it is accompanied by copies of the proposals for a compromise or a draft settlement in relation to the affairs of the company, if there are any. It is also accompanied by a report of an independent expert, who is either the company's auditor, or a person, who has the qualifications to be appointed as an auditor or examiner of the company.

32.27 The court does not decide on the application, without having first given the chance to hear the company's representatives or any creditor of the company who has expressed his request to be heard by the court on the subject matter.

32.28 Law 62(I)/2015, provides also for the adoption of interim relief measures. From the date of the filing to the decision on the admissibility of the examinership procedure, no liquidation process can be commenced against the company. Equally, seizures at the hands of a third party, sequestrations, and any other form of seizure or enforcement against the assets of the company are suspended, unless the examiner agrees on their continuation. Among the powers of the examiner are the convening of the general meetings of the board and the setting of the agenda and the general meetings of the company, entering in suggestions or resolutions and reporting to these meetings, as well as entering into agreements on claims against the company.

32.29 Upon appointment, the examiner draws up, as soon as possible, a proposal for a compromise or a draft settlement. The proposal is examined in a meeting of the members of the company or the creditors or any category of members or creditors invited to do so. The court, upon receiving the examiner's report and upon a hearing, may confirm, with or without amendments, or reject the proposals. If these proposals are confirmed by court, they are binding for the company, as well as for any creditor or third party affected by the proposal.

32 This person has to agree to this appointment.

C. TREATMENT OF EXECUTORY CONTRACTS

Neither in Chapter 113 as well as the Law of Contracts, known in the Cypriot law as Chapter 149,[33] is there any particular provision that deals with the treatment of executory contracts when one of the parties enters into liquidation, or an examiner is appointed. **32.30**

Pursuant to article 39 of the Law of Contract entitled 'Effect of refusal of party to perform promise wholly', it is generally provided that when a party to a contract becomes insolvent and fails to perform his part of the obligation (or declares that he will not perform), the counter-party may terminate the contract, unless he has signified, by words or conduct, his acquiescence in its continuance.[34] **32.31**

Thus, in the case of both liquidation and examinership, as processes implemented against insolvent companies, the aforementioned general provision applies, unless there is a relevant special provision which applies only to certain contracts. **32.32**

Additionally, explicit respective provision on termination of the contract, upon specific notification, in case of an order for the liquidation of the company as contracting party, can be provided for and is indeed provided for in practice, through contractual clauses. These are commonly known as *ipso facto* clauses, which under Cypriot law are valid and enforceable. **32.33**

In any case, any claim of the creditor against the debtor, even where linked to the non-performance or termination of an executory contract, should follow from now on the process of verification of each claim and whether they will be satisfied depends on the one hand on whether they are secured or not and on the other hand from the existing assets of the company. Furthermore, as provided for by article 298 of Chapter 113,[35] in every liquidation all debts **32.34**

33 This Law is interpreted according to the principles of legal interpretations prevailing in England and the expressions used in it are presumed to be used with the meaning given to them by the English law and are to be equally interpreted as long as this interpretation is not contrary to the content of the text and as long as no other notion is explicitly provided for.

34 This is the translation in English of the text of article 39, made by the author of the present report.

35 It is noted that according to Chapter 113, article 298B, in the winding up procedure of an insolvent company the same rules shall prevail and be observed with regard to the respective rights of secured and unsecured creditors and to debts provable and to the valuation of annuities and future and contingent liabilities as are in force for the time being under the law of bankruptcy with respect to the estates of persons adjudged bankrupt. Thus, all persons who in any such case would be entitled to prove for and receive dividends out of the assets of the company may come in under the winding up and make such claims against the company as they respectively are entitled to. The provisions of article 35 of the bankruptcy law shall apply by analogy in cases of debt set-off.

payable on a contingency, and all claims against the company, present or future, certain or contingent, ascertained or sounding only in damages, shall be admissible to proof against the company, a just estimate being made, so far as possible, of the value of such debts or claims as may be subject to any contingency or sound only in damages, or for some other reason do not bear a certain value.

32.35 Nevertheless, article 233 of Chapter 113 is relevant to the effect of company liquidation on contracts, in relation to the general powers and liabilities of the liquidator, which among others, provides that the liquidator shall have power, with the sanction either of the court or of the committee of inspection to make any compromise or arrangement with creditors or persons claiming to be creditors, or having or alleging themselves to have any claim, present or future, certain or contingent, ascertained or sounding only in damages against the company, or whereby the company may be rendered liable. The liquidator may also take any security for the discharge of any responsibility, as well as to sell the real and personal property and things in action of the company by public auction or private contract, with power to transfer the whole thereof to any person or company or to sell the same in parcels. The liquidator can also act and execute, in the name and on behalf of the company, all deeds, receipts and other documents, and for that purpose to use, when necessary, the company's seal and to draw, accept, make and endorse any bill of exchange or promissory note in the name and on behalf of the company, with the same effect with respect to the liability of the company as if the bill or note had been drawn, accepted, made or endorsed by or on behalf of the company in the course of its business. Finally, the liquidator can deal with all such other things as may be necessary for winding up the affairs of the company and distributing its assets. From the aforementioned it is stated that the liquidator has the power to enter into contracts for the company under liquidation for a wide range of contracts.

32.36 The liquidation influences any conveyance, charge, mortgage, delivery of goods, payment, execution or other act relating to property made or done by or against a company within six months before the commencement of its winding up which,[36] had it been made or done by or against an individual within six months before the presentation of a bankruptcy petition on which he is adjudged bankrupt, would be deemed in his bankruptcy a fraudulent preference, shall in the event of the company being wound up be deemed a

36 Any time period during which the company is under the protection of the court, is not taken into consideration.

fraudulent preference of its creditors and be invalid accordingly.[37] Additionally, any conveyance or assignment by a company of all its property to trustees for the benefit of all its creditors shall be void to all intents.

The influence of the insolvency process to a certain kind of contracts is located in case of appointment of an examiner to a company, for leasing contracts, as well as proposals for a compromise or a draft settlement may not include, without written consent of the tenant, provision for deletion or reduction of the amount of any rent or other periodic payment that is retained according to land leasing, which should be paid upon the date when the compromise or the draft settlement enters into force. **32.37**

Finally, insolvency affects, in the Cypriot law, the employment contracts[38] between an insolvent employer and his employees. Within this framework, law 25 (I) of 2001[39] for the protection of the employees' rights in case of insolvency of their employer, was established for the harmonization of the Cypriot law with the Directive 80/987/EEC relating to the protection of employees in the event of the insolvency of their employer and in particular in **32.38**

37 Where, in the case of a company wound up, anything made or done after the commencement of this Law is void under section 301 as a fraudulent preference of a person interested in property mortgaged or charged to secure the company's debt, then (without prejudice to any rights or liabilities arising apart from this provision) the person preferred shall be subject to the same liabilities, and shall have the same rights, as if he had undertaken to be personally liable as surety for the debt to the extent of the charge on the property or the value of his interest, whichever is the less.

38 Cypriot labour law contains statute law and common law rules. There is no actual definition of the employment contract in Cypriot law. See, A. Emilianides and Chr. Ioannou, *Labour Law in Cyprus, International Encyclopedia of Laws/Labour Law and Industrial Relations* (Wolters Kluwer Law International 2016) 141 (in English):

> A contract of employment is a contract and, as such, the conditions for its conclusion are gorerned by the provisions of the Contract Law, Cap.149, to the extent that there are no conflicting provisions in other specific legislation. Accordingly, a contract of employment may be either express or implied if the circumstances prove that the employee is actually employed by the employer despite the lack of an express agreement. No formality is required for the conclusion of the employment contract.

Cypriot law distinguishes between employees of the private and the public or semi public sector. The most typical categories of employment in Cyprus is an employment contract of indeterminate or indefinite duration. Other common categories of employment are fixed term (labour) contracts and part-time employment. A fixed term worker is defined in section 20 of Law 98(I)/2003. In addition, a relevant law is the Termination of Employment Law 24/1967. Employees are further classified by reference to their field of work and there is specific legislation governing cetegories of employees, such as hotel employees, shop employees, office employees etc. See further, Emilianides and Ioannou, ibid., 122–41 (in English). S. Giannakourou, *Cypriot Labour Law* (Nomiki Bibliothiki Publications Athens 2016) 29–31, 36–7, 95–7 (in Greek). The Regulation Rome I does not define the notion of an individual employment contract nor does it distinguish such a contract from a collective employment contract or from similar contracts such as a contract to supply services.

39 As this law was modified, by laws 14(I)/2006, 89(I)/2006, 20(I)/2008 and 13(I)/2014.

order to guarantee payment of their outstanding claims.[40] For this reason, a fund is created, which will guarantee the payment of the claims in question.[41] In the aforementioned law, the 'insolvent employer' is a legal or natural person for which there has been an application at the relevant court for the issue of a receiving decree (for an individual) or a liquidation decree (for a legal entity) and such a decree has either been issued by the respective court or the court has determined that the employer has ceased any activity and there were not enough assets to justify the issue of such a decree. As it is also defined in article 3 of the law in question, an employee of an insolvent employer is entitled to payment by the fund, provided that he has worked for at least 26 continuous weeks before the date of his employer's insolvency. The calculation of the payment in question, that is how many wages, is set out in article 4 of the abovementioned law.

D. REFORMS – PAST AND CURRENT

(1) Major reforms of current insolvency legislation in Cyprus since 2005

32.39 The legislation for the winding up of companies, that is the law of companies, Chapter 113, which is basically the insolvency law for the companies registered in Cyprus underwent important amendments in 2015 through five consecutive laws. More specifically, the laws in question are the following:

32.40 Law 61(1)/2015, which has amended the law on bankruptcy for individuals (Chapter 5) and is not examined in this chapter, which deals with legal entities. This law aims at the modernization of bankruptcy law of Cyprus, through the amendment of the existing legal framework on the bankruptcy of individuals, since the process followed up until then was deemed to be insufficient and time-consuming. It is noted that the law on bankruptcy (Chapter 5) has undergone small amendments with laws 2(I)/2008, 74(I)/2008, 206 (I)/2012 and 80 (I)/2016.

32.41 Law 62(I)/2015,[42] which has added to Chapter 113 (law of companies) the part IVA regarding the institution of the examiner of the company (examinership) and whose regulations have been mentioned above. The examinership process, is intended to provide 'a breathing space' to a company which faces

40 T.E. Synodinou and V. Argyropoulou, *Cypriot Private Law, Interpretation per article-Case Law* (Sakkoulas Publications Athens –Thessaloniki 2014) 625 (in Greek). Giannakourou (n 39) 241–8.

41 Law 25(I) of 2001, article 7.

42 Published in the Official Gazette of the Republic of Cyprus on 7/5/2015.

insolvency. During this period, the company is placed 'under the court's protection', while an insolvency practicioner appointed by the court assesses the company's business and, if appropriate, compiles a rehabilitation plan, based on a voluntary arrangement. The principal function of the examiner is to formulate and secure agreement on a restructuring plan and, unless the order the examiner provides otherwise, the power to manage that the business will remain 'in the hands of the directors', following the appointment of an examiner. This procedure is available to any registered company in Cyprus apart from banks and insurance companies, which are subject to special procedures. Generally, the aim of this law is to reinforce the framework of company loans in order to reduce the size of non-performing loans for the avoidance of further damage to the credit institutions. This proposal was not actually widely accepted, particularly by the bank sector of Cyprus, since it was seen as a method of malversation and not as tool for the reinforcement of companies. Within this framework, the conclusion of settlements, which make a company able to reduce and pay its debts, is sought after, through the introduction of the institution of the examiner, at the same time taking into consideration the interests of the creditors and the guarantors. In practice, there is not even one appointed examiner of any company, so far, in Cyprus.

Law 63(I)/2015, which is about the reform of the legal framework in relation **32.42** to the process of the compulsory liquidation of companies,[43] that is, the reform of Chapter 113, which is also mentioned above. Law 120(I)/2015 is also a law that deals with the liquidation of an insolvent company and has introduced article 298B in Chapter 113.[44]

Law 64(I)/2015, as amended by law 197(I)/2015. Law 64(I)/2015, has **32.43** introduced the institution of Insolvency Consultants and is part of the 'generation' of laws which have modernized the insolvency processes in the Cypriot legislation. The aforementioned law was also passed after consultation of the Ministers' Council with the European Commission and the International Monetary Fund and upon updating of the European Central Bank and the European Stability Mechanism. In law 64(I)/2015, an 'insolvency consultant' means any person who, according to law, is authorized to exercise the profession of the Insolvency Consultant and 'Insolvency Service' means the Official Recipient or any other department or service of the Ministry of Energy, Commerce, Industry and Tourism appointed by the Minister to carry out the tasks assigned to him by the legislation in force. Additionally, a person

43 Ibid.
44 Ibid., fn 32.

is considered to act as an insolvency consultant,[45] if, among other things, he acts as a liquidator, temporary liquidator, recipient, receiver or examiner, in relation to a company. This natural, not legal person, must have a valid license of an insolvency consultant and be registered at the respective register kept by the Insolvency Service. In addition, an insolvency consultant must have malpractice insurance. In practice, there are many licensed and registered insolvency consultants now in Cyprus, (mostly trained attorneys at law and accountants) and this institution seems to be one that actually works in the insolvency field of Cyprus.

32.44 Law 65 (I)/2015 on the insolvency of individuals (personal plans of payment and decree for the exemption from debts), which aims to safeguard the rights of society and the treatment of non-performing loans in such a way that restores the proper functioning of the financial system.[46] More specifically, these measures aim at the protection of the debtors that have greatly suffered from the financial crisis and the establishment of fair and sustainable payment plans for the safeguarding of the reasonable rights of creditors and guarantors. The Insolvency Service supervises the processes and the implementation of the insolvency settlements related to individuals. The law in question is not further analysed in this chapter, since it is about bankrupt individuals and not insolvent legal entities. However, it is noted that article 79 of the law in question for court protection with a decree of 'non sustainable debtor' also includes a company unable to pay its debts and for which a liquidation process is about to commence and also in its assets there is immovable property which is considered to be a principal place of business.[47]

32.45 All five aforementioned laws were not established by the legislator, as a result of inner national processes and consultations or by pressure from companies or other factors such as labour or business unions, banks, etc, but as an immediate 'legislative consequence' of the updated Memorandum of Understanding signed between the Republic of Cyprus, the International Monetary Fund, the European Commission and the European Central Bank. This Memorandum provides that, within the framework of a complete reform that introduces appropriate processes of insolvency for natural and legal persons, among others, the profession and the authorization of the Insolvency Consultant, in

45 An insolvency practitioner appointed by the court, assesses the company's business and, if appropriate, compiles a rehabilitation plan, based on a voluntary arrangement.

46 For the general analysis of this law, see L. Kaoutzani, *Insolvency Law for Natural Persons (N. 65(I)/2015), Summary and Main Points* (Nicosia 2015) (in Greek).

47 See L. Kaoutzani, Insolvency Law for Natural Persons (N. 65(I)/2015), Summary and Main Points, (Nicosia 2015) 65–66 (in Greek).

order to secure the effective implementation of legislations that govern the insolvency procedures for natural and legal persons.

Without prejudice to all those mentioned above, in part B(1) of this chapter, none of the aforementioned recent legislative amendments is about the introduction of a new rule or an amendment of an existing rule particularly in relation to the effect of the liquidation processes on the executory contracts of the insolvent company. **32.46**

Of the aforementioned laws, those which introduced the potential of contractual agreements negotiated by the parties in solvent times are: a) Law 62(I)/2015, where through the institution of the examiner (examinership) of a company the conclusion of settlements which make a company able to reduce and pay its debts, is sought after, through the introduction of the institution of the examiner, at the same time taking into consideration the interests of the creditors and the guarantors; b) Law 63(I)/2015 that has amended, among others, article 233 of Chapter 113, in relation to the general powers and responsibilities of the liquidator. This article provides, among others, that the liquidator has the power, with the sanction either of the court or of the committee of inspection to make any compromise or arrangement with creditors or persons claiming to be creditors, or having or alleging themselves to have any claim. The law gives the power to the liquidator to enter into compromise with creditors and for debts of the company, which may come from a contract that was not executed by the company; c) Law 65 (I)/2015 on the insolvency of natural persons, in which suggestions by the debtor to the creditors, through the Insolvency Consultant, for personal plans of payment which, if the creditor consents, are considered to be consensual personal plans of payment, are provided for. **32.47**

E. CONCLUDING REMARKS

Within the framework of the Cypriot legislation, a company which cannot pay its created debts can be put under compulsory liquidation by the court or an examiner can be appointed. There is no possibility for negotiations between the debtor and creditors out of court. The relevant legislation has been modernized as one of the consequences of the Memorandum concluded between the Republic of Cyprus and its international lenders and not upon inner processes and consultations with the business world and other market factors. However, the legislative reform, even if it is aimed at the speeding up of the processes and the rescue of businesses and companies, which, despite the financial difficulties, show signs of sustainability, does not seem to **32.48** succeed. The reason is that, in reality, the delays in the judicial process of the compulsory liquidation of a company, significantly affect the effectiveness of the process. By way of example, because of congestion in the courts, the hearing date for a petition for the appointment of an examiner can be as late as three months after the date of presentation of the petition. With an overall time limit of four months for examinership, this severely impairs the effectiveness of the process. Consequently, further reforms may be needed in order to make the changes work in practice.

33

NATIONAL REPORT FOR INDIA

Indrajit Dube

A. INTRODUCTORY NOTE

India enacted a comprehensive law on corporate insolvency in 2016.[1] Before the enactment of new law, the creditors enforced their rights against the debtor company under different legislations. India also notably did not have a provision like s 365 of the US Bankruptcy Code. Thus, the executory contract[2] or similar principles were not developed by Indian courts/tribunals in adjudicating the creditors' claim against the debtor company. The Calcutta High Court in 1963 referred to the concept in a winding up proceedings.[3] There was no mention thereafter in any judgements. It is of interest as to why executory principle was not significant to Indian courts, and whether and to what extent such contracts would be treated under the present IBC 2016. **33.01**

1 The Insolvency and Bankruptcy Code 2016 [hereafter called IBC.]

2 See Jesse M Fried, 'Executory Contracts and Performance Decisions in Bankruptcy' (1996) 46 *Duke Law Journal* 517, 517.

> This article analyses the treatment in bankruptcy of a debtors' 'executory contracts' – contract under which the debtor still owes performance at the time of debtor files for bankruptcy. Under the laws of most countries, including the United States, the bankruptcy trustee generally disposes of executory the contract in one of two ways: she either (1) seeks performance of the contract; or to 'rejects' the contract, in which case any resulting damage claim is treated as pre-bankruptcy and unsecured clam. Since such claims are typically paid only a fraction of their face amount, the usual consequence of rejection is that an injured party receives much less than full compensation.

See also, Michael T Andrew, 'Executory Contracts Revisited: A Reply to Professor Westbrook' (1991) 62 *U. Colo. L. Rev.* 1.

3 In *Re: Bengal Textiles Association* [1963] AIR 112 (Cal) it was held that the official liquidator cannot enforce the executory contract.

33.02 The modern Indian legal system was transplanted by the British during its colonial rule.[4] Insolvency law for organisations[5] was no exception. Although, India had well-framed 'organisational law' including insolvency management before British colonisation. For a long time, even after independence, India followed the British legacy in this matter. Changing phases of the economy in post-independent India developed indigenous corporate insolvency process.

33.03 In the pre-independence majority, business was controlled by the families. The laws of that time[6] did not differentiate between personal property and business property. The creditor had access to the individual and family wealth for business debt. The native framework of organisational and insolvency law caused concern to British traders managing business debt and business insolvency against native creditors and traders.[7] To overcome the difficulty, the British colonial government enacted two insolvency legislations namely the Presidency Town Act 1909 and Provincial Act 1907.[8] Both pieces of legislation were identical with only a difference of territorial operations. The first enactment was for presidency towns where English common law was effective. The latter statute was for provinces and princely states where different traditional laws were in force.[9] The basic pillars of the statutes were the insolvent's disqualification from entering into a contract and the bankrupt's criminal liability. The Acts were also used for business insolvency because the traditional law in India never distinguished between business property and the personal property of the trader.[10] Until recently the Acts were in force although they had been subjected to various amendments over time. It served the British traders well but lost its relevance with changing times and economic conditions.

4 See, Ron Harris, 'The English East India Company and the History of Company Law' (2005) in Ella Gepken-Jager, Gerard van Solinge, Levinus Timmears (eds) *VOC 1602–2002 – 400 Years of Company Law, Series Law of Business and Finance* (Kluwer Legal Publishers 2005) 219.

5 Author means insolvency laws relating to company, partnership, cooperatives and societies.

6 There was no uniform legal system governing Indian territory at that time. So, certain parts were under the control of the British Colonial Government and so the common law applied, other parts were under the Islamic Kings so sariat law would prevail and remaining parts were governed by Hindu customary law. See generally Sailendra Nath Banerjee, 'An Outline of the Law and Practice Relating to Bankruptcy in British India' (1933) *Journal of the National Association of Referees in Bankruptcy* 139.

7 See, Federation of Chambers of Commerce of the British Empire, 'Bankruptcy Law in British Empire: Report of a Special Committee of the Federation of Chambers of Commerce of the British Empire' (1932); Banerjee (n 6).

8 See generally, Indrajit Dube, Corporate Insolvency Law: Efficiency and Efficacy from a Cross Border Perspective. <https://ssrn.com/abstract=1141931>.

9 See also, Banerjee (n 7).

10 Enactment of different 'organisation law' brought changes in application of this act during British rule and post-Independent period.

B. EVOLUTION OF CORPORATE INSOLVENCY LAW IN INDIA

Business organisations' insolvency (namely, corporate insolvency) were not in focus in the Indian legal system due to the ownership model in post-independence. Most of the businesses in India were organised under the different business forms, i.e., proprietorship, partnership, cooperatives, societies, public/private trust (foundations) and companies. Except for proprietorship, all other business forms were governed by respective legislation either enacted by the federal government,[11] or the provincial government.[12] Most informal businesses were non-companies, and any recovery of the debt by creditors was subjected to insolvency laws (i.e., presidency and provincial) and adjudicated under regular judicial process. For business organisations, governing statutes provided the provisions for dissolution or liquidation of business at insolvency by the creditors. **33.04**

The government of post-independent India was to recover quickly from the devastated economic impacted by war and colonialism.[13] A high-level committee was set up to outline plans for economic recovery and to foster growth.[14] Two critical opinions advanced by the committee was the strict control of the government on economy and enactment of a well-organised Company Act with firm government control. The company was identified as the vehicle of economic development.[15] The centralised agency was proposed to oversee the affairs of registrar companies (including financing and liquidation of the company). Following the report of the committee, the Companies Act 1956[16] (CA 1956) was enacted. **33.05**

Post-1956 witnessed the massive growth of incorporation of government companies influenced by the success of the Soviet Russia economic model. By 1961 the government held 61 per cent[17] of the equity in all incorporated **33.06**

11 Known as 'Central Government' in India.

12 Known as 'State Government' in India.

13 See generally, 'Shastri Committee Report on Company Act Amendment, 1957' (Ministry of Finance, Government of India 1957) <http://reports.mca.gov.in/Reports/21-Shastri%20committee%20report%20on%20Company%20act%20amendment,%201957.pdf> accessed 27 December 2017.

14 See generally, 'Bhabha Committee, Report on Company Law Committee, 1952' (1952) <http://reports.mca.gov.in/Reports/22-Bhabha%20committee%20report%20on%20Company%20law%20committee,%201952.pdf> accessed 19 December 2017.

15 'Symposium on New Company Law, 1957' <http://reports.mca.gov.in/Reports/33-Symposium%20on%20new%20Company%20Law,%201957.pdf> accessed 6 January 2016.

16 Act No. 1 of 1956.

17 See also, 'Working Group on Company Law Administration, 1968 (Mazumdar Committee Report)' (Administrative Reform Commission 1968) <http://reports.mca.gov.in/Reports/28-Mazumdar%20committee%20report%20working%20group%20on%20company%20law%20Administration,%201968.pdf> accessed 7 January 2016.

companies. During this period the government policies tilted towards to a socialistic pattern of the economy but the private incorporation of registrar companies was allowed under the act of 1956. The business families and neo-riches of the 'war economy' mainly promoted these private companies. Industries (Development and Regulation) Act 1952 empowered the government to decide sectors to grant a licence for private incorporation. The objective of sectoral allocations was to minimise economic concentrations. A highly centralised economic system was put in place by the government of that time.

33.07 Faster industrialisation was the primary objective of CA 1956.[18] The government[19] incorporated companies in almost all sectors to foster inclusive growth and development in an economically fragmented society. The primary emphasis was on manufacturing which catered to the domestic need. So, the focus was on growth and the social demand instead of efficiency building in the industrial process. Industrial sickness and insolvency were undermined by the government as evidenced by the policies and legislative mandate of that time. The different sections[20] of the CA 1956 include the provision of 'public interest'[21] in operation and management of the company. Insolvency of the business was the last option for the government. Strict industrial allocations rules reduced competition within the sector. In some instances, there were limited players in the sector, and if private incorporations became 'sick', the government had no option but to take over the management.[22] The management of the private company was taken over to protect the interest of workforces.

33.08 The concepts of 'compromise'[23] and 'company when deemed unable to pay its debts'[24] were only the protective provisions for creditors under CA 1956. These two provisions conferred to the creditors[25] the right to apply to

18 See, Matthew J Kust, 'The Corporation and the Public Interest in India' (1967) 2 *Studies in Law and Economic Development* 35, 55.

19 Include different layers of government i.e., local government, state (provincial) government and central (federal) government.

20 The Companies Act 1956, ss 81, 89, 108B, 205, 210A, 219, 243, 247, 269, 300, 388A, 394, 397, 398, 408, 497, 509.

21 See, Kust (n 18). The term 'public interest' was construed widely. It included the interest of all stakeholders i.e., beyond the interest of shareholders and creditors of the company.

22 See generally, Ananya Mukherjee Reed, 'Corporate Governance Reforms in India' (2002) 37 *Journal of Business Ethics* 249, 252.

23 The Companies Act (n 20), ss 391, 392 and 393.

24 Ibid., s 434.

25 Ibid., s 391 (1) 'Where a compromise … is proposed – (a) between a company and its creditors or any class of them.'

the court[26] to restructure the debts and approve the scheme.[27] The compromise was an agreement between the company and the class of creditors. The liability of performance against each other in future was part of the scheme. The court might issue the directions for modification of the scheme if party/parties failed to perform his/their respective obligations.[28] Once the scheme had been approved by the court, the parties to the agreement were bound to each other. Unsuccessful implementation of the scheme might lead to winding up. The second provision 'company when deemed unable to pay its debt' was a weapon for the creditor to pressurise the debtor company to pay the debt immediately. The creditor might file a winding up application in court on non-payment and recover the debt through liquidation. This right was available to both secured and unsecured creditors.[29] There was scope for negations by secured creditor or class of creditors under 'compromise'.

(1) Bank nationalisations and its impact on insolvency

Bank nationalisations in the 70s was an important milestone from a corporate insolvency perspective. Through the nationalisation of financial services[30] major industrial/business creditors were put under the control of governments. During this time banks' lending procedures were closely monitored by the Central Bank.[31] The enforcement of credit agreements by financial institutions was difficult due to: the policies of that time; inadequate provisions in **33.09**

26 Later the same power conferred to National Company Law Tribunal under Part 1B. The establishment of tribunal conceived to deal with only company matters for faster disputer resolution. But this part of the Act was never notified due to the litigation about the constitutional validity of the amendment act. The Companies Act (n 20).

27 While approving the scheme the court should satisfy itself that, the meeting was to be held and conducted between the class of creditors, and respective shareholders; that the compromise was a real compromise; that it was accepted by a competent majority; that the majority was acting in good faith and for common advantage of the whole class; that what they did was reasonable, prudent and proper; that the court should satisfy itself as to (a) whether the provisions of the statue have been complied with; (b) whether the scheme is reasonable and practical or whether there is any reasonable objection to it; (c) whether the creditors acted honestly and in good faith and had sufficient information; (d) whether the court ought in the public interest the decisions of the creditor and shareholders.

Lakshimi Commercial Bank Ltd., Re, [1948] 18 Com Cases 265 reaffirmed thereafter in several cases including *CHPL Enterprises P. Ltd., In re* (2000) 2 Comp LJ 218 (AP). Cited by, Justice YV Chandrachud and Dr SM Dugar (eds), *A Ramaiya Guide to the Companies Act, vol* 2 (16th edn, Wadhwa Nagpur 2006) 3230–32.

28 The Companies Act (n 20), s 392 (b).

29 This provision generally availed by the small creditor.

30 All the major bank of the country was taken under goverment control. Banking Companies (acquisition and transfer of undertakings) Act 1970, ss 3 and 7.

31 Known as Reserve Bank of India.

governing laws;[32] and the dispute settlement system. During this period, the economic development was slow,[33] and by the 80s, the economy was almost at a halt.[34] A large number of companies were sick[35] in the public as well as the private sectors. India's balance of payment was negative and industrial production was hit very severely.[36]

33.10 To militate against industrial insolvency, the federal government enacted the Sick Industrial Companies (Special Provision) Act 1985.[37] The act established the 'Board for Industrial and Financial Reconstruction' (BIFR). It was responsible for inquiring into the affairs of the underperforming company,[38] negotiating with different creditors and developing the scheme of revival for the companies. The outcome of the negotiations was the formation of an executory contract between the consortium of creditors, promoters and the sick company. This included the fresh financing of the company, a change in management, selling the company or its assets, merging it with another company, and changing the company charter.[39] The BIFR monitored the implementation of the agreement. Parties to the agreement had a limited right to enforcement of the agreement. This enactment failed to produce the desired result. The act was in force until December 2016[40] until replaced by IBC 2016.[41]

(2) Economic reform and insolvency

33.11 A large number of public and private sector industries were defaulting on their loan repayments. An increasing number of litigations was pending in different

32 The Companies Act (n 20).

33 Known as Hindu rate of growth.

34 See generally, Valerie Cerra and Sweta Chaman Saxena, 'What Caused the 1991 Currency Crisis in India?' (2002) IMF Staff Papers 395.

35 The word 'sick' was used as a synonym for insolvency.

36 Caroline Van Zile, 'India's Mandatory Corporate Social Responsibility Proposal: Creative Capitalism Meets Creative Regulation in the Global Market' (2011) 13 *APLPJ* 269, 285.

37 Act No. 1 of 1986, popularly known as SICA.

38 The Act was only enacted for production (i.e., manufacturing companies of different sectors, food processing, etc.) companies. It excluded all the service companies and financial companies. Insolvency of financial companies (i.e., banking and non-banking) were dealt under Banking Regulation Act, 1949.

39 Known as memorandum of associations and articles of associations.

40 The Act was repealed in the year beginning 1st January 2004 by Sick Industrial Companies (Special Provisions) Repeal Act, 2003. This repealed Act of SICA was never notified. Part VIA of Company Act 1956 incorporates the similar provisions of SICA i.e., Revival and Rehabilitation of Sick Industrial Companies from ss 424A–424L by Companies (Second Amendment) Act, 2002. Even, Part VIA was never notified after incorporations.

41 Act of 31 of 2016, notified on 31st November 2016. All pending cases before the BIFR and Appellate Authority were transfered to National Company Law Tribunal and Appellate Tribunal established under Companies Act 2013.

subordinate[42] and High Courts[43] of the country. This trend which started in the late 70s[44] became acute by the beginning of 90s. The federal government in post-90s[45] initiated economic reforms through institutional transformations in the financial sector.[46] The Recovery of Debt due to Bank and Financial Institution Act 1993 (RDBFI) was passed to facilitate recovery of debt by financial institutions and banks. The Act established a special tribunal and an appellate tribunal. Section 19 of the Act excluded the jurisdictions of a civil court and created a provision for appointment of a receiver.[47] The receiver had power to take possession or custody of property, take over the management, defend and file any suit or litigation in the tribunal to realise, manage, protect, reserve and improve the property, collect rents and profits, and execute documents.[48] This was an attempt to curb accumulated debt of borrower companies to the financial institutions and banks. Further, this law was a departure from earlier policy to protect and takeover sick (insolvent) companies for 'public interest'.[49] Settling the credit dispute through negotiation between the parties (i.e., creditors and borrower companies) was beyond the focus of this Act. The tribunal failed to reduced the number of litigations on debt recovery against the government as well as privately owned companies.

Post-90s the market needed more liquidity to support growth. Piling up debt **33.12**
in public sector financial institutions and the banks became a serious cause for concern. Banking reform committee[50] recommended the liberalisation of

42 The creditors (financial institution and bank) recovered debt by filing money suits to recover debts due to the company in the District Court and below (depend on their pecuniary jurisdictions. These courts are also known as subordinate courts) under Civil Procedure Code 1908. This remedy was availed mostly by unsecured creditors.

43 High Courts are the constitutional courts. Every State (province) capital has a High Court. High Courts were also, until recently, the court of first instance in matters of dispute between the company and creditor. The National Company Law Tribunal has conferred the same power under Companies Act 2013 and Insolvency and Bankruptcy Code 2016.

44 In 1981, a committee headed by Mr T Tiwari had examined the legal difficulties faced by banks and financial institutions and suggested remedial measures including amendment in law and setting up a Special Tribunal for recovery of dues of the banks and financial institutions.

45 See generally, Kaushik Basu, *India's Emerging Economy: Performance and Prospects in the 1990s and Beyond* (MIT Press 2004).

46 The Central (federal) government under the chairmanship of Mr M. Narasimham appointed a committee on 14th August 1991 to examine and recommend the structure, organisation, functions and procedures of the financial systems and to recommend improvements in their efficiency and productivity. It also included how to manage debt due to bank and financial institutions by the companies.

47 The same as administrator in other jurisdictions.

48 The Recovery of Debt due to Banks and Financial Institutions Act (n 48), s 19 (18) (d).

49 Although, large numbers of earlier policies and the law regarding insolvency were in operation during this period.

50 'Committee on Financial System' (Reserve Bank of India 1991); 'Committee on Banking Sector Reforms' (Reserve Bank of India 1998). Committee on Financial System Reforms was of the opinion that the reason for a non-performing asset (NPA) in a commercial bank was the 'priority sector lending' (PSL). PSL stands for favouring group of industry in a particular segment. The government wanted to focus on a few sectors to

the recovery of debt system. It advocated the securitisation of bad loans, repacking of loans through asset reconstructions and enforcement of security without the intervention of the court. The federal government passed legislation named Securitisation and Reconstruction of Financial Assets and Enforcement of Security Interest Act 2002 (SARFAEAI) to give effect to those recommendations. The Act incorporated provision to take over the NPA[51] by Assets Management Company (AMC) from the banks and financial institutions. The Asset Reconstruction Company (ARC) had acquisition rights,[52] i.e., taking over or changing the management of the business of the borrower,[53] the sale or lease of a part or all of the business of the borrower, rescheduling of payment of debt, enforcement of security interest, settlement of dues, taking possession of secured assets. The creditors' are empowered to enforce security interest to take possession of securities, appoint a manager to manage the security, ask any debtors of the borrower to pay after giving the notice for 60 days without the intervention of tribunal and court. Both RDBFI and SARFAEAI were a good attempt to liberalise and expedite the recovery of the debt and streamline the insolvency process in the country.

33.13 The Reserve Bank of India (RBI) as the owner of the public-sector banks[54] set up a committee[55] to pledge reform relating to banking insolvency. This led to several amendments in the Banking Regulations Act 1949[56] and incorporated separate sections regarding banking and financial institutions' insolvency. Under the amended provisions, the RBI will initiate moratorium and restructure the bank/financial institute with large NPA. This amendment separated the insolvency process of the banking and financial companies from other companies.

33.14 In 2013 the Indian Parliament adopted the new Companies Act 2013 and replaced the CA 1956. The new Act had almost similar provisions regarding the creditors' rights as CA 1956. But the Act focused on building efficient

---

cater for the domestic need. Subsequently, the Committee on Banking Sector reforms highlighted the need for zero NPA in all the banking companies in India. The committee recommended creation of assets reconstruction companies (ARC) to take over the bad loans of the banks and increase the liquidity to the commercial banks. It also suggested an apt system to identify and classify the NPAs and recommended introduction of new legislation.

51 'NPA', stands for Non-Performing Assets. NPA means bad loans, those securities failing to generate revenues for bank/financial institutes.

52 See Securitisation and Reconstruction of Financial Assets and Enforcement of Security Interest Act (n 53), ss 5 and 9.

53 Debtor company.

54 Until early 2000 Reserve Bank of India discharged the roles of owner of Public Sector Bank and Money Market Regulator.

55 See, 'Report of the Advisory Group on Bankruptcy Laws' (2001).

56 This is the governing law for all Scheduled Bank and the Financial Institute.

adjudicatory institutions. The Act established the National Company Law Tribunal (NCLT) and the Appellate Tribunal (NCLTA),[57] dedicated tribunals to deal with all company related disputes.[58] Offices of the company liquidator, established under CA 1956, were conferred with substantial powers[59] in the protection of assets of liquidating the company. On pronouncement of liquidation, the company liquidator will take control and custody of the liquidating companies' property, and the property will be deemed as the property of the tribunal. The number of amendment carried out in different acts to confer powers on NCLT to adjudicate any matter of creditor/s' claim against the company and in matters of corporate insolvency.

Thus, until the enactment of IBC 2016, multiple legislations were applied to deal with individual insolvency,[60] non-corporate business organisations, production (manufacturing sector companies) and the financial sector (i.e., banking) companies. The majority of company (i.e., non-financial) insolvencies are dealt under the winding up provisions. The company liquidator (or administrator/receiver) has very limited rights to negotiate with the debtors of the insolvent company. The governing statutes did not provide any provisions for bankruptcy property. This created hurdles for the insolvency and liquidation process as far as the company liquidator was concerned. Multiple courts or tribunals used to entertain litigation relating to insolvency. Provisions of the different legislation led to a complex and conflicting outcome and dragged out the insolvency process for years. It led to asset loss and hindered creditor effort to recover assets. The law was unclear about how to deal with the conflicting groups or classes of creditors. In addition to that, the law for the non-corporate business organisation was subject to other laws. **33.15**

---

57 Companies Act 2013, s 225 (2):

> Substituted by the Insolvency and Bankruptcy Code 2016: (2) the provisional liquidator or the Company Liquidator, as the case may be, shall be appointed from a panel maintained by the Central Government consisting of the name of chartered accountants, advocates, company secretaries, cost accountants or firm or bodies corporate having search chartered accountants, advocates, cost accountants and such other professional as may be notified by the Central Government from a firm or a body corporate a persons having a combination of such professionals as may be prescribed and having at least 10 years'experience in company matters.

<http://www.manupatrafast.in/ba/fulldisp.aspx?iactid=12340> accessed 24 November 2017.

58 See, 'Report of High Level Committee on Law Relating to Insolvency of Companies' (2000). Justice V. B. Eradi Committees set up to draw the outline to strengthen the Corporate Insolvency Law. But discussion of the committee became focused only on the difficulty faced by the 'liquidator' (government appointed) in the liquidation process. A major reason identified by the committee was the difficulty faced by the creditor in adjudicating the corporate insolvency process in a regulator court (i.e., High Court). It suggested setting up the National Company Law Tribunal (NCLT) which would be a one-stop adjudicatory forum for company law disputes. Also, it suggested introducing the insolvency professional and liquidator.

59 Companies Act 2013 (n 57), s 290.

60 Sole traders.

33.16 The present government set up a committee,[61] in order to ease the doing of business, to recommend a comprehensive law on insolvency and bankruptcy. On the recommendation of the committee, new legislation was enacted to facilitate and quicken the corporate insolvency processes. The present act applies to an individual[62] as well as non-corporate business[63] and corporate insolvency. The provision relating to insolvency professionals[64] incorporated under this Act to oversee the insolvency process in the country. The Act brought an amendment into Company Act 2016, RDBFI 1993, and SARFAESI 2002 to align with the objectives of the IBC. It introduced the time-bound insolvency process, the creditors control over the debtor assets and provides immunity to the debtor from the claim of a creditor and the cases filed by them during insolvency proceedings. The Act provided for establishment of the insolvency resolution professional and insolvency resolution firm.[65] The law also set up an insolvency and bankruptcy board of India to regulate the insolvency resolution professional and firm.

C. INSOLVENCY FRAMEWORK

33.17 The IBC introduced creditor primacy within the corporate insolvency realm. The majority of business creditors are the commercial and industrial banks, and other financial institutions (i.e., mutual, insurance, and pension funds). In the majority of cases, the government has significant control over these institutions as a controlling shareholder. Although, in the last 20 years a number of privately owned institutions have emerged in the financial market, their influence and market holding comparatively is still less than public financial institutions. The objective of the IBC was to maximise creditors' control over the operation of the insolvent company, protect their interest and dispose of insolvency in a time bound manner. Another objective was to bring efficiency to the market economy and reduce NPAs[66] in banks and financial institutions.

33.18 The code created the provisions for Insolvency Resolution Professional (RP) and Insolvency Professional Agency, and Insolvency regulator, i.e., The Insolvency and Bankruptcy Board of India (IBBI).[67] The code attempted to

61 'Report of High Level Committee on Law Relating to Insolvency of Companies' (n 59).
62 Sole traders.
63 Partnership, cooperatives, associations of persons (e.g., clubs), etc.
64 The Insolvency and Bankruptcy Board of India.
65 This professional equivalent to the insolvency trustee or insolvency administrator of other jurisdictions.
66 Getting control over the bad loan.
67 The Insolvency and Bankruptcy Code 2016 (n 1), s 207.

bring required expertise in different market segments.[68] It lays down eligibility requirements and registration procedures for RPs with the regulator. The RP shall possess the qualification and experience in the field of finance, law, management, insolvency and other associated fields.[69] Insolvency Professional Agencies will grant membership to the person who has fulfilled all the requirements set out in its bylaw on payment of membership fees. It will lay down the standards of professional conduct of its members; safeguard the right, privileges and the interests of the insolvency professionals; suspend or cancel the membership of insolvency professionals; redress the grievances of the consumer against the insolvency professionals; publish information about dysfunctions, lists of members, performance of its members and such other information.

Corporate insolvency is envisaged as a two-step process under the code, i.e., insolvency resolution process (IRP) and liquidations. During the resolution process, RP will make an effort to restore the financial state of the company and carry on the business. The financial creditor or operational creator[70] can initiate the resolution process against the default company in NCLT. The NCLT will appoint RP/s to administer the insolvency process. The RP will take over the management and operate the business as an ongoing concern. In the second stage, the RP will identify the financial creditors and constitute a creditors' committee. The decision of the creditors' committee will be binding on the debtor's company and other creditors. The creditors' committee will decide upon the revival of the company or proceed with the liquidation of the company within 180 days. The significant change also introduced by IBC in the priority of the claim that of the previous regime. After the payment of the cost of insolvency, secured creditor and worker dues, government dues are paid. Earlier government dues used to get priority over all the claimant, and there was no provision for payment of the cost of insolvency. **33.19**

The code provided for the separate insolvency resolution process for individuals and unlimited partnerships. The code envisages two distinct processes in cases of individuals' insolvency, i.e., automatic fresh start and insolvency resolution. The Debt Recovery Tribunal (DRT) incorporated under RDBFI is designated as an adjudicatory forum for individual insolvency. **33.20**

---

68 Manufacturing, Financial, Services and sub-sectors.

69 The Insolvency and Bankruptcy Code 2016 (n 1), s 204.

70 The Insolvency and Bankrupcy Code 2016 (n 1), s 5 (20), 'Operational Creditor' means a person to whom an operational debt is owed and includes any person to whom such debt has been legally assigned or transferred. Section 5 (21), 'operational debt' means a claim in respect of the provision of goods or services including employment or a debt in respect of repayment of dues arising under any law for the time being in force payable to the Central Government, any State Government or any local authority.

33.21 The IBBI incorporated as a regulator to oversee the functioning of insolvency intermediaries, i.e., insolvency resolution professionals, insolvency professional agencies, information utilities and regulating the insolvency process. The information utilities (IU) are a notable feature in the code to create infrastructure towards collecting, collating, authenticating and disseminating financial information of the debtor company in the centralised electronic database. Such information will be available to creditors, resolution professionals, and other stakeholders in the insolvency process. IU were created to bring down the asymmetry of information in the insolvency process.

D. THE TREATMENT OF EXECUTORY CONTRACTS IN INDIA

33.22 The author is of the view that the adoption of executory contract principles will be beneficial to protect creditors as well as other stakeholders' interest during insolvency in India. This part of the chapter will concentrate on identifying the legislative provisions which can be interpreted to create a framework to enforce 'executory contract'.

33.23 The 'interim resolution professional' has power 'to enter into a contract on behalf of the corporate debtor or to amend or modify the contracts or transactions which were entered into before the commencement of corporate insolvency resolution process'.[71] The resolution professional has a duty to 'take immediate custody and control of all assets of the corporate debtor', and 'exercise rights for the benefit of the corporate debtor'. Also, the resolution professional[72] will continue to have the same powers and duty as of the 'interim resolution professional'.[73] The resolution professional may 'enter into a contract on behalf of the corporate debtor or to amend or modify the contracts or transactions which were entered into before the commencement of corporate insolvency resolution process'.[74] The professionals can 'apply to the tribunal for the avoidance of transactions'[75] entered by the debtor company before filing the insolvency petitions.[76] If a preference has been given to a

71 Management of operations of corporate debtor as going concern, Section 20 (b) The Insolvency and Bankruptcy Code 2016 (n 1).

72 Once the insolvency resolution order has been passed the same interim resolution professional is appointed as resolution professional unless the creditors' committee demand the appointment of a new agency as insolvency resolution professional.

73 The Insolvency and Bankruptcy Code 2016 (n 1), s 23(2).

74 Ibid., s 20 (1) (b).

75 The insolvency resolution professional will have the same power as is vested in the liquidator under Chapter III of Part II of IBC 2016.

76 The Insolvency and Bankruptcy Code 2016 (n 1), s 25 (2) (j).

particular transaction by a corporate debtor,[77] the insolvency professional may apply to the tribunal by avoiding the transactions on the ground of the preferential treatment.[78] The liquidator[79] also can apply to the tribunal for the avoidance of transaction on the ground of preferential treatment. The provisions in the law provide extensive power to RP to take a call on executory contract.

The corporate insolvency jurisprudence in India earlier evolved around the public interest.[80] Protection of the creditor interest and bringing back the liquidity to market after liquidation of the company was always looked at through the prism of social perspective, i.e., by protecting the interests of different stakeholders. Providing superior rights to the creditors or creditors' committee during insolvency is a newer understanding in India, as was introduced by IBC 2016.[81] The law designates debtor property as insolvency property which is a sharp departure from the earlier public interest concept. The present code envisages the influence of market power over the insolvency process as equally, if not more, important than that of the government in the management of corporate insolvency. **33.24**

This policy shift in corporate insolvency conferred on the insolvency resolution professional tremendous power to bargain with the debtor of the insolvent company. In some instances, the powers are statutory, and their exercise needs the consent of the creditors' committee[82] and may be subject to the instructions of the tribunal. The professional can negotiate, re-negotiate, rescind, avoid and contract which will be detrimental to the insolvency property. The objective is to maximise the value of the insolvency property. **33.25**

---

77 The insolvent company.

78 Section 43 (1); Sub-section (2)

> A corporate debtor shall be deemed to have given a preference, if – (a) there is a transfer of property or an interest thereof of the corporate debtor for the benefit of a creditor or surety or a guarantor for or on account of an antecedent financial debt or operational debt or other liabilities owed by the corporate debtor; and (b) the transfer under clause (a) has the effect of putting such creditor or a surety or a guarantor in a beneficial position it would have been in the event of a distribution of assets being made in accordance with section 53. Sub – section '(4) A preference shall be deemed to be given at a relevant time, if … (b) a preference is given to a person other than related party during the period of one year preceding the insolvency commencement date.

79 On the failing of insolvency process or before completion of the process the tribunal may order for the liquidation of the company. On the passing of the liquidation order of the debtor company either the existing resolution professional or new resolution professional will be appointed as liquidator. The certain power of the liquidator may be exercised by the resolution professional.

80 *Supra.*

81 The finance minister on different occasions mentioned that this measure is to bring down the NPA (Non performing Assets – financial assets) in the government's own banks and financial institutions.

82 The Insolvency and Bankruptcy Code 2016 (n 1), s 21.

33.26 It is time to wait and see how the tribunals interpret the provisions. Will they borrow the principles of 'executory contract' from other jurisdictions to further strengthen the choice of contract by the insolvency resolution professional and pave the way to bargain hard for the protection of the creditors' interest in the insolvency property? A quick scrutiny of the judgments and litigation before the tribunals reveals that present insolvency litigations are concerned more with trying to balance the tension between promoters[83] and creditors about the insolvency process and the issue of who is better placed to secure control of the company. Time will lead to the finer issues of the executory contract being properly addressed, with the maturity of new insolvency jurisprudence in India.

E. CONCLUDING REMARKS

33.27 The code has aimed to identify the early financial failure and maximise the asset value of the insolvent company. IBC streamlined the process of insolvency resolution and liquidation. It consolidated fragmented insolvency approach; institutional divide to address corporate insolvency; address the lack of adequate insolvency expert professional in the different industrial segment, and provide the framework to resolve the insolvency within a time bound manner.

33.28 A recent media report[84] pointed out, 525 insolvency petitions filed in different NCLT benches, and out of that 30 companies liquidated, 10 have a resolution plan approved, 36 have been closed by the appeal and others are under review. The lenders have been able to recover 1854.40 crores out of the total claims of 5530.30 crores. This amounts to one-third of the total outstanding debt.

33.39 Indian creditors (i.e., the banking industry) are set to change the corporate landscape after the introduction of IBC 2016. The companies will no longer be able to avoid paying the dues to the creditors. The insolvency resolution process has equipped the creditors with adequate power to dictate terms to the defaulter company and to have their say in running the company during the resolution process. The creditors' committee shall supervise the resolution

83 Controlling shareholders.

84 Tamal Bandyopadhyay, 'Indian Bankers Set to Rewrite Corporate History – Livemint' <http://www.livemint.com/Opinion/dFbpJCab7TPzd25ddCRdQK/Indian-bankers-set-to-rewrite-corporate-history.html> accessed 16 March 2018.

process and approve the plan for the revival of the company. The adjudicatory forum, i.e., NCLT has a limited role in the approval of the plan after considering the collective interest of all the constituents of the company.

34

NATIONAL REPORT FOR SOUTH AFRICA

Clement Marumoagae

A. INTRODUCTION

34.01 In South Africa, the insolvency of a natural person results in the sequestration of their estate, while corporate insolvency may lead to the liquidation of that company. The idea behind sequestration and liquidation is to ensure equitable distribution of the insolvent's available assets, which often results in fewer creditors being paid while others receive only part of what they are owed or end up not being paid at all. The Master of the High Court appoints trustees to sequestrate natural persons (and partnerships) estates, while liquidators are appointed to dissolve juristic (or legal) persons.[1]

34.02 'Insolvency' is traditionally described as the situation in which the debtor is unable to pay all his, her or its creditors in full. Insolvency law aims to promote collaborative collection and realisation of available assets in the insolvent estate with the aim of distributing the proceeds thereof between creditors.[2] The sequestration or liquidation order is only made by the court when it is clear that such an order will be to the advantage of the creditors.[3] Such an order

1 See *Ex parte: Master of the High Court of South Africa (North Gauteng)* [2011] (5) SA 311 (GNP) para 28.

2 See *Richter NO* v *Riverside Estates (Pty.) Ltd* [1946] OPD 209 at 223.

3 See generally *Sangiorgio NO and Another v Duyn* Unreported case number: 9285/2002 of 27 February 2004 available at http://www.saflii.org/za/cases/ZAWCHC/2004/11.html [Last accessed 06 November 2018].

brings about the *concursus creditorum*,[4] which entails that the rights of all the creditors as a group are taken as more important than those of any individual creditor.

It has been held that, to give effect to the *concursus creditorum*, the trustee or liquidator must decide whether it would be for the benefit of the community of creditors[5] to honour the obligations inherited by the insolvent estate, which include executory contracts.[6] **34.03**

There are no clear legislative guidelines on executory contracts in South Africa. Hence, trustees and liquidators look to the courts for guidance on how to deal with these contracts. **34.04**

This chapter discusses the treatment of executory contracts under South African law. First, this chapter provides a general overview of insolvency law in South Africa. Secondly, it highlights some of the statutory provisions, which deal with executory contracts. The chapter then proceeds to evaluate the manner in which South African courts have adjudicated disputes arising from executory contracts once the trustee or liquidator has assumed office. In particular, this chapter aims to illustrate the important role of trustees and liquidators when confronted with executory contracts during the process of sequestration. **34.05**

B. BRIEF OVERVIEW OF SOUTH AFRICA LEGAL FRAMEWORK

South Africa does not have a unitary legislation regulating insolvency law. Various statutes provide procedures for natural persons and partnerships on one side and legal persons on the other. Nonetheless, the Insolvency Act ('IA 1936') is the main source of South African Insolvency Law and its actual **34.06**

4 See *Richter NO v Riverside Estates (Pty) Ltd* (n 2), 223 where *concursus creditorum* was described as 'community of creditors'. See also *Ward v Barrett NO & another NO* [1963] (2) SA 546 (A) at 552 and *Walker v Syfret* [1911] AD 141.

5 The Constitutional Court in *Stratford and Others v Investec Bank Ltd and Others* [2015] 36 *ILJ* 583 (CC) para 44 held that:

> [t]he correct approach in evaluating advantage to creditors is for a court to exercise its discretion [and] assess whether the sequestration will result in some payment to the creditors as a body; that there is a substantial estate from which the creditors cannot get payment except through sequestration; or that some pecuniary benefit will result for the creditors.

6 Ellerine Brothers (Pty) Ltd v McCarthy Ltd [2014] (4) SA 22 (SCA) para 11.

administrative processes.[7] The IA 1936 through its definition of who can be sequestrated expressly excludes corporate entities from its scope.[8] The liquidation processes relating to corporate insolvency in South Africa are generally included in the 2008 Companies Act[9] ('CA 2008') and the repealed 1973 Companies Act[10] ('CA 1973'), parts of which are still enforceable. In particular, the provisions relating to corporate insolvency procedures contained in the CA 1973 were not repealed, while the CA 2008 provides detailed provisions dealing with business rescue.[11]

34.07 The CA 2008 also amended parts of the Close Corporations Act,[12] by changing the regulatory framework applicable to close corporations and effectively prohibiting the registration of new close corporations. Existing close corporations can be converted into companies.[13] The IA 1936 provides procedural steps, which are also applicable to companies and close corporations. For instance, section 44(1) of the IA 1936 enjoins creditors to prove their claims before the expiration of the period of three months from the conclusion of the second meeting of the creditors of the estate. This provision also applies to companies.[14] Some parts of the IA 1936 are equally enforceable – from the winding-up of insolvent companies, to the appointment of, and control over, liquidators and provisional liquidators.[15] Such provisions were imported into the company law framework by section 339 of the CA 1973.[16]

34.08 There are instances where South African courts have also questioned the parallel regulation of sequestration and liquidation processes, because of the similarities existing between these procedures.[17] In 1999, the South Africa Law Reform Commission published a discussion paper inviting comments on the review of the insolvency law in South Africa. This discussion paper

7 24 of 1936. See the University of Pretoria's Law Faculty's Final Report Containing Proposals on a Unified IA 1936 (January 2000) vii available at http://www.justice.gov.za/master/m_docs/insolve-unified-insolvency-report-up.pdf [Last accessed 06 November 2018].

8 See IA 1936, s 2.

9 71 of 2008.

10 61 of 1973.

11 Boraine A and Van Wyk J 'The application of "repealed" sections of the Companies Act 61 of 1973 to liquidation proceedings of insolvent companies' (2013) *De Jure* 644, 646.

12 69 of 1984.

13 Companies Act 71 of 2008, sch 3, item 2. See also *Herman and Another v Set-Mak Civils* [2013] (1) SA 386 (FB) para 4.

14 See *Mayo NO v De Montlehu* [2016] (1) SA 36 (SCA) para 19.

15 See CA , s 339.

16 *Ex parte: Master of the High Court of South Africa (North Gauteng)* (n 1) para 8.

17 See *Woodley v Guardian Assurance Company of SA Ltd* [1976] (1) SA 758 (W) at 763E–F.

contained the Draft Insolvency Bill and Explanatory Memorandum,[18] which recognised the:

> strong support for uniform provisions for all corporate and individual insolvencies, at least as regards the administration of the liquidation process, with nuances for banks, insurance companies and others where such differences are justified by structural requirements.[19]

The legislature is currently working on the revised and consolidated unified Insolvency Bill, which is expected to unify Insolvency Law in South Africa. It would be beneficial to have a clear and easy to navigate unitary insolvency legislation which adequately deals with all insolvency processes irrespective of whether natural persons or juristic persons are involved.[20] While the proposed unified legislation might not necessarily eradicate uncertainties and ambiguities relating to the administration of insolvent estates, it will nonetheless, lead to increased efficiency in their administration generally.[21]

C. TREATMENT OF EXECUTORY CONTRACTS

In South Africa, the phrase 'executory contracts' while recognised under our insolvency law, is nonetheless, not widely used. Instead, the phrase 'uncompleted contracts' has received both judicial[22] and academic[23] endorsement and appears to be used to refer to what in other jurisdictions may be referred to as 'executory contracts'. It is difficult to provide a precise definition of what may amount to an executory contract in South Africa in respect of insolvency law. Nonetheless, an executory contract may be described as a contract which has not been performed at all, or which has alternatively only been partially performed by the time of the appointment of either the trustee or the liquidator. Thus, an executory contract refers to a situation wherein a person or entity has been put under insolvency processes due to his or its inability to **34.09**

18 South African Law Commission 'Review of the Law of Insolvency' Discussion Paper 86 (Volume 1) Project 63 (29 October 1999).

19 Ibid., para 5.1.

20 *Keay* A. 'To *unify* or *not* to *unify* insolvency legislation: *international. experience* and the *latest South African proposals*' (1999) De Jure 62, 79.

21 University of Pretoria's Law Faculty's Final Report Containing Proposals on a Unified Insolvency Act (January 2000) para 3.7 available at http://www.justice.gov.za/master/m_docs/insolve-unified-insolvency-report-up.pdf [Last accessed 06 November 2018].

22 See *Ellerine Brothers* (n 6) para 12, *Smith & another v Parton NO* [1980] (3) SA 724 (D) 728H–729A and *Tangney & others v Zive's Trustee* [1961] (1) SA 449 (W) 452–3, *Edkins v Registrar of Deeds, Johannesburg and Others* [2012] (6) SA 278 (GSJ) para 5.

23 See also Sharrock R, Van der Linde K, and Smith A Hockly, *Insolvency Law* (9th ed., 2012) 87 and Bertelsmmann *et al, Mars, The Law of Insolvency in South Africa* (9th ed., 2008) 222.

satisfy his or its debts, it is a contract to which they are a party, but only one or none of the parties has performed the terms of such a contract.[24] In other words, either the insolvent or the other party to the contract at the time of the appointment of the liquidator or the trustee has not performed at all or only provided a portion of the required performance and is yet to complete the required performance in full.

34.10 As such, for the purposes of this chapter, executory contracts should be understood as those contracts, which can arise from a variety of transactions such as: lease agreements; credit agreements; acquisition of immovable and employment contracts before sequestration or liquidation.

(1) Common law approach

34.11 The common law as interpreted and applied by the courts provides general principles regulating to instances where performance under an already concluded contract has not been rendered at the time the trustee or liquidator assumes office.

34.12 As confirmed in *Nedcor Investment Bank v Pretoria Belgrave Hotel (PTY) Ltd* ('*Nedcor*'), the starting point is that an executory contract 'does not terminate automatically on the company being placed in liquidation'.[25] This means that contracting parties cannot legally put a clause in their contract, which would suspend or put an end to the parties' contract on the sequestration or liquidation of one of the parties. In other words, in South Africa, the so-called ipso facto clauses are generally unenforceable.

34.13 However, as Sharrock *et al* correctly caution, 't]he proposition that insolvency does not suspend or put an end to the insolvent's executory contracts must be qualified to some extent'.[26] The general rule expressed in *Nedcor* is not applicable to all executory contracts in South Africa. For instance, section 38(1) of the IA 1936 specifically provides that '[t]he contracts of service of employees whose employer has been sequestrated are suspended with effect from the date of the granting of a sequestration order'. Similarly, in *Goodricke & Son V Auto Protection Insurance Co Ltd (In Liquidation)*,[27] the court accepted in the context of attorney and client mandate contract that 'the relationship of

24 See Countryman V., 'Executory contracts in bankruptcy: Part I' (1973) 57 *Minnesota Law Review* 439–91, 460.

25 *Nedcor Investment Bank v Pretoria Belgrave Hotel (PTY) Ltd* 2003 (5) SA 189 (SCA) para 6. See also *Bryant & Flanagan (Pty) Ltd v Muller and Another NNO* [1978] (2) SA 807 (A) at 812.

26 Sharrock *et al* (n 23) 91.

27 1968 (1) SA 717 (A) at 722H.

an attorney and his client is based on mandatum with some features which are peculiar to this particular kind of agency, [thus] when any change of status of the principal occurs, which includes the latter's insolvency, the mandate is automatically terminated'. However, it has been argued that this position was an overgeneralisation, in that:

> The agent cannot bind the principal to the contract which the principal himself would not have the power to conclude. However, if the mandate pertains to a matter in which the insolvent may act without the consent of his trustee, the mandate does not terminate automatically.[28]

It appears however, that the nature of the mandate itself and the ability of the insolvent to act independently from the trustee or liquidator in relation to that contract of mandate will determine whether or not the sequestration or liquidation brings an end to the mandate concerned. As such, given the fact that sequestration or liquidation of the debtor does not result in the termination of a contract, it follows that parties should not as a matter of law put clauses in their contracts, which will have the effect of either suspending or terminating contracts when either of them is declared insolvent. **34.14**

In South Africa, the general principles which should guide trustees dealing with executory contracts have been stated by the courts over a period of time. It has been held that: **34.15**

> [t]he trustee may elect to abide by the contract and must make such election within a reasonable time, failing which he will be taken to have abandoned it and the other party can treat it as at an end. If, however, the trustee elects to abide by the contract, he steps into the shoes of the insolvent and is obliged to the other party to perform whatever is required of the insolvent in terms of the contract, including unfulfilled past obligations of the insolvent.[29]

Executory contracts remain valid notwithstanding the fact that one of the parties has been declared insolvent. Sequestration, while not terminating the executory contract, nonetheless, empowers the trustee to elect whether or not to abide by such a contract. It has been argued that the trustee is not *per se* **34.16**

---

28 See Bertelsmmann (n 23) 245 and authorities cited there. However, in *Klein No v South African Transport Services And Others* [1992] (3) SA 509 (W), Zulman J was not convinced by this criticism and held that '[i]t seems to me, however, that, even on the basis of the reasoning and test put forward by the learned author later in para 8.22 at 161, to the effect that it is necessary to examine the particular mandate before concluding whether it terminated upon insolvency, if one examines the mandate *in casu*, that mandate must have terminated on insolvency'.

29 *Smith* (n 22) 728D see also decisions cited by the court.

empowered to terminate executory contracts owing to the insolvent's sequestration, but merely shields the trustee who stepped into the insolvent's shoes not to be compelled to render performance in terms of such contracts.[30] In insolvency cases, the emphasis shifts on ensuring the highest possible return for creditors.

34.17 It is crucial for all the creditors to be treated fairly. To ensure fairness, creditors should be paid in accordance with their ranking. The law should devise measures to prevent one or more creditors' claims being satisfied to the prejudice of others.[31] Creditors are able to prove their claims at purposely convened meetings. For instance, section 40(1) of the IA 1936 provides that upon appointment, the Master shall immediately convene a first meeting of the creditors to allow them to prove their claims and elect a trustee. Section 364(1)(a) of the CA 1973 also makes provision for a meeting of creditors of the company to be convened after the liquidation order has been made by the court, in order for such creditors to prove their claims. Once creditors have proven their claims, they will be in a position to collectively guide the activity of the trustees and liquidators to pursue their interests.

34.18 The CA 1973 provides for the protection of creditors from the conduct of liquidators and trustees. Section 386(1)(a)–(e) of CA 1973 grants to the liquidators the power to carry out on their own, without prior authorisation, administrative functions. Section 386(4)(a)–(i) of the CA 1973 describes the powers which liquidators should exercise only upon approval from the creditors. As such, a liquidator should receive guidance from the body of creditors for instance when agreeing 'to any reasonable offer of composition made to the company by any debtor and to accept payment of any part of a debt due to the company in settlement thereof or to grant an extension of time for the payment of any such debt'.[32] They should also receive guidance when contemplating to 'compromise or admit any claim or demand against the company, including an unliquidated claim'.[33]

34.19 Due to the fact that the decision to accept payments, make an offer to pay, admit or demand a claim may relate to executory contracts, as a general rule liquidators should first obtain guidance from the general body of creditors on how to deal with such executory contracts. Liquidators should not only obtain guidance, but also abide by the directives of the body of creditors in order to ensure that the ultimate decision relating to the manner in which executory

30 Sharrock *et al* (n 23) 87.
31 See *Walker* (n 4) 160.
32 CA 1973, s 386(4)(b).
33 Ibid., s 386(4)(c).

contracts should be dealt with is not prejudicial to the interests of the general body of creditors.[34] It is in the creditors' collective interests to participate in the process of realising the assets of the insolvent person or company. In these meetings, creditors will be able to express their views on among others, whether or not executory contracts should be honoured by the trustee or liquidator.

After having received the guidance from the creditors, liquidators and trustees must act accordingly. However, absent any indication from the creditors, trustees and liquidators will act in accordance with their common law or statutory powers by electing either to abide by or repudiate such contracts. Liquidators and trustees are entitled by virtue of their appointment to terminate executory contracts, and cannot be coerced to perform in terms of such contracts when they have decided not to honour them.[35] However: **34.20**

> a trustee who elects to abide by an executory contract entered into prior to insolvency cannot demand performance of any remaining obligations under the contract from the other party unless the trustee is prepared to perform in full and tenders complete performance of all the insolvent's obligations, including unfulfilled past ones, under the contract.[36]

It is crucial for liquidators and trustees to decide promptly how they wish to proceed with executory contracts, failing which they will be regarded as having abandoned such contracts.[37] Once the liquidator or trustee has repudiated the contract then the creditor can either accept or reject the repudiation. Acceptance of the repudiation enables the creditor to prove concurrent claims for damages suffered as a result of breach of contract. The creditors' acceptance of the liquidator's repudiation of the executory contract will prevent the creditor from enforcing specific performance of that contract against the liquidator.[38] The creditor of an executory contract either way is directed to line up with concurrent creditors who have proved their claims for monetary compensation. However, when the liquidator has decided to honour the executory contract, he or she must carry out the obligations originally included in such a contract.[39] Should the trustee or liquidator inform the creditor that he or she will honour an executory contract, he or she cannot later decide not to honour that contract. **34.21**

34 *Chater Developments v Waterkloof Marina Estates and Another* 2015 (5) SA 138 (SCA) paras 9–11.

35 See *Thomas Construction (Pty) Ltd (in liquidation) v Grafton Furniture Manufactures (Pty) Ltd* 1988 (2) SA 546 (A) 566–7.

36 *Goodricke & Son v Auto Protection Insurance Co Ltd* 1968 (1) SA 717 (A) at 723 G.

37 *Smith* (n 22) 728D.

38 See *Ward* (n 4) 552H–553(B).

39 *Smith* (n 22) 728D.

(2) Statutory provisions relating to executory contracts

34.22 Sections 35 to 37 and section 84 of the IA 1936 deal with specific contracts or transactions where performance either by the insolvent or the third party or even both the insolvent and the third party are still outstanding after the court has granted a sequestration order and the trustee has been appointed.

Immovable properties

34.23 Where the insolvent person acquired an immovable property but such property was not transferred to him or her, the trustee must make a decision whether or not to complete such a transaction. Section 35 of the IA 1936 enables the trustee to either enforce or abandon an executory contract involving an immovable property. The trustee has six weeks to make his or her election, failing which the other party may apply to the court for the cancellation of that contract as well as the restoration of possession of such property. The decision to enforce the contract would mean both the insolvent estate and the third party will be bound to perform any outstanding obligations arising from that contract. While the third party can request the cancellation of the contract and restoration of the immovable property, it appears that they cannot request the court to order specific performance in order to enforce the contract. In other words, the trustee's decision to repudiate such a contract means that the third party cannot demand performance from the trustee, and can only sue the insolvent estate for any damages which they can prove to have suffered as a concurrent creditor.

34.24 Acquisition of immovable property by credit agreement before sequestration is also affected by the Alienation of Land Act.[40] Prior to 1971, purchasers of immovable properties were not entitled under common law to insist that such properties be transferred to them when the sellers were declared insolvent.[41] In 1971, the now repealed Sale of Land on Instalments Act,[42] 'made provision for a right vesting in the purchaser to take transfer of the land purchased on instalments, subject to conditions provided by that Act'.[43] This was repealed by the Land Alienation Act.

---

40 68 of 1981.

41 *Sarrahwitz v Martiz N.O. and Another* [2015] (8) BCLR 925 (CC) para 33. See also *Glen Anil Finance (Pty) Ltd v Joint Liquidators, Glen Anil Development Corporation (Pty) Ltd (In Liquidation)* [1981] (1) SA 171 (A) 183 G.

42 72 of 1971.

43 *Sarrahwitz v Maritz NO* (819/2012) [2013] ZAECGHC 10 (07 February 2013) para 15. See also *Sarrahwitz* (n 41) para 33.

It has been held that the protection previously offered by the Sale of Land on Instalments Act 'applies with equal force in respect of sections 21 and 22 of the Alienation of Land Act as read with the definition of the term "contract" provided for by section 1 of that Act'.[44] The Constitutional Court has cautioned that the protection offered by the Sale of Land on Instalments Act which was retained by sections 21 and 22 of the Land Alienation Act, was not intended for everyone irrespective of their socio economic status. The Constitutional Court made it clear that these provisions were meant to protect 'vulnerable people who have no other place they could call home or lack the resources to acquire another, when the one they had is lost to the seller's insolvency'.[45] **34.25**

It is doubtful whether the Sale of Land on Instalments Act or Alienation of Land Act distinguishes between poor and rich creditors when it comes to insisting on transferring the property upon the insolvency of the seller. In the interest of certainty, it is preferable that a buyer who purchases a property on instalments irrespective of his or her socio-economic status is able to enjoy the protection that is available under sections 21 and 22 of the Alienation of Land Act. **34.26**

The Constitutional Court's view that 'Parliament saw the need to afford protection to those vulnerable and financially-constrained buyers by ensuring that they could still obtain transfer of the residential property when the seller becomes insolvent' is – in the author's opinion – too restrictive.[46] Actually, the legislature sought to protect any buyer irrespective of their financial muscle who chose to pay for an immovable property through instalments. Nonetheless, the Constitutional Court correctly held that: **34.27**

> [t]he purpose for the creation of the exception was to protect the interests of individuals who would have spent ... money they had to secure residential property, in terms of an instalment sale agreement, when the seller of that property became insolvent. There was a risk of the purchaser having to endure the real hardship and misfortune of losing both the house and the money already paid, as a result of the common law position.[47]

Basically, where there is a credit sale agreement of an immovable property and the seller's estate is sequestrated, the trustee must notify the purchaser of such **34.28**

44 Ibid., *Sarrahwitz* (2013) para 17. The Constitutional Court has indirectly confirmed this in *Sarrahwitz* (n 41) para 34.
45 Ibid., para 35.
46 Ibid., para 38.
47 Ibid.

agreement in order for the purchaser to exercise his or her right to take transfer of the immovable property.[48]

34.29 There are circumstances where the insolvent can purchase a movable property before sequestration of their estate, but fail to pay the purchase price in full after the property has been delivered. In such circumstances, section 36 (1) of the IA 1936 provides that:

> the seller may, after the sequestration of the purchaser's estate, reclaim that property if within ten days after delivery thereof, he has given notice in writing to the purchaser or to the trustee of the purchaser's insolvent estate or to the Master, that he reclaims the property.

The trustee will evaluate the claim and decide whether to return the property or dispute the seller's right to reclaim such movable property.[49] Should the trustee decide not to return the movable property to the seller, they will not be entitled to reclaim that property directly from the trustee. The seller can only reclaim such property by instituting legal proceedings for the restoration of such movable property within 14 days after the trustee's notification of intention not to return the property to the seller.[50]

34.30 In terms of section 36(2) of the IA 1936, the insolvent and the seller's contract 'shall be deemed to provide for the payment of the purchase price upon delivery of the property in question to the purchaser, unless the seller has agreed that the purchase price or any part thereof shall not be claimable before or at the time of such delivery'. The insolvent buyer and the seller's contract will be regarded as an executory contract if the movable property was delivered to the insolvent buyer and – notwithstanding, the agreement that the purchase price would be payable at the time of delivery or anytime thereafter – the insolvent buyer nonetheless, fails to pay the purchase price in full. If the insolvent buyer did not pay anything towards the acquisition of such movable property, it might not be difficult for the seller to obtain their movable property back. However, it is worth noting that 'a seller shall not be entitled to recover any property which he [or she] sold and delivered to a purchaser whose estate was sequestrated after the sale, only by reason of the fact that the purchaser failed to pay the purchase price'.[51]

---

48 See Land Alienation Act, ss 21 and 22.
49 IA 1936, s 36(1).
50 Ibid.
51 Ibid., s 36(4).

These provisions provide the trustee of the insolvent buyer's estate with the power to refuse to restore the movable property to the seller if the seller's request for restoration is merely based on the fact that the insolvent buyer failed to pay the purchase price in full. 'The trustee of the purchaser's insolvent estate shall not be obliged to restore any property reclaimed by the seller ... unless the seller refunds to him [or her] every part of the purchase price which he [or she] has already received.'[52] 34.31

Lease agreements

Section 37 of the IA 1936 provides that a 34.32

> lease entered into by any person as lessee shall not be determined by the sequestration of his estate, but the trustee of his insolvent estate may determine the lease by notice in writing to the lessor: Provided that the lessor may claim from the estate, compensation for any loss which he may have sustained by reason of the non-performance of the terms of such lease.

In terms of section 386(4)(g) of the CA 1973, the liquidator of a company has the same powers conferred to the trustee of the insolvent estate referred to in section 35 and 37 of the IA 1936 with regard to immovable properties acquired by the company and lease agreements entered into by the company before liquidation.

Despite section 37 of the IA 1936, there was a need for South African courts to clarify whether the continuation of lease agreements could be affected by the insolvency of one of the parties to such agreements. In *Ellerine Brothers (Pty) Ltd v McCarthy Ltd*,[53] Tois let certain business premises from Ellerine and sub-let the portion of the property to McCarthy. Tois failed to keep up with rental payments and Ellerine cancelled the lease agreement. Six days before Ellerine could cancel the lease agreement, one of Tois's creditors' launched an application to liquidate Tois, which was to be heard on the day Ellerine delivered a letter which informed Tois of the cancellation of the lease agreement. The matter was subsequently postponed to allow for the filing of answering and replying papers. During this period, Ellerine and Tois's liquidators entered into a cession agreement, wherein '[a]s consideration for the rental payable by the insolvent to Ellerine under the lease, the liquidator ceded to Ellerine the insolvent's rights to the rental payable by McCarthy 34.33

52 IA 1936, s 36(3).
53 2014 (4) SA 22 (SCA).

under the sub-lease'.[54] In terms of the said cession, it was agreed that the lease was still operative and that the liquidator had elected to continue with the lease.

34.34 Relying on the cession, Ellerine sued McCarthy for the amounts due in terms of the sub-lease.[55] The court clarified that on the insolvency of the lessee ordinary election common law principles relating to executory contracts are applicable.[56] The declaration of insolvency by the court and the coming into effect of *concursus creditorum* do not impact the continued existence of the parties' rights and obligations under the lease agreement. As such, nothing prevents the trustee or the liquidator from executing the insolvent's part of the contract which ought to have been carried out between the date the court granted the sequestration or liquidation order and the date the trustee or liquidator decides to honour the contract.[57] It has been held that '[i]t is only in the event of the liquidator making an election not to abide by the executory contract that the lessor, because of the *concursus*, cannot compel performance. Absent such an election, the terms of the lease remain in place and the liquidator must comply with it'.[58]

Credit agreements

34.35 It is also possible that an insolvent may have been required under a contract for the sale of goods to make payment by instalments. In terms of section 84 (1) of the IA 1936:

> [i]f any property was delivered to a person ... under a transaction that is an instalment agreement ... such a transaction shall be regarded on the sequestration of the debtor's estate as creating in favour of the other party to the transaction ... a hypothec over that property whereby the amount still due to him [or her] under the transaction is secured.

34.36 According to Smith '[t]his section specially provides for the situation in which an insolvent buys movable goods under an instalment agreement and his [or her] estate is later sequestrated. Under this agreement, all or part of the price is deferred and is to be paid by periodic payments'.[59] The buyer would receive the movable property subject to the condition that they should pay instalments usually on a monthly basis. However, ownership is in principle reserved until

54 *Ellerine Brothers* (n 6) para 4.
55 Ibid., para 5.
56 Ibid., para 10 (footnotes omitted).
57 Ibid., para 12.
58 Ibid., para 13.
59 Smith A 'Insolvency Law' (2013) *Annual Survey of South African Law* 578–632, 609.

payment is made in full. Should the buyer be declared insolvent, the seller who ordinarily should possess the ownership of the item sold, would not retain ownership due to the security established by section 84 (1) of the IA 1936 in their favour. The effect of section 84(1) of the IA 1936 is that ownership will pass to the buyer's insolvent estate and vest in the trustee or the liquidator and the seller will have a secured claim in terms of the hypothec credited by this section in their favour. In *Ukubona 2000 Electrical CC and Another v City Power Johannesburg (Pty) Ltd*[60] it was held that: '[w]here the creditor/seller is the owner of the goods, ownership over the goods of necessity passes to the trustee of the buyer's insolvent estate. The reason is that no-one may have a hypothec over his [or her] own property'.[61]

Section 84(1) of the IA 1936 further provides that: '[t]he trustee of the debtor's insolvent estate shall, if required by the creditor, deliver the property to him, and thereupon the creditor shall be deemed to be holding that property as security for his claim ...'. **34.37**

Market participation and master agreements

Sections 35A and 35B of the IA 1936 deal with insolvent persons who participate in financial markets and those who enter into master agreements respectively before their sequestration. A person becomes a market participant by constituting, maintaining, and providing infrastructure transferred by or on behalf of a seller. He or she must also have brought together buyers and sellers of securities or matched the orders for securities of multiple buyers and sellers.[62] His or her market participation might also have made him or her 'a person authorised by a licensed exchange with which it is associated to perform clearing services or settlement services or both clearing services and settlement services in terms of the exchange rules' or a person to whom a regulated person provides security services.[63] On sequestration of such a market participant, those to whom he or she owes some performance in respect of any transaction are entitled to terminate the transaction or revoke settlement instructions. The trustee of the insolvent estate of the market participant will be bound by such termination or revocation. Unlike section 35 of the IA 1936, section 35A does not entitle the trustee to decide whether to repudiate or enforce executory obligations arising from transactions relating to exchange of securities. **34.38**

60 (155/03) [2004] ZASCA 65 (1 June 2004) para 14.

61 See also *Williams Hunt (Vereniging) Ltd v Slomowitz* 1960 (1) SA 499 (T) 501 E-G and *Van Zyl NO v Bolton* 1994 (4) SA 648 (C) 652 E-G.

62 Securities Services Act 36 of 2004, s 1.

63 Financial Markets Act 19 of 2012, s 1.

34.39 Section 35B (1) of the IA 1936 deals with master agreements which are entered in 'accordance with standard terms published by the International Swaps and Derivatives Association, the International Securities Lenders Association, the Bond Market Association or the International Securities Market Association'.[64] If the insolvent was a party to a master agreement, upon their sequestration 'all unperformed obligations of the parties in this agreement terminate or may be terminated' or 'become or may become due immediately'.[65] The 'values of the unperformed obligations are determined or may be determined' in order 'to calculate the net amount payable upon sequestration'.[66] This section does not provide direction in relation to the trustee's role regarding master agreements. It appears, however, that guidance will be sought from the agreement itself. It does not appear as if the trustee has an election under this section.

34.40 The trustee or liquidator should also deal with employment contracts which were in existence before the employer's sequestration or liquidation. When the employer's estate is sequestrated or liquidated, the trustee or the liquidator must consult and engage with the insolvent employer's employees in order to explore appropriate measures to save or rescue the whole or part of the business of the insolvent employer.[67]

Employment contracts

34.41 In terms of section 38(1) of the IA 1936 '[t]he contracts of service of employees whose employer has been sequestrated are suspended with effect from the date of the granting of a sequestration order'.[68] Such employees are not required to render services in terms of their employment contracts and are not entitled to any remuneration in terms of such contracts.[69] In terms of section 38(4) of the IA 1936, the trustee or liquidator is entitled to terminate the employees' contracts of employment after consulting them. In terms of section 38(11) of the IA 1936, 'an employee whose contract of service terminates or has been terminated … is entitled to claim severance benefits from the estate of the insolvent employer in accordance with section 41 of the Basic Conditions of Employment Act … 75 of 1997'.[70]

---

64 IA 1936, s 35B(2)(a).

65 Ibid., s 35B(2)(a)(i)(aa) and (bb).

66 Ibid., s 35B(2)(a)(ii) and (iii).

67 Ibid., s 38 (6).

68 See *Stratford and Others v Investec Bank Ltd and Others* 2015 (3) BCLR 358 (CC) para 34. See also H Chitimira 'Furnishing employees with the petition for sequestration – constitutional and related issues: Stratford and Others v Investec Bank Limited and Others 2015 (3) SA 1 (CC)' (2017) 1 *SA Merc LJ* 153–71.

69 IA 1936, s 38(2)(a).

70 *Mabaso and Others v Barnard NO and Others* (6962/2011, 15956/2012) [2012] ZAGPPHC 187 (31 August 2012) para 12.

D. LACK OF REFORMS

No insolvency rules provide adequate guidance for executory contracts. In *Bryant & Flanagan (Pty) Ltd v Muller and Another*[71] it was held that '[t]he IA 1936 … does not provide generally for the effects of insolvency on executory or partly performed contracts entered into by insolvents before the sequestration of their estates … one must look to principles developed over the years in a series of judgments'. **34.42**

It is recommended that all the provisions dealing with unperformed obligations after the sequestration of the insolvent's estate should be reviewed. In particular, there should be a uniform approach to different transactions which were entered into by the insolvent before their sequestration. The trustee must be provided the same powers irrespective of the nature of the executory transaction. It is submitted that the trustee after consultation with the creditors must at all times have a right to elect either to enforce or repudiate any executory contract. The trustee's election irrespective of the nature of the contract must be to the collective advantage of creditors. **34.43**

Since 1987, the South African Insolvency law has been under review and the South African Law Reform Commission has investigated how this area of law can be improved and has published its recommendations in various working papers and reports.[72] Notwithstanding, the work done by the South African Law Reform Commission and the recommendations the commission has made, the legislature has not shown any interest in changing the South African Insolvency law. The University of Pretoria's faculty of law has also made proposals on how South African insolvency law can be improved, but most importantly that there should be a uniform legislation which should regulate the entire insolvency law industry in South Africa.[73] It is unfortunate however, that while recommendations and proposals have been made regarding insolvency law generally, nonetheless, none of the proposed reforms have dealt with executory contracts. The manner in which executory contracts either once the trustee or liquidator has been appointed or before liquidation after the appointment of the business rescue practitioner should be dealt with has not been part of the reform discussions. It is hoped that this chapter will provoke some thoughts on how executory contracts can be regulated in South **34.44**

71 [1977] 2 All SA 107 (N) 111.

72 See Discussion Paper 86 'Review of Insolvency Law' Volume 1 Project 63 which incorporated the Draft Insolvency Bill and Explanatory Memorandum available at http://salawreform.justice.gov.za/dpapers/dp86.pdf. See also *Report* on *review* of the *Law of Insolvency (2000) available at* http://www.justice.gov.za/salrc/reports/r_prj63_insolv_2000apr.pdf [Last accessed 06 November 2018].

73 University of Pretoria (n 7) para 3.7.

Africa. The legislature has however, made provision during the business rescue proceedings for the practitioner either partially or conditionally to suspend, for the duration of the business rescue proceedings, any obligation of the company that arises under an agreement to which the company was a party at the commencement of the business rescue proceedings; and would otherwise become due during those proceedings.[74]

E. CONCLUDING REMARKS

34.45 This chapter discussed the manner in which executory contracts are dealt with in South Africa. It was shown that executory contracts are regulated by the common law. However, there are specific sections in the IA 1936 which provide some guidance on how the courts can deal with executory obligations once the insolvent has been sequestrated.

34.46 In order for the courts to deal with these contracts adequately, there is a need for uniform legislative provision dealing with executory contracts. The phrase 'executory contracts' within the ambit of insolvency law should be defined in order to clarify the circumstances under which contracts could be classified as executory. It should further provide guidance whether wholly executory contracts should be dealt with in the same manner as partially completed contracts.

34.47 Most importantly, such provision should make it clear whether the trustee or liquidator can legitimately repudiate a partially completed contract in the same manner in which he can, with a wholly executory contract.

34.48 In conclusion, executory contracts have not yet received adequate legislative, judicial and academic attention. As such, these contracts are generally not regarded as controversial in South Africa, save where the courts are called to deal with them on a case-by-case basis. In all the discussion papers issued by the South African Law Reform Commission relating to insolvency law, there appears to be no dedicated attention to executory contracts. It is hoped, however, that this chapter will spark academic debate which hopefully will eventually craft the jurisprudence relating to executory contracts in South Africa.

74 CA 2008, s 136(2)(a).

35

NATIONAL REPORT FOR THE UNITED ARAB EMIRATES AND ITS FREE ZONES

Christian Chamorro-Courtland*

A. INTRODUCTION

This report considers the treatment of executory contracts[1] upon the default of a debtor company under the three main jurisdictions in the United Arab Emirates ('UAE'). Depending on the financial situation of the business, a default could result in the commencement of restructuring[2] or liquidation procedures. The analysis will focus on the enforceability of *ipso facto* clauses[3] 35.01

* The author would like to thank Marc H. Cohen and Adrian Low for their research assistance.

1 Executory contracts are contracts that at the commencement of an insolvency proceeding have not yet been fully performed by both the insolvent debtor and the counterparty. For the purpose of this report, the definition of an executory contract is broad in scope.

2 The terms 'reorganization' and 'restructuring' are used interchangeably.

3 '*Ipso facto* clauses are common place in commercial contracts. They allow a party to automatically terminate a contract where a specified insolvency event has occurred, such as where a liquidator, receiver or administrator is appointed or a deed of company arrangement is entered into. There is a sentiment in some quarters that *ipso facto* clauses are a major impediment to distressed companies being able to turn their situation around. The opposing view is that the other contracting party should be able to protect their commercial interests.' Graham Roberts and Rocco Russo, 'Australia: Insolvency Insights: Proposed Outlawing of Ipso Facto Termination Clauses' (9 Oct. 2016). http://www.mondaq.com/404.asp?404;http://www.mondaq.com:80/australia/x/533774/Insolvency+Bankruptcy/Insolvency+insights+Proposed+outlawing+of+ipso+facto+termination+clauses&login=true [Last accessed on 1 January, 2017].

For example, the company's trade creditors may refuse to provide goods and services even though they are still being paid. The operation of these clauses further diminishes the value of a business entering upon the commencement of restructuring proceedings where a moratorium[4] is imposed.

35.02 The UAE has a unique legal system because it has three jurisdictions with their own separate insolvency regimes. Businesses have the option to choose between the Dubai International Financial Centre ('DIFC') and the Abu Dhabi Global Market ('ADGM'),[5] which are located in free zones, and the new federal insolvency legislation,[6] which applies in the rest of the UAE. This chapter will consider these three regimes separately.

35.03 This chapter fills a gap in the legal literature by providing a detailed comparative analysis on the treatment of executory contracts on the insolvency of a business in the various UAE jurisdictions. In order to provide some context, it provides a summary of the insolvency procedures available to a business in distress under the previous insolvency regime; yet the main focus is on the insolvency regime in the DIFC and the new UAE federal insolvency legislation. Furthermore, it provides an exhaustive description on the treatment of executory contracts negotiated by the parties during solvency should one of the parties enter into insolvency proceedings, with a particular focus on *ipso facto* clauses and close-out netting. It extensively examines the factors that shaped the insolvency regimes in the UAE and considers areas where the law requires further reform.

B. INSOLVENCY LAW

35.04 The UAE has had some form of insolvency legislation since 1993 under the Commercial Code[7] and the Commercial Companies Law.[8] Under this antiquated civil law legal framework:

> a petition for bankruptcy [could] be initiated by a trader, a public prosecutor, a court, or a creditor. From the lender's perspective, a trader [would] have committed a criminal office (sic) of bankruptcy by default if it [had] suspended payment for more

---

insolvency and may reduce the scope for a successful restructure or prevent the sale of the business as a going concern, with consequential impact on the returns to creditors in any subsequent liquidation.

Australian Government, National Innovation and Science Agenda, *Improving Bankruptcy & Insolvency Laws*, Proposals Paper (Apr. 2016) 17.

4 The terms 'moratorium' and 'automatic stay' are used interchangeably.

5 This chapter will not discuss the insolvency regime used in the ADGM, as this is still a brand new jurisdiction and it has closely modelled its laws on those of the UK.

6 Federal Decree Law No. 9 of 2016 on Bankruptcy. The quotes from this legislation used in this report are from an unofficial translation from Arabic.

7 Federal Law No. 18 of 1993 [hereinafter 'Commercial Code'].

8 Federal Law No. 2 of 2015.

> than 30 days and failed to file a petition for bankruptcy within the 30 days period … Upon the declaration of bankruptcy, a moratorium [came] into effect such that no proceedings [could] be brought by a creditor against the debtor.[9]
>
> On the making of a bankruptcy declaration a bankruptcy judge, an inspector and a trustee in bankruptcy [were] all appointed … The trustee [had] the *option to complete any uncompleted contractual obligations of the debtor or to terminate onerous contracts* … In all cases, a creditors' committee [would] be appointed. The committee [had] established powers and rights to require relevant information and [would] consult with the bankruptcy trustee on most issues.[10]

The former insolvency regime was intended to facilitate the liquidation of an insolvent business. However, there are various reasons why this legislation was rarely used by failing businesses.[11] First, it is possible that the law was not applied because 'there are no specialist courts or courts that necessarily have any bankruptcy experience'.[12] Therefore, the owners of failing businesses would have been reluctant to file for bankruptcy with judges inexperienced in handling insolvency proceedings. **35.05**

Second, under the Commercial Code, 'a trader which is unable to pay its debts [was required to] apply to be declared bankrupt within 30 days. Failure to do so constitute[d] the criminal offence of 'bankruptcy by default', and [could] result in fines and potential imprisonment'.[13] Hence, rather than report that the business was insolvent, a large number of business owners would flee the UAE to avoid fines and incarceration.[14] **35.06**

---

9 Renata Rai and Yi Ling Wong, 'An Overview of the UAE Insolvency Regime and its Effectiveness' (Jun/Jul. 2016) Al Tamimi & Co. [hereinafter 'Rai and Wong'].

10 World Bank, Hawkamah/World Bank/OECD/INSOL International: Study on Insolvency Systems in the Middle East and North Africa (Dec. 1, 2009) at 54 [hereinafter 'World Bank, Insolvency Systems'] [emphasis added].

11 'Gary Watts, partner and regional head of corporate commercial at law firm Tamimi & Co, points out that the UAE already has insolvency laws – 'though it is fair to say that nobody makes use of them'. When questioned by Arabian Business, several lawyers said they were aware of just one significant corporate insolvency administered in the UAE under the existing law – the *White Bay* case concerning property developer Al Murjan Real Estate in Umm Al Quwain in 2011.' Sarah Townsend, 'Rising from the Ashes: The UAE's Insolvency Dilemma' (6 Feb., 2016) *Arabian Business* [hereinafter 'Townsend'].

12 World Bank, *Insolvency Systems*, see above fn 10 at 54.

13 Adrian Low, 'United Arab Emirates: New UAE Insolvency Law – What you need to Know' (8 Nov. 2016) Clyde & Co [hereinafter 'Low'].

14

> For small businesses, the difference between being able to restructure in difficult times is the difference between make or break. Last autumn [2015], UAE Banks Federation chairman Abdul Aziz Al Ghurair warned that an increasing number of small business owners are fleeing the UAE leaving behind an estimated $1.4bn of unpaid debt. This is bound to be alarming for a country that is working hard to encourage entrepreneurship and economic diversification in an era of persistently low oil prices.

Townsend, see above fn 11. This observation conflicts with comments made by Rai and Wong, who have remarked that '[i]n practice, however, we have not seen this offence pursued by the relevant authorities'. Rai and Wong, see above fn 9.

35.07 Third, the law provided limited recourse[15] for companies temporarily struggling with their finances to restructure their business.[16] 'The practice of formal restructuring is still rare in the Middle East, largely due to the stigma associated with public admission of corporate failings, and the anti-sharia implications of borrowing large sums of money.'[17] Hence, UAE businesses viewed the insolvency regime unfavourably because it favoured creditors over debtors. In the case of large businesses, the stigma of failing led to informal arrangements for restructuring because maintaining a good reputation was seen as particularly important.[18] The restructuring process was often 'camouflaged as refinancing negotiations'.[19] It is possible that the insolvency regime in the UAE favoured creditors over debtors because there is an inherent discord between the concept of restructuring and sharia law. 'The Quran essentially says that to voluntarily forgive a debtor is not just a breach of the law, but a sin.'[20] Therefore, religious law may have had a role in shaping the underlying policies of the former UAE insolvency framework.

35.08 The shortcomings of the previous insolvency framework encouraged two UAE free zones with their own financial centres – the DIFC and the ADGM – to introduce insolvency legislation in their own jurisdictions. It also led the UAE federal government to replace the Commercial Code with a new federal insolvency regime in 2016 that is applicable throughout the entire country.

C. AVAILABLE PROCEDURES AND TREATMENT OF EXECUTORY CONTRACTS

35.09 The Dubai International Financial Centre[21] is a financial centre located in Dubai with a common law jurisdiction, its own legislation, its own court system, and its own financial regulator – the Dubai Financial Services Authority ('DFSA').[22] The DIFC aims to become the leading financial centre

15 Struggling businesses had 'limited recourse to restructure debts and start again on a stronger footing.' ibid.

16 'The concept of business reorganizations is not known in the UAE.' World Bank, *Insolvency Systems*, see above fn 10 at 54.

17 Townsend, see above fn 11.

18 'Historically, creditors' rights in recovery of debts have been the focus of the insolvency regime in the UAE whilst debtor friendly restructuring options under the legislative framework are not a viable option due, in our view, to the stringent statutory requirements. Instead, informal consensual restructurings prevail.' Rai and Wong, see above fn 9.

19 Townsend, see above fn 11.

20 Ibid, quoting Didier Bruère-Dawson, partner at Brown Rudnick law firm.

21 The DIFC is recognized as a financial free zone under Federal Law No. 8 of 2004 Concerning Financial Free Zones, Federal Decree No. 35 of 2004, and Dubai Law No. 9 of 2004.

22 The DFSA regulates 'Authorized Firms', which include banks, insurance companies, investment banks, asset managers, and fund administrators providing financial services in the DIFC.

in the region. Its success stems from being established in a 'free zone', which exempts registered businesses from the UAE's commercial, corporate and civil laws.[23] The DIFC also has its own insolvency legislation, which is modelled on UK insolvency legislation.[24] The legislation includes provisions for the reorganization and liquidation of a failing business.

(1) Voluntary arrangement (restructuring)

The DIFC Insolvency Law[25] allows the directors of a company to propose 'a scheme of arrangement of its affairs'[26] to its creditors, which is a type of restructuring known as a 'voluntary arrangement'. The directors of a company will appoint a nominee who will summon meetings of shareholders and creditors to decide whether to approve the proposed voluntary arrangement. It allows the directors of the company to apply to the DIFC court[27] to 'obtain a moratorium for the Company'.[28] 'During the period for which a moratorium is in force for a Company,'[29] 'no other proceedings and no execution or other legal process may be commenced or continued, and no distress may be levied, against the Company or its Property except with the leave of the Court and subject to such terms as the Court may impose'.[30] This will require certain creditors to continue performing their executory contracts with the distressed company. **35.10**

The World Bank has observed that reorganization proceedings 'are not widely used in practice' in the DIFC because '[a] critical limitation on the usefulness of the procedure is that the creditors cannot bind the preferential or secured creditors to any reduction in their rights'.[31] This means that preferential and secured creditors are able to enforce their executory contracts with the debtor company upon entering a scheme of arrangement, as the Insolvency Law[32] includes certain exceptions to any moratorium that is granted by the court. For instance, a company would not be eligible to apply for a moratorium if it is a debtor under a security interest;[33] if its property is subject to the clearing rules **35.11**

23 'These zones and Financial Activities shall also be subject to all federal laws with the exception of federal civil and commercial laws.' Federal Law No. 8 of 2004, art 3(2).
24 Insolvency Act 1986 (c. 45) (UK).
25 Insolvency Law, DIFC Law No. 3 of 2009.
26 Ibid., s 8(1).
27 DIFC Insolvency Regulation (1 Oct., 2008), s 3.1.1.
28 Insolvency Law, DIFC Law No. 3 of 2009, s 9(1).
29 DIFC Insolvency Regulation, s 3.5.
30 Ibid., s 3.5(h).
31 World Bank, *Insolvency Systems*, see above fn 10 at 21.
32 Insolvency Law, DIFC Law No. 3 of 2009.
33 DIFC Insolvency Regulation, s 3.4.2(b).

of an authorized clearing system;[34] if it is the subject of any form of insolvency procedure;[35] or if it has incurred a liability under an agreement of USD $20 million or more.[36] Therefore, creditors are placed in a privileged position to decide whether the debtor must perform a particular executory contract, or they can decide whether they would like to terminate a particular contract.

35.12 The World Bank has also argued reorganizations are uncommon at the DIFC because '[t]he provisions for creditor voting are rather vague. Nevertheless, a dissenting creditor has the right to appeal against a reorganisation plan and the court must approve any amendments to the plan'.[37] Overall, it appears that creditors have more power than debtors during a voluntary arrangement, and creditors will have more control on whether executory contracts are enforced or terminated in these situations.

(2) Liquidation

35.13 In cases where the company is liquidated, it appears that creditors are in a weaker position vis-à-vis the failing business.

35.14 In practice, it is not easy for a recalcitrant debtor to obstruct the commencement of insolvency proceedings. The court may also grant provision relief to protect the estate. It is equally straightforward for the directors of an insolvent company to commence winding up by an application to the court. Whether it is a creditor or the directors of the debtor who makes the application, the commencement of proceedings immediately prohibits any unauthorized subsequent disposition of the debtor's estate. The estate does not for these purposes, however, extend to secured creditors whose rights are unfettered by the commencement of winding up. Under Part 5 of the law, the court has the power to set aside certain transactions that are contrary to the creditors' interests and in this connection, it provides for a lesser criteria where the other party is connected to the debtor.[38]

---

34 Ibid., s 3.4.2(c).

35 Ibid., s 3.4.2(d).

36 Ibid., s 3.4.2(f). Other reasons for not using reorganization procedures in the DIFC are because:

> the law does not require that a decision regarding a proposed reorganisation is reached within any specific time; it does not provide for any independent analysis of the proposed plan and it does not require that the anticipated return to creditors will be equal to that that they would obtain in liquidation.

World Bank, *Insolvency Systems*, see above fn 10 at 21.

37 Ibid.

38 Ibid., at 20.

The Insolvency Law[39] also permits the appointed liquidator to terminate any 'unprofitable contracts'.[40] Therefore, on the one hand, some creditors will find that the liquidator is able to cherry-pick and terminate executory contracts that are onerous. On the other hand, secured creditors will be able to enforce their security interests by terminating an executory contract under which the secured transaction arose. **35.15**

(3) Close-out netting

The DIFC Netting Law[41] enforces close-out netting, even during a moratorium. Close-out netting is a tool that is related to *ipso facto* clauses, as it allows a party to a *financial contract* that is still executory to *terminate* it if a default event occurs. Close-out netting involves *calculating* the termination values of the obligations of each of the parties and *setting-off* the termination values to arrive at a net amount payable by the net debtor to the net creditor. Jurisdictions around the world have passed special legislation that provides 'safe harbours' that carve-out financial contracts from insolvency legislation.[42] **35.16**

The aim has been to ensure that financial contracts are not affected by a moratorium and can be terminated upon the major default of a counterparty. This exemption is deemed necessary because close-out netting is regarded as an essential tool that allows market participants to terminate their executory contracts and minimize their losses upon the default of their counterparty. It is intended to prevent counterparties from spreading their losses to other counterparties and exacerbating contagion and systemic risk in financial markets that are interconnected.[43] Therefore, although close-out netting is **35.17**

39 Insolvency Law, DIFC Law No. 3 of 2009.

40 Ibid., s 68(2)(a).

41 Netting Law, DIFC Law No. 2 of 2014, s 8

> The provisions of a netting agreement will be enforceable in accordance with their terms, including against an insolvent party, and, where applicable, against a guarantor or other person (including a guarantor or other person that is insolvent) providing security for a party and will not be stayed, avoided or otherwise limited by (a) the appointment of, or any application for the appointment of, a liquidator, or any action of a liquidator, (b) any provision of law relating to bankruptcy, liquidation (including any compulsory winding up procedure or proceeding), reorganisation, composition with creditors, receivership, conservatorship or any other insolvency proceeding to which a party may be subject, or (c) any other provision of law that may be applicable to an insolvent party, subject to the conditions contained in the applicable netting agreement.

42 Section 6(2) of the Netting Law states that the Netting Law prevails over any conflicting provisions of the DIFC Insolvency Law. Therefore, the courts would not be able to prevent the enforcement of close-out netting clauses by imposing a moratorium upon the default of debtor counterparty.

43 However, the effectiveness of carve-out statutes has not been universally embraced in the academic community. Professor Stephen J. Lubben has argued that the financial contracts should not receive a special carve-out because:

specifically provided for, the DIFC Insolvency Law[44] and Insolvency Regulation[45] are silent on the enforceability of *ipso facto* clauses upon the commencement of a voluntary arrangement or a liquidation.[46]

(4) The shortcomings of the DIFC

35.18 The DIFC has had a comprehensive set of insolvency laws for businesses registered in the DIFC since 2009. Furthermore, since 2011, businesses that are not registered in the DIFC are allowed to apply to the DIFC courts to resolve their legal disputes.[47] Therefore, UAE businesses could have substituted the deficient former UAE insolvency law with the DIFC law. However, there are two reasons why distressed UAE businesses have not fully embraced the DIFC insolvency regime. First, some local UAE businesses may be reluctant to have their cases heard by the DIFC courts, as court proceedings are conducted in English instead of Arabic, and the majority of legislation and regulations are only written in English and modelled on English common law.

35.19 Second, the DIFC's insolvency legislation, for the reasons mentioned above, is inadequate for reorganizing large companies. This inadequacy became apparent to the UAE government in 2009, when Dubai World experienced financial difficulties as a result of the global financial crisis. This government-owned conglomerate announced that it was going to restructure debts of USD $24.9 billion owed by its subsidiaries in the Dubai World Group.[48] The Dubai World Group has a unique legal status because it was created as a 'decree corporation', yet its debts were not guaranteed by the UAE government. This meant that Dubai World could not seek protection under the Commercial Code.[49] Furthermore, the DIFC's insolvency legislation was not used to reorganize Dubai World because it favours creditors over debtors, which could

---

> the safe harbours encourage a rush to sell derivatives, and buy replacement derivatives, upon a firm's financial distress. It seems manifestly implausible that this situation reduces systemic risk. If instead the automatic stay applied, the ripples of panic and market disruption that are currently generated would be at least moderated by the pause that a bankruptcy filing would bring, perhaps creating enough space for a distressed firm to transfer its business to a new, more stable owner. In short, systemic risk would be reduced.

Stephen J. Lubben, 'Repeal the Safe Harbours' (2010) 18 *American Bankruptcy Institute Law Review* 319, 322.

44 Insolvency Law, DIFC Law No. 3 of 2009.

45 DIFC Insolvency Regulation (1 Oct., 2008).

46 *Ipso facto* clauses will be discussed further below.

47 Dubai Law No. 16 of 2011 on Amending Some Provisions of Law No. 12 of 2004 Concerning the Dubai International Financial Centre Courts.

48 Townsend, see above fn 11.

49 Linklaters, Briefing Note Dubai World Restructuring Decree No. 57 of 2009 (Dec. 2009) at 7 [hereinafter, 'Linklaters'].

hinder the restructuring process. Consequently, the Ruler of Dubai signed Decree No. 57:[50]

> bringing into effect bespoke insolvency protection regulations to govern any future formal reorganisation and restructuring of Dubai World and any of its direct or indirect subsidiaries.[51] ... The Government's intention was to develop a law that would permit a restructuring of the obligations of Dubai World and its subsidiaries in accordance with international best practices following a fair, equitable and transparent legal process.[52]

This ad hoc legislation established an independent tribunal of three judges who were from the DIFC and applied a modified version of the DIFC Insolvency Law[53] and Insolvency Regulation[54] to restructure companies within the Dubai World Group.[55] The Decree is 'in essence, a hybrid[56] of the English and US corporate rescue systems, with clear influences from both (although the process is perhaps closest to Chapter 11 [of the US Bankruptcy Code]).'[57] **35.20**

The government decided to base the law of the Decree on the insolvency laws, rules and regulations of the DIFC because it determined that such laws, rules and regulations were comprehensive and reflected international standards. In addition, such laws, rules and regulations were in English rather than Arabic, which the government determined would facilitate a complex financial re-organization involving investors and professionals from all over the world. However, the government determined that the existing DIFC laws, rules and regulations needed additional modifications to allow them to work effectively for a reorganization involving an enterprise as large and complex as Dubai World. The modifications included provisions to provide for an *automatic stay or moratorium*, provisions to allow the tribunal to approve priority financing during the course of a *reorganization*, provisions enabling Dubai World and its **35.21**

50 Decree No. 57 of 2009, Establishing a Tribunal to Decide the Disputes Related to the Settlement of the Financial Position of Dubai World and its Subsidiaries. The Decree was signed on 13th of December 2009 [hereinafter 'Decree No. 57].

51 Ibid., 1.

52 Ibid., 7.

53 Insolvency Law, DIFC Law No. 3 of 2009.

54 DIFC Insolvency Regulation (1 Oct., 2008).

55 Dubai World used Decree 57 again in 2014 to 'ensure an orderly process in the restructuring of US$15 billion of debts'. Frank Kane, 'Dubai World Restructuring Set to Adopt Bankruptcy Law' *The National* (Dec. 3, 2014).

56 Hybrid Insolvency Procedures are informal procedures indirectly assisted by the court or other public bodies by means of limited, temporary stay on enforcement actions. They are able to produce binding effects on a minority of creditors, if approval by a majority (in number and proportion) of creditors has been reached, and approved to the satisfaction of the court/public body.

57 Linklaters, see above fn 49 at 3. 11 USC Bankruptcy Code (US).

subsidiaries to continue to benefit from existing contracts, and provisions enabling the formation of appropriate classes of creditors and provisions specifying the approvals required for a voluntary company arrangement.[58]

35.22 The Decree[59] permitted companies from the Dubai World Group to apply to the tribunal for a voluntary arrangement, which triggered an automatic moratorium.

> Where the board of the Corporation notify the Tribunal in writing … together with such other documents as may be prescribed by the registrar of the Tribunal that they intend to make a proposal to the Corporation's creditors for a voluntary arrangement … , the Tribunal shall convene and an automatic moratorium *shall immediately apply to all creditors, secured or unsecured* and *without their consent*, in respect of such Corporation and its assets wherever located from the time of the Voluntary Arrangement Notification until the conclusion of proceedings or such earlier time as ordered by the Tribunal for cause. The moratorium shall have effect as specified in the DIFC Insolvency Regulations (as modified by this Schedule) and shall also preclude a creditor of such Corporation from exercising any *right of set-off* in respect of any obligation due from such Corporation.[60]

35.23 Hence, this provision distinguished the Decree from the DIFC's Insolvency Law, as it limited the ability of creditors (including secured creditors) to terminate executory contracts and exercise insolvency set-off with Dubai World. This provision was broad and presumably rendered *ipso facto* clauses void, including possibly close-out netting provisions.[61] Although Decree No. 57 was effective in reorganizing Dubai World, the Decree was not extended to other businesses in the UAE. Consequently, in 2016, the UAE federal government passed new insolvency legislation in order to modernize the existing patchwork regime.

D. REFORMS

35.24 The UAE federal government deemed that it was critical to introduce an effective insolvency regime for the entire country in order to promote

58 Ibid., 8 [emphasis added].

59 Decree No. 57 of 2009.

60 Ibid., art 8 [emphasis added].

61 Insolvency set-off and close-out netting are related concepts. 'The key difference between close-out netting and set-off is that close-out netting could take place across a number of transactions, regardless of when payments would otherwise have become due'. Clifford Chance, 'New UAE Bankruptcy Law: Analysis and Highlights' (7 Dec., 2016) 8.

economic growth. In 2016, the government enacted new insolvency legislation for two main reasons. First, in 2014, the UAE government became concerned that many medium and large businesses would be negatively affected by the global decrease in oil prices, as the UAE economy is reliant on oil revenues. A regime that permits reorganization was deemed necessary in order to rescue distressed businesses that were expected to make a recovery. It was evident that the existing legislation (including the Commercial Code, the DIFC Insolvency Legislation and Decree No. 57) did not strike the right balance between creditors and debtors or permit the reorganization of decree companies.

Second, a major policy of the UAE government is to encourage more foreign direct investment and foreign businesses to establish in the UAE. This goal has been hindered because the UAE has received poor ratings in international rankings for being able to handle company insolvencies. Although the UAE is ranked 26th out of 109 countries in the world for ease of doing business by the World Bank, it is only ranked 104th for resolving insolvency.[62] **35.25**

The World Bank's Doing Business 2016: Measuring Regulatory Quality and Efficiency report, published in October, claims that the lack of a modern restructuring law is one of the biggest barriers to effective business in the UAE. The report found it is relatively easy for people to set up a company in the UAE compared to other GCC states, yet they face difficulties when confronted with debtors in financial trouble, and further challenges if they run into a sticky financial situation themselves. The report claims that in the UAE it takes on average 3.2 years to complete an insolvency process with costs amounting to 20 per cent of the debtor's estate and an average recovery rate for creditors of 29 cents on the dollar, compared with average figures for OECD countries: 1.7 years, 9 per cent and 72.3 cents on the dollar.[63] **35.26**

Effective frameworks for insolvency and creditor right systems foster greater access to credit at more affordable prices; establish the legal framework within which corporate restructuring takes place; operate as a safety valve for corporate distress by enabling parties to salvage viable businesses or transfer assets efficiently to better uses; and serve to promote good corporate governance.[64] **35.27**

---

62 World Bank, *Ease of Doing Business*, 2016. http://www.doingbusiness.org/rankings [Last accessed on 1 January, 2017].

63 Townsend, see above fn 11.

64 World Bank, *Insolvency Systems*, see above fn 10 at 2.

35.28 Overall, '[t]he lack of a modern, comprehensive bankruptcy law has long been cited as a major shortfall of the UAE's business climate'.[65] The legislative gap encouraged lawyers and businesses to lobby[66] the UAE government to introduce insolvency legislation so that businesses can restructure internally in a controlled environment. Consequently, the UAE government responded by introducing a new insolvency regime in 2016.

(1) The new insolvency legislation

35.29 The new insolvency legislation, which has been in the works since 2009, has replaced the patchwork of UAE insolvency legislation. The new law, Federal Decree Law No. 9 of 2016 on Bankruptcy,[67] came into force on 29 December, 2016 and it provides a formal insolvency procedure.[68] The new law is based on Chapter 11 of the US Bankruptcy Code,[69] which deals with reorganizing a distressed company. The new legislation contains four key provisions:

> a broad moratorium on litigation actions by creditors once a bankruptcy case has been filed; ability to implement restructuring based on a two-thirds creditor majority so minority interests cannot derail the process; debtor's privilege of interim funding and management so long as secured creditors are adequately protected, and decriminalisation of bounced cheques.[70]

More specifically, the new legislation sets out three main procedures for a business in financial difficulty:

1. *Protective composition*: this is a debtor-led, court-sponsored process, designed to facilitate the rescue of a business which is in financial difficulty but not yet insolvent. The scheme requires the approval of both a majority in number and two-thirds by value of the unsecured creditors. The scheme must be implemented within three years of court approval, which may be extended for a further three years with creditor approval;

65 John Everington, 'Q&A: What You Need to Know About the UAE Bankruptcy Law' (Sept. 6, 2016) The National.

66 'Arcapita's story is often used by lawyers and other parties lobbying Arab governments to introduce insolvency legislation similar to Chapter 11.' Townsend, see above fn 11.

67 Federal Decree Law No. 9 of 2016.

68 Formal Insolvency Procedures are collective proceedings (involving all creditors) subject to the control or supervision of a court and/or an insolvency administrator, which means that the debtors can lose control of their assets or are greatly restricted in their actions. This procedure implies an automatic moratorium (stay of individual enforcement actions) and can result in either restructuring (where this is possible) or, more often, liquidation.

69 Townsend, see above fn 11. 11 USC Bankruptcy Code (US).

70 Ibid.

2. *Insolvency with restructuring*: where a debtor is insolvent but the court determines that the business is capable of rescue, it may approve a restructuring scheme. Such a scheme is similar to the protective composition described above, requiring the same levels of creditor approval, but a longer period of five years (extendable by a further three years) is allowed for implementation;
3. *Insolvency and liquidation*: where a protective composition or restructuring scheme is not appropriate or approved or is terminated, or a debtor is acting in bad faith to evade its financial obligations, the court will order the insolvent winding-up of the business.[71]

Protective composition

Only the debtor can apply for protective composition. 'In order for the preventive composition application to be accepted, the debtor shall not be in default for more than (30) thirty consecutive business days due to [their] unstable financial position or in the condition of account receivable.'[72] The protective composition scheme imposes a moratorium on creditors.[73] However, secured creditors are allowed to enforce their security interests against the debtor as their debts fall due.[74] The appointed trustee will have to take certain actions and make certain dispositions on behalf of the debtor, including the termination or maintenance of certain executory contracts.[75] According to Article 34: **35.30**

1. … the issue of commencement decision *shall not rescind or terminate any effective contract* between the debtor and the contracting party. The *contracting party shall perform his contractual obligations* unless he obtains a judgment of stay of execution, due to the failure of the debtor to perform his obligations, before the date of issue of the procedures' commencement decision.

71 Low, see above fn 13.
72 Federal Decree Law No. 9 of 2016, art 6(2).
73 Ibid., art 32(1).
74 Ibid., art 32(2).
75 Ibid., art 26(3):

> During the performance of his duties, the trustee may make the following actions and dispositions on behalf of the debtor, whenever such actions and dispositions fulfill the purpose of the [protective] composition, having attained the consent of the debtor or the permission of the Court: a. Hold any of properties of the debtor in possession … ; d. Collect any monies or rights on behalf of the debtor; e. Conclude or maintain any insurance policies necessary to continue the practice of business of the debtor; f. Pay any amounts or discharge any claims that must be paid or discharged as part of executing the [protective] composition scheme; g. Hire any properties of the debtor or terminate lease contracts and lease any properties, if necessary; h. Enter on behalf of the debtor into any arrangement, quittance or settlement with one or more of creditors of the debtor; i. Obtain any guarantee which the debtor neglected to obtain or renew.

2. At request of the trustee, *the court may order the rescission of an effective contract* to which the debtor is a party, if necessary to enable the debtor to transact his business; or if such rescission would fulfill interest [*sic*] of all creditors of the debtor and would not fatally prejudice the interests of the party contracting with the debtor.[76]

35.31 Hence, there are limitations on when the debtors and creditors may terminate executory contracts. In all cases, debtors and creditors must obtain the approval of the court before they are allowed to terminate an executory contract. This means that *ipso facto* clauses would likely be void upon the commencement of protective composition proceedings.[77]

Restructuring

35.32 A restructuring scheme is similar to a protective composition procedure, but with a longer duration. The restructuring process involves the trustee[78] creating a draft restructuring scheme[79] which requires the court's approval.[80] The following articles outline the treatment of executory contracts during the restructuring process:

> Article (161): The trustee may, during the management of procedures, request the debtor to do everything necessary to maintain interests of his business. The trustee may further *request the debtor to perform the effective contracts* to which the debtor is a party'.
>
> Article 164: 1. The trustee shall ensure that the debtor is capable to perform his obligations.
>
> 2. In the framework of implementing the restructuring scheme, the trustee may pay any amount that must be paid by the debtor to the party with whom the debtor

---

76 Ibid., art 34.

77 'Other key tools of [protective composition] seek to build upon useful features of US bankruptcy law: … ipso facto provisions which prevent counterparties from using insolvency-linked contractual termination provisions, provided the debtor performs its executory obligations.' Clifford Chance, see above fn 61 at 5. This poorly written paragraph suggests that *ipso facto* clauses are void upon the commencement of protective composition, as Federal Decree Law No. 9 of 2016 on Bankruptcy is modelled on Chapter 11 of the Bankruptcy Code; 11 USC Bankruptcy Code (US).

78 Federal Decree Law No. 9 of 2016, art 126.

79 Ibid., art 101.

80 Ibid, art 101(2):

> The restructuring scheme draft shall indicate the following: a. The possibility of the debtor's business to re-generate profits; b. Activities of the debtor that must be suspended or terminated; c. Terms and conditions of settlement of any liabilities; d. Any performance bonds might be requested from the debtor, if any; e. Any proposal to purchase all or part of business of the debtor, if any; f. Grace periods and payment deductions; g. The possibility of converting the debt to share capital of any project; h. The possibility to consolidate, create, redeem, sell or replace any guarantees, if necessary, to implement the scheme draft; i. Propose a period or periods to repay the whole debt.

> *contracted under an enforceable contract*, unless the contracting party grants the debtor a term for payment.
>
> 3. If the trustee fails to perform or continue the performance of the contract, the other contracting party may apply to the court to *rescind the contract*. This shall not result in the suspension of procedures.
>
> Article 165: 1. The decision of initiating restructuring procedures shall not result in the abatement of any term agreed on for the repayment of a debt owed by the debtor. *Every contractual provision to the contrary shall be null and void.*
>
> 2. Initiating the restructuring procedures *shall not result in the rescission or termination of any effective contract* between the debtor and third party, unless the contract is based on personal considerations. The party contracting with the debtor shall perform his contractual obligations, unless he entered plea of non-performance for the failure of the debtor to perform his obligations, before the date of issue of decision of initiating procedures.
>
> 3. At request of the trustee, *the court may order the rescission of any effective contract* to which the debtor is a party, if necessary to enable the debtor to transact his business; or if such rescission would fulfill interest of all creditors of the debtor and would not substantially prejudice the interests of the party contracting with the debtor.[81]

Overall, these articles can be summed up as follows: Upon the commencement of restructuring procedures, the trustee must ensure that executory contracts are performed by the debtor; a creditor can apply to the court to terminate an executory contract if the debtor is unable to perform; the trustee, with the permission of the court, may terminate contracts that prevent the debtor from operating its business; the trustee may also terminate contracts if it is for the benefit of creditors; and *ipso facto* clauses are deemed null and void during the restructuring process. Hence, the new restructuring procedure is quite flexible, as it allows the trustee to tailor the scheme to the needs of each debtor company. **35.33**

Liquidation

A company is required to initiate liquidation proceedings with the court if it 'ceases repayment of [its] debts on the maturity dates for over (30) thirty consecutive business days due to [its] shaken financial position or being in the condition of account receivable'.[82] Whereas the previous legislation permitted creditors to apply to have a debtor company declared bankrupt regardless of the amount owed, the new legislation makes its more complicated for creditors to file an application. A creditor can only initiate liquidation proceedings if it **35.34**

81 Federal Decree Law No. 9 of 2016, arts 166 and 167 deal specifically with the treatment of executory contracts regarding leases, investment contracts and employment contracts.

82 Federal Decree Law No. 9 of 2016, art 68(1).

is owed at least AED 100,000[83] and it has not been paid within 30 days of notifying the debtor of the claim.[84]

35.35 If the court accepts an application to liquidate a company;

> a moratorium on creditor action (excluding enforcement of secured claims which may occur with permission of the court) will immediately apply and the court will place the debtor under the control of [a trustee][85] ... Following the commencement of bankruptcy, the [trustee] takes over the management of the debtor's business and is bestowed with *wide powers* in relation to the preservation of assets and the continuation (or otherwise) of the business.[86]

The trustee is responsible for liquidating all the properties of the debtor.[87] Consequently, the trustee will determine which executory contracts to perform and which ones to terminate. It is also likely that creditors will be unable to enforce *ipso facto* clauses upon the commencement of the liquidation process, except in the case of secured claims.

(2) Insolvency set-off and close-out netting

35.36 After the commencement of bankruptcy, the Commercial Code[88] permitted insolvency set-off for debts that were 'associated' with each other.[89] Article 183 of the new insolvency legislation also permits insolvency set-off:

> between a creditor and debtor if it had been *contractually agreed prior to insolvency*, but not in respect of debts which arise after the commencement of an insolvency procedure ... ; and provides for a creditor to submit a claim for the 'post set-off' amount to the insolvent party's estate or, if the creditor owes the insolvent party the 'post set-off' sum, then the creditor would pay this sum to the insolvency estate.[90]

35.37 Therefore, insolvency set-off is type of *ipso facto* clause that is enforceable between the creditor and the debtor. However, it appears that the new law only permits insolvency set-off to be exercised in protective composition and

83 This is USD $27,248.
84 Federal Decree Law No. 9 of 2016, art 69.
85 Clifford Chance, see above fn 61 at 6; Federal Decree Law No. 9 of 2016, art 126.
86 Ibid., Clifford Chance, at 7 [emphasis added].
87 Federal Decree Law No. 9 of 2016, art 132.
88 Federal Law No. 18 of 1993.
89 Ibid., art 688. Clifford Chance, see above fn 61 at 7.
90 Clifford Chance, Ibid. [emphasis added].

restructuring procedures.[91] There is no mention whether insolvency set-off can be exercised upon the commencement of liquidation proceedings.[92]

Furthermore, the new law does not mention the enforceability of close-out netting clauses, which could create legal uncertainty when a trustee deals with the executory financial contracts of a large distressed company.[93] A trustee handling a protective composition, restructuring or liquidation may be allowed to cherry-pick and terminate unprofitable contracts with creditors, whereas creditors could be required to perform their executory contracts with the distressed company.[94] This may exacerbate systemic risk during a financial crisis as creditors may not be allowed to terminate executory financial contracts with the distressed company to minimize their losses. Consequently, the new law is not equipped to handle the insolvency of large companies that have large volumes of unperformed financial contracts. **35.38**

(3) *Ipso facto* clauses

The following section will consider whether *ipso facto* clauses are enforceable under the existing insolvency regimes in the UAE, including the DIFC and ADGM. There are two broad approaches that jurisdictions can take in the treatment of *ipso facto* clauses. On the one hand, jurisdictions that permit the enforcement of *ipso facto* clauses argue that the parties should be able to freely contract to protect themselves upon the occurrence of a default event. In England, for example, *ipso facto* clauses are enforceable under the Insolvency Act 1986[95] upon the commencement of administration.[96] Although a **35.39**

---

91 Federal Decree Law No. 9 of 2016, art 183(2).

92 'Whereas the [protective composition] provisions in the New Law include a carve out to allow terminations required to effect Article 183 set-off, an equivalent is not expressly provided for rescue within bankruptcy procedures'. Clifford Chance, see fn 61 above at 8.

93 Ibid., 3.

94 Ibid., 8:

> In all of the three procedures available under the New Law, the insolvent party's [trustee] has powers to review the sums which are submitted as claims on the insolvent estate. This power would make it possible for lump sum close-out amounts to be picked apart across multiple transactions, with the effect that the creditor has to pay the gross amount of all or some of the 'in the money' transactions to the insolvency estate, whilst filing a claim separately for the claims under the 'out of the money' transactions.

95 Insolvency Act 1986 (c. 45)(UK).

96 Australia in an example of a jurisdiction that currently permits the enforcement of *ipso facto* clauses; however, the Australian government is planning to reform the *Corporations Act 2001* in order to make *ipso facto* clauses void during a corporate restructuring:

> The proposed law reform will provide a moratorium shelter when a company restructures. The change will make *ipso facto* clauses that have the purpose of allowing contracts to be terminated solely due to an insolvency event unenforceable if a company is undertaking a restructure ... The Government proposes that any term of a contract or agreement which terminates or amends any contract or agreement (or any term of any contract or agreement) by reason only that an 'insolvency event' has occurred, would be void.

moratorium is imposed when the company files for administration, it does not extend to *ipso facto* clauses,[97] meaning 'that parties may terminate contracts with the debtor during its administration'.[98]

35.40 There is an overriding reluctance to encroach upon the parties' rights to contract freely on such terms as they see fit, in spite of the existing interferences that are an inescapable aspect of any statutory insolvency or restructuring regime. Where there is an alleged conflict between contractual provisions and elements of insolvency law, however, the courts have proved more willing to honour the contract as freely entered into by the parties involved.[99]

35.41 On the other hand, jurisdictions that do not recognize and enforce *ipso facto* clauses argue that this is necessary to increase the chance of successfully restructuring a business.[100] For example, in the US, Chapter 11 of the Bankruptcy Code 'prevents creditors from terminating contracts of an insolvent party if the relevant debtor seeks protection under Chapter 11'.[101] The filing of Chapter 11 triggers an automatic stay that 'is broad in scope and applies to almost all types of creditor actions against the debtor or the property of the estate'.[102] Section 365(e) of the Bankruptcy Code states that:

> an executory contract ... may not be terminated or modified, and any right or obligation under such contract ... may not be terminated or modified, at any time after the commencement of the case solely because of a provision in such a contract ... that is conditioned on ... the commencement of a case under this title.[103]

35.42 This treatment of *ipso facto* clauses in these jurisdictions can be used to determine whether these clauses are enforceable in the UAE under the two

---

> Any provision in an agreement that has the effect of providing for, or permitting, anything that in substance is contrary to the above provision would be of no force or effect.

Australian Financial Markets Association, *Insolvency Law Reform – Ipso Facto Moratorium Proposal* Member News (May 2016) 2.

97 Insolvency Act 1986 (c. 45)(UK), s 11(3)(d).

98 Slaughter & May, 'Insolvency Law and Contract: Policy and Practice in the US and UK' (July 2012) 3.

99 Ibid., 6.

100

> The justification for these types of provisions is to ensure important contracts are maintained so that goodwill is preserved while the company is under bankruptcy protection. This is intended to maximize the chances of the insolvent company continuing as a going concern, or otherwise, its value to third parties.

Australian Financial Markets Association, see above fn 96 at 1.

101 Ibid. 11 USC Bankruptcy Code (US).

102 Slaughter & May, see above fn 98 at 3.

103 Ibid., 4. The New York Bankruptcy Court in *Lehman Brothers Financing Inc. v BNY Corporate Trustee Services Ltd* 422 B.R. 407 (Bankr. SDNY 2011) held that an attempt to enforce an *ipso facto* clause 'would violate the automatic stay under section 362(a)(3) of the Bankruptcy Code'. Ibid.

main insolvency regimes. On the one hand, the DIFC Insolvency Law[104] and Insolvency Regulation[105] are silent on the enforceability of *ipso facto* clauses between creditors and the debtor in the case of a voluntary arrangement or liquidation. Since the DIFC legislation is modelled on the UK Insolvency Act,[106] it is presumed that, notwithstanding the moratorium, *ipso facto* clauses can be enforced between the parties during a voluntary arrangement and liquidation.

On the other hand, the new UAE federal insolvency legislation,[107] which is modelled on the US Bankruptcy Code,[108] contains language indicating that *ipso facto* clauses are void upon the commencement of restructuring procedures and selectively void upon the commencement of liquidation. Consequently, the availability of multiple insolvency regimes in the UAE means that businesses can choose where to establish their business. Businesses that prefer a creditor-friendly regime can establish in the DIFC or the ADGM, whereas the businesses that prefer a debtor-friendly regime can establish anywhere else in the UAE. **35.43**

E. CONCLUDING REMARKS

This chapter has highlighted the shortcomings of the previous insolvency framework under the Commercial Code,[109] which prompted the DIFC and the ADGM to introduce insolvency legislation in their own jurisdictions. However, the DIFC has two major shortcomings: first, it operates mainly in English and on common law principles as opposed to Arabic and on sharia law principles. Second, the Dubai World restructuring demonstrated that the DIFC insolvency regime was inadequate for handling the restructuring of large companies because it empowers creditors to terminate executory contracts with a distressed company, thereby jeopardizing the restructuring process. For instance, the DIFC's legislation permits the enforceability of close-out netting clauses. It is also probable that during restructuring proceedings the DIFC courts would uphold *ipso facto* clauses that were negotiated between the parties during solvency, as this regime is modelled on UK insolvency regime. These shortcomings led the UAE government to pass ad **35.44**

104 Insolvency Law, DIFC Law No. 3 of 2009.
105 DIFC Insolvency Regulation (1 Oct., 2008).
106 Insolvency Act 1986 (c. 45)(UK).
107 Federal Decree Law No. 9 of 2016.
108 11 USC Bankruptcy Code (US).
109 Federal Law No. 18 of 1993.

hoc legislation in the form of Decree No. 57[110] in order to be able to successfully restructure Dubai World. This bespoke legislation restricted the ability of creditors to terminate executory contracts with Dubai World upon the commencement of restructuring proceedings. However, Decree No. 57[111] did not apply to other businesses in the UAE.

35.45 The shortcomings of the former UAE and DIFC insolvency regimes, coupled with the desire of the UAE government and local businesses to boost national competitiveness and international attractiveness, led the UAE government to replace the Commercial Code[112] with a new insolvency regime in 2016.[113] The purpose of the reform was to introduce an updated insolvency regime that incorporated best practices and could handle the restructuring of large businesses during an economic shock. Nevertheless, the new insolvency regime remains untested, and it remains to be seen how it will be applied in practice. There is still scepticism about the ability of local judges, who are generally inexperienced in handling restructuring and liquidation proceedings, to properly apply the new law.[114]

35.46 It is also unclear whether close-out netting clauses will be enforceable under the new insolvency legislation, which could negatively impact companies with large volumes of executory contracts during a financial crisis. The new law, which is modelled on the US insolvency regime, makes clear that *ipso facto* clauses will not be enforced by the general UAE courts[115] upon the commencement of restructuring proceedings. Furthermore, it is unclear whether the UAE courts would have the necessary records and accounts to successfully restructure a distressed UAE business. 'Perhaps more worrying is [Bharat Gupta's] observation that many UAE businesses do not even keep detailed financial accounts, making it impossible to find a record of all of the assets and draw up a viable restructuring plan.'[116] Therefore, further reforms in accounting practices and corporate governance will be necessary in the UAE in order to ensure that the new law can be implemented properly.

110 Decree No. 57 of 2009.
111 Ibid.
112 Federal Law No. 18 of 1993.
113 Federal Decree Law No. 9 of 2016.
114 Bharat Gupta, senior director at Alvarez & Marsal Middle East, whose parent company helped draft Chapter 11 in the US 'warns that a shortage of competent specialist judges could cause the system to fail even if the law is enacted ... The key will be for [the UAE] to find ways of attracting good judges from private practice'. Townsend, see above fn 11.
115 There are currently no specialist insolvency courts in the UAE.
116 Townsend, see above fn 11.

Overall, the UAE offers a great opportunity for local and international businesses, as it provides them with a choice of which jurisdiction to use for initiating restructuring or liquidation proceedings. Businesses that prefer a creditor-friendly regime can establish in the DIFC or the ADGM, whereas businesses that prefer a debtor-friendly regime can establish anywhere else in the UAE. However, more of the road needs paving before UAE businesses can experience a smooth ride during insolvency. **35.47**

INDEX

Note: the abbreviation ECs refers to executory contracts.